THE

Sourcebook

BUILDERS

DECORATORS

REMODELERS

by Jay Fruin

First Edition

Microtronics, Massapequa Park, New York

JAN 2 3 1996

No part of this book may be reproduced without the express written consent from the Publisher. Every precaution has been taken in the preparation of this book to present accurate information, the author and publisher assume no responsibility for any errors or omissions. No liability is assumed for any damages resulting from the use of the information contained in this book.

Any mention of product names in this book are copyright and registered trademarks of their respective owners.

Published by:

Microtronics
P.O. Box 200
Massapequa Park, NY 11762-0200 USA
(516) 783-5793

E-mail: 72647.1463@compuserve.com

Copyright © 1995 All Rights Reserved
First Edition 1995

CIP/LC 94-96168
ISBN 0-9645594-0-4

Cover Design by John O'Malley
Cover Photos by Stephen Simpson and Mark Scott, FPG International

ACKNOWLEDGEMENTS

Sincere thanks go to Rita Rovery for doing the research, mailings, and office stuff while learning everything there is to know about publishing a book. To Peggy Fruin for her help in evaluating the idea, getting things organized, and generally getting things done. To John O'Malley for his sound graphics advice, patience, and fine end product. To Bill Beyer at Beyer Graphics and Tom Dunk at Quantum Imaging for their help in turning 3 floppy disks into a book.

Software products used to create the book;

Microsoft Foxpro 2.6 for Windows
Corel Ventura 5.0 for Windows
Corel Database Publisher 4.2 for Windows
Adobe Photoshop 3.0 for Windows

John O'Malley used the following to create the cover artwork.
Adobe Phototshop 3.0 for Macintosh
QuarkXPress for Macintosh

Hardware used to create the book;

IBM compatible 486/66 PC
Apple Macintosh Quadra 650
Relysis Reli 4816 Image Scanner
Apple LaserWriter Select 360

ACKNOWLEDGEMENTS

Adobe Photoshop 3.0 is a registered trademark of Adobe Systems Incorporated.

Corel Ventura and Corel Database Publisher are registered trademarks of Corel Corporation.

IBM is a registerd trademark of International Business Machines Corporation.

Macintosh and LaserWriter Select 360 are registered trademarks of Apple Computer Corporation.

Microsoft Foxpro 2.6 and Windows are registered trademarks of Microsoft Corporation.

QuarkXPress is a registered trademark of Quark Incorporated.

Preface

Welcome to The Complete Sourcebook for Builders, Decorators, and Remodelers. We hope you find the book a useful tool in finding sources for all kinds of building and decorating products. Our goal in creating it was to give both professionals and do-it-yourselfers a handy reference guide to aid in the search for primary and alternate sources for building and decorating products. It is particularly helpful when looking for unique or hard to find items.

The idea for the book came as a result of research we had done for our own building and remodeling projects. As do-it-yourselfers, we learned that the success of a project often hinges on the materials used. Knowing where and what to buy is critical. Finding all the alternatives in a building/decorating project is time-consuming and difficult. New products come out every day and the only way to keep on top of them is to buy every building and decorating magazine you can find. Even when we contracted to build a house, we found that our architect and builder faced the same problem in sourcing products. New products, sometimes using new technology, can save hundreds if not thousands of dollars over the course of a project.

As an example, when we built our house the architect included a column detail. When it came time to buy the columns our builder went to the lumber yard and researched all the alternatives. As an experienced builder, he knew how tough the local weather was on columns. At first, the alternatives he came upon were variations using wood as the material. Finally, he happened on a new company making columns out of fiberglass and marble chips. These columns were cheaper and would stand up to the harshest weather conditions. We liked this alternative and decided to use them. Now, every time I walk by one of those columns I admire how nice they look and confirm that they were the right material for the job.

The Complete Sourcebook puts that kind of information at your fingertips, helping you to;

Save Time

Having the information right in front of you, and organized in a way that you can find suppliers quickly, ends up saving alot of time. Whether you are looking for unique decorating items, or want competitive bids from several vendors on commodity items.

Save Money

The more alternatives sources you know about, the greater the opportunity to save money. You can use the information in our book to price shop products with multiple suppliers, or to investigate different material alternatives, often discovering price advantages to one material over another.

Improve Quality

Our culture is becoming more and more aware of quality, and quality is most evident in the use of detail. Detail items are often not the easiest things to find. Often these items are unique, like a specialty tile or a cornice molding. One way of acquiring uniqueness in a detail is to use products that have not yet been discovered by the mass market. Finding a manufacturer of unique items is easier than ever with our book and you are sure to have more sources to choose from.

One other thing, we decided early on that we would list all appropriate companies, regardless of size, in the directory for free. That way we would be able to present you with the largest possible group of sources. We didn't discriminate on style either, so you'll find sources for everything from Country to Contemporary, Modern to Victorian and beyond.

A bit about the format of the book. We constructed a reference book that is easy to use, allowing you to quickly find a source. In order to do this we cross-referenced each company as to the key things they do or sell. The cross-reference, in the back of the book, gives you a quick way of finding suppliers by product or product type. But recognizing that people like to "channel surf" we loosely grouped companies by their major area of focus. So we have twelve chapters providing that loose grouping in alphabetical order.

Our database of companies constantly changes. Companies tend to come and go. Since the research and planning for the book took about two years our database was constantly being updated to stay on top of the current status of companies. Once a company is entered into our database we do regular mailings to insure that the information in the book is as accurate as possible.

How did we do it?

Well, we began by casually accumulating catalogs and flyers from companies selling products that we had an interest in. These were mostly companies that sold products we felt we would use in our own projects. As time went by, we became more serious about creating a comprehensive sourcebook, so we left our personal tastes aside and constructed a computerized database of company listings. Our research effort expanded and we developed many contacts in trade associations throughout North America and Europe that helped us in bringing you a comprehensive listing of sources. For each company listed we created cross-reference entries for the primary products or services that that company provides. We then used Corel Ventura desktop publishing software to extract the information in the database, putting it in our printed format. In order to create the Index we did some custom programming and manual reformatting to put the Index in the most usable form. We brought our Ventura files to a graphics service bureau where they transferred the printed images to film negatives. The film negatives were then transferred to metal plates for the final printing process.

What are we doing next?

Well, later this year we will publish a computerized CD-ROM version of The Complete Sourcebook with over 6,000 pages of brochures and catalogs from many of the companies in the book. The CD-ROM will give you even greater access to vast amounts of product information quickly and efficiently. Please fill out the registration card in the back of the book so that we can advise you of the availability of the CD-ROM as well as updated versions of the book. Also, if we forgot a company that you know about, please fill out the other postcard in the back of the book and we will go about adding them to our database.

Jay Fruin

Table of Contents

One
Architectural Components 1-38

Two
Bathroom 1-13

Three
Building Supply 1-102

Four
Doors 1-18

Five
Flooring 1-11

Six
Furniture 1-87

Seven
Garden Supply 1-8

Eight
Home Decoratoring 1-78

Nine
Home Security 1-4

Ten
Kitchen 1-11

Eleven
Lighting 1-36

Twelve
Windows 1-28

Index
Cross Reference 1-99

Architectural Components

A A Abbingdon Affilliates, Inc.

Victorian and Art Deco - Tin Ceiling and Wall

2149 Utica Ave.
Brooklyn, NY 11234

Mail Order Available

Credit Cards Accepted

Phone 718-258-8333

FAX 718-338-2739

A.F. Schwerd Manufacturing Co.

Manufacturer - Architectural Wood Columns, Posts

3215 McClure Ave.
Pittsburgh, PA 15212

Catalog/Information Available Free

Phone 412-766-6322

A.J.P. Coppersmith

Order Direct - Nationwide Shipping - Reproduction Colonial Lighting Fixtures

20 Industrial Pkwy.
Woburn, MA 01801

Send $3.00 for Catalog/Information

Credit Cards Accepted

Phone 617-932-3700

Toll Free 800-545-1776

FAX 617-932-3704

ABN

*Algemene Nederlandse Bond Van Natuursteenbewerkendebedrijven
President - M. Olthof Member-European International Federation Of Natural Stone Industry*

Postbus 216
P-B 1440 AE Purmerend
Netherlands

Phone 011-31-299020303

FAX 011-31-299071014

ACCRA Wood Products Ltd.

Architectural Designer Wood Moulding, Parquet Flooring In Maple, Beech, Oak, Birch, Mahogany

6150 Lougheed Highway
Barnaby, BC V5B 2Z9
Canada

Phone 604-294-9885

Toll Free 800-663-8012

FAX 604-294-6212

ADI Corporation

Manufacturer - Marble, Granite & Wood Mantels, Surrounds, Countertops

5000 Nicholson Ct.
North Bethesda, MD 20895

Mail Order Available

Phone 301-468-6856

FAX 301-468-0562

AFG Industries, Inc.

Manufacturer - Architectural Glass
PO Box 929
Kingsport, TN 37662

Phone 615-229-7200

FAX 615-229-7459

Abaroot Manufacturing Company

Columns, Posts, Newels
21757-1/2 S. Western Ave.
Torrance, CA 90501

Phone 213-320-8172

Ability Woodwork Co. Inc.

Architectural Woodwork
5596 N. Northwest Hwy.
Chicago, IL 60630

Phone 312-775-1585

Abitibi-Price

Manufacturer - Hardwood, Moulding, Siding
3250 W. Big Beaver Rd.
Troy, MI 48089

Phone 313-649-3300

Toll Free 800-521-4250

FAX 313-649-3139

Accent Millwork Inc.

Decorative Architectural Wood Products
285 North Amboy Rd.
Conneaut, OH 44030

Phone 216-593-6775

FAX 216-593-6927

Accurate Lock & Hardware Co.

Architectural Hardware & Custom Locks
Annie Place
Stamford, CT 06902

Phone 203-348-8865

FAX 203-348-5234

Acorn Structures Inc.

Home Plans/Designs
PO Box 1445
Concord, MA 01742

Phone 508-369-4111

Acrymet Industires Inc.

Manufacturer - Glass Block
42-05 10th Street
Long Island City, NY 11101

Phone 718-786-7654

Adkins Architectural Antiques

Architectrual Antiques - Mantels, Doors, Windows, Lighting & Plumbing Fixtures
3515 Fannin Street
Houston, TX 77004

Phone 713-522-6547

FAX 713-529-8253

Adornments for Architecture

Architectural Ornaments - Cupolas, Steeples, Weathervanes, Windmills, Lighting Rods, Sundials
Bernhardt R. Seifert
309 Hollow Rd. Dept. TB
Staatsburg, NY 12580

Phone 914-889-8390

FAX 914-889-8350

Albion Design

Manufacturer - Worldwide Shipping - Spiral Staircases
Dales Manor Business Park
Babraham Road, Sawston, Cambridge
CB2 4LH
Great Britain

Phone 011-44-233-836128

FAX 011-44-223-837117

Algoma Hardwoods, Inc.

Manufacturer - Architectural Doors
1001 Perry St.
PO Box 118
Algoma, WI 54201

Phone 414-487-5221

Toll Free 800-678-8910

FAX 414-487-3636

Architectural Components

Allen Iron Works & Supply – American Moulding & Millwork Co.

Allen Iron Works & Supply

Iron Stairs, Columns, Railings

1000 Pinson Valley Pkwy.
Birmingham, AL 35217

Catalog/Information Available Free

Mail Order Available

Credit Cards VISA/MC

Phone 205-841-5574

Allied Bronze Corp.

Ornamental & Architectural Metal Work

25-11 Hunterspoint Ave.
Long Island City, NY 11101

Phone 718-361-8822

Alpine Moulding

Manufacturer - Moulding

155 Industrial Drive
Burlington, WI 53105

Mail Order Available

Toll Free 800-870-0336

FAX 414-767-0411

Aluma Trim

Moulding

239 Richmond St.
Brooklyn, NY 11208

Phone 718-647-5700

FAX 718-235-4557

American Architectural Art Company

Architectural Accents

PO Box 904
Adamstown, PA 19501

Phone 215-775-8876

American Custom Millwork Inc.

Order Direct Worldwide - Architectural Moulding, Millwork

3904 Newton Rd.
PO Box 3608
Albany, GA 31706

Send $5.00 for Catalog/Information

Mail Order Available

Phone 912-888-3303

FAX 912-888-9245

American General Products

Manufacturer - Distributor - Spiral & Circular Stairs

1735 Holmes Rd.
PO Box 395
Ypsilanti, MI 48197

Catalog/Information Available Free

Phone 313-483-1833

Toll Free 800-782-4771

American Millwork Inc.

Manufacturer - Millwork, Moulding, Jambs

11615 N.E. 116th
Kirkland, WA 98034

Phone 206-823-6060

Toll Free 800-854-3956

FAX 206-823-8343

American Moulding & Millwork Co.

Manufacturer - Millwork, Moulding, Panels, Country Pine Furniture

PO Box 8220
Stockton, CA 95208

Phone 209-946-5800

Toll Free 800-441-8231

FAX 209-946-5813

Architectural Components

The Complete Sourcebook

1 - 3

American Ornamental Corporation

Steel Spiral Staircases
5013 Kelley St.
PO Box 21548
Houston, TX 77026
Catalog/Information Available Free
        Phone 713-635-2385
        Toll Free 800-231-3693
        FAX 713-635-2386

American Wood Column Corp.

Manufacturer - Door Trim & Facing, Wood Columns, Pedestals, Moulding, Doors
913 Grand St.
Brooklyn, NY 11211
Catalog/Information Available Free
Mail Order Available
        Phone 718-782-3163
        FAX 718-387-9099

Amherst Woodworking & Supply Inc.

Manufacturer - Moulding, Architectural Paneling, Mantels, Bookcases
PO Box 718
Hubbard Ave.
Northampton, MA 01061
Mail Order Available
        Phone 413-584-3003
        FAX 413-585-0288

Anderson-McQuaid Company Inc.

Architectural Millwork
170 Fawcett St.
Cambridge, MA 02138
        Phone 617-876-3250
        FAX 617-876-8928

Andreas Lehman Fine Glasswork

Custom Victorian Architectural Glass - New designs can be created and traditional designs can be reproduced
1793 12th St.
Oakland, CA 94607
Catalog/Information Available Free
        Phone 510-465-7158
        FAX 510-465-7158

Andrews Custom Woodworking

Moulding, Turnings, Furniture
181 Chief Looking Glass Rd.
Florence, MT 59833
        Phone 406-273-2423

Anthony Wood Products Inc.

Order Direct - Nationwide Shipping - Victorian Woodwork
PO Box 1081
Hillsboro, TX 76645
Send $3.00 for Catalog/Information
Mail Order Available
Credit Cards Accepted
        Phone 817-582-7225
        FAX 817-582-7620

Antique Emporium

Antique Architectural, Fixtures, Cabinetry & Accessories
7805 Loraine Ave.
Cleveland, OH 44102
        Phone 216-651-5480

Anything Fiberglass

Architectural Details
Rte. 1, PO Box 608-A 4
Cedar Creek, TX 78612
Mail Order Available
        Phone 512-247-4044

Apache Building Products

Manufacturer - Decorative or Reflective Ceiling Panels
2025 E. Linden Ave.
Linden, NJ 07036
        Phone 908-353-3370

Aqualand Manufacturing Inc.

Manufacturer - Spiral Stairs
PO Box 9
Woodruff, WI 54568
        Phone 715-356-3800
        FAX 715-356-4469

Arcadia Mfg. Inc.

Manufacturer - Architectural Aluminum, Windows, Glass Sliding Doors
21 Cross Street
New Canaan, CT 06840

Phone 203-966-0134
FAX 203-972-0712

Architectural Antiques

Antique Building Components
801 Washington Ave. N
Minneapolis, MN 55401

Phone 612-332-8344
FAX 612-332-8344

Architectural Antiques Exchange

Architectural Antiques - Building Components
709-15 North Second St.
Philadelphia, PA 19123

Phone 215-922-3669
FAX 215-922-3680

Architectural Antiques West

French Doors
14201 S. Main
Los Angeles, CA 90061

Mail Order Available

Phone 213-516-1039

Architectural Antiquities

Architectural Components - Brass Lighting Fixtures, Hardware, Victorian Plumbing Fixtures, Fireplace Mantels, Doors, Windows, Stained Glass
John Jacobs
Harborside, ME 04642

Phone 207-326-4938

Architectural Artifacts

Architectural Components - Lighting Fixtures, Stained Glass Windows, Mantels
4325 North Ravenswood
Chicago, IL 60613

Mail Order Available

Phone 312-348-0622
FAX 312-348-6118

Architectural Cataloguer, USA

Architectural Building Components
PO Box 8270
Galveston, TX 77553

Send $4.50 for Catalog/Information

Phone 409-763-4969

Architectural Components

Doors, Windows, Frames, Sashes, Mouldings
26 N. Leverett Rd.
Montague, MA 01351

Send $5.00 for Catalog/Information

Phone 413-367-9441
FAX 413-367-9461

Architectural Crystal Ltd.

Lighting Fixtures - Lamps, Chandeliers
A&D Bldg. 150 East 58th St.
New York, NY 10155

Send $10.00 for Catalog/Information

Phone 212-935-1655
Toll Free 800-648-2012

Architectural Elements

Architectural Components & Hardware
503 150th St.
Amery, WI 54001

Phone 715-268-2694
FAX 715-268-2694

Architectural Grille

Custom Finished Grilles
51 T Fourth St.
Brooklyn, NY 11231

Phone 718-858-7607
FAX 718-834-8393

Architectural Heritage

Fireplace Surrounds, Antique Garden Statuary, Antique Oak & Mahogany Paneling

Taddington Manor, Taddington
Nr Cutsdean, Cheltenham, Glos
GL54 5RY
Great Britain

Phone 011-44-38-673414

FAX 011-44-38-673414

Architectural Iron Company

Manufacturer - Custom & Stock Items - 18th & 19th Wrought Iron Work

PO Box 126
Schocopee Rd.
Milford, PA 18337

Send $4.00 for Catalog/Information

Mail Order Available

Credit Cards Check/Money Order

Phone 717-296-7722

Toll Free 800-442-4766

FAX 717-296-4706

Architectural Lathe & Mill

Architectural Building Components - Columns, Posts

2819 Chartres
New Orleans, LA 70117

Phone 504-482-0980

Architectural Paneling

Available only to Designers - Architects Reproduction English, French Paneling, Cabinets, Ceilings, Mantels

Anthony Lombardo
979 Third Ave.
New York, NY 10022

Send $10.00 for Catalog/Information

Phone 212-371-9632

FAX 212-759-0276

Architectural Rarities Ltd.

Lighting Fixtures

10650 Country Rd. 81
Maple Grove, MN 55369

Send $4.00 for Catalog/Information

Toll Free 800-328-9493

Architectural Salvage Company

Architectural Antiques - Doors, Hardware, Stained Glass, Woodwork, Mantels, Lighting Fixtures, Columns

103 W. Michigan Ave.
PO Box 401
Grass Lake, MI 49240

Catalog/Information Available Free

Phone 517-522-8516

Architectural Systems, Inc.

Architectural Building Components

304 Old Mill Rd.
Exton, PA 19341

Phone 215-363-0466

Architectural Timber & Millwork

Manufacturer - Antique Plank Flooring, Moulding, Beams

35 Mt. Warner Road
Hadley, MA 01035

Phone 413-586-3045

FAX 413-586-3046

Aristocrat Products Inc.

Manufacturer - Plaster Cornices, Columns, Medallions, Surrounds

8215 Roswell Rd. Bldg. 600
Atlanta, GA 30550

Mail Order Available

Phone 404-913-1272

FAX 404-913-1269

Armstrong World Industries Inc.

Manufacturer - Decorative Ceiling Panel, Crown Moulding, Chair Rail Moulding

PO Box 3001
Lancaster, PA 17064

Toll Free 800-233-3823

Art Directions

Call for Local Representative, or Ordering - Architectural Lighting Fixtures - Brass, Copper, Aluminum

6120 Delmar Blvd.
St. Louis, MO 63112

Send $2.00 for Catalog/Information

Phone 314-863-1895

FAX 314-863-3278

Art Marble and Stone

Mantels, Glass Doors, Fireplace Accessories

5862 Peachtree Industrial Blvd.
Atlanta, GA 30341

Catalog/Information Available Free

Toll Free 800-476-0298

Artefact-Architectural Antiques

18th & 19th Century Architectural Antiques and Hardware

790 Edison Furlong Rd.
Furlong, PA 18925

Phone 215-794-8790

Artefacts Architectural Antiques

Architectural Components - Antique Hardware, House Parts

17 King St.
St. Jacobs, ON N0B 2N0
Canada

Phone 519-664-3760

Artistry in Veneers Inc.

Architectural Veneers

450 Oak Tree Ave.
S. Plainfield, NJ 07080

Send $1.00 for Catalog/Information

Phone 908-668-1430

FAX 908-668-4317

Arvid's Historic Woods

Wood Mantels, Windows, Doors, Moulding

2820 Rucker Ave.
Everett, WA 98201

Send $5.95 for Catalog/Information

Phone 206-252-8374

Toll Free 800-627-8437

FAX 206-258-4334

Atlantic Stairworks

Spiral Stairs

Box 244
Newburyport, MA 01950

Send $2.00 for Catalog/Information

Phone 508-462-7502

Axon Products

Mantels and Surrounds

171 Eugenia Dr.
Ventura, CA 93003

Catalog/Information Available Free

B & B Products

Manufacturer - Architectural Door Hardware, Railings

5091 G St.
Chino, CA 91710

Phone 714-590-9529

BD Mantels Ltd.

Fireplace Surrounds

Unit B2, Ford Airfield Ind Est
Ford Arundel, W Sussex BN18 0HY
Great Britain

Phone 011-44-903-717770

Baldinger Architectural Lighting, Inc.

Architectural Lighting

19-02 Steinway St.
Astoria, NY 11105

Phone 718-204-5700

FAX 718-721-4986

Architectural Components

Ballard Designs

Mouldings, Mantels, Custom Headboards
1670 DeFoor Ave. NW
Atlanta, GA 30318-7528
Send $3.00 for Catalog/Information
Credit Cards Accepted
Phone 404-351-5099

Barnett Millworks, Inc.

Mouldings, Door Units, Window Units, Millwork
PO Box 389
Theodore, AL 36590
Phone 205-653-7710
FAX 205-653-6123

Baydale Architectural Metalwork Ltd.

Doors, Windows
Banks Rd, Darlington
Co Durham DL1 1YB
Great Britain
Phone 011-44-325/460203
FAX 011-44-325/381918

Bendix Mouldings

Mouldings
37 Ramland Road South
Orangeburg, NY 10962
Send $1.00 for Catalog/Information
Mail Order Available
Phone 914-365-1111
Toll Free 800-526-0240
FAX 914-365-1218

Best Moulding Corporation

Moulding - Pine, Douglas Fir, Red Oak
PO Box 10148
Albuquerque, NM 87184
Phone 505-898-6770
FAX 505-898-1301

Bjorndal Woodworks

Manufacturer - Millwork, Doors, Cabinets, Furniture
Route 1, Box 110
Colfax, WI 54730
Phone 715-962-4389

Booth-Muirie Ltd.

Ceiling Panels & Tiles, Moulding
870 South St.
Glasgow G14 0SY
Great Britain
Phone 011-44-41/9581173
FAX 011-44-41/9591183

Boston Turning Works

Manufacturer - Order Direct - Trade Discounts - Columns, Posts, Finials
42 Plympton St.
Boston, MA 02118
Mail Order Available
Credit Cards Accepted
Phone 617-482-9085
FAX 617-482-0415

Botrea Stairs

Stairs, Stair Components
Subsid. of Saxondell Ltd.
Higher Botrea, Newbridge, Penzance
Cornwall TR20 8PS
Great Britain
Phone 011-44-736/78714
FAX 011-44-736/788141

Bow House

House Plans/Designs
92 Randall Road
Bolton, MA 01740
Phone 508-779-6464
FAX 508-779-2272

Boyertown Planing Mill Co.

Manufacturer - Architectural Millwork
2nd & Franklin St.
PO Box 180
Boyertown, PA 19512
Phone 215-367-2124

The Complete Sourcebook

Bradley Custom Mantels & Woodworking

Manufacturer - Mantels

518 13th Avenue
Prospect Park, PA 19076

Mail Order Available

Phone 215-586-3528

FAX 215-586-0864

Bright Wood Corp.

Pine & Hem-Fir Mouldings and Millwork

PO Drawer 828
Madras, OR 97741

Phone 503-475-2243

FAX 503-475-7086

Brill & Walker Associates Inc.

Architectural Components - Mouldings, Mantels, Bookcases, Cabinets

PO Box 731
Sparta, NJ 07871

Send $4.00 for Catalog/Information

Phone 201-729-8876

FAX 201-729-5149

Brown Moulding Company

Wood Columns, Posts, Spindles, Dowels, Stair Parts

PO Box 170
Montevallo, AL 35115

Phone 205-665-2546

FAX 205-665-1803

Browne Winther & Co. Ltd.

Beams, Fireplace Surrounds, Decorative Moulding, Stair Parts Door Facings

Nobel Rd., Eley Est.
Edmonton, London N18 3DX
Great Britain

Phone 011-44-81/8033434

FAX 011-44-81/8070544

Burt Millwork Corp.

Manufacturer - Millwork, Moulding, Doors, Windows

1010 Stanley Ave.
Brooklyn, NY 11208

Mail Order Available

Phone 718-257-4601

FAX 718-649-4398

By-Gone Days Antiques Inc.

Architectural Antiques, Mantels, Hardware

3100 South Blvd.
Charlotte, NC 28209

Phone 704-527-8717

FAX 704-527-0232

C. G. Girolami & Sons

Manufacturer - Factory Direct - Architectural Ornaments, Moulding, Columns, Fireplaces

944 N. Spaulding Ave.
Chicago, IL 60651

Send $5.00 for Catalog/Information

Mail Order Available

Phone 312-227-1959

CMF Colonial Moulding

Moulding - Wood, Brass, Chrome

30 Cit Avenue #15
Hyannis, MA 02601-1723

Phone 508-778-6382

FAX 508-778-6385

Cape Cod Cupola Co., Inc.

Nationwide Shipping USA and Canada - Cupolas, Weathervanes

78 State Rd.
North Dartmouth, MA 02747

Send $2.00 for Catalog/Information

Mail Order Available

Credit Cards MC/VISA/Money Order

Phone 508-994-2119

The Complete Sourcebook

Cape May Millworks

Victorian Windows, Doors, Moulding
1042 Shunpike Rd.
Cape May, NJ 08204

Phone 609-884-0408

Cascade Wood Products Inc.

Manufacturer - Architectural Columns, Oak Staircases, Hemlock Staircases
8399 14th Street
PO Box 2429
White City, OR 97503

Phone 503-826-2911

Toll Free 800-423-3311

FAX 503-826-1393

Cassidy Brothers Forge, Inc.

Manufacturer - Custom Metal Railings, Spiral Stairways
U.S. Rt.1
Rowley, MA 01969

Send $1.00 for Catalog/Information

Phone 508-948-7303

FAX 508-948-7629

Center Lumber Company

Architectural Millwork, Lumber, Moulding
PO Box 2242
85 Fulton St.
Patterson, NJ 07509

Send $25.00 for Catalog/Information

Phone 201-742-8300

FAX 201-742-8303

Chadsworth, Inc.

Manufacturer - Architectural Components
PO Box 53268
Atlanta, GA 30355

Send $5.00 for Catalog/Information

Phone 404-876-5410

Toll Free 800-394-5177

FAX 404-876-4492

Chelsea Decorative Metal Co.

Ship Nationwide - Antique Metal Ceiling
9603 Moonlight Dr.
Houston, TX 77096

Mail Order Available

Credit Cards Bank/Certified Check

Phone 713-721-9200

FAX 713-776-8661

Cheyenne Company

Architectural Woodwork, Custom Cabinet Work
123 East Mineola Ave.
Valley Stream, NY 11580

Phone 516-561-8840

Cider Hill Woodworks

Architectural Wood Carving, Mantels, Finials, Newel Posts
90 Cider Hill Road
York, ME 03909

Catalog/Information Available Free

Phone 207-363-6388

CinderWhit & Company

Spindles, Columns Newel Posts
733 Eleventh Avenue South
Wahpeton, ND 58074

Catalog/Information Available Free

Send $3.00 for Catalog/Information

Mail Order Available

Credit Cards VISA/MC

Phone 701-642-9064

FAX 701-642-4204

Classic Architectural Specialties

Architectural Ornaments
3223 Canton St.
Dallas, TX 75226

Send $6.00 for Catalog/Information

Mail Order Available

Phone 214-748-1668

Toll Free 800-662-1221

FAX 214-748-7149

Classic Ceilings

Tin Ceilings, Paintable Wallcover, Mouldings, Medallions

902 E. Commonwealth Ave.
Fullerton, CA 92631

Send $3.00 for Catalog/Information

Toll Free 800-992-8700

FAX 714-870-5972

Classic Mouldings Inc.

Manufacturer - Architectural Plaster Ornaments - Mantels, Moulding, Niches, Cornices, Brackets, Columns

226 Toryork Dr.
Weston, ON M6L 1Y1
Canada

Mail Order Available

Phone 416-745-5560

FAX 416-745-5566

Cleveland Wrecking

Antique Building Components

3170 East Washington Blvd.
Los Angeles, CA 90023

Catalog/Information Available Free

Phone 213-269-0633

Clifton Moulding Corporation

Manufacturer - Moulding

PO Box 77
Clifton, TX 76634

Phone 817-675-8641

FAX 817-675-6727

Coastal Millworks Inc.

Architectural Mouldings, Antique Flooring, Millwork

1335 Marietta Blvd. NW
Atlanta, GA 30318

Phone 404-351-8400

FAX 404-355-7555

Collingdale Millwork Co.

Windows, Doors, Mouldings, Stairs

PO Box 1408
Collingdale, PA 19023

Phone 215-586-8000

FAX 215-586-0233

Colonial Antiques

Antique Building Components

5000 West 96th St.
Indianapolis, IN 46268

Catalog/Information Available Free

Phone 317-873-2727

Colonial Cupolas Inc.

Cupolas

5902 Buttonwood Dr.
PO Box 38
Haslett, MI 48840

Send $3.00 for Catalog/Information

Mail Order Available

Phone 517-339-4320

Conner's Architectural Antiques

Nationwide Shipping - Lighting, Hardware, Doors, Iron Fencing, Stained Glass

701 "P" St.
Lincoln, NE 68508

Mail Order Available

Phone 402-435-3338

Consolidated Pine, Inc.

Manufacturer - Pine Moulding

PO Box 428
Prineville, OR 97754

Phone 503-447-5635

FAX 503-447-6525

Constantine's

Architectural Accents, Hardware, Lumber, Woodwork

2050 Eastchester Rd.
Bronx, NY 10461

Send $1.00 for Catalog/Information

Mail Order Available

Toll Free 800-223-8087
FAX 718-792-2110

Continental Woodworking Co.

Manufacturer - Architectural Components, Flooring, Furniture, Mantels

4562 Worth St.
Philadelphia, PA 19124

Mail Order Available

Phone 215-537-5800
FAX 215-743-3179

Corning Moulding Corporation

Pine, Douglas Fir, White Fir, Cedar Door Jambs, Moulding

PO Box 187
Corning, CA 96021

Phone 916-824-4220
Toll Free 800-824-4108

Cotswold Architectural Products Ltd.

Door and Window Hardware, Locks

Manor Park Ind Est, Manor Rd.
Cheltenham, Glos GL51 9QU
Great Britain

Phone 011-44-242/233993
FAX 011-44-242/221146

Country Cupolas

Order Direct - Cupolas, Decorative Metalcraft - Weathervanes, Mailboxes, Door Hardware

Route 113
East Conway, NH 04037

Mail Order Available

Credit Cards Accepted

Phone 603-939-2698

Country Wood Products Inc.

Manufacturer - Moulding

656 Fourth St.
Adudbon, MN 56511

Phone 218-439-3385
FAX 218-439-3771

Crockett Log & Timber Frame Homes

Builder-Dealer - Log, Timber Frame, Panel Homes - Ranch, Cape, Saltbox, Chalet - Call for a Builder-Dealer near you.

Route 12, Galen Road
Westmoreland, NH 03467

Catalog/Information Available Free

Phone 603-399-7725
FAX 603-399-7132

Crossland Studio

Architectural Antiques, Furniture

118 East Kingston Ave.
Charlotte, NC 28203

Phone 704-332-3032

Crosswinds Gallery

Cupolas

980 East Main Rd.
Portsmouth, RI 02809

Catalog/Information Available Free

Phone 401-683-7974
FAX 401-253-2830

Crown Plastering

Architectural Details - Mouldings, Columns, Pedestals, Niches

385 Merrick Ave.
East Meadow, NY 11554

Phone 516-489-8200
FAX 516-489-1893

Architectural Components

Cumberland Woodcraft Co. – Danbury Stairs Corp.

Cumberland Woodcraft Co.

Order Direct - Reproduction Victorian Woodwork - Mouldings, Doors, Panels

PO Box 609
10 Stover Drive
Carlisle, PA 17013

Send $4.50 for Catalog/Information

Mail Order Available

Credit Cards MC/VISA

Phone 717-243-0063
Toll Free 800-367-1884
FAX 717-243-6502

Curvoflite Inc.

Manufacturer - Order Direct - Architectural Millwork, Spiral Staircases, Mouldings, Paneling, Cabinets

205 Spencer Ave.
Chelsea, MA 02150

Catalog/Information Available Free

Mail Order Available

Phone 617-889-0007
FAX 617-889-6339

Custom & Historic Millwork

Architectural Millwork

5310 Tennyson St.
Denver, CO 80212

Phone 303-480-1617
FAX 303-480-5006

Custom Decorative Mouldings

Manufacturer - Decorative Moulding

PO Box F, Rt. 13
Greenwood, DE 19950

Catalog/Information Available Free

Mail Order Available

Toll Free 800-543-0553
FAX 302-349-4816

Custom Hardwood Productions

Architectural Millwork

917 York Street
Quincy, IL 62301

Phone 217-224-7013
FAX 217-224-5733

Custom Wood Turnings

Manufacturer - Columns, Mouldings, Posts

156 Main Street
Ivoryton, CT 06442

Send $5.50 for Catalog/Information

Mail Order Available

Phone 203-767-3236
FAX 203-767-3238

Custom Woodturnings

Nationwide Shipping - Posts, Spindles, Stair Parts, Posts, Architectural Ornaments

4000 Telephone Rd.
Houston, TX 77087

Phone 713-641-6254
Toll Free 800-554-9608

Customwood Mfg. Co.

Manufacturer - Arichitectural Woodwork - Grilles, Panels, Doors Doorpulls, Shutters

PO Box 26208
Albuquerque, NM 87125

Phone 505-344-1691
Toll Free 800-735-0854
FAX 505-883-2894

Dahlke Stair Co.

Curving Wood Staircase

PO Box 418
Glastonbury, CT 06033

Send $2.00 for Catalog/Information

Phone 203-434-3589

Danbury Stairs Corp.

Wood Stairs & Railings

39B Mill Plain Rd.
Danbury, CT 06811

Phone 203-743-5567

Architectural Components

The Complete Sourcebook

1 - 13

Danny Alessandro Ltd./Edwin Jackson Inc.

Reproduction & Antique Mantels

8409 Santa Monica Blvd.
Los Angeles, CA 90069

Mail Order Available

Phone 213-654-6198
FAX 213-654-5153

DeAurora Showrooms Inc.

Moulding & Mirrors

12-131 Merchandise Mart
Chicago, IL 60654

Phone 312-644-4430
FAX 312-644-9415

Deck House

House Plans/Designs

930 Main St.
Acton, MA 01720

Send $20.00 for Catalog/Information

Phone 203-438-4066
Toll Free 800-727-3325
FAX 203-438-0046

Decorative Plaster Supply Co.

Architectural Ornaments

633 West Virginia St.
Milwaukee, WI 53204

Mail Order Available

Phone 414-272-3657

Decorators Supply Corp.

Architectural Ornamentation

3610-12 S. Morgan St.
Chicago, IL 60609-1586

Phone 312-847-6300
FAX 312-847-6357

Decorum Inc.

*Architectural Antiques, Lighting, Bath,
Kitchen Fixtures, Reproduction Hardware*

235-237 Commercial St.
Portland, ME 04101

Catalog/Information Available Free

Mail Order Available

Phone 207-775-3346
FAX 207-775-3038

Detail Millwork Inc.

Manufacturer - Reproduction Woodwork

160 Riverview Ave.
Waltham, MA 02154

Phone 617-983-2241
FAX 617-893-1855

Dickinsons Architectural Antiques

*Period Bathrooms, Fireplaces, Doors,
Lighting*

140 Corve Street
Ludlow Shropshire
Great Britain

Phone 011-44-584/876207

Dimension Lumber & Milling

Hardwood & Softwood Moulding

517 Stagg St.
Brooklyn, NY 11237

Phone 718-497-1680
FAX 718-366-6531

Dimitrios Klitsas

*Architectural Ornaments, Furniture,
Chests, Panels, Frames*

Fine Wood Sculptor
705 Union St.
West Springfield, MA 01089

Phone 413-732-2661

Diversified Millwork

Manufacturer - Moulding, Jambs, Frames

9843 S. Titan Ct, Unit B
Littleton, CO 80125

Phone 303-791-7466
FAX 303-791-0749

Architectural Components

Double D Mouldings Inc. – Emsworth Fireplaces Ltd.

Double D Mouldings Inc.

Manufacturer - Mouldings, Door Jambs

12580 Ashland Ave.
Red Bluff, CA 96080-9273

Phone 916-824-0414

FAX 916-824-0163

Dovetail Antiques

Nationwide Shipping - Antique Wicker Furniture

474 White Pine Rd.
Columbus, NJ 08022

Send $5.00 for Catalog/Information

Phone 609-298-5245

Draper & Draper

Fireplace Mantels

29 Hibernia Rd.
Salt Point, NY 12578

Phone 212-679-0547

FAX 212-679-0549

Drummond Woodworks

Reproduction Moulding, Medallions, Mantel Accents

327 Bay St. South
Hamilton
Ont., L8P 3J7
Canada

Toll Free 800-263-2543

Drums Sash & Dove Co.

Architectural Woodwork

PO Box 207
Drums, PA 18222

Send $1.00 for Catalog/Information

Mail Order Available

Phone 717-788-1145

FAX 717-788-3007

Duke City Moulding Company

Pine, Douglas Fir Moulding

PO Box 26266
Albuquerque, NM 87125

Phone 505-842-8500

FAX 505-842-1522

Duvinage Corporation

Manufacturer - Distributor - Spiral Staircases

60 West Oak Ridge Drive
Hagerstown, MD 21740

Phone 301-733-8255

Toll Free 800-541-2645

FAX 301-791-7240

E. F. Bufton & Son Builders

Oak Posts & Beams

Box 58l
So. Lancaster, MA 01561

Send $5.00 for Catalog/Information

Mail Order Available

Phone 617-365-7633

Eaton-Gaze Ltd.

Plaster Cornices, Ceiling Centres , Moulding

86 Teesdale St.
Bethnal Green, London E2 6PU
Great Britain

Phone 011-44-71/7397272

FAX 011-44-71/7397159

Empire Moulding Co.

Mouldings

721-733 Monroe St.
Hoboken, NJ 07030

Phone 201-659-3222

FAX 201-659-2259

Empire Woodworks

Victorian Millwork & Wood Products

PO Box 717
Blanco, TX 78606

Send $3.00 for Catalog/Information

Phone 512-833-2116

Emsworth Fireplaces Ltd.

Fireplace Surrounds and Accessories

Unit 3, Station Approach, North St.
Emsworth, Hants PO10 7PN
Great Britain

Phone 011-44-243/373431

Architectural Components

The Complete Sourcebook

1 - 15

Entol Industries

Architectural Mouldings, Medallions, Rosettes

8180 NW 36th Ave.
Miami, FL 33147

Send $1.50 for Catalog/Information

Mail Order Available

Phone 305-696-0900

FAX 305-696-1045

Eric Schuster Corp.

Moulding

45 Wood St.
Paterson, NJ 07509

Phone 201-278-4440

Executive Woodsmiths Inc.

Mantels, Mouldings

215 Foster Ave.
Charlotte, NC 28203

Send $5.00 for Catalog/Information

Phone 704-527-9090

Toll Free 800-951-9090

FAX 704-529-0007

Fancy Front Brassiere Co.

Millwork, Screen Doors

PO Box 2847
Roseville, CA 95746

Send $2.00 for Catalog/Information

Phone 916-791-7733

Fastenation

Plaster Ceiling Buttons for Ceiling Restoration

PO Box 1364
Marblehead, MA 01945

Catalog/Information Available Free

Mail Order Available

Credit Cards Check

Phone 617-846-6444

FAX 617-539-0534

Feature Fires Ltd.

Fireplace Surrounds and Accessories

32 High St.
Northwood, Middx
HA6 1BN
Great Britain

Phone 011-44-923/826699

Federal Millwork Corp.

Millwork, Cabinetry, Grilles, Mouldings

3300 SE 6th Ave.
Fort Lauderdale, FL 33316

Phone 305-522-0653

FAX 305-522-3299

Felber Ornamental Plastering Corp.

Architectural Plaster Ornaments - Cornices, Niches, Ceilings, Sculpture

PO Box 57, 1000 W. Washington St.
Norristown, PA 19404

Send $3.00 for Catalog/Information

Mail Order Available

Phone 610-275-4713

Toll Free 800-392-6896

FAX 610-275-6636

Fibertech Corporation

Manufacturer - Fiberglass Architectural Components

250 S. Depot St.
Pendleton, SC 29670

Phone 803-646-9990

FAX 803-646-7213

Fischer & Jirouch Company

Architectural Plaster Ornaments - Brackets, Centerpieces, Cornice, Grilles, Mouldings, Niches

4821 Superior Ave. NE
Cleveland, OH 44103

Send $15.00 for Catalog/Information

Mail Order Available

Phone 216-361-3840

FAX 216-361-0650

Architectural Components

Floral Glass & Mirror, Inc. — Fypon Molded Millwork

Floral Glass & Mirror, Inc.

Architectural Glass
895 Motor Parkway
Hauppauge, NY 11788

Phone 516-234-2200
Toll Free 800-647-7672
FAX 516-234-8866

Florida Mantel Shoppe

Mantels
3800 NE 2nd Ave.
Miami, FL 33137

Send $3.00 for Catalog/Information
Mail Order Available

Phone 305-576-0225

Florida Victorian Arch. Antiques

Antique Building Components
112 W. Georgia Avenue
Deland, FL 32720

Catalog/Information Available Free

Phone 904-734-9300

Florida Wood Moulding & Trim

*Architectural Columns, Moulding &
Exterior Shutters*
10780 47th St. North
Clearwater, FL 34622

Send $5.00 for Catalog/Information

Phone 813-572-1983
FAX 813-572-1983

Foreign & Domestic Woods, Inc.

Moulding & Jambs
PO Box 449
Bowling Green, VA 22427

Phone 804-633-5001
FAX 804-633-4406

Forester Moulding & Lumber

Manufacturer - Moulding
52 Hamilton St.
Leominister, MA 01453

Mail Order Available

Phone 508-840-3100
FAX 508-534-8356

Foster Mantels

Mantels
30489 San Antonio St.
Hayward, CA 94544

Toll Free 800-285-8551

Frank E. Wilson Lumber Co. Inc.

Moulding & Millwork
PO Box 1277
Elkins, WV 26241

Phone 304-636-3000
FAX 304-636-9465

Frederick Wilbur, Carver

*Architectural Moulding, Mantels and
Furniture*
PO Box 425
Lovingston, VA 22949

Mail Order Available

Phone 804-263-4827
FAX 804-263-5958

Fritz V. Sterbak Antiques

*Architectural Antiques Marble & Wood
Fireplaces, Victorian Stained Glass,
Ornamental Iron*
123 Market Street
Harve de Grace, MD 21078

Phone 410-939-1312

Fypon Molded Millwork

*Manufacturer - Millwork, Entrances,
Moulding, Windows, Trim*
22 West Pennsylvania Ave.
PO Box 365
Stewartstown, PA 17363

Send $2.00 for Catalog/Information

Phone 717-993-2593
Toll Free 800-537-5349
FAX 717-993-3782

**Architectural
Components**

The Complete Sourcebook

Garland Woodcraft Co. Inc. — Great Gatsby's Auction Galley
Architectural Components

Garland Woodcraft Co. Inc.

Manufacturer - Millwork, Cabinetry
451 South Driver St.
Durham, NC 27703
Mail Order Available

Phone 919-596-8236
FAX 919-596-5077

Geneva Designs

Moulding
2231 Lockport Rd.
Lockport, IL 60441

Phone 815-727-4683
FAX 815-727-4684

Gibco Services Inc.

Moulding, Flooring
725 S. Adams Rd. L-59
Birmingham, MI 48009

Phone 313-647-3322
FAX 313-647-8720

Glass Blocks Unlimited Inc.

Manufacturer - Glass Block
126 East 16th Street
Costa Mesa, CA 92627

Phone 714-548-8531

Glazing Products Corp.

Moulding
78th & 68th Rds.
Box 168
Middle Village, NY 11379

Phone 718-894-7979

Glostal Systems Ltd.

Architectural Glass
Ashchurch
Tewkesbury, Glos GL20 8NB
Great Britain

Phone 011-44-684/297073
FAX 011-44-684/293904

Goddard Manufacturing

Manufacturer - Wholesale Prices - Spiral Staircases Wood or Wrought Iron
Box 502
Logan, KS 67646
Catalog/Information Available Free

Phone 913-689-4341
Toll Free 800-536-4341

Gossen Corp.

Manufacturer - Crown Moulding
2030 W. Bender Rd.
Milwaukee, WI 53209

Phone 414-228-9805
Toll Free 800-558-8984
FAX 414-228-9077

Gotham Inc.

Wood Architectural Ornaments
78 Centennial Rd., Unit 6
Orangeville, Ontario L9W 1P9
Canada
Mail Order Available
Credit Cards VISA

Phone 519-942-2041
FAX 519-942-3352

Governor's Antiques & Arch. Materials

Architectural Antiques, Wood Flooring
6240 Meadowbridge Rd.
Mechanicsville, VA 23111

Phone 804-746-1030
FAX 804-730-8308

Great Gatsby's Auction Galley

Architectural Antiques - Chandeliers, Furniture, Gazebos, Stained Glass Windows, Entryways
3070 Peachtree Industrial Blvd.
Atlanta, GA 30341
Catalog/Information Available Free

Toll Free 800-428-7297
FAX 404-457-7250

Architectural Components

Gregor's Studios

Manufacturer - Reproduction 18th Century Mantels

1413 Dragon St.
Dallas, TX 75207

Send $12.00 for Catalog/Information

Phone 214-744-3385

FAX 214-748-4864

Gunther Mills Inc.

Custom Millwork

55 Randall Ave.
Bridgeport, CT 06606

Mail Order Available

Phone 203-339-3223

H & Brothers

Spiral Staircase

4835 S. Western Ave.
Chicago, IL 60609

Send $3.50 for Catalog/Information

Mail Order Available

Phone 312-247-2948

H.I.C. Millwork Inc.

Manufacturer - Architectural Millwork

7107 Crossroads Blvd.
Brentwood, TN 37207

Mail Order Available

Phone 615-371-8080

FAX 615-377-3385

Haas Woodworking Company Inc.

Columns, Millwork, Moulding, Posts

64 Clemintina St.
San Francisco, CA 94105

Phone 415-421-8273

FAX 415-543-6928

Hallelujah Redwood Products

Victorian Style Woodwork

Box 669
Mendocino, CA 95460

Mail Order Available

Phone 707-937-4410

Hallidays America Inc.

Architectural Mantels, Bookcases, Cabinets, Mouldings

PO Box 731
Sparta, NJ 07871-0731

Phone 201-720-8876

FAX 201-729-5149

Hampton Decor

Architectural Ornaments, Moulding

30 Fisk St.
Jersey City, NJ 07305

Send $4.00 for Catalog/Information

Phone 201-433-9002

Hartman-Sanders Co.

Architectural Columns, Cornices, Entryways

4340 Bankers Circle
Atlanta, GA 30360

Catalog/Information Available Free

Phone 404-449-1561

Toll Free 800-241-4303

Heritage Hardwoods

Red Oak Moulding, Jambs

W. Anderson Ave.
Shawano, WI 54166

Phone 715-526-2146

FAX 715-524-0329

Heritage Mantels Inc.

Reproduction Mantels

PO Box 240
Southport, CT 06490

Send $3.00 for Catalog/Information

Mail Order Available

Phone 203-335-0552

FAX 203-335-8886

The Complete Sourcebook

Heritage Woodcraft

Architectural Ornaments
1230 Oakland St.
Hendersonville, NC 28792

Send $2.00 for Catalog/Information

Mail Order Available

Phone 704-692-8542

Hicksville Woodworks Co.

Millwork, Screen Doors
265 Jerusalem Ave.
Hicksville, NY 11801

Send $3.00 for Catalog/Information

Phone 516-938-0171

Hill & Lumber & Hardware Co.

Millwork, Lumber, Plywood
1259 Brighton Ave.
Albany, CA 94706

Phone 415-525-1000

Horesfeathers Architectural Antiques

Architectural Antiques - Doors, Lighting, Mantels
346 Connecticut St.
Buffalo, NY 14213

Phone 716-882-1581

FAX 716-882-1581

House of Moulding

Manufacturer - Hardwood/Softwood - Mouldings, Handrails, Corbels
15202 Oxnard St.
Van Nuys, CA 91411

Phone 818-781-5300

Toll Free 800-327-4186

FAX 808-994-7848

Hyde Park Fine Art of Mouldings

Manufacturer - Moulding, Ceilings, Surrounds
29-16 40th Ave.
Long Island City, NJ 11101

Mail Order Available

Phone 718-706-0504

FAX 718-706-0507

Hyde Park Raised Panel

Hardwood Raised Panel
Robert Linder Inc.
150 East 49th Street
New York, NY 10017

Phone 212-759-8404

Toll Free 800-299-2923

FAX 212-759-8361

Investment Antiques & Collectibles

Architectural Antiques, Stained Glass
123 Market St.
Havre de Grace, MD 21078

Phone 301-939-1317

FAX 301-939-9433

Irreplaceable Artifacts

Mouldings, Mantels, Windows, Grilles, Doors
14 Second Ave.
New York, NY 10003

Phone 212-777-2900

FAX 212-780-0642

Italian Glass Block Designs Ltd.

Manufacturer - Glass Block
3911 South Mariposa Street
Englewood, CO 80110

Phone 303-762-9330

J. A. du Lac Company

Portfolio Cupolas, Exterior Embellishments
381 Notre Dame
Gross Pointe, MI 48230

Phone 313-886-6802

J. P. Weaver Co.

Architectural Ornaments
941 Air Way
Glendale, CA 91201
Mail Order Available

Phone 818-841-5700
FAX 818-841-8462

J. Zeluck Inc.

Architectural Windows & Doors
5300 Kings Hwy.
Brooklyn, NY 11234

Phone 718-251-8060
FAX 718-531-2564

Jeffries Wood Works Inc.

Made to Order - Posts, Columns, Turnings, Spindles
8807 Valgro Rd.
Knoxville, TN 37920
Mail Order Available

Phone 615-573-5876
FAX 615-573-6367

K & G

Architectural Millwork
144 Anawanda Lake View Rd.
Roscoe, NY 12776
Mail Order Available

Phone 914-482-4648
FAX 914-482-4648

Kaatskill Post & Beam

Posts, Beams, Frames
Zabel Hill Road
Box 128A
Feura Bush, NY 12067
Send $5.00 for Catalog/Information

Phone 518-768-2642

Kentucky Millwork Inc.

Architectural Millwork
4200 Reservoir Ave.
Louisville, KY 40213
Send $2.00 for Catalog/Information

Phone 502-451-3456
FAX 502-451-6027

Kneeshaw Woodworking Installations Inc.

Architectural Woodwork and Cabinetry
156 Beers St.
Keyport, NJ 07735

Phone 908-264-6630

Kolbe & Kolbe Millwork Co. Inc.

Manufacturer - Windows & Doors
1323 S. Eleventh Ave.
Wausau, WI 54401

Phone 715-842-5666
FAX 715-842-3642

Kolson

Architectural and Decorative Hardware
653 Middle Neck Rd.
Great Neck, NY 11023

Phone 516-487-1224
Toll Free 800-783-1335
FAX 516-487-1231

Konceptual Design

Architectural Hardware - Bronze & Brass
PO Box 99
No. Quincy, MA 02171

Phone 617-773-2021
FAX 617-773-2037

La France Architectural Stone & Design

Tile
2008 S. Sepulveda Blvd.
Los Angeles, CA 90025

Phone 310-478-6009
FAX 310-312-9943

Architectural Components

Larkin Company

Mantels, Mouldings - Walnut, Mahogany, Cherry

210 Carter Drive, Ste. 4
West Chester, PA 19382

Send $7.00 for Catalog/Information

Phone 215-696-9096
FAX 215-692-8708

Lewis Brothers Lumber Co. Inc.

Millwork, Hardwood Lumber

PO Box 334
Aliceville, AL 35442

Phone 205-373-2496
FAX 205-373-2122

Lianga Pacific, Inc.

Lauan, Red Oak Mouldings, Jambs

PO Box 1355
Tacoma, WA 98401

Phone 206-383-4761
FAX 206-572-8427

Logan Co.

Spiral Stairs

200 Cabel St.
Louisville, KY 40206

Mail Order Available

Phone 502-587-1316

Lynn Lumber Company

Architectural Mouldings

180 Commercial St.
Lynn, MA 01905

Send $1.00 for Catalog/Information

Mail Order Available

Phone 617-592-0400

MacBeath Hardwood Co.

Mouldings, Sills, Thresholds, Plywood, Millwork

2150-52 Oakdale Ave.
San Francisco, CA 94124

Phone 415-647-0782

Mad River Woodworks

Order Direct - Nationwide Shipping - Custom Millwork, Architectural Ornaments, Moulding, Trim, Shingles, Brackets, Screen Doors

189 Taylor Way
PO Box 1067
Blue Lake, CA 95525

Send $3.00 for Catalog/Information

Mail Order Available

Credit Cards Accepted

Phone 707-668-5671
Toll Free 800-446-6580
FAX 707-668-5673

Maine Architectural Millwork, Inc.

Architectural Reproductions - Millwork, Ornaments

Front St.
S. Berwick, ME 03908

Mail Order Available

Phone 207-384-2020

Maizefeld Mantels

Mantels

PO Box 336
Port Townsend, WA 98368

Mail Order Available

Phone 206-385-6789

Mantels of Yesteryear Inc.

Restored Antique Mantels

70 W. Tennessee Ave.
PO Box 908
McCaysville, GA 30555

Phone 706-492-5534

Maple Grove Restorations

Manufacturer - Order Direct - Wood Shutters, Raised Panels, Fireplace Surrounds Oak, Cherry, Walnut, Pine

PO Box 9194
Bolton, CT 06043

Catalog/Information Available Free

Mail Order Available

Credit Cards MC/VISA/AMEX/Check

Phone 203-742-5432

Marion H. Campbell

Antique Woodwork, Mantels, Furniture
39 Wall Street
Bethlehem, PA 18018
Send $1.00 for Catalog/Information
Mail Order Available
Phone 215-837-7775

Mark A. Knudsen

Staircase Spindles
1100 E. Country Line Rd.
Des Moines, IA 50320
Catalog/Information Available Free
Mail Order Available
Phone 515-285-6112

Marley Mouldings

Moulding
PO Box 610
Marion, VA 24354
Phone 703-783-8161
FAX 703-783-8169

Marshall Galleries, Inc.

17th Century & 18th Century Mantels
8420 Melrose Ave.
Los Angeles, CA 90069
Mail Order Available
Phone 213-852-1964
FAX 213-852-0486

Materials Unlimited

Architectural Millwork, Stained, Leaded, Beveled Glass, Antique Furniture
2 W. Michigan Ave.
Ypsilanti, MI 48197
Mail Order Available
Phone 313-483-6980
FAX 313-482-2626

Maurer & Shepherd Joyners Inc.

Manufacturer - Colonial Woodworking - Doors, Entryways, Moulding, Raised Panel Walls, Windows
122 Naubuc Avenue
Glastonbury, CT 06033
Send $5.00 for Catalog/Information
Phone 203-633-2383

McDan Woodworking

Custom Interior and Exterior Moulding, Panel Doors
374 East Broad St.
Gibbstown, NJ 08027
Phone 609-423-5337
FAX 609-224-0968

Medallion Millwork, Inc.

Pine, Douglas Fir, White Fir Moulding, Jambs
4722 Skyway Dr.
Marysville, CA 95901
Phone 916-743-7161
Toll Free 800-535-0050
FAX 916-741-1926

Medford Moulding Company

Pine Moulding, Jambs
PO Box 596
Medford, OR 97501
Phone 503-826-2181
FAX 503-826-6797

Mercer Products Co.

Moulding
4455 Dardanelle Dr.
Orlando, FL 32808
Phone 407-578-2900
Toll Free 800-832-5398

Metropolitan Artifacts, Inc.

Architectural Antiques
4783 Peachtree Rd.
Atlanta, GA 30341
Catalog/Information Available Free
Phone 404-986-0007

Architectural Components

Michael Farr Custom Woodworking,Inc.

Mouldings, Raised Panel Doors

R.D. #2 Box 140
Millville, PA 17846

Send $1.00 for Catalog/Information

Phone 717-458-4295

Michael's Fine Colonial Products

Custom Moulding, Doors, Windows, Shutters

PO Box 272
Salt Point, NY 12578

Mail Order Available

Phone 914-677-3960
FAX 914-677-5964

Midwestern Wood Products

Hardwood Ceiling Panels

1500 West Jefferson St.
PO Box 434
Morton, IL 61550

Toll Free 800-441-7493

Millwork Specialties

Wood Stairs

2197 Canton Rd.
Marietta, GA 30066

Mail Order Available

Toll Free 800-729-2906

Mitchell Moulding Co.

Wood Mouldings

1509 Circle Ave.
Forest Park, IL 60130

Phone 708-366-2690
FAX 708-366-5918

Moorwood

Mouldings & Restoration Mouldings

22 Cottage Street
Middletown, NY 10940

Catalog/Information Available Free

Phone 914-341-1924

Mt. Taylor Millwork, Inc.

Pine, Douglas Fir, Red Oak Moulding, Jambs

PO Box 2307
Milan, NM 87021

Phone 505-287-9469
FAX 505-287-9468

Mylen

Manufacturer - Order Direct - Oak & Steel Spiral Stairs

650 Washington St.
Peekskill, NY 10566

Send $0.50 for Catalog/Information

Phone 914-739-8486
Toll Free 800-431-2155
FAX 914-739-9744

Myro Inc.

Moulding

8440 N. 87th St.
Milwaukee, WI 53224

Phone 414-354-3678
FAX 414-354-3618

NMC Focal Point

Architectural Moulding, Columns, Niches, Arches

PO Box 93327
Atlanta, GA 30377

Send $2.00 for Catalog/Information

Phone 404-351-0820
Toll Free 800-662-5550
FAX 404-352-9049

Nashotah Moulding Co., Inc.

Wood Mouldings

528 Industrial Dr.
PO Box 317
Hartland, WI 53209

Phone 414-367-2191
FAX 414-367-8011

Architectural Components
National Forest Products, Inc. – Oakwood Classic & Custom Woodwork

National Forest Products, Inc.

Hardwood Mouldings, Door Jambs
1727 Stocker St.
N. Las Vegas, NV 89030

Phone 702-649-4488

FAX 702-649-8150

National Woodworks, Inc.

Fax 205-252-7157 Ext.230 - Millwork, Window & Exterior Door Units
PO Box 5365
Birmingham, AL 35207

Phone 205-252-7157

Navajo Forest Products Ind.

Pine Moulding, Jambs
PO Box 1280
Navajo, NM 87238

Phone 505-777-2211

FAX 505-777-2415

Nevers Oak Fireplace Mantels

Manufacturer - Fireplace Mantels
933 Rancheros Dr. Suite B
San Marcos, CA 92060

Mail Order Available

Phone 619-745-8841

Newman Brothers Inc.

Ornamental Metal Work
5609 Center Hill Ave.
Cincinnati, OH 45216

Mail Order Available

Phone 513-242-0011

FAX 513-242-0015

Nor-Cal Moulding Company

Pine, Douglas Fir Moulding
PO Box 2720
3663 Feather River Blvd.
Marysville, CA 95901

Phone 916-741-1046

Toll Free 800-828-8308

FAX 916-741-1099

Northern Moulding Co.

Moulding, Paneling, Trim
3524 Martens St.
Franklin Park, IL 60131

Phone 708-678-2220

FAX 708-678-3771

Nose Creek Forest Products, Ltd.

Manufacturer - Moulding and Door Frames
647 46th Ave. NE
Calgary, Alberta
T2E 8J6
Canada

Phone 403-276-9501

FAX 403-277-3694

Nostalgia

Architectural Antiques
307 Stiles Ave.
Savannah, GA 31401

Send $2.50 for Catalog/Information

Credit Cards VISA/MC

Phone 912-232-2324

Toll Free 800-874-0013

Oak Leaves Studio

Custom Doors, Mantels, Entrys, Architectural Wood Sculptures
PO Box 2356
Carmel Valley, CA 93924

Send $1.00 for Catalog/Information

Phone 408-659-0652

Oakwood Classic & Custom Woodwork

Manufacturer - Doors, Mantels, Flooring, Moulding
517 West Commercial St.
East Rochester, NY 14445

Mail Order Available

Phone 716-381-6009

FAX 716-383-8053

Architectural Components

The Complete Sourcebook

Old Kentucky Wood Products

Millwork, Custom Woodwork, Hardwood Lumber

858 Contract St.
Lexington, KY 40505

Phone 606-255-2976

Old World Moulding & Finishing Co.

Hardwood Paneling, Cabinetry & Moulding

115 Allen Blvd.
Farmingdale, NY 11735

Send $3.00 for Catalog/Information

Mail Order Available

Phone 516-293-1789

FAX 516-293-1908

Olde Theatre Architectural Salvage

Architectural Antiques

2045 Broadway
Kansas City, MO 64108

Catalog/Information Available Free

Phone 816-283-3740

FAX 816-283-3051

Oregon Fir Millwork, Inc.

Moulding, Lumber, Jambs

PO Box 2556
White City, OR 97503

Phone 503-826-9210

Toll Free 800-347-9210

FAX 503-826-1633

Ornamental Mouldings

Victorian Hardwood Moulding

1907 Nuggett Rd.
PO Box 4257
High Point, NC 27263

Catalog/Information Available Free

Toll Free 800-779-1135

FAX 919-431-9120

Ornamental Mouldings, Ltd.

Moulding, Millwork, Decorative Wood Ornaments

289 Marsland Dr., Box 336
Waterloo
Ont., CAN N2J 4A4
Canada

Phone 519-884-4080

FAX 519-884-9692

Ostermann & Scheiwe, USA, Inc.

Douglas Fir, White Fir, Cedar Moulding, Jambs

PO Box 669
Spanaway, WA 98387

Phone 206-847-1951

Toll Free 800-344-9663

FAX 206-847-8586

Outwater Plastic Industries

Trade Only - Architectural Ornaments - Mouldings, Niches, Columns, Ceiling Medallions

4 Passaic St.
Woodbridge, NJ 07075

Phone 201-472-3580

Toll Free 800-888-0880

FAX 800-888-3315

P. W. Plumly Lumber Corporation

Oak, Ash, Cherry and Walnut Flooring, Moulding

Box 2280
Winchester, VA 22601

Phone 703-662-3891

FAX 703-662-0467

Pagliacco Turning & Milling

Columns, Posts

PO Box 225
Woodacre, CA 94973

Send $6.00 for Catalog/Information

Mail Order Available

Phone 415-488-4333

FAX 415-488-9372

Architectural Components

Palmer Creek Hand-Hewn Wood Products – Ponderosa Mouldings

Palmer Creek Hand-Hewn Wood Products

Arichitectural Materials - Archways, Mantles, Doors, Shelving

PO Box 3313
Santa Rosa, CA 95402

Mail Order Available

Phone 707-578-0870

FAX 707-578-5406

Paniflex Corp.

Millwork, Wardrobes, Closet Doors

430 165th St.
Bronx, NY 10456

Phone 212-993-1270

Partelow Custom Wood Turnings

Manufacturer - Order Direct - USA & Canada Nationwide - Mouldings, Mantels, Posts, Finials, Columns

156 Main St.
PO Box 338
Ivoryton, CT 06442

Credit Cards Certified Check/Money Order

Phone 203-767-3236

FAX 203-767-3238

Perkins Architectural Millwork

Moulding, Stair Parts, Interior Hardwood Doors, Beveled Glass Doors, Mantels, Shutters

Route 5, Box 264
Longview, TX 75601

Send $5.00 for Catalog/Information

Mail Order Available

Phone 903-663-3036

Piedmont Home Products Inc.

Manufacturer - Spiral Stairs

PO Box 269
Ruckersville, VA 22968

Mail Order Available

Phone 804-985-8909

FAX 804-985-8910

Piedmont Mantel & Millwork

Mantels

4320 Interstate Dr.
Macon, GA 31210

Send $3.00 for Catalog/Information

Mail Order Available

Phone 912-477-7536

FAX 912-477-7342

Pilkington Glass Ltd.

Architectural Glass, Insulation

Prescot Rd., St. Helens
Merseyside WA10 3TT
Great Britain

Phone 011-44-744/692000

FAX 011-44-744/613049

Pinecrest

Mantels, Doors, Shutters

2118 Blaisdell Ave.
Minneapolis, MN 55404-2415

Send $10.00 for Catalog/Information

Mail Order Available

Phone 612-871-7071

Toll Free 800-443-5357

FAX 612-871-8956

Pittcon Industries Inc.

Manufacturer - Drywall, Wainscot Panels, Georgian Panels, Moulding

6409 Rhode Island Ave.
Riverdale, MD 20737-1098

Catalog/Information Available Free

Send $2.50 for Catalog/Information

Phone 301-927-1000

Toll Free 800-637-7638

Ponderosa Mouldings

Pine, Douglas Fir, White Fir Mouldings, Jambs

PO Box 518
Redmond, OR 97756

Phone 503-548-2171

FAX 503-923-0135

Architectural Components

The Complete Sourcebook

Port-O-Lite Corporation

Pine, Custom Hardwood Mouldings and Decorative Millwork

10 Railroad Ave.
PO Box 630
West Swanzey, NH 03469

Phone 603-352-3205

FAX 603-352-8073

Pridgen Cabinet Works, Inc.

Architectural Woodwork & Cabinets

PO Box 32
Whiteville, NC 28472

Phone 919-642-7175

Queen City Architectural Salvage

Architectural Antiques - Hardware, Lighting, Doors, Fencing

PO Box 16541
4750 Brighton Blvd.
Denver, CO 80216

Phone 303-296-0925

FAX 303-296-0925

R & R Lumber & Building Supply Corp.

Distributor - Architectural Supply

37 Harrison Avenue
Brooklyn, NY 11211

Phone 718-963-3890

Toll Free 800-963-3890

FAX 718-384-4803

Ralph H. Simpson Co.

Architectural & Ornamental Iron Work

1680 N. Ada
Chicago, IL 60622

Phone 312-278-5510

Ranchwood Mfg.

Fireplace Mantels

5 Cotton Land
Dotsero, CO 81637

Phone 303-524-9705

Randall Bros. Inc.

Architectural Millwork, Lumber

665 Marietta St. NW
PO Box 1678
Atlanta, GA 30371

Phone 404-892-6666

Raymond Enkeboll Designs

Order Direct - Architectural Ornaments, Moulding, Mantels, Arches, Posts, Brackets, Columns

16506 Avalon Blvd.
Carson, CA 90746

Send $25.00 for Catalog/Information

Mail Order Available

Credit Cards Accepted

Phone 310-532-1400

Toll Free 800-745-5507

FAX 310-532-2042

Readybuilt Products Co.

Manufacturer - Wood Mantels, Metal Fireplaces

PO Box 4425
1701 McHenry St.
Baltimore, MD 21223-0425

Send $2.50 for Catalog/Information

Phone 301-233-5833

Toll Free 800-626-2901

FAX 301-566-7170

Red Rose Millwork

Millwork, Red Cedar

Rt. 5 Box 387
Lexington, VA 24450

FAX 703-463-7303

Reeves Design Workshop Ltd.

Woodwork, Cabinetry

7085 Ridge Rd.
Marriotsville, MD 21104

Mail Order Available

Phone 301-781-6228

Architectural Components
Register & Grille Manufacturing Co. Inc. – Rocky Mountain Forest Products

Register & Grille Manufacturing Co. Inc.

Architectural Grilles - Aluminum, Steel, Brass

202 Norman Ave.
Brooklyn, NY 11222

Phone 718-383-9090

Toll Free 800-521-4895

FAX 718-349-2611

Reliance Industries Inc.

Moulding
PO Box 129
Richland, IA 52585

Mail Order Available

Phone 319-456-6030

FAX 319-456-6031

Rennovator's Supply

Architectural Supply

7523 Renovator's Old Mill
Miller Falls, MA 01349

Catalog/Information Available Free

Phone 413-659-2211

Toll Free 800-659-2211

FAX 413-659-3113

Replico Products Inc.

Manufacturer - Polymer Decorative Ceiling Medallions, Cornices, Brackets, Shutters, Surrounds, Columns, Mantels, Mouldings, Ornaments

3675 36e/th Ave. , P.A.T.
Montreal, Quebec
H1A 3K1
Canada

Phone 514-642-6171

FAX 514-642-6177

Rich Woodturning Inc.

Posts, Columns, Medallions, Spiral Stairs
98 NW 29th St.
Miami, FL 33127

Mail Order Available

Phone 305-573-9142

FAX 305-576-1653

River Bend Turnings

Newell Posts, Finials, Balusters - Ash, Beech, Cherry, Maple, Oak
Box 364 RD#1 River Rd.
Wellsville, NY 14895

Mail Order Available

Phone 716-593-3495

FAX 607-356-3304

Riverside Millwork Co. Inc.

Millwork, Flooring, Door & Window Units
77 Merrimack St.
Penacook, NH 03301

Phone 603-753-6318

Riverview Millworks Inc.

Architectural Woodwork, Doors & Moulding
9157 Lem Turner Rd.
Jacksonville, FL 32208

Phone 904-764-9571

FAX 904-764-2680

Roberts Consolidated

Moulding
600 N. Baldwin Park Blvd.
Industry, CA 91749

Phone 813-369-7311

Robillard

Custom Millwork & Mouldings
PO Box 16
South Berwick, ME 03908

Mail Order Available

Phone 207-384-9541

Rocky Mountain Forest Products

Manufacturer - Pine Moulding
PO Box 777
667 W. Flint
Laramie, WY 82070

Phone 307-745-8924

Toll Free 800-421-3725

FAX 307-742-2510

The Complete Sourcebook

1 - 29

Roger Pearson

Marble Fireplace Surrounds
Hockley Lane
Wingerworth, Chesterfield
S42 6QG
Great Britain
Phone 011-44-246/276393

Rogue River Millwork

Pine - Columns, Posts, Hand Rails, Jambs, Moulding
PO Box 2429
White City, OR 97503
Phone 503-826-2911
FAX 503-826-1393

S. A. Bendheim Co. Inc.

Nationwide Shipping - Restoration 1900 Architectural Glass
61 Willet Street
Passaic, NJ 07055
Mail Order Available
Credit Cards MC/VISA
Phone 201-471-1733
Toll Free 800-221-7379
FAX 201-471-3475

Saco Manufacturing & Woodworking

Architectural Columns
39 Lincoln Street
Saco, ME 04072
Phone 207-284-6613

Sacramento Valley Moulding Co.

Pine, Douglas Fir, Cedar Moulding, Jambs
PO Box 70
Crescent Mills, CA 95934
Phone 916-284-7121
FAX 916-284-6748

Salas & Co.

Architectural Millwork
502 Riverside Drive
San Antonio, TX 78223
Phone 210-733-1269
FAX 210-733-9663

Salter Industries

Manufacturer - Order Factory Direct - Oak or Brass Spiral Stairs
PO Box 183
Eagleville, PA 19048
Catalog/Information Available Free
Mail Order Available
Credit Cards Accepted/Bank Check/Money Order
Phone 215-631-1360
Toll Free 800-368-8280
FAX 215-631-9384

Samuel B. Sadtler & Co.

Marble Mantels & Surrounds, Reproduction Door Hardware
340 South Fourth St.
Philadelphia, PA 19106
Mail Order Available
Phone 215-923-3714
FAX 215-923-3714

San Francisco Victoriana

Victorian Style Moulding, Ornaments
2245 Palou Ave.
San Francisco, CA 94124
Send $5.00 for Catalog/Information
Mail Order Available
Credit Cards VISA/MC
Phone 415-648-0313

Schlesser Co., Inc.

Manufacturer - Mouldings, Jambs, Frames
2501 N. Columbia Blvd.
Portland, OR 97217
Phone 503-285-8323
FAX 503-289-4756

Schoenherr Iron Work

Ornamental Iron, Brass Railings & Accessories
21471 Schoenherr
Warren, MI 48089
Phone 313-777-4141

Seneca Millwork Inc.

Architectural Millwork & Moulding
635 W. Tiffen St.
PO Box 429
Fostoria, OH 44830
Phone 419-435-6671

Shatterproof Glass Corp.

Architectural Glass
4815 Cabot Ave.
Detroit, MI 48210
Phone 313-582-6200

Sierra Pacific Industries Millwork Div.

Wood Moulding, Jambs
PO Box 496028
Redding, CA 96049-6028
Phone 916-275-8812
FAX 916-275-4811

Silverton Victorian Millworks

Order Direct - Millwork - Base Moulding, Casings, Crowns, Corner Blocks, Doors, Gingerbread, Wainscot
PO Box 2987
Durango, CO 81302
Send $4.00 for Catalog/Information
Mail Order Available
Credit Cards Accepted
Phone 303-259-5915
Toll Free 800-933-3930
FAX 303-259-5919

Smith Millwork, Inc.

Wood Moulding, Millwork
920 Robbins St.
Lexington, NC 27292
Phone 704-249-8171
FAX 704-243-2688

Softub Inc.

Manufacturer - Home Portable Spas
21100 Superior St.
Chatsworth, CA 91311
Phone 818-407-4646
Toll Free 800-554-1120

Southern Accents Architectural Antiques

Architectural Antiques
308 Second Ave. SE
Cullman, AL 35055
Mail Order Available
Phone 205-737-0554
FAX 205-734-4799

Southern Millwork, Inc.

Mouldings, Millwork, Cabinetry, Doors, Frames
525 S. Troost
Tulsa, OK 74120
Phone 918-585-8125
FAX 918-585-8129

Southern Staircase Co.

Custom Stairways & Spiral Staircase in many Styles
7561 Industrial Ct.
Alpharetta, GA 30201
Phone 404-664-5571
FAX 404-664-7521

Spiral Manufacturing

Spiral Staircases
17251 Jefferson Highway
Baton Rouge, LA 70817
Catalog/Information Available Free
Phone 504-753-8336
Toll Free 800-535-9956
FAX 504-753-8351

Spiral Stairs of America

*Manufacturer - Order Direct - Spiral
Staircases - Iron, Steel, Wood*
1718 Franklin Ave.
Erie, PA 16510
Catalog/Information Available Free

Phone 814-898-3700
Toll Free 800-422-3700
FAX 814-899-9139

Sporthill Inc.

Architectural Furnishings
PO Box 468
Reading Ridge, CT 06876
Send $5.00 for Catalog/Information
Mail Order Available

Phone 203-938-3148
FAX 203-938-4127

Spurwink Spiral Stairs

Spiral Staircases
PO Box 1397
Portland, ME 04104
Catalog/Information Available Free

Toll Free 800-528-7787

Stair Building & Millwork Co. Inc.

*Wood Railings, Circular Stairs, Spiral
Stairs*
51 Kennedy Ave.
Blue Point, NY 11715

Phone 516-363-5000

Stair-Pak Products Co. Inc.

Manufacturer - Oak Spiral Stairs
2575 Rt. 22 West
PO Box 3428
Union, NJ 07083
Mail Order Available

Phone 980-688-1200
FAX 908-688-1209

Stairways Inc.

*Manufacturer - Order Direct Wholesale -
Spiral Staircases - Wood, Steel,
Aluminum, Brass, Stainless*
4166 Pinemont
Houston, TX 77018
Catalog/Information Available Free

Phone 713-680-3110
Toll Free 800-231-0793
FAX 713-680-2571

Starling Inc.

Wood Columns & Posts
Eden Church Rd.
PO Box 937
Denham Springs, LA 70727-0937

Phone 504-664-3361
FAX 504-664-9982

States Industries Inc.

*Manufacturer - Hardwood Architectural
Panel*
29545 Enid Road, East
PO Box 7037
Eugene, OR 97401
Catalog/Information Available Free

Phone 503-688-7871
Toll Free 800-537-0419
FAX 503-689-8051

Steptoe & Wife Antiques Ltd.

Spiral Staircases
322 Geary Ave.
Toronto, Ontario
M6H 2C7
Canada
Send $3.00 for Catalog/Information

Phone 416-530-4200
FAX 416-530-4666

Stuart Post & Lumber Co.

Posts & Lumber
Hwy. 70
PO Box 240
Millerton, OK 74750

Phone 405-746-2459

Architectural Components

Style-Mark, Inc. – Tennessee Moulding & Frame Inc.

Style-Mark, Inc.

Architectural - Brackets, Mouldings, Entrance Systems

960 W. Barre Rd.
Archbold, OH 43502

Catalog/Information Available Free

Toll Free 800-446-3040

FAX 419-445-4440

Sunset Moulding Co.

Moulding, Millwork

PO Box 326
Yuba City, CA 95992

Phone 916-695-1801

FAX 916-695-2560

Sunshine Architectural Woodworks

Fireplace Mantels

Rt. 2 Box 434
Fayetteville, AR 72701

Send $3.00 for Catalog/Information

Mail Order Available

Phone 501-521-4329

Sunshine Woodworks

Mantels, Mouldings, Raised Paneling, Shutters

2169 Sunshine Drive
Fayetteville, AR 72703

Send $5.00 for Catalog/Information

Phone 501-521-4329

FAX 501-521-8863

Superior Architectural Cornices

Manufacturer - Plaster Moulding

PO Box 184
Sewickley, PA 15143

Mail Order Available

Phone 412-766-0676

FAX 412-734-5411

Taco

Architectural Glass Railing and Components

50 N.E. 179th St.
Miami, FL 33162

Phone 305-652-8566

Toll Free 800-223-3449

FAX 305-653-1174

Taconic Architectural Woodworking

Architectural Woodwork, Cabinets

Box 1183 Rd 1 Burr Pond Rd.
Sudbury, VT 05733

Phone 802-247-3743

Tafcor Inc.

Millwork, Wood Mouldings

PO Box 222
Berrien Springs, MI 49103

Phone 616-471-2351

FAX 616-471-4282

Tallahassee Mouldings & Millwork

Architectrual Moulding & Mantels

679 Industrial Dr.
Tallahassee, FL 32310

Mail Order Available

Phone 904-222-7082

Tatem Mfg. Co. Inc.

Custom Woodworking

PO Box 25189
Greenville, SC 29616

Phone 803-281-0087

FAX 803-288-2944

Tennessee Moulding & Frame Inc.

Moulding

1188 Antioch Pike
Nashville, TN 37211

Phone 615-833-4540

FAX 615-834-1742

Architectural Components

The Complete Sourcebook

1 - 33

Tewa Moulding Corporation

Pine, Red Oak Moulding
PO Box 10291
Albuquerque, NM 87184

Phone 505-898-0420
FAX 505-898-9636

The Balmer Studios Inc.

Architectural Ornaments - Mouldings, Ceiling Centers, Niches
9 Codeco Court
Don Mills, ON M3A 1B6
Canada

Send $25.00 for Catalog/Information

Phone 416-449-2155

The Bank Architectural Antiques

Mantel Trim, Flooring, Doors, Shutters
1824 Felicity St.
New Orleans, LA 70113

Catalog/Information Available Free

Toll Free 800-274-8883

The Color People

Architectural Color Consultants - Exterior Color Schemes - Victorian, Colonial, Art Deco
1522 Blake Street, Suite 300
Denver, CO 80202

Mail Order Available

Phone 303-534-4600
FAX 303-534-1310

The Emporium

Architectural Antiques
2515 Morse St.
Houston, TX 77019

Send $3.00 for Catalog/Information

Phone 713-528-3808

The Iron Shop

Order Factory Direct - Spiral Staircases - Cast Iron in many Styles and Finishes, Oak Sprial Stairs
Box 547
400 Reed Road
Broomail, PA 19008

Catalog/Information Available Free

Credit Cards Accepted/Bank Check/Money Order

Phone 215-544-7100
Toll Free 800-523-7427
FAX 215-544-7297

The James Wood Company

Manufacturer - Paneling, Millwork Moulding
2916 Reach Road
PO Box 3547
Williamsport, PA 17701

Mail Order Available

Phone 717-326-3662
FAX 717-322-8842

The Porch Factory

Victorian Interior & Exterior Millwork
PO Box 231
White House, TN 37188

Send $2.00 for Catalog/Information

Phone 615-672-0998

The Salamander and the Web

Architectural Components
PO Box 1834
Topeka, KS 66601-1834

Mail Order Available

Toll Free 800-984-3932
FAX 913-232-3308

Architectural Components

The Wood Factory

Nationwide Shipping - Custom Woodwork, Moulding, Screen Doors, Trim, Fence Pickets

111 Railroad St.
Navasota, TX 77868

Send $2.00 for Catalog/Information

Mail Order Available

Credit Cards VISA/MC/Check/Money Order

Phone 409-825-7233

FAX 409-825-1791

Thunderbird Moulding Company

Pine, Douglas Fir, White Fir Moulding

6001 Power Inn Rd.
Sacramento, CA 95824

Phone 916-381-4200

FAX 916-381-0803

Timberpeg

Post & Beam Home Designs

PO Box 1500
Claremont, NH 03743

Send $15.00 for Catalog/Information

Phone 603-542-7762

FAX 603-542-8925

Trimcraft Inc.

Moulding, Door Frames, Jambs

1335 Neptune Drive
Boynton Beach, FL 33426

Phone 407-732-1116

FAX 407-736-7991

Unique Spiral Stairs & Millwork Inc.

Spiral Stairs, Millwork

RFD 3, Box 4500
Winslow, ME 04901

Phone 207-873-6214

United Plastics Corp.

Manufacturer - Vinyl Ceiling Panels

513 Independent Rd.
Oakland, CA 94621

Phone 510-569-6700

FAX 510-638-9100

United Stair Corp.

Pre-Fab Wood Staircases

Highway 35
Keyport, NJ 07735

Catalog/Information Available Free

Mail Order Available

Phone 201-583-1100

United States Woodworking, Inc.

Architectural Woodwork, Wood Windows & Doors

35 Engineers Rd.
Hauppage, NY 11788

Phone 516-234-4910

Universal Window Corp.

Millwork

5001 N. Graham St.
Charlotte, NC 28213

Phone 704-596-6152

FAX 704-598-9016

Urban Archaeology

Architectural Antiques, Reproduction Bathroom Fixtures, Lighting

285 Lafayette St.
New York, NY 10012

Mail Order Available

Phone 212-431-6969

FAX 212-941-1918

Urban Artifacts

Architectural Antiques, Furniture, Windows, Doors

4700 Wissahickon Ave.
Suite 111
Philadelphia, PA 19144

Phone 215-844-8330

Toll Free 800-621-1962

FAX 215-844-8687

The Complete Sourcebook

Uroboros Glass Studios Inc.

Manufacturer - Tiffany Glass, Architectural Glass

2139 N. Kerby
Portland, OR 97227

Phone 503-284-4900
FAX 503-284-7584

Valley Mouldings Inc.

Wood Moulding

4201 Williams St. SE
Albuquerque, NM 87105

Phone 505-877-3000

Valley Planing Mill Inc.

Millwork, Doors, Mantels, Plywood, Lumber

1210 Hickory Farm Lane
Appleton, WI 54914

Phone 414-739-4712

Vermont Frames

House Plans Post & Beam Frame Homes - Foam Laminate Building System

Box 102
Hinesburg, VT 05461

Catalog/Information Available Free

Phone 802-453-4438
FAX 802-453-2339

Vetter Stone Co.

Architectural Building Stone - Marble Interior & Exterior

PO Drawer 38
Kasota, MN 56050

Phone 507-345-4568
FAX 507-345-4777

Vicor Corp.

Architectural Woodwork

52 Walnut Ave.
Elgin, IL 60120

Phone 708-695-7770

Vintage Wood Works

Order Direct - Victorian and Country Architectural Details

Highway 34 South, Box R
Quinlan, TX 75474

Send $2.00 for Catalog/Information

Mail Order Available

Credit Cards MC/VISA/DISCOVER

Phone 903-356-2158
FAX 903-356-3023

Visador Co.

Manufacturer - Beveled Leaded Glass for Entryways, Fiberglass & Marble Columns, Stairs & Stair Parts, Spiral Staircases

940 Visador Rd.
Jasper, TX 75951

Phone 409-384-2564
FAX 409-384-8409

W. F. Norman Corporation

Manufacturer - Factory Direct - Architectural Ornaments, Ceilings, Siding, Metal Roofing Shingles

PO Box 323
214 N. Cedar St.
Nevada, MO 64772

Send $3.00 for Catalog/Information

Mail Order Available

Phone 417-667-5552
Toll Free 800-641-4038
FAX 417-667-2708

Walter H. Weaber Sons, Inc.

Moulding, Jambs in Red Oak, White Oak, Poplar and Ash

R.D. #4 Box 1255
Lebanon, PA 17042

Phone 717-867-2212
FAX 717-867-1711

Western Moulding Company, Inc.

Pine Moulding, Jambs

PO Box 70
Snowflake, AZ 85937

Phone 602-536-2131
FAX 602-536-2133

Architectural Components
Westlake Architectural Antiques — Woodcraft Architectural Millwork Inc.

Westlake Architectural Antiques

*Architectural Antiques - Mantels, Doors,
Stained Glass, Chandeliers*

3315 Westlake Dr.
Austin, TX 78746

Send $5.00 for Catalog/Information

Phone 512-327-1110

William Jackson Co.

Fireplace Mantels

210 East 58th St.
New York, NY 10022

Phone 212-753-9400

Williams & Hussey Machine Co. Inc.

Wood Mouldings

PO Box 1149
Wilton, NH 03086

Phone 603-654-6828

Toll Free 800-258-1380

FAX 603-654-5446

Willis Lumber Company Inc.

*Manufacturer - Moulding, Paneling,
Flooring, Doors*

545 Millikan Ave.
PO Box 84
Washington, OH 43160

Mail Order Available

Phone 614-335-2601

Toll Free 800-346-3527

FAX 614-335-5757

Windham Millwork Inc.

Architectural Millwork, Moulding

PO Box 1358
Windham, ME 04062

Send $5.00 for Catalog/Information

Phone 207-892-3238

FAX 207-892-5905

Windsor Mill, Inc.

*Redwood Moulding, Jambs and Millwork,
Doors*

PO Box 39
Windsor, CA 95492

Phone 707-546-6373

FAX 707-838-7978

Winter Seal of Flint, Inc.

*Manufacturer - Windows and Glass
Sliding Doors*

18161 E 8 Mile Road
Eastpointe, MI 48021-3219

Phone 313-634-8261

Wm. H. Jackson Co.

Fireplace Furnishings & Mantels

210 East 58th St.
New York, NY 10022

Phone 212-753-9400

FAX 212-753-7872

Wohners Inc.

*Manufacturer - Architectural Components
- Mantels, Ornaments, Doors, Shelves*

29 Bergen Street
Englewood, NJ 07631

Send $5.00 for Catalog/Information

Phone 201-568-7307

FAX 201-568-7415

Woodcraft Architectural Millwork Inc.

Architectural Millwork

2323 Dean Ave.
Des Moines, IA 50317

Phone 515-262-5633

Architectural Components

The Complete Sourcebook

Architectural Components

Wooden Nickel Architectural Antique

Architectural Antiques - Mantels, Stained Glass, Victorian Furinture, Beveled Glass Entryways

1400-1414 Central Parkway
Cincinnati, OH 45210

Catalog/Information Available Free

Phone 513-241-2985
FAX 513-241-0842

Woodstone Company

Manufacturer - Order Direct - Architectural Woodwork, Windows, Doors

PO Box 223
Westminster, VT 05158

Send $3.00 for Catalog/Information

Mail Order Available

Phone 802-722-9217
Toll Free 800-682-8223
FAX 802-722-9528

Worthington Group, Ltd.

Manufacturer - Order Factory Direct - Architectural Products, Moulding, Columns, Domes

PO Box 868
Troy, AL 36081-0868

Mail Order Available

Credit Cards Accepted

Phone 205-566-4537
Toll Free 800-872-1608
FAX 205-566-5390

Wright's Stained Glass

Architectural Stained Glass Custom Frame Work - Oak, Ash, Cherry, Walnut

330 Winchester Ave.
Martinsburg, WV 25401

Catalog/Information Available Free

Mail Order Available

Phone 304-263-2502
FAX 304-267-2705

Yakima Manufacturing Co.

White Fir Moulding, Jambs

PO Box 1427
Yakima, WA 98907

Phone 509-248-2601
FAX 509-248-8627

Yellowstone Woodworks

Pine, Douglas Fir Moulding, Jambs

Div. of Brand S Corp.
PO Box 119
Livingston, MT 59047

Phone 406-222-8181
Toll Free 800-336-4306
FAX 406-222-8545

York Spiral Stairs

Manufacturer - Order Direct - Spiral Staircases - Red Oak, Mahogany in many Styles

Rt. 32 North
Vassalboro, ME 04962

Catalog/Information Available Free

Mail Order Available

Phone 207-872-5558
FAX 207-872-6731

Yuba River Moulding & Millwork, Inc.

Pine, Douglas Fir Moulding, Frames, Jambs

PO Box 1078
Yuba City, CA 95991

Phone 916-742-2168
FAX 916-742-7140

Zimmerman's Millwork & Cabinet

Millwork, Cabinets

159 Maxwell St.
Fayetteville, NC 28304

Phone 919-433-2051

The Complete Sourcebook

Bathroom

A-Ball Plumbing Supply

Discounts on large orders - Plumbing Fixtures - Contemporary, European, Nostalgic Basins, Tubs, Shower Heads, Faucets, Fittings, Kitchen Sinks

12210 SE 21st Ave.
Milwaukee, OR 97222

Catalog/Information Available Free

Mail Order Available

Credit Cards VISA/MC

Phone 503-228-0026
Toll Free 800-228-0134
FAX 503-228-0030

AAA Plumbing Pottery Corp.

Manufacturer - Plumbing Fixtures

PO Box 1340
Gadsden, AL 35902

Phone 205-538-7804
FAX 205-538-7807

ARDCO, Inc.

Curved Glass Shower Enclosures

Advanced Glass Products Div.
12400 S. Laramie Ave.
Chicago, IL 60658

Phone 708-388-4300

Absolute Accessories

Manufacturer - Bathroom Accessories

3261 Bolero Dr.
Chamblee, GA 30341

Phone 404-270-5770

Abundant Energy, Inc.

Design Guide - Glazing System for Sunrooms, Solariums

PO Box 307
Pine Island, NY 10969

Phone 914-258-4022
Toll Free 800-426-4859
FAX 914-258-4023

Ace Shower Door Co. Inc.

Manufacturer - Tub Enclosures, Shower Enclosures, Shower Doors, Sliding Mirror Doors

5 Skillman St.
Roslyn, NY 11576

Phone 516-484-4080
Toll Free 800-645-6374
FAX 516-621-8271

Allgood Shower Door Corp.

Shower Doors and Enclosures

981 W. 3rd St.
San Bernardino, CA 92410

Phone 714-889-3541
FAX 714-889-6181

Almost Heaven Hot Tubs

Retail & Wholesale Hot Tubs, Spas, Saunas

Rt. 5
Renick, WV 24966

Mail Order Available

Credit Cards VISA/MC/AMEX

Phone 304-497-2473
FAX 304-497-2698

American Shower Door Corp.

Manufacturer - Shower Doors & Enclosures

6920 E. Slauson Ave.
City of Commerce, CA 90030-0010

Phone 213-726-2478
Toll Free 800-421-2333
FAX 213-726-7469

American Standard

Bathroom Fixtures

One Centennial Plaza
PO Box 6820
Piscataway, NJ 08854-6820

Catalog/Information Available Free

Mail Order Available

Phone 908-980-3000
Toll Free 800-442-1902
FAX 908-980-3335

Antique Baths & Kitchens

Victorian Style Bath & Kitchen Fixtures

2220 Carlton Way
Santa Barbara, CA 93109

Send $2.00 for Catalog/Information

Mail Order Available

Phone 805-962-8598

Aqata Limited

Shower Enclosures

Unit 10, Sketchley Lane Ind, Est.
Hinckley, Leics LE10 3EN
Great Britain

Phone 011-44-455/251909
FAX 011-44-455/25176

Aqua Glass Corporation

Manufacturer - Tub & Shower Doors

PO Box 412
Industrial Park
Adamsville, TN 38310

Phone 901-632-0911

Aston Matthews

Bathrooms - Basins, Mixers, Showers, Faucets

141-147A Essex Road
Islington, London N1 25N
Great Britain

Phone 011-44-71-2267220
FAX 011-44-71-3545951

Barber Wilsons & Co. Ltd.

Showers, Taps, Mixers, Valves

Crawley Rd., Westbury Ave.
Wood Green, London N22 6AH
Great Britain

Phone 011-44-81-8883461

Barclay Products Co.

Antique Bathroom Accessories

424 N. Oakley Blvd.
Chicago, IL 60612

Catalog/Information Available Free

Phone 312-243-1444

Basco

Bathroom Cabinets, Doors, Tub & Shower Doors, Mirrors, Curved Glass Shower Doors

7201 Snider Rd.
Mason, OH 45040

Phone 513-573-1900
Toll Free 800-543-1938
FAX 513-573-1919

BathEase

Manufacturer - Plumbing Fixtures

2537 Frisco Drive
Clearwater, FL 34621

Phone 813-791-6656

Bathroom Jewlery

Bathroom Fixtures

16030 Arthur Street
Cerritos, CA 90701

Phone 310-407-2707
Toll Free 800-285-0885
FAX 310-407-2725

Bathroom

Bathroom Machineries — Cheviot Products Inc.

Bathroom Machineries

Victorian Bathroom Accessories, Restored Original Antique Plumbing Fixtures

495 Main St., Box 1020
Murphys, CA 95247

Send $3.00 for Catalog/Information

Mail Order Available

Credit Cards VISA/MC/AMEX

Phone 209-728-2031
FAX 209-728-2320

Baths From The Past Inc.

Victorian & Traditional Style Bathroom Fixtures and Faucets

83 East Water St.
Rockland, MA 02370

Send $5.00 for Catalog/Information

Mail Order Available

Credit Cards Accepted/Check

Phone 617-871-8530
Toll Free 800-697-3871
FAX 617-871-8533

Beach Craft, Inc.

Fiberglass Shower Stalls, Tubs

701-A Collier St.
Hannibal, MO 63401

Phone 314-221-4146

Black Country Heritage Ltd.

Bathroom Accessories

Britannia Ho, Mill St.
Brierley Hill, Worcs DY5 2TH
Great Britain

Phone 011-44-384/480810
FAX 011-44-384/482866

Blackhawk Marble Mfg.

Bathroom Fixture & Accessories

3342 Illinois Rt 26 S.
Freeport, IL 61032

Phone 815-223-5666
FAX 815-233-5273

Boston Tile Company

Tile

852 Providence Highway
Dedham, MA 02026

Phone 617-461-0406
FAX 617-329-4895

Brass & Traditional Sinks Ltd.

Solid Fireclay Sinks, Brass Accessories

Devauden Green
Chepstow, Gwent NP6 6PL
Great Britain

Phone 011-44-291/650738
FAX 011-44-291/650827

Broadway Industries

Bathroom Fixtures, Hardware

601 West 103rd St.
Kansas City, MO 64114

Send $5.00 for Catalog/Information

Credit Cards VISA/MC

Phone 816-942-8910
Toll Free 800-225-6365

Carlos Shower Doors Inc.

Shower Doors, Enclosures, Wardrobe Closet Doors, Mirrors, Windows

300 Kentucky St.
Bakersfield, CA 93305

Phone 805-327-5594
FAX 805-327-1628

Century Shower Door, Inc.

Manufacturer - Shower Doors

250 Lackawanna Avenue
West Paterson, NJ 07424

Toll Free 800-524-2578

Cheviot Products Inc.

Distributor - Bathroom Fixtures

200-1594 Kebet Way
Port Cogquitlam, B.C. V3C 5W9
Canada

Phone 604-464-8966
FAX 604-464-8993

Bathroom

The Complete Sourcebook

2 - 3

Clivus Multrum, Inc.

Manufacturer - Worldwide Shipping - Composting Toilet

1 Eliot Square
Cambridge, MA 02138

Catalog/Information Available Free

Mail Order Available

Phone 617-491-0051
Toll Free 800-425-4887
FAX 617-491-0053

Coastal Industries, Inc.

Manufacturer - Shower Doors, Enclosures

Shower Door Div.
3700 St. Johns Ind. Pkwy. W,PO Box 16091
Jacksonville, FL 32245

Phone 904-642-3970

Dina Division

Manufacturer - Marble Bathroom Accessories

303 Coons Blvd.
Oswego, KS 67356

Mail Order Available

Phone 316-795-4941
FAX 316-795-4998

Diston Industries Inc.

Shower & Mirror Closet Doors

3293 E. 11 Ave.
Hialeah, FL 33013

Phone 305-691-4141
FAX 305-691-0361

DuraGlaze Service Corp.

Antique Plumbing, Sinks, Bathtubs

2825 Bransford Ave.
Nashville, TN 37204

Phone 615-298-1787

EFRON America

Manufacturer - Shower Enclosures

2050 Henderson Dr.
Sharon Hill, PA 19079-1400

Phone 215-461-4700
Toll Free 800-543-3766
FAX 215-461-6200

Enerjee International

Heating Systems

32 S. Lafayette Ave.
Morrisville, PA 19067

Mail Order Available

Phone 215-295-0557
FAX 215-736-2328

F & M Plumbing Supply

Bathroom Fixtures

631 E. 9th
New York, NY 10009-6043

Phone 212-674-0545

FV America Corporation

Luxury Faucets & Bathroom Accessories

4000 Porett Drive
Gunree, Ill 60031

Phone 708-244-1234
FAX 708-244-1259

Franklin Brass Mfg. Co.

Bathroom Accessories

PO Box 5226
Culver City, CA 90231-5226

Phone 213-306-5944

Fuji Hardware Co., Ltd.

Glass for Shower Doors or Enclosures, Skylights, Windows

Valdes Associates
W9546 Hwy.18
Cambridge, WS 53523

Bathroom

G.M. Ketcham Co., Inc. — Hiawatha, Inc.

G.M. Ketcham Co., Inc.

Manufacturer - Glass Shower Enclosures, Medicine Cabinets

7331 William Ave., Suite 600
Allentown, PA 18106

Phone 215-391-9500
Toll Free 800-538-2446
FAX 215-391-9595

Garofalo Studio

Tub & Shower Enclosures, Doors, Panels, Wall Hanging Units

55 Florida St.
Farmingdale, NY 11735-6302

Phone 516-752-0215

Gemini Bath & Kitchen

Bath & Kitchen Faucets

3790 E. 44th St.
Suite 228
Tucson, AZ 85713

Toll Free 800-262-6252

Gilmer Potteries, Inc.

Manufacturer - Ceramic Bathroom Accessories

PO Box 1173
105 Warren Ave.
Gilmer, TX 75644

Phone 903-843-2509
FAX 903-843-3310

Global Mid-South Mfg. Co.

Bathroom Fixtures and Accessories

13901 SW 142 Ave.
Miami, FL 33186-6799

Phone 305-251-5585

Granite Lake Pottery

Order Direct - Pottery Bathroom Sinks, Tile

Route 9, PO Box 236
Munsonville, NH 03457

Mail Order Available

Credit Cards Bank Check

Phone 603-847-9908
Toll Free 800-443-9908

H & M Marble

Marble Bathroom Accessories

Div. of Eilers Products Ltd.
455 German School Rd., Paris
Ont, CAN N3L 3E1
Canada

Phone 519-442-4641
FAX 519-442-4641

H & W Plastics Inc.

Fiberglass - Bathtubs, Showers, Whirlpool Bath

PO Box 249
Moyock, NC 27958

Phone 919-435-6376

Hans Grohe Ltd.

Bathroom Accessories, Shower Enclosures, Taps, Mixers, Valves

Unit D2, Sandown Park Trading Est.
Royal Mills, Esher, Surrey
KT10 8BL
Great Britain

Phone 011-44-372/465655
FAX 011-44-372/470670

Harden Industries

Manufacturer - Shower, Bath & Kitchen Washerless Faucets

13813 S. Main St.
Los Angeles, CA 90061

Send $5.00 for Catalog/Information

Mail Order Available

Phone 310-532-7850
Toll Free 800-877-7850
FAX 310-532-9699

Hiawatha, Inc.

Manufacturer - Bathroom - Shower Door Hardware

4450 West 78th St. Circle
Bloomington, MN 55435

Phone 612-835-6850
FAX 612-835-2218

Bathroom

The Complete Sourcebook

2 - 5

Ideal-Standard Ltd.

Bathroom Accessories, Baths, Basins, Countertops, Bidets, Shower Enclosures, Taps, Mixers, Valves

PO Box 60, National Avenue
Kingston-upon Hull
HU5 4JE
Great Britain

Phone 011-44-482/46461
FAX 011-44-482/445886

Imperial Shower Door Co.

Shower Door Enclosures

2421 S. Susan St.
Santa Ana, CA 92704

Phone 714-957-3830
FAX 714-957-3839

Interbath Inc.

Manufacturer - Bathroom Shower Heads & Hardware

665 N. Baldwin Park Blvd.
City of Industry, CA 91746

Toll Free 800-800-2132

International Supply Co.

Bath Equipment and Supplies

2001C Kahal
Honolulu, HI 96819-2251

Phone 808-845-9788

J. M Mills

Shower & Window Curtains

Box 33-D
Islip, NY 11751

Send $4.95 for Catalog/Information

Mail Order Available

Jacuzzi Inc.

Steambath & Shower Combinations, Whirlpool Baths & Spas

100 N. Wiget Lane
PO Drawer J
Walnut Creek, CA 94596

Phone 415-938-7070
Toll Free 800-678-6889
FAX 415-938-3025

Jado Bathroom & Hardware Mfg. Co.

Faucets

4690 Calle Quetal
Camarillo, CA 93011

Phone 805-482-2666

Kallista

Whirlpool Baths, Shower Systems, Faucets, Sinks

Two Henry Adams St. #115
San Francisco, CA 94103

Phone 510-895-6400
FAX 510-895-6990

Kimstock Inc.

Fiberglass Tub, Shower Enclosures, Stalls

226 N. Lincoln Ave.
Corona, CA 91720-1893

Phone 714-546-6850

Kohler Awning, Inc.

Awnings

365 Nagel Dr.
Buffalo, NY 14225

Phone 716-685-3333

Kraft

Plumbing - Bathroom Fixtures, Hardware

306 East 61st St.
New York, NY 10021

Send $10.00 for Catalog/Information

Phone 212-838-2214
FAX 212-644-9254

LaMont Ltd.

Manufacturer - Bathroom Accessories - Wicker Bath Shelves & Hampers

N. Bluff Rd., PO Box 399
Burlington, IA 52601-0399

Phone 319-753-5131
FAX 319-753-0946

Bathroom

Lasco Bathware

Manufacturer - Bath Fixtures
3255 East Miraloma Avenue
Anaheim, CA 92806
Toll Free 800-877-0464

Lenape Products, Inc.

Bathroom Fixtures
PO Box 117
Pennington, NJ 08534-0117
Phone 609-737-0206
FAX 609-737-0625

Lippert Corp.

Vanity Tops, Bath Tubs, Showers
PO Box 219-A
Menomonee Falls, WI 53051
Phone 414-255-2350
FAX 414-255-2304

M & H Design & Home Center

Bath Equipment & Supplies
460 Black Horse Pike
Blackwood, NJ 08012-1051
Phone 609-228-1300

MDM Marble Co. Inc.

Bath Tubs, Vanity Tops
3040 Industrial 33rd St.
Fort Pierce, FL 33450
Phone 407-465-6700

Marcello Marble & Tile PLS

Bathroom Fixtures & Accessories
796 Boston Post Rd.
Marlborough, MA 01752-3703
Phone 508-481-6336

McPherson Inc.

Flush Up Basement Toilet
Box 15133
Tampa, FL 33684
Phone 813-876-6392

Merit Cabinet Distributors

Custom Vanities, Cabinets, Formica Tops, Marble Tops,
40 Vreeland Ave.
Totowa, NJ 07512
Phone 201-256-3748
FAX 201-256-4683

Meynell Valves Ltd.

Shower - Taps, Mixers, Valves
Bushbury
Wolverhampton WV10 9LB
Great Britain
Phone 011-44-902/28621
FAX 011-44-902/26500

Midland Manufacturing Corp.

Manufacturer - Sliding Shower & Tub Doors
162 E. Industry Ct.
Deer Park, NY 11729
Catalog/Information Available Free
Phone 516-586-5400

Milano Marble Co., Inc.

Marble Vanity & Table Tops, Bathtubs, Wall Panels
2525 National Dr.
Garland, TX 75041
Phone 214-271-5444

Miracle Method Bathroom Restoration

Reproduction Hardware & Faucets
701 Center St.
Ludlow, MA 01056
Send $4.00 for Catalog/Information
Mail Order Available
Phone 413-589-0769
FAX 413-583-3276

Mission Pipe & Supply

Bathroom Fixtures
32107 Alipaz
San Juan Capistrano, CA 92675
Phone 714-493-4591

The Complete Sourcebook

Monarch Metal Products Corp.

Bathroom Lighting Fixtures
1901 Estes Ave.
Elk Grove, IL 60007
Phone 708-437-5600

Nope

Shower Curtain - Waterproof Cotton
PO Box 39179
Baltimore, MD 21212
Credit Cards Accepted
Toll Free 800-323-2811

Nordic Showers

Steam Showers, Saunas, Enclosures
Holland Road
Oxted Surrey
RH8 9BZ
Great Britain
Phone 011-44-883/71611
FAX 011-44-883/716970

Ohmega Salvage

Antique - Faucets, Sinks, Tubs, Toilets
2407 San Pablo Ave.
Berkely, CA 94702
Phone 510-843-7368

Old & Elegant Distributing

Faucets, Sinks, Door Knobs, Tile, Hardware
10203 Main St. Lane
Bellevue, WA 98004
Mail Order Available
Phone 206-455-4660

Ole Fashion Things

Nationwide Shipping - Clawfoot Bathtubs, Pedestal Lavatories, Plumbing Hardware, Architectural Ornaments
402 Southwest Evangeline
Lafayette, LA 70501
Send $6.00 for Catalog/Information
Mail Order Available
Credit Cards VISA/MC/Money Order
Phone 318-234-4800

Omega Too

Antique & Reproduction Sinks, Tubs, Windows, Ornaments, Lighting
2204 San Pablo Ave.
Berkeley, CA 94702
Mail Order Available
Phone 510-843-7363

PE O'Hair & Co.

Bathroom Fixtures
6300 District Blvd.
Bakersfield, CA 93313
Phone 805-398-0811

Pacific Faucets

Manufacturer - Faucets
8966D Benson Avenue
Montclair, CA 91763
Phone 714-982-9281

Perkins & Powell

Bathroom Accessories, Furniture, Door & Window Hardware
Div. of Samuel Heath & Sons PLC
Cobden Wks, Leopold St., Birmingham
B12 0UJ
Great Britain
Phone 011-44-21/7722303
FAX 011-44-21/7723334

Peter Goldberger

Designer Hardware - Faucets, Doorknobs, Bath Accessories
34 Wildwood Road
NW Rochester, NY 14616
Phone 914-834-1182

Phylrich International

Plumbing & Porcelain Fixtures
1000 No. Orange Drive
Los Angeles, CA 90038
Catalog/Information Available Free
Send $15.00 for Catalog/Information
Phone 213-467-3143
Toll Free 800-421-3190
FAX 213-871-8021

Bathroom

Pipe Dreams — SEPCO Industries Inc.

Pipe Dreams

Will service overseas customers -
Edwardian, Victorian, Modern Bathrooms
Tubs, Sinks, Tile, Shower, Toilets

72 Gloucester Rd.
London   SW7 4QT
Great Britain

Catalog/Information Available Free

Phone 011-44-71/2253978

FAX 011-44-71/5898841

Plastic Creations Inc.

Manufacturer - Acrylic Whirlpool Baths

1023 S. Hamilton St.
Dalton, GA 30720

Catalog/Information Available Free

Phone 706-278-7090

Toll Free 800-868-0254

Porcher Ltd.

Manufacturer - Bathroom & Kitchen
Fixtures, Faucets

3618 E. LaSalle
Phoenix, AZ 85040

Toll Free 800-359-3261

Price Pfister Inc.

Manufacturer - Brass Plumbers' Supply -
Kitchen & Bath Faucets, Showerheads,

13500 Paxton Street, PO Box 4518
Pacoima, CA 91331

Phone 818-896-1141

FAX 818-897-4047

Quintessentials

Bath Fixtures

515 Amsterdam Ave.
New York, NY 10024

Phone 212-877-1919

FAX 212-721-6172

Rapetti Faucets

Manufacturer - Faucets

George Blocher Ltd.
Zero High Street
Plainville, MA 02762

Toll Free 800-688-5500

Raphael Ltd.

Manufacturer - Luxury Bathroom Faucets
& Sinks , Showerheads

PO Box 390
Brookfield, WI 53008

Phone 414-461-5400

Toll Free 800-727-4235

Reflections USA

Manufacturer - Custom Designed
Shower Enclosures

65 Sea Cliff Ave.
Glen Cove, NY 11542

Phone 516-676-0010

Toll Free 800-759-9992

FAX 516-676-1471

Rockingham Plumbing Supply

Bathroom Fixtures

507 Mill Rd.
Rockingham, NC 28379-4238

Phone 919-895-5208

Roman Limited

Bath & Shower Enclosures, Screens

Hurworth Road,Aycliffe Industrial Estate
Newton Aycliffe, County Durham
DL5 6UD
Great Britain

Phone 011-44-325/311318

FAX 011-44-325/319889

SEPCO Industries Inc.

Manufacturer - Decorative Plumbing
Accessories - Faucets, Showerheads

491 Wortman Ave.
Brooklyn, NY 11208

Phone 718-257-2800

FAX 718-257-2144

The Complete Sourcebook

Sherle Wagner

Bathroom Fixtures, Wallcover, Ceramic Tile

60 East 57th St.
New York, NY 10022

Send $5.00 for Catalog/Information

Mail Order Available

Phone 212-758-3300

Sherwood Shower Door Co.

Shower Doors & Enclosures

420 E. Colorado St.
Glendale, CA 91205

Phone 818-240-5371

Shower-Rite Corp.

Cut Glass Tub Doors with Chrome, Brass, or Antique Brass

7519 S. Greenwood Ave.
Chicago, IL 60619

Phone 312-483-5400

Showerlux U.S.A.

Shower Enclosures

1 Permalume Place NW
PO Box 20202
Atlanta, GA 30318

Phone 800-387-7194

Toll Free 800-333-8326

FAX 416-752-8209

Showerlux UK Ltd.

Shower Enclosures

Freepost, Sibree Rd.
Coventry CV3 4BR
Great Britain

Phone 011-44-203/639400

Solid Surface Products Inc.

Order Direct - Bathroom Vanity Top & Sink

PO Box 1461
Cornelius, NC 28031

Catalog/Information Available Free

Mail Order Available

Credit Cards Accepted

Toll Free 800-891-8677

St. Thomas Creations Inc.

Luxury Bathroom Fixtures

9270 Trade Place, Suite 100
San Diego, CA 92126

Phone 619-530-1940

Toll Free 800-767-2284

FAX 619-530-1893

Sterling Plumbing Group

Tub & Shower Enclosures

2900 Golf Road
Rolling Meadows, IL 60008

Phone 708-734-4626

Toll Free 800-248-3266

FAX 708-734-4767

Sunflower Shower Company

Order Direct - Victorian Style Showerhead

PO Box 4218
Seattle, WA 98104

Catalog/Information Available Free

Mail Order Available

Phone 206-722-1232

FAX 206-722-1321

Sunrise Specialty

Nationwide Shipping - Victorian Bathroom Fixtures - Clawfoot Tubs, Water Closets, Pedestal Sinks, Faucets, Shower Heads

5540 Doyle St.
Emeryville, CA 94068

Send $2.00 for Catalog/Information

Mail Order Available

Phone 510-654-1794

Toll Free 800-444-4280

FAX 510-654-5775

Swan Mfg. Co.

Glass Shower Doors

65 Kingston Ave.
Columbus, OH 43207

Phone 614-443-6593

FAX 614-443-1033

Bathroom

T & S Brass & Bronze Works Inc.

Faucets, Fittings, Plumbing Specialties
Rte. 4, Old Buncombe Rd.
Travelers Rest, SC 29690

Phone 803-834-4102
FAX 803-834-3518

The Broadway Collection

Bathroom Hardware in many Styles
1010 West Santa Fe
PO Box 1210
Olathe, KS 66061-1210

Send $5.00 for Catalog/Information

Phone 913-782-6244
FAX 913-782-0647

The Chicago Faucet Company

Bathroom & Kitchen Faucets
2100 South Nuclear Dr.
Des Plaines, IL 60018

Phone 708-803-5000
FAX 708-298-3101

The Faucet Factory

Reproduction Faucets, Sinks, Tubs
19 Thompson Street
Winchester, MA 01890

Send $5.00 for Catalog/Information

Toll Free 800-270-0028

The Fixture Exchange

*Shipped Direct - Plumbing Fixtures -
Tubs, Pedestal Sinks, Door Hardware,
Architectural Columns*
PO Box 307
Bainbridge, GA 31717

Send $5.00 for Catalog/Information

Mail Order Available

Credit Cards MC/VISA/AMEX

Phone 912-246-4938
FAX 912-246-1186

The Sink Factory

Bathroom Fixtures, Faucets, Accessories
2140 San Pablo Ave.
Berkeley, CA 94702

Send $3.00 for Catalog/Information

Mail Order Available

Phone 510-540-8193
Toll Free 800-653-4926
FAX 510-540-8212

The Soft Bathtub Co.

Manufacturer - Plumbing Fixtures
International Cushioned Products
202-8360 Bridgeport Rd.
Richmond, British Columbia
Canada

Toll Free 800-882-7638

Thermo Spas Inc.

Manufacturer - Spas, Bathtubs, Saunas
155 East St.
Wallingford, CT 06492

Catalog/Information Available Free

Toll Free 800-231-8000

Tomlin Industries Inc.

Vanity Tops, Acrylic Shower Stalls & Tubs
623 Colby Dr.
Waterloo
Ont., CAN N2V 1B4
Canada

Phone 519-884-5290
FAX 519-746-3114

Trevi Showers

Shower Accessories, Taps, Mixers, Valves
PO Box 60, National Ave.
Kingston-upon Hull
HU5 4JE
Great Britain

Phone 011-44-482/470788
FAX 011-44-482/445886

The Complete Sourcebook

Triton PLC

Bathroom Accessories, Hardware, Baths
Triton Ho, Newdegate St
Nuneaton, Warwickshire
CV11 4EU
Great Britain

Phone 011-44-203/344441
FAX 011-44-203/349828

Tub-Master Corp.

Manufacturer - Plumbing Fixtures
413 Virginia Drive
Orlando, FL 32803

Toll Free 800-327-1911

Universal Bath Systems

Bath Liner & Wall Surround System
165B Front St.
Chicopee, MA 01013

Phone 413-592-4791
Toll Free 800-553-0120
FAX 413-592-6876

Valley Fibrebath Ltd.

Tubs, Showers
Comp. 65 Pallisade
Armstrong
B.C., CAN V0E 1B0
Canada

Phone 604-546-8701

Vassallo Precast Mfg. Corp.

Terrazzo Shower Floors
103 Jersey
West Babylon, NY 11704-1206

Phone 516-643-5986

Villeroy & Boch (USA) Inc.

Bathroom Fixtures & Tile
Interstate 80 at New Maple Ave.
Pine Brook, NJ 07058

Phone 201-575-0550
FAX 201-575-1279

Villeroy & Boch AG

*Manufacturer - Bathroom Fixtures,
Ceramic Wall & Floor Tile*
10120
Mettlach 1 D-W-6642
Germany

Phone 011-49-684/811
FAX 011-49-684/81266

Villeroy & Boch Ltd.

*Manufacturer - Bathroom Fixtures,
Ceramic Tile*
267 Merton Rd.
London SW18 5JS
Great Britain

Phone 011-44-81/8714028
FAX 011-44-81/8703720

Vintage Plumbing

Bathroom Fixtures
9645 Sylvia Ave.
Northridge, CA 91324

Mail Order Available

Phone 818-772-1721

Vitistor's Catalog

*Antique and Reproduction Bathroom
Fixtures*
19 West Bradford Ave.
Sonora, CA 95370

Catalog/Information Available Free

Mail Order Available

Phone 209-728-2031

W. T. Weaver & Sons

Bathroom Fixtures & Hardware
1208 Wisconsin Ave.
Washington, DC 20007

Send $2.50 for Catalog/Information

Phone 202-333-4200
FAX 202-333-4154

Bathroom

Water Faucets – Wirth-Salander Studios

Water Faucets

Manufacturer - Faucets

3001 Fedhill, Building 5
Suite 108
Costa Mesa, CA 92626

Toll Free 800-243-4420

Water Saver Faucet Co.

Faucets, Shower Heads

701 W. Erie
Chicago, IL 60610

Phone 312-666-5500

FAX 312-666-8597

Watercolors Inc.

Manufacturer - Bathroom Fixtures

Garrison-on-Hudson
Garrison, NY 10524

Send $5.00 for Catalog/Information

Phone 914-424-3327

FAX 914-424-3169

Western Pottery Co. Inc.

Bathroom Fixtures

11911 Industrial Ave.
South Gate, CA 90280

Phone 213-636-8124

FAX 213-630-5040

Wirth-Salander Studios

Handpainted - One of a kind Tile & Sinks

132 Washington St.
South Norwalk, CT 06854

Phone 203-852-9449

FAX 203-866-5390

Bathroom

The Complete Sourcebook

2 - 13

Building Supply

18th Century Hardware Co. Inc. — A.E. Gombert Lumber Co.

Building Supply

18th Century Hardware Co. Inc.

Order Direct - Nationwide Shipping - Reproduction Hardware - Will duplicate any item, pattern

131 East Third St.
Derry, PA 15627

Send $4.00 for Catalog/Information

Mail Order Available

Credit Cards   Check

Phone 412-694-2708

A & B Industries Inc.

Brass & Bronze Hardware

1261 Andersen Dr., Suite C
San Rafael, CA 94901

Phone 415-258-9300

A & M Wood Specialty Inc.

Shipping to Canada & USA, Hardwood, Plywood, Veneers

358 Eagle St. N
PO Box 32040, Cambridge
Canada

Credit Cards VISA/Check

Phone 519-653-9322
Toll Free 800-265-2759
FAX 519-653-3441

A & S Window Associates, Inc.

Steel Windows and Doors

88-19 76th Ave.
Glendale, NY 11385

Phone 718-275-7900

A Touch of Brass

Registers, Hardware, Stair Rods

9052 Chevrolet Drive
Ellicott City, MD 21042

Catalog/Information Available Free

Phone 410-666-5961
Toll Free 800-272-7734
FAX 410-750-7275

A. Johnson Co.

Lumber

Route 116
Bristol, VT 05443

Phone 802-453-4884

A. Moorhouse Co.

Roof Trusses

PO Box 96
Glidden, IA 51401

Phone 712-659-3795

A.A. Used Boiler Supply Co.

Reconditioned Cast Iron Gas & Oil Burners

8720 Ditmas Ave.
Brooklyn, NY 11236

Phone 718-385-2111

A.E. Gombert Lumber Co.

Pine Mouldings, Flooring, Paneling

PO Box 58
North Tonawanda, NY 14120

Phone 716-692-4500

The Complete Sourcebook

A.J.P. Weslock Industries Co.

Door Hardware

13344 S. Main St.
Los Angeles, CA 90061

Phone 213-327-2770

FAX 213-324-4624

A/S Johs. Gronseth & Co.

*Member - European International
Federation of Natural Stone Industry*

Stenindustri
PO Box 81 Skoyen
N-0212 0SL0
Norway

Phone 011-47-22-50/4350

FAX 011-47-22-50/1915

AAA Aluminum Products Ltd.

*Manufacturer - Wholesale - Canada &
USA Nationwide Shipping - Aluminum
Patio Covers, Awnings*

1710 Gilmore Ave.
Burnaby,B.C.
CAN V5C 4T3
Canada

Phone 604-298-7241

Toll Free 800-543-5546

FAX 604-294-2411

ABC Glass Block Company

American and German Glass Block

3560 N. Bronco St.
Las Vegas, NV 89108-4833

Phone 702-644-3008

FAX 702-644-7731

ACIF Ceramiche S.R.L.

*Imported Tile - Bath & Kitchen - Floor and
Wall*

US Agent Mr. Giuseppe Adriani
3811 NE. 2nd Ave.
Miami, FL 33137

Phone 305-573-4418

FAX 305-573-4605

ALCOA Building Products

Roofing, Vinyl Siding

PO Box 3900
Peoria, IL 61612-3900

Toll Free 800-962-6973

AMOCO Foam Products Co.

Manufacturer - Foam Insulation

400 Northridge
Rd., Suite 1000
Atlanta, GA 30350

Phone 404-587-0535

Toll Free 800-241-4402

ARMAC Brassfounders Group Ltd.

*Brass & Bronze Victorian & Edwardian
Window and Door Hardware*

60, Staniforth St.
Birmingham B4 7DN.
Great Britain

Phone 011-44-21-3594821

FAX 011-44-21-3594698

ASC Pacific Inc.

Manufacturer - Metal Roofing Systems

2110 Enterprise Blvd.
West Sacramento, CA 95691

Phone 916-372-6851

Toll Free 800-726-2727

AWNCO Inc.

Awnings

9301 S. Western Ave.
Chicago, IL 60620

Phone 312-239-1511

AWSCO

Manufacturer - Round Top Windows

4301 N. Western Ave.
Dayton, OH 45427

Phone 513-263-1053

Building Supply

Abatron Inc.

Building Restoration Compounds
5501 95th Ave.
Kenosha, IL 53144

Catalog/Information Available Free

Mail Order Available

Credit Cards MC/VISA/AMEX

Phone 708-426-2200

FAX 708-426-5966

Abet Laminati

Laminate Surfacing - Walls, Countertops, Flooring
100 Hollister Rd.
Teterboro, NJ 07608

Phone 201-941-0462

Toll Free 800-228-2238

FAX 201-941-0008

Able Fabricators Inc.

Roof Trusses
N. 1407 Elm
Spokane, WA 99201

Phone 509-326-0427

Absolute Bathroom Boutique

Manufacturer - Plumbing Fixtures
Bridgewater Commons
400 Commons Way
Bridgewater, NJ 08807

Phone 908-725-5400

Absolute Coatings Inc.

Manufacturer - Wood Finish & Stains in Gloss and Satin for Floors, Doors, Furniture, Cabinets, Railings
38 Portman Road
New Rochelle, NY 10801

Phone 914-636-0700

Toll Free 800-221-8010

FAX 914-636-0822

Accents In Stone

Wholesale - Marble & Granite - Countertops, Showers, Floors, Walls, Surrounds, Moulding, Trim, Saddles
3123 Lee Place
Bellmore, NY 11710

Phone 516-781-2799

FAX 516-781-0203

Accurate Aluminum Products, Inc.

Manufacturer - Aluminum - Downspouts, Gutters, Patio Covers
370 Lemon Lane
Casselberry, FL 32707

Phone 407-831-1606

Acme Brick Co.

Glass Block System
PO Box 425
Ft. Worth, TX 76101

Toll Free 800-932-2263

Acme Plumbing Specialties

Plumbing Specialties
315 Franklin Ave.
Franklin Square, NY 11010

Phone 516-326-1700

Acorn Manufacturing Co. Inc.

Cabinet, Door & Shutter Hardware
PO Box 31
Mansfield, MA 02048

Mail Order Available

Phone 508-339-4500

Toll Free 800-835-0121

Actiengesellschaft

Manufacturer - Ceramic Wall Tile
Norddeutsche Steingutfabrik
700018 Bremen 70 D-W-2820
Germany

Phone 011-49-421/661011

Building Supply

The Complete Sourcebook

3 - 3

AcuTruss Industries Ltd.

Roof Trusses

4109 25th Ave.
Vernon, B.C. CAN V1T 7G9
Canada

Phone 604-545-3215

FAX 604-542-6370

Adam Lumber Inc.

Roof Trusses

40 Allen St.
Waterloo, Que, CAN J0E 2N0
Canada

Phone 514-539-1858

FAX 514-539-2585

Adams Stair Works Carpentry Inc.

Order Direct - Stair Parts

1975 Johns Drive
Glenview, IL 60025

Credit Cards VISA/MC

Phone 708-657-7127

FAX 708-657-6802

Addkison Hardware Co. Inc.

Door & Cabinet Hardware

126 E. Amite St.
PO Box 102
Jackson, MS 39205

Toll Free 800-821-2750

FAX 601-354-1916

Adelmann & Clark Inc.

Designer Hardwoods, Lumber, Paneling, Trim, Millwork

Rt. 93 & 328
PO Box 478
McArthur, OH 45651

Phone 614-596-5271

FAX 614-596-4456

Adonis Forest Products, Inc.

Hardwood Lumber

PO Box 35
New Martinsville, WV 26155

Phone 304-334-3012

Advance Technologies, Inc.

Sunrooms, Solariums

PO Box 617
Clifton Park, NY 12065

Aetna Plywood, Inc.

Plywood, Particle Board, Hardboard

1731 N. Elston Ave.
Chicago, IL 60622

Phone 312-276-7100

Aexcel Corp.

Paint, Primers, Finish, Coatings, Enamels

PO Box 780
Mentor, OH 44061

Phone 216-974-3800

FAX 216-974-3808

Agrob-Wessel-Servais AG

Manufacturer - Ceramic Wall & Floor Tile

2540 Siemensstr 6-12
Bonn1 D-W-5330 Germany
Germany

Phone 011-49-228/64820

FAX 011-49-2286482366

Ailene Lumber Inc.

Roof & Floor Trusses

2241 Industrial Blvd.
Abilene, TX 79602

Phone 915-698-4465

Albany Hardware Specialty Mfg. Co. Inc.

Manufacturer - Shed, Garage Lock

PO Box 71, Hwy 14 North
Viroqua, WI 54665

Catalog/Information Available Free

Phone 608-637-8427

FAX 608-637-8427

Building Supply

Albany Woodworks Inc. – Alter Design Inc.

Albany Woodworks Inc.

Antique Building Materials, Heart Pine Flooring, Doors, Cabinetry, Paneling, Beams

PO Box 729
Albany, LA 70711

Phone 504-567-1155

FAX 504-567-2417

Albeni Falls Building Supply

Building Supply

114 Albeni Falls
Newport, WA 99156

Phone 208-437-3153

Albert Gunther

French Terracotta Wall & Floor Tile

36 W. Biddle St.
Baltimore, MD 21201

Send $1.00 for Catalog/Information

Mail Order Available

Phone 301-837-7437

Alfa Ceramiche

Imported Ceramic Tile - Bath & Kitchen - Wall & Floor

C/O Riwal Ceramiche S.R.L.
Via Ghiarola Nuova 101, 41042 Fiorano
Italy

Phone 011-39-536/851503

FAX 011-39-536/851502

All American Wood Register Co.

Wood Registers

239 E. Main St.
Cary, IL 60013

Catalog/Information Available Free

Phone 708-639-0393

FAX 708-639-0157

All-Phase Electric Supplies

Electric Supplies

4625 Clay SW
Wyoming, MI 49508-3068

Phone 616-538-5520

Allentown Paint Division

Paint

PO Box 597
Allen & Graham
Allentown, PA 18105

Phone 215-433-4273

FAX 215-433-6116

Allied Building Products Corp.

Roofing, Siding, Wallboard, Skylights, Lumber, Vinyl Replacement Windows

15 East Union Ave.
East Rutherford, NJ 07073

Phone 201-935-0800

Alpine Engineer Products Inc.

Manufacturer - Wood Roof & Floor Trusses, I-Beams & Headers, Hardware

National Headquarters
PO Box 2225
Pompano Beach, FL 33061

Phone 305-781-3333

Toll Free 800-735-8055

Alro Plumbing Specialty Co. Inc.

Plumbing Specialties

410 Flushing Ave.
Brooklyn, NY 11205

Phone 718-875-5166

Alside

Manufacturer - Vinyl Siding, Shutters

3773 State Road
PO Box 2010
Akron, OH 44309

Phone 216-929-1811

Alter Design Inc.

Beveled Glass

PO Box 131, 6 Pumpkin Pine Rd.
Natick, MA 01760

Phone 508-653-7399

Building Supply

The Complete Sourcebook

3 - 5

Alumax Aluminum Corp.

Building Products - Gutters, Downspouts, Window Wells

Home Products Div.
PO Box 4515
Lancaster, PA 17604

Phone 717-299-3711

Aluminum Industries of Arkansas

Vinly & Aluminum Siding

300 Phillips Rd.
North Little Rock, AR 72117

Catalog/Information Available Free

Toll Free 800-521-1234

Amaru Tile

Distributor - Ceramic Italian Tile Monocottura, Bicottura, Terracotta, Handmade, Inserts, Borders, Special Pieces (Floor, Wall, Kitchen/Bath)

73 Sherwood Avenue
Farmingdale, NY 11735

Phone 516-752-8999
Toll Free 800-242-8991
FAX 516-752-8991

Amdega Ltd.

Manufacturer - Sunrooms

PO Box 713
Glenview, IL 60025

Phone 708-729-7212
Toll Free 800-922-0110
FAX 708-729-7214

American Building Component

Floor & Roof Trusses

6250 Dougherty Rd.
Dublin, CA 94566

Phone 415-828-0400

American Building Components

Building Components

6975 Danville Rd.
Nicholasville, KY 40356

Phone 606-887-4406

American Building Restoration

Restoration Products

9720 South 60th St.
Franklin, WI 53132

Toll Free 800-346-7532

American China

Manufacturer - Plumbing Fixtures

3618 East LaSalle
Phoenix, AZ 85040

Toll Free 800-551-0208

American Energy Technologies Inc.

Solar Water Heaters

Box 1865
Green Cove Springs, FL 32043

Phone 904-284-0552

American Glass & Mirror Corp.

Glass & Mirrors

3026 N. Cicero Ave.
Chicago, IL 60646

Phone 312-286-8484
FAX 312-286-8478

American Home Supply

Brass Hardware, Antique Locks, Doorknobs

191 Lost Lane Lane
Campbell, CA 95008

Send $2.00 for Catalog/Information

Mail Order Available

Credit Cards Accepted

Phone 408-246-1962

American International

Distributor - Ceramic Italian Tile Monocottura, Bicottura, Terracotta, Inserts, Borders, Steps for Floor, Wall, Kitchen/Bath

850 Pratt Boulevard
Elk Grove Village, IL 60007

Phone 708-364-5400
FAX 708-364-5404

Building Supply

American Marazzi Tile — Androck Hardware Corp.

American Marazzi Tile

Manufacturer - Ceramic Tile
359 Clay Road
Sunnyvale, TX 75182
　　　　　　Phone 214-226-0110
　　　　　　FAX 214-226-5629

American Marble Co., Inc.

Marble Floor Tile, Vanity Tops, Tubs
2516 3rd Ave. S.
Birmingham, AL 35233
　　　　　　Phone 205-328-0384
　　　　　　FAX 205-328-0387

American Olean Tile Co.

Manufacturer - Ceramic Tile
1000 Cannon Ave.
PO Box 271
Lansdale, PA 19446
　　　　　　Phone 215-855-1111
　　　　　　Toll Free 800-678-1112
　　　　　　FAX 215-393-2784

American Solar Network

Solar Water Heater
5840 Gibbons Dr.#H
Carmichael, CA 95608-6903
Mail Order Available
Credit Cards Check/Money Order
　　　　　　Phone 916-481-7200
　　　　　　FAX 916-481-7203

American Tack & Decorative Hardware

Decorative Hardware
25 Robert Pitt Dr.
Monsey, NY 10952
　　　　　　Phone 914-352-2400
　　　　　　FAX 914-425-3554

American Thermal Products Inc.

Manufacturer - Wholesale - Insulation
9220 Bonita Beach Rd. #111
Bonita Springs, FL 33923
　　　　　　Phone 813-992-0566
　　　　　　FAX 813-992-9152

Amerock Corporation

Window Hardware, Decorative Hardware
Window Hardware Division
PO Box 7018, 4000 Auburn St.
Rockford, IL 61125-7018
　　　　　　Phone 815-961-7600
　　　　　　FAX 815-961-7670

Amsterdam Corporation

Dutch Handpainted Tiles
150 East 58th St., 9th floor
New York, NY 10155
Send $3.00 for Catalog/Information
Mail Order Available
　　　　　　Phone 212-644-1350
　　　　　　FAX 212-935-6291

An Affair of the Hearth

Fireplace Collectibles
PO Box 95174
Oklahoma City, OK 73143
Catalog/Information Available Free
Credit Cards VISA/MC
　　　　　　Toll Free 800-755-5488

Andrews & Sons (Marbles & Tiles)

Ceramic Tile, Marble, Granite
324-330 Meanwood Rd.
Leeds LS7 2JE
Great Britain
　　　　　　Phone 011-44-532/624751

Andrews Distributing Co.

Heat Pumps
5411 Trebor Lane
Knoxville, TN 37914-6438
　　　　　　Phone 615-522-1221

Androck Hardware Corp.

Hardware
711 19th St.
Rockford, IL 61104
　　　　　　Phone 815-229-1144

Building Supply

The Complete Sourcebook　　　　　　*3 - 7*

Angelo Amaru Tile & Bath Collection

Ceramic Tile Collection - Bicottura, Terracotta, Handmade, Steps, Specialty Pieces for Wall, Floor, Kitchen/Bath

8017 Tilghman St.
Allentown, PA 18104

Phone 215-821-4883

FAX 215-821-4055

Anglo-American Brass Co.

Reproduction Brass Hardware

4146 Mitzi Drive
San Jose, CA 95117

Catalog/Information Available Free

Mail Order Available

Phone 408-246-0203

Ann Sacks Tile & Stone

Distributor - Ceramic Tile Terracotta, Handmade, Steps for Floor, Wall, Kitchen/Bath

8120 NE 33rd Drive
Portland, OR 97211

Phone 503-222-2605

Toll Free 800-488-8453

FAX 503-222-4410

Anthony Forest Product Co.

Manufacturer - Lumber, Beams, Flooring, Paneling, Log Cabin Siding

PO Box 1877
El Dorado, AR 71730

Phone 501-862-3414

Toll Free 800-221-2326

FAX 501-862-6502

Antiche Ceramiche D'Talia (ACIT) S.R.L.

Imported Tile Floor & Wall - Bath & Kitchen

US Agent Arturo Mastelli
115 Ocean Lane Drive
Key Biscayne, FL 33149

Antioch Building Materials

Building Supplies

PO Box 870
Antioch, CA 94509

Phone 415-432-3828

Antique Builders Hardware

Antique Hardware

10317 Meandering Way
Ft. Smith, AR 72903

Send $2.00 for Catalog/Information

Mail Order Available

Phone 501-452-4185

Antique Hardware Store

Retail - Antique Bath Fixtures, Hardware, Lighting Fixtures

9730 Easton Rd., Rt. 611
Kintnersville, PA 18930

Send $2.00 for Catalog/Information

Mail Order Available

Credit Cards Accepted

Phone 215-847-2447

Toll Free 800-422-9982

FAX 215-847-5628

Apache Products Company

Polyisocyanurate Insulations

905 23rd Ave.
Meridian, MS 39301-5018

Apex Gutter Systems Ltd.

Gutters, Mouldings, Rooflights

Esgair Farm Est.
Llanbrynmair, Powys SY19 7DU
Great Britain

Phone 011-44-650/521496

FAX 011-44-650/521505

Appalachian Stove & Fab

Manufacturer - Wood & Gas Stoves, Fireplace Equipment

329 Emma Rd.
Asheville, NC 28806-3822

Phone 704-253-0164

FAX 704-254-7803

Building Supply

Aquatek Systems, Inc.

Manufacturer - Ground Water Heat Pump

30 Manhan St.
Waterbury, CT 06722

Phone 203-574-1162

Architectural Antique Warehouse

_Architectural Antiques - Plumbing
Fixtures, Lighting, Mirrors, Mantels,
Columns, Ceilings_

PO Box 3065, Station D
Ottawa ON K1P 6H6
Canada

Phone 613-526-1818

FAX 613-526-1093

Arden Forge

18th & 19th Century Hardware

301 Brinton's Bridge Rd.
West Chester, PA 19382

Phone 215-399-1530

Arius Tile Co.

Retail - Floor & Mural Tiles

PO Box 5497
Santa Fe, NM 87502

Send $3.00 for Catalog/Information

Mail Order Available

Credit Cards Accepted

Phone 505-988-8966

Toll Free 800-362-7487

Armstar

Marble Floor Tiles & Wall Panels

Box 820
Lenior City, TN 37771

Phone 615-986-4040

Arnold-Missouri Corp.

Manufacturer - Ceramic Tile

3905 Forest Park Blvd.
St. Louis, MO 63108

Phone 314-371-2200

FAX 314-371-2214

Arsco Manufacturing Co.

Manufacturer - Radiator Enclosures

3564 Blue Rock Rd.
Cincinnati, OH 45247

Catalog/Information Available Free

Phone 513-385-0555

Toll Free 800-543-7040

FAX 513-741-6292

Art on Tiles

Ceramic Tile

20 Smugglers Way
Wandsworth, London SW18 1EQ
Great Britain

Phone 011-44-81/8713965

Art-Line Design

Decorative Hardware

PO Box 743126
Dallas, TX 75374

Phone 214-964-7151

FAX 214-964-8816

Artglass By Misci

Stained Glass

20 Cary Ave.
Revere, MA 02151

Phone 617-284-9433

Artistic Brass

Brass Hardware

1400 Ardmore Avenue
Southgate, CA 90280

Phone 213-564-1100

Ashfield Stone Quarry

_Mica, Granite, Stone for Floor Tile,
Mantels, Countertops, Patios, Steps_

Hawley Rd.
Ashfield, MA 01330

Catalog/Information Available Free

Phone 413-628-4773

Building Supply

The Complete Sourcebook

_3 - 9_

Assimagra

President - M. L'ing. Joad Daude Member - European International Federation of Natural Stone Industry
rua Rodriquez Sampaio 110, 1 Dt
P - 1100 Lisboa
Portugal

Phone 011-351-52-00-38
FAX 011-351-113525227

Associated Foam Manufacturers

Manufacturer - Polystyrene Insulation
PO Box 246
Excelsior, MN 55331

Catalog/Information Available Free

Phone 612-474-0809
Toll Free 800-255-0176
FAX 612-474-2074

Association of Greek Heavy Clay Mftrs.

Member - Federation Europeenne Des Fabricants De Tuiles Et De Briques
Fragini 7
GR-546 24 Thessaloniki
Greece

Phone 011-30-31-222192

Associazione Nazionale degli Industriali

Member -The Tile & Brick European Association
Via Allessandro Torlonia, 15
00161 Roma
Italy

Phone 011-39-6861376
FAX 011-39-68442758

Assomarmi

Member -The European International Federation of Natural Stone Industry
M. Feilice Chiro, President
Via Nizza 59
I-00198 Roma
Italy

Phone 011-39-6-860-959
FAX 011-39-6-8840959

Atas International Corp.

Manufacturer - Roofing
6612 Snowdrift Rd.
Allentown, PA 18106

Phone 610-395-8445
FAX 610-395-9342

Atlas Roofing Corporation

Polyisocyanurate Insulation - Member - Polyisocyanurate Insulation Manufacturers Association
1121 East Main Street, Suite 200
St. Charles, IL 60174

Phone 708-584-1623

Austin Hardware West

Hardware
1455 Linda Way
Sparks, NV 89431-6126

Phone 702-359-3031
Toll Free 800-648-1150
FAX 702-359-6954

Authentic Designs

Colonial and Early American Lighting Fixtures
42 The Mill Road
West Rupert, VT 05776

Send $3.00 for Catalog/Information
Credit Cards VISA/MC

Phone 802-394-7713

Avonite

Countertops
1945 Highway 304 S.
Belen, NM 87002

Phone 505-864-3800
Toll Free 800-428-6648
FAX 505-864-7790

Awnings by Shuster

Awnings
PO Box 570
Vandergrift, PA 15690

Phone 412-567-5689

Axeman-Anderson Co.

Heat - Baseboard, Hot Water Radiators
300 E. Mountain Ave.
South Williamsport, PA 17701

Phone 717-326-9114

Aye Attracting Awnings

Blinds, Shades, Shutters, Draperies
2180 Country Club Rd.
Spartanburg, SC 29302

Phone 803-583-2180

Aylward Products Co.

Building Supply
4509 W. Harry
Wichita, KS 67209-2735

Phone 316-942-6712

B. F. Gilmour Co.

Hardware, Plumbing and Heating Supply
152 41st St.
Brooklyn, NY 11232

Phone 718-788-0700

B. Lilly & Sons Ltd.

Door & Window Hardware
Baltimore Rd.
Birmingham B42 1DJ
Great Britain

Phone 011-44-21357-1761
FAX 011-44-21357-9029

BMC West Building Materials

Building Supply
2069 Washington Blvd.
Ogden, UT 84401

Phone 801-621-7763

BRE Lumber

*Lumber and Flooring - Ash, Maple,
Mahogany, Red Oak, White Oak,
Teakwood, Cherry and many more*
10741 Carter Rd.
Traverse City, MI 49684

Mail Order Available

Credit Cards VISA/MC/Check/Money
Order

Phone 616-946-0043
FAX 616-946-6221

Backwoods Solar Electric Systems

*Manufacturer - Order Direct - Solar
Heating, Lighting Products*
8530 Rapid Lightning Creek Rd.
Sandpoint, ID 83864

Send $3.00 for Catalog/Information

Mail Order Available

Credit Cards Accepted

Phone 208-263-4290

Badger Tiles

Ceramic Tile
125 Main Rd.
Long Hanborough, Witney, Oxon
OX8 8JX
Great Britain

Phone 011-44-993/882280

Badgerland Building Material

Building Supply
W229 N2510 Duplainville Rd.
Waukesha, WS 53186

Phone 414-548-9599

Baja Products Ltd.

Manufacturer - Plumbing Fixtures
4065 North Romero Road
Tucson, AZ 85705

Toll Free 800-845-2252

Baldwin Hardware

Door and Cabinet Hardware
Decorative Warehouse
500 Executive Blvd.
Elmsford, NY 10523

    Toll Free 800-992-1330

Baldwin Hardware Corp.

Victorian Lamps, Decorative Hardware, Door Hardware
841 Wyomissing Blvd., Box 82
Reading, PA 19603

Send $0.75 for Catalog/Information

Mail Order Available

    Phone 215-777-7811

Baltarbo Tegelbruk AB

Member of The Swedish Brick and Tile Manufacturers Association
Box 56
S-776 00 Hedemora
Sweden

    Phone 011-46-225-10158
    FAX 011-46-152636

Baraboo Tent & Awning

Canvas Awnings
PO Box 57
Baraboo, WI 53913

    Phone 608-356-8303

Bard Manufacturing Company

Manufacturer - Ground Water Heat Pump
PO Box 607
Bryan, OH 43506

    Phone 419-636-1194

Barker Metalcraft

Radiator Covers, Grilles
1701 W. Belmont
Chicago, IL 60657

Catalog/Information Available Free

    Phone 312-248-1115
    Toll Free 800-397-0129
    FAX 312-929-2281

Barrel Builders

Hot Tub Kits & Solar Energy Panels
1085 Lodi Lane
St. Helena, CA 94574

Catalog/Information Available Free

Mail Order Available

    Phone 707-963-7914

Barrett Hardware Co.

Hardware
324 Henderson
Joliet, IL 60432-2537

    Phone 815-726-4341

Basic Coatings

Manufacturer - Wood Floor Finish
2124 Valley Drive
Des Moines, IA 50321

    Phone 515-288-0231
    FAX 515-288-0615

Baukeramik U.

Manufacturer - Ceramic Wall & Floor Tile
Steinzeugroehrenwerk P. Teeuwen GmbH &Co
An der Burg 1-7
Geilenkirchen 4 D-W-5130
Germany

    Phone 011-49-245180035

Bay Cities Metal Products

Gutter Fittings, Roof Flashings
2323 E. Manville St.
Compton, CA 90292

    Phone 213-603-9047
    FAX 213-603-0978

Bay City Paint Company

Specialty Paint and Brushes
2279 Market St.
San Francisco, CA 94114

    Phone 415-431-4914

Building Supply

Beachwood Lumber & Mfg. — Bellegrove Ceramics Ltd.

Beachwood Lumber & Mfg.

Roof Trusses
RFD 4
Warsaw, IN 46580
>Phone 219-858-9325

Bear Creek Lumber

Wholesale Distributor - Ship Direct Nationwide - Hard-to-Find Specialty Lumber, Frames, Beams
Bair Industrial Plaza
PO Box 669
Winthrop, WA 98862

Send $2.00 for Catalog/Information

Mail Order Available
>Phone 509-997-3110
>Toll Free 800-597-7191
>FAX 509-997-2040

Beautyware Plumbing Products

Plumbing Supplies
4350 West Cypress St., Ste 800
Tampa, FL 33607
>Phone 813-878-0178

Beaver Industries

Order by Phone - Underground Downspout Kits, Vinyl Fencing
890 Hersey St.
Saint Paul, MN 55114

Catalog/Information Available Free
>Phone 612-644-9933
>Toll Free 800-828-2947

Beckett, R.W. Corp.

Oil Burners
PO Box 1289
Elyria, OH 44036
>Phone 216-327-1060

Beech River Mill Company

Shutters - Interior and Exterior, Doors
Old Rt. 16 , Box 263
Centre Ossipee, NH 03814

Send $3.00 for Catalog/Information
>Phone 603-539-2636
>FAX 603-539-2636

Behr Process Corp.

Paint, Varnish, Stains
3400 Segerstrom Ave.
Santa Ana, CA 92704
>Phone 714-545-7101
>FAX 714-241-1002

Bel Vasaio Ltd.

Decorative Tile
PO Box 189
E. Orleans, MA 02643-0189

Send $2.00 for Catalog/Information

Mail Order Available

Credit Cards Accepted
>Toll Free 800-962-7061

Bel-Mar Paint Corp.

Paint, Stains
2790 W. 3rd Court
Hialeah, FL 33010
>Phone 305-887-6554
>FAX 305-888-7316

Beldes, Inc.

Manufacturer - Chimney Guard
PO Box 2808
Westport, CT 06880
>Toll Free 800-456-8803

Belfi Bros. & Co., Inc.

Tile, Marble
4310 Josephine
Philadelphia, PA 19124
>Phone 215-289-2766

Bellegrove Ceramics Ltd.

Ceramic Tile, Mosaic Tile
Bellegrove Ho, Salisbury Rd.
Watling St, Dartford, Kent
DA2 6EL
Great Britain
>Phone 011-44-322/277877

Building Supply

The Complete Sourcebook

3 - 13

Belwith International

Decorative Hardware
18071 Arenth Ave.
Industry, CA 91748

>Phone 212-889-8400
>FAX 212-725-5813

Bender Roof Tile Ind.Inc.

Manufacturer - Roof Tile
3100 SE County Rd.
PO Box 190
Belleview, FL 32620

>Phone 904-245-7074
>FAX 904-245-1873

Benton Harbor Awning & Tent

Awnings
2275 M-139
Benton Harbor, MI 49022

>Phone 616-925-2187

Berbaum Millwork Inc.

Millwork, Woodwork, Wood Doors, Cabinets
201 W. Winsconsin Ave. #510
Milwaukee, WI 53259-0001

>Phone 414-352-9168

Bergen Bluestone Co. Inc.

Natural Stone - Marble, Granite, Slate, Quartzite
404 Rt. 17
PO Box 67
Paramus, NJ 07652

>Phone 201-261-1903
>Toll Free 800-955-7625

Bergen Brick & Tile Co.

Wholesale Lumber
685 Wyckoff Ave.
Wyckoff, NJ 07481

>Phone 201-891-3500

Berger Building Products Corp.

Vinyl Siding, Roof Drainage Products
805 Pennsylvania Blvd.
Feasterville, PA 19047

>Phone 215-355-1200
>FAX 215-355-7738

Berjen Metal Industries

Radiator Enclosures
645 New York Ave.
Huntington, NY 11743

>Phone 516-673-7979
>FAX 516-673-7989

Berke Door & Hardware, Inc.

Wood, Metal Doors, Builder's Hardware
8255 Belvedere Ave.
Sacramento, CA 95826

>Phone 916-452-7331
>FAX 916-452-7573

Berkheiser Lumber Co. Inc.

Wholesale Lumber
1825 Proper
Corinth, MS 38834-5133

>Phone 601-286-5564

Berridge Manufacturing Co.

Manufacturer - Victorian, Classic Metal Roofing
1720 Maury St.
Houston, TX 77026

>Toll Free 800-231-8127

Bertin Studio Tiles

Handmade Ceramic Tile
10 St. John Place
Port Washington, NY 11050

>Phone 516-944-6964

Bessler Stairway Co.

Manufacturer - Wholesale to Distributors - Disappearing Stairways
110 Auction Ave.
Memphis, TN 38105

>Phone 901-522-9017
>FAX 901-523-1832

Building Supply

Better Trees — **Boise Moulding & Lumber**

Better Trees

Black Locust Lumber

7894 W. Maple Rapids Rd.
St Johns, MI 48879

Phone 517-682-4637

Bettina Elsner Artistic Tiles

Tile

11812 143rd Street
Largo, FL 34644

Phone 813-596-3038

Bill Koehler Co.

Plywood, Hardboard, Mouldings

Box 95
Hanover, PA 17331

Phone 814-238-0158

Bird, Inc.

Asphalt & Fiberglass Shingle

Roofing Division
1077 Pleasant St.
Norwood, MA 02062

Phone 617-551-0656

Bisazza Mosaico S.P.A.

Mosaic Tile - Floor, Wall, Bath

US Agent Renato Bisazza Inc.
88-R Wells Ave.
Newton, MA 02159

Phone 617-332-2570

FAX 617-332-2756

Blackland Moravian Tile Works

Embossed Painted Tiles

46 Ocean Drive
Key Largo, FL 33037

Send $1.25 for Catalog/Information

Mail Order Available

Phone 305-852-5865

Blakeson Inc.

English Fireplaces

2320 Pear Orchard
Little Rock, AR 72211

Send $5.00 for Catalog/Information

Phone 501-221-9441

FAX 501-221-9441

Blenko Glass Company Inc.

Stained Glass

Box 67
Milton, WV 25541

Catalog/Information Available Free

Phone 304-743-9081

FAX 304-743-0547

Blount Lumber Co.

Millwork, Lumber

PO Box 220
Lacona, NY 13083

Phone 315-387-3451

Blue Ox Millworks

Reproduction Millwork

Historical Park
X Street
Eureka, CA 95501

Send $6.00 for Catalog/Information

Phone 707-444-3437

Toll Free 800-248-4259

FAX 707-444-0918

Bohemia Plumbing Supply Co. Inc.

Plumbing and Heating Supply

1595 Lakeland Ave.
Bohemia, NY 11706

Credit Cards VISA/MC/AMEX

Phone 516-567-1551

Boise Moulding & Lumber

Manufacturer - Cabinetry, Doors Flooring, Millwork, Moulding, Windows

116 East 44th Street
Boise, ID 83714

Phone 208-322-6066

FAX 208-322-6633

Building Supply

The Complete Sourcebook

Bona Decorative Hardware

Decorative Hardware
3073 Madison Rd.
Cincinnati, OH 45209
Send $2.00 for Catalog/Information
Mail Order Available
Credit Cards Accepted

Phone 513-321-7877
FAX 513-321-7879

Bonus Books

Guide to Solar Energy
160 E. Illinois St.
Chicago, IL 60611

Toll Free 800-225-3775

Bootz Plumbingware

Plumbing Supplies
PO Box 6165
Evansville, IN 47712

Phone 812-428-6321

Boral Bricks, Inc.

Manufacturer - Brick
PO Box 1957
Agusta, GA 30913

Phone 404-722-6831
Toll Free 800-533-9292

Boston Valley Pottery

Custom Terracotta Roof Tiles
6860 South Abbott Rd.
Orchard Park, NY 14217

Phone 716-649-7490
FAX 716-649-7688

Boulder Art Glass Co.

Custom Stained Glass
1920 Arapahoe
Boulder, CO 80302
Send $3.00 for Catalog/Information
Mail Order Available

Phone 303-449-9030

Boulton & Paul PLC

Victorian, Edwardian, Georgian - Doors, Frames, Doorsets, Kitchen Units, Roof Windows, Stairs, Vanity Units, Windows, Window Accessories
Riverside, Norwich
Norfolk NR1 1EB
Great Britain

Phone 011-44-603/660133
FAX 011-44-603/626972

Bower's Awning & Shade

Awnings
366 N. 9th St.
Lebanon, PA 17042

Phone 717-273-2351

Bradco Supply Corp.

Roofing Materials
1303 N. Hamburg St.
Baltimore, MD 21230-1914

Phone 301-332-1134

Brady & Sun

Wood Frame Solariums
97 Webster St.
Worcester, MA 01603

Toll Free 800-888-7177

Brass Accents

Decorative Hardware - Brass, Bronze, Chrome
1000 S. Broadway
Salem, OH 44460

Phone 216-332-9500
FAX 216-337-8775

Brass Tacks Hardware Ltd.

Bathroom Accessories, Door & Window Hardware Decorative Grilles
177 Bilton Rd., Perivale
Greenford, Middx UB6 7HG
Great Britain

Phone 011-44-81/5669669
FAX 011-44-81/5669339

Building Supply

Brent Materials Co. – Bulldog Home Hardware

Brent Materials Co.

Lumber

741 Northfield Ave.
West Orange, NJ 07052
Phone 201-325-3030

Briar Hill Stone Co.

Sandstone Sills, Lintels, Steps

12470 State Route 520, Box 457
Glenmont, OH 44628

Send $2.00 for Catalog/Information

Mail Order Available
Phone 216-377-5100
FAX 216-377-5110

Bridge Lumber Co.

Lumber, Plywood, Drywall

515 Union Ave.
Brooklyn, NY 11211
Phone 718-387-0143

Brooklyn Tile Supply Co.

Ceramic Tile

184 4th Ave.
Brooklyn, NY 11217

Mail Order Available
Phone 718-875-1789
FAX 718-875-1791

Brown Stove Works Inc.

Manufacturer - Stoves, Ranges

PO Box 2490
Cleveland, TN 37320
Phone 615-476-6544
Toll Free 800-251-7485
FAX 615-476-6599

Bruce Post Company Inc.

Redwood Posts for Decks and Stoops

PO Box 332
Chestertown, MD 21620

Mail Order Available

Credit Cards Accepted
Phone 410-778-6181
FAX 410-556-6432

Bryant Stove Works

Antique Wood Burning Stoves & Ranges

PO Box 2048, Rich Rd.
Thorndike, ME 04986

Mail Order Available
Phone 207-568-3665

Buesche Inc.

Decorative Hardware

17955 Sky Park Circle Ste. H
Irvine, CA 92714
Phone 714-250-3055
FAX 714-261-7857

Builders Bargains

Building Supply

501 E. Randolph Rd.
Hopewell, VA 23680-5247
Phone 804-458-3030

Builders Brass Works Corp.

Manufacturer - Builders' Brass Supplies - Door Hardware

3474 Union Pacific Ave.
Los Angeles, CA 90023
Phone 213-269-8111
FAX 213-269-1872

Builders Square

Building Supplies

6740 W. Greenfield Ave.
Milwaukee, WS 53214-4900
Phone 414-771-5370

Building Products of America Corp.

Building Supplies

430 W. Merrick Rd.
Valley Stream, NY 11580
Phone 516-568-0222

Bulldog Home Hardware

Hardware

4533 Old Lamar Ave.
Memphis, TN 38118
Phone 901-365-0479

The Complete Sourcebook

3 - 17

Bundesverband der Deutschen

Member - Federation Europeene Des Fabricants De Tuiles Et De Briques
Ziegelindustrie e.v.
Schaumburg-Lippe-Strasse 4
Germany
　　　　Phone 011-49-228/213031
　　　　FAX 011-49-228/224057

Burnham

Home Heating Units - Baseboard, Hot Water Radiators
PO Box 3079
Lancaster, PA 17604
　　　　Phone 717-397-4701

Burnham Corp.

Greenhouses, Skylights, Solariums, Glass Enclosures
Lord & Burnham Div.
2 Main St., PO Box 255
Irvington on Hudson, NY 10533
　　　　Phone 914-591-8800

Busby Gilbert Tile Co.

Tile
16021 Arminta St.
Van Nuys, CA 91406
　　　　Phone 818-780-9460

Butler Stove Co.

Fireplace Fronts, Inserts, Standing Stoves
Rte. 1
PO Box 36
Gooding, ID 83330
Catalog/Information Available Free
　　　　Phone 208-934-5142

C & H Roofing Inc.

Cottage Style, Red Cedar Roofing Shingle
PO Box 2105
Lake City, FL 32056
　　　　Toll Free 800-327-8115
　　　　FAX 904-755-2353

CBS Home Express

Building Supply
Hwy 71
Coushatta, LA 71019-8124
　　　　Phone 318-932-6761

CGM Inc.

Manufacturer - Specialty Building Products - Crack Filler, Tile Grout, Concrete Patch, Silicone Sealer
1463 Ford Rd.
Bensalem, PA 19020
Catalog/Information Available Free
　　　　Phone 215-638-4400
　　　　Toll Free 800-523-6570
　　　　FAX 215-638-7949

CPN Inc.

Manufacturer - Floor & Wall Building Supply
705 Moore Station Industrial Park
Prospect Park, PA 19076
　　　　Toll Free 800-437-3232
　　　　FAX 610-534-1006

CW Design Inc.

Glass & Mirrors
1620 Terrace Drive
Roseville, MN 55113
　　　　Phone 612-631-2010
　　　　FAX 612-631-2031

Caberboard Ltd.

Wood, Particle Board, Floor Systems
Cowie, Stirlingshire
FK7 7BQ
Great Britain
　　　　Phone 011-44-786/812921
　　　　FAX 011-44-786/815622

Cabot Stains

Manufacturer - National Dealer List - Quality Wood Stains
100 Hale St.
Newburyport, MA 01950

Phone 508-465-1900
Toll Free 800-877-8246
FAX 508-462-0511

Cadet Mfg. Co.

Manufacturer - 800# for Nearest Distributor - Electric Baseboard, Wall Heaters
PO Box 1675
Vancouver, WA 98668

Phone 206-693-2505
Toll Free 800-442-2338
FAX 206-694-6939

Cal-Shake, Inc.

Manufacturer - Azteca Clay Roofing
PO Box 2048
5355 N. Vincent Ave.
Irwindale, CA 91706

Catalog/Information Available Free

Phone 818-969-3451
Toll Free 800-736-7663
FAX 818-969-7520

Calendar Tiles Ltd.

Ceramic Tile
Prettywood Complex, Bury New Rd.
Heap Bridge, Bury BL9 7HY
Great Britain

Phone 011-44-61/7052272

California Builders Hardware

Hardware
1850 Bates Ave.
Concord, CA 94520-1253

Phone 415-680-7557

California Redwood Association

Redwood Paneling
405 Enfrente Drive, Suite 200
Novato, CA 94949

Phone 415-382-0662

California Tile Supply

Distributor - Ceramic Tile Monocottura, Bicottura, Handmade, Special Pieces for Wall, Floor, Kitchen/Bath
1230 Allec Street
Anaheim, CA 92805

Phone 714-491-1585
FAX 714-491-1796

California Wholesale Tile

Ceramic Tile
1656 So. State College Blvd.
Anaheim, CA 92806

Phone 714-937-0591
FAX 714-937-3916

Cambridge Smithy

Custom Wrought Iron Work, Metal Antique Restoration, Hardware
Peter Krusch
RR1, Box 1280
Cambridge, VT 05444

Phone 802-644-5358

Cambridge Tile Mfg. Co.

Ceramic Floor & Wall Tile
145 Caldwell Dr.
Cincinnati, OH 45216

Phone 513-948-0500

Campbellsville Industries

Reproduction Victorian Roofing, Columns, Cupolas, Gazebos
PO Box 278, Taylor Blvd.
Campbellsville, KY 42718

Catalog/Information Available Free

Phone 502-465-8135
Toll Free 800-467-8135
FAX 502-465-6839

Cancos Tile Corporation

Distributor - Ceramic Italian Tile Monocottura, Bicottura, Terracotta, Handmade, Inserts, Borders, Special Pieces for Floor, Wall Kitchen/Bath
1050 Portion Road
Farmingville, NY 11738

Phone 516-736-0770

The Complete Sourcebook

Candy Tiles Ltd.

Ceramic Tiles
Heathfield, nr Newton
Abbot, Devon TQ12 6RF
Great Britain
Phone 011-44-626/832641

Cangelosi Marble & Granite

Marble & Granite
1402 Pike Rd.
Missouri City, TX 77489
Phone 713-499-7521

Cannon Rainwater Systems Ltd.

Gutters, Flashing
Cannon Ho, Stores Rd.
Derby DE2 4BD
Great Britain
Phone 011-44-332/360589
FAX 011-44-332/290301

Capital City Awning

Awnings
577 N. Fourth St.
Columbus, OH 43215
Phone 614-221-5404

Carl Schilling Stoneworks

Stone Restoration
PO Box 607
62 Main Street
Proctor, VT 05765
Phone 802-459-2200
FAX 802-459-2948

Carolina Components Corp.

Wood Trusses, Windows, Doors and Stairways
PO Box 58515
Raleigh, NC 27658
Phone 919-876-8955

Carolina Truss Mfg. Co., Inc.

Roof, Floor Trusses
PO Box 2052
Monroe, NC 28110
Phone 704-283-8179

Carrier Corp.

Home Heating Units
318 First St.
Liverpool, NY 13088
Phone 315-432-6000
Toll Free 800-227-7437

Carroll Awning Co. Inc.

Awnings
2955 Frederick Ave.
Baltimore, MD 21223
Toll Free 800-999-5617

Castle Wholesalers Inc.

Wholesale Hardware
31728 Bladensburg Rd. NE
Washington DC, 20018
Phone 202-529-8005

Causeway Lumber Co.

Roof Trusses
2601 S. Andrews Ave.
PO Box 21088
Fort Lauderdale, FL 33335
Phone 305-763-1224

Cecil Ellis Sauna Corp.

Saunas
PO Box 204
Middlefield, CT 06455

Catalog/Information Available Free

Mail Order Available

Cedar Plus

Manufacturer - Cedar Shake & Shingle
PO Box 515
Sumas, WA 98925
Toll Free 800-663-8707
FAX 604-820-3879

Building Supply

Cedar Shake & Shingle Bureau – Century Fireplace Furnishings Inc.

Cedar Shake & Shingle Bureau

Manufacturer - Guide to Cedar Shake & Shingle

515-116th Ave. NE, Suite 275
Bellevue, WA 98004

Catalog/Information Available Free

Send $2.50 for Catalog/Information

Phone	206-453-1323
FAX	206-455-1314

Cedar Valley Shingle Systems

Shingle & Siding

943 San Felipe Rd.
Hollister, CA 95023

Catalog/Information Available Free

Mail Order Available

Phone	408-636-8110
Toll Free	800-521-9523
FAX	408-636-9035

Cedir S.P.A.

Marco Busanelli - Monocottura for Walls, Bicottura for Floor, Wall, Bath

Via Emilia Ponente 2070
48104 Castelbolognese (RA)
Italy

Phone	.........011-39-546/50558
FAX	.........011-39-546/55600

Cedit S.P.A.

Luchino Visconti - Monocottura, Bicottura, Inserts, Borders for Floor & Wall

Via Vallassina 21
22040 Lurago D'erba (CO)
Italy

Phone	.........011-39-31/699051
FAX	.........011-39-31/699441

Celadon Ceramic Slate

Manufacturer - Roofing Tile

750 E. Swedesford Rd.
Valley Forge, PA 19842

Toll Free	800-782-8777
FAX	610-341-7055

Celotex Corp.

Manufacturer - Sales Office List - Acoustical Ceilings, Insulation Board, Foam Sheathing, Roofing Systems

PO Box 31602
Tampa, FL 33631

Phone	813-873-1700
Toll Free	800-235-6839
FAX	813-873-4103

Celsisus Energy Company

Manufacturer - Ground Water Heat Pump

3126 Dixie Highway
Erlenger, KY 41018

Cemar International S.P.A.

Alessandro Capitani - Monocottura, Bicottura for Floor, Wall, Bath

Via Crociale, 1
41053 Maranello (MO)
Italy

Phone	.........011-39-536/941200
FAX	.........011-39-536/943469

Central Brass Mfg. Co.

Plumbing Fixtures, Trim, Brass Goods

2950 East 55th St.
Cleveland, OH 44127

Phone	216-883-0220
Toll Free	800-338-9414

Central Distributors Inc.

Distributor - Ceramic Tile

117 College Ave.
Des Moines, IA 50314

Phone	515-244-8103
FAX	515-244-8103

Century Fireplace Furnishings Inc.

Fireplace Accessories

856 N Main St.
PO Box 248
Wallingford, CT 06492

Phone	203-265-1686
Toll Free	800-284-4328

Building Supply

The Complete Sourcebook

3 - 21

Century Insulation Mfg.

Manufacturer - Insulation
Industrial Park
PO Box 160
Jackson, MS 39365
Phone 601-774-8285

Ceramic Radiant Heat

Wood/Coal Stoves
Pleaseant Drive
Lochmere, NH 03252
Credit Cards VISA/MC
Phone 603-524-9663
Toll Free 800-343-0991

Ceramica Candia S.P.A.

*Imported Italian Ceramic Tile -
Monocottura, Bicottura, Wall, Flooring for
Kitchen & Bath*
US Agent Israel Yaker
763 Stelton Street
Teaneck, NJ 07665
Phone 201-837-0420
FAX 201-837-1470

Ceramica Colli Di Sassuolo S.P.A.

Exporter - Bicottura - Wall, Kitchen & Bath
Via Viazza 1 Tronco 42
41042 Fiorano Modenese (Modena)
Italy
Phone 011-39-536/843855
FAX 011-39-536/920039

Ceramica Del Conca S.P.A.

*Guiliano Cava - Monocottura, Bicottura,
Porcelain, Mosaic, Steps for Wall, Bath*
Via Croce 8
47040 San Clemente (FO)
Italy
Phone 011-39-541/996636
FAX 011-39-541/996038

Ceramica Ilsa S.P.A.

*Exporter - Monocottura, Bicottura, Special
Pieces for Wall, Floor, Kitchen/Bath*
Via Nazionale 5
17043 Carcare (Savona)
Italy
Phone 011-39-19/518761
FAX 011-39-19/517166

Ceramica Panaria S.P.A.

*Exporter - Monocottura, Bicottura, Steps,
Special Pieces for Floor, Wall,
Kitchen/Bath*
Via Panaria Bassa 22/A
41034 Finale Emila (Modena)
Italy
Phone 011-39-535/95111
FAX 011-39-535/90503

Ceramiche Atlas Concorde S.P.A.

*Monocottura, Bicottura, Procelain,
Mosaic, Inserts, Borders for Floor & Wall -
Kitchen & Bath*
Via Canaletto, 141
41040 Spezzano DI Fiorano (MO)
Italy
Phone 011-39-536/840811
FAX 011-39-536/843094

Ceramiche Brunelleschi S.P.A.

*Exporter - Monocottura, Terracotta, Steps,
Inserts, Borders, Special Pieces for Floor,
Wall, Kitchen/Bath*
Via Della Stazione 1 Fraz. Sieci
50069 Pantassieve (Firenze)
Italy
Phone 011-39-55/8309651
FAX 011-39-55/8328356

Ceramiche Cuoghitalia S.P.A.

*Monocottura, Bicottura, Inserts, Borders,
Steps for Floor, Wall, Bath*
Via Ghiarola Nuova, 162/164
41042 Fiorano Modenese (MO)
Italy
Phone 011-39-536/830006
FAX 011-39-536/830148

Building Supply

Ceramiche Edilcuoghi S.P.A. – Charles Rupert Designs

Ceramiche Edilcuoghi S.P.A.

Exporter - Monocottura, Bicottura, Inserts, Handmade, Majolica, Borders, Steps for Floor, Wall, Bath

Via Radici In Piano 675
41049 Sassuolo (Modena)
Italy

Phone 011-39-536/800101
FAX 011-39-536/806909

Ceramiche Edilgres-Sirio S.P.A.

Exporter - Monocottura, Bicottura for Wall, Floor, Bath

Via Cirocond.Le S. Francesco 122
41042 Fiorano Modenese (MO)
Italy

Phone 011-39-536/830004
FAX 011-39-536/832426

Ceramografia Artigiana S.P.A.

Mosaic, Inserts, Borders, Handmade for Wall, Bath and Interiors

Via Radici In Monte, 11
42010 Roteglia (RE)
Italy

Phone 011-39-536/851454
FAX 011-39-536/851216

Cerdomus Ceramiche S.P.A.

Renzo Caponervi - Monocottura, Bicottura, Terracotta, Handmade, Inserts, Borders for Floor, Wall, Bath

Via Emilia Ponente 1000
48104 Castelbolognese (RA)
Italy

Phone 011-39-546/50210
FAX 011-39-546/50010

Cerim Ceramiche S.P.A.

Exporter - Monocottura, Bicottura, Procelain, Inserts, Steps, Special Pieces for Floor, Wall, Kitchen/Bath

S.S. 610 Selice 1
40027 Mordano (Bologna)
Italy

Phone 011-39-541/57111
FAX 011-39-541/51049

Cersosimo Lumber Co.

Lumber

20 North Main St.
Norwalk, CT 20385

Phone 203-852-0060

CertainTeed Corp.

Manufacturer - Asphalt & Fiberglass Shingle, Insulation, Windows and Glass Sliding Doors

PO Box 860
Valley Forge, PA 19482

Catalog/Information Available Free

Phone 610-341-7000
Toll Free 800-782-8777
FAX 610-341-7055

Certainly Wood

Veneers and Plywood

11753 Big Tree Rd.
East Aurora, NY 14052

Catalog/Information Available Free

Phone 716-655-0206

Champion International Corp.

Exterior & Interior Plywood, Hardboard, Particleboard, Lumber

One Champion Plaza
Stamford, CT 06921

Phone 203-358-7000

Champion Irrigation Products

Plumbing Fixtures and Lawn Sprinklers

1460 Naud
Los Angeles, CA 90012

Phone 213-221-2108

Charles Rupert Designs

Reproduction Tile & Wallpaper

2004 Oak Bay Avenue
Victoria, B.C. V8R 1E4
Canada

Mail Order Available

Phone 604-592-4916
FAX 604-592-4999

The Complete Sourcebook

3 - 23

Charles Street Supply Co.

Nationwide Delivery - Plaster Washers - Plaster Wall and Ceiling Kits

54 Charles Street
Boston, MA 02114

Catalog/Information Available Free

Mail Order Available

Credit Cards Accepted/Check/Money Order

Phone 617-367-9046

Toll Free 800-382-4360

FAX 617-367-0682

Chartwell Group Ltd.

Lamps & Chandeliers

501 West Green Dr.
High Point, NC 27260

Phone 919-841-5222

Chester Granite Co.

Manufacturer - Granite, Marble Sills & Lintels

Algerie Road
Blandford, MA 01008

Mail Order Available

Phone 413-269-4287

FAX 413-269-7738

Chesterfield Awning Co.

Awnings

16999 Van Dam Rd.
South Holland, IL 60473

Phone 708-596-4434

China Diesel Imports

12,000, 8,000m 20,000 Watt Generators for Home Primary Power Source or Backup Source Order Direct

15749 Lyons Valley Rd.
Jamul, CA 91935

Catalog/Information Available Free

Mail Order Available

Phone 619-669-1995

FAX 619-669-4829

Circle Redmont Inc.

Glass Block, Insulated Glass, Skylights, Sunrooms

PO Box 4053
Wallingford, CT 06492

Phone 203-265-3888

FAX 203-265-6517

Cirecast

Cast Iron, Bronze, Steel Hardware

380 7th St.
San Francisco, CA 94103

Send $3.50 for Catalog/Information

Mail Order Available

Phone 415-863-8319

FAX 415-863-7721

Cisa-Cerdisa-Smov

Exporter - Monocottura, Bicottura, Klinker, Porcelain, Mosaics, Terracotta, Inserts, Borders for Floor, Wall, Kitchen/Bath

S.S 467, 42
41042 Fiorano Modenese (Modena)
Italy

Phone 011-39-536/866300

FAX 011-39-536/807477

Cisco

Plumbing Supplies and Fixtures

1502 West Cherry
Chanute, KS 66720

Credit Cards Check/Money Order

Phone 316-431-9290

FAX 316-431-7354

City Awning of South Bend

Awnings

1731 S. Franklin St.
South Bend, IN 46613

Phone 219-289-9266

Building Supply

Classic Accents

Nationwide Delivery - Brass Switch Plates
12869 Eureka, PO Box 1181
Southgate, MI 48195
Send $1.00 for Catalog/Information
Mail Order Available
Credit Cards VISA/MC

Phone 313-282-5525
FAX 313-282-5158

Classic Products

*Manufacturer - Roofing - Rustic Shingle
Roofing in Antique Brown, Cedar Red,
Charcoal Gray, Chocolate Brown, Pavilion
Green, Sierra Brown, White*
8510 Industry Park Dr.
PO Box 701
Piqua, OH 45356
Catalog/Information Available Free

Phone 513-773-9840
Toll Free 800-543-8938
FAX 513-773-9261

Climate Master Inc.

Manufacturer - Ground Water Heat Pump
PO Box 25788
Oklahoma City, OK 73125

Phone 405-745-6000

Cline Glass Company

Distributor - Stained Glass
1135 SE Grand Ave.
Portland, OR 97214
Send $5.00 for Catalog/Information

Phone 503-233-5946
Toll Free 800-547-8417
FAX 503-239-3766

Co-Em S.R.L.

Ceramic Tile - Inserts, Borders, Steps
US Agent S.M.E.
25 Indian Rd, Apt. 6h
New York, NY 10034

Coast Trim Company

Wooden Roof Gutters
4200 Ross Rd.
Sebastapol, CA 95472
Mail Order Available

Phone 707-546-2271

Coastal Canvas & Awning

Canvas Awnings
PO Box 1493
Savannah, GA 31402

Phone 912-236-2416

Coastal Lumber Co.

Lumber
PO Drawer 1207
Uniontown, PA 15401

Phone 412-438-3527

Coker's Wholesale Building Supply

Wholesale Building Supply
Old Lake City Hwy.
Kingstree, SC 29556

Phone 803-382-2396

Cold Spring Granite Co.

Granite
202 South 3rd Ave.
Cold Spring, MN 56320

Phone 612-685-3621
FAX 612-685-8490

Colonial Building Supply

Building Supply
189 W. 200 S
Bountiful, UT 84010-6217

Phone 801-295-9471
FAX 801-295-8381

Colonial Marble Products Ltd.

*Marble, Granite, Onyx - Vanity Tops,
Mantels, Floor Tiles*
304 E. Bank St.
Petersburg, VA 23803

Phone 804-861-3199
FAX 804-733-4936

Building Supply

The Complete Sourcebook

3 - 25

Colonial Stair & Woodwork Co.

Manufacturer - Wood Stairs
PO Box 38
Jeffersonville, OH 43128

Phone 614-426-6326
FAX 614-426-9295

Color Tile Ceramic Mfr. Co.

Ceramic Tile
PO Box 1039
Cleveland, MS 38732

Phone 601-843-2756
FAX 601-846-0416

Color Tile Inc.

Manufacturer - Ceramic Tile
515 Houston St.
Fort Worth, TX 76102

Phone 817-870-9400

Command-Aire Corporation

Manufacturer - Ground Water Heat Pump
PO Box 7916
Waco, TX 76714

Phone 817-840-3244

Commercial Gutter Systems

Manufacturer - Gutters
5621 East "DE" Avenue
Kalamazoo, MI 49004
Mail Order Available

Phone 616-382-2700
FAX 616-343-3141

Complete Carpentry Inc.

Building Supply
Rough & Finish Carpenters
2325 W. Granville Rd.
Columbus, OH 43235

Phone 614-889-8341

Concrete Technology Inc.

Manufacturer - Exterior & Interior Concrete Resurfacing
1255 Starkey Road
Largo, FL 34641

Toll Free 800-447-6573

Condar Company

Fireplace Supply
Box 287, 10500 Industrial Drive
Garrettsville, OH 44231

Phone 216-527-4343
FAX 216-527-4346

Conklin Metal Industries

Manufacturer - Metal, Steel, Copper Roofing
PO Box 1858
Atlanta, GA 30301
Send $3.00 for Catalog/Information

Phone 404-688-4510
FAX 404-533-7439

Conklin's Authentic Antique Barnwood

Order Direct - Wholesale Dealer - Hand Hewn Beams, Planks, Flooring, Flagstone, Wall Stone
Rd. 1, Box 70
Susquehanna, PA 18847
Mail Order Available

Phone 717-465-3832
FAX 717-465-3832

Conrolled Acoustics Corp.

Lumber
12 Wilson St.
Hartsdale, NY 10530

Phone 914-428-7740

Conservation Building Products Ltd.

Baths, Bricks, Doors, Paneling, Sinks, Fireplaces, Roof Tiles, Oak Beams
Forge Lane
Cradley Heath, Warley, West Midlands
B64 5AL
Great Britain

Phone 011-44-384/64219
FAX 011-44-384/410625

Building Supply

Consolidated Electrical Distributor

Electrical Supplies

608 N. Grape
Medford, OR 97501-2417

Phone 503-779-1447
FAX 503-779-0537

Contact Lumber Company

Pine, Hem-Fir, Lauan, Cutstock, Door Frames, Moulding, Window and Door Components

1881 S.W. Front Ave.
Portland, OR 97201-5199

Phone 503-228-7361
Toll Free 800-547-1038
FAX 503-221-1340

Continental Ceramic Tile

Italian Tile

2030 Grant Ave.
Philadelphia, PA 19115

Phone 215-676-1118

Continental Clay Company

Manufacturer - Brick & Tile

PO Box 1013
Kittanning, PA 16201

Phone 412-543-2611

Cook & Dunn Paint Corp.

Manufacturer - Paint , Stains

700 Gotham Parkway
Carlstadt, NJ 07072

Phone 201-507-8887

Cooper Stair Co.

Wooden Stairs

1331 Leithton Rd.
Mundelein, IL 60060

Catalog/Information Available Free

Mail Order Available

Phone 312-362-8900

Cooperativa Ceramica D'Imola Soc. A.R.L.

Monocottura, Bicottura, Procelain, Inserts, Handmade, Steps Borders for Floor, Wall, Bath

US Agent Wally Silva
WVS Enterprises, 2350 Coral Way
Miami, FL 33145

Phone 305-858-4744
FAX 305-858-0264

Country Plumbing

Antique and New Plumbing Supplies

5042 7th St.
Carpinteria, CA 93013

Phone 805-684-8685

Crate Fires

Gas Fireplaces

PO Box 351
Athens, GA 30603

Phone 706-353-8281
FAX 706-353-8312

Crawford's Old House Store

Reproduction Hardware, Lighting, Plumbing Fixtures

550 Elizabeth St.
Waukesha, WI 53186

Catalog/Information Available Free

Credit Cards VISA/MC/AMEX/Check

Phone 414-542-0685
Toll Free 800-556-7878

Creative Structures

Manufacturer - Wood Frame Solariums

1765 Walnut Lane
Quakerstown, PA 18951

Phone 215-538-2426
Toll Free 800-873-3966
FAX 215-538-7308

Building Supply

The Complete Sourcebook

Crest Distributors

Distributor - Ceramic Tile - Monocottura, Bicottura, Handmade, Special Pieces for Wall, Floor, Kitchen/Bath

1136 Lansdale Ave.
Central Falls, RI 02863

Phone 401-723-9774

FAX 401-723-4889

Crest/Good Mfg. Co., Inc.

Plumbing Supplies

325 Underhill Blvd.
Syosset, NY 11791

Phone 516-921-7260

FAX 516-921-4607

Crispaire

Manufacturer - Ground Water Heat Pump

PO Box 400
Cordele, GA 31015

Phone 912-273-3636

Croonen KG

Manufacturer - Ceramic Floor Tile

Gasstrasse 23
W-2000 Hamburg 50
Germany

Phone 011-49-40/8908140

Cross Industries

Manufacturer - Vinyl Decorative Lattice Panels

3174 Marjan Dr.
Atlanta, GA 30341

Catalog/Information Available Free

Phone 404-451-4531

Toll Free 800-521-9878

FAX 404-457-5125

Crossville Ceramics

Manufacturer - Ceramic Tile

PO Box 1168
Crossville, TN 38557

Phone 615-484-2110

Toll Free 800-843-3880

FAX 615-484-8418

Crown Boiler

Manufacturer - Baseboard, Hot Water Radiators

PO Box 14818
Philadelphia, PA 19134

Phone 215-535-8900

Crown City Hardware

Decorative Hardware - 16th-19th Century

1047 N. Allen Ave.
Pasadena, CA 91104

Send $6.50 for Catalog/Information

Mail Order Available

Phone 818-794-1188

FAX 818-794-1439

Croy-Marietta Hardwoods Inc.

Hardwood Lumber

PO Box 643
Marietta, OH 45750

Phone 614-373-1013

FAX 614-373-6892

Cummings Stained Glass Studios Inc.

Stained Glass

PO Box 427
North Adams, MA 01247

Mail Order Available

Phone 413-664-6578

FAX 413-664-6570

Curran Glass & Mirror Co.

Beveled, Leaded, Etched Glass

30 N. Maple St.
Florence, MA 01060

Send $1.00 for Catalog/Information

Phone 413-584-5761

Custom Canvas Awning, Inc.

Custom Canvas Awnings

Route 287 Lakewood Dr.
Greenville, SC 29607

Phone 803-277-5998

Building Supply

Custom Hardware Mfg., Inc. – Daniels-Olsen Building Products

Custom Hardware Mfg., Inc.

Bath Specialties
PO Box 846
Keokuk, IA 52632

Phone 319-524-7119

D & B Tile Distributors

*Distributor - Ceramic Italian Tile -
Monocottura, Bicottura, Terracotta,
Inserts, Borders, Steps for Floor, Wall,
Kitchen/Bath*
5800 Radman Street
Hollywood, FL 33023

Phone 305-983-6373

FAX 305-966-5641

D & D Natural Stone and Marble

Granite and Marble for Kitchen & Baths
811 Sivert
Wood Dale, IL 60191

Phone 708-860-7840

D'Mundo Tile

Ceramic Tile
36-660 Bankside Dr.
Cathedral City, CA 92234

Phone 619-328-4646

FAX 619-321-7472

D.C. Mitchell Reproductions

Brass Locks, Hardware, Knockers
8 Hadco Rd.
Newark, DE 19713

Mail Order Available

Phone 302-998-1181

FAX 302-994-0178

DS Locksmithing Company

*Reproduction Victorian & Colonial Locks
Hardware*
220 E. Sixth St.
Jacksonville, FL 32206

Mail Order Available

Phone 904-356-5396

Dado Ceramica S.R.L.

*Monocottura, Bicottura, Klinker, Inserts,
Borders, Steps for Floor, Wall, Bath*
US Distributor Nemo Tile Inc.
177-02 Jamaica Ave.
Jamaica, NY 11432

Phone 718-291-5969

FAX 718-291-5992

Dal-Tile

Ceramic Tile, Granite, Marble, Slate
7834 Hawn Freeway
Dallas, TX 75217

Phone 214-398-1411

Toll Free 800-933-8453

FAX 214-944-4457

Dale Incor, Inc.

Steel Studs, Building Components
1001 N.W. 58 Court
Fort Lauderdale, FL 33309

Phone 305-772-6300

FAX 305-772-7124

Daly's Wood Finishing Products

Wood Finish Systems
3525 Stoneway N.
Seattle, WA 98103

Phone 206-633-4200

Toll Free 800-735-7019

FAX 206-632-2565

Daniels Co., Inc.

Home Heating Furnaces
PO Box 868
Montpelier, VT 05602

Phone 802-223-2801

Daniels-Olsen Building Products

Building Supplies
815 W. Blackhawk
Sioux Falls, SD 57104-0371

Phone 605-336-3588

The Complete Sourcebook

3 - 29

De Best Mfg. Co., Inc.

Plumbing Repair Parts, Bath Decorative Trim

117 E. 162nd St.
PO Box 2002
Gardena, CA 90247

Mail Order Available

Phone 213-323-2981
Toll Free 800-972-4081
FAX 213-327-1921

Dean Custom Awnings

Custom Awnings

50 N. Madison Ave.
Spring Valley, NY 10977

Phone 914-425-1193

Deco-Trol

Central Air Grilles - Brass, Chrome

802 North I-35E
Denton, TX 76201

Catalog/Information Available Free

Toll Free 800-678-1977

Decorative Hardware Studio

Decorative Hardware - Trade Only

160 King Street
PO Box 627
Chappaqua, NY 10514

Send $10.00 for Catalog/Information

Mail Order Available

Phone 914-238-5251
FAX 914-238-4880

DeepRock

Water Well System

7222 Anderson Rd., PO Box 1
Opelika, AL 36803-0001

Mail Order Available

Phone 205-749-3377
Toll Free 800-633-8774
FAX 205-749-5601

Deer Creek Pottery

Reproduction Victorian, Spanish, Art Deco Tile

305 Richardson St.
Grass Valley, CA 95945

Phone 916-272-3373
FAX 916-272-9671

Delaware Quarries, Inc.

Building Stone - Granite, Slate, Limestone

River Road , Route 32
Lumberville, PA 18933

Mail Order Available

Phone 215-297-5647
FAX 215-297-8133

Delphi Stained Glass

Distributor - Stained, Beveled Glass

2116 E. Michigan Ave.
Lansing, MI 48912

Send $5.00 for Catalog/Information

Mail Order Available

Phone 517-482-2617
Toll Free 800-248-2048
FAX 517-482-4028

Delray Awnings, Inc.

Awnings

80 No. Congress Ave.
Delray Beach, FL 33445

Phone 406-727-6538

Designer Ceramics

Ceramic Tile, Marble, Mosaic

Ceramics Ho, 139 Wigan Rd., Euxton
Chorley, Lancs PR7 6JJ
Great Britian

Phone 011-44-257/273114
FAX 011-44-257/262386

Building Supply

Designs in Tile — Donald Durham Co.

Designs in Tile

Interior & Exterior Hand-painted Ceramic Tile - Nationwide Shipping

PO Box 358
Mt. Shasta, CA 96067

Send $3.00 for Catalog/Information

Mail Order Available

Phone 916-926-2629
FAX 916-926-2629

Deutscher & Sons, Inc.

Hardware, Plumbing and Heating Supply

105-07 150th St.
Jamaica, NY 11435

Phone 718-291-5600

Deutscher Naturwerstein

President - M. Henschel Member - Eurpoean International Federation of Natural Stone Industry

Verband E. V. (DNV)
4, Sanderstrasse
D-8700 Wurzburg
Germany

Phone 011-49-931/12061
FAX 011-49-931/14549

Devine Lumber Do-It-Center

Building Supply

115 W. Hondo Ave.
Devine, TX 78016-2920

Phone 512-663-2867

Diamond Wood Products, Inc.

Hardwood Lumber

90253 Prairie Rd.
PO Box 2009
Eugene, OR 97402

Phone 503-689-2581
FAX 503-689-9937

Dibiten USA

Roofing

4301 E. Firestone Blvd.
South Gate, CA 90280

Phone 213-564-7220
Toll Free 800-342-4836
FAX 213-564-9732

Dickson Elbertson Mills, Inc.

Awnings

22599 Western Ave.
Torrence, CA 90501

Phone 213-212-3311

Distepro USA Inc.

Decorative Hardware

PO Box 212
Huntington Station, NY 11746-0174

Toll Free 800-521-0003
FAX 516-424-3736

Dize Company

Awnings

PO Box 937, 1512 S. Main St.
Winston-Salem, NC 27102

Phone 910-722-5181
Toll Free 800-642-0606
FAX 910-761-1334

Domus Linea S.P.A.

Importer - Terracotta Tile

US Agent G.A.M. Robert E. Ceramic Tiles
950 Mockingbird Lane 615
Plantation, FL 33324

Phone 305-591-3744
FAX 305-591-1289

Donald Durham Co.

Manufacturer - Building Repair Compounds

PO Box 804
Des Moines, IA 50304

Building Supply

The Complete Sourcebook

3 - 31

Dorning Roofing & Insulation Co.

Manufacturer - Roofing and Insulation
422 S. Edgemont Cir. NW
Huntsville, AL 35811-1372
Phone 205-539-2251

Dovre

Cast Iron Stoves and Fireplaces
401 Hanks Ave.
Aurora, IL 60505
Phone 312-844-3353
Toll Free 800-368-7387
FAX 708-844-3238

Dow Chemical USA

Manufacturer - Exterior Insulation System (Styrofoam)
2020 Willard H
Dow Center
Midland, MI 48674
Phone 517-636-1000
Toll Free 800-441-4369

Dryvit Systems, Inc.

Stucco Style Siding
1 Energy Way
PO Box 1014
West Warwick, RI 02893
Toll Free 800-556-7752

Duncan Enterprises

Manufacturer - Paint
5673 East Shields Avenue
Fresno, CA 93727
Phone 209-291-4444

Dundee Manufacturing Co.

Building Supplies
Building Specialty Products Div.
4756 N. Ann Arbor Rd.
Dundee, MI 48131
Phone 313-529-2431

Durking Awning Corp.

Awnings
17 Federal Rd.
Danbury, CT 06810
Phone 203-748-2142

Dutch Products & Supply Co.

Delft BorderTile, Reproduction Colonial Brass Lighting Fixtures, Lamp Posts, Fencing
166 Lincoln Ave.
Yardley, PA 19067
Send $1.00 for Catalog/Information
Phone 215-493-4873
FAX 215-493-4873

Dwight Lewis Lumber Co., Inc.

Lumber
190 Park Street
Williamsport, PA 17701
Catalog/Information Available Free
Phone 717-326-7471
Toll Free 800-233-8450

E B Bradley Co.

Hardware
7825 Arjons Rd.
San Diego, CA 92126-4368
Phone 619-549-8181
Toll Free 800-292-9791
FAX 619-549-4833

E.L. Hilts & Company

Building, Roofing Supply
2551 Hwy. 70 West
PO Box 1789
Hickory, NC 28603
Toll Free 800-354-4587
FAX 704-328-2835

Building Supply

EDLCO — Elon Inc.

EDLCO

Hardwoods, Softwoods, Plywood - Ash, Birch, Cherry, Maple, Oak, Mahogany

PO Box 5373
Asheville, NC 28813-5373

Send $2.00 for Catalog/Information

Mail Order Available

Phone 704-255-8765
Toll Free 800-554-1722

EK Hardware Co., Inc.

Hardware Specialties

4 Warren St.
New York, NY 10007

Phone 212-227-8117

EPRO, Inc.

Handmade Sandstone Tile

156 East Broadway
Westville, OH 43081

Phone 614-882-6990
FAX 614-882-4210

Eagle

Multi-Fuel Furnace Central Heating System

PO Box 130894
2000 W. Country Rd.
Roseville, MN 55113

Catalog/Information Available Free

Phone 612-633-5044

East Coast Tile Imports Inc.

Distributor - Ceramic Tile - Monocottura, Bicottura for Wall, Floor, Kitchen/Bath

35 State Street
Ludlow, MA 01056

Phone 413-583-4246
FAX 413-589-7920

Edwards Engineering

Manufacturer - Baseboard, Hot Water Radiators

101 Alexander Ave.
Pompton Plains, NJ 07444

Toll Free 800-526-5201

Electric Glass Co.

Beveled Glass , Stained Glass Panels & Lampshades

One E. Mellen St.
Hampton, VA 23663

Send $3.00 for Catalog/Information

Mail Order Available

Phone 804-722-6200
FAX 804-723-4329

Electrical Wholesale

Wholesale Electrical Supply

2415 Gilchrist Rd.
Akron, OH 44305-4407

Phone 216-733-7400
FAX 216-733-6209

Elite Fireplace Facings Inc.

Fireplace Facings

PO Box 16124
Shawnee, KS 66216

Mail Order Available

Phone 913-631-5443
Toll Free 800-932-8812

Elixer Vinyl Siding

Manufacturer - Vinyl Siding

304 E. Main St.
Leola, PA 17540

Elof Hansson, Inc.

Lumber

201 E. 42nd St.
New York, NY 10017

Phone 212-949-1700

Elon Inc.

Imported Mexican Clay, Ceramic Tile

5 Skyline Drive
Hawthorne, NY 10532

Send $1.00 for Catalog/Information

Mail Order Available

Phone 914-347-7800

Building Supply

The Complete Sourcebook

3 - 33

Endicott Clay Products Co.

Manufacturer - Face Brick
PO Box 17
Fairbury, NE 68352
Phone 402-729-3315
FAX 402-729-5804

Endicott Tile Ltd.

Manufacturer - Ceramic Tile
PO Box 645
Fairbury, NE 68352
Phone 402-729-3323
FAX 402-729-5804

Enduro Fabric Awnings

Fabric Awnings
9350 South Point
Houston, TX 77054
Phone 713-796-2322

Energy Etcetera

Woodstove and Fireplace Accessories
PO Box 451
Bayside, NY 11361
Credit Cards VISA/MC

Energy Pioneers

Wood Heating Products
Box 163
Williamson, NY 14589
Send $2.00 for Catalog/Information
Mail Order Available

Englander Wood Stoves

Wood Stoves
PO Box 206
Monroe, VA 24574
Phone 804-929-0120

Enhanced Glass Corp.

Glass Units
1701-A W. Loop 340
Waco, TX 76712
Phone 817-666-3536
FAX 817-666-1481

Enterprise Industries, Inc.

Steel Trusses
275 E. Industry Ave.
Frankfort, IL 60423
Phone 815-469-6611

Enterprise Lumber Co.

Lumber
3210 Smokey Point Dr., Suite 201
Arlington, VA 98223
Mail Order Available
Phone 206-435-1111
FAX 206-651-2137

Epifanes USA

Finishes, Varnishes
1218 SW 1st Ave.
Fort Lauderdale, FL 33315
Phone 305-467-8325
FAX 305-523-9490

Eurocobble

European Cobblestone
4265 Lemp Avenue
Studio City, CA 91604
Mail Order Available
Phone 213-877-5012
FAX 818-766-6363

Evergreen Lumber and Molding

Pine, Red Oak Moulding
PO Box 10518
Santa Ana, CA 92711-0518
Phone 714-921-8088
FAX 714-921-8087

Evergreen Slate Co.

Samples Sent Upon Request - Roof Slate
68 East Potter Ave.
PO Box 248
Granville, NY 12382
Catalog/Information Available Free
Phone 518-642-2530
FAX 518-642-9313

FBAMTP

President - M. Dascotte Member - European International Federation of Natural Stone Industry - Federation Belge Des Associates De Maitres Tallerus De Pierres

a.s.b.l.,Galerie du Centre -Bur.220/222 rue des Fripiers
1000 Bruxelles
Belgium

Phone 011-32-2-2230647

FAX 011-32-2-2230538

FFPM

President - M. Paul Henry Member - European International Federation of Natural Stone Industry

Fed. Francaise DE LA Pierre ET DU Marbre
Rue Alfred Roll 3
F-75 849 Paris Cedex 17
France

Phone 011-33-440-14701

FAX 011-33-405-40328

FHP Manufacturing

Manufacturer - Ground Water Heat Pump

Division of Harrow Products Inc.
601 NW 65th Court
Ft. Lauderdale, FL 33309

Phone 305-776-5741

FNMMB

Federation Natonale Des Maitres Marbriers De Belgique President M.g. Heris - Member - European International Federation of Natural Stone Industry

a.s.b.l.
Rue due Lombard, 34-42
1000 Bruxelles
Belgium

Phone 011-32-2-5136532

Fabricated Wood Products

Roof & Floor Trusses

I-35, PO Box 154
Owatonna, MN 55060

Phone 507-451-1019

Fabulon Products

Manufacturer - Floor Finish

75 Tonawanda St.
Buffalo, NY 14027

Phone 716-873-2770

Toll Free 800-876-7220

FAX 716-874-1464

Fafco Inc.

Solar Heating Equipment

2690 Middlefield Rd.
Redwood City, CA 94063

Phone 415-363-2690

FAX 415-363-2890

Fahrenheat Heating Products

Heating Products

470 Beauty Spot Rd. E.
Bennettsville, SC 29512

Phone 803-479-4006

Fayston Iron & Steel Works

Door Hardware, Fireplace Equipment, Staircases

Box 91 D
Fayston, VT 05673

Send $1.00 for Catalog/Information

Phone 802-496-2574

Fellenz Antiques

Antique Hardware, Lighting Fixtures, Bathroom Fixtures

2224 Cherokee
St. Louis, MO 63118

Phone 314-776-8363

Fergene Studio

Fireplace Tile

4320 Washington St.
Gary, IN 46408

Send $1.00 for Catalog/Information

Mail Order Available

Phone 219-884-1119

Fiberfine of Memphis Inc.

Home Insulation
PO Box 9055
Memphis, TN 38109
Phone 901-789-0440

FibreCem Corporation

Manufacturer - Roofing Shingle & Slate
PO Box 411368
Charlotte, NC 28246
Phone 704-527-2727
Toll Free 800-346-6147
FAX 704-588-2096

Fibreboard Box & Millwork Corp.

Lumber, Moulding, Millwork
PO Box 430
Red Bluff, CA 96080-0430
Phone 916-527-9113
FAX 916-529-0180

Fields Corporation

Manufacturer - Roofing
2240 Taylor Way
Tacoma, WA 98421
Phone 206-869-0070

Fierst Distributing Co.

Ceramic Tile
746 Trumbull Dr.
Pittsburgh, PA 15205
Phone 412-429-9300
FAX 412-276-5166

Fine Paints of Europe

Interior & Exterior European Paint
PO Box 419
Woodstock, VT 05091-0419
Send $5.00 for Catalog/Information
Mail Order Available
Credit Cards MC/VISA
Phone 802-457-2468
Toll Free 800-332-1556
FAX 802-457-3984

Finishing Products

Wood Finish
8165 Big Bend
St. Louis, MO 63119
Send $2.00 for Catalog/Information
Phone 314-481-0700

Finlay Forest Industries Ltd.

Lumber
PO Box 250
Mackenzie
B.C. CAN V0T 2C0
Canada
Phone 604-997-3201
FAX 604-997-5133

Firebird Inc.

Hand Painted Tile
335 Snyder Ave.
Berkeley Heights, NJ 07922
Send $2.00 for Catalog/Information
Phone 908-464-4613
FAX 908-464-4615

Firestone Building Products Co.

Manufacturer - Insulation
525 Congressional Blvd.
Carmel, IN 46032-5607
Phone 317-575-7000
Toll Free 800-428-4442
FAX 317-575-7100

Flame & Hearth Fireplaces

Fireplaces
3321 S Rte 31
Crystal Lake, IL 60012-1404
Phone 815-455-0320

Flexicore Co., Inc.

Roofing & Flooring
367 W. 2nd St.
Dayton, OH 45402
Phone 513-226-8700

Building Supply

Flood Company — Foothill Hardware & Lumber

Flood Company

Manufacturer - Wood Finish for Decking, Fencing, Wood Siding

1212 Barlow Road
PO Box 399
Hudson, OH 44236-0399

Phone 216-650-4070
Toll Free 800-321-3444
FAX 216-650-1453

Flora & Fauna

Decorative Hardware

38001 Old Stage Rd.
PO Box 578
Gualala, CA 95445

Phone 707-884-3363
FAX 707-884-1515

Florano Ceramic Tile Design Center

Italian Tile

1400 Hempstead Tpk.
Elmont, NY 11003

Phone 516-354-8453

Florence Corp.

Lumber

1647 E. Jericho Turnpike
Huntington, NY 11743

Phone 516-499-6200

Florian Tiles

Hand-Painted Ceramic Tile

The Stables, Waterston Manor
Lower Waterston, Dorchester, Dorset
DT2 7SP
Great Britain

Phone 011-44-30/5848600

Florida Brick & Clay Co.,Inc.

Ceramic Tile

1708 Furkey Creek Rd.
Plant City, FL 33567

Phone 813-754-1521
FAX 813-754-5469

Florida Ceramic Tile Center

Distributor - Ceramic Tile - Monocottura, Bicottura - Wall, Floor, Kitchen/Bath

665 South Orcas
Seattle, WA 98108

Phone 206-767-9819
FAX 206-767-0217

Florida Plywoods, Inc.

Particle Board, Plywood

Box 458
Greenville, FL 32331

Phone 904-948-2211

Florida Tile Industries, Inc.

Manufacturer - Ceramic Tile

One Sikes Blvd., PO Box 447
Lakeland, FL 33802

Phone 813-687-7171
Toll Free 800-352-8453
FAX 813-683-8936

Focus Ceramics Ltd.

Ceramic & Mosaic Tile

Div of Focus Industires, Unit 5
Hamm Moor La., Weybridge Trading Est
Weybridge, Surrey KT15 2SD
Great Britain

Phone 011-44-932/854881

Foil-Sulate Div.

Wall & Building Insulation

Dynamic Development Co.
PO Box 582
El Toro, CA 92630

Phone 714-768-5798

Foothill Hardware & Lumber

Hardware and Lumber

11748 S. Foothill Blvd.
Yuma, AR 85365-5812

Phone 602-342-1400

Building Supply

The Complete Sourcebook

3 - 37

Building Supply

Forest Siding Supply Inc.

Building Supply, Siding
2035 E. Ovid Ave.
Des Moines, IA 50313-4742
Phone 515-265-9826

Four Seasons

Sunrooms, Patio Rooms, Atriums
5005 Veterans Memoral Hwy.
Holbrook, NY 11741
Catalog/Information Available Free
Phone 516-563-4000
Toll Free 800-368-7732

Frampton Industries Inc.

Lumber
PO Box 09718
Columbus, OH 43209
Phone 614-239-9861

Frank Scolaro Mrable Co. Inc.

Marble
340 Jackson Ave.
Bronx, NY 10454
Phone 212-585-1133

Franklin Art Glass Studios

Distributor - Stained Glass
222 E. Sycamore St.
Columbus, OH 43206
Mail Order Available
Phone 614-221-2972
Toll Free 800-848-7683
FAX 614-221-5223

Frazier Park Lumber & Hardware

Lumber & Hardware
3320 Mount Pinos Way
Frazier Park, CA 93225
Phone 805-245-3301

Fred Beyer Co.

Manufacturer - Glass Block
7810 S. Claremont
Chicago, IL 60620
Phone 312-778-4300

Freundlich Supply Co.

Hardware, Plumbing and Heating Supply
1550 Coney Island Ave.
Brooklyn, NY 11230
Phone 718-338-2409

Frizelle Enos Co.

Wood Stoves & Accessories
265 Petaluma Ave.
Sebastopol, CA 95472
Mail Order Available
Credit Cards VISA/MC
Phone 707-823-6557

Fuller O'Brien Paints

Manufacturer - Interior/Exterior Victorian Paint
2001 W. Washington Ave.
PO Box 17
South Bend, IN 46624
Toll Free 800-338-8084
FAX 219-232-8407

G S Energy Industries Inc.

Solar Heaters
108 Jefferson Ave.
Des Moines, IA 50314
Phone 515-243-7570

GAF Building Materials Corp.

Manufacturer - Fiberglass Roofing Shingle
1361 Alps Rd.
Wayne, NJ 07470
Phone 201-628-3000
FAX 201-628-3865

GMT Floor Tile, Inc.

Ceramic Tile
1255 Oak Point Ave.
Bronx, NY 10474
Catalog/Information Available Free
Phone 212-991-8500

GS Roofing Products Co., Inc.

Manufacturer - Roofing
5525 MacArthur Blvd.
Suite 900
Irving, TX 75038

Phone 214-580-5600

GTE Products Corp.

Ceramic Tile
Glass Products
135 Commerce Way
Portsmouth, NH 03801

Phone 603-436-8900

FAX 603-436-8483

Gabbianelli S.R.L.

Bicottura, Inserts, Borders, Handmade for Wall, Bath & Kitchen
US Agent Atlantic Trading Co. LTd.
506 Industrial Drive
Lewisberry, PA 17339

Phone 717-938-5648

FAX 717-938-8749

Garbe Industries Inc.

Brass Hardware
4137 S. 72nd East Ave.
Tulsa, OK 74145
Mail Order Available

Phone 918-627-0284

FAX 918-665-6731

Gas Appliance Manufacturers

Heating, Gas Forced-Air
1901 N. Moore St.
Suite 1100
Arlington, VA 22209

Gaston's Wood Finishes & Antiques

Finish, Hardware, Furniture
2626 North Walnut St.
Bloomington, IN 47408
Send $2.50 for Catalog/Information
Mail Order Available

Toll Free 800-783-2845

Gate Roofing Manufacturing Inc.

Manufacturer - Roofing
914 Hall Park Drive
PO Box 716
Green Cove Springs, FL 32043

Phone 904-284-7571

Gawet Marble & Granite Inc.

Marble & Granite Counter Tops, Vanity Tops, Fireplace Surrounds
Rt. 4 West, PO Box 219
Center Rutland, VT 05736
Mail Order Available

Toll Free 800-323-6398

General Building Products Corp.

Building Supply & Lumber
2599 Route 112
Medford, NY 11763

Phone 516-654-3500

Genova Products

Gutters, Downspouts, Vinyl Plumbing Products
7034 E. Court St.
Davison, MI 48423
Mail Order Available

Phone 313-744-4500

FAX 313-744-1653

Gentron Corp.

Decorative Tempered Glass
PO Box 416
Sweetwater, TN 37874

Phone 615-337-3522

FAX 615-337-7979

Georgia Marble Company

Manufacturer - Marble Tile, Natural Stone Products
Blue Ridge Ave.
PO Box 9
Nelson, GA 30151

Phone 404-735-2591

Toll Free 800-334-0122

Georgia Pacific Corp. – Glidden Co.

Building Supply

Georgia Pacific Corp.

Manufacturer - Decorative Paneling, Gypsum, Hardwood Plywood, Insulation, Lumber, Metal Products, Millwork, Roofing, Siding

133 Peachtree NE
PO Box 105605
Atlanta, GA 30303

Send $1.00 for Catalog/Information

Phone 404-652-4000

Toll Free 800-284-5347

Gerard Roofing Technologies

Roofing Materials

Gerard Corporate Headquarters
955 Columbia St.
Brea, CA 92621-2927

Toll Free 800-841-3213

Gerber Plumbing Fixtures Corp.

Plumbing Fixtures

4656 West Touhy Ave.
Chicago, IL 60646

Phone 708-675-6570

Gercomi Corp.

Glass Tiles - 40 Designs, 14 Colors

4474 NW 74th Ave.
Miami, FL 33166

Gibraltar

Manufacturer - Countertops, Vanity Laminate

Wilson Plastics Co.
600 General Bruce Dr.
Temple, TX 76501

Phone 817-778-2711

Toll Free 800-433-3222

FAX 817-778-1822

Gilchrist Timber Co.

Pine Lumber

PO Box 638
Gilchrist, OR 97737

Phone 503-433-2222

FAX 503-433-9581

Gilmer Wood Co.

Wood, Lumber

2211 NW St.Helens Rd.
Portland, OR 97210

Phone 503-274-1271

Glashaus Inc.

Glass Block - Warhouse Westbury, NY - Distributor Glass Block Source Aurburn, Wa - Glass Block for Shower and Windows

415 W. Golf Rd., Suite 13
Arlington Heights, IL 60005

Phone 708-640-6910

FAX 708-640-6955

Glass Block Co.

Glass Block for Windows or Shower

1316 E. Slauson Ave.
Los Angeles, CA 90011

Phone 213-585-6368

FAX 213-587-4421

Glass Houses

Conservatories

53 Ellington St.
London N7 8PN
Great Britain

Phone 011-44-71/6076071

FAX 011-44-71/6096050

Glen Raven Mills Inc.

Patio Covers and Awnings

1831 North Park Ave.
Glen Raven, NC 27215

Phone 919-227-6211

Toll Free 800-441-5118

Glidden Co.

Wood Floor Finish

925 Euclid Ave.
Cleveland, OH 44115

Phone 216-344-8216

Toll Free 800-221-4100

FAX 216-344-8150

Building Supply

Glo King Woodstoves

Woodstoves
PO Box 179
Florence, OR 97439-0006

Catalog/Information Available Free

Toll Free 800-366-0682
FAX 503-997-8968

Globe Building Materials Inc.

Manufacturer - Roofing
2230 Indianapolis Blvd.
Whiting, IN 46394

Phone 219-473-4500

Globe Marble & Tile

Marble, Granite
7348 Bellaire Ave.
N. Hollywood, CA 91605

Phone 818-982-4040
FAX 818-982-6881

Gold Bond Building Products

*Manufacturer - Building Products -
Wallboard, Wall Panels, Ceilings*
2001 Rexford Rd.
Charlotte, NC 28211

Catalog/Information Available Free

Phone 704-365-7300

Good Time Stove Co.

Cast Iron Stoves & Parts
Rt. 112, PO Box 306
Goshen, MA 01032

Send $2.00 for Catalog/Information

Mail Order Available

Phone 413-268-3677
FAX 413-268-9284

Goodwin Lumber

*Manufacturer - Order Direct - Heart Pine
Lumber and Red Cypress, Flooring,
Paneling, Beams*
Rt. 2, Box 119
Micanopy, FL 32667

Catalog/Information Available Free

Mail Order Available

Phone 904-373-9663
Toll Free 800-336-3118
FAX 904-466-0608

Grandpa Snazzy's Hardware

Antique Hardware
1832 S. Broadway
Denver, CO 80210

Mail Order Available

Phone 303-778-6508

Granite Creations Inc.

Granite
75 Autumn
Cranston, RI 02910-5332

Phone 401-781-0670
FAX 401-294-3084

Granite Design

Granite & Marble Countertops
PO Box 130
Watertown, SD 57201

Phone 605-886-6942
Toll Free 800-843-3305
FAX 605-886-6943

Granitech Corp.

Granite Panels, Tiles
PO Box 1780
600 South 23rd St.
Fairfield, IA 52556

Phone 515-472-6161
FAX 515-472-6100

Building Supply

The Complete Sourcebook

3 - 41

Grant Plywood & Dimension Co.

Plywood
521 Rte. 211 E
Philadelphia, PA 10940

Phone 914-692-4222
FAX 914-692-4257

Granville Manufacturing Co. Inc.

Wood Building Products
Rt. 100, PO Box 15
Granville, VT 05747

Mail Order Available

Phone 802-767-4747
FAX 802-767-3107

Grate Fires Inc.

English Style Gas & Coal Fireplaces
PO Box 351
Athens, GA 30603

Mail Order Available

Phone 706-353-8281
FAX 706-353-8312

Green River

Manufacturer - Cedar Shake & Shingle
PO Box 515
Sumas, WA 98295

Toll Free 800-663-8707
FAX 604-820-3879

Greeter Building Center

Building Supply
26 College
Monteagle, TN 37356

Phone 615-924-2048

Groff & Hearne Lumber

Lumber
858 Scotland Rd.
Quarryville, PA 17566

Mail Order Available

Credit Cards VISA/MC/DISCOVER

Phone 717-284-0001
Toll Free 800-342-0001
FAX 717-284-2400

Groupement National de l'Industrie

Member - Federation Europeenne Des Fabricants De Tuiles Et De Briques - Tile & Brick
Rue des Poissonniers
13, Boite 22
Belgium

Phone 011-32-2/511 2581
FAX 011-32-2/5132640

Gruppo Elba S.P.A.

Monocottura, Bicottura for Floor, Wall, Bath
US Agent Mediterranean Exports
3401 N.W. 7th Street
Miami, FL 33125

Phone 305-541-4800
FAX 305-541-4843

GutterCrest Ltd.

Gutters
Maesbury Rd, Oswestry
Shropshire SY10 8NN
Great Britain

Phone 011-44-691/650749
FAX 011-44-691/658077

Gutterfast Ltd.

Gutters
Keepers Corner, Redehall Rd.
Smallfield, Horley, Surrey
RH6 9RH
Great Britain

Phone 011-44-342/716433
FAX 011-44-342/712109

Gyp-Crete Corporation

Manufacturer - Radiant Heating System
920 Hamel Rod
Hamel, MN 55340

Phone 800-356-7887
Toll Free 612-478-2431

H & R Johnson Tiles

Victorian Wall & Floor Tile
410 W. 53rd St., Apt. 728
New York, NY 10019

Phone 212-245-2295

H. B. Fuller Co./TEC Incorporated

Manufacturer - Exterior Insulation System, Terrazzo Flooring, Ceramic & Marble Mortars

315 South Hicks Rd.
Palatine, IL 60067

Phone 708-358-9500

Toll Free 800-323-7407

FAX 708-358-9510

H. H. Robertson Co.

Building Supply

400 Holiday Dr.
Pittsburgh, PA 15220

Phone 412-928-7519

H. M. Stauffer & Sons Inc.

Lumber, Building Materials, Millwork

PO Box 38
Leola, PA 17450

Phone 717-656-2811

H. Verby Co. Inc.

Lumber

186-14 Jamaica Ave.
Jamaica, NY 11423

Phone 718-454-5522

HCP Solar Div.

Solar Heating Systems

Sealed Air Corp.
3433 Arden Rd.
Hayward, CA 94545

Phone 415-887-7000

Hager Hinge Co.

Hinges & Builders' Hardware

Victor & Thomas Sts.
St. Louis, MO 63104

Phone 314-772-4400

FAX 314-772-0744

Hall Hardware Co.

Hardware

PO Box D
Belfast, ME 04915

Catalog/Information Available Free

Mail Order Available

Credit Cards VISA/MC

Phone 207-338-1170

Hamilton Cedar Products Inc.

Cedar Shakes

3206 Hamilton Cemetary Rd.
Sedro Wooley, WA 98284

Phone 206-826-3785

Hamrick Truss, Inc.

Wood Trusses

PO Box 576M
Clearwater, FL 33517

Phone 813-442-3161

Hancock Gross Inc.

Plumbing Specialties

PO Box 8892
Trenton, NJ 08650

Phone 609-443-8180

Handcraft Tile Inc.

Quarry Floor & Wall Tile

1696 S. Main St.
Milpitas, CA 95035

Phone 408-262-1140

Harco Chemical Coatings

Manufacturer - Wood, Cement Floor Finish

208 Dupont St.
Brooklyn, NY 11222

Phone 718-389-3777

FAX 718-389-2032

Hardware + Plus Inc.

*Hardware, Lighting, Mouldings,
Wallcoverings, Plumbing Fittings*

701 E. Kingsley Rd.
Garland, TX 75041

Send $20.00 for Catalog/Information

Mail Order Available

Phone 214-271-0319
Toll Free 800-522-7336
FAX 214-271-9726

Harrison Hardwood Mfg. Inc.

Lumber

Hwy. 84 E.
Ferriday, LA 71334

Phone 318-757-3132

Hart & Cooley

*Manufacturer - Registers - Classics
Collection*

500 E. 8th Street
Holland, MI 49423

Phone 616-392-7855
FAX 800-223-8461

Hart Fireplace Furnishings

Fireplace Accessories

2549 Charlestown Rd.
New Albany, IN 47150

Phone 812-944-7723
FAX 812-944-7739

Hartwood Ltd.

Lumber, Plywood

East Golden Lane
PO Box 323
New Oxford, PA 17350

Credit Cards VISA/MC

Phone 717-624-4323
FAX 717-624-4365

Hastings Tile & Il Bagno Collection

*Distributor - Ceramic Italian Tile -
Monocottura, Bicottura, Terracotta,
Inserts, Borders, Steps for Floor, Wall,
Kitchen/Bath*

230 Park Avenue South
New York, NY 10003

Phone 212-674-9700
FAX 212-674-8083

Hayes Equipment Corp.

Woodstoves

PO Box 526
Unionville, CT 06085

Send $1.00 for Catalog/Information

Mail Order Available

Heart Truss & Engineering

Steel Roof Trusses

1830 N. Grand River
Lansing, MI 48906

Phone 517-372-0850

Hearthstone Hardware Co.

Reproduction Iron Hardware

Rt. 1, Box 170
Round Hill, VA 22141

Send $1.00 for Catalog/Information

Mail Order Available

Phone 804-973-3155

Heat Controller, Inc.

Manufacturer - Ground Water Heat Pump

PO Box 1089, 1900 Wellworth
Jackson, MI 49204-1089

Phone 517-787-2100

Heat-Fab Inc.

*Manufacturer - Stainless Steel Chimney
Liners & Stove Pipes*

38 Haywood St.
Greenfield, MA 01301

Phone 413-774-2356
Toll Free 800-772-0739
FAX 413-773-3133

Heat-N-Glo Fireplace Products Inc.

Manufacturer - Fireplace Products
6665 W. Hwy 13
Savage, MN 55378

Toll Free 800-669-4328
FAX 612-890-3525

Heatilator Inc.

Fireplaces, Chimneys, Wood Burning Stoves
1915 W. Saunders St.
Mount Pleasant, IA 52641

Phone 319-385-9211
Toll Free 800-321-7344
FAX 319-385-9225

Heating Research Co.

European Antique Cast Iron Stoves
Acworth Rd.
Acworth, NH 03601

Send $3.00 for Catalog/Information
Mail Order Available

Phone 603-835-6109

Heatway

Radiant Heat
3131 West Chestnut Expressway
Springfield, MO 65802

Toll Free 800-255-1996
FAX 417-864-8161

Heckler Brothers

Central Heating Supply & Repair Parts
4105 Steubenville Pike
Pittsburgh, PA 15205

Mail Order Available

Phone 412-922-6811

Helen Williams - Delft Tiles

Imported Antique Delft Tile
12643 Hortense St.
Studio City, CA 91604

Phone 818-761-2756

Henegan's Wood Shed

Exotic, Native Hard and Soft Woods, Table Slabs, Veneers
7760 Southern Blvd.
West Palm Beach, FL 33411

Send $1.00 for Catalog/Information

Phone 407-793-1557

Henssgen Hardware Corp.

Hardware
PO Box 2078
38 Everts Ave
Glen Falls, NY 12801

Phone 518-793-3593

Herbert H. Sabbeth Corp.

Lumber
55 N. Industry Court
Deer Park, NY 11729

Phone 516-242-0303

Heritage Energy Systems

Wood Burning Stoves, Fireplace Inserts
23 Balsam St.
Collingwood
Ont, CAN L9Y 4H7
Canada

Phone 705-445-7655

Hewi, Inc.

Door Hardware, Railing Systems, Cabinet Hardware, Bathroom Accessories
2851 Old Tree Dr.
Lancaster, PA 17603

Phone 717-293-1313
FAX 717-293-3270

High Point Glass & Decorative Co.

Decorative Glass
PO Box 101
High Point, NC 27261

Phone 919-884-8035

Hilltop Slate Co.

Roofing Tile

PO Box 201, Rte 22A
Middle Granville, NY 12849

Phone 518-642-2270

FAX 518-642-1220

Hines of Oxford

Tapestry Cushions & Wall Hangings - International Shipping

Tapestry Importers
Weavers Barn, Windmill Rd., Headington
OX3 7DE
Great Britain

Send $20.00 for Catalog/Information

Mail Order Available

Phone 011-44-865/741144

Hipkiss & Co. Ltd.

Door Hardware, Builders' Hardware

40-45 George St.
Birmingham B3 1QA
Great Britain

Phone 011-44-21/2365342

FAX 011-44-21/2364174

Hippo Hardware & Trading Co.

Hardware, Lighting, Plumbing

1040 E. Burnside
Portland, OR 97214

Send $2.00 for Catalog/Information

Mail Order Available

Phone 503-231-1444

FAX 503-231-5708

Hiskson Corporation

Weather Resistant Lumber

Perimeter 400 Center, Suite 680
1100 Johnson Ferry Rd.,NE
Atlanta, GA 30342

Catalog/Information Available Free

Historic Housefitters

Period Hardware, Lighting Fixtures

Farm to Market Rd.
Brewster, NY 10509

Send $3.00 for Catalog/Information

Phone 914-278-2427

FAX 914-278-7726

Historic Paints Ltd.

18th & 19th Century Authentic Paints

Burr Tavern
Route 1, Box 474
East Meredith, NY 13757

Phone 607-433-0229

Toll Free 800-664-6283

Hjelmeland Truss Corp.

Floor & Roof Trusses

Hwy. 169 N
PO Box 713
Algona, IA 50511

Phone 515-295-7701

Hodkin & Jones (Sheffield) Ltd.

Fireplaces and Accessories, Decorative Moulding

Callywhite La., Dronfield
Shefffield S18 6XP
Great Britain

Phone 011-44-246/290888

FAX 011-44-246/290292

Hoff Forest Products, Inc.

Lumber, Door Jambs, Frames, Sash Parts, Mouldings

420 W. Franklin Rd.
PO Box 208
Meridian, ID 83642

Phone 208-888-6798

FAX 208-888-5031

Building Supply

Holden Register, Inc.

Residential Heating Grilles
3 Hoffman St.
Kitchener
Ont., CAN N2M 3M5
Canada

Phone 519-576-6260

FAX 519-576-0115

Hollywood Disappearing Attic Stair Co.

Attic Stairs
9525 White Rock Trail
Dallas, TX 75238

Phone 214-348-7240

Homasote Company

Manufacturer - Polyisocyanurate Insulation
PO Box 7240
West Trenton, NJ 08628

Phone 609-883-3300

FAX 609-530-1584

Home Electric Supply

Wholesale - Electrical Supplies
1308 Jackson St.
Salem, IN 47167

Phone 812-883-3606

Home Improvement Supply

Building Supplies
85 Smith Ave.
Mansfield, OH 44950-2854

Phone 419-531-2176

Home Quarters Warehouse

Building Supply
1517 Sams Circle
Chesapeake, VA 23320-4694

Phone 804-543-1171

Home Warehouse Inc.

Building Supply
PO Box 3298
410 Green Bag Rd.
Sabraton, WV 26505

Phone 304-291-1006

Homestead Paint & Finishes

Wholesale Prices - Authentic Milk Paint & Finish
111 Mulpus Rd.
PO Box 1668
Lunenburg, MA 01462

Catalog/Information Available Free

Mail Order Available

Credit Cards Check/Money Order

Phone 508-582-6426

Horton Brasses

Brass Hardware - Cabinet & Furniture
Nooks Hill Rd., PO Box 120
Cromwell, CT 06416

Send $3.00 for Catalog/Information

Mail Order Available

Phone 203-635-6400

FAX 203-635-6473

House of Fara Inc.

Hardwood Trim & Decorative Moulding
520 Eggerbrecht Rd.
PO Box 164
La Porte, IN 46350

Phone 219-362-8544

Housecraft Associates

Building Restoration Epoxies
7 Goodale Rd.
Newton, NJ 08769

Catalog/Information Available Free

Mail Order Available

Phone 201-579-1112

FAX 201-579-1112

Hudevad Britain

Heating Systems
Hudevad HO, 130-132 Terrace Rd.
Walton-on-Thames, Surrey
KT12 2EA
Great Britain

Phone 011-44-932/247835

FAX 011-44-932/247694

Building Supply

The Complete Sourcebook

Hughes Roof Truss Co. Ltd.

Roof Trusses
71 Thompson St.
Ajax
Ont, CAN L1S 1R3
Canada

Phone 416-431-1931
FAX 416-683-6559

Humes

Manufacturer - Roof Tile & Shake
10650 Poplar Ave.
Fontant, CA 92335

Phone 714-350-4238

Huntington/Pacific Ceramics, Inc.

*Distributor - Beveled Edge Tile for Walls,
Counterops, Shower - Monocottura,
Bicottura for Wall, Floor, Kitchen/Bath*
3600 Conway
Fort Worth, TX 76111

Phone 817-838-2323
FAX 817-831-7168

Hurd Lumber Co.

Lumber
Box 631
East Lebanon, ME 04027

Phone 207-477-2620

Hurd Millwork Company

*Manufacturer - Dealer List - Wood
Windows and Patio Sliding Doors*
575 S. Whelen Ave.
Medford, WI 54451

Phone 715-748-2011
Toll Free 800-223-4873
FAX 715-748-6043

Hutch Mfg. Co.

Fireplace Accessories
PO Box 569
Bloomfield Hill, MI 48303

Phone 313-645-1000
FAX 313-645-1001

Hutcherson Tile

*Distributor - Ceramic Italian Tile
Monocottura, Bicottura, Terracotta,
Inserts, Borders, Steps for Floor, Wall,
Kitchen/Bath*
130 Mitchell Road
Houston, TX 77037

Phone 713-447-6354
FAX 713-820-0124

Hy-Ko Products Co.

Decorative Hardware
24001 Aurora Rd.
Bedfor Heights, OH 44146

Phone 216-232-8223
FAX 216-232-8227

Hydrotherm Inc.

Home Heating Units
Rockland Ave.
Northvale, NJ 07647

Phone 201-768-5500

I. C. R. S.P.A. (Appiani)

*Monocottura, Bicottura, Inserts,
Handmade, Steps, Borders for Floor &
Wall - Kitchen & Bath*
US Agent Ernesto Machado
Polygon Plaza, 2050 Center Ave. Ste.200
Fort Lee, NJ 07024

Phone 201-585-0992
FAX 201-585-0993

IKO Manufacturing Inc.

Roofing
120 Hay Rd.
Wilmington, DE 19089

Phone 302-764-3100
FAX 302-764-5852

IMPO Glaztile

Ceramic Tile
7600 County Line Rd.
Burr Ridge, IL 60521

Phone 708-655-4676
FAX 708-655-4696

Building Supply

ITT Rayonier Inc.

Manufacturer - Wood, Lumber, Building Materials

1177 Summer St.
Stamford, CT 06904

Phone 203-348-7000

Idaho Quartzite Corp.

Natural Stone Tile

1404 Broadway Ave.
Boise, ID 83706

Phone 208-343-2580
FAX 208-336-2076

Ideal tile of Manhatttan Inc.

Italian Tile

405 East 51st St. (Ist Ave.)
New York, NY 10022

Phone 212-759-2339

Idowa Timber

Roof Trusses

900 W. Risinger Rd.
Fort Worth, TX 76140

Phone 817-293-1001

Illahe Tileworks

Manufacturer - Interior & Exterior Tile

695 Mistletoe Rd.
Ashland, OR 97520

Mail Order Available

Phone 503-488-5072

Imperial Marble, Inc.

Table Tops, Window Sills, Bathroom Items, Vanity Tops

4637 NE 48th Terrace
Kansas City, MO 64119-3612

Phone 816-221-3574
FAX 816-221-5172

Imported European Hardware

Imported European Hardware

4320 W. Bell Drive
Las Vegas, NV 89118

Send $3.00 for Catalog/Information

Mail Order Available

Credit Cards Accepted

Phone 702-871-0722
Toll Free 800-779-7458
FAX 702-871-0991

Impronta S.P.A.

Monocottura, Bicottura, Terracotta, Inserts, Borders, Steps for Floor, Wall, Bath

US Agent Architectural Imports
4573 Ponce De Leon Blvd.
Coral Gables, FL 33146

Phone 305-661-1112
FAX 305-979-2660

Independent Lumber Co.

Lumber

12435 S. Hawthorne Blvd.
Hawthorne, CA 90250-4403

Phone 213-489-2565

Indiana Wood Products, Inc.

Lumber

5822 County Rd. 43
PO Box 1168
Middlebury, IN 46540

Phone 219-825-2129
FAX 219-825-2129

International Granite & Marble

Granite & Marble

2038 83rd St. N.
Bergen, NJ 07047

Iron Intentions Forge

Reproduction 18th Century Hardware

1112 Lucabaugh Mill Rd.
Westminster, MD 21157

Phone 410-876-6299

Building Supply

The Complete Sourcebook

Island Lumber Co., Inc.

Building Supply
Polpis Rd.
Nantucket, MA 02554
Phone 508-228-2600

Italian Tile Center

Buyers Guide to Italian Tile & US Distributors
499 Park Avenue
New York, NY 10022
Catalog/Information Available Free
Phone 212-980-1500
FAX 212-758-1050

J. H. Hamlen & Son

Lumber
PO Box 327
Little Rock, AR 72203
Phone 501-375-3233

J. H. Monteath

Wood
Box 143
South Amburg, NJ 00887
Mail Order Available
Phone 201-292-9333

J. H. Wood Shake Inc.

Wood Shingles
PO Box 68
Lebam, WA 98554
Phone 206-934-5323

Jacobsen Energy Industries, Inc.

Manufacturer - Ground Water Heat Pump
805 W. Fifth St.
Lansdale, PA 19446
Phone 215-361-1700

Jali Ltd.

Ceiling Systems, Radiator Covers, Shutters, Panels, Gazebo Components
Apsley Ho, Chartham
Canterbury, Kent
CT4 7HT
Great Britain
Phone 011-44-277/831710
FAX 011-44-227/831950

Jameco Industries Inc.

Plumbing Supply & Fixtures
248 Wyandanch Ave.
Wyandanch, NY 11798
Phone 516-643-5300
FAX 516-643-5305

Jameson Home Products

Electronic Thermostats
2820 Thatcher Rd.
Downers Grove, IL 60515
Toll Free 800-445-8299

Jasper Wood Products Co., Inc.

Plywood, Hardwood
PO Box 271
Jasper, IN 47546
Phone 812-482-3454

Johnson Paint Co. Inc.

Paint
355 Newbury St.
Boston, MA 02115
Send $1.00 for Catalog/Information
Mail Order Available
Phone 617-536-4838
FAX 617-536-8832

Johnsonius Precision Millwork

Wood, Millwork, Flooring
PO Box 275
McKenzie, TN 38201
Catalog/Information Available Free
Phone 901-352-5656

Johnston & Rhodes Bluestone Co.

Natural Stone & Lumber

1 Bridge St.
East Branch, NY 13576

Mail Order Available

Phone 607-363-7595

FAX 607-363-7894

Jones & Barclay Ltd.

Hardware & Door Locks

63 Bath Row
Birmingham B15 1LY
Great Britain

Phone 011-44-21/6432647

Julius Seidel & Company

Manufacturer - Roofing Tile, Cedar Shake, Shingle

3514 Gratiot St.
St. Louis, MO 63103

Phone 314-772-4000

Toll Free 800-325-1923

FAX 314-772-4010

KPT, Incorporated

Ceramic Tile

State Road 54 East
PO Box 468
Bloomfield, IN 47424

Phone 812-384-3563

FAX 812-384-4222

Kakabeka Timber Ltd.

Tongue & Groove Wood Paneling, Wood Flooring

PO Box 278
Kakabeka Falls
Ont., CAN P0T 1W0
Canada

Phone 807-473-9311

FAX 807-473-9488

Kalk-og Teglvaerksforeningen af 1893

Member - Federation Europeenne Des Fabricants De Tuiles Et De Briques

Norre Voldgade 34
DK-1358 Kobenhavn K
Denmark

Phone 011-45-33-143414

FAX 011-45-33-141233

Kallwall's Solar Components Center

Solar Heating Products

Box 237
Manchester, NH 03105

Send $2.50 for Catalog/Information

Mail Order Available

Phone 603-668-8186

Kanebridge Corp.

Hardware, Plumbing and Heating Supply

360 Franklin Turnpike
Mahwah, NJ 07430

Phone 201-825-1776

Kawartha Wood Products Ltd.

Hardwood Lumber

2495 Hanes Rd.
Mississauga
Ont., CAN L4Y 1Y7
Canada

Phone 416-663-9800

Kayne & Son Custom Forged Hardware

Hardware, Fireplace Accessories

100 Daniel Ridge Rd.
Candler, NC 28715

Send $4.00 for Catalog/Information

Mail Order Available

Phone 704-667-8868

FAX 704-665-8303

Building Supply

The Complete Sourcebook

3 - 51

Kebring Hardware

Decorative Hardware
16 Quaker Place
Milford, CT 06460
Phone 203-878-2043

Keen Building Components Inc.

Roof & Floor Trusses
115 Young St. Box 210
Fredericksburg, VA 22401
Phone 703-371-2655

Kelly & Hayes Electrical Supply Inc.

Electrical Supplies
1042 Atlantic Ave.
Brooklyn, NY 11238
Phone 718-638-7761
FAX 718-789-1542

Kemp & George

Decorative Hardware, Bath Accessories, Lighting
PO Box 510
Madison, VA 22727-0510

Credit Cards Accepted
Phone 703-672-1712
Toll Free 800-456-0788

Keniston Tile & Design

Tile
269 Commercial St.
Portland, ME 04101

Send $5.00 for Catalog/Information
Phone 207-775-2238

Kennedy Electrical Supply

Electrical Supplies
221-18 Merrick Blvd.
Jamaica, NY 11413
Phone 718-527-5600

Kent Trusses Ltd.

Roof & Floor Trusses
PO Box 190
Sundridge
Ont., CAN P0A 1Z0
Canada
Phone 705-384-5326

Keokuk Stove Works

Antique Coal, Gas, Wood Stoves
1201 High Street
Keokuk, IA 52632
Phone 319-524-6202
FAX 319-524-7388

Kickapoo Diversified Products Inc.

Wood Burning Stoves
Main St., PO Box 127
La Farge, WI 54639
Phone 608-625-4431

Kilian Industries Ltd.

Floor Trusses
PO Box 1800
Morinville
Alta, CAN T0G 1P0
Canada
Phone 403-939-4101

Kimberly Black

Braided Rugs
PO Box 472927
Charlotte, NC 28247

Send $3.00 for Catalog/Information
Phone 704-846-6099
Toll Free 800-296-6099

Kinsman Company

Aluminum Gutter Guards
River Road
Point Pleasant, PA 18950

Catalog/Information Available Free
Toll Free 800-733-5613

Klingenberg Dekoramik GmbH

Manufacturer - Ceramic Wall & Floor Tile
1020
Klingeberg D-W-8763
Germany

Phone 011-49-9372/1311
FAX 011-49-9372131220

Koninkijk Verbond van Nederlandse

Member - Federation Europeenne Des Fabricants De Tuiles Et De Briques
Baksteenfabrikanten
Hoofdstraat 8, Postbus 51, NL-6994 ZH
Netherlands

Phone 011-31-830959110
FAX 011-31-830951077

Kountry Kraft Hardwoods

Hardwoods
RR1
Lake City, IA 51449
Mail Order Available

Phone 712-464-8140

Kraftile Company

Natural Clay Tile
800 Kraftile Rd.
Fremont, CA 94536

Phone 415-793-4432
FAX 415-791-2953

Kris Elosvolo

Italian Tile - Monocottura, Bicottura, Terracotta, Inserts, Borders, Steps for Floor, Wall, Bath
US Agent of Impronta S.P.A
31431 Sundance Drive.
S.J. Capistrano, CA 92675

Kunico Truss & Prefab Ltd.

Floor & Roof Trusses
1276 32nd St., PO Box 34
Medicine Hat
Alta., CAN T1A 7E5
Canada

Phone 403-527-4732
FAX 403-527-2658

L'esperance Tile Works

Kitchen & Bathroom Reproduction Tile
237 Sheridan Ave.
Albany, NY 12210
Mail Order Available

Phone 518-465-5586
FAX 518-465-5586

La Luz Canyon Studio

Handpainted Mural Ceramic Tile
PO Box 683
La Luz, NM 88337

Phone 505-434-0112

LaFaenza America Inc.

US Agent for Ceramiche Lafaenza S.p.a. Italian Tile Monocttura, Bicottura, Handmade for Floor, Wall, Bath
63 Harlington Court
Kensington, CA 94707

Phone 415-524-5278
FAX 415-524-0588

Lakeland Builders Supply

Building Supply
9700 Dixie Hwy.
Clarkston, MA 48106

Phone 313-625-8995

Lampe Lumber Co.

Roof Trusses
PO Box 1098
Tulare, CA 93274

Phone 209-688-6611
FAX 209-688-9267

Landmark Truss, Inc.

Roof Trusses
3222X NE 24th St.
Oscala, FL 32670

Phone 904-732-5002

Latco Ceramic Tile

Manufacturer - Wall & Floor Ceramic Tile
2943 Gleneden St.
Los Angeles, CA 90039

Phone 213-664-1171
FAX 213-665-6971

Laticrete International Inc.

Ceramic Tile
1 Laticrete Park N
Bethany, CT 06525

Phone 203-393-1111
FAX 203-393-1684

Laufen International, Inc.

Manufacturer - Ceramic Tile
4942 E. 66th St., North
PO Box 6600
Tulsa, OK 74156

Phone 918-428-3851
Toll Free 800-331-3651
FAX 918-428-1279

Lawrence R. McCoy & Co. Inc.

Lumber
120 Front St.
Worcester, MA 01608

Phone 508-798-7575
FAX 617-798-7516

Leatherback Industries

Manufacturer - Roofing
111 Hillcrest Rd.
Hollister, CA 95023

Phone 408-637-5841

Leduc Truss

Roof & Floor Trusses
4507 61st Ave.
Leduc
Alta, CAN T9E 6M3
Canada

Phone 403-986-0334

Lehman Hardware

*Order Direct - Amish Lamps,
Woodstoves, Victorian Gas & Electric
Stoves*
PO Box 41
4779 Kidron Rd.
Kidron, OH 44636

Send $2.00 for Catalog/Information

Mail Order Available

Phone 216-857-5441
FAX 216-857-5785

Lemee's Fireplace Equipment

Fireplace Equipment
815 Bedford St.
Bridgewater, MA 02324

Send $2.00 for Catalog/Information

Phone 508-697-2672

Lemire Lumber Co. Inc.

Hardwood Lumber
21 Vimy N
Sherbrooke
Que., CAN J1J 3M3
Canada

Phone 819-562-7466
FAX 819-564-2672

Lennox International Inc.

Home Heat Units
2100 Lake Park Blvd.
Richardson, TX 75080

Phone 214-497-5258

Leonardo 1502 Ceramica S.p. A.

Italian Ceramic Tile
Via G. Di Vittorio
24 - 40020 Casalfiumanese Bologna
Italy

Phone 011-39-542/664111
FAX 011-39-542/665170

Building Supply

Leslie-Locke Inc. – Lone Star Ceramics Company

Leslie-Locke Inc.

Manufacturer - Skylights, Ventalation Products, Window Guards, Ornamental Iron Railings & Columns, Fencing, Ductwork

4501 Circle 75 Parkway
Suite 6300
Atlanta, GA 30339

Catalog/Information Available Free

Phone 404-953-6366
Toll Free 800-755-9392
FAX 404-953-6366

Levesque Plywood Ltd.

Plywood, Particleboard

Prince St.E, PO Box 10
Hearst
Ont., CAN P0L 1N0
Canada

Phone 705-362-4242
FAX 705-372-1549

Liberty Cedar

Wood Roofing

535 Liberty Lane
W. Kingston, RI 02892

Mail Order Available

Phone 401-789-6626
Toll Free 800-882-3327
FAX 401-789-0320

Lifetile

Manufacturer - Roof Tile

Boral Concrete Products
3511 No. Riverside Ave.
Rialto, CA 92376

Phone 714-822-4407

Lifetime Rooftile Co.

Manufacturer - Roof Tile

1805 High Grove Lane
Naperville, IL 60540

Phone 815-357-8600
Toll Free 800-359-4166

Lindal Cedar Sunrooms

Cedar Sunrooms, Flooring

PO Box 24426
Seattle, WA 98124

Phone 206-725-0900
Toll Free 800-426-0536

Livingston Systems Inc.

Solar Collectors, Solar Equipment

State Rd. 1 South
10 Paul R. Foulke Pky.
Hagerstown, IN 47346

Phone 317-489-4359

Livos PlanChemistry

Finishes for Floors

2641 Cerrillos Rd.
Santa Fe, NM 87501

Liz's Antique Hardware

Antique Hardware - Door, Window, Furniture, Lighting, Bath Accessories Original circa 1850-1950 - Will match photo or template.

453 South La Brea
Los Angeles, CA 90036

Mail Order Available

Phone 213-939-4403
FAX 213-939-4387

Lochinvar Water Heater Corp.

Manufacturer - Water Heaters

2005 Elm Hill Pike
Nashville, TN 37210

Phone 615-889-8900
FAX 615-885-4403

Lone Star Ceramics Company

Ceramic Tile

PO Box 810215
Dallas, TX 75381-0215

Phone 214-247-3111
FAX 214-247-3113

Building Supply

The Complete Sourcebook

3 - 55

Loredo Truss Co. Inc.

Trusses
PO Box 140006
Austin, TX 78414-0006
Phone 512-926-9518

Louisiana-Pacific Corporation

Manufacturer - Wood Siding Products, Vinyl Windows & Patio Doors, All Wood Windows & Patio Doors, Joists - Floor & Roof Applications, Nature Guard Insulation
111 Southwest 5th Ave.
Portland, OR 97204

Catalog/Information Available Free
Phone 503-221-0800
FAX 503-796-0204

Ludowici Celadon Co. Inc.

Manufacturer - Order Direct - Roof Tiles
4757 Tile Plant Rd.
PO Box 69
New Lexington, OH 43764

Mail Order Available
Phone 614-342-1995
Toll Free 800-945-8453
FAX 614-342-5175

Lumber Specialties

Floor & Roof Trusses
1301 3rd Ave. N.E.
Dyersville, IA 52040
Phone 319-875-2858

M & H Truss Co. Inc.

Roof Trusses, Beams, Headers
4510 NE 52nd Ave.
Gainesville, FL 32609
Phone 904-376-5204

M & S Systems

Building Products
2861 Congressman Lane
Dallas, TX 75220
Phone 214-358-3196

M. L. Condon Company Inc.

Lumber, Custom Millwork, Doors, Stair Railings, Moulding, Columns
238 Ferris Ave.
White Plains, NY 10603

Send $2.00 for Catalog/Information
Phone 914-946-4111
FAX 914-946-3779

M. Wolchonok & Son Inc.

Reproduction Hardware
155 E. 52nd St.
New York, NY 10023

Mail Order Available
Phone 212-755-2168

Mac The Antique Plumber

Antique Plumbing Supplies
6325 Elvas Ave.
Sacramento, CA 95819

Send $6.00 for Catalog/Information

Mail Order Available

Credit Cards MC/VISA
Phone 916-454-4507
Toll Free 800-916-2284
FAX 916-454-4150

MacDonald Stained Glass

Stained Glass, Lamps, Sconces, Windows
Lobster Cove Rd.
Boothbay Harbor, ME 04538
Phone 207-633-4815

Majestic Co.

Manufacturer - Woodburning & Gas Fireplaces & Accessories - Marble & Slate Surrounds
1000 E. Market Street
Huntington, IN 46750-2579
Phone 219-356-8000
Toll Free 800-525-1898
FAX 219-356-9672

Building Supply

Malm Fireplaces Inc.

Fireplaces
368 Yolanda Ave.
Santa Rosa, CA 95401

Phone 707-546-8955
FAX 707-571-8036

Mammoth

Manufacturer - Ground Water Heat Pump
13120-B County Road 6
Minneapolis, MN 55441

Phone 612-559-2711

Mannington Ceramic Tile

Manufacturer - Ceramic Tile
PO Box 1777
Lexington, NC 27293-1777

Phone 704-249-3931
FAX 704-249-8928

Mansfield Plumbing Products

Manufacturer - Plumbing Products
150 First St.
Perryville, OH 44864

Phone 419-938-5211
FAX 419-938-6234

Manufacturers Lumber & Millwork, Inc.

Lumber & Millwork
PO Box 133
Auburn, MA 01501

Catalog/Information Available Free

Phone 508-832-3291

Manufacturers Wholesale

Roofing Materials - Wholesale
1458 Furnace
Montgomery, AL 36104-1602

Phone 205-262-0344

Manville Manufacturing Corporation

Manufacturer - Plumbing Fixtures
342 Rockwell Avenue
Pontiac, MI 48341-2458

Phone 313-334-4583

Manville/Schuller

Manufacturer - Roofing, Asphalt & Fiberglass Shingle
Roofing Systems Division
717 17th St., PO Box 5108
Denver, CO 80217

Phone 303-978-2000
Toll Free 800-654-3103
FAX 303-978-2318

Marble & Tile Imports

Granite, French Limestone, Marble - Countertops, Fireplace Facings, Dining Tables
1290 Powell St.
Emeryville, CA 94608

Phone 415-420-0383
FAX 415-428-1251

Marble Concepts

Marble Tile
400 Northern Blvd.
Great Neck, NY 11021

Catalog/Information Available Free

Phone 516-487-4679

Marble Institute of America

Marble, Slate, Granite, Limestone, Onyx
33505 State St.
Farmington, MI 48335

Phone 313-476-5558
FAX 313-476-1630

Marble Modes Inc.

Granite and Marble
15-25 130th St.
College Point, NY 11356

Phone 718-539-1334
Toll Free 800-826-6637
FAX 718-353-8564

Building Supply

The Complete Sourcebook

3 - 57

Marble Technics Ltd.

Marble Paneling
A & D Building
150 E. 58th St.
New York, NY 10155
Send $1.00 for Catalog/Information
Mail Order Available
Phone 212-750-9189

Marble Unlimited

Marble
1963 Alpine Way
Hayward, CA 94545
Phone 415-785-9940

Marion Plywood Corp.

Plywood
Corner of Garfield & Parkview Sts.
PO Box 497
Marion, WI 54950
Phone 715-754-5231
FAX 715-754-2582

Marjam Supply Company

Building Supply - Moulding, Flooring, Lumber
20 Rewe St.
Brooklyn, NY 11211
Phone 718-388-6465

Marlborough Ceramic Tiles

Ceramic Tile
Elcot La.
Marlborough, Wilts
5NB 2AY
Great Britain
Phone 011-44-672/512422

Marley Roof Tiles, Canada Ltd.

Manufacturer - Roof Tile
281 Alliance Rd.
Milton
ON L9T 4N9
Canada
Toll Free 800-521-5832
FAX 416-878-8334

Marque Enterprises

Plumbing Window Trap
3630 McCall Rd., Suite D
Englewood, FL 34224
Phone 813-475-0164

Marquette Lumber Co. Inc.

Lumber
3201 Cardinal Drive.
PO Box 3040
Vero Beach, FL 32964
Phone 407-231-5252
FAX 407-231-7560

Marsak Cohen, Cohen Corp.

Hardware, Plumbing & Heating Supply
623 Medford State Road
Patchogue, NY 11772
Phone 516-475-0306

Martin Industries Inc.

Woodburning Stoves, Fireplace Inserts, Heat Pumps
301E Tennessee St.
PO Box 128
Florence, AL 35631
Phone 205-767-0330

Martin-Senour Paints

Manufacturer - Paint
101 Prospect Avenue NW
Cleveland, OH 44115
Toll Free 800-542-8468
FAX 216-566-2666

Maruhachi Ceramics of America Inc.

Manufacturer - Roof Tile
1985 Sampson Ave.
Corona, CA 91719
Phone 714-736-9590
FAX 714-736-6052

Marwin Co.

Disappearing Stairs, Bi-Folding Doors
PO Box 9126
Columbia, SC 29290

Phone 803-776-2396
FAX 803-776-5852

Maryland Lumber Co.

Lumber, Building Materials
2600 W. Franklin St.
Baltimore, MD 21223

Phone 301-233-3333

Masco Corporation

Plumbing Fixtures
55 East 111th St.
PO box 40980
Indianapolis, IN 46280

Phone 317-848-1812

Master Shield

Vinyl Siding
1202 N. Bowie Dr.
Weatherford, TX 76086

Mastic Corp.

Insulated & Solid Vinyl Siding
131 S. Taylor St.
PO Box 65
South Bend, IN 46624

Phone 219-288-4621

Maui Trading Co.

Kiln Dried Wood & Custom Furniture
Box 263
Kula, HI 96790

Phone 808-878-2705

Maurice L. Condon Co.

Oak, Cherry, Maple, Birch, Teak, Walnut Wood
246 Ferris Ave.
White Plains, NY 10603

Send $1.00 for Catalog/Information

Phone 914-946-4111

Mays Lumber Co.

Roof Trusses
Hwy. 3 & 7 W.
PO Box 849
Broken Bow, OK 74728-0849

Phone 405-584-9709

McCloskey Corp.

Finishes for Floors
7600 State Rd.
Philadelphia, PA 19136

Phone 215-624-4400

McIntyre Tile Co. Inc.

Handcrafted Ceramic Tile
55 W. Grant St.
PO Box 14
Healdsburg, CA 95448

Phone 707-433-8866
FAX 707-433-0548

McLaughlin Roof Trusses Ltd.

Roof Trusses
R.R. 1, Upper Woodstock
N.B., CAN E0J 1Z0
Canada

Phone 506-375-8884

McMillen Lumber Co.

Lumber
203 Center St.
Sheffield, PA 16347

Phone 814-968-3241
FAX 814-968-3843

Meeco Mfg. Co.

Fireplace, Stove & Heating Products
11325 Roosevelt Way N.E.
PO Box 75086
Seattle, WA 98125-0086

Phone 206-364-9393
FAX 206-361-9393

Meissen-Keramik GmbH

Manufacturer - Ceramic Tile
Neumarkt 5
0-8250 Meissen
Germany
> Phone 011-49-3521820
> FAX 011-49-352/182346

Merit Metal Products Corp.

*Decorative Brass Hardware - Over 600
items offered for Doors, Cabinets,
Furniture, Registers*
Mr. Harvey Scribner
242 Valley Rd.
Warrington, PA 18976

Send $10.00 for Catalog/Information
> Phone 215-343-2500
> FAX 215-343-4839

Met-Tile, Inc.

*Spanish Style - Galvanized Steel Roofing
System*
1745 Monticell Ct.
PO Box 4268
Ontario, CA 91761
> Phone 714-947-0311

Metco Tile Distributors

*Ceramic Tile - Monocottura, Bicottura,
Floor, Wall for Kitchen & Bath*
291 Arsenal Street
Watertown, MA 02172
> Phone 617-926-1100
> FAX 617-926-9714

Meyer Furnace Co.

House Heating & Cooling Units
1300 SW Washington St.
Peoria, IL 61602
> Phone 309-673-6351
> FAX 309-673-6358

Mid-State Truss Co., Inc.

Roof Trusses
PO Box 74-P
Lakeland, FL 33802
> Phone 813-665-1309
> FAX 813-294-4588

Midwest Custom Brass

Brass Fixtures
34691 N. Wilson
Ingleside, IL 60041

Send $1.00 for Catalog/Information

Mail Order Available
> Phone 312-546-2200

Midwest Dowel Works, Inc.

*Wood Dowels - Oak, Walnut, Hickory,
Maple, Cherry, Mahogany, Teak*
4631 Hutchinson Rd.
Cincinnati, OH 45248

Send $1.00 for Catalog/Information

Mail Order Available
> Phone 573-574-8488

Midwest Lumber & Supply

Building Supplies
916 D St. S.
Fort Smith, AR 72901-4506
> Phone 501-783-8971

Mill & Timber Products, Ltd.

*Western Red Cedar Lumber, Siding &
Paneling*
12770-116th Ave.
Surrey
B.C., CAN V3V 7H9
Canada
> Phone 604-580-2781

Millen Roofing Company

Manufacturer - Slate & Tile Roofing
2247 North 31 St.
Milwaukee, WI 53208

Mail Order Available
> Phone 414-442-1424
> FAX 414-442-1526

Building Supply

Miller Shingle Co., Inc. – Monier Roof Tile Inc.

Miller Shingle Co., Inc.

Manufacturer - Wood Shingles
208-20 102nd Ave. NE
Granite Falls, WA 98252
Phone 206-691-7727

Minnco Inc.

Plumbing Fixtures
1197 Baltimore-Annapolis Blvd.
PO Box 310
Arnold, MD 21012
Phone 301-544-7399

Minton Corley Collection

Furniture, Mirrors Chairs, Tables
2903 Shotts St.
Fort Worth, TX 76107
Phone 817-332-8993

Minuteman International Co.

Fireplace Doors, Surrounds and Accessories
75 Sawyer Passway
Fitchburg, MA 01420

Send $5.00 for Catalog/Information

Mail Order Available
Phone 508-343-7475

Mission Tile West

Handcrafted & Painted Ceramic Tile
853 Mission St.
S. Pasadena, CA 91030

Mail Order Available
Phone 818-799-4595
FAX 818-799-8769

Mohawk Industries Inc.

Woodburning Stoves
173 Howland Ave.
Adams, MA 01220
Phone 413-743-3648

Mojave Granite Co.

Manufacturer - Granite
1651 Miller Ave.
Los Angeles, CA 90063
Phone 213-268-3164

Moller's Building & Home Centers

Building Material
821 Hampshire
Quincy, IL 62301-3041
Phone 217-223-4281

Monadnock Forest Products, Inc.

Hardwood Lumber
Prescott Rd.
Jaffrey, NH 03452
Phone 603-532-4471
FAX 603-532-8759

Monarch Radiator Enclosures

Steel Radiator Enclosures
2744 Arkansas Drive
Brooklyn, NY 11234

Send $1.00 for Catalog/Information

Mail Order Available
Phone 201-796-4117
FAX 201-796-7717

Monarch Tile Inc.

Manufacturer - Ceramic Tile
5225 Phillips Hwy.
Jacksonville, FL 32207-7934
Phone 904-733-0727
FAX 904-733-0766

Mongold Lumber Co., Inc.

Lumber, Millwork
Rte. 1, Box 6
Elkins, WV 26241
Phone 304-636-2081
FAX 304-636-4000

Monier Roof Tile Inc.

Manufacturer - Roof Tile
750 Tile City Dr. South #200
Orange, CA 92668
Phone 714-750-5366
FAX 714-750-0751

Building Supply

The Complete Sourcebook

3 - 61

Monitor products

Kerosene Heaters
PO Box 3408
Princeton, NJ 08543
Send $1.00 for Catalog/Information
Phone 201-329-0900

Monroe Coldren & Sons

18th & 19th Century Hardware, Shutters, Doors, Mantels
723 E. Virginia Ave.
West Chester, PA 19380
Mail Order Available
Phone 610-692-5651

Moretti-Harrah Marble Co.

Marble Floor & Wall Tile
PO Box 330
Sylacauga, AL 35150
Phone 205-249-4901

Morris Paint & Varnish Co.

Paint & Varnish
120 Main St.
East St. Louis, IL 62201
Phone 618-271-6692

Mosaic Supplies Inc.

Italian Imported Tile - Bicottura, Inserts, Borders, Handmade for Wall, Bath
2274-76 Flatbush Ave.
Brooklyn, NY 11234
Phone 718-253-5800
FAX 718-285-1864

Motawi Tileworks

Order Direct - Handmade Embossed Ceramic Tile
3301 Packard Rd.
Ann Arbor, MI 48108
Catalog/Information Available Free
Mail Order Available
Credit Cards MC/VISA
Phone 313-971-0765

Mount Baker Plywood Inc.

High Grade Plywood
PO Box 997
Bellingham, WA 98227
Phone 206-733-3960

Murmac Paint Mfg. Co.

Paint
1300 Harvey St.
Beloit, WI 53511
Phone 608-362-1900

Murray Bros. Lumber Co. Ltd.

Lumber
PO Box 70
Madawaska
Ont., CAN K0J 2C0
Canada
Phone 613-637-2840

Mutual Screw & Supply

Hardware, Plumbing & Heating Supply
68 W. Passaic St.
Rochelle Park, NJ 07662
Phone 201-845-5700

Mystica & Company Inc.

Decorative Hardware
1265 Birchrun Rd.
Chester Springs, PA 19425
Mail Order Available
Phone 610-469-0535
FAX 610-469-0999

NHC Inc.

Manufacturer - Hearth Stone Wood or Gas Stoves
PO Box 1069
Morrisville, VT 05661
Catalog/Information Available Free
Phone 802-888-5232
Toll Free 800-827-8683
FAX 802-888-7249

NRG Barriers, Inc.

*Polyisocyanurate Insulation - Member -
Polyisocyanurate Insulation
Manufacturers Association*

15 Lund Road
Saco, ME 04072

Nailite International Inc.

*Manufacturer - Acrylium Siding, Cedar
Shakes, Brick & Stone Panels*

1251 NW 165th St.
Miami, FL 33169

Phone 305-620-6200

Toll Free 800-328-9018

Nashville Sash & Door Co.

Building Supply

3040 Sidco Dr.
Nashville, TN 37204

Phone 615-254-1371

National Association of Master Masons

*President - M. Frank Stephens Member -
European International Federation of
Natural Stone Industry*

Crown Buildings, High Street
G-B Aylesbury, Buckinghamshire
HP20 1SL
Great Britain

Phone 011-44-296/434750

FAX 011-44-296/431332

National Ceramics

Ceramic & Mosaic Tile

Sheepscar Way, Scott Hill Rd.
Leeds
LS7 3JD
Great Britain

Phone 011-44-532/625162

National Ceramics of Florida

*Italian Ceramic Tile - Monocottura,
Bicottura, Floor, Wall for Kitchen & Bath*

7800 NW 34th St.
Miami, FL 33122

Phone 305-591-8326

FAX 305-592-7596

National Concrete Masonry Assoc.

Interlocking Foundation Blocks

PO Box 781
2302 Horse Pen Rd.
Herndon, VA 22070

National Home Products

Indoor & Outdoor Solar Clothes Dryers

30-46 S. Keystone Ave.
Emmaus, PA 18049-0306

Phone 215-967-2184

National Solar Supply

Solar Equipment

2331 Adams Dr. N.W.
Atlanta, GA 30318

Phone 404-352-3478

Native American Hardwoods

Many Species of Wood

Street Address Not Available
Hamberg, NY 10475

Toll Free 800-688-7551

Nemo Tile Company, Inc.

*Distributor - Ceramic Italian Tile
Monocottura, Bicottura, Terracotta,
Handmade, Inserts, Borders, Special
Pieces, Hand-decorated (Floor, Wall
Kitchen/Bath)*

177-02 Jamaica Avenue
Jamaica, NY 11432

Phone 718-291-5969

FAX 718-291-5992

Nepco, Inc.

Manufacturer - Ground Water Heat Pump

PO Box 331
Monroeville, PA 15146

Phone 412-856-5440

Nevada County Building Supply

Building Supply

12461 La Barr Meadows Rd.
Grass Valley, CA 95949-9582

Phone 916-273-0937

New Buck Corporation

Standing Stoves - Wood, Gas, Coal
1265 Bakersfield Highway
Spruce Pine, NC 28777

Catalog/Information Available Free

Phone 704-765-6144
Toll Free 800-438-2825

New England Brassworks

Brass Hardware
214 Elmwood St.
N. Attleboro, MA 02760

Mail Order Available

Phone 508-699-9322

New England Slate Company

Roofing Slate, Floor & Wall Slate
RD 1, Burr Pond Rd.
Sudbury, VT 05733

Mail Order Available

Phone 802-247-8809
FAX 802-247-0089

New England Tool Company

Architectural Metalwork, Home Accessories
PO Box 30
Chester, NY 10918

Send $2.00 for Catalog/Information

Phone 914-782-5332
FAX 914-651-7857

New-Aire Mfg. Co., Inc.

Fireplaces, Stoves, Inserts
PO Box 603
Joplin, MO 64802

Phone 417-782-1260

Nexton Industries Inc.

Decorative Hardware
51 South 1st St.
Brooklyn, NY 11211

Mail Order Available

Phone 718-599-3837

Nicola Ceramics & Marble

Marble & Granite - Kitchen, Baths, Tables, Steps, Fireplaces Vanitytops
2515 Merrick Rd.
Bellmore, NY 11710

Phone 516-783-5965
FAX 516-783-5991

Nonweiler Co.

Enamels, Lacquers & Paint
PO Box 1007
Oshkosh, WI 54902-1007

Phone 414-231-0850
FAX 414-231-8085

Norges Teglindustrieforening

Member - Federation Europeennee Des Fabricants De Tuiles Et De Briques
c/o Mur-Sentret
Forsningsveien 3B
Norway

Phone 011-47-2/0965888
FAX 011-47-2/601192

North American Stone Co. Ltd.

Interlocking Stone for Driveways or Patios
287 Armstrong Ave.
Georgetown, Ontario
Canada

Phone 416-453-1438

North Coast Shake Co.

Shake & Shingles
PO Box 12
Aloha, WA 98525

Phone 206-276-4562

North Country Lumber Co. Inc.

Lumber & Flooring
PO Box 915
Mellen, WI 54546

Phone 715-274-4311
FAX 715-274-2304

Building Supply

North Fields Restorations – O'Brien Bros. Slate Company

North Fields Restorations

Antique Pine, Oak, Chestnut Lumber

PO Box 741, 672 Wethersfield St.
Rowley, MA 01969

Catalog/Information Available Free

Phone 508-948-2722

FAX 508-948-7563

North Hoquiam Cedar Products Inc.

Cedar Shake & Shingles

902 Monroe St.
PO Box 118
Hoquiam, WA 98550

Phone 206-538-1350

Northern Michigan Truss Co.

Roof & Floor Trusses

M 33 Hwy.
PO Box 24
Cheboygan, MI 49721

Phone 616-627-7832

Northland Hardwood Lumber Co.

Hardwood Lumber

County Rd. 9
PO Box 1411
Bemidji, MN 56601

Phone 218-751-0550

FAX 218-751-5924

Northwest Builders Hardware

Builders' Hardware

5204 E. Lake Sammamish Rd. SE
PO Box 1008
Issaquah, WA 98027-1008

Phone 206-391-3700

FAX 206-391-2070

Northwest Hardwoods Inc.

Hardwood Lumber

2 Lincoln Center
10220 S.W. Greenburg
Portland, OR 97223

Phone 503-248-9200

Nouveau Glass Art

Stained Glass

7907 Argyll Rd.
Edmonton, Alta
Edmonton T6C 4A9
Canada

Phone 403-468-9399

Novatile Ltd.

Ceramic Tile

Unit 25, Dawley Trading Est
Stallings La, Kingswinford, W Midlands
DY6 7BL
Great Britain

Phone 011-44-384/270786

Nuove Ceramiche Ricchetti, S.r.l.

Italian Ceramic Tile

Via Radici in Piano, 428
41049 Sassuolo Modena
Italy

Phone 011-39-536/800050

FAX 011-39-536/807355

Nutone

Manufacturer - Vacumn System, Security Systems, Bath & Wall Heaters

Madison & Red Bank Rd.
Cincinnati, OH 45227

Send $3.00 for Catalog/Information

Phone 513-527-5100

Toll Free 800-543-8687

Nuttle Lumber

Wood Trusses

7th & Lincoln Sts.
Denton, MD 21629

Phone 301-479-2500

O'Brien Bros. Slate Company

Roofing Slate

57 North St.
Granville, NY 12832

Mail Order Available

Phone 518-642-2105

Building Supply

The Complete Sourcebook

3 - 65

O'Dette Energies of Canada Ltd.

Wood & Coal Burning Stoves

595 O'Connor Dr.
Kingston
Ont., CAN K7P 1J9
Canada

Phone 613-384-1459

OK Truss Co. Inc.

Roof Trusses

PO Box 1171
Tavares, FL 32778

Phone 904-742-1616

Ohio Hardwood Lumber Co.

Hardwood Lumber

PO Box 2205
Youngstown, OH 44504-0205

Phone 216-759-0353

Old Carolina Brick Company

Manufacturer - Brick

475 Majolica Rd.
Salisbury, NC 28147

Mail Order Available

Phone 704-636-8850
FAX 704-636-0000

Old Country Ceramic Tile

Imported Italian Ceramic Tile Bicottura for Kitchen & Bath

27 Urban Ave.
Westbury, NY 11590

Phone 516-334-6161
FAX 516-338-8781

Old Fashioned Milk Paint Co.

Manufacturer - Authentic Milk Paint

436 Main St.
Groton, MA 01450

Mail Order Available

Phone 508-448-6336
FAX 508-448-2754

Old Home Building & Restoration

Antique Building Materials

PO Box 384
West Suffield, CT 06093

Mail Order Available

Phone 203-668-2445

Old World Hardware Co.

Reproduction Victorian Hardware, Bathroom Fixtures

103 N. Texas
DeLeon, TX 76444

Send $6.00 for Catalog/Information

Credit Cards MC/VISA

Phone 817-893-3862
FAX 817-893-3846

Olderman Mfg. Corp.

Plumbing Supplies

PO Box 917
Bridgeport, CT 06601

Phone 203-333-3146

Ole Country Barn

Order by Phone - Colonial, Victorian Style Paint - Interior, Exterior

PO Box 279
Niles, MI 49120

Toll Free 800-682-2276
FAX 616-684-5619

Olympic Structures Inc.

Wood Roof & Floor Trusses

1850 93rd Ave. SW
Olympia, WA 98502

Phone 206-943-5433

Omar's Built-In Vacuum Systems

Built-in Vacuum Systems

19501 144 Ave. N.E.
Suite A-600
Woodinville, WA 98072

Phone 206-487-3730

Building Supply

Omnia Industries – PDC Home Supply

Omnia Industries

Manufacturer - Fine Brass Door
Hardware & Locks
5 Cliffside Drive
Box 330
Cedar Grove, NJ 07009

Phone 201-239-7272

FAX 201-239-7272

Ontario Hardwood Products Ltd.

Hardwood, Lumber
188 Perth Ave.
Toronto
ON M5V 1B6
Canada

Phone 416-535-3191

Onyx Enterprises of America

Ceramic Tile
6816 - 13th Ave.
Brooklyn, NY 11219

Phone 718-331-4049

FAX 718-837-0957

Optiroc AB

Member - The Swedish Brick and Tile
Manufacturers Association
Box 991
S-191 29 Sollentuna
Sweden

Phone 011-46-8/920050

FAX 011-46-35158

Orbit Mfg. Co.

Factory Direct - Baseboard Heaters, Wall
Unit Heaters, Cabinet Heaters
Ridge Park & Park Ave.
Perkasie, PA 18944

Mail Order Available

Phone 215-257-0727

FAX 215-257-7399

Orignial Style

Ceramic Tile
Div of Stovax Ltd., Falcon Rd.
Sowton Ind Est, Exeter
EX2 7LF
Great Britain

Phone 011-44-392/216923

Ostara-Fliesen Gmbh & Co. KG

Manufacturer - Ceramic Tile - Wall, Floor,
Glazed, Unglazed
2364 Struemper Str 12
Meerbusch 2 D-W-4005
Germany

Phone 011-49-2159-5210

FAX 011-49-2159521207

Owens Corning Fiberglass Corp

Manufacturer - Roofing Materials
Roofing Products Division
Fiberglas Tower, 17th Fl.
Toledo, OH 43659

Phone 419-248-8000

P. B. Trusses Ltd.

Roof Trusses
PO Box 189
Stony Mountain
Man., CAN R0C 3A0
Canada

Phone 204-344-5404

P. E. Guerin Inc.

Decorative Hardware, Bathroom
Accessories
23 Jane St.
New York, NY 10014

Send $20.00 for Catalog/Information

Mail Order Available

Phone 212-243-5271

FAX 212-727-2290

PDC Home Supply

Building Material
Industrial Drive
Rockmart, GA 30153-9276

Phone 404-684-8691

Building Supply

The Complete Sourcebook

3 - 67

PGL Building Products

Building Supplies
5900 Arctic Blvd.
Anchorage, AK 99518-1675
Phone 907-562-2131

Pabco Roofing Products

Manufacturer - Roofing Products
1014 Chesley Ave.
Richmond, CA 94801
Phone 415-234-2130

Pacific Burl and Hardwood

*Black Walnut, Redwood, Maple,
Mandrone Wood Samples*
6790 Williams Highway
Grants Pass, OR 97527-9428
Catalog/Information Available Free
Phone 503-479-1854

Pacific Post & Beam

Frames, Beams and Posts
PO Box 13708
San Luis Obispo, CA 93406
Send $3.00 for Catalog/Information
Phone 805-543-7565

Panhellenic Marble Association

*President - M. G. Papadopoulos Member
- European International Federation of
Natural Stone Industry*
1, Eleon Str.
G - 145 64 N. Kifisia - Athens
Greece
Phone 011-30-80/72940
FAX 011-30-81/236894

Paris Ceramics

Ceramic, Terracotta, Limestone Tile Floors
31 East Elm St.
Greenwich, CT 06830
Catalog/Information Available Free
Phone 203-862-9538
FAX 203-629-5484

Parks Corporation

Manufacturer - Paint
PO Box 5
Somerset, MA 02726
Toll Free 800-225-8543

Pasvalco

Natural Stone & Marble
100 Bogert Street
Closter, NJ 07624
Toll Free 800-222-2133
FAX 210-768-5927

Path Enterprises, Inc.

Beveled & Stained Glass
7717 Portland Ave. E.
Tacoma, WA 98404
Phone 206-535-4000
FAX 206-535-6889

Paulis Co.

Roof Trusses
4834 Old Philadelphia Rd.
Aberdeen, MD 21001
Phone 301-272-6600

Paxton Hardware Ltd.

Period Hardware
7818 Bradshaw Rd., PO Box 256
Upper Falls, MD 21156
Send $4.00 for Catalog/Information
Phone 410-592-8505
FAX 410-592-2224

Payless Cashways

Building Supplies
5200 S. Western St.
Amarillo, TX 79109-6184
Phone 806-359-8501

Building Supply

Pecora Corporation

Manufacturer - Sealants, Caulking Compounds, Waterproofing Products

165 Wambold Rd.
Harleysville, PA 19438

Phone 215-723-6051
FAX 215-721-0286

Peerless Pottery

Manufacturer - Plumbing Fixtures

PO Box 145
Rockport, IN 47635-0145

Phone 812-649-6430
FAX 812-649-6429

Pelnick Wrecking Company, Inc.

Antique Building Components

1749 Erie Blvd. East
Syracuse, NY 13210

Catalog/Information Available Free

Phone 315-472-1031

Penn Big Bed Slate Co. Inc.

Manufacturer - Roofing & Flooring Slate

PO Box 184
8450 Brown St.
Slatington, PA 18080

Mail Order Available

Phone 610-767-4601
FAX 610-767-9252

Penna Supply & Mfg. Co.

Manufacturer - Roofing Material

827 N. 12th
Allentown, PA 18102-1358

Phone 215-434-5295

Penrod Co.

Lumber

PO Box 2100
Virginia Beach, VA 23450

Phone 804-498-0186
FAX 804-498-1075

Perfection Metal & Supply Co.

Manufacturer - Window, Door Screens and Frames

PO Box 8010
Birmingham, AL 35218

Phone 205-787-9661
FAX 205-787-9666

Perfection Truss Co. Inc.

Roof & Floor Trusses

5305 William St. S.E.
PO Box 27427
Albuquerque, NM 87125

Phone 505-877-0770
FAX 505-873-2438

Peter Josef Korzilius Soehne GmbH & Co

Manufacturer - Ceramic Tile - Kitchens & Baths

Krugbaeckerstr 3
Mogendorf D-W-5431
Germany

Phone 011-49-2623/6090
FAX 011-49-2623609102

Pewabic Pottery Co.

Handmade Ceramic Tile

10125 Jefferson Ave. E.
Detroit, MI 48214

Phone 313-822-0954
FAX 313-822-6266

Pfanstiel Hardware Co.

Brass & Bronze Decorative Hardware

Rt 52
Jeffersonville, NY 12748

Send $7.50 for Catalog/Information

Mail Order Available

Phone 914-482-4445

Phillips Industries Inc.

Manufacturer - Window, Door Screens and Frames

3221 Magnum Drive, PO Box 2327
Elkhart, IN 46515

Phone 219-295-0000

FAX 219-296-0147

Phoenix Products Inc.

Faucets

583 Miller Rd.
Avon Lake, OH 44145

Phone 216-933-8100

FAX 216-933-6252

Phyllis Kennedy Restoration Hardware

Restoration Hardware

9256 Holyoke Court
Indianapolis, IN 46268

Send $3.00 for Catalog/Information

Mail Order Available

Phone 317-872-6366

Pickens Hardwoods

Imported and Domestic Hardwoods

PO Drawer 1127
Clinton, MS 39060-1127

Send $2.00 for Catalog/Information

Phone 601-924-4301

Pilgram Fireplace Equipment Co.

Fireplace Equipment

720 Harbour Way S.
Richmond, CA 94804

Phone 415-529-2050

FAX 415-237-6541

Pine Products Corp.

Pine Lumber

PO Box 460
Prineville, OR 97754

Phone 503-447-6212

FAX 503-447-7149

Pine River Lumber Co. Ltd.

Lumber

PO Box 96
Long Lake, WI 54542

Phone 715-674-6411

FAX 715-674-6202

Pioneer Roofing Tile Inc.

Tile Roofing Shake in many styles and colors

10650 Poplar Avenue
Fontana, CA 92337

Phone 909-350-4238

FAX 909-350-2298

Pittsburgh Corning

Glass Block

800 Presque Isle Dr.
Pittsburgh, PA 15239

Send $2.95 for Catalog/Information

Phone 412-327-6100

Toll Free 800-624-2120

FAX 412-327-5890

Plain and Fancy Ceramic Tile

Ceramic Tile

1855 Griffin Rd.
Schaefferstown, PA 17088

Phone 717-949-6571

FAX 717-949-2114

Plumb-Craft Mfg.

Plumbing Fixtures

24455 Aurora
Bedford, OH 44146

Phone 216-439-1834

Ply-Gem Mfg.

Manufacturer - Hardboard and Plywood Paneling, Marble Tiles

201 Black Horse Pike
Haddon Heights, NJ 08035

Catalog/Information Available Free

Phone 609-546-0704

FAX 609-546-0539

Building Supply

Plywood Mfg. Of California Inc. – Primrose Distributing

Plywood Mfg. Of California Inc.

Plywood
2201 Dominquez St.
Torrance, CA 90501
Phone 213-328-7986

Porcelanosa

Ceramic Tile
1301 S. State College Blvd.
Anaheim, CA 92806
Phone 714-772-3183
FAX 714-772-9851

Porter Paints

Manufacturer - Paint
400 South 13th Street
PO Box 1439
Louisville, KY 40201-1439
Phone 502-588-9200

Porter-Cable Corp.

Manufacturer - Professional Power Tools
4825 Highway 45 North
PO Box 2468
Jackson, TN 38302-2468
Phone 901-668-8600
FAX 901-664-0525

Portland Stove Company

Manufacturer - Stoves
PO Box 2468
Jackson, TN 38302
Send $2.00 for Catalog/Information
Phone 901-668-8600
FAX 901-664-0525

Praire Marketing

Monocottura, Bicottura, Procelain, Inserts, Borders for Floor, Wall, Bath
2200 E. Devon Ave.
Elk Grove Village, IL 60007
Phone 312-593-1432
FAX 312-593-0401

Pratt & Lambert

Manufacturer - Paint
PO Box 22
Buffalo, NY 14240
Phone 716-873-6000
Toll Free 800-289-7728
FAX 716-873-9920

Precision Hardware Inc.

Builders Hardware
10053 W. Fort St.
Detroit, MI 48209
Phone 313-843-1850
FAX 313-843-5011

Precision Multiple Controls, Inc.

Manufacturer - Photocontrols, Time Switches for Outdoor Lighting, Hot Water Heaters
33 Greenwood Avenue
Midland Park, NJ 07432
Phone 201-444-0600
FAX 201-445-8575

PriceKing Building Supply Inc.

Building Supply, Custom Millwork
2324 McDonald Ave.
Brooklyn, NY 11223
Phone 718-265-5000
FAX 718-449-6057

Primrose Distributing

18th & 19th Century Authentic Interior & Exterior Paint
5445 Rose Road
South Bend, IN 46628
Phone 219-234-6728
Toll Free 800-222-3092
FAX 219-234-1138

Building Supply

The Complete Sourcebook

Progressive Building Products

Solariums, Skylights, & Greenhouses
PO Box 849
Franklin, NC 28734-0849
Mail Order Available
Credit Cards VISA/MC

Phone 916-924-3532
FAX 916-924-3017

Pryor Truss Co.

Trusses
W. Hwy. 20
PO Box 830
Pryor, OK 74362

Phone 918-825-1715

Puccio Marble & Onyx

Marble & Onyx Floors, Bathrooms
661 Driggs Ave.
Brooklyn, NY 11211
Mail Order Available

Phone 718-387-9778

Pukall Lumber Co.

Manufacturer - Of quality Lumber & Wood products; retail store, design services - Wholesale & Retail - Nationwide Shipping
10894 Hwy. 70E
Woodruff, WI 54568
Credit Cards Accepted

Phone 715-356-3252

Pumphouse

Water Pumps - Sump, Sewage, Pool, Repair Parts
177 Cortland Rd. SE
Warren, OH 44484
Catalog/Information Available Free

Toll Free 800-947-8677

Putnam Rolling Ladder Company Inc.

Order Direct - Custom Solid Wood Rolling Ladders for the home
32 Howard St.
New York, NY 10013
Send $1.00 for Catalog/Information

Phone 212-226-5147
FAX 212-941-1836

Quality Marble Inc.

Marble Decorative Tile
3860 70th Ave. N.
Pinellas Park, FL 33565

Phone 813-527-1676
FAX 813-527-7317

Quality Marble Ltd.

Granite & Marble
Unit 1, Fountayne Ho, Fountayne Rd.
London N15 4QL
Great Britain

Phone 011-44-81/8081110

Quality Truss

Roof Trusses
PO Box 669
Inola, OK 74036

Phone 918-836-4449

Quality-Line Truss Mfg. Co.

Trusses
PO Box 146
Big Cabin, OK 74332

Phone 918-783-5227

Quarry Slate Industries Inc.

Roof Slate
PO Box 197
Poultney, VT 05764

Phone 802-287-9871

Building Supply

Quarry Tile Company

Ceramic Tile

Spokane Industrial Park
Bldg. #12
Spokane, WA 99216

Phone 509-924-1466

FAX 509-928-0352

Radco Products Inc.

Solar Water Heater

2877 Industrial Pkwy
Santa Maria, CA 93455

Phone 805-928-1881

Radiant Technology

Manufacturer - Hot Water Radiant Heating - Adaptable to new contruction, and retrofit with little or no change in existing or planned architectural design.

11A Farber Drive
Bellport, NY 11713

Catalog/Information Available Free

Phone 516-286-0900

FAX 516-286-0947

Rainhandler

Rainhandler Gutters

Savetime Corp.
2710 North Avenue
Bridgeport, CT 06604

Mail Order Available

Phone 203-382-2991

Toll Free 800-942-3004

FAX 203-382-2995

Raleigh Inc.

Roofing Tile

6506 Bus U.S. Rte 20
PO Box 448
Belvidere, IL 61008

Phone 815-544-4141

FAX 815-544-4866

Rams Imports

Monocottura, Klinker, Porcelain, Inserts, Borders, Steps for Floor, Wall, Bath

Russell Slaight
1356 North Federal Highway
Pompano Beach, FL 33062

Phone 305-786-9397

FAX 305-786-9614

Raven Industries Inc.

Manufacturer - Energy Saving Housewrap - Insulation

PO Box 1007
Sioux Falls, SD 57117-1007

Phone 605-336-2750

Toll Free 800-227-2836

Re-Bath Corporation

Manufacturer - Plumbing Fixtures

1055 South Country Club Dr.
Building #2
Mesa, AZ 85210-4613

Toll Free 800-426-4573

Read Bros. Building Supply

Roof Trusses

PO Box 786
Jacksonville, AL 36265

Phone 205-492-7678

Real Goods Trading Corp.

Solar Energy Products

966 Mazzoni St.
Ukiah, CA 95482

Mail Order Available

Toll Free 800-762-7325

Red Clay Tile Works

Manufacturer - Handmade Tile

75 Meade Ave.
Pittsburgh, PA 15202

Mail Order Available

Phone 412-734-2222

The Complete Sourcebook

Red Deer Truss Systems — Restoration Works

Building Supply

Red Deer Truss Systems

Roof Trusses

PO Box 400
Penhold
Alta, CAN T0M 1R0
Canada

Phone 403-886-4414

Reed Bros.

Garden Furniture, Armoires, Credenzas, Headboards

Turner Station
Sebastopol, CA 95472

Send $10.00 for Catalog/Information

Mail Order Available

Phone 707-795-6261
FAX 707-829-8620

Regal Manufacturing Co.

Sunrooms, Skylights, Mirror Doors

PO Box 14578
Portland, OR 97214

Phone 503-230-0444

Reid Building & Truss Co.

Steel Trusses

Rt. 10 Box 216
Cullman, AL 35055

Phone 205-747-2753

Reinke Shakes

Manufacturer - Metal Roofing

3321 Willowwood Circle
Lincoln, NE 68506

Toll Free 800-228-4312

Remodeler's Supply Co.

Hardware & Fixtures

Box 92 Hwy. 18
Garrison, MN 56450

Send $2.00 for Catalog/Information

Mail Order Available

Renaissance Decorative Hardware Co.

Brass Hardware

PO Box 332
Leonia, NJ 07605

Send $2.50 for Catalog/Information

Mail Order Available

Phone 201-568-1403

Renaissance Roofing Inc.

Roofing Material

PO Box 5024
Rockford, IL 61109

Mail Order Available

Phone 815-897-5695
FAX 815-874-2957

Restoration Hardware

Victorian Hardware

438 Second St.
Eureka, CA 95501

Send $3.00 for Catalog/Information

Mail Order Available

Phone 707-443-3152

Restoration Resource

Antique Building Components

Suite 605
Post Road East
Westport, CT 06880

Catalog/Information Available Free

Phone 203-259-2533

Restoration Works

Plumbing Fixtures, Brass Hardware

810 Main St.
Buffalo, NY 14202

Send $3.00 for Catalog/Information

Mail Order Available

Credit Cards Accepted

Phone 716-856-8000
Toll Free 800-735-3535
FAX 716-856-8040

The Complete Sourcebook

Building Supply

Rheem Mfg Co.

Manufacturer - Water Heaters

Rheem Water Heater Div.
101 Bell Rd., PO Box 244020
Montgomery, AL 36124

Phone 205-279-8930

Rho Sigma Inc.

Solar Energy Controls & Heaters

1800 W. 4th Ave.
Hialeah, FL 33010

Phone 305-885-1911

Richard Blaschke Cabinet Glass

Antique Cabinet & Window Glass

670 Lake Avenue
Bristol, CT 06010

Mail Order Available

Phone 203-584-2566

Richard Burbidge Ltd.

Fireplaces and Accessories, Decorative Moulding, Stairs, Stair Components

Whittington Rd.
Oswestry, Shropshire
SY11 1HZ
Great Britain

Phone 011-44-691/655131

FAX 011-44-691/657694

Richmond Ceramic Tile Distributors Inc.

Italian Tile

31 North Bridge St.
Staten Island, NY 10309

Phone 718-317-8500

Richmond Foundry & Mfg. Co.

Plumbing Specialties

3514 Mayland Ct.
Richmond, VA 23233

Phone 804-273-0466

Richmond Plywood Corp.

Plywood

13911 Vulcan Way
Richmond B.C.
CAN V6V 1K7
Canada

Phone 604-278-9111

FAX 604-278-2617

Ridgway Roof Truss Co. Inc.

Wood Roof & Floor Trusses

PO Box 1309L
Gainesville, FL 32602

Phone 904-376-4436

Rimbey Truss Systems Inc.

Roof Trusses

R.R. 3
Rimbey
Alta., CAN T0C 2J0
Canada

Phone 403-843-6052

Rinnai America Corp.

Gas Furnace

1662 Lukken Industrial Dr. West
LaGrange, GA 30240

Phone 704-884-6070

Toll Free 800-621-9419

Rising & Nelson Slate Company

Roofing Slate

PO Box 98, Main Street
West Pawlet, VT 05775

Mail Order Available

Phone 802-645-0150

FAX 802-645-1974

Riteway Mfg. Co. Inc.

Wood Burning Heaters

1680 Country Club Rd.
Harrisonburg, VA 22801

Phone 703-434-3800

FAX 703-434-5589

Building Supply

The Complete Sourcebook

Ritter & Son Hardware

Brass Hardware, Weathervanes, Garden Accessories
38401 Hwy. 1S
Gualala, CA 95445
Send $1.00 for Catalog/Information
Mail Order Available
Credit Cards VISA/MC
Phone 707-884-3363
Toll Free 800-358-9120
FAX 707-884-1515

Riverside Roof Truss Inc.

Roof Trusses
PO Box 2276
Danville, VA 24541
Phone 804-793-0217

Ro-Tile Inc.

Ceramic Tile
1615 South Stockton St.
Lodi, CA 95240
Phone 209-334-1380
Toll Free 800-334-3200
FAX 209-334-3136

Rockford-Eclipse

Brass Plumbing Valves
Div. of Esclipse Inc.
1665 Elmwood Rd.
Rockford, IL 61103
Phone 815-877-3031
FAX 815-877-3335

Rocktile Specialty Products Inc.

Natural Stone Tile
220 S. Ave. A
Boise, ID 83702
Phone 208-342-7700
Toll Free 800-545-7735
FAX 208-342-7880

Romet Inc.

Insulation & Insulation Materials
PO Box 1678
Conroe, TX 77305
Phone 409-539-5244

Roofage

Manufacturer - Acrylic Roofing System
PO Box 20784
Lehigh Valley, PA 18002-0784
Catalog/Information Available Free
Phone 610-866-9288
Toll Free 800-722-7019
FAX 610-868-6110

Roofmaster Products Company

Roofing Supply
750 Monterey Pass Rd.
Monterey Park, CA 91754-3668
Mail Order Available
Toll Free 800-421-6174
FAX 213-261-8799

Royal Brass Mfg. Co.

Brass Plumbing Products
1420 E. 43rd St.
Cleveland, OH 44103
Phone 216-361-3175
FAX 216-361-0788

Royal-Apex Mfg. Co. Inc.

Rain Drainage Products
639 South Ave.
Plainfield, NJ 07062
Phone 201-753-6414
FAX 201-753-4183

Rubens & Locke

Manufacturer - Plumbing Fixtures
Hanover Park
3 Lebanon Street
Hanover, NH 03755
Toll Free 800-333-3448

Building Supply

Rufkahr's

Reproduction Hardware
4207 Eagle Rock Court
St. Charles, MO 63304

Send $2.00 for Catalog/Information

Mail Order Available

Credit Cards MC/VISA/DISCOVER
Toll Free 800-545-7947

Rustic Home Hardware

Reproduction Early American Hardware & Fireplace Equipment
Rd #3
Hanover, PA 17331

Send $2.00 for Catalog/Information

Mail Order Available
Phone 717-632-0088

SRI

Floor & Roof Trusses
5179 Mountville Rd.
Frederick, MD 21701
Phone 301-874-5660

Samson Industries Inc.

Solar Collectors
175 Sea Cliff Ave.
Glen Cover, NY 11542
Phone 516-759-1010

San Do Designs

Handpainted Ceramic Tile
2104 E. 7th Ave.
Tampa, FL 33605

Mail Order Available
Phone 813-247-6817

Sanders Building Supply Inc.

Building Supply
595 Ferdon Blvd.
Crestview, FL 32536-2766
Phone 904-682-3317

Sandy Pond Hardwoods

Lumber and Flooring
921-A Lancaster Pike
Quarryville, PA 17566

Mail Order Available

Credit Cards VISA/MC
Phone 717-284-5030
Toll Free 800-546-9663
FAX 717-284-5739

Santa Catalina

Distributor - Monocottura, Porcelain, Inserts, Borders, Steps for Floor, Wall, Bath
1600 East Babbit Ave.
Anaheim, CA 92805
Phone 714-385-9095
FAX 714-939-9063

Santa Fe Trading Co.

Tile
1415 Vernon St.
Anaheim, CA 92805
Phone 714-778-6403

Santile International Corp.

Manufacturer - Plumbing Fixtures
6687 Jimmy Carter Blvd.
Norcross, GA 30071
Phone 404-416-6224

Sav On Discount Material

Building Supply
1454 Hwy 95 Bus
Payette, ID 83661-5351
Phone 208-642-4792

Sayville Plumbing Go.

Hardware, Plumbing & Heating Supply
620 Montauk Hwy.
Bayport, NY 11705
Phone 516-589-0216

Building Supply

The Complete Sourcebook

Schmitt Builders Supply

Building Supply
1631 Paterson Plank Rd.
Secaucus, NJ 07094

Phone 201-866-1600

Schubert Lumber Co.

Roof & Floor Trusses
1601 Third Creek Rd.
Knoxville, TN 37921

Phone 615-584-4664

Scotch Lumber Co.

Lumber
PO Box 38
Fulton, AL 36446

Phone 205-636-4424

Seelye Equipment Specialists

Solar Energy Equipment
913 State St.
Charlevoix, MI 49720

Phone 616-547-9430
Toll Free 800-678-9430
FAX 616-547-5522

Sequence USA Co. Ltd.

Decorative Hardware
PO Box 51010
Durham, NC 27717-1010

Phone 919-489-1146
FAX 919-489-8948

Sequoia Industries Inc.

Saunas & Hot Tubs
2394 Bailey Ave.
Buffalo, NY 14215

Phone 716-893-7204

Setzer Forest Products

Lumber, Moulding, Door and Window Frames
2570 3rd St.
Sacramento, CA 95818

Phone 916-442-2555
Toll Free 800-824-8506

Shaker Workshops

Rockers, Chairs, Tables
PO Box 1028
Concord, MA 01742

Send $1.00 for Catalog/Information

Mail Order Available

Credit Cards VISA/MC/AMEX/DISCOVER

Phone 617-646-8985
Toll Free 800-840-9121
FAX 617-648-8217

Shakertown Corp.

Manaufacturer - Representative List - Cedar Shakes & Shingles, Roofing Supplies
1200 Kerron Street
Winlock, WA 98596

Catalog/Information Available Free

Phone 206-785-3501
Toll Free 800-426-8970
FAX 206-785-3076

Shamokin Trail Shingle Co.

Manufacturer - Oak Roofing Shingle
PO Box 122
Luthersburg, PA 15848

Phone 814-583-5342
FAX 814-583-5145

Shelly Tile Inc.

Tile and Marble
D & D Bldg.
979 Third Ave.
New York, NY 10022

Phone 212-832-2255
FAX 212-832-0434

Shingle Mill Inc.

Manufacturer - Wood Roofing Shingle
PO Box 134
6 Cote Ave.
S. Ashburnham, MA 01466

Mail Order Available

Phone 508-827-4889

Building Supply

Shoffner Industries Inc. – Solar Additions Inc.

Shoffner Industries Inc.

Roof Trusses

Alamance Battleground Rd.
PO Box 97
Burlington, NC 27215

Phone 919-226-9356

Sholton Assoc.

Glass Block for Windows & Showers

6915 S.W. 57th Ave., Suite 206
Coral Gables, FL 33143

Toll Free 800-272-9400

Shutter Shop

Louvers, Colonial Raised Panels - Interior and Exterior

PO Box 11882
Charlotte, NC 28209

Send $2.00 for Catalog/Information

Phone 704-334-8031

Sign of the Crab

Manufacturer - Plumbing Fixtures

3756 Omec Circle
Ranco Cordova, CA 95742

Phone 916-630-2722

FAX 916-638-2725

Sikes Corp

Ceramic & Glazed Tile

One Sikes Blvd.
Lakeland, FL 33801

Phone 813-687-7171

Silver State Components

Roof & Floor Trusses

1208 Wagner
North Las Vegas, NV 89030

Phone 702-399-1000

Simplex Products Division

Manufacturer - Housewrap Insulation

Barricade Building Wrap
PO Box 10
Adrian, MI 49221-0010

Phone 517-263-8881

Simpson Tile Co.

Decorative Ceramic Tile

7657 North Ave.
Lemon Grove, CA 92045

Phone 619-461-2464

Sioux Chief Mfg. Co. Inc.

Plumbing Specialties

Old 71 Hwy. S
PO Box 397
Peculiar, MO 64078

Phone 816-758-6104

FAX 816-758-5950

Sky Lodge Farm

Cedar Roofing Shingle

46 Wendell Road
Shutesbury, MA 01072

Phone 413-259-1271

Snelling's Thermo-Vac, Inc.

Order Direct - Nationwide Shipping - Decorative Ceiling Tile

PO Box 210
130 Front St.
Blanchard, LA 71009

Mail Order Available

Credit Cards Certified/Bank Check

Phone 318-929-7398

FAX 318-929-3923

Snyder General Corp.

Manufacturer - Ground Water Heat Pump

13600 Industrial Park
Minneapolis, MN 55441

Solar Additions Inc.

Add on Solar Room Kits

Box 241
Greenwich, NY 12834

Send $5.00 for Catalog/Information

Phone 518-692-9673

Toll Free 800-833-2300

Building Supply

The Complete Sourcebook

3 - 79

Solar Depot

Solar Electric Systems, Water Heaters, Equipment and Supply
61 Paul Drive
San Rafael, CA 94903

Phone 415-499-1333

Solar Development Inc.

Solar Water Heater
3607-A Prospect Avenue
Riviera Beach, FL 33404

Phone 407-842-8935
FAX 407-842-8967

Solar Heating & Air Conditioning Corp.

Solar Energy Supply
331 Thornton Ave.
St. Louis, MO 63119

Phone 314-961-7538

Solar Innovations Inc.

Solar Energy Supply
412 Longfellow Blvd.
Lakeland, FL 33801

Phone 813-665-7085

Solar Oriented Environmental Systems

Manufacturer - Ground Water Heat Pump
10634 SW 187th St.
Building D
Miami, FL 33157

Solar Water Heater

Solar Water Heater
111-G Carpenter Dr.
Sterling, VA 22170

Send $1.00 for Catalog/Information

Solarmetrics Inc.

Solar Energy Supply
3160 Ft. Denaud Rd.
Labelle, FL 33935

Phone 813-674-1901
Toll Free 800-356-4751
FAX 813-674-1904

Sonoma Spas

Redwood Home Spas
5845 193rd Ave. SW
Rochester, WA 98579

Phone 206-273-5923
Toll Free 800-772-4762

South & Jones Lumber Co.

Building Supply
N of Evanston
Evanston, WY 82930

Phone 307-789-2398

South & Sons Panels Inc.

Insulated Building Panels
142 Industrial Dr.
Franklin, OH 45005

Phone 513-746-3544
FAX 513-746-9706

South Coast Lumber Co.

Lumber
PO Box 670
Brookings, OR 97415

Phone 503-469-2136

South Coast Shingle Company Inc.

Shingles
2220 East South St.
Long Beach, CA 90805

Mail Order Available

Phone 310-634-7100
Toll Free 800-540-7626
FAX 213-634-0559

South Side Roofing Co. Inc.

Tile & Slate Roofing
290 Hanley Industrial Court
St. Louis, MO 63144-1588

Mail Order Available

Phone 314-968-4800
FAX 314-968-4804

Southampton Brick & Tile Co.

Italian Tile

1540 North Highway
Southampton, NY 11968

Phone 516-283-8088

Southeast Hardware Mfg. Co.

Manufacturer - Decorative Hardware

14060 S. Anderson St.
Paramount, CA 90723

Send $22.50 for Catalog/Information

Phone 213-231-9301

FAX 213-636-8152

Southern Components Inc.

Roof & Floor Trusses

7360 Julie Frances
PO Box 29010
Shreveport, LA 71149

Phone 318-687-3330

FAX 318-686-5159

Southern Maryland Aluminum Prod. Co.

Roofing, Gutters, Siding

1268 Central Ave.
Davidsonville, MD 21035

Phone 301-798-4300

FAX 301-261-4859

Southland Building Inc.

Building Supply

2115 McClellan
Shreveport, LA 71103-3723

Phone 318-538-8000

Specification Chemicals Inc.

Plaster Wall Restoration Compound and Covering

824 Keeler
Boone, IA 50036

Mail Order Available

Credit Cards Check/Money Order

Phone 515-432-8256

Toll Free 800-247-3932

FAX 515-432-8366

Spiegelwerk Wilsdruff GmbH

Manufacturer - Ceramic Tile, Wall Mirrors

Tharandter Strasse 8
Postfach 1/33
0-8224 Wilsdruff
Germany

Phone 011-49-352048073

FAX 011-49-35204341

Staco Roof Tile Manufacturing

Manufacturer - Roof Tile

3530 E. Elwood
Phoenix, AZ 85040

Phone 602-437-0297

FAX 602-437-5006

Stained Glass Overlay Inc.

Decorative Stained Glass

1827 N. Case St.
Organge, CA 92665

Phone 714-974-6124

Toll Free 800-944-4746

FAX 714-974-6529

Stair Parts Ltd.

Wood Stairs & Parts

2197 Canton Rd.
Marietta, GA 30066

Mail Order Available

Phone 404-427-0124

Toll Free 800-827-8247

FAX 404-425-6140

Stair Specialist Inc.

Stairs

2257 W. Columbia Ave.
Battle Creek, MI 49017

Send $4.00 for Catalog/Information

Phone 616-964-2351

FAX 616-964-4824

Building Supply

Staloton - Die keramiker H.H.

Manufacturer - Ceramic Tile - Wall, Floor, Bricks, Decorative Garden Ornaments

Hensiek GmbH & Co. KG
2769 Ackerhagen 14
Buende 1 D-W-4980
Germany

Phone 011-49-5223/4016

Stamford Wrecking

Antique Building Components

One Barry Place
Stamford, CT 06902

Catalog/Information Available Free

Phone 203-324-9537

Standard Brands Paint Co.

Paint

4300 W. 190th St.
Torrance, CA 90509

Phone 213-214-2411

Standard Building Systems

Trusses

PO Box C
Point of Rocks, MD 21777

Phone 301-874-5141

Standard Paint Co.

Paint, Varnishes

8225 Lyndon Ave.
Detroit, MI 48238

Phone 313-931-3300

FAX 313-931-3314

Standard Tile Distributors Inc.

Italian Tile

105 Hamilton Street
New Haven, CT 06511-5812

Phone 203-777-3637

Star Bronze Co.

Manufacturer - Environmentally Friendly Finish, Stains

PO Box 2206
Alliance, OH 44601

Phone 216-823-1550

Toll Free 800-321-9870

FAX 216-823-2658

Starbuck Goldner Tile

Handmade Ceramic Tile

315 West Fourth St.
Bethlehem, PA 18015

Mail Order Available

Phone 215-866-6321

Stark Truss Co. Inc.

Roof Trusses

1556 Perry Dr. SW
PO Box 80469
Canton, OH 44708

Phone 216-478-2100

FAX 216-477-2805

State Industries Inc.

Water Heaters, Solar Heaters

500 Bypass Rd.
Ashland, TN 37015

Phone 615-792-4371

Stenindustriens Landssammenslutning

Norwegian Natural Stone - Granite, Slate, Marble, Soapstone

Federation of Norwegian Stone Industries
Torvet 11
Posboks 231, 3251 Larvik
Norway

Phone 011-47-33/186699

FAX 011-47-33/181816

Stern-Williams Co. Inc.

Plumbing Fixtures

PO Box 8004
Shawnee Mission, KS 66208

Phone 913-362-5635

FAX 913-362-6689

Building Supply

Stone Door & Truss

Roof Trusses & Garage Doors
Rte. 5
PO Box 13 A
Florence, SC 29502

Phone 803-669-0205

Stone Federation

*President M. Erik Brookes Member -
European International Federation of
Natural Stone Industry*
82 New Cavendish St.
London W1M 8AD
Great Britain

Phone 011-44-5805588

FAX 011-44-42861983

Stone Mfg. Co.

Fireplace Furnishings
1636 W. 135th St.
PO Box 1325
Garden, CA 90249

Phone 213-323-6720

Stone Products Corporation

*Manufacturer - Cultured Stone - Granite,
Cobblefield, Brick, Fieldstone, Flintstone,
Riverrock*
PO Box 270
Napa, CA 94559-0270

Phone 707-255-1717

Toll Free 800-255-1727

FAX 707-255-5572

Stonelight Tile Co.

Old World Style Ceramic Tile
1651 Pomona Ave.
San Jose, CA 95110

Phone 408-292-7424

FAX 408-292-7427

Stoneware Tile Company

Ceramic Tile
PO Box 73
Summitville, OH 43962

Phone 216-223-1511

FAX 216-223-1414

Strabruken AB

*Member - The Swedish Brick and Tile
Manufacturers Association*
Box 4505
S-191 04 Sollentuna
Sweden

Phone 011-46-8/920030

FAX 011-46-35713

Structural Slate Co.

*Manufacturer - Window Sills, Fireplace
Facings, Slate Flooring, Slate Roofing*
222 E. Main St.
PO Box 187
Pen Argyl, PA 18072

Phone 215-863-4141

FAX 215-863-7016

Structural Stoneware Inc.

Ceramic Tile
PO Drawer 119
Minerva, OH 44657

Phone 216-868-6434

Stuc-O-Flex International Inc.

Exterior Stucco Finish
17639 NE 67th Court
Redmond, WA 98052-4944

Mail Order Available

Toll Free 800-548-1231

FAX 206-869-0107

Stulb's Old Village Paints

*Authentic Historic Colors - Interior &
Exterior Paint*
PO Box 1030
Fort Washington, PA 19034

Send $2.00 for Catalog/Information

Mail Order Available

Credit Cards VISA/MC

Phone 215-654-1770

FAX 215-654-1976

The Complete Sourcebook

Suburban Manufacturing Company

Heating Units
PO Box 399
Dayton, TN 37321
Phone 615-775-2131

Summitville Tiles Inc.

Manufacturer - Floor, Wall, Decorative Tile
PO Box 73, State Route 644
Summitville, OH 43962
Send $3.00 for Catalog/Information
Phone 216-223-1511
FAX 216-223-1414

Sun House Tiles

Fireplace Tile
9986 Happy Acres West
Bozeman, MT 59715
Mail Order Available
Phone 406-587-3651

Sun Ray Solar Heaters

Solar Collectors
1943 Friendship Dr.
El Cajon, CA 92020
Phone 619-284-0844

SunEarth Inc.

Manufacturer - Solar Thermal Collectors
4315 Santa Ana St.
Ontario, CA 91761
Phone 909-984-8737
FAX 909-988-0477

Sunbilt Solar Products

Solariums
109-10 180th St.
Jamaica, NY 11433
Catalog/Information Available Free
Phone 718-297-6040
FAX 718-297-3090

Sunburst Stained Glass Co. Inc.

Manufacturer - Beveled, Stained, Etched Glass, Door Panels, Windows
20 West Jennings St.
Newburgh, IN 47630
Send $3.00 for Catalog/Information
Mail Order Available
Toll Free 800-982-1521

Sundance II Fireplace Distributors

Fireplace Supplies
16629 Yucca
Hesperia, CA 92345
Phone 619-244-3366

Sunelco

Manufacturer - Solar Electricity - Solar Modules, Batteries, Outdoor Lighting
PO Box 1499
Hamilton, MT 59840
Send $5.00 for Catalog/Information
Credit Cards MC/VISA/AMEX/DISCOVER
Phone 406-363-6924
Toll Free 800-338-6844
FAX 406-363-6046

Sunheating Mfg. Co.

Solar Water Heater
Box 1120
San Juan Pueblo, NM 87566
Phone 505-852-2622

Sunrise Stained Glass

Stained Glass
3350 Boca Raton Blvd.
Boca Raton, FL 33431
Phone 407-368-8808

Sunshine Rooms Inc.

Manufacturer - Solariums, Skylights (Support Services & Factory Direct Program)
3333 N. Mead
PO Box 4627
Wichita, KS 67204-4627
Phone 316-838-0033
Toll Free 800-222-1598

Suomen Tiiliteollisuusliitto r.y.

Member - Federation Europeenne Des Fabricants De Tuiles Et De Briques

Laturinkuja 2, Pl 6
SF-02601 Espoo
Finland

Phone 011-358-519133
FAX 011-358-514017

Superior Clay Corp.

Flue Linings

PO Box 352
Urichsville, OH 44683

Catalog/Information Available Free

Mail Order Available

Phone 614-922-4122
Toll Free 800-848-6166
FAX 614-922-6626

Superior Fireplace Co.

Manufacturer - Wood & Gas Fireplace Systems

4325 Artesia Avenue
Fullerton, CA 92633

Phone 714-521-7302
FAX 714-994-5382

Superior Truss & Components Inc.

Roof Trusses

State Hwy. 68
PO Box 366
Minneota, MN 56264

Phone 507-872-5195
FAX 507-872-5185

Supply Line

Plumbing & Building Supplies

2400 Button Gwinnet Dr.
Doraville, GA 30340

Catalog/Information Available Free

Mail Order Available

Credit Cards VISA/MC

Phone 404-447-5400
Toll Free 800-241-6822

Supradur Manufacturing Corp.

Manufacturer - Roofing Shingles & Siding

PO Box 908
411 Theodore Fremd Ave.
Rye, NY 10580

Phone 914-967-8230
Toll Free 800-223-1948
FAX 914-967-8344

Supro Building Products Corp.

Glass Block

48-08 70th St.
Woodside, NY 11377

Phone 718-429-5110

Sveriges Stenindustriforbund

Member - European International Federation of Natural Stone Industry

The Swedish Stone Industries Federation
Box 106, S-12122 Johanneshov
Sweden

Phone 011-46-8818600
FAX 011-46-8818602

Swedecor Ltd.

Ceramic, Marble, Mosaic Tile

41-47 Scarborough St., Hull
HU3 4TG
Great Britain

Phone 011-44-482/29691

T. G. Schmeiser Co. Inc.

Fireplaces

3160 California
PO Box 1047
Fresno, CA 93714

Phone 209-268-8128

TARM USA, Inc.

Multi-Fuel Boiler - Wood, Coal, Oil, Gas, Electricity

Box 265 Main Street
Lyme, NH 03768

Toll Free 800-782-9927
FAX 603-795-4740

TEMCO – Terra Designs, Inc.

Building Supply

TEMCO

Vent Gas Fireplace
301 S. Perimeter Park Drive
Nashville, TN 37211
Catalog/Information Available Free
Phone 615-831-9393
FAX 615-831-9127

TJ International Inc.

Building Material
380 E. Park Ctr.
Boise, ID 83707
Phone 208-345-8500

Tacoma Truss Systems

Trusses
20617 Mountain Hwy. E.
Tacoma, WA 98387
Phone 206-847-2204

Tafco Corp.

Glass Block for Windows and Showers
5024 N. Rose St.
Schiller Park, IL 60176
Phone 708-678-8425

Talarico Hardwoods

Wood
Rd. #3 Box 3268
Mohnton, PA 19540
Phone 215-775-0400
Toll Free 800-373-6097

Talebloo Oriental Rugs

Oriental Rugs
4130 Magazine Street
New Orleans, LO 70115
Phone 504-899-8114
FAX 504-899-8800

Taney Stair Products Inc.

Stairs, Stair Parts
5130 Allendale Lane
Taneytown, MD 21787
Phone 301-756-6671

Tarkett Ceramic Inc.

Italian Imported Tile
200 S. Harbour City Blvd.
Melbourne, FL 32901
Phone 407-984-0505
FAX 407-984-0503

Tarmac Roofing Systems Inc.

Manufacturer - Roofing
1401 Silverside Rd.
Wilmington, DE 19810
Phone 302-475-7974

Tatko Brothers Slate Company

Floor & Roof Slate
PO Box 198
Middle Granville, NY 12849
Mail Order Available
Phone 518-642-1640

Taylor Manufacturing, Inc.

Stoves
PO Box 518
Elizabethtown, NC 28337
Toll Free 800-545-2293

Technical Glass Products

Replacement Glass for Woodstoves and Fireplaces
2425 Carillon Point
Kirkland, WA 98033
Toll Free 800-426-0279

Tegola USA

Manufacturer - Metal Roofing Shingles
PO Box 300443
Denver, CO 80203-0443
Toll Free 800-545-4140

Terra Designs, Inc.

Manufacturer - Handpainted Tile
Rt. 202
Far Hills, NJ 07931
Send $1.00 for Catalog/Information
Phone 908-234-0440
FAX 908-781-1810

Building Supply

3 - 86

The Complete Sourcebook

Tetco

Manufacturer - Water Heat Pumps

1290 U.S. 42 North
Delaware, OH 43015

                        Phone 614-363-5002
                        FAX 800-468-3826

Textruss Inc.

Trusses

12201 Dorsett
Austin, TX 78759

                        Phone 512-836-4830

The 18th Century Company

Antique Building Material & Hardware

105 Commorce Circle
Durham, CT 06433

                        Phone 203-349-9512

The 3E Group Inc.

Paints & Sealers for Restoration and Renovation

850 Glen Ave.
PO Box 392
Moorestown, NJ 08057

                        Phone 609-866-7600

The Adams Company

Fireplace Accessories

100 East 4th St.
Dubuque, IA 52001

Catalog/Information Available Free

                        Phone 319-583-3591
                        Toll Free 800-553-3012
                        FAX 319-583-8048

The Antique Hardware Store

Reproduction Fixtures and Hardware

43 Bridge St.
Frenchtown, NJ 08825

                        Toll Free 800-422-9982

The Antique Plumber

Reproduction Fixtures and Hardware

885 57th St.
Sacramento, CA 95819

                        Phone 916-454-4507

The Berea Hardwoods Co.

Wood

125 Jacqueline Drive
Berea, OH 44017

                        Phone 216-243-4452

The Brass Knob

Architectural Antiques

2311 18th St. NW
Washington, DC 20009

Mail Order Available

Credit Cards Accepted

                        Phone 202-332-3370
                        FAX 202-332-5594

The Brick Development Association

Member - Federation Europeenne Des Fabricants De Tuiles Et De Briques - Technical Literature Available

Woodside House, Winkfield, Windsor
Great Britain
Great Britain

                        Phone 011-44-344/885651
                        FAX 011-44-344/890129

The Brickyard Inc.

Brick - Will match existing construction

PO Box A
Harrisonville, MO 64701

Catalog/Information Available Free

Send $10.00 for Catalog/Information

                        Phone 816-887-3366
                        FAX 816-887-5757

The Coldren Company

Reproduction Hardware, Shutters

PO Box 668
100 Race St.
North East, MD 21901

Mail Order Available

                        Phone 410-287-2082
                        FAX 410-287-2082

The Country Iron Foundry

Fireplace - Firebacks
PO Box 600
Paoli, PA 19301
Send $2.00 for Catalog/Information

Phone 215-296-7122

The Decorative Tile Works

Decorative Ceramic Tile
Jackfield Tile Museum
Ironbridge, Telford, Stropshire
TF8 7AW
Great Britain

Phone 011-44-952/88412

The Dize Co.

Decorative Hardware
1512 S. Main St.
Winston-Salem, NC 27127

Phone 919-722-5181
FAX 919-761-1334

The Dorris Lumber & Moulding Co.

Lumber & Moulding
2601 Redding Ave.
Sacramento, CA 95820

Phone 916-452-7531
Toll Free 800-824-5823
FAX 916-452-0377

The Durable Slate Company

Slate Roofing
1050 North Fourth Street
Columbus, OH 43201

Phone 614-299-5522
Toll Free 800-666-7445

The Merchant Tiler

Decorated Wall Tile, Terracotta, Slate
Twyford Mill, Oxford Road
Adderbury, Oxon
OX17 3HP
Great Britain

Phone 011-295/812179

The Muralo Company Inc.

Manufacturer - Interior & Exterior Paints
148 East 5th St.
Bayonne, NJ 07002

Phone 201-437-0770
FAX 201-437-2316

The Natural Choice Catalog/ECO Design Co

Manufacturer - All Natural Interior & Exterior Paints, Stains, Finishes
1365 Rufina Circle
Santa Fe, NM 87501
Mail Order Available
Credit Cards VISA/MC

Phone 505-438-3448

The Northern Roof Tile Sales Co.

Roof Tiles
PO Box 275
Millgrove, Ontario
L0R 1V0
Canada

Phone 905-627-4035
FAX 905-627-9648

The Plywood Depot

Plywood
PO Box 897
Gaylord, MN 55334
Mail Order Available

The Reggio Register Co. Inc.

Manufacturer - Decorative Brass Grilles & Registers
PO Box 511
Ayer, MA 01432
Send $1.00 for Catalog/Information
Mail Order Available
Credit Cards VISA/MC/DISCOVER

Phone 508-772-3493
FAX 508-772-5513

Building Supply

The Roof, Tile & Slate Co.

Roofing Tile & Slate, Slate Flooring

1209 Carrol
Carrollton, TX 75006

Mail Order Available

Toll Free 800-446-0220

FAX 214-242-1923

The Shop

Victorian Historic Tiles for Fireplaces, Bathrooms, Kitchens Wallpapers & Borders

Charles Rupert
2004 Oak Bay Avenue, Victoria, B.C.
CAN V8R 1E4
Canada

Send $5.00 for Catalog/Information

Mail Order Available

Phone 604-592-4916

The Stone & Marble Supermarket

Marble, Onyx Sink Tops, Table Tops, Steps, Slate Sills

177-01 Liberty Ave.
Jamaica, NY 11434

Phone 718-297-8400

The Structural Slate Co.

Manufacturet - Slate - Flooring, Trim, Roofing, Fireplace Surrounds

222 East Main St., PO Box 187
Pen Argyl, PA 18072

Phone 215-863-4141

FAX 215-863-7016

The Stulb Company

Historic Milk Paint

PO Box 597
Allentown, PA 18105

Toll Free 800-221-8444

FAX 215-433-6116

The Sun Electric Co.

Sunelso Solar Electricity

PO Box 1499
100 Skeels St.
Hamilton, MT 59840

Send $3.95 for Catalog/Information

Toll Free 800-338-6844

The Tile Collection

Italian Tile

4031 Bigelow Blvd.
Pittsburgh, PA 15213

Phone 412-621-1051

The Tileworks

Ceramic Tile

2700 Grand Ave.
Des Moines, IA 50312

Phone 515-246-8304

FAX 515-246-1871

The Willette Corporation

Ceramic Tile

Joyce Kilmer Ave. & Reed St.
PO Box 28
New Brunswick, NJ 08903-0028

Phone 908-545-2723

FAX 908-545-2763

The Wise Company

Reproduction Brass Hardware, Fixtures

PO Box 118
Arabi, LA 70032

Send $4.00 for Catalog/Information

Mail Order Available

Credit Cards VISA/MC

Phone 504-277-7551

Building Supply

The Complete Sourcebook

The Woodbury Blacksmith & Forge Co.

Early American Hardware & Firebacks - Nationwide Delivery

161 Main Street
PO Box 268
Woodbury, CT 06798

Send $3.00 for Catalog/Information

Mail Order Available

Phone 203-263-5737

Thermal Control Co.

Wood & Coal Stoves, Wrought Iron Products

Howe Caverns Rd.
Howes Cave, NY 12092

Catalog/Information Available Free

Credit Cards VISA/MC

Phone 518-296-8517

Thermal Energy Systems Inc.

Manufacturer - Water Heaters

805 West Fifth Street
Landsdale, PA 19446

Phone 215-361-1700
FAX 215-361-1845

Thermo-Rite Mfg. Co.

Glass Fireplace Screens, Enclosures

1355 Evans Ave.
PO Box 1108
Akron, OH 44309

Phone 216-633-8680

Thermomax USA Ltd.

Solar Heat Equipment

6702 Rajpur Place
PO Drawer 82
Victoria B.C. CAN V8X 3X1
Canada

Toll Free 800-776-5277
FAX 612-223-8604

Thompson Lumber Co.

Lumber & Building Products

140 Washington Ave. S
Hopkins, MN 55343-8495

Phone 612-535-7827
FAX 612-535-5526

Thorn Lumber Co.

Building Supply, Roof & Floor Trusses

310 N. Raleigh St.
Martinsburg, WV 25401

Phone 304-267-8955

Tile & Marble Designs

Manufacturer - Ceramic Tile

3801 San Bernardo Ave.
Loredo, TX 78041-4404

Phone 512-724-2179

Tile Creations

Ceramic Tile

806 Moonlit Ln.
Acworth, GA 30101

Phone 404-924-1412

Tile Emporium International

Marble, Tile, Bathroom Accessory

1432 Lincoln Blvd.
Santa Monica, CA 90404

Phone 213-393-0499
FAX 213-451-0085

Tile Mart International

Ceramic Tile

615 Medord Ave.
Patchogue, NY 11772

Phone 516-475-0800

Building Supply

Tile Promotion Board – Tri State Truss Co.

Tile Promotion Board

Ceramic Tile

900 East Indiantown Rd.
Suite 211
Jupiter, FL 33477

Catalog/Information Available Free

Phone	407-743-3150
Toll Free	800-881-8453
FAX	407-743-3150

Tile West Distributors

*Italian Ceramic Tile - Monocottura,
Bicottura, Floor, Wall for Kitchen & Bath*

3757 E Broadway Rd. #2-3
Phoenix, AZ 85040-2951

Phone	602-894-5500
FAX	602-894-9601

Tile and Designs Inc.

Italian Tile

229 Spahr St.
Pittsburgh, PA 15232

Phone 412-362-8454

Tile with Style

Ceramic, Marble, Mosaic Tile

270 Kentish Town Rd.
London NW5 2AA
Great Britain

Phone 011-44-71/4859455

Tilepak America Inc.

Ceramic Tile

188-G Frank West Circle
Stockton, CA 95206

Phone	209-982-5294
FAX	209-982-5105

Tilton Truss Mfrs. Inc.

Roof Trusses

PO Box 267
Woodinville, WA 98072

Phone 206-483-8585

Timber Tech Truss Systems Ltd.

Roof Trusses

1405 31st St. N
Lethbridge
Alta., CAN T1H 5G8
Canada

Phone 403-328-5499

Timber Top Truss Ltd.

Roof & Floor Trusses

Station Rd., Industrial Park
Grand Falls
N.B., CAN E0J 1M0
Canada

Phone 506-473-5722

Timber Truss Housing Systems Inc.

Wood Building Components

525 McClelland St.
PO Box 996
Salem, VA 24153

Phone	703-387-0273
FAX	703-389-0849

Tower Paint Mfg.

Wallcover

620 W. 27th St.
Hialeah, FL 33010

Phone 305-887-9583

TradeCom International Inc.

*Cabinets, Built-in Central Vacuum
Systems, Bathroom Accessories*

33900 Curtis Blvd. #208
Eastlake, OH 44095

Phone	216-942-4468
FAX	216-942-2526

Tri State Truss Co.

Roof & Floor Trusses

1198 51st St. N.E.
PO Box 3810
Cleveland, TN 37320

Phone	615-472-3389
FAX	615-476-9198

The Complete Sourcebook

3 - 91

Tri-City Lumber/Building Supplies

Lumber & Building Supply
1202 W. Washington St.
Petersburg, VA 23803-3923
Phone 804-733-0660

Triangle Brass Mfg. Co. Inc.

Door Builders' Hardware
3520 Emery St.
PO Box 23277
Los Angles, CA 90023
Phone 213-262-4191
Toll Free 800-637-8746

Trimall Interior Products Inc.

Building Supplies - Lumber, Interior & Exterior Doors, Cabinets & Countertops
PO Box 317
Pelican Rapids, MN 56572-0317
Phone 218-863-4123
Toll Free 800-446-7595
FAX 218-863-4124

Tru-Test General Paint & Chemical

Wood Floor Finish
Div. of Cotter Co.
201 Jandus Rd.
Cary, IL 60013

Tru-Truss Inc.

Roof Trusses
1219 Carpenter Rd.
Lacey, WA 98503
Phone 206-491-8024

Trus Joist Corporation

Manufacturer - Silent Flooring Building Materials
PO Box 60
Boise, ID 83707
Phone 208-375-4450
Toll Free 800-338-0515

Trusses Inc.

Roof & Floor Trusses
1150 W. Coyote
Casper, WY 82601
Phone 307-234-7416
FAX 307-473-2653

Tuff-Kote Company

Building Repair Compounds
210 Seminary Avenue
Woodstock, IL 60098
Mail Order Available
Toll Free 800-827-2056
FAX 815-338-9105

U.S. Brass Turning Co. Inc.

Brass Fittings
35 Melville Park Rd.
Melville, NY 11747
Phone 516-293-9494
FAX 516-293-9499

U.S. Ceramic Tile Co.

Wall & Floor Tile
10233 Sandyville Rd. SE
East Sparta, OH 44626
Phone 216-866-5531

U.S. Electricar Co.

Solar Energy Supply
1981 West Redlands Blvd.
Redlands, CA 92373-8030
Send $5.00 for Catalog/Information
Mail Order Available
Phone 909-793-2891
Toll Free 800-283-5328
FAX 909-798-2865

U.S. Fiber Corp.

Building Insulation
PO Box 337
Ronda, NC 28670
Phone 919-835-2048

Building Supply

UCSMB – United States Mahogany Corp.

UCSMB

*President M. Jean Van Den Wildenberg
Member - European International
Federation of Natural Stone Industry*

2, Raborive
G - 4920 Aywaille
Belgium

Phone 011-32-41/845393
FAX 011-32-41/846794

UGIMA

*President - G.A. Da Mommio Member -
European International Federation of
Natural Stone Industry*

Via Sette Luglio 16 bis
I-54033 Carrara (Massa)
Italy

Phone 011-39-58570396
FAX 011-39-58575187

USG Corporation

Manufacturer - Texture Coated Siding

101 S. Wacker Drive
Chicago, IL 60606

Phone 312-606-4122

Ultraflo Corp.

Plumbing Fixtures

4515 Columbus Ave.
PO Box 2294
Sandusky, OH 44870

Phone 419-626-8182

Uniflor

Roof & Floor Trusses

105 Hwy. 20 E., PO Box 340
Fonthill
Ont., CAN L0S 1E0
Canada

Phone 416-892-2641

United Ceramic Tile Corp.

Ceramic Tile

923 Motor Parkway
Happauge, NY 11788

United Coatings Co.

Wood Floor Finish

980 North Michigan Avenue
Chicago, IL 60611

Phone 312-944-5400

United House Wrecking, Inc.

Antique Building Components

535 Hope St.
Stamford, CT 06906

Catalog/Information Available Free

Mail Order Available

Phone 203-348-5371
FAX 203-961-9472

United Solar Technology Inc.

Solar Collectors

121 W. Front St.
Statesville, NC 28677

Phone 704-873-7959

United States Ceramic Tile Co.

Manufacturer - Ceramic Tile

10233 Sandyville Rd. SE
PO Box 338
E. Sparta, OH 44626

Phone 216-866-5531
FAX 216-866-5340

United States Gypsum Company

Manufacturer - Building Supply

101 So. Wacker Dr.
Chicago, IL 60606-4385

Phone 312-606-4122
Toll Free 800-874-4968

United States Mahogany Corp.

Hardwoods, Plywood

746 Lloyd Rd.
Aberdeen Township, NJ 07747

Phone 201-583-6300
FAX 201-583-6303

Building Supply

The Complete Sourcebook

3 - 93

United Wholesale Distributors

Roofing Materials
1021 W 1st Ave.
Mesa, AZ 85210-8401
Phone 602-969-4151

Universal Forest Products

Roof & Floor Trusses
PO Box 217
Auburndale, FL 33823-0217
Phone 813-965-2566

Universal Rundle Corp.

Plumbing Fixtures
PO Box 960
New Castle, PA 16103
Phone 412-658-6631

Urban Glassworks

Carved Glass Panels, Glass Furniture
3617 Blackburn Rd. SE
Calgary
Alta., CAN T2G 4A3
Canada
Phone 403-243-2201

Valley Builders Supply

Building Supply
295 S. State
Rigby, ID 83442-1425
Phone 208-745-8757

Valley Lumber & Hardware

Building Supply
223 Elmira Rd.
Ithaca, NY 14850-5301
Phone 607-272-0603

Valley Marble & Slate Corp.

Marble, Slate (Support Services)
15 Valmar Drive
New Milford, CT 06776-4396
Phone 203-354-3955
FAX 203-354-0149

Valley Truss Co.

Roof Trusses
316 E. 42nd
Boise, ID 83704
Phone 208-376-1521

Van Dyke's Restorers

Brass Hardware, Lamps, Moulding
PO Box 278
Woonsocket, SD 57385
Send $1.00 for Catalog/Information
Mail Order Available
Credit Cards MC/VISA
Phone 605-796-4425
Toll Free 800-843-3320
FAX 605-796-4085

Vande Hey-Raleigh Manufacturing Inc.

Manufacturer - Roof Tile
1665 Bohm Dr.
Little Chute, WI 54140
Phone 414-766-1181
Toll Free 800-236-8453
FAX 414-766-0776

Vaughan & Sons Inc.

Building Material, Doors, Lumber
PO Box 1001
San Antonio, TX 78294
Phone 512-222-1311

Vaughn Mfg. Corp.

Solar Water Heaters
386 Elm St.
Box 5431
Salisbury, MA 01950
Phone 508-462-6683

Verband Schweiz. Ziegel

Member - Federation Europeenne Des Fabricants De Tuiles Et De Briques

Obstgartenstrasse 28
Postfach 217
Switzerland

Phone 011-41-1-3619659
FAX 011-41-1-3610205

Vermont Antique Lumber Co.

Beams, Flooring, Lumber

PO Box 51
Mattituck, NY 11952

Toll Free 800-298-5579
FAX 516-298-5579

Vermont Castings

Woodstoves and Fireplaces

PO Box 501
Bethel, VT 05032

Phone 802-728-3181
Toll Free 800-227-8683
FAX 802-728-3940

Vermont Marble Co.

Interior & Exterior Custom Marble

5 PSI Plaza
Proctor, VT 05765

Phone 802-459-3311
Toll Free 800-451-4468
FAX 802-459-2948

Vermont Soapstone Co.

Soapstone for Fireplaces & Countertops

Stoughton Pond Road, PO Box 168
Perkinsville, VT 05151-0168

Phone 802-263-5404
FAX 802-263-9451

Vestal Mfg.

Fireplace Equipment, Building Supply

PO Box 420
Sweetwater, TN 37874

Phone 615-337-6125
FAX 615-337-2003

Victory Tile & Marble

Tile & Marble

68796 Perez Rd.
Cathedral City, CA 92234-7253

Phone 619-321-6000

Villaume Industries Inc.

Roof & Floor Trusses

2926 Lone Oak Circle
St. Paul, MN 55121

Phone 612-454-3610
FAX 612-454-4765

W. R. Outhwaite & Son

Rope Bannisters

Hawes
North Yorkshire DL8 3HM
Great Britain

Phone 011-44-969/667487

WSI Distributors

Brass Hardware

PO Box 1235
St. Charles, MO 63302

Send $2.00 for Catalog/Information

Phone 314-946-5811

Wal-Vac Inc.

Manufacturer - Central Vacuum Systems

318 Mart St. SW
Grand Rapids, MI 49548

Phone 616-241-6717

Walker & Zanger

Distributor - Ceramic Italian Tile - Marble, Granite, Natural Stone (Floor, Wall, Kitchen/Bath)

8901 Bradley Avenue
Sun Valley, CA 91352

Phone 818-504-0235
FAX 818-504-2057

Walker Industries

Bathroom Fixtures
7460 Highway 70 S
Nashville, TN 37221-1701
Send $5.80 for Catalog/Information
Phone 615-646-5084

Wallace Supply & Wholesale Distributor

Building Supply
Box 216 RR 2
Indian Mound, TN 37079-9544
Phone 615-232-7187

Walter Norman & Co.

Manufacturer - Wood Radiator Enclosures
PO Box 148037
Chicago, IL 60614-8037
Mail Order Available
Phone 312-281-1088
FAX 312-281-1089

Wanda Mfg. Co. Inc.

Central Vacuum System
PO Box 637
Comanche, OK 73529
Phone 405-439-5550

Wandplattenfabrik Engers GmbH

Manufacturer - Ceramic Wall Tile
210140
Neuwied 21 D-W-5450
Germany
Phone 011-49-262/24033
FAX 011-49-2622/13009

Ward Clapboard Mill Inc.

Clapboard Siding
PO Box 1030
Waitsfield, VT 05660
Catalog/Information Available Free
Mail Order Available
Credit Cards MC/VISA
Phone 802-496-3581
FAX 802-496-3294

Warren Truss Co. Inc.

Roof & Floor Trusses
10 Aleph Dr.
Newark, DE 19702
Phone 302-368-8566

Wasatch Solar Engineering

Solar Skylights
1164 North St.
Ogden, VT 84404
Send $1.00 for Catalog/Information
Mail Order Available
Phone 801-792-8532

Wascana Wood Components Ltd.

Roof & Floor Trusses
Pilot Butte
Sask
CAN 0SG 3Z0
Canada
Phone 306-561-2545

Watco Mfg. Co.

Plumbing Specialties
1220 S. Powell Rd.
Independence, MO 64057
Phone 816-796-3900
FAX 816-796-0875

Waterlox Chemical & Coating Corp.

Manufacturer - Paint & Varnish
9808 Meech Ave.
Cleveland, OH 44105
Phone 216-641-4877
Toll Free 800-321-0377
FAX 216-641-7213

Wayne Tile Company

Ceramic Tile - Monocottura, Bicottura, Floor, Wall for Kitchen & Bath
1459 Route 23
Wayne, NJ 07470
Phone 201-694-5480
FAX 201-694-5455

Building Supply

Weems Roof Truss Co. – Western Oregon Tile Supplies

Weems Roof Truss Co.

Roof Trusses
Rte. 2 Hwy. 11 E
Mosheim, TN 37818
　　　　　Phone 615-422-4439

Weil-McLain

Home Heating Units - Baseboard, Hot Water Radiators
Blaine Street
Michigan City, IN 46360
　　　　　Phone 219-879-6561

Welawood Inc.

Lumber
PO Drawer 86
West Lafayette, OH 43845
　　　　　Phone 614-545-6120
　　　　　FAX 614-545-5109

Wellington Hall, Ltd.

Wall Systems
Wellington Walls
PO Box 1354
Lexington, NC 27292
　　　　　Phone 704-249-4931

Wendover Woodworks

Wood
39 Liberty St.
Newburyport, MA 01950

Wendricks Roof Trusses

Roof Trusses
R.R. No. 1
Hermansville, MI 49847
　　　　　Phone 906-498-2397

Wesco Cedar Inc.

Manufacturer - Cedar Shake & Shingles
PO Box 2566
Eugene, OR 97402
　　　　　Phone 503-688-5020
　　　　　Toll Free 800-547-2511
　　　　　FAX 503-688-5024

West Forest Wood Products

Manufacturer - Red Cedar Shake
PO Box 1500
Coos Bay, OR 97420
　　　　　Phone 503-269-9597

West Michigan Nail Co.

Building Supply
PO Box 2434
2964 Clydon SW
Grand Rapids, MI 49501-2434
　　　　　Phone 616-538-8000

Westar Timber Ltd.

Lumber
1800-1176 W. Georgia St.
Vancouver, B.C.
CAN V6E 4B7
Canada
　　　　　Phone 604-685-2452
　　　　　FAX 604-683-0511

Westbury Conservatories

Custom Conservatories
Martels, High Easter Rd.
Branston, Essex
CM6 1NA
Great Britain
　　　　　Phone 011-44-371/876576

Western Archrib

Manufacturer - Arches, Trusses, Beams
750 Johnson N , PO Box 580
Boissevain, Man.
CAN R0K 0E0
Canada
　　　　　Phone 204-534-2486
　　　　　FAX 204-534-2236

Western Oregon Tile Supplies

Ceramic Tile
2603 SE Grand
Portland, OR 97202-1026
　　　　　Phone 503-232-2252

Building Supply

The Complete Sourcebook

Western Red Cedar Lumber Association

Red Cedar Siding, Decking
#203 - 457 Main Street
Farmingdale, NY 11735

Phone 516-643-9725
FAX 516-643-7252

Western Tile

Tile - Counters, Floors
3780 Santa Rosa Ave.
Santa Rosa, CA 95407

Phone 707-585-1501

Western Wood Fabricators Inc.

Roof Trusses
8485 Roslyn
PO Box 479
Commerce City, CO 80037-0479

Phone 303-286-7511

Westinghouse Electric Supply

Electric Supplies
24 Parkway Blvd.
York, PA 17404-2722

Phone 717-843-0891
FAX 717-843-1149

Westview Products, Inc.

Manufacturer - Sunrooms and Skylights
PO Box 569
1350 S.E. Shelton Street
Dallas, OR 97338

Phone 503-623-5174
FAX 503-623-3382

Weyerhaeuser Company

Manufacturer - Hardboard Siding in many different Styles
Weyerhaeuser Rd., PO Box 9
Klamath Falls, OR 97601

Phone 503-883-4853
Toll Free 800-547-5201
FAX 503-884-7282

White Brothers

Lumber
PO Box 14084
Oakland, CA 94614-2084

Phone 415-261-1600

White City Plywood Co.

Plywood
8380 Agate Rd.
White City, OR 97503

Phone 503-826-2281

Whitechapel Ltd.

American & English Hardware
PO Box 136
3650 West Highway 22
Wilson, WY 83014

Send $2.00 for Catalog/Information

Mail Order Available

Credit Cards VISA/MC/Check/Money Order

Phone 307-739-9478
Toll Free 800-468-5534
FAX 307-739-9458

Whitson Lumber Co. Inc.

Lumber
5701 California Ave.
PO Box 90247
Nashville, TN 37209

Phone 615-350-7260
FAX 615-350-7265

Wiggins & Son Inc.

Building Materials & Hardware
PO Box 9
Estill, SC 29918

Phone 803-625-2288

Wilco Building Material Distributors

Building Supplies
PO Box 48235
Doraville, GA 30362-8325

Phone 404-448-0100

Wilcox Lumber Inc.

Lumber
RR1, PO Box 3180
Arlington, VT 05250

Phone 802-375-2782

Wilh. Gail'sche Tonwerke KG a.A.

Manufacturer - Ceramic Wall Tile
5510
Giessen D-W-6300
Germany

Phone 011-49-641/7031

Wilkening Fireplace Co.

Ceramic Glass, Airtight Fireplace Doors
HCR 73 Box 625
Walker, MN 56484

Phone 215-547-1988

Toll Free 800-367-7976

Willamette Industries Inc.

Manufacturer - Plywood, Veneer, Particleboard, Laminated Beams
#1 East Saginaw Rd.
PO Box 277
Eugene, OR 97472

Phone 503-465-1655

FAX 503-465-1664

Willard Brothers Woodcutters

Wood
300 Basin Rd.
Trenton, NJ 08619

Phone 609-890-1990

Willet Stained Glass Studios

Stained Glass
10 E. Moreland Ave.
Philadelphia, PA 19118

Phone 215-247-5721

FAX 215-247-2951

Williams & Sons Slate & Tile Inc.

Slate & Tile
6596 Sullivan Trail
Wind Gap, PA 18091

Phone 215-863-4161

FAX 215-863-8128

Williams Lumber & Hardware

Lumber & Hardware
116 W. Woodford
Lawrenceburg, KY 40342

Phone 502-839-4261

Williamsburg Blacksmiths Inc.

Reproduction Wrought Iron Hardware
Rt. 9, PO Box 1776
Williamsburg, MA 01096

Send $5.00 for Catalog/Information

Mail Order Available

Phone 413-268-7341

Wilsonart

Manufacturer - Decorative Interior Finish Laminates
600 South General Bruce Drive
Temple, TX 76504

Phone 817-778-2711

Toll Free 800-433-3222

FAX 817-770-2384

Winburn Tile Manufacturing Co.

Manufacturer - Ceramic Tile
PO Box 1369
Little Rock, AR 72203

Phone 501-375-7251

Winther Browne

Manufacturer - Radiator Covers, Moulding
Fine Wood Carvings & Mouldings
Nobel Rd., Eley Estate, Edmonton
London N18 3DX
Great Britain

Phone 011-44-81/8033434

FAX 011-44-81/8070544

Wm. D. Bowers Lumber Co.

Roof and Floor Trusses
10620 Woodsboro Pike
Woodsboro, MD 21798
Phone 301-898-3200
FAX 301-845-8067

Wm. Zinsser & Co. Inc.

Manufacturer - Paint
39 Belmont Drive
Somerset, NJ 08875-1285
Phone 908-469-8100

Wolohan Lumber & Improvement

Lumber & Building Supply
2395 St. Johns Rd.
Lima, OH 45804-3862
Phone 419-227-2512

Wolverine Technologies Inc.

*Manufacturer - Vinyl Siding in many
different Styles and Colors*
Four Parklane Blvd.
Dearborn, MI 48126
Catalog/Information Available Free
Phone 313-337-7100
Toll Free 800-542-2152
FAX 313-337-7109

Wood Kote

Wood Floor Finish
PO Box 17192
Portland, OR 97217
Phone 503-285-8371
FAX 503-285-8374

Wood Structures Inc.

Roof & Floor Trusses
Alfred Rd. Business Pk.
PO Box 347
Biddeford, ME 04005
Phone 207-282-7556

Wood World

Lumber, Plywood, Moulding, Power Tools
13650 Floyd Rd., Suite 101
Dallas, TX 75243
Mail Order Available
Credit Cards MC/VISA/DISCOVER
Phone 214-669-9130
Toll Free 800-451-4086

Woodcrafters Supply

Lumber, Veneers, Mouldings
7703 Perry Hwy (Rt.19)
Pittsburgh, PA 15237
Phone 412-367-4330

Woodstock Soapstone Co., Inc.

Decorative Woodstoves
Airpark Rd., Box 37H
West Lebanon, NH 03784
Mail Order Available
Phone 603-298-5955
Toll Free 800-866-4344
FAX 603-298-5958

Woodward-Wanger Co.

Plumbing Supply
PO Box 5647
Philadelphia, PA 19129
Phone 215-226-4900

Woodworkers

*Order Direct - Worldwide Shipping -
Exotic & Domestic Hardwood*
5402 S. 40th St.
Phoenix, AZ 85040
Mail Order Available
Credit Cards VISA/MC/DISCOVER
Phone 602-437-4415
Toll Free 800-423-2450
FAX 602-437-3819

Woodworking Specialties

Cabinets
1300 Cameron Rd.
Hope Hills, NC 28348-2426
Phone 919-424-4146

Building Supply

World Innovations Ltd. – Yxhult AB

World Innovations Ltd.

Door Hardware
Box 184
Alliance
Alta., CAN T0B 0A0
Canada

Phone 403-879-3697
FAX 403-879-3900

World's End Tiles

Manufacturer - Handcrafted Designer Ceramic Tile
Silverthorne Rd.
Battersea, London
SW8 3HE
Great Britain

Phone 011-44-71/7208358
FAX 011-44-71/6271435

Worthy Works Inc.

Decorative Hardware
1220 Rock St.
Rockford, IL 61101-1437

Phone 815-968-5858
FAX 815-968-5959

Wrightway Mfg. Co.

Plumbing Supply
750 Northgate Pky.
Wheeling, IL 60090-2660

Phone 708-520-9080

Wyoming Lumber & Supply Co.

Building Supply
110 Park St.
Pineville, WV 24874

Phone 304-732-7911

Yankee Hearth

Fireplace Accessories
PO Box 124
Wheelwright, MA 01094
Send $0.25 for Catalog/Information

Yellow Jacket Solar

Alternative Energy Components & Systems
Box 253M
Yellow Jacket, CO 81335
Send $2.00 for Catalog/Information
Mail Order Available

Phone 303-562-4884

York International Corp.

Gas Furnaces, Heating and Ventilation Equipment
PO Box 1592
York, PA 17405

Phone 717-771-7890

Yost Mfg. & Supply Inc.

Manufacturer - Order Direct - Nationwide Delivery - Gutters, Leaders
1018 Hartford Tpke., Rt 85
Waterford, CT 06385
Mail Order Available

Phone 203-447-9678
Toll Free 800-872-9678
FAX 203-444-9678

Youngstown Roof Truss Co.

Roof Trusses
397 S. Meridan
Youngstown, OH 44509

Phone 216-792-2323

Yulix Inc.

Ceramic Tile
812 Fifth Ave.
Oakland, CA 94606

Phone 415-834-8800
FAX 415-790-2572

Yxhult AB

Member - The Swedish Brick and Tile Manufacturers Association
Street Address Not Available
S-69200 Kumla Sweden,
Sweden

Phone 011-46-19/86000
FAX 011-46-72733

Building Supply

The Complete Sourcebook

Zappone Manufacturing

Manufacturer - Roofing Shingle

2928 N. Pittsburg
Spokane, WA 99207

Mail Order Available

Phone 509-483-6804
FAX 509-483-8050

Zeidler Forest Industries Ltd.

Lumber, Plywood

4828 89th St., PO Box 4370
Edmonton
Alta., CAN T6E 1N9
Canada

Phone 403-468-3311
FAX 403-468-5918

Doors

A-J Industries Inc.

Aluminum Doors & Windows
1217 Oak St.
Bloomer, WI 54724
Phone 715-568-2204

Academy Mfg. Co. Inc.

Aluminum Screen Doors
1519 W. 132nd St.
Gardena, CA 90249
Phone 213-321-8900

Acorn Antique Doors

Manufacturer - Antique & Reproduction Georgian & Victorian Doors in Pine, Oak
The High Street, Twyford, nr
Winchester, Hampshire S021 1RJ
Great Britain
Catalog/Information Available Free
Phone 011-44-962-777500

Albert Marston & Co. Ltd.

Door and Window Hardware
Wellington Works
Planetary Rd. Willenhall, West Midlands
SV13 3ST
Great Britain
Phone 011-44-90-2305511
FAX 011-44-90-2305290

Alexander Moulding Mill Co., Inc.

Pre Hung Door Units
PO Box 312
Hamilton, TX 76531
Phone 817-386-3187
FAX 817-386-3675

Allister Door Control Systems Inc.

Manufacturer - Door Control Systems
PO Box 10
Exton, PA 19341
Phone 215-363-7450
Toll Free 800-441-9300

American Door Co. Inc.

Manufacturer - Folding Doors
PO Box 626
Mishawaka, IN 46544
Phone 219-259-5281
FAX 219-255-7671

American Door Co. of Michigan Inc.

Manufacturer - Doors & Windows
PO Box 1
Walkerton, IN 46574
Phone 219-586-3192

Apex Doors Ltd.

Garage Doors
Crown Lane, Horwich
Bolton BL6 5HP
Great Britain
Phone 011-44-204-68151
FAX 011-44-204-690955

Artistic Doors and Windows

Doors and Windows
60 Brunswick Ave.
Edison, NJ 08817
Phone 908-287-2500

Atlas Roll-lite Door Co.

Manufacturer - Prepainted Steel Garage Door
PO Box 593949
Orlando, FL 32859-3949

Phone 407-857-0680
FAX 407-859-9770

Atrium Door and Window Co.

Atrium Doors and Windows
PO Box 226957
Dallas, TX 75222

Toll Free 800-527-5249

Bassett & Findley Ltd.

Doors, Moulding, Stair Components
Talbot Road North
Wellingborough, Northants NN8 1QS
Great Britain

Phone 011-44-933/224898
FAX 011-44-933/227731

Bel-Air Door Co.

Carved Wood Doors
314 S. Date Ave.
PO Box 829
Alhambra, CA 91802

Send $2.00 for Catalog/Information

Mail Order Available

Phone 213-283-3731

Benchmark

Manufacturer - Doors
12842 Pennridge
Bridgeton, MO 60344-9982

Toll Free 800-523-5261

Bend Millwork Systems Inc.

Manufacturer - Wood Doors, Entry Systems
PO Box 5249
Bend, OR 97708

Phone 503-382-4411
Toll Free 800-547-6880
FAX 503-382-1292

Bennett Industries Inc.

Manufacturer - Distributor List (Wholesale & Retail) Interior & Exterior - Panel and French Doors, Oak Paneled Leaded Glass Doors
1530 Palisade Avenue
Fort Lee, NJ 07024

Catalog/Information Available Free

Phone 201-947-5340
FAX 201-947-3908

Berea Prehung Door, Inc.

Interior & Exterior Doors - Metal, Wood - Stock or Custom
2648 Medina Rd.
Medina, OH 44256

Phone 216-725-7541

Besam Ltd.

Doors, Locks
Washington Ho, Brooklands Clo
Sunbury-on-Thames, Middx TW16 73Q
Great Britain

Phone 011-44-932/765888
FAX 011-44-932/812235

Bevel Glass & Mirror

Beveled Windows, Doors, Mirrors
4846 Potomac St.
St. Louis, MO 63116

Phone 314-353-1160

Billings Sash & Door Co.

Doors, Millwork
RR1 Box 113
Wadena, MN 56482

Phone 218-631-9249

Bison Manufacturing

Manufacturer - French Doors
PO Box 19849
1445 W. Belt North
Houston, TX 77043

Phone 713-467-6700

Doors

Black Millwork Co. Inc. – Cline Aluminum Doors Inc.

Black Millwork Co. Inc.

Doors, Windows, Screens, Rooflights

Andersen Ho, Dallow St.
Burton-on-Trent, Staffs DE14 2PQ
Great Britain

Phone 011-44-283/511122

FAX 011-44-283/510863

Bostwick Doors UK Ltd.

Doors

Mersey Ind Est.
Stockport, Cheshire SK4 3ED
Great Britain

Phone 011-44-61/4427227

Bright Star Woodworking

French Doors

14618 Tyler Foote Rd.
Nevada City, CA 95959

Phone 916-292-3514

Buell Door Company

Doors

5200 E. Grand Ave.
Dallas, TX 75223

Phone 214-827-9260

CECO Corp.

Manufacturer - Steel Doors

750 Old Hickory Blvd. #150
Brentwood, TN 37027-4502

Cal-Wood Door Inc.

Wood Doors, Frames

PO Box 1656
Santa Rosa, CA 95402

Phone 707-584-9663

FAX 707-584-4963

Cascade Mill & Glass Works

Screen Doors

21 Pkwy, Hwy 23
PO Box 316
Ouray County, CO 81427

Send $2.00 for Catalog/Information

Mail Order Available

Phone 303-325-4780

Castlegate, Inc.

Fiberglass & Steel Entry Systems, Patio Doors in many styles and colors

Entry Systems
PO Box 76, 911 East Jefferson Street
Pittsburg, KS 66762

Toll Free 800-835-0364

Catnic Ltd.

Doors, Locks

Pontgwindy Est,
Caerphilly, M Glam CF8 2WJ
Great Britain

Phone 011-44-222/885955

FAX 011-44-222/863178

Century Wood Door Limited

Wood Doors and Frames

1600 Britannia Rd., E.
Mississauga
Ont, CAN L4W 1J2
Canada

Phone 416-670-2030

FAX 416-673-9891

Cherry Creek Enterprises Inc.

Beveled Glass For Doors, Cabinets, Windows

3500 Blake St.
Denver, CO 80204

Send $2.00 for Catalog/Information

Mail Order Available

Phone 303-892-1819

Toll Free 800-338-5725

Cline Aluminum Doors Inc.

Aluminum Doors, Frames and Louvers

112 32nd Ave.
W. Bradenton, FL 33205-8096

Phone 813-746-4104

FAX 813-746-5153

The Complete Sourcebook

4 - 3

Clopay Corporation – Defiance Forest Products

Doors

Clopay Corporation

Manufacturer - Garage Doors
312 Walnut St., Suite 1600
Cincinnati, OH 45202

Phone 513-381-4800
Toll Free 800-225-6729
FAX 513-762-3861

Cole Sewell Corp.

Manufacturer - Custom Solid Core Storm Doors
2288 University Ave.
St. Paul, MN 55114

Phone 612-646-7873
Toll Free 800-328-6596

Combination Door Company

Wood Windows, Screen Doors, Basement Doors, Garage Doors
1000 Morris St.
PO Box 1076
Fond du Lac, WI 54936-1076

Catalog/Information Available Free

Phone 414-922-2050
FAX 414-922-2917

Cotswood Door Specialists Ltd.

Mahogany Doors
5 Hampden Way
Southgate N14 5DJ
Great Britain

Phone 011-44-81/3689635
FAX 011-44-81-3688345

Craftline

Wood Doors
Div. of Vega Industries Inc.
1125 Ford St.
Maumee, OH 43537

Phone 419-893-3311
FAX 419-893-0735

Crawford Door Ltd.

Doors
Whittle Rd, Meir
Strok-on-Trent ST3 7AQ
Great Britain

Phone 011-44-782/599899
FAX 011-44-782/599989

Creative Openings

Colonial, Victorian Screen Doors
PO Box 4204
Bellingham, WA 98227

Send $4.00 for Catalog/Information

Phone 206-671-6420

Crestline

French Patio Doors
1725 Indian Wood Circle
Maumee, OH 43537

Toll Free 800-552-4111

Crown Door Corp.

Wood Doors
5110 W. Clifton Ave.
PO Box 15277
Tampa, FL 33634

Phone 813-884-3456
FAX 813-882-0914

Curriers Co.

Steel Doors & Frames
905 S. Carolina
PO Box 1648
Mason City, IA 50401

Phone 515-423-1334
FAX 515-424-8305

Defiance Forest Products

Manufacturer - Wood Doors, Jambs & Frames
PO Box 1696
Tacoma, WA 98401

Phone 206-272-7090
FAX 206-272-7385

The Complete Sourcebook

Doors

Delmar Hardware Mfg. Ltd. – Dor-Win Manufacturing

Delmar Hardware Mfg. Ltd.

Door Hardware

1275 Eglinton Ave. E
Missssauga
Ont, CAN L4W 2Z2
Canada

Phone 416-625-6455

Delta Door Co., Inc.

Wood Doors

433 W. Scotts
Stockton, CA 95203

Phone 209-948-0637
FAX 209-948-0341

Dexter Lock

Manufacturer - Door Locks and Hardware

300 Webster Rd.
Auburn, AL 36830

Phone 205-826-3300
FAX 205-887-6932

Donat Flamand, Inc.

Door & Window Frames

90 Rue Industrielle St.
Apollinaire
Que, CAN G0S 2E0
Canada

Phone 418-692-0868
FAX 418-881-2514

Door Systems Inc.

Doors

333 Byberry Rd.
Hatboro, PA 19040

Phone 215-672-8087

DoorCraft Manufacturing Co.

Wood Doors

A Jeld-Wen Co.
3201 N.W. Lower River Rd.
Vancouver, WA 98666

Phone 206-696-4031
FAX 206-693-8429

Doorcraft Mfg. Ltd.

Wood Garage Doors

465 Wilsey Rd.
Fredericton
N.B. CAN E3B 5N6
Canada

Phone 506-450-3031
FAX 506-453-0699

Doorland 2000 Inc.

Manufacturer - Wood Doors

140 Hanlan Rd.
Woodbridge, ON L4L 3P6
Canada

Send $3.00 for Catalog/Information

Mail Order Available

Toll Free 800-265-0379
FAX 905-850-5193

Doorman Hardware

Manufacturer - Door Hardware

1158 Tower Lane
Bensenville, IL 60106

Phone 312-766-1621
Toll Free 800-323-4615

Doormen

Wood Doors

220 Main St.
Hempstead, NY 11550

Phone 516-486-0300

Doors, Incorporated

Wood Doors

1760-B North Ardenwood Dr.
Baton Rouge, LA 70806

Phone 504-926-2470
FAX 504-926-4301

Dor-Win Manufacturing

Manufacturer - Doors, Windows

109 Midland Ave.
Elmwood Park, NJ 07407

Phone 201-478-3500
FAX 201-791-1962

Doors

The Complete Sourcebook

Dunbarton Corp.

Steel Door Frames, Aluminum Frames, Sliding Closet Doors
510 Murray Rd.
Dothan, AL 36302

                  Phone 205-794-0661
                  FAX 205-794-9184

Duraflex Systems Ltd.

Doors, Windows
Duraflex Ho, Tewkesbury Rd.
Cheltenham, Glos GL51 9PP
Great Britain

                  Phone 011-44-242/580868
                  FAX 011-44-242/577302

EMCO

Manufacturer - Doors
PO Box 853, 2121 East Walnut St.
Des Moines, IA 50317

                  Phone 515-265-6101
                  Toll Free 800-777-3626

ENJO Doors and Windows

Manufacturer - Doors & Windows
16 Park Ave.
Staten Island, NY 10302

                  Phone 718-447-5220
                  Toll Free 800-437-3656
                  FAX 718-442-7041

Eagle Plywood & Door Mftrs. Inc.

Wood Doors
450 Oak Tree Ave.
S. Plainfield, NJ 07080

                  Phone 908-769-7650
                  FAX 908-668-4317

Eggers Industries

Wood Doors, Frames
1819 E. River St.
PO Box 88
Two Rivers, WI 54241

                  Phone 414-793-1351
                  FAX 414-793-2958

Elegant Entries

Exterior and Interior Doors
240 Washington St.
Auburn, MA 01501

Catalog/Information Available Free

                  Phone 508-755-5237
                  Toll Free 800-343-3432
                  FAX 508-832-6874

Elite Interior Doors

Interior Doors
Commerce Drive
Mount Vernon, OH 43050

                  Phone 614-397-3403

Entrances Inc.

Manufacturer - Doors, Windows, Shutters
Robert Bonneau
164 Poocham Road
Westmoreland, NH 03467

Catalog/Information Available Free

Mail Order Available

                  Phone 603-399-7723
                  FAX 603-399-4943

Erebus Limited

Door Locks & Hardware
377 Lichfield Rd.
Wednesfield, Wolverhampton WV11 3HD
Great Britain

                  Phone 011-44-90-2737282
                  FAX 011-44-90-2864684

Eugenia's Place

Antique Door Hardware
3522 Broad St.
Chamblee, GA 30341

Catalog/Information Available Free

Mail Order Available

Credit Cards MC/VISA/Money Order

                  Phone 404-458-1677
                  Toll Free 800-337-1677

Doors

F. E. Schumacher Co., Inc.

Wood Doors and Frames

200 Mill St., S.E.
PO Box 10
Hartville, OH 44632

Phone 216-877-9307

Feather River Wood & Glass Co.

Glass Paneled Doors

PO Box 447
9296 Midway
Durham, CA 95938

Catalog/Information Available Free

Mail Order Available

Phone 916-095-0752

Toll Free 800-284-3007

FAX 916-895-0752

Fenebee Inc.

Doors & Windows

130 Rue Michener
St. Joseph-De-Beauce
Que, CAN G0S 2V0
Canada

Phone 418-397-6886

Fenestra Corp.

Steel Doors & Frames

PO Box 8189
Erie, PA 16505

Phone 814-838-2001

FAX 814-838-2009

Fenestra Wood Door Div.

Wood Doors

2501 Universal Dr.
Oshkosh, WI 54904

Phone 414-233-6161

Fiberlux, Inc.

Sliding Glass Doors

59 South Terrace Ave.
Mt. Vernon, NY 10550

Phone 914-664-7111

Toll Free 800-342-7111

Filmore Thomas & Co., Inc.

Wood Doors

350 County Center St.
PO Box 218
Lapeer, MI 48446

Phone 313-664-2400

FAX 313-664-9911

Fineman Doors Inc.

Solid Hardwood Entry Interior Doors

16020 Valley Wood Rd.
Van Nuys, CA 91401

Mail Order Available

Phone 818-990-3667

FAX 818-990-4406

Frank Allart & Co., Ltd.

Brass Door & Window Hardware

36 Sherborne St.
Birmingdal B16 8DB
Great Britain

Phone 011-44-21/4542977

FAX 011-44-21/4562234

Fraser Woods Inc.

Manufacturer - Solid Hardwood Doors, Furnishings, Flooring

217 Overton - Broad Rd.
Shreveport, LA 71106

Phone 318-798-3098

G & T Woodworking Ltd.

Doors & Windows

PO Box 150
Millville
N.B. CAN E0H 1M0
Canada

Phone 506-463-2241

G. R. Theriault Ltd.

Doors & Windows

547 Rue Tobique
Grand Falls
N.B. CAN E0J 1M0
Canada

Phone 506-228-4530

FAX 506-228-4974

The Complete Sourcebook

4 - 7

GT Doors & Locks

Victorian Door Locks
5901 Sherman
Downers Grove, IL 60516

Catalog/Information Available Free

Phone 708-963-1919
Toll Free 800-831-5616
FAX 708-963-1994

Garran Mfg. Ltd.

Doors & Windows
4040 228th St.
Langley
B.C., CAN V3A 7B9
Canada

Phone 604-534-2990
FAX 604-534-5384

General Products Co. Inc.

Manufacturer - Steel Doors & Frames in many styles
PO Box 7387
Fredericksburg, VA 22404

Catalog/Information Available Free

Phone 703-898-5700
FAX 703-898-5802

Glass Craft Specialties, Inc.

Beveled Glass Door & Cabinet Inserts
2409 Center St.
Houston, TX 77007-6006

Phone 713-868-4276
FAX 713-868-9136

Graham Mfg. Corp.

Manufacturer - Wooden Flush Doors
1920 E. 26th St.
Marshfield, WI 54449

Phone 715-387-2581
FAX 715-387-0739

Grand Era Reproductions

Victorian, Country Screen & Storm Doors, Arbors, Gates, Brackets
PO Box 1026
Lapeer, MI 48446

Send $2.00 for Catalog/Information

Mail Order Available

Credit Cards VISA/MC

Phone 313-664-1756
Toll Free 800-258-3822
FAX 313-664-8957

Grande Entrance Door Company

Douglas Fir Doors
PO Box 5249
Bend, OR 97708

Toll Free 800-821-1016

Great Paines Glassworks

Decorative Glass for Doors, Windows, Shower Doors, Table Tops
2861 Walnut Street
Denver, CO 80205

Mail Order Available

Toll Free 800-338-5408
FAX 303-294-0163

Haley Bros.,Inc.

Wood Doors and Frames
6291 Orangethorpe Ave.
Buena Park, CA 90620

Phone 714-670-2112
FAX 714-994-6971

Hazelmere Industries Ltd.

Mantel Pieces, Overhead Garage Doors
2-5422 175 St.
Surrey BC V35 4C3
Canada

Mail Order Available

Phone 604-574-3304
FAX 604-574-7814

Doors

Hendricks Woodworking

Custom Wood Doors, Moulding

RD 2, Box 227-1B
Kempton, PA 19529

Catalog/Information Available Free

Phone 215-756-6187

FAX 215-756-6171

Hillaldam Coburn Topdor Ltd.

Sliding Door Systems

Unit 27, Barwell Business Park
Leatherhead Rd., Chessington Surrey
KT9 2NY
Great Britain

Phone 011-44-13/975151

FAX 011-44-13/914914

Iberia Millwork

*French Doors, Interior/Exterior Wood
Shutters, Custom Millwork*

500 Jane St.
New Iberia, LA 70560

Catalog/Information Available Free

Mail Order Available

Phone 318-365-5644

FAX 318-365-3923

Ideal Door Co.

Overhead Garage Doors

PO Box 106
Baldwin, WI 54002

Phone 715-684-3223

FAX 715-684-2247

Ideal Wood Products

Wood Doors

890 Central Court
New Albany, IN 47150

Toll Free 800-626-6271

FAX 812-945-9256

International Wood Products

Hardwood Doors

10883 Thornment Rd.
San Diego, CA 92123

Send $1.00 for Catalog/Information

Toll Free 800-468-3667

FAX 800-426-8655

Iowa Des Moines Door & Hardware

Steel Frames & Doors

1450 Delaware Ave.
PO Box 3052
Des Moines, IA 50317

Phone 515-262-9822

J. Legge & Co. Ltd.

Door Locks, Latches

Moat St.
Willenhall, West Midlands
WV13 1TD
Great Britain

Phone 011-44-90/2366332

FAX 011-44-90/2608211

JJJ Specialty Co.

Wood Doors and Frames

113 27th Ave. N.E.
Minneapolis, MN 55418

Phone 612-788-9688

FAX 612-788-2002

Jack Wallis Doors

*Manufacturer - Retail & Wholesale -
Custom Doors, Entryways*

Rt. 1 Box 22A
Murray, KY 42071

Send $4.00 for Catalog/Information

Phone 502-489-2613

FAX 502-489-2187

Doors

Jeld-Wen

Manufacturer - Interior, Exterior, Entrance Doors Casements, Basement, Double Hung, Sliding, Stationery - 800# for Nearest Distributor

3303 Lakeport Blvd.
PO Box 1329
Klamath Falls, OR 97601-0268

Phone 503-882-3451
Toll Free 800-877-9482
FAX 503-885-7454

Jessup Door Company

Manufacturer - Wood Doors - Interior/Exterior, French Doors

300 E. Railroad St.
Dowagiac, MI 49047

Phone 616-782-2183
FAX 616-782-3505

Johnson Metal Products

Steel Doors

305 Industrial Parkway
Richmond, IN 47374

Phone 317-962-8515

Josiah Parkes and Sons Ltd.

Door Hardware and Locks

Union Works
Gower St. Willenhall, West Midlands
WV13 1JX
Great Britain

Phone 011-44-90/2366931
FAX 011-44-90/2366888

Karona Inc.

Raised Panel Doors, Louvered Doors

PO Box 128
One Karona Dr.
Grandville, MI 49418

Phone 616-532-5901
Toll Free 800-253-9233

Kaylien

Sculptured Wood & Glass Panel Doors, Decorative Metal-Faced Doors

8520 Railroad Avenue
PO Box 711599
Santee, CA 92072-2599

Catalog/Information Available Free

Phone 619-448-0544
Toll Free 800-748-5627
FAX 619-448-5196

Keller Industries Inc.

Patio, Storm Doors, Tub Enclosures, Windows

18000 State Rd.9
Miami, FL 33162

Phone 305-651-7100
FAX 305-653-9986

Kenmore Industries

Carved Door Fan-Lights, Entries

1 Thompson Square
Boston, MA 02129

Send $3.00 for Catalog/Information

Mail Order Available

Phone 617-242-1711
FAX 617-242-1982

Kirby Millworks

Solid Oak Doors, Moulding

PO Box 898
Ignacio, CO 81137

Phone 303-563-9436

Klamath Doors

Manufacturer - Doors

PO Box 10266
Portland, OR 97210-9879

Toll Free 800-877-9482

Korona

Exterior and Interior Doors

PO Box 128
Grandville, MI 49468

Doors

Kwikset Corp.

Manufacturer - Designer Door Hardware

516 E. Santa Ana St.
PO Box 4250
Anaheim, CA 92803-4250

Phone 714-535-8111
FAX 714-533-9547

Laflamme & Frere, Inc.

Wood Windows & Doors

51 Rue Industrielle
Lotbiniere
Que., CAN G0S 2E0
Canada

Phone 418-881-3950
FAX 418-881-2691

Lamson-Taylor Custom Doors

*Manufacturer - Order Direct - Nationwide
Delivery - Custom Wood Doors*

5 Tucker Rd.
South Acworth, NH 03607

Send $2.00 for Catalog/Information

Mail Order Available

Phone 603-835-2992
FAX 603-835-2992

Landmark Doors

Doors

28 Marcy Ave.
Brooklyn, NY 11211

Mail Order Available

Phone 718-834-8534

Landquist & Son, Inc.

Wood Doors and Frames

1900 W. Hubbard St.
Chicago, IL 60622

Phone 312-226-1768

Leicester Joinery Co.

*Doors, Windows, Door and Window
Hardware, Frames*

Unit 5, Ashville Way
Whetstone, Leicester
LE8 3NU
Great Britain

Phone 011-44-533/866866
FAX 011-44-533/750058

Lynden Door, Inc.

Wood Doors and Frames

177 West Main St.
PO Box 326
Lynden, WA 98264

Phone 206-354-5676
FAX 206-354-3738

Madawaska Doors Inc.

Solid Wood Doors

PO Box 850
Bolton, Ontario
CAN L7E 5T5

Phone 905-859-4622
Toll Free 800-263-2358
FAX 905-859-4654

Magnet Trade

*Doors, Windows, Door and Window
Furniture, Stairs, Roof Windows, Locks,
Faucets, Moulding*

Div. of Magnet Ltd., Roydings Ave.
Keighley, W Yorkshire
BD21 4BY
Great Britain

Phone 011-44-535661133
FAX 011-44-535610363

Manufacturers Glass

*Worldwide Shipping - Glass - Beveled,
Leaded, Door and Entryways*

650 Reed St.
Santa Clara, CA 95050

Send $3.00 for Catalog/Information

Mail Order Available

Phone 408-748-1806
FAX 408-748-0160

Doors

The Complete Sourcebook

Mar-Flo, Inc. – Nottingham Gallery

Doors

Mar-Flo, Inc.

Custom - Interior and Exterior Doors
8 Fox Court
Dumont, NJ 07628
Phone 201-742-4765

Masonite Corp.

*Manufacturer - Doors, Facings,
Hardboard Siding*
1 South Wacker Dr.
Chicago, IL 60606
Phone 312-750-0900
Toll Free 800-848-3673
FAX 312-263-5808

Maywood Inc.

Manufacturer - Wood Doors
PO Box 30550
900 E. 2nd 79101
Amarillo, TX 79120-0550
Phone 806-374-2835
FAX 806-374-3821

Millwork Supply Company

Wood Doors, Windows, Mantels, Moulding
2225 1st Ave. S.
Seattle, WA 98134
Mail Order Available
Phone 206-622-1450
FAX 206-292-9176

Mohawk Flush Doors, Inc.

Wood Doors and Frames
PO Box 112
Northumberland, PA 17857
Phone 717-473-3557
FAX 717-473-3737

Morgan Distribution

French Doors
128 McQueen St.
West Columbia, SC 29169

Morgan Manufacturing

*Manufacturer - Interior & Exterior Wood
Doors, French Doors*
601 Oregon St., PO Box 2446
Oshkosh, WI 54903
Phone 414-235-7170
Toll Free 800-435-7464
FAX 414-235-5773

Morgan-Bockius Studios Inc.

*Stained, Beveled, Etched Glass, Wood
Doors*
1412 York Rd.
Warminster, PA 18974
Phone 215-672-6547

National Screen Company, Inc.

Door & Window Screens
PO Box 1608
Suffolk, VA 23434
Phone 804-539-2378

Nord Company

*Manufacturer - Interior & Exterior Wood
Doors, Posts, Columns, Mouldings*
PO Box 1187
Everett, WA 98206
Phone 206-259-9292
FAX 206-252-3269

North Central Door Co.

Wood & Steel Garage Doors
PO Box 575, 955 First Street NE
Bemidji, MN 56601
Phone 218-751-6962

Nottingham Gallery

Antique Glass Doors & Windows
339 Bellvale Rd.
Warwick, NY 10990
Mail Order Available
Phone 914-986-1487

Doors

Nu-Air Mfg. Co. — Pixley Lumber Co.

Nu-Air Mfg. Co.

Patio Doors & Windows

8105 Anderson Rd.
PO Box 15436M
Tampa, FL 33684

Phone 813-885-1654

Olde South Door

Manufacturer - Oak & Mahogany Doors

3209 E. Albermarle Rd.
Midland, NC 28107

Toll Free 800-289-1024

FAX 704-888-5060

Omega Garage Door

Garage Doors

215 Me Clurg Rd.
Boardman, OH 44512

Phone 216-758-7528

Oregon Wooden Screen Door Co.

Nationwide Shipping - Wood Screen Doors & Brass Hardware

2767 Harris Street
Eugene, OR 97405

Send $3.00 for Catalog/Information

Mail Order Available

Phone 503-485-0279

FAX 503-484-0353

Overhead Door Corp.

Manufacturer - Wood and Steel Insulated Doors

6750 LBJ Freeway
PO Box 809046
Dallas, TX 75380-9046

Phone 214-233-6611

Toll Free 800-543-2269

FAX 214-233-0367

Peachtree Doors, Inc.

Distributor List - Doors - French, Glass Sliding, Insulated, Custom - Doublehungs, Bow, Bay, Casement

PO Box 5700
Norcross, GA 30091

Phone 404-497-2000

Toll Free 800-447-4700

Pease Industries, Inc.

Manufacturer - Steel Doors

7100 Dixie Highway
Fairfield, OH 45014

Send $1.00 for Catalog/Information

Phone 513-870-3600

Toll Free 800-543-1180

FAX 513-870-3672

Perma-Door

Wood and Steel Doors

631 N. First Street
PO Box 457
West Branch, MI 48661

Phone 517-345-5110

Toll Free 800-543-4456

Philips Home Products

Manufacturer - Garage Door Openers

22790 Lake Park Blvd.
Alliance, OH 44601

Phone 216-829-3600

Toll Free 800-654-3643

FAX 216-829-3636

Pixley Lumber Co.

Interior & Exterior Wood Door Units

715 W. Will Rogers Blvd.
PO Box 308
Claremore, OK 74018

Phone 918-341-4223

The Complete Sourcebook

Portes Belhumeur Inc.

Doors
891 Rue St. Viateur
Berthierville
Que., CAN J0K 1A0
Canada

Phone 514-836-6255

Premdor Inc.

Manufacturer - Interior Doors
4120 Yonge Street, #420
Willowdale
Ont., CAN M2P 2B8
Canada

Phone 416-250-8933

Quality Door & Millwork

Doors, Millwork
2540 Midpard Dr.
Montgomery, AL 36109

Phone 205-277-4123

Rare Wood

Antique Doors, Shutters, Hardware
106 Ferris St.
Brooklyn, NY 11231

Send $1.50 for Catalog/Information

Mail Order Available

Phone 718-875-9037

Ray Tenebruso

Manufacturer - Doors, Shutters, Windows
2842 Gaston Rd.
Cottage Grove, WI 53527

Mail Order Available

Phone 608-839-4518

Raynor Garage Doors

Manufacturer - Garage Doors
101 East River Rd.
PO Box 448
Dixon, IL 61021-0448

Phone 815-288-1431
Toll Free 800-545-0455
FAX 815-288-3720

Red-E-Built Products

Doors
PO Drawer 5131
Mansfield, OH 44901

Phone 419-522-0276

Restorer's Supply

Doors, Mantels
PO Box 311
Boston, MA 02199

Mail Order Available

Phone 617-247-0740

Ridge Doors

Garage Doors
New Rd.
Monmouth Junction, NJ 08852

Phone 201-329-2311
Toll Free 800-631-5656

Rural Hall Inc.

Raised Panel Doors - Oak, Ash, Birch, Maple, Walnut, Cherry
PO Box 831
Rural Hall, NC 27045

Phone 919-969-6886

SNE Enterprises, Inc.

Wood Doors
Div. Plygen Ind.
PO Box 8007
Wausau, WI 54402-8007

Phone 715-845-1161
FAX 715-847-6603

Sauder Door Corporation

Wood Doors and Frames
PO Box 727
733 6th St. S.
Kirkland, WA 98033

Phone 206-822-6006
Toll Free 800-752-6892
FAX 206-822-3877

Doors

Scherr's Cabinets — Sovereign Group Ltd.

Scherr's Cabinets

Raised Panel Doors
Hwy. 2 East, Rt. #5
Box 12
Minot, ND 58701

Send $1.00 for Catalog/Information
Credit Cards Accepted

Phone 701-839-3384
FAX 701-852-6090

Schuco International

Doors, Windows
Whitehall Ave.
Kingston, Milton Keynes
MK10 0AL
Great Britain

Phone 011-44-908/282111
FAX 011-44-908/282124

Semling-Menke Company, Inc.

Wood Doors and Frames
South Nast St.
PO Box 378
Merrill, WI 54452

Phone 715-536-9411

Sheppard Millwork, Inc.

Order Direct - Custom Doors, Moulding, Casings, Stair Parts
21020 70th Ave. West
Edmonds, WA 98020

Mail Order Available

Phone 206-771-4645
FAX 206-672-1622

Simpson Door Company

Manufacturer - Wood Doors
31919 First Ave.
Federal Way, WA 98003

Phone 206-495-3291
Toll Free 800-952-4057
FAX 206-495-3295

Somerset Door & Column Co.

Doors & Columns
PO Box 755
S. Edgewood Ave.
Somerset, PA 15501

Catalog/Information Available Free

Phone 814-445-9608
Toll Free 800-242-7916
FAX 814-443-1658

Southeastern Aluminum Products Inc.

Doors
PO Box 6427
Jacksonville, FL 32236

Phone 904-781-8200
FAX 904-695-9541

Southwest Door Company Inc.

Manufacturer - Doors
219 North 3rd Avenue
Tucson, AZ 85705

Phone 602-624-1434

Southwood Door Company

Windows and Doors
110 West Donald St.
PO Box 560
Quitman, MS 39355

Phone 601-776-2164
FAX 601-776-2144

Sovereign Group Ltd.

Doors, Windows, Shutters, Moulding
Vale St.
Nelson, Lancs
BB9 0TA
Great Britain

Phone 011-44-282/618171
FAX 011-44-282/692733

The Complete Sourcebook

4 - 15

Sovereign Wright

Door & Window Frames, Doors, Windows
9 Telford Pl.
South Newmoor Ind Est, Irvine, Ayrshire
KA11 4HW
Great Britain

Phone 011-44-294/211227
FAX 011-44-294/213604

Spanish Pueblo Doors Inc.

Santa Fe Style Doors
PO Box 2517
Santa Fe, NM 87504

Mail Order Available

Phone 505-473-0464

Specialty Woodworks Co.

Wood Doors & Cabinets
PO Box 1450
212 Pennsylvania
Hamilton, MT 59840

Mail Order Available

Phone 406-363-6353
FAX 406-363-6373

Stanley Door Systems

Manufacturer - Door Systems, Garage Doors, Entryways, Home Security
1225 E. Maple Road
Troy, MI 48084-5600

Phone 810-528-1400
Toll Free 800-521-2752

Steldor Ltd.

Steel Doors & Frames
975 Logan Ave.
Winnipeg
Man., CAN R3C 2X4
Canada

Phone 204-774-4533
FAX 204-786-5899

Steves & Sons

Wood Doors and Frames
PO Drawer S
San Antonio, TX 78211

Phone 512-924-5111
FAX 512-924-0470

Stripling-Blake Lumber Co. Inc.

Pre-Hung Door Units
3400 Steck Ave.
Austin, TX 78759

Phone 512-465-4200
FAX 512-465-4222

Swish Products Ltd.

Doors, Windows, Moulding
Building Products Div.
Lichfield Rd Ind Est, Tanworth, Staffs
B79 7TW
Great Britain

Phone 011-44-82764242
FAX 011-44-82759816

Taylor Brothers Inc.

Victorian & Chippendale Storm Doors
905 Graves Mill Rd.
Lynchburg, VA 24506

Send $2.00 for Catalog/Information

Mail Order Available

Phone 804-237-8100
Toll Free 800-288-6767
FAX 804-237-4227

Taylor Building Products

Steel Entry and Patio Doors
631 North First St.
West Branch, MI 48661

Phone 517-345-5110

Temple Products, Inc.

Paneled and Carved Wood Doors
PO Box 1008
Temple, TX 76503

Toll Free 800-634-3667

Doors

The Bilco Co.

Manufacturer - Basement Doors
PO Box 1203
New Haven, CT 06505

Phone 203-934-6363

FAX 203-933-8478

The London Door Company

Oak, Pine, Mahogany Doors

165 St. John's Hill
London SW11 1TQ
Great Britain

Phone 011-44-71/2237243

The Old Wagon Factory

*Victorian Wood Storm Doors, Benches,
Shutters, Planters*

PO Box 1427
Clarksville, VA 23927

Send $2.00 for Catalog/Information

Phone 804-374-5717

FAX 804-374-4646

The Smoot Lumber Co.

Doors, Windows, Millwork, Moulding

629520 Edsall Rd.
Alexandria, VA 22312

Mail Order Available

Phone 703-823-2100

FAX 703-823-8787

The Yorkshire Door Company Ltd.

*Victorian Panel Doors, Fitted Bedroom &
Kitchen Furniture*

Cottingley Bar
Bradford Road, Bingley, West Yorkshire
BD16 1PD
Great Britain

Phone 011-44-274/568532

FAX 011-44-274/551573

Thermal Profiles, Inc.

Sliding Glass Doors

300 Smith St.
Keasbey, NJ 08832

Phone 201-738-1665

Touchstone Woodworks

*Order Direct - Nationwide Shipping -
Mahogany Storm Doors & Gingerbread*

PO Box 112
Ravenna, OH 44266

Mail Order Available

Phone 216-297-1313

Urban Ore

Doors

1333 Sixth St.
Berkeley, CA 94710

Phone 510-559-4450

V-T Industries Inc.

*Wood Doors, Custom Countertops,
Decorative Laminate*

1000 Industrial Park
PO Box 490
Holstein, IA 51205-0490

Phone 712-368-4381

Toll Free 800-827-1615

FAX 712-368-4667

Vancouver Door Co. Inc.

Wood Doors

203 5th St. NW
Puyallup, WA 98371

Phone 206-845-9581

Velux America Inc.

Manufacturer - Doors & Windows

PO Box 5001
Greenwood, SC 29648

Phone 803-941-4700

Toll Free 800-888-3589

FAX 800-388-1329

Wallace-Crossly Corp.

Glass Sliding Doors

3501 N.W. 46th St.
Miami, FL 33142

Wayne-Dalton Corporation — Young Manufacturing Co.

Doors

Wayne-Dalton Corporation

Steel Garage Doors
PO Box 67
Mount Hope, OH 44660

Phone 216-674-7015

Weslock National

Manufacturer - Door Hardware & Locks
1334 So. Main St.
Los Angeles, CA 90015

Phone 310-327-2770
Toll Free 800-541-2430
FAX 310-324-4624

Western Oregon Doors, Inc.

Wood Doors and Frames
PO Box 1960
Winston, OR 97496

Phone 503-679-6791
FAX 503-679-5063

Wholesale Door Company

Wood Doors & Frames
PO Box 190
Snohomish, WA 98290

Phone 206-568-0515
FAX 206-568-0754

Windsor Door

Distributor List - Garage Doors, Rolling Shutters
PO Box 8915
Little Rock, AR 72219

Phone 501-562-1872

Wing Industries Inc.

Interior French Doors, Glass & Wood Bi-Fold Doors, Mirrored Closet Doors, Octagon & Oval Fashion Windows
PO Box 38347
Dallas, TX 75238

Phone 214-699-9900
Toll Free 800-341-9464

Woodgrain Millwork, Inc.

Wood Doors, Windows and Frames
300 N.W. 16th St.
PO Box 650
Fruitland, ID 83619

Phone 208-452-3801

Woodland Industries, Inc.

Wood Doors
401 Dabbs House Rd.
Richmond, VA 23223

Phone 804-222-2622
FAX 804-222-4861

Woodpecker Products Inc.

Doors, Shutters
1010 N. Cascade
Montrose, CO 81401

Mail Order Available

Phone 303-249-2616
Toll Free 800-524-7055
FAX 303-249-2392

Young Manufacturing Co.

Door Frames
521 South Main St.
Beaver Dam, KY 42320

Phone 502-274-3306
FAX 502-274-9522

4 - 18

The Complete Sourcebook

Flooring

A Candle In The Night

Oriental & Turkish Rugs
181 Main Street
Brattleboro, VT 05302

Phone 802-257-0471

AGA Corporation

Flooring
251 Industrial Park Rd.
PO Box 246
Amasa, MI 49903

Phone 906-822-7311

Aged Woods

Antique Heart Pine Flooring
2331 East Market St.
York, PA 17402

Catalog/Information Available Free

Phone 717-840-0330

Toll Free 800-233-9307

FAX 717-840-1468

Anderson Hardwood Flooring

Hardwood Flooring
Old Laurens Rd.
PO Box 1155
Clinton, SC 29325

Phone 803-833-6250

FAX 803-833-6664

Antique Pine Co.

Antique Pine Flooring
PO Box 447
Lacombe, LA 70445

Arizona Tile

Marble Flooring
1245 W. Elliott St. #111
Tempe, AZ 85284

Phone 602-940-9555

FAX 602-438-8516

Arkansas Oak Flooring Co.

Oak & Pine Flooring
Box 7227
Pine Bluff, AR 71611

Phone 501-534-3110

FAX 501-534-2132

Authentic Pine Floors Inc.

Wide Plank Pine Flooring
4042 Highway 42
PO Box 206
Locust Grove, GA 30248

Toll Free 800-283-6038

FAX 404-914-2925

B.A. Mullican Lumber & Manufacturing Co.

Manufacturer - Oak, Maple Flooring and Trim
Box 4069
Maryville, TN 37802

Phone 615-984-3789

FAX 615-977-8431

Bangkok International

Hardwood Flooring - Teak, Rosewood, Birch, Ash, Mahogany, Oak

4562 Worth St.
Philadelphia, PA 19124

Catalog/Information Available Free

Phone 215-537-5800

FAX 215-743-3179

Biwood Flooring

Manufacturer - Flooring

5744 Nanjack Circle
Memphis, TN 38115

Phone 901-795-3567

FAX 901-795-5348

Boen Hardwood Flooring

Wood Flooring

Rt. 2 - Hollie Drive
Bowels Industrial Park
Martinsville, VA 24112

Phone 703-638-3700

FAX 703-638-3066

Bonakemi USA, Inc.

Wood Floor Finish

14805 E. Moncrieff Pl.
Aurora, CO 80011

Phone 303-371-1411

FAX 303-371-6958

Broad-Axe Beam Co.

Nationwide Shipping - Wide Pine Flooring, Hand Hewn Beams

Rd. 2, PO Box 417
Brattleboro, VT 05301

Send $2.00 for Catalog/Information

Mail Order Available

Phone 802-257-0064

Bruce Hardwood Floors

Manufacturer - Hardwood Flooring & Cabinets

16803 Dallas Pkwy
PO Box 660100
Dallas, TX 75248

Phone 214-931-3100

Toll Free 800-722-4647

Carlisle Restoration Lumber

Nationwide Delivery - Eastern White Pine, Wide Board Flooring

HCR 32 Box 679
Stoddard, NH 03464-9712

Catalog/Information Available Free

Mail Order Available

Credit Cards Accepted

Phone 603-446-3937

FAX 603-446-3540

Carver Tripp

Wood Floor Finish

Parks Corp.
1083 County St., PO Box 5
Somerset, MA 02726

Phone 508-679-5938

FAX 508-674-8404

Castle Burlingame

Antique Wood Flooring

10 Stone St.
N. Plainfield, NJ 07060

Send $7.50 for Catalog/Information

Mail Order Available

Phone 908-757-3160

Centre Mills Antique Floors & Hewn Beams

(Wholesale Only) Antique Flooring & Hewn Beams - Chestnut, Oak, Heart Pine, White Pine, Hemlock

PO Box 16
Aspers, PA 17304

Mail Order Available

Phone 717-334-0249

FAX 717-334-6223

Flooring

Century Floors Inc. — Domco Floors

Century Floors Inc.

Imported Ceramic Tile
15 East 16th St.
New York, NY 10003

Send $10.00 for Catalog/Information

Phone 212-627-8300

Country Floors

Manufacturer - American Special Order Tiles - Imported Ceramic & Terracottas
15 East 16th St.
New York, NY 10003

Send $14.00 for Catalog/Information

Phone 212-627-8300
FAX 212-627-7742

Craftsman Lumber Co.

Manufacturer - Order Direct - Pine Flooring, Paneling, Railroad Siding
436 Main St.
PO Box 222
Groton, MA 01450

Catalog/Information Available Free

Mail Order Available

Credit Cards Accepted

Phone 508-448-5621

Cumberland Lumber & Manufacturing Co.

Wood Flooring, Moulding, Thresholds
202 Red Rd.
McMinnville, TN 37110

Phone 901-774-9672
FAX 901-774-9684

DeSoto Hardwood Flooring Company

Oak, Maple, Cherry, Walnut Strip Flooring
977 Sledge Ave.
Memphis, TN 38104

Phone 901-774-9672
FAX 901-774-9684

Deft, Inc.

Wood Floor Finish
17451 Von Karmen Ave.
Irvine, CA 92714

Phone 714-474-0400
FAX 714-474-7269

Diamond "W" Floor Covering

Wood Flooring
2901 S. Tanager St.
Los Angeles, CA 90040

Phone 213-685-7400
FAX 213-685-6323

Diamond K. Co., Inc.

Wide Plank Flooring, Barnwood Beams, Hand-hewn Beams, Quarrystone Fireplace
130 Buckland Rd.
South Windsor, CT 06074

Catalog/Information Available Free

Mail Order Available

Phone 203-644-8486

Dixon Lumber Company

Manufacturer - Oak, Maple Flooring
152 Boyer Rd., PO Box 907
Galax, VA 24333

Phone 703-236-9963
FAX 703-236-9490

Domco Floors

Vinyl Flooring
Domco Industries Ltd.
1001 Yamaska St. E.
Farnham PQ J2N 1J7
Canada

Phone 514-293-3173
Toll Free 800-237-7800
FAX 514-393-6644

Flooring

The Complete Sourcebook

5 - 3

Dura Seal

Manufacturer - Wood Floor Finish

Div. of Minwax Co.
102 Chestnut Ridge Plaza
Montvale, NJ 07645

Phone 201-391-0253
Toll Free 800-526-0495

E. T. Moore Company

Heart Pine Flooring, Furniture

3100 North Hopkins Rd.
Richmond, VA 23224

Catalog/Information Available Free

Phone 804-231-1823
FAX 804-231-0759

Erie Flooring & Wood Products

Hardwood & Parquet Flooring

PO Box 430
West Lorne
Ont, CAN N0L 1P0
Canada

Phone 519-768-1200

Felix Huard Inc.

Flooring & Lumber

121 St. Alphonse Rue
Luceville
Que, CAN G0K 1E0
Canada

Phone 418-739-4894
FAX 418-739-3457

Fired Earth Tiles PLC

*Worldwide Delivery - Natural Floor
Coverings, Ceramic Tile, Marble, Granite*

Twyford Mill, Oxford Road
Adderbury, Oxon
OX17 3HP
Great Britain

Mail Order Available

Phone 011-44-1295812088
FAX 011-44-1295810832

Flooring Distributors

Ceramic Tile

Div. of Lowy Enterprises
4101 Geraldine Ave.
St. Louis, MO 63115

Phone 314-383-2055
FAX 314-383-2005

Floors By Juell

Wood Floors

8137 North Austin Ave.
Morton Grove, IL 60053

Mail Order Available

Phone 708-965-6900
FAX 708-965-8808

Floortown

Flooring, Carpeting

PO Box 646
Marblehead, MA 01975-0646

Mail Order Available

Phone 617-599-6544

Galleher Hardwood Co.

Manufacturer - Hardwood Flooring

12906 Telegraph Rd.
Santa Fe Springs, CA 90670

Phone 213-944-8885
FAX 213-941-3929

Guyon

Flooring, Ceiling Beams

Rear 20, Del Run Rd.
Manheim, PA 17545

Send $2.00 for Catalog/Information

Mail Order Available

Phone 717-664-2485

Hardwood Flooring & Paneling Inc.

Hardwood Flooring & Paneling

13851 Station Rd.
PO Box 15
Burton, OH 44021

Phone 216-834-1710
FAX 216-834-0243

Flooring

Harmony Exchange

Flooring & Paneling

Rt. 2, Box 843
Boone, NC 28607

Mail Order Available

Credit Cards VISA/MC

Phone 704-264-2314
Toll Free 800-968-9663
FAX 704-264-4770

Harris-Tarkett, Inc.

*Manufacturer - Distributor List -
Hardwood Flooring in many different
styles and Finishes*

PO Box 300
2225 Eddie Williams Rd.
Johnson City, TN 37604-0300

Phone 615-928-3122
Toll Free 800-842-7816
FAX 615-928-9445

Hartco/Tibbals Flooring Company

*Manufacturer - Flooring - Parquet,
Herringbone, Basket Weave*

900 S. Gay Street, Suite 2102
Knoxville, TN 37902

Catalog/Information Available Free

Phone 615-544-0767
FAX 615-544-2071

Hayes Forest Products, Inc.

Hardwood Flooring

PO Box 196
Calico Rock, AR 72159

Phone 501-297-3701

Historic Floors of Oshkosh

Sample Wood Flooring

PO Box 572
Oshkosh, WI 54902

Catalog/Information Available Free

Send $25.00 for Catalog/Information

Phone 414-233-5066
FAX 414-233-7644

Hoboken Floors Inc.

Wood Flooring

70 Demarets Drive
Wayne, NJ 07470

Phone 201-694-2888
FAX 201-694-6885

Hunt County Hardwoods, Inc.

Plank Flooring

PO Box 987
Warrentown, VA 22186

Catalog/Information Available Free

Phone 703-347-4338

Imperial Black Marble Co.

Black Marble Flooring

PO Box 103
Thorn Hill, TN 37881

Phone 615-767-2888
FAX 615-531-2954

J. L. Powell & Company Inc.

Heart Pine Flooring

107 Powell Bldg.
600 S. Madison
Whiteville, NC 28472

Send $15.00 for Catalog/Information

Mail Order Available

Phone 919-642-8989
Toll Free 800-227-2007
FAX 919-642-3164

Kentucky Wood Floors

Manufacturer - Wood Flooring

PO Box 33276
Louisville, KY 40232

Send $2.00 for Catalog/Information

Phone 502-451-6024
Toll Free 800-235-5235
FAX 502-451-6027

L.D. Brinkman & Co. Inc.

Wood Flooring

PO Box 569450
Dallas, TX 75356-9450

Phone 214-579-3500

The Complete Sourcebook

5 - 5

Lamb Flooring & Trim Co.

Manufacturer - Flooring & Moulding
1332 Sunnybrooke Ct.
Pulaski, TN 38478
Mail Order Available

Phone 615-363-8150

FAX 615-363-1298

Launstein Hardwood

Manufacturer - Hardwood Flooring
384 S. Every Rd.
Mason, MI 48854
Mail Order Available

Phone 517-676-1133

FAX 517-676-6379

Lebanon Oak Flooring

Red Oak Flooring
PO Box 669
Lebanon, KY 40033

Phone 502-692-2128

FAX 502-692-2128

Leslie Brothers Lumber Company

Hardwood Flooring
PO Box 609
Cowen, WV 26206
Mail Order Available

Phone 304-226-3844

FAX 304-226-3726

Linden Lumber Company

Oak, Pine Flooring
Drawer 480369
Linden, AL 36748

Phone 205-295-8751

Toll Free 800-251-8751

FAX 205-295-8088

Linoleum City

Linoleum
5657 Santa Monica Blvd.
Hollywood, CA 90038
Mail Order Available

Phone 213-469-0063

FAX 213-465-5866

Livermore Wood Floors

Manufacturer - Order Direct - Wood Flooring - Cherry, Oak, Maple, Ash, Wide Pine, Walnut, Birch
PO Box 146
East Livermore, ME 04228
Mail Order Available

Phone 207-897-5211

Madison Flooring Company

Flooring & Moulding
Box 26A
Madison, VA 22727

Phone 703-948-4498

FAX 703-948-3339

Mannington Wood Floors

Manufacturer - Flooring
1327 Lincoln Drive
High Point, NC 27260-9945
Send $5.00 for Catalog/Information

Phone 919-884-5600

FAX 919-884-8171

McMinnville Manufacturing Co.

Oak Flooring
Box 151
McMinnville, TN 37110

Phone 615-473-2131

FAX 615-473-2342

Flooring

Memphis Hardwood Flooring Co. – Overseas Hardwoods Co. Inc.

Memphis Hardwood Flooring Co.

Manufacturer - Oak Flooring
1551 North Thomas St.
PO Box 38217
Memphis, TN 38107

Catalog/Information Available Free

Phone 901-526-7306
Toll Free 800-346-3010
FAX 901-525-0059

Midwestern Terrazzo corp.

Terrazzo Flooring
2601 N. Sherman Dr.
Indianapolis, IN 46218

Phone 317-547-5424
FAX 317-547-5425

Miller & Company, Inc.

Oak Flooring, Moulding
Box 779
Selma, AL 36701

Phone 205-874-8271
FAX 205-875-9109

Missouri Floor Co.

Oak Flooring
2438 Northline Industrial Blvd.
Maryland Heights, MO 63042

Phone 314-432-2260

Missouri Hardwood Flooring Co.

Oak Flooring
114 N. Gay Ave.
St. Louis, MO 63105

Phone 314-727-2267
FAX 314-727-2264

Monticello Flooring & Lumber Co.

Oak, Maple Flooring, Trim
Box 637
Monticello, KY 42633

Phone 606-348-5941
FAX 606-348-3636

Mountain Lumber Co.

*Antique Heart Pine Flooring, Moulding,
Mantels - Call for samples*
PO Box 289
Ruckersville, VA 22968-0289

Catalog/Information Available Free

Mail Order Available

Phone 804-985-3646
Toll Free 800-445-2671
FAX 804-985-4105

National Floor Products Co., Inc.

Manufacturer - Luxury Vinyl Flooring
PO Box 354
Florence, AL 35631

Phone 205-766-0234

National Hardwood Floors

Hardwood Floors
14595 Delano
Van Nuys, CA 91411

Toll Free 800-848-5556
FAX 818-988-4955

New England Hardwood Supply Co.

Hardwood Flooring, Moulding
100 Taylor St., PO Box 2254
Littleton, MA 01460

Mail Order Available

Phone 508-486-8683
FAX 508-486-9045

Nora Flooring

Synthetic Rubber Flooring
4201 Wilson Ave.
Madison, IN 47250

Phone 812-273-1852

Overseas Hardwoods Co. Inc.

Hardwood Flooring
PO Box 11501
Mobile, AL 36611

Phone 205-457-7616
FAX 205-457-7633

Flooring

The Complete Sourcebook

5 - 7

Partee Flooring Mill

Oak Flooring
Box 667
Magnolia, AR 71753

Phone 501-234-4082
FAX 501-234-8123

Peace Flooring Co. Inc.

Hardwood Parquet Flooring & Flooring Adhesive
520 W. Garland
PO Box 87
Magnolia, AR 71753

Phone 501-234-2310
FAX 501-234-5145

Pine Floors Inc.

Heart Pine Flooring
PO Box 206
Locust Grove, GA 30248

Toll Free 800-283-6038

Pine Plains Woodworking Inc.

Flooring, Moulding
RR 1, Box 74
Pine Plains, NY 12567

Mail Order Available

Phone 518-398-7665
FAX 518-398-7666

Plancher Beauceville Inc.

Hardwood Flooring
202 12E Ave. St.Louis, PO Box 116
Beauceville
Que., CAN G0M 1A0
Canada

Phone 418-774-3365

Plaza Hardwood Inc.

Manufacturer - Hardwood Flooring
5 Enebro Court
Santa Fe, NM 87505

Mail Order Available

Phone 505-466-7885
FAX 505-466-0456

Potlatch Corporation

Oak Flooring, Plank Paneling
Box 916
Stuttgart, AR 72160

Toll Free 800-777-5265
FAX 501-673-4360

Quality Woods Ltd.

Wood Flooring - Teak, Rosewood
63 Flanders Bartley Rd.
Flanders, NJ 07836

Phone 201-584-7554
FAX 201-584-3875

Razorback Hardwood, Inc.

Oak, Ash Flooring, Lumber, Trim
Rt. 4 Box 96-A
Monticello, AR 71655

Phone 501-367-2436
FAX 501-367-2968

River City Woodworks

Antique Pine Flooring, Lumber, Wood Beams, Moulding, Doors, Stair Parts
825 9th Street
New Orleans, LA 70115

Send $3.25 for Catalog/Information

Phone 504-899-7278

Robbins Hardwood Flooring

Manufacturer - Hardwood Flooring
4785 Eastern Avenue
Cincinnati, OH 45226

Phone 513-871-8510
FAX 513-871-8069

Robbins Inc.

Oak, Maple Flooring, Lumber, Trim
Box 999
Warren, AR 71671

Phone 501-226-6711
FAX 501-226-6427

Flooring

Searcy Flooring, Inc.

Oak, Maple Flooring
Box 906
Searcy, AR 72143

Phone 501-268-8694
FAX 501-279-2440

Shaw Marble Works

Marble Flooring
5012 S. 38 St.
St. Louis, MO 63116

Phone 314-481-5860
FAX 314-352-5801

Smith Flooring, Inc.

Oak Flooring
Box 99
Mountain View, MO 65548

Phone 417-934-2291
FAX 417-934-2295

Somerset Wood Products, Inc.

Oak Flooring
Box 1355
Somerset, KY 42502

Phone 606-561-4146
FAX 606-561-6337

Stanley Knight

Hardwood Flooring
226 Boucher St., PO Box 1150
Meaford
Ont., CAN N0H 1Y0
Canada

Phone 519-538-3300
FAX 519-538-5020

Stuart Flooring Corp.

Wood Flooring
Box 947
Stuart, VA 24171

Phone 703-694-4547
FAX 703-694-4953

Stuart Lerman Inc.

Wood Flooring
2495 Walden Ave.
Buffalo, NY 14225

Phone 716-681-3780
FAX 716-681-9371

Sykes Flooring Products

Hardwood Flooring
PO Box 999
Warren, AR 71671

Phone 501-226-6711
FAX 501-226-6427

Sylvan Brandt Inc.

Flooring, Doors, Hardware, Antique Glass
651 East Main Street
Lititz, PA 17543

Mail Order Available

Phone 717-626-4520
FAX 717-626-5867

Tarkett Inc.

Vinyl Flooring and Ceramic Tile
PO Box 264
800 Lanidex Plaza
Parsippany, NJ 07054

Catalog/Information Available Free

Phone 201-428-9000
FAX 201-428-8017

The Amtico Co., Ltd.

Vinyl Flooring
Kingfield Rd.
Coventry CV6 5PL
Great Britain

Phone 011-44-203/861400
FAX 011-44-203/861552

The Complete Sourcebook

The Burruss Company

Oak, Pine, Maple, Ash, Walnut, Cherry Flooring

Box 6
Brookneal, VA 24528

Phone 804-376-2666
Toll Free 800-334-2495
FAX 804-376-3698

The Floor Shop

Hardwood Flooring

Mirage Hardwood Flooring
154 Wicksteed Ave.
Toronto, Ont.
Canada

Phone 416-421-7651

The Joinery Company

Factory Direct - Antique Heart Pine Flooring, Millwork, Raised Paneled Doors, Beams, Mouldings, Windows, Cabinetry

PO Box 518
Tarboro, NC 27886

Send $5.00 for Catalog/Information

Mail Order Available

Phone 919-823-3306
Toll Free 800-227-3959
FAX 919-823-0818

The Natural Woodflooring Company

Beech, Mahogany, Maple, Oak, Pine, Teak Flooring

20 Smugglers Way
London SW18 1EQ
Great Britain

Phone 011-44-81/8719771

The Roane Co.

Wood Flooring

PO Box 3297
Cerritos, CA 90701-3297

Phone 310-404-3464
Toll Free 800-273-6499
FAX 310-404-8028

The Woods Company

Local & Nationwide Shipping - Antique Flooring, Beams, Moulding

2357 Boteler Rd.
Brownsville, MD 21715

Mail Order Available

Phone 301-432-8419
FAX 301-432-8439

Thompson Oak Flooring Co.

Oak Flooring

946 Mesena Rd. NW
Thomson, GA 30824

Phone 404-595-2577
FAX 404-595-1039

Toli International

Vinyl Flooring

55 Mall Drive
Commack, NY 11725

Phone 516-864-4343
Toll Free 800-446-5476
FAX 516-864-9710

Treework Services Ltd.

Hardwood Flooring - Oak, Elm, Ash

Cheston Combe
Blackwell, NR. Bristol
BS19 3JQ
Great Britain

Phone 011-44-275/464466

Valley Flooring Distributors

Flooring

320 W Ocean Ave.
Lompoc, CA 93436-6737

Phone 805-735-3371

Flooring

Vintage Lumber & Construction Co. – Zickgraf Hardwood Company

Vintage Lumber & Construction Co.

Antique Pine & Oak Flooring

1 Council Drive
PO Box 104
Woodsboro, MD 21798

Catalog/Information Available Free

Mail Order Available

Phone 301-845-2500
Toll Free 800-499-7859
FAX 301-845-6475

Vintage Pine Company

Manufacturer - Heart Pine Flooring, Architectural Components

PO Box 85
Prospect, VA 23960

Catalog/Information Available Free

Mail Order Available

Phone 804-574-6531

White River

Hardwood Flooring

1187 Happy Hollow Rd.
Fayetteville, AK 72701

Phone 501-442-6986

Woodhouse

Antique Pine & Oak Flooring - Samples Available

PO Box 7336
Rocky Mount, NC 27804

Phone 919-977-7336
FAX 919-641-4472

Woods American

Flooring, Paneling, Mouldings, Siding

123 South Main St.
Brownsville, MD 21725

Catalog/Information Available Free

Phone 301-432-8419

Yawkey-Bissell Hardwood Flooring Co.

Hardwood Flooring

PO Box 37
White Lake, WI 54491

Phone 715-882-2011
FAX 715-882-2904

Zickgraf Hardwood Company

Oak, Maple Flooring

Box 1149
Franklin, NC 28734

Toll Free 800-243-1277
FAX 704-524-5581

Flooring

The Complete Sourcebook

Furniture

A K Exteriors

*Wholesale Prices - Cast Aluminum
Furniture & Fixtures*
298 Leisure Lane
Clint, TX 79836
Send $4.00 for Catalog/Information

Phone 915-851-2594

A-1 Mfg. Co. Inc.

Furniture
3255 W. Osborn Rd.
Phoenix, AZ 85017

Phone 602-269-9731

A. Brandt Co., Inc.

Furniture
PO Box 391
Fort Worth, TX 76101

Phone 817-926-5141

A. Liss & Co.

Furniture, Shelving
35-03 Bradley Ave.
Long Island City, NY 11101
Send $3.00 for Catalog/Information
Credit Cards VISA/MC/AMEX

Phone 718-392-8484
Toll Free 800-221-0938

A.L.F. Uno Spa

Manufacturer - Italian Furniture
Via S. Pio X, 17
31010 Francenigo Di Gaiarine (TV)
Italy

Phone 011-39-434/769111
FAX 011-39-434/769245

AEL Furniture Group

Bedroom Furniture
Unit 4, Riverside Ind Est
Morson Rd, Enfield, Middx
EN3 4TH London
Great Britain

Phone 011-44-81-4432322

AMCOA Inc.

Beveled Glass Table Tops
6301 N.E. 4th Ave.
Miami, FL 33138

Phone 305-751-2202
Toll Free 800-327-7514
FAX 305-751-0672

ARM Industries Inc.

Patio and Lawn Furniture
PO Box 1900
Brandon
Man, CAN R7A 6N8
Canada

Phone 204-728-9594

Abacus Mfg. Ltd.

Furniture
369 Danforth Rd.
Scarborough
Ont., CAN M1L 3X8
Canada

Phone 416-694-3487

Accademia

Italian Furniture
Via Indipendenza, 4
33044 Manazno (UD)
Italy
> Phone 011-39-432/754439
> FAX 011-39-432/755066

Acerbis International Spa

Italian Furniture
Via Brusaporto, 31
24068 Seriate (Bergamo)
Italy
> Phone 011-39-35/294222
> FAX 011-39-362/971359

Acme Furniture Mfg. Inc.

Upholstered Furniture, Chairs, Ottomans, Sectionals, Rockers
450 Sheppard St.
PO Box 396, Winnipeg
Man, CAN R3C 2J2
Canada
> Phone 204-633-9840
> FAX 204-694-6521

Acmetrack Ltd.

Bedroom Furniture
Acme Ho, Garland Rd.
East Grinstead, W Sussex
RH19 1DR
Great Britain
> Phone 011-44-342-410955

Acrylic Innovations Inc.

Custom Acrylic Furniture, Table Bases, Architectural Accents
1304 Dragon St.
Dallas, TX 75207
> Phone 214-742-4435
> FAX 214-761-0702

Action Industries Inc.

Furniture - Reclining Chairs
Box 1627
Tupelo, MS 38802-1627
> Phone 601-566-7211
> Toll Free 800-447-4700

Adam A. Weschler & Sons

Antique Furniture & Artworks
905-9 East St. NW
Washington, DC 20004
Mail Order Available
> Phone 202-628-1281

Adams Wood Products, Inc.

Queen Ann Furniture Kits
974 Forest Dr.
Morristown, TN 37814
Catalog/Information Available Free
> Phone 615-587-2942
> FAX 615-586-2188

Adden Furniture Inc.

Furniture
26 Jackson St.
Lowell, MA 01852
> Phone 508-454-7848
> FAX 508-453-1449

Addington-Beamon Lumber

Building Supply
814 Chapman Way
Newport News, VA 23602-1302
> Phone 804-875-1850

Adirondack Designs

Order Direct - Wholesale - Redwood Furniture - Chairs, Benches, Swings, Planters
PO Box 656
350 Cypress St.
Fort Bragg, CA 95437
Mail Order Available
Credit Cards Accepted
> Phone 707-964-4940
> Toll Free 800-222-0343
> FAX 707-964-2701

Adirondacks Store & Gallery

Oak and Maple Outdoor Furniture
PO Drawer 991
Lake Placid, NY 12946
> Phone 518-523-2646

Advance Modular Concepts

Furniture
Woodcraft Designs
Danville, PA 17821
Toll Free 800-343-4766

Airon SRL

Italian Furniture
Via don Struzo 10
20050 Triuggio (MI)
Italy
Phone 011-39-362/930231
FAX 011-39-362/971359

Albert M. Lock & Son

Furniture
1609 Memorial Ave.
Williamsport, PA 17705
Phone 717-326-2461
FAX 717-322-5372

Alfresco Porch Swing Company

Redwood Outdoor Furniture - Porch Swing, Adirondack Chair
PO Box 1336
Durango, CA 81302

Catalog/Information Available Free
Phone 303-247-9739

Alivar SRL

Italian Furniture
Strada Statale 429, KM, 42.5
50021 Barberino Val D'Elsa (FI)
Italy
Phone 011-39-55/8078272
FAX 011-39-55/8078269

Allibert

Outdoor Furniture - Chairs, Lounges, Umbrellas, Tables
9800 West Kincey Avenue
Suite 110
Huntersville, NC 28078
Phone 704-948-0440
Toll Free 800-258-5619
FAX 704-948-0190

Allied Manufacturing Co. (London) Ltd.

Bedroom Furniture
Sarena Ho, Grove Pk
Colindale, London NW9 0EB
Great Britain
Phone 011-44-81-2058844

Allmilmo Ltd.

Livingroom, Diningroom Furniture
48 The Broadway
Thatcham, nr Newbury, Berks RG13 4HP
Gret Britain
Phone 011-44-635/868181

America's Finest Furniture

Name Brand Furniture
Box 7421
Futureland Station
High Point, NC 27264
Phone 919-884-0163

American Drew

Wood Furniture
PO Box 3
High Point, NC 27261

Send $2.00 for Catalog/Information
Phone 919-889-0333

American Furniture Co.

Colonial Furniture
1500 Industrial Rd.
Marion, VA 24354

Send $0.25 for Catalog/Information
Phone 703-783-8173

American Furniture Galleries

Victorian and French Reproduction Furniture
PO Box 60
Montgomery, AL 36101

Send $1.00 for Catalog/Information
Phone 205-262-0381
Toll Free 800-547-5240

The Complete Sourcebook

6 - 3

American Liberty Furniture

Victorian Furniture
American Enterprise Plaza
PO Box 5698
Greenville, SC 29606

Send $2.00 for Catalog/Information
Toll Free 800-388-4310

American Starbuck

Order Direct - Pine, Walnut, Oak Pencil Post Beds
PO Box 15376
Lenexa, KS 66215

Catalog/Information Available Free

Mail Order Available

Credit Cards VISA/MC
Phone 913-894-1567
Toll Free 800-245-7188

Amish Country Collection

Early American Bedroom Furniture
Rd. 5 Sunset Valley Rd.
New Castle, PA 16105

Send $5.00 for Catalog/Information
Phone 412-458-4811
Toll Free 800-232-6474
FAX 412-658-4496

Amish Furniture Collection

Amish Style Furniture
Beth Schneider
PO Box 111
New Wilmington, PA 16142

Mail Order Available
Phone 412-946-8799

Anderson Furniture

Finished & Unfinished Wood Furniture
Hwy. 11, Box 229
Atkins, VA 24311

Mail Order Available
Phone 703-783-3336

Angel House Designs

Reproduction Furniture
Box 1 Rt. 148
Brookfield, MA 01506

Send $2.00 for Catalog/Information

Mail Order Available
Phone 508-867-2517

Anger Mfg. Co., Inc.

Oak Bar Stools, Swings, Picture Frames
Hwy. 62 W.
PO Box 1075
Pocahontas, AR 72455

Send $1.00 for Catalog/Information
Phone 501-892-4419

Anglo Nordic Marketing (UK) Ltd.

Bedroom, Livingroom, Diningroom Furniture
59 New Kings Rd.
London SW6 4SE
Phone 011-44-71/7362031

Anthropologie

Home Furnishings - Furniture, Antiques, Crafts
201 W. Lancaster Ave.
Wayne, PA 19087
Phone 215-687-4141

Antiquaria

Victorian Style Furniture
60 Dartmouth St.
Springfield, MA 01109

Send $4.00 for Catalog/Information
Phone 413-781-6927

Antiquarian Traders

Antique Furniture, Architectural Parts
4851 S. Alameda St.
Los Angeles, CA 90058

Send $15.00 for Catalog/Information
Phone 213-687-4000
FAX 213-232-3767

Furniture

Antique Furniture Copies

Antique Reproduction Furniture
Corn Hill Rd.
Machiasport, ME 04655
Send $3.00 for Catalog/Information

Antique Furniture Workroom

Antique Furniture
225 E. 24th St.
New York, NY 10010
Mail Order Available
Phone 212-683-0551

Antiquity

Custom Furniture
715 Genesee St.
Delafield, WI 53018
Send $5.00 for Catalog/Information
Phone 414-464-4911
FAX 414-392-2282

Aram Designs Ltd.

*Bedroom, Livingroom, Diningroom
Furniture, Lighting*
3 Kean St., Covent Garden
London WC2B 4AT
Great Britain
Phone 011-44-71-2403933

Arc Linea Arredamenti SPA

Italian Furniture
Via Pasubio 50
36030 Caldogno (VI)
Italy
Phone 011-39-444/394111
FAX 011-39-444/394262

Archbold Furniture Co.

Manufacturer - Furniture
PO Box 159
Archbold, OH 43502
Phone 419-445-0850
FAX 419-445-1844

Arflex

Italian Furniture
Via Monterosa 27
20051 Limbiate (MI)
Italy
Phone 011-39-2/9961241
FAX 011-39-2/9963933

Arkitektura Inc.

Reproduction Furniture
379 West Broadway, 4th Fl.
New York, NY 10012
Send $45.00 for Catalog/Information
Phone 212-334-5570

Arrben Di O. Benvenuto

*Worldwide Shipping - Italian Furniture -
Leather Chairs, Armchairs, Tables*
Z.I.P.R. Via Forgaria 6
33078 S. Vito Al Tagliamento (PN)
Italy
Phone 011-39-43485091
FAX 011-39-43485092

Art In Iron

*Wrought Iron Furniture - Beds, Tables,
Shelving*
291 Jane Street
Toronto
Ont., M6S 3Z3
Canada
Phone 416-762-7777

Arte de Mexico

Wrought Iron Furniture, Lighting
5356 Riverton Ave.
North Hollywood, CA 91601
Send $15.00 for Catalog/Information
Phone 818-769-5090
FAX 818-769-9425

Furniture

The Complete Sourcebook

Artesanos Imports, Inc.

Furniture, Mexican Tile, Lighting and Mirrors
222 Galisteo St.
Santa Fe, NM 87501

Catalog/Information Available Free

Mail Order Available

Credit Cards Accepted

Phone 505-983-5563
FAX 505-982-0860

Artistic Upholstery Ltd.

Livingroom, Diningroom Furniture
Bridge St., Long Eaton
Nottingham NG10 4QQ
Great Britain

Phone 011-44-602/734481

Ashby & Horner Joinery Ltd.

Manufacturer - Interior Decoration & Restoration Bedroom, Livingroom, Diningroom Furniture
795 London Rd., West Thurrock
Grays, Essex RM16 1LH
Great Britain

Catalog/Information Available Free

Phone 011-44-708-866841
FAX 011-44-708-861872

Ashely Manor

Furniture
PO Box 477
1010 Surrett Dr.
High Point, NC 27261

Send $10.00 for Catalog/Information

Phone 919-882-8131
Toll Free 800-582-1401
FAX 919-889-5532

Ashley Furniture Industries

Furniture
350 Madison St.
Arcadia, WI 54612

Phone 608-323-3377

Atelier SRL

Italian Furniture
Via Vivai S.N.
22066 Mariano Comense (CO)
Italy

Phone 011-39-31/743323
FAX 011-39-31/746233

Athens Furniture

Manufacturer - Wood Furniture - Bedroom, Cabinets, Curios, Tables
10 Matlock Ave.
Athens, TN 37303

Phone 615-745-1833
FAX 615-745-1833

Atlanta Furniture Craftsmen

Solid Wood Furniture
1780 Hembree Rd.
Alpharetta, GA 30201

Phone 404-552-2558

Atlantic Furniture Sytems

Manufacturer - Furniture - Home/Office
PO Box 151777
Tampa, FL 33684

Phone 813-874-6989
Toll Free 800-877-3274
FAX 813-875-5868

Avanti Furniture Corp.

Furniture
497 Main St.
Farmingdale, NY 11735

Phone 516-293-8220
FAX 516-293-9335

B & B Italia Spa

Italian Furniture
B & B Italia USA Inc.
150 East 58th Street, A&D Building
New York, NY 10155

Phone 212-758-4046
Toll Free 800-872-1697
FAX 212-758-2530

Furniture

B & I Furniture

Furniture

611 N. Broadway
Milwaukee, WI 53202

Catalog/Information Available Free

Phone 414-272-6082

Toll Free 800-558-8662

Backwoods Furnishings

Rustic Furniture - Chairs, Benches, Beds

Box 161, Route 28
Indian Lake, NY 12842

Catalog/Information Available Free

Phone 518-251-3327

Baker Chair Co.

Furniture - Chairs, Sofas, Tables

PO Box 1286
Lenoir, NC 28645

Phone 704-758-5521

Baker Furniture

Furniture

1661 Monroe Ave. NW
Grand Bay, MI 49505

Send $7.50 for Catalog/Information

Mail Order Available

Phone 616-361-7321

Baleri Italia

Italian Furniture

Via S. Bernardino, 39
24040 Lallio (BG)
Italy

Phone 011-39-35692690

FAX 011-39-35691454

Bales Furniture Mfg.

Wall Beds, Chest Beds, Dressers, Book Cases

153 Utah Ave.
S. San Francisco, CA 94080

Catalog/Information Available Free

Phone 415-742-6210

Ball and Ball

Reproduction Furniture & Historic Lighting

463 W. Lincoln Hwy.
Exton, PA 19341

Send $5.00 for Catalog/Information

Mail Order Available

Credit Cards Accepted

Phone 610-363-7330

Toll Free 800-363-7330

FAX 610-363-7639

Banana River Open Air Furniture

Manufacturer - Outdoor Furniture

1380 W New Haven Ave.
West Melbourne, FL 32904-3902

Phone 407-984-0973

Barbary Coast Furniture Co.

Manufacturer - Furniture

1177 Campbell Ave.
San Jose, CA 95126

Phone 408-554-1444

Barclay Furniture Associates Inc.

Upholstered Livingroom Furniture

88 Chicopee St.
Chicopee, MA 01013

Phone 413-592-3262

Bargain John's Antiques

Antique Furniture

700 South Washington
PO Box 705
Lexington, NE 68850

Phone 308-324-4576

Barlow Tyrie

Outdoor Teakwood Furniture

1263 Glen Ave., Suite 230
Morrestown, NJ 08057

Phone 609-273-7878

Toll Free 800-451-7467

FAX 609-273-9199

The Complete Sourcebook

Barnes & Barnes

Brand Name Furniture - Discounted Prices - Chairs, Loveseats, Sofas, Ottomans

190 Commerce Ave.
Yadkin Park
Southern Pines, NC 28387

Catalog/Information Available Free

Credit Cards Accepted

Toll Free 800-334-8174
FAX 910-692-3381

Barnett Products Co.

Chairpads, Rocking Chair Cushions, Decorative Pillows, Wicker Furniture Cushions

PO Box 7803
Macon, GA 31209

Phone 912-781-7048

Bartley Collection

Reproduction Furniture Kits

29060 Airpark Drive
Easton, MD 21601

Catalog/Information Available Free

Credit Cards Accepted

Phone 301-820-7722
Toll Free 800-787-2800
FAX 301-820-7059

Bassett Furniture Industries Inc.

Furniture

PO Box 626
Bassett, VA 24055

Mail Order Available

Phone 703-629-6000

Bausman & Company, Inc.

Bench Made Furniture

1520 South Bon View
Ontario, CA 91761

Phone 714-947-0139
FAX 714-947-4508

Bazzani Alberto di F. Bazzani & C. SAS

Italian Furniture - Bazzani Alberto Di F. Bazzani & C. SAS

Via Pusterla, 37
20030 Bovisio (MI)
Italy

Phone 011-39-362/591001
FAX 011-39-362/591002

Beachley Furniture Co., Inc.

Furniture

Box 978
Hagerstown, MD 21740

Phone 301-733-1910
Toll Free 800-344-1887
FAX 301-733-5354

Bedlam Brass

Brass Beds

530 River Drive
Garfield, NJ 07026-3818

Send $1.00 for Catalog/Information

Phone 201-546-5000
FAX 201-478-7900

Bedquarters

Factory Direct - Beds, Sofabeds, Wall Beds, Wall Systems

PO Box 7791
FDR Station
New York, NY 10150-1914

Phone 212-371-6355
FAX 212-879-8304

Beds By Benzcian, Inc.

Beds

6509 Woodshed Circle
Charlotte, NC 28270

Phone 704-841-1122
Toll Free 800-582-9147
FAX 704-841-1194

Bedspreads By Thomas

Bedspreads, Decorative Fabric

5820 Washington Ave.
Houston, TX 77007

Phone 713-864-8086

Toll Free 800-345-8281

Bernhardt Furniture Co.

Manufacturer - Furniture

PO Box 740
1839 Morganto Blvd.
Lenoir, NC 28645

Phone 704-758-9811

Toll Free 800-345-9875

Best Furniture Distributors, Inc.

Order by Phone - Furniture

16 W. Main, PO Box 489
Thomasville, NC 27360

Toll Free 800-334-8000

Bevan Funnel Limited

Manufacturer - Distributor - Nationwide Shipping - English 17th & 18th Century Reproduction Furniture

PO Box 1109
High Point, NC 27261

Catalog/Information Available Free

Phone 910-889-4800

Toll Free 800-334-8349

FAX 910-889-7037

Bevan Funnell Ltd.

International Shipping - Bedroom, Livingroom, Diningroom Furniture

Beach Rd.
Newhaven, E Sussex BN9 0BZ
Great Britain

Phone 011-44-273/513762

Bevis Custom Furniture

Custom Furniture

PO Box 2280
Florence, AL 35630

Phone 205-766-6497

Toll Free 800-766-7886

Bielecky Brothers, Inc.

Rattan Furniture

306 East 61st Street
New York, NY 10021

Phone 212-753-2355

Big Country

Reproduction Wood Furniture

242 Long John Silver Dr.
Wilmington, NC 28405

Catalog/Information Available Free

Toll Free 800-344-4072

Big Table Furniture

Manufacturer - Scandanavian Pine - Post, Bunk, Platform Beds

56 Great Western Road
London W9 3NT
Great Britain

Credit Cards Accepted

Phone 011-44-71-2215058

Billing Croft of Salem

Custom Shaker Style Furniture

302 Essex St.
Salem, MA 01970

Phone 508-744-7140

FAX 508-744-5511

Blackwelder's Industries, Inc.

Furniture - Oak, Cherry, Pine

U.S. Highway 21 N.
Statesville, NC 28677

Send $7.50 for Catalog/Information

Credit Cards Accepted

Phone 704-872-8921

Toll Free 800-438-0201

FAX 704-872-4491

Blake Industries

Manufacturer - Distributor - Indoor and Outdoor Teak Furniture
PO Box 155
Abington, MA 02351
Catalog/Information Available Free

Phone 617-337-8772
FAX 617-335-3004

Blanton & Moore Co.

Furniture, Millwork
Hwy. 21 S.
PO Box 70
Barium Springs, NC 28010

Phone 704-528-4506
FAX 704-528-6519

Blue Canyon Woodworks

Manufacturer - Order Direct - Southwestern Style Furniture, Antique Reproductions, Doors, Gates
1310 Siler Rd., #1
Santa Fe, NM 87501
Mail Order Available

Phone 505-471-0136

Bograd's

Custom Furniture - Kindel, Century, Karges, Stickley, Ahenkel
288 Main St.
Paterson, NJ 07505

Phone 201-278-4242

Bombay Company

Antique Reproduction Furniture
PO Box 161009
Fort Worth, TX 76161-1009
Catalog/Information Available Free

Toll Free 800-829-7789
FAX 817-347-8291

Bonaldo SPA

Italian Furniture
Via Straelle, 3
35010 Villanova Di Camposampie (PD)
Italy

Phone 011-39-49/5563159
FAX 011-39-49/9220359

Bonaventure Furniture Ind.

Furniture
894 Bloomfield Ave.
Montreal
PQ CAN H2V 3S6
Canada

Phone 514-270-7311
FAX 514-270-7978

Boston & Winthrop

Handpainted Children's Furniture
2 East 93rd St.
New York, NY 10128
Catalog/Information Available Free
Mail Order Available

Phone 212-410-6388

Boudoir Furniture Mfg. Corp.

Bedroom Furniture
1224 W. 130th St.
Gardena, CA 90247

Phone 213-769-1985
FAX 213-769-0618

Boyd R. Smith

Chairs
3301 DeBord Rd.
Chillicothe, OH 45601
Send $1.00 for Catalog/Information
Mail Order Available

Phone 614-663-2750

Furniture

Boyles Furniture

Up To %50 Discount - Furniture - 18th Century, Contemporary, Traditional, Country English - Bedroom, Livingroom, Diningroom

616 Greensboro Rd.
High Point, NC 27260

Catalog/Information Available Free

Mail Order Available

Credit Cards Check/Money Order

    Phone 919-884-8088

    FAX 919-884-1534

Bracewell Furniture Co.

Furniture

PO Box 867
Conover, NC 28613

    Phone 704-464-1441

Bradington Young

Manufacturer - Upholstered Furniture, Recliners

4040 10th Ave. Dr. SW
Hickory, NC 28602-9080

    Phone 704-328-5702

    FAX 704-328-1104

Brady Furniture Co.

Furniture

PO Box 129
Rural Hall, NC 27045

    Phone 919-969-6816

    FAX 919-969-9365

Braman Furniture Mfg.

Manufacturer - Furniture

2930 9th Ave. N
Lethbridge
Alta CAN T1H 5E4
Canada

    Phone 403-329-3299

Brass Bed Factory

Contemporary and Traditional Brass Beds

442 Harding Way West
Galion, OH 44833

Send $1.00 for Catalog/Information

    Phone 419-468-3861

Brass Bed Shoppe

Solid Brass and White Iron Beds

12421 Cedar Road
Cleveland, OH 44106

Catalog/Information Available Free

    Phone 216-371-0400

    FAX 216-292-0026

Brass Beds Direct

Order Direct Wholesale - Solid Brass Beds

4866 W. Jefferson Blvd.
Los Angeles, CA 90016

Catalog/Information Available Free

    Phone 213-737-6865

    Toll Free 800-727-6865

Brayton International Inc.

Furniture

PO Box 7288
High Point, NC 27261

    Phone 919-434-4151

Brentwood Manor Furnishings

Nationwide Shipping - Name Brand Furniture, Draperies, Upholstery Fabric

317 Virginia Ave.
PO Box 332
Clarksville, VA 23927

Catalog/Information Available Free

Credit Cards Accepted

    Phone 804-374-4297

    Toll Free 800-225-6105

    FAX 804-374-9420

Furniture

The Complete Sourcebook

Bridgewater

Furniture
Div. of Ethan Allen
PO Box 66
Bridgewater, VA 22812

Phone 703-828-2546

Bristol House

Furniture
2100 E. 38th St.
Box 58812
Los Angeles, CA 90058

Phone 213-232-4161
FAX 213-233-8020

British Antique Replicas

Manufacturer - Wholesale & Retail Prices - Nationwide Shipping - Reproduction Furniture
School Close, Queen Elizabeth Ave.
Burgess Hill, West Sussex RH15 9RX
Great Britain

Phone 011-44-245577
FAX 011-44-232014

British-American Marketing Services Ltd.

Teak Garden Furniture
118 Pickering Way
Lionville, PA 19353

Toll Free 800-344-0259

Brooks Furniture Mfg. Inc.

Manufacturer - Wood Furniture
U.S. Hwy. 131, Rt.2
Tazewell, TN 37879

Phone 615-626-5261

Bros's SRL

Italian Furniture
Via Nazionale, 61
33048 S. Giovanni Al Natisone (UD)
Italy

Phone 011-39-432/757651
FAX 011-39-432/757562

Brown Jordon Furniture

Outdoor Furniture
9860 Gidley St.
PO Box 5688
El Monte, CA 91734

Send $4.00 for Catalog/Information

Mail Order Available

Phone 818-443-8971
FAX 818-575-0126

Broyhill Furniture Ind. Inc.

Furniture
Broyhill Park
Lenoir, NC 28645

Phone 704-758-3111
Toll Free 800-272-2769

Brunati SRL

Italian Furniture
Via Oberdan, 47
20030 Lentate S/Seveso (MI)
Italy

Phone 011-39-362/557827
FAX 011-39-362/557930

Budoff Outdoor Furniture

Outdoor Furniture
PO Box 530
Monticello, NY 12701

Toll Free 800-548-0204

Builtright Chair Co. Inc.

Chairs
PO Drawer 1609, 901 Corner St.
Statesville, NC 28677

Phone 704-873-6541
FAX 704-873-7511

Bulluck Furniture Co.

Manufacturer - Lighting - Lamps
PO Box 671
Rocky Mount, NC 27802

Phone 919-446-3266

Furniture

Burcham Furniture Manufacturing, Inc.

Manufacturer - Pine Livingroom Furniture, Oak Glider Rockers

Rt. 14, Box 574
Florence, AL 35630

Phone 205-766-5051
Toll Free 800-345-3850

Butcher Block & More Furniture

Oak Furniture

1600 S. Clinton St.
Chicago, IL 60616

Phone 312-421-1138

Butler Specialty Co.

Occasional & Accent Furniture

8200 S. Chicago Ave.
Chicago, IL 60617

Phone 312-221-1200
FAX 312-221-5892

C. H. Southwell

Antique Furniture Shaker Style, Reproductions

PO Box 484
Suttons Bay, MI 49682

Phone 616-271-3416

C. Neri, Antiques

Antique Furniture & Lighting

313 South St.
Philadelphia, PA 19147

Send $5.00 for Catalog/Information

Phone 215-923-6669

CM Comini Modonutti SRL

Italian Furniture

Via Planez 42
33043 Cividale Del Friuli (UD)
Italy

Phone 011-39-432/731993
FAX 011-39-432/731981

Cabin Creek Furniture

Pine Bedroom Furniture, Shaker Furniture

PO Box 427
Wake Forest, NC 27587

Phone 919-556-1023

Caldwell Chair Company

Furniture Diningrooms - Oak Reproductions

PO Box 679
Haleyville, AL 35565

Phone 205-486-9424
Toll Free 800-526-6065
FAX 205-486-8243

California Marble Co.

Marble Furniture

616 S. Marengo Ave.
Alhambra, CA 91803

Phone 818-282-9156

Calligaris SPA

Italian Furniture

Viale Trieste, 12
33044 Manzano (UD)
Italy

Phone 011-39-432/750767
FAX 011-39-432/750104

Camel International SRL

Italian Furniture

Via Benedetti, 34
31010 Francenigo (Tv)
Italy

Phone 011-39-434/767878
FAX 011-39-434/767976

Cameo Mica Furniture Manufacturer

Manufacturer - Furniture

212 Maple Ave.
Rockville Centre, NY 11570-4315

Phone 516-764-8403

Furniture

The Complete Sourcebook

Candlertown Chairworks

Handmade - Chairs, Barstools, Benches
PO Box 1630
Candler, NC 28715

Send $2.00 for Catalog/Information

Credit Cards VISA/MC

Phone 704-667-4844

Cane & Basket Supply Company

*Nationwide Shipping - Caning Supplies
(Do-it-Yourself Repair Kits)*

1283 South Cochran Ave.
Los Angeles, CA 90019

Mail Order Available

Credit Cards Accepted

Phone 213-939-9644
FAX 213-939-7237

Cappellini International Interiors SPA

Italian Furniture

Via Marconi, 35
31010 Francenigo (TV)
Italy

Phone 011-39-31/761717
FAX 011-39-31/763322

Carl Forslund

Furniture

3676 Patterson Ave. SE
Grand Rapids, MI 49512-4023

Send $2.00 for Catalog/Information

Phone 616-459-8101

Carleton Furniture Group Ltd.

*Bedroom, Livingroom, Diningroom
Furniture*

Monkhill, Pontefract
W Yorkshire WF8 2NS
Great Britain

Phone 011-44-977/700770

Carlton Mfg. Inc.

Upholstered Furniture

55786 Bullard Road
Elkhart, IN 46516

Phone 219-295-5051
FAX 219-293-8513

Carolina Furniture Works, Inc.

Furniture

PO Box 1120
Brooklyn St.
Sumter, SC 29150

Phone 803-775-6381

Carolina Interiors

Name Brand Furniture

115 Oak Ave.
Kannapolis, NC 28081

Mail Order Available

Phone 704-933-1888
Toll Free 800-438-6111
FAX 704-938-2990

Carolina Strand Co., Inc.

Upholstered Furniture

PO Box 1829
Conway, SC 29526

Phone 803-347-3170

Carrier Furniture Inc.

Manufacturer - Wood Furniture

825 Boul
Industriel, Cranby
Que, CAN J2J IA5
Canada

Phone 514-378-4617
FAX 514-378-1928

Carson's Furniture

Contemporary Style Furniture

PO Box 150
High Point, NC 27261-0150

Send $5.00 for Catalog/Information

Phone 919-887-3544

Casa Stradivari

Furniture
221 Mckibbin St.
Brooklyn, NY 11206
Send $3.00 for Catalog/Information
Phone 718-386-0048

Cassina SPA

Italian Furniture - USA 212-245-2121
Via Busnelli, 1
20036 Meda (MI)
Italy
Phone 011-39-362/3721
FAX 011-39-362/342246

Cassina USA Inc.

Manufacturer - Italian Furniture
200 Mckay Road
Huntington Station, NY 11746
Phone 516-423-4560

Castle Mount

Diningroom, Livingroom Furniture
Hudson St.
Deddington, Oxon OX5 45W
Great Britain
Phone 011-44-869/38506

Catherine Ann Furnishings

Wicker Indoor/Outdoor Furniture
615 Loudonville Rd.
Latham, NY 12110
Catalog/Information Available Free
Phone 518-785-4175

Cattelan Italia SPA

Italian Furniture
Via Pilastri 15-ZI, Ovest
36010 Carre (VI)
Italy
Phone 011-39-445/314076
FAX 011-39-445/314289

Cedar Design Ltd.

Lawn and Patio Furniture
5206 20th Ave. NW
Calgary
Alta, CAN T3B 0V8
Canada
Phone 403-288-5945

Cedar Rock Home Furnishings

Name Brand Furniture
PO Box 515
Hudson, NC 28638
Phone 704-396-2361

Century Furniture

Manufacturer - Furniture
401 11th St. NW
Hickory, NC 28601
Phone 704-328-1851
Toll Free 800-852-5552

Chaircraft Inc.

Chairs
Rte. 13, 127 North
Hickory, NC 28601
Phone 704-495-8291
FAX 704-495-8661

Channel Hall

Furniture
1468 S. Military Hwy.
Chesapeake, VA 23320
Send $5.00 for Catalog/Information
Mail Order Available

Chapin Townsend Furniture

18th Century Furniture
PO Box 628
West Kingdom, RI 02892
Send $2.00 for Catalog/Information
Phone 401-783-6614

The Complete Sourcebook

Charles P. Rogers

Brass Beds
899 First Ave.
New York, NY 10022
Send $1.00 for Catalog/Information
Phone 212-935-6900
Toll Free 800-272-7726
FAX 212-935-6900

Charles Webb Furniture

Wood Furniture
51 McGraff Hwy.
Somerville, MA 02143
Send $2.00 for Catalog/Information
Mail Order Available
Phone 617-776-7100

Charleston Iron Works

White Iron Beds
1720 Sam Rittenberg Blvd.
Charleston, SC 29407
Catalog/Information Available Free
Mail Order Available
Phone 803-763-1965
Toll Free 800-999-4233

Charmaster

*Manufacturer - Order Factory Direct -
Furnace - Wood Heat & Gas*
2307 O Highway 2 West
Grand Rapids, MN 55744
Mail Order Available
Phone 218-326-6788
Toll Free 800-542-6360
FAX 218-326-2636

Chatsworth Interiors

Order by Phone - Name Brand Furniture
PO Box 9592
Hickory, NC 28603
Toll Free 800-951-3621

Cherry & Deen Furniture

Reproduction Furniture
1214 Goshen Mill Rd.
Peach Bottom, PA 17563
Send $2.00 for Catalog/Information
Phone 717-548-3254

Cherry Hill Furniture,Carpet & Interiors

*Order Direct - Nationwide Shipping -
Furniture, Rugs, Carpet, Floorcovering*
PO Box 7405
Furnitureland Station
High Point, NC 27264
Catalog/Information Available Free
Mail Order Available
Phone 910-882-0933
Toll Free 800-328-0933
FAX 910-882-0900

Cidue

Italian Furniture
Via S. Lorenzo, 32
36010 Carre' (VI)
Italy
Phone 011-39-445/381133
FAX 011-39-445/679002

Ciro Coppa

*Adirondack Chairs, End Tables,
Loveseats, Coffee Tables, Screen Doors*
1231 Paraiso Ave.
San Pedro, CA 90731
Catalog/Information Available Free
Phone 213-548-5332

Clapper's

Garden Furniture
1121 Washington St.
West Newton, MA 02165
Phone 617-244-7909

Furniture

Clark Casual Furniture Inc.

Manufacturer - Rattan Furniture
214 Industrial Road
Greensburg, KY 42743

Phone 502-932-4273
FAX 502-932-4275

Classic Choice

*Order Factory Direct - Furniture - Sofas,
Sofa Beds, Recliner Chairs, Wing Chairs,
Chairs - Many Styles and Fabrics*
Unit 1 Brynmenyn Industrial Estate
Bridgend, Mid Glamorgan
CF32 9TD
Great Britain

Catalog/Information Available Free

Credit Cards Accepted

Phone 011-44-656/725111
FAX 011-44-656/725404

Classic Gallery Inc.

Furniture
211 Fraley Rd.
PO Box 1030
High Point, NC 27263

Phone 919-886-4191
Toll Free 800-334-7397
FAX 919-841-7122

Classic Leather

Leather Furniture
Box 2404
Hickory, NC 28603

Phone 704-328-2046
FAX 704-324-6212

Clayton Marcus Co., Inc.

Furniture
Hwy. 127 N.
Hickory, NC 28601

Phone 704-495-8211

Clear Lake Furniture

Furniture
250 Whipple Road
Tewksbury, MA 01876

Send $5.00 for Catalog/Information

Toll Free 800-758-8767

Cochrane Furniture Co.

*Manufacturer - Bedroom & Diningroom
Furniture*
PO Box 220
Lincolnton, NC 28092

Phone 704-732-1151

Coffey Discount Furniture

*Discounted Prices - Nationwide Delivery -
Major Brand Furniture*
PO Box 141
Granite Falls, NC 28630

Catalog/Information Available Free

Credit Cards Bank Check/Money Order

Phone 704-396-2900
FAX 704-396-3050

Cohasset Colonials

Colonial Style Beds & Chairs
10 Churchill Rd.
Hingham, MA 02043-1589

Send $3.00 for Catalog/Information

Mail Order Available

Credit Cards Accepted

Phone 617-740-4224
Toll Free 800-288-2389
FAX 617-740-4554

Collection Reproductions

*Reproduction European Furniture -
Wood, Iron*
PO Box 6436
301 44th St.
Corpus Christi, TX 78405

Phone 512-887-0082
FAX 512-887-6750

Furniture

The Complete Sourcebook

6 - 17

Colombo Mobili SNC

Italian Furniture
Via Verdi, 23
20030 Meda (MI)
Italy
Phone 011-39-362/340572
FAX 011-39-362/340580

Colonial Designs Furniture

18th Century Reproduction Furniture
PO Box 1429
Havertown, PA 19083
Send $2.00 for Catalog/Information
Phone 215-446-0835

Colonial Furniture Shops, Inc.

Colonial Furniture
Box 12007
Winston-Salem, NC 27117-2007
Send $1.00 for Catalog/Information
Phone 919-788-2121
Toll Free 800-334-5250

Colonial Williamsburg

Reproduction Furniture
PO Box 3532
Williamsburg, VA 23187
Send $18.90 for Catalog/Information
Phone 804-220-7463
Toll Free 800-446-9240

Color-Tex Distributors

Factory Direct - Name Brand Furniture
1102 Doris Avenue
High Point, NC 27260
Toll Free 800-442-9049

Comoexport-Divisione Di Cantu

Worldwide Shipping - Branch Offices - America, Asia, Austrailia, South America, Central America - Major Brand Italian Furniture - Sofas, Tables, Chairs, Beds
Via Cavour, 27
22063 Cantu' (CO)
Italy
Phone 011-39-31710290
FAX 011-39-31711859

Concepts International

Furniture
10 Andrews Rd.
Hicksville, NY 11801
Phone 516-822-0090
Toll Free 800-223-7587
FAX 516-933-6930

Concepts in Comfort

Furniture
9 Circus Time Rd.
South Portland, ME 04106
Mail Order Available
Phone 207-775-4312

Conexport

Italian Furniture
Via Della Scuola 13
06087 Ponte San Giovanni (PG)
Italy
Phone 011-39-75/5990798
FAX 011-39-75/397067

Continental Chair Co.

Chairs
PO Box 2809
Hickory, NC 28603
Phone 704-322-4225

Continental Custom Made Furniture

Custom Furniture
171 E. Hunting Park Ave.
Philadelphia, PA 19124
Phone 215-457-1900

Coppa Woodworking

Order Direct - Adirondack Chairs, Loveseats, Tables, Screen Doors
1231 Paraiso Ave.
San Pedro, CA 90731
Mail Order Available
Credit Cards Accepted/Check/Money Order
Phone 310-548-4142
FAX 310-548-6740

Furniture

Cornucopia, Inc.

Furniture - Early American, Windsor Chairs, Rockers, Tables, Braided Rugs

PO Box 1
Harvard, MA 01451-0001

Send $2.00 for Catalog/Information

Credit Cards Accepted

Phone 508-772-0023

FAX 508-772-9857

Corsican

Manufacturer - Metal Furniture

2417 East 24th Street
Los Angeles, CA 90058

Send $50.00 for Catalog/Information

Mail Order Available

Phone 213-587-3101

FAX 213-589-2769

Country Bed Shop

Nationwide Shipping - 17th & 18th Century Furniture - Pencil Post Beds, Tables, Chairs, Chests

329 Richardson Rd., RR 1
Box 65
Ashby, MA 01431

Send $4.00 for Catalog/Information

Mail Order Available

Phone 508-386-7550

FAX 508-386-7263

Country Casual

Trade & Retail Prices - Garden Teakwood Furniture, Mahogany Furniture

17317 Germantown Rd.
Germantown, MD 20874 -2999

Send $5.00 for Catalog/Information

Mail Order Available

Credit Cards VISA/MC

Phone 301-540-0040

Toll Free 800-284-8325

FAX 301-540-7364

Country Crossroads Furniture

Country Style Furniture

Rt.1, Box 201
Edgemoor, SC 29712

Send $2.00 for Catalog/Information

Credit Cards Accepted

Phone 803-328-8076

Toll Free 800-476-7845

Country Furniture Shop

18th Century Reproduction Furniture

Box 125, Rt. 20E
Madison, NY 13402

Send $3.00 for Catalog/Information

Phone 315-893-7404

Country Pine Furniture

Handcrafted Early American Furniture

Rte. 11 Wilmont-Andover Town Line
PO Box 153
Wilmont Flat, NH 03287-0153

Phone 603-735-5778

Country Store

Willow Furniture

PO Box 17696
Whitefish Bay, WI 53217

Send $2.00 for Catalog/Information

Mail Order Available

Phone 414-263-1919

Country Workshop

Hardwood Finished and Unfinished Furniture

95 Rome St.
Newark, NJ 07105

Send $1.00 for Catalog/Information

Mail Order Available

Credit Cards Accepted

Phone 201-589-3407

Toll Free 800-526-8001

Furniture

The Complete Sourcebook

6 - 19

Craft House

Reproduction Furniture & Home Furnishings
1 South England St.
Williamsburg, VA 23185

Catalog/Information Available Free

Credit Cards VISA/MC

Phone 804-229-1000

Crate & Barrel Furniture

Furniture - Seaside Collection
646 N. Michigan Ave.
Chicago, IL 60611

Phone 312-787-5900

Crawford Furniture Mfg. Corp.

Furniture
Allen Extension
Jamestown, NY 14701

Phone 716-661-9100
FAX 716-483-2634

Creative Designs

Custom Cabinetry
387 Manhattan Ave.
Greenpoint Brooklyn, NY 11211

Phone 718-389-1120
FAX 718-389-1158

Creative Furniture Systems

Furniture
4301 S. Upton Ave.
Minneapolis, MN 55410

Mail Order Available

Phone 612-929-3250

Cricket on the Hearth, Inc.

Furniture - English Reproductions
PO Box 14373
Savannah, GA 31416

Send $5.00 for Catalog/Information

Phone 912-354-0529
FAX 912-354-0554

Cumberland Furniture

Furniture
30-20 Thompson Ave.
Long Island City, NY 11101

Phone 718-937-6300
FAX 718-784-3860

Curran Upholstered Furniture

Upholstered Furniture
1410 Danmar Ave.
High Point, NC 27260

Phone 919-889-2818
Toll Free 800-334-8192
FAX 919-885-7457

Custom Furniture Corp.

Custom Furniture
721 South Hamilton St.
High Point, NC 27260

Phone 919-885-0912
FAX 919-885-5954

Customcraft

Furniture
1110 Arroyo Ave.
San Fernando, CA 91340

Phone 818-365-6811
Toll Free 800-624-6792

Cymann Designs

Contemporary Furniture
305 East 63rd St. 6th Fl
New York, NY 10021

Send $40.00 for Catalog/Information

Phone 212-758-6830
FAX 212-758-6735

Cypress Street Center

Outdoor Furniture
350 Cypress St.
Fort Bragg, CA 95437

Catalog/Information Available Free

Mail Order Available

Phone 707-964-4940
Toll Free 800-222-0343

D & L Mfg., Co.

Diningroom Furniture, Stools
2200 Aisquith St.
Baltimore, MD 21218

Phone 301-889-4477

DHM Cabinetmakers Inc.

Furniture, Millwork
RT 4 Box 173
Floyd, VA 24091

Send $4.00 for Catalog/Information

Phone 703-745-3825
Toll Free 800-346-2210
FAX 703-745-3875

DHU Designs, Inc.

Furniture

475 Garyray Dr.
Weston, Ontario
CAN M9L 1P9
Canada

Phone 416-746-4488

DMI Furniture, Inc.

Furniture

101 Bullitt Lane, Suite 205
Louisville, KY 40222

Phone 502-426-4351
FAX 502-429-6285

Dan Wilson & Company

Outdoor Furniture

PO Box 566
Fuquay-Varina, NC 27526

Send $2.00 for Catalog/Information

Mail Order Available

Phone 919-552-4945

Dana Robes Wood Craftsmen

Nationwide Shipping - Reproduction Shaker Furniture- Hardwoods - Cherry, Maple, Ash, Butternut

PO Box 707, Lower Shaker Village
Enfield, NH 03748

Send $3.00 for Catalog/Information

Mail Order Available

Phone 603-632-5385
Toll Free 800-722-5036
FAX 603-632-5377

Dancan Mfg. Ltd.

Furniture

224-52175 Range Rd.
Sherwood Park
Alta, CAN T8C 1B5
Canada

Phone 403-922-3287

Dapha Limited

Furniture

109 Lane Avenue
High Point, NC 27260

Phone 919-889-3312
Toll Free 800-284-4063
FAX 919-886-5729

David Edward Ltd.

Manufacturer - Furniture

1407 Parker Rd.
Baltimore, MD 21227

Phone 301-242-2222
FAX 301-242-0111

David W. Lamb Cabinetmaker

Reproduction Queen Anne, Shaker, Chippendale Furniture

Rt.2, Box 745
Canterbury, NH 03224

Phone 603-783-9912

Davis Cabinet Company

Custom Solid Cherry Wood Victorian Bedroom Furniture

PO Box 60444
505 Crutcher St.
Nashville, TN 37206

Send $3.00 for Catalog/Information

Mail Order Available

Phone 615-244-7100
FAX 615-244-7103

Davis Furniture Industries, Inc.

Furniture

2401 S. College Dr.
High Point, NC 27261

Phone 919-889-2009
FAX 919-889-0031

Deacon & Sandys

Country English Furniture, Oak Paneling, Windows and Doors

Hillrest Farm Oast
Cranbrook, Kent TN17 3QD
Great Britain

Phone 011-44-580/713775

Dean & Brook Ltd.

Bedroom, Livingroom, Diningroom Furniture

Grange Rd.
Batley, W Yorkshire WF17 6LN
Great Britain

Phone 011-44-923/477175

Decker Antique Reproductions

Reproduction Appalachian Furniture

PO Box 5688, Rt. 26 Dry Gap Pike
Knoxville, KY 37918

Send $3.00 for Catalog/Information

Phone 615-689-2371

Decor-Rest Furniture Ltd.

Manufacturer - Furniture - Livingroom

17 Milvan Dr.
Weston
Ont, CAN M9L 1Y8
Canada

Phone 416-745-6800
FAX 416-745-3655

Decorative Crafts Inc.

Furniture & Accessories - To the Trade

50 Chestnut St.
Greenwich, CT 06830

Phone 203-531-1500
Toll Free 800-431-4455
FAX 203-531-1590

Deep River Trading Company

Major Brand Furniture - Contemporary, Country, French, Reproduction 18th Century, Victorian

2436 Willard Rd.
High Point, NC 27260

Mail Order Available

Phone 910-885-2436

Del Tongo (UK) Ltd.

Bedroom, Livingroom, Diningroom Furniture

73 Clerkenwell Rd.
London EC1R 5BU
Great Britain

Phone 011-44-71/8317595

Delta Furniture Inc.

Furniture

9225 Pascal-Gagnon St.
Leonard
Que, CAN H1P 1Z4
Canada

Phone 514-329-1889
FAX 514-329-3522

Furniture

Deltacrafts Mfg. Ltd. – Directional of North Carolina Inc.

Deltacrafts Mfg. Ltd.

Buffets, Cabinets, Wall Units

99 River Dr.
Georgetown
Ont, CAN L7G 4T1
Canada

Phone 416-877-6948

Dependable Furniture Mfg. Co.

Furniture

45 Williams Ave.
San Francisco, CA 94124

Phone 415-822-3232
FAX 415-822-2515

Derby Desk Company

Antique Roll Top Desks

140 Tremont St.
Brighton, MA 02135

Catalog/Information Available Free

Phone 617-787-2707

Design Furniture Mfg. Ltd.

Teak Bedroom & Wall Units

2360 Midland Ave.
Agincourt
Canada

Phone 416-291-8858
FAX 416-291-8858

Design Gallery Milano

Italian Furniture

Via Manzoni 46
20121 Milano (MI)
Italy

Phone 011-39-2/798955
FAX 011-39-2/784082

Design Systems International

Furniture

296 Exeter Rd.
London
Ont, CAN N6L 1A3
Canada

Phone 519-652-9882
FAX 519-471-0864

Designer Gallery Ltd.

Furniture

735 Orangethorpe
Placentia, CA 92670

Phone 714-993-3970
FAX 714-993-0668

Designer Repros

Brass & Iron Beds

2417 East 24th St.
Los Angeles, CA 90058

Send $5.00 for Catalog/Information

Phone 213-587-4223

Designer Window Decor/Truview

Window Treatments - Blinds

10990 Petat St. #200
Dallas, TX 75238

Phone 214-343-2601

Deutsch

Rattan Furniture

31 E. 32nd St.
New York, NY 10016

Send $3.00 for Catalog/Information

Mail Order Available

Phone 212-683-8746
Toll Free 800-223-4550

Dimas Manufacturing Inc.

Furniture

227 Guayama St.
Hato Rey, PR 00918

Phone 809-751-1057
FAX 809-250-7342

Direct Furniture

Major Brand Furniture

PO Box 629
High Point, NC 27261

Directional of North Carolina Inc.

Furniture

PO Box 2005
High Point, NC 27261

Phone 919-841-3209

The Complete Sourcebook

6 - 23

Directions Inc.

Furniture
50 West Canyon Crest Rd.
Alpine, UT 84004
Phone 801-763-0954

Distinction Furniture Corp.

Furniture
I-40 Exit 33, PO Box 397
Conover, NC 28613
Phone 704-464-6476
FAX 704-464-9240

Dixie Furniture Co.

Furniture
PO Box 758
Foley, AL 36536
Phone 205-943-5681

Dominion Chair, Ltd.

Wood - Tables, Chairs, Rockers, Stools
PO Box 200
Brass River, N.S.
CAN B0M 1B0
Canada
Phone 902-647-2350

Don Ruseau Inc.

Furniture
413 E. 53rd St.
New York, NY 10022
Phone 212-753-0876

Doolings of Santa Fe

Southwestern Style Furniture
525 Airport Rd.
Santa Fe, NM 87501
Send $5.00 for Catalog/Information
Phone 505-471-5956
Toll Free 800-835-0107
FAX 505-471-1568

Door Store

Chairs, Desks, Furniture
1 Park Ave.
New York, NY 10016
Catalog/Information Available Free
Mail Order Available
Credit Cards VISA/MC
Phone 212-753-2280

Doors, Inc.

Oak Vanities, Mirrors, Oak Wall Units
127 Hartman Rd., Box A
Wadsworth, OH 44281
Phone 216-336-3558

Dor-Val Mfg. Ltd.

Furniture
2760 Laurentian Blvd.
St. Laurent
Que, CAN H4K 2E1
Canada
Phone 514-336-7780
FAX 514-745-2640

Drexel Heritage

Manufacturer - Furniture
101 North Main St.
Drexel, NC 28619
Phone 704-433-3000
Toll Free 800-447-4700

Driade SPA

Italian Furniture
Via Padana Inferiore, 12
29012 Fossadello di Caorso (PC)
Italy
Phone 011-39-523/821648
FAX 011-39-523/822628

Dried Flower Creations

Craft Supplies - Dried Flowers
PO Box 96-0880
Miami, FL 33296-0880
Phone 305-386-2355

Furniture

Dunhill Furniture Corp.

Furniture
10810 St. Louis Dr.
El Monte, CA 91731
Phone 213-283-4218

Dutailer Inc.

Furniture
298 Chaput St.
St-Pie De Bagot
Que, CAN J0H 1W0
Canada
Phone 514-772-2403
FAX 514-772-5055

Dynasty Wood Products Inc.

Solid Wood Furniture
4315 61st Ave. SE
Calgary, Alberta
CAN T2C 1Z6
Canada
Phone 403-236-3220
FAX 403-279-9516

E. J. Evans

Danish Furniture
1611 Lincoln Blvd.
Venice, CA 90294
Phone 213-821-6400

E.C. Hodge Ltd.

Bedroom, Livingroom, Diningroom Furniture
Norton Rd.
Stevenage, Herts SG1 2BB
Great Britain
Phone 011-44-438/357341

ETA Wood Concepts

Order Direct - Furniture - Entertainment Centers
23565 Reedy Drive
Elkhart, IN 46514
Mail Order Available
Credit Cards VISA/MC/AMEX
Phone 219-262-3457
Toll Free 800-382-6000
FAX 219-262-1078

Edgar B Furniture

Furniture
PO Box 849
Clemmons, NC 27012
Send $15.00 for Catalog/Information
Credit Cards Accepted
Phone 919-766-6321
Toll Free 800-225-6589

Edra SPA

Italian Furniture
Via Toscana, 11
56030 Perignano (PI)
Italy
Phone 011-39-587/616660
FAX 011-39-587/617500

Edward P. Schmidt Cabinetmaker

Reproduction Furniture, Wall Units, Doors
205 North Easton Rd.
Glenside, PA 10938
Phone 215-886-8774

Eldrid Wheeler

18th Century Reproduction Furniture
60 Sharp St.
Hingham, MA 02043
Send $5.00 for Catalog/Information
Mail Order Available
Phone 617-337-5311
FAX 617-337-2863

The Complete Sourcebook

Elk Valley Woodworking Inc.

Columns - Cedar, Pine, Oak, Rewood, Mahogany - Custom Cabinets, Tables
Rt.1 Box 88
Carter, OK 73627
Send $2.00 for Catalog/Information

Phone 405-486-3337
FAX 405-486-3491

Ellenburg's Furniture

Major Brand - Victorian, Shaker, Wicker, Rattan Furniture
Box 5638
Statesville, NC 28687
Send $6.00 for Catalog/Information

Mail Order Available

Credit Cards Accepted

Phone 704-873-2900
Toll Free 800-841-1420

Elm Industries

Major Brand Outdoor Furniture
1539 Race St.
Cincinnati, OH 45210

Phone 513-241-7927
FAX 513-241-0160

Elmo Guernsey

Rustic Style Beds
7706 Northway
San Antonio, TX 78213
Send $5.00 for Catalog/Information

Phone 210-341-4290

Emerson Leather Co.

Leather Furniture
816 13th St. N.E.
Hickory, NC 28601

Phone 704-328-1701

Empire State Chair Co., Inc.

Furniture
Foot of Liberty St.
Haverstraw, NY 10927

Phone 914-429-5700

Ephraim Marsh

Reproduction 18th Century Furniture
PO Box 266
Concord, NC 28025
Send $5.00 for Catalog/Information

Credit Cards Accepted

Phone 704-782-0814
Toll Free 800-992-8322
FAX 704-782-0436

Ercol Furniture Ltd.

Furniture- Will Export
Ercol Buildings, London Road
High Wycombe, Buckinghamshire
England HP13 7AE
Great Britain

Catalog/Information Available Free

Phone 011-44-494/521261
FAX 011-44-494/462467

Ernest Thompson Furniture

Southwestern Style Furniture & Custom Doors
2618 Coors Rd. SW
Albuquerque, NM 87105
Send $8.00 for Catalog/Information

Mail Order Available

Credit Cards VISA/MC/AMEX

Phone 505-873-4652
Toll Free 800-568-2344
FAX 505-877-7185

Erwin-Lambeth, Inc.

Furniture
201 Holly Hill Rd.
Thomasville, NC 27360

Phone 919-476-7751

Esse SRL

Italian Furniture
Via Treviso, 83
30037 Scorze' (VE)
Italy

Phone 011-39-41/445111
FAX 011-39-41/445600

Essential Items

Custom Stools & Ottomans
Church House
Plungar, Notts NG13 0JA
Great Britain

Phone 011-44-949/61172
FAX 011-44-602/843254

Ethan Allen, Inc.

Furniture, Rugs, Lamps, Accessories
Ethan Allen Drive
Danbury, CT 06810

Send $5.00 for Catalog/Information

Phone 203-743-8000

Eudy Cabinet Shop Inc.

Cabinets & Furniture
PO Box 559
Stanfield, NC 28163

Phone 704-888-4454

European Furniture Importers

European Furniture
2145 W. Grand Ave.
Chicago, IL 60612

Catalog/Information Available Free

Mail Order Available

Credit Cards VISA/MC/DISCOVER

Toll Free 800-283-1955
FAX 312-633-9308

Evertidy Furniture Ltd.

Bedroom Furniture
Culwell Trading Est
Hobgate Clo, Heath Town, Wolverhampton
WW10 0PB
Great Britain

Phone 011-44-902/456567

Expressions Custom Furniture

Custom Furniture
3636-1 10, Service Rd., Suite 103
Metairie, LA 70001

Phone 504-834-9222
Toll Free 800-544-4519
FAX 504-837-7613

FDY Furniture Mfg. Ltd.

Furniture
11430 142 St.
Edmonton
Alta, CAN T5M 1V1
Canada

Phone 403-452-8275

Fabian Furniture Mfg. Co. Ltd.

Furniture
East Victoria St., Box 359
Clinton
Ont, CAN N0M 1L0
Canada

Phone 519-482-7961

Fairchild of Calfornia

Furniture
8146 Byron Rd.
Whittier, CA 90606

Phone 213-698-7988
FAX 213-698-4959

Fairfield Chair Co.

Manufacturer - Chairs
1331 Harpo Ave. SW
PO Box 1710
Lenoir, NC 28645

Phone 704-758-4411

Fama SPA

Italian Furniture
Via Filiberto 2/BIS
45011 Adria (RO)
Italy

Phone 011-39-426/900200
FAX 011-39-426/900400

Fancher Chair Co. Inc.

Chairs
PO Box 8
S. Work St.
Falconer, NY 14733

Phone 716-665-4313
FAX 716-665-5168

Fancher Furniture Co.

Furniture
PO Box 351
100 Rochester St.
Salamanca, NY 14779
Phone 716-945-5500
FAX 716-945-5658

Faneuil Furniture Hardware Co. Inc.

Brass - Furniture Hardware, Door & Bath Hardware
163 Main St.
Salem, NH 03079
Send $3.00 for Catalog/Information
Phone 603-898-7733
FAX 603-898-7839

Felice rossi SRL

Italian Furniture
Via Sempione 17
21011 Casorate Sempione (VA)
Italy
Phone 011-39-331/295031
FAX 011-39-331/768449

Ferretti F.LLi Di Ferretto SPA

Italian Furniture
Via Volterrano, 60
56033 Capannoli (PI)
Italy
Phone 011-39-587/639111
FAX 011-39-587/609146

Ficks Reed Co.

Rattan Furniture
4900 Charlemer Dr.
Cincinnati, OH 45227
Phone 513-271-9011

Fine Arts Furniture Co.

Living Room Tables
1129 S. Bridge
Belding, MI 48809
Phone 616-794-1700

Fine Woodworking by Living Tree

Custom Manufacturer - Furniture, Cabinetry, Architectural Millwork, Doors
Rt. 213 W
RD1, Box 302A
Stone Ridge, NY 12484
Mail Order Available
Phone 914-687-9636
FAX 914-687-9698

Finkel Outdoors Products Inc.

Outdoor Furniture
317 S. Elm St.
PO Box 280
Owosso, MI 48867
Phone 517-723-7881

Flanders Industries Inc.

Outdoor Patio Furniture
PO Box 1788
Fort Smith, AR 72902
Catalog/Information Available Free
Toll Free 800-843-7532
FAX 501-783-2694

Flexform

Manufacturer - Italian Furniture - Tables, Chairs, Sofas, Beds, Lamps
Via Einaudi, 23/25
20036 Meda (MI)
Italy
Phone 011-39-362/74426
FAX 011-39-362/73055

Flexform

Italian Furniture
900 Broadway, Int. 902
New York, NY 10003
Phone 212-477-3188
FAX 212-477-4862

Flexsteel Industries

Manufacturer - Furniture
Brunswick Industrial Block
PO Box 877
Dubuque, IA 52001
Phone 319-556-7730

Furniture

Florida Furniture Industries — Frank & Son Inc.

Florida Furniture Industries

Manufacturer - Furniture
PO Box 610
Palatka, FL 32177
Phone 904-328-3444

Florida Headboard & Furniture Mfg. Co.

Manufacturer - Furniture
4401 N.W. 37 Ave.
Miami, FL 33142
Phone 305-638-4277

Fly By Nite Futons

Futons - Wool or Cotton Filled
199 Mississippi Street
Colorado Springs, CO 94107
Phone 415-255-9225

Fly Line

Italian Furniture
Via Terrenato, 7
36010 Carre' (VI)
Italy
Phone 011-39-445/314070
FAX 011-39-445/314308

Fong Brothers Company

Teakwood Chairs
5731 South Alameda St.
Los Angeles, CA 90058
Phone 213-583-6481
FAX 213-583-8650

Fontaine Bros. Inc.

Furniture
14 Leamy St.
Gardner, MA 01440
Phone 508-632-1831

Fontana Arte SPA

Italian Furniture & Lighting
Via Alzaia Trieste, 49
20094 Corsico (MI)
Italy
Phone 011-39-2/45100087
FAX 011-39-2/4476861

Foreign Traders

Spanish Colonial Furniture
202 Galisteo St.
Santa Fe, NM 87501
Send $5.00 for Catalog/Information
Mail Order Available
Phone 505-983-6441

Foremost Furniture

Furniture
8 West 30th St., 10th Fl.
New York, NY 10001
Phone 212-889-6347

Foster Bros. Mfg. Co.

Furniture
2025 S. Vandeventer St.
St. Louis, MO 63110
Phone 314-773-3441

Foster Manufacturing

Furniture & Home Accessories
414 N. 13th St.
Phildelphia, PA 19108
Mail Order Available
Phone 215-625-0500

Founders Furniture Co.

Furniture
PO Box 339
Thomasville, NC 27360
Phone 919-475-1361

Fran's Basket House

Wicker Furniture & Accessories
295 Route 10
Succasuna, NJ 07876
Credit Cards Accepted
Phone 201-584-2230
Toll Free 800-372-6799

Frank & Son Inc.

Occasional Furniture
PO Box 1252
Conway, SC 29526
Phone 803-347-3155

Furniture

The Complete Sourcebook

6 - 29

Franklin Custom Furniture

Country Western Style Furniture

193 East Main St.
Franklin, NC 28734

Phone 704-369-7881

Frederick Duckloe & Bros.

*Windsor Furniture - Chairs, Rockers,
Benches, Tables*

PO Box 427
Portland, PA 18351

Send $5.00 for Catalog/Information

Phone 717-847-6172

French Country Living

French Country Furniture

10205 Colvin Run Road
Great Falls, VA 22066

Phone 703-759-2245

Frisco Mfg. Co.

Furniture

PO Box 40
Highway 21 South
Frisco City, AL 36445

Phone 205-267-3111
Toll Free 800-888-5603

Fulgini Orilio & F.LLI SPA

Italian Furniture

Via Fermo, 32
61100 Pesaro (PS)
Italy

Phone 011-39-721/402088
FAX 011-39-721/25786

Furnitrad Inc.

Furniture

2650 Boul Vanier
S. Hyacinthe
Que, CAN J2S 6L9
Canada

Phone 514-773-2517
FAX 514-773-6425

Furniture Collections of Carolina

Major Brand Furniture

Route 8, Box 128
Hickory, NC 28602

Catalog/Information Available Free

Mail Order Available

Phone 704-294-3593
Toll Free 800-736-0542

Furniture Craft

Early American Furniture, Accessories

PO Box 1800
Largo, FL 34649-1800

Send $1.00 for Catalog/Information

Mail Order Available

Credit Cards VISA/MC

Phone 813-530-1621

Furniture Design Imports

*Many Major Brands and Imported
Furniture*

925 West Main St.
Forest City, NC 28043

Phone 704-245-0630

Furniture Forge

Furniture

23507 - 49th Ave. SE
Bothell, WA 98021

Phone 206-481-3535

Furniture Mart Design Center

Major Brand Furniture

2220 Highway 70 SE
Hickory, NC 28602

Toll Free 800-462-6278

Furniture That Exceeds Your Expectations

Hardwood Furniture

226 Crescent Street
Jamestown, NY 14701

Send $10.00 for Catalog/Information

Phone 716-487-1165

Furniture

Futon Furnishings

Futons
Lincoln Road, East Finchley
London N2 Great Britain
Great Britain
Credit Cards Accepted
Phone 011-44-81/4447249

G & G Furniture

Order by Phone - Furniture
10 E. Main Street
Thomasville, NC 27360
Toll Free 800-221-9778

Gaby's Shoppe

Wrougth Iron Furniture
1311 Dragon Street
Dallas, TX 75207
Send $25.00 for Catalog/Information
Phone 214-748-6644
Toll Free 800-299-4229
FAX 214-748-7701

Galeria San Ysidro, Inc.

Western Style Furniture
PO Box 17913
El Paso, TX 79917-7913
Phone 915-858-5222

Gallery of H B

Water Beds
6394 Euclid
Marlette, MI 48453
Catalog/Information Available Free
Phone 517-635-7970

Garcia Imports

Furniture
871 Willow St.
PO Box 5066
Redwood City, CA 94063
Send $25.00 for Catalog/Information
Phone 415-367-9600
Toll Free 800-346-8811
FAX 415-366-9390

Genada Imports

Danish Modern Furniture
PO Box 204
Teaneck, NJ 07666
Send $1.00 for Catalog/Information
Credit Cards Accepted
Phone 201-790-7522

General Mica Corp.

Furniture
13901 SW 142nd Ave.
Miami, FL 33186-6734
Phone 305-949-7247
FAX 305-940-7302

Georgia Chair Co.

Furniture
456 Industrial Blvd.
Gainesville, GA 30501
Phone 404-536-1366
Toll Free 800-833-4158

Georgian Furnishings Co., Ltd.

Fine Furniture
5400 Jefferson Highway
New Orleans, LA 70123
Phone 504-733-4141
FAX 504-733-7718

Georgian Reproduction

Reproduction Furniture
1524 Spring Hill Rd. #GG
McLean, VA 22102-3005
Phone 919-884-1171
Toll Free 800-334-3890
FAX 919-841-4936

Gerald Curry-Cabinetmaker

18th Century Reproduction Furniture
Pound Hill Rd.
Union, ME 04862
Catalog/Information Available Free
Phone 207-785-4633

Furniture

The Complete Sourcebook

6 - 31

Gilliam Furniture Inc.

Furniture
PO Box 1610
Statesville, NC 28677

Phone 704-872-6515

Giovanni Erba & C. SNC

Italian Furniture
Via Carlo Cattaneo, 91
PO Box 137
20035 Lissone (MI)
Italy

Phone 011-39-39/490632
FAX 011-39-39/491582

Glober Mfg. Co.

Occasional Tables, Curios, Buffets
10 W. Main St.
Carpentersville, IL 60110

Phone 708-428-3933
FAX 708-428-3013

Gold Medal Inc.

Furniture
1500 Commerce Rd.
Richmond, VA 23216

Phone 804-233-4337
FAX 804-230-2347

Good Tables Inc.

Bedrooms, Occasional Tables, Wall Units
1118 E. 223rd St.
Carson, CA 90745

Phone 213-775-8541
FAX 213-835-6039

Gordon's Inc.

Furniture
815 Love St.
PO Box 1676
Johnson City, TN 37601

Phone 615-928-2191

Grand Manor Furniture Inc.

Manufacturer - Furniture - Sofas, Chairs
PO Box 1286
Lenoir, NC 28645

Phone 704-758-5521

Grand River Workshop

Furniture Kits - Oak Roll Top Desks, Bookcases, Cupboards
PO Box AP
Des Moines, IA 50302

Send $2.00 for Catalog/Information

Mail Order Available

Phone 515-265-3239
Toll Free 800-373-1101

Grange Furniture, Inc.

Cherry & Rattan Furniture - Tables, Chairs, Beds, Dressers, Armoire, Mirrors
200 Lexington Ave.
New York, NY 10016

Send $10.00 for Catalog/Information

Phone 212-685-9494
Toll Free 800-472-6431
FAX 212-213-5132

Great American Log Furniture

Log Furniture
PO Box 3360
Ketchum, ID 83340

Send $4.00 for Catalog/Information

Toll Free 800-624-5779

Great Meadows Joinery

Reproduction Shaker Style Furniture
PO Box 392
Wayland, MA 01778

Send $4.00 for Catalog/Information

Mail Order Available

Credit Cards MC/VISA

Phone 508-358-4370
FAX 508-358-4370

Furniture

Great Western Furniture Mfg. Co.

Manufacturer - Furniture
515 W. Mississippi
Denver, CO 80223 -3120

Phone 303-733-5563
FAX 303-733-5566

Green Brothers Furniture Co.

Furniture
PO Box 87
North Wikesboro, NC 28659

Phone 919-838-2091

Green Country Furniture Mfg. Co.

Furniture
501 Division St.
Fort Smith, AR 72904

Phone 501-783-2771

Green Enterprises

Victorian Porch Furniture
43 S. Rogers St.
Hamilton, VA 22068

Send $1.50 for Catalog/Information

Mail Order Available

Credit Cards VISA/MC

Phone 703-338-3606

Greystone Victorian Furniture

Victorian Reproduction Furniture
PO Box 60
Montgomery, AL 36101-0060

Send $5.00 for Catalog/Information

Toll Free 800-552-3236

Griffon Furniture Ltd.

French Manufacturer - Bedroom, Livingroom, Diningroom Furniture
188 Campden Hill Rd.
London W8 7TH
Great Britain

Phone 011-44-71/2216741

Grindstaff's Interiors

Major Brand Furniture
927 BD West Main St.
Forest City, NC 28043

Catalog/Information Available Free

Phone 704-245-0630

Guy Vincent Custom Furniture and Crafts

Oak Furniture & Crafts
Rt. 2 Box 3596
Abbeville, LA 70510

Credit Cards Accepted

Phone 318-893-9271

H. Morris & Co. Ltd.

Livingroom & Diningroom Furniture
66 Grey Swan Ave.
Glasgow G435 9TS
Great Britain

Phone 011-44-41-6349000

H.U.D.D.L.E.

Childrens' Furniture
11159 Santa Monica Blvd.
Los Angeles, CA 90025

Send $2.00 for Catalog/Information

Credit Cards VISA/MC

Phone 213-836-8001

Habersham Plantation Corp.

17th & 18th Maple, Pine, Oak Furniture
171 Collier Rd.
PO Box 1209
Toccoa, GA 30577

Send $12.00 for Catalog/Information

Toll Free 800-241-0716

Hale Co.

Early American Dining Furniture
PO Box 356
East Windsor Hill, CN 06028

Phone 802-375-6511

The Complete Sourcebook

Hale Mfg. Co. – Hedstrom Corp.

Furniture

Hale Mfg. Co.

Wood Bookcases

PO Box 751
Herkimer, NY 13350

Phone 315-866-4250
Toll Free 800-873-4253
FAX 315-866-6417

Haliburton & White Ltee.

Furniture

85 Rue Montpellier
Montreal
Que, CAN H4N 2G3
Canada

Phone 514-748-6554
FAX 514-748-0326

Hamilton Furniture

Major Brand Furniture

506 Live Oak
Beaufort, NC 28516

Catalog/Information Available Free

Toll Free 800-488-4720

Hamlet Furniture Ltd.

Bedroom, Livingroom, Diningroom Furniture

Waverley Rd.
Yate, Bristol BS17 5QT
Great Britain

Phone 011-44-454/139090

Hammary Furniture Co.

Manufacturer - Furniture

PO Box 760
Lenoir, NC 28645

Phone 704-728-3231
FAX 704-728-5063

Harden Furniture Inc.

Furniture, Wall Sytems

Mill Pond Way
McConnellsville, NY 13401-1844

Send $2.00 for Catalog/Information

Phone 315-245-1000
FAX 315-245-2884

Harden Mfg. Co.

Furniture

Route 5, Box 289
Haleyville, AL 35565

Phone 205-486-7872
Toll Free 800-548-3034

Hart Furniture

Furniture

PO Box 760
Collierville, TN 38017

Phone 901-853-8595
FAX 901-854-0614

Harts Mfg. Co., Inc.

Bedroom Furniture

141 Eastley St.
Collierville, TN 38017

Phone 901-853-8595
FAX 901-854-0614

Harvest House Furniture

Order by Phone - Furniture

Highway 109, South PO Box 1440
Denton, NC 27239

Credit Cards Accepted

Phone 704-869-5181
Toll Free 800-334-3552

Heath Craft Wood Works

Furniture Kits

Heath Co.
Benton Harbor, MI 49022

Catalog/Information Available Free

Mail Order Available

Credit Cards VISA/MC

Phone 616-982-3200

Hedstrom Corp.

Indoor/Outdoor Furniture

PO Box 432
Sunnyside Rd.
Bedford, PA 15522

Phone 814-623-9041
Toll Free 800-934-3949

Furniture

Heirloom Reproductions – Historic Charleston Reproductions

Heirloom Reproductions

Order Direct - French & Victorian Reproduction Furniture
1834 West 5th St.
Montgomery, AL 36106

Send $2.00 for Catalog/Information

Mail Order Available

Credit Cards MC/VISA/Check/Money Order

Phone 205-263-3511
Toll Free 800-288-1513
FAX 205-263-3313

Hekman Furniture

Antique Reproduction Furniture
1400 Buchanan St. SW
Grand Rapids, MI 49507

Phone 616-452-1411
Toll Free 800-253-9249
FAX 616-452-0688

Henkel-Harris

Reproduction 18th Century Furniture
Box 2170
Winchester, VA 22601

Send $10.00 for Catalog/Information

Mail Order Available

Phone 703-667-4900

Henredon

Furniture
Henredon Rd., Hwy.70
Morgantown, NC 28655

Send $5.00 for Catalog/Information

Phone 704-437-5261
Toll Free 800-444-3682

Heron-Parigi

Italian Furniture
PO Box 13
50032 Borgo San Lorenzo (FI)
Italy

Phone 011-39-55/8457444
FAX 011-39-55/8456341

Hickory Chair Co.

Furniture
PO Box 2147
Hickory, NC 28601

Send $5.00 for Catalog/Information

Mail Order Available

Phone 704-328-1801
FAX 704-328-8954

Hickory Furniture Co.

Furniture
PO Box 998
Hickory, NC 28601

Phone 704-322-8624

Hickory Furniture Mart

Furniture Buying Guide
2220 Highway 70 SE
Hickory, NC 28602

Catalog/Information Available Free

Phone 704-322-3510
Toll Free 800-462-6278

Hickory White

Manufacturer - Furniture
PO Box 1600
300 Oak St.
High Point, NC 27261

Phone 919-885-2222
FAX 919-885-1200

Highland House of Hickory Inc.

Manufacturer - Furniture
207 20th St. S.E.
Hickory, NC 28601

Phone 704-328-5251

Historic Charleston Reproductions

Reproduction Furniture & Decorative Accessories
105 Broad St.
Charleston, SC 29402

Catalog/Information Available Free

Credit Cards VISA/MC/AMEX

Phone 803-723-8292

Furniture

The Complete Sourcebook

6 - 35

Hitchcock Chair Co.

Furniture
Village Center
Riverton, CT 06065

Phone 203-379-8531

Holder Pearce

Bedroom, Livingroom, Diningroom Furniture
18 Grove Rd.
Eastbourne, E. Sussex
BN21 4TR
Great Britain

Phone 011-44-323/26565

Holiday Pool & Patio

Name Brand Patio Furniture
PO Box 727
Hwy 231
Hudson, NC 28638

Mail Order Available

Phone 704-728-2664

Hollingsworth

Antique Reproduction Pencil Post Beds
PO Box 2592
Wilmington, NC 28402

Catalog/Information Available Free

Mail Order Available

Phone 919-251-0280

Holloways

Conservatory Furniture - English, Victorian Style
Lower Court
Suckley, Worcs WR6 5DE
Great Britain

Phone 011-44-886/884665

Holton Furniture Co.

Major Brand Furniture
805 Randolph Street, PO Box 280
Thomasville, NC 27361-0280

Catalog/Information Available Free

Phone 919-472-0400
Toll Free 800-334-3183

Homecrest Industries, Inc.

Manufacturer - Outdoor Furniture
PO Box 350
Wadena, MN 56482

Phone 218-631-1000
Toll Free 800-346-4852
FAX 218-631-2609

Homestead Furniture

Country Style Furniture Reproductions
114 Commerce Drive
Hesston, KS 67072

Send $3.00 for Catalog/Information

Phone 919-472-0400
Toll Free 800-334-3183

Homeway Furniture Co.

Furniture - Nationwide Delivery - Discounted Prices
121 W. Lebanon St.
PO Box 1548
Mount Airy, NC 27030

Send $10.00 for Catalog/Information

Mail Order Available

Phone 919-786-6151
Toll Free 800-334-9094
FAX 919-786-1822

Horchow Home Collection

Indoor & Outdoor Furniture, Decorative Accessories
221 E. Walnut Hill Lane
Irving, TX 75039

Send $5.50 for Catalog/Information

Credit Cards Accepted

Toll Free 800-456-7000

Horm SRL

Italian Furniture
Via Delle Crede
33170 Pordenone (PN)
Italy

Phone 011-39-434/572610
FAX 011-39-434/572622

Furniture

Hostess Furniture Ltd.

Bedroom, Livingroom, Diningroom Furniture

Vulcan Rd, Bilston,
W Midlands   WV14 7JR
Great Britain

Mail Order Available

Phone 011-44-902/493681

House Dressing Furniture

Major Brand Furniture

3608 West Wendover Ave.
Grennsboro, NC 27407

Catalog/Information Available Free

Mail Order Available

Phone 910-294-3900

Toll Free 800-322-5850

FAX 910-294-0004

House of Brougham Collection

Early American Bedroom Furniture

Upper Canada Furniture Co.
406 Silvercreek Parkway, Guelph
Ontario N1H 138
Canada

Catalog/Information Available Free

Howard Miller Clock Company

Furniture, Grandfather Clocks, Curios

860 East Main
Zeeland, MI 49464

Send $2.00 for Catalog/Information

Phone 616-772-9131

Howe Furniture Corp.

Furniture

151 Woodward Ave.
South Norwalk, CT 06854-4730

Phone 203-853-4600

Howerton Antique Reproductions

Reproduction Furniture

PO Box 215
120 Buffalo Rd.
Clarksville, VA 23927

Send $3.00 for Catalog/Information

Mail Order Available

Phone 804-374-5715

Toll Free 800-443-4755

Hudson's Discount Furniture

Major Brand Discounted Furniture

PO Box 2547
940 Highland Ave. NE
Hickory, NC 28601

Catalog/Information Available Free

Mail Order Available

Phone 704-322-4996

FAX 704-322-6953

Hughes Furniture Industries, Inc.

Furniture

PO Box 486
701 S. Stout St.
Randleman, NC 27317

Phone 919-498-8700

FAX 919-498-8750

Hunt Country Furniture

Wood Furniture

Webatuck Craft Village
PO Box 500
Wingdale, NY 12594

Send $2.00 for Catalog/Information

Credit Cards VISA/MC/AMEX

Phone 914-832-6522

The Complete Sourcebook

Hunt Galleries, Inc.

Furniture - Chairs, Ottomans, Benches, Sectionals, Sofas, Beds
PO Box 2324 , 2920 Hwy. 127 N
Hickory, NC 28603

Send $5.00 for Catalog/Information

Mail Order Available

Credit Cards VISA/MC

Phone 704-324-9934
Toll Free 800-248-3876

Huntingburg Wood Products co.

Furniture
1008 N. Chestnut St.
Huntingburg, IN 47542

Phone 812-683-2789

Hyde Park Antiques, Ltd.

Antique English Furniture
836 Broadway
New York, NY 10003

Catalog/Information Available Free

Mail Order Available

Phone 212-477-0033

Hyperion Wall Furniture Ltd.

Bedroom, Livingroom, Diningroom Furniture
166 Oatlands Dr.
Weybridge, Surrey
Great Britain

Phone 011-44-932/844783

Hyphen Fitted Furniture

Bedroom Furniture
Unit 12, Deeside Ind Pk
Deeside, Clwyd
CH5 2NY
Great Britain

Phone 011-44-244/816758

I. P. E. SPA

Italian Furniture
Via Roma, 57
40069 Bologna (BO)
Italy

Phone 011-39-51/755128
FAX 011-39-52/755207

Images of America Inc.

Furniture
829 Blair St., PO Box 1127
Thomasville, NC 27360

Phone 919-475-7106
FAX 919-476-3016

Imperial of Morristown

Furniture
PO Box 707
Morristown, TN 37814

Phone 615-586-2821

Indian Ocean Trading Co.

Teak Garden Furniture, Umbrellas
47 Rudloe Road
London SW12 0DR
Great Britain

Phone 011-44-81/6754808
FAX 011-44-81/6754652

Interior Furnishings, Ltd.

Major Brand Furniture
PO Box 1644
Hickory, NC 28603

Send $2.00 for Catalog/Information

Mail Order Available

Phone 704-328-5683

Interna Furniture Design Ltd.

Furniture
76 Signet Dr.
Weston
Ont., CAN M9L 1T2
Canada

Phone 416-741-4211
FAX 416-749-2374

International Woodworking

Cedar Furniture
588 Claude St.
Wiarton
Ont., CAN N0H 2T0
Canada
         Phone 519-534-1692

Irving & Jones Fine Garden Furnishings

Garden Furniture
Village Center
Colebrook, CT 06021
Send $2.00 for Catalog/Information
         Phone 203-379-9219

Isabel Brass Furniture

Brass Beds
200 Lexington Ave.
New York, NY 10016
Send $4.00 for Catalog/Information
         Phone 212-689-3307
         Toll Free 800-221-8523

J & C Crafts

Cabinets
20316 NE 58th
Vancouver, WA 98682-9610
         Phone 206-892-4274

J D Furniture Mfg. Ltd.

Furniture
Bay 25, 4416 61st Ave.
Calgary
Alta., CAN T2C 1Z5
Canada
         Phone 403-236-0092

J. T. Ellis & Co. Ltd.

Bedroom, Livingroom, Diningroom Furniture
Silver St.
Huddersfield
HD5 9BA
Great Britain
         Phone 011-44-484/514212

J.A.G. International Inc.

Iron Canopy Bed
1525 Dragon
Dallas, TX 75207
Send $2.00 for Catalog/Information
Credit Cards Accepted
         Phone 214-761-9540

JMW Gallery

Will assist in Special Item searches - Antiques, Period Mission Furniture, American Art Pottery
144 Lincoln St.
Boston, MA 02111
Catalog/Information Available Free
         Phone 617-338-9097

Jackelope Furniture

Santa Fe Style Furnishings, Pottery
2823 Cerrillos Rd.
Santa Fe, NM 87501
         Phone 505-471-8539
         FAX 505-471-6710

Jackson Sales, Inc.

Furniture
PO Box 429
106 8th Ave.
Springfield, TN 37172
         Phone 615-384-6134
         Toll Free 800-251-3025
         FAX 615-384-8477

James Lea-Cabinetmaker

Reproduction 18th Century Furniture
9 West Street
Rockport, ME 04856
Send $5.00 for Catalog/Information
Mail Order Available
         Phone 207-236-3632

James M. Taylor & Co.

Manufacturer - Mission & Shaker Style Furniture & Cabinetry

39 Frost Hill Rd.
York, ME 03909

Send $5.00 for Catalog/Information

Mail Order Available

Phone 207-439-1176
FAX 207-439-4205

Janis Aldridge, Inc.

17th-19th Century Furniture & Accessories

2900 M Street NW
Washington DC,   20007

Phone 202-338-7710

Jarabosky

Manufacturer - Wood Furniture made from Exotic Woods

PO Box 112, Halifax
West Yorkshire HX5 OSZ
Great Britain

Phone 011-44-422/311922

Jasper Cabinet Co.

Furniture Cabinets

PO Box 69
126 S. Jackson
Jasper, IN 47546

Phone 812-482-4747
FAX 812-482-4240

Jeffco

Furniture

1 N. Broadway, #711
White Plains, NY 10601

Phone 914-682-0303

Jeffrey P. Greene, Furniture Maker

18th Century Style Furniture

1 West Main St.
Wickford, RI 02852

Send $5.00 for Catalog/Information

Mail Order Available

Phone 401-295-1200

Jesper Furniture USA

Manufacturer - Home/Office Furniture

275 Route 46 W.
Fairfield, NJ 07004

Phone 201-808-3310
Toll Free 800-537-7372
FAX 201-808-3312

John Alan Designs

Custom Settees

120-22 Walcot St.
Bath, England
Great Britain

Phone 011-44-235/466963

John Congdon, Cabinetmaker

Reproduction Furniture

PO Box 206
Charlotte, VT 05445

Mail Order Available

Phone 802-425-2522
FAX 802-425-2522

John Michael Furniture

Order by Phone - Name Brand Furniture

3136 Hickory Blvd.
Hudson, NC 28638

Phone 704-728-2944
Toll Free 800-669-3801

John Minter Furniture Ltd.

Hand Painted Furniture

Monks Hill
Smarden, Kent
TN27 8QJ
Great Britain

Phone 011-44-233/77541

John Pulsford Associates Ltd.

Bedroom, Livingroom, Diningroom Furniture

32 Britannia St.
London WC1X 9JF
Great Britain

Phone 011-44-71/8373399

John Widdicomb Co.

Furniture

601 5th N.W.
Grand Rapids, MI 49504

Phone 616-459-7173
FAX 616-459-5873

Johnny's Cabinet Shop

Cabinets

301 Broad
Pilot Point, TX 76258

Phone 817-686-2417

Jones Brothers

Furniture

PO Box 991
Smithfield, NC 27577

Mail Order Available

Phone 919-934-4162
FAX 919-934-4162

Jones' Oak Furniture

*Oak End Tables, Sofa Tables, Coffee
Tables*

PO Box 400
Talbott, TN 37877

Send $3.00 for Catalog/Information

Credit Cards Accepted

Phone 615-581-6031
Toll Free 800-752-5543

Jr Ross Ltd.

Quality Solid Wood Stools

PO Box 5228
High Point, NC 27262

Send $1.00 for Catalog/Information

Toll Free 800-444-2245

K & C Southwest Interiors

Manufacturer - Furniture

9852 E Alpaca St.
South El Monte, CA 91733-3102

Phone 818-350-8043

Kane Masterbuilt Furniture Co.

Furniture

5851 N.W. 35th Ave.
Miami, FL 33142

Phone 305-633-0542
FAX 305-635-3695

Karges Furniture Co., Inc.

Reproduction Furniture

1501 W. Maryland St.
PO Box 6517
Evansville, IN 47712

Phone 812-425-2291
Toll Free 800-252-7437

Kartell SPA

Italian Furniture

Via Delle Industrie, 1
61100 Pesaro (PS)
Italy

Phone 011-39-2/900121
FAX 011-39-9053316

Keller Manufacturing Co.

Manufacturer - Furniture

Box 8
Corydon, IN 47112

Phone 812-738-2222

Kenneth D. Lynch & Sons, Inc.

Wrought Iron Outdoor Furniture

84 Diane Blvd., PO Box 488
Wilton, CT 06897

Phone 203-762-8363
FAX 203-762-2999

Kenneth Winslow Furniture

Furniture - Chairs, Tables, Sofas, Beds

464 Broome St.
New York, NY 10003

Mail Order Available

Phone 212-219-9244
FAX 212-219-9332

Kesterport Ltd.

Bedroom, Livingroom, Diningroom Furniture
Kestrel Ho, 111 Heath Rd.
Twickenham
TW1 4AH
Great Britain
Phone 011-44-81/8916401

Key City Furniture Co., Inc.

Manufacturer - Furniture
PO Box 1049
503 C. Street
North Wilkesboro, NC 28659
Phone 919-838-4191

Kimball Furniture Reproductions

Victorian Furniture Reproductions
1600 Royal St., PO Box 460
Jasper, IN 47549-1001
Phone 812-482-1600
Toll Free 800-482-1616
FAX 812-482-8300

Kincaid Galleries

Solid Wood Furniture
430 S.Main St.
High Point, NC 27260
Phone 919-883-1818

King Brothers Woodworking Inc.

Cabinets, Doors, Millwork, Builders' Hardware
3711 First St.
PO Box 3024
Union Gap, WA 98903
Phone 509-453-4683
FAX 509-457-7854

King Hickory Furniture Co. Inc.

Furniture
1028 15th St. Dr. NE
Hickory, NC 28601
Phone 704-324-7449

Kings River Casting

Chairs, Benches, Posts, Tables
1350 North Ave.
Sanger, CA 93657
Mail Order Available
Phone 209-875-8250
FAX 209-875-5974

Kingsdown Inc.

Furniture
3rd & Holt Sts.
Mebane, NC 27302
Phone 919-563-3531

Kingsley Furniture Co. Inc.

Furniture
102 Park St.
La Porte, IN 46350
Phone 219-326-0550

Kingsley-Bate, Ltd.

Handcarved Garden Furniture - Teak, Mahogany
5587B Guniea Rd.
Fairfax, VA 22032
Send $1.00 for Catalog/Information
Mail Order Available
Phone 703-978-7200
FAX 703-978-7222

Kirby Mfg. Co. Inc.

Furniture
Lenoir City Industrial Park
PO Box 483
Lenoir City, TN 37771
Phone 615-986-5102

Kisabeth Furniture

Furniture
5320 Glenview Dr.
Fort Worth, TX 76117
Phone 817-281-7560
FAX 817-498-9248

Furniture

Kittinger Co.

Furniture

1893 Elmwood Ave.
Buffalo, NY 14207

Phone 716-876-1000
Toll Free 800-876-2378
FAX 716-876-8521

Klein Design Inc.

Solid Oak Rockers, Chairs, Loveseats,
Sofas, Side Tables

99 Sadler St.
Gloucester, MA 01930

Phone 508-281-5276
Toll Free 800-451-7247

Knight Galleries

Order by Phone - Furniture

PO Box 1254
Lenoir, NC 28645

Toll Free 800-334-4721

Knipp & Co. Inc.

Custom Wood Furniture, Architectural
Millwork

3401 S. Hanover St.
Baltimore, MD 21225

Phone 301-355-0440
FAX 301-355-2866

Kopil & Associates Timeless Furniture

Manufacturer - Cherry Custom Furniture

PO Box 411
Jonesville, VT 05466

Phone 802-434-4400
FAX 802-434-5639

Kraemer Furniture Designs

Waterbeds & Bedroom Furniture

PO Box 33
1350 Main St.
Plain, WI 53577

Send $2.75 for Catalog/Information

Kramer Brothers

Victorian Iron Garden Furniture

PO Box 255
17 Dell Street
Dayton, OH 45404

Catalog/Information Available Free

Phone 513-228-4194
FAX 513-228-4194

Kroehler Furniture Co.

Furniture

552 Ontario St.
Stratford
Ont., CAN N5A 6T4
Canada

Phone 519-271-2340
FAX 519-273-0175

L & J.G. Stickley, Inc.

Manufacturer - Solid Oak & Cherry
Furniture - Livingroom, Bedroom

PO Box 480
Stickley Drive
Manlius, NY 13140-0480

Send $5.00 for Catalog/Information

Mail Order Available

Phone 315-682-5500
FAX 315-682-6306

L'Image Design

Furniture

7100 Warden Ave.
Markham
Ont., CAN L3R 5M7
Canada

Phone 416-475-7703

La Lune Collection

Trade Only - Furniture

930 E. Burleigh
Milwaukee, WI 53212

Send $25.00 for Catalog/Information

Phone 414-263-5300
FAX 414-263-5508

Furniture

The Complete Sourcebook

La-Z-Boy Furniture

Furniture - Sofas, Loveseats

1284 N. Telegraph
Monroe, MI 48161

Phone 313-242-1444
Toll Free 800-843-6735

Ladd Furniture Industries, Inc.

Furniture

1 Plaza Center
High Point, NC 27261

Phone 919-889-0333
FAX 919-899-5839

Lanark Furniture Corp.

Manufacturer - Furniture - Livingroom

140 Wendell Ave.
Weston
Ont., CAN M9N 3R2
Canada

Phone 416-247-1777
FAX 416-247-3091

Lane Company, Inc.

Early American Furniture, Shaker Furniture

American Folk Art Collection
PO Box 151
Alta Vista, VA 24517-0151

Send $5.00 for Catalog/Information

Phone 804-369-5641
Toll Free 800-447-4700

Lanier Furniture Company

Handcrafted Solid Wood Shaker Style Furniture

PO Box 3576
Wilmington, NC 28406

Catalog/Information Available Free

Mail Order Available

Credit Cards VISA/MC/Check

Toll Free 800-453-1362
FAX 919-392-1045

Lanzet (UK) Ltd.

Bedroom Furniture

Unit 20, Headley Park 10
Headley Rd. East, Woodley, Berks
RG5 4SW
Great Britain

Phone 011-44-734/695707

Larkspur Furniture Co.

Outdoor Furniture - Hardwood Chairs, Ottomans

274 Magnolia Ave.
Larkspur, CA 94939

Send $1.00 for Catalog/Information

Mail Order Available

Toll Free 800-959-8174

Larry & Alley, Inc.

Furniture

PO Box 4823
Martinsville, VA 24115

Phone 703-632-6403

Lawing's

Name Brand Furniture

Rt. 1 Box 40
Hudson, NC 28638

Toll Free 800-765-8183

Lazy Lawyer Co. Inc.

Wood Desks

29422 Josephine Dr.
Elberta, AL 36530

Phone 205-986-7233

LeFort

18th Century Reproduction Furniture

293 Winter Street
Hanover, MA 02339

Send $10.00 for Catalog/Information

Mail Order Available

Phone 617-826-9033

Furniture

Leather Furniture Sales, Inc.

Leather Furniture
PO Box 2911
Hickory, NC 28603

Send $3.00 for Catalog/Information

Leather Interiors

*Leather Furniture - Contemporary,
Traditional*
Box 9305
Hickory, NC 28603

Mail Order Available

Phone 704-552-0778

Toll Free 800-627-4526

Leboff International Ltd.

Livingroom, Diningroom Furniture
Lock Field Ave., Brinsdown
Enfield, Middx
EN3 7TG
Great Britain

Phone 011-44-81/8043352

Lee Industries Inc.

Furniture
701 N. Albany
Chicago, IL 60622

Phone 312-722-7070

FAX 312-826-7373

Lee L. Woodard Sons Inc.

Wrought Iron Furniture
George St.
PO Box 188
Maxton, NC 28364

Phone 919-844-3653

Legendary Furniture of Ezra G.

Furniture
5606 E. St. Rt. 37
Delaware, OH 43015

Send $3.00 for Catalog/Information

Mail Order Available

Phone 614-369-1817

Lehigh Furniture

Manufacturer - Furniture - Bedroom
PO Box 640
Marianna, FL 32446

Phone 904-526-2811

Lenore Mulligan Designs, Inc.

Southwestern Style Furniture
333 South Clark Drive
Beverly Hills, CA 90211

Send $10.00 for Catalog/Information

Phone 310-358-9012

FAX 310-358-9037

Leonard's Reproductions & Antiques

Reproduction Furniture
600 Taunton Ave.
Seekonk, MA 02771

Send $4.00 for Catalog/Information

Mail Order Available

Credit Cards Accepted

Phone 508-336-8585

FAX 508-336-4884

Leverwood Ltd.

*Bedroom, Livingroom, Diningroom
Furniture*
145 Low St.
Sunderland
SR1 2AB
Great Britain

Phone 011-44-91/5657116

Lewis Mittman, Inc.

Manufacturer - Reproduction Furniture
214 East 52nd St.
New York, NY 10022

Phone 212-888-5580

FAX 212-371-5061

Lewittes Furniture Enterprises Inc.

Furniture
420 Great Neck Rd.
Great Neck, NY 11021

Phone 516-482-2550

The Complete Sourcebook

Lexington Furniture Industries

Reproduction Victorian Style Furniture
PO Box 1008
Lexington, NC 27293

Phone 704-898-6162
Toll Free 800-544-4694

Lexterten Ltd.

*Bedroom, Livingroom, Diningroom
Furniture*
Patricia Way, Pyson Rd. Ind Est
Broadstairs, Kent
CT10 2LE
Great Britain

Phone 011-44-843/868841

Liberty Hall

Reproduction Pine Furniture
PO Box 236
104 Fremont Street
Burgaw, NC 28425

Catalog/Information Available Free

Phone 919-259-3493

Limelight Bedrooms

Bedroom Furniture
1st Avenue, Unit 27
Pensnett Tradding Est, Kingswinford
West Midlands DY6 7PP
Great Britain

Phone 011-44-384/400434

Lincoln House Furniture

Leather Furniture
3105 Sulphur Springs Rd. NE
Hickory, NC 28601

Send $5.00 for Catalog/Information

Phone 704-322-4478

Lineas Sas Di Asgnaghi Giannarturo & Co.

Italian Furniture
Via Dei Celuschi, 4/12
20036 Meda (MI)
Italy

Phone 011-39-362/72600
FAX 011-39-362/70277

Link-Taylor Corp.

Manufacturer - Furniture
PO Box 1537
Lexington, NC 27292

Phone 704-352-2121

Lion House Antique (Copies)

Reproduction Furniture
16-18 New Street
Chipping Norton, Oxon
OX7 5LJ
Great Britain

Phone 011-44-6086643294
FAX 011-44-608641940

Lisa Victoria Beds

Brass Beds
17106 South Crater Rd.
Petersburg, VA 23805

Send $4.00 for Catalog/Information

Mail Order Available

Phone 804-862-1491

Lister Teak, Inc.

Teak Outdoor Furniture
561 Exton Commons
Exton, PA 19341

Phone 215-524-9770
Toll Free 800-345-8325

Little Colorado Inc.

Solid Wood Juvenile Furniture
15866 W. 7th Ave.
Golden, CO 80401

Send $2.00 for Catalog/Information

Credit Cards Accepted

Phone 303-278-2451
Toll Free 800-776-7337

Lloyd Loom Catalogue

Woven Fibre Furniture
Elmley Heritage
Stone House, Elmley Lovett, Droitwich
Worchester WR9 0PS
Great Britain

Phone 011-44-299/851447

Furniture

Lloyd/Flanders

Wicker Indoor/Outdoor Furniture
3010 Tenth Street
PO Box 550
Menominee, MI 49858

Catalog/Information Available Free

Mail Order Available

Phone 906-863-4491
Toll Free 800-526-9894
FAX 906-863-6700

Loftin-Black Furniture Co.

Major Brand Furniture - Nationwide Shipping
111 Sedgehill Dr.
Thomasville, NC 27360

Credit Cards Accepted

Phone 919-472-6117
Toll Free 800-334-7398
FAX 919-472-2052

Louis Interiors Inc.

Furniture
120 Orfus Rd.
Toronto
Ont., CAN M6A 1L9
Canada

Phone 416-785-9909
FAX 416-785-0301

Louisiana Cypress Ltd.

Louisiana Cypress Furniture
PO Box 53253
New Orleans, LA 70153

Catalog/Information Available Free

Lyon-Shaw

Wrought-Iron Furniture
PO Box 2069
Salisbury, NC 28145

Phone 704-636-8270
FAX 704-633-9350

M. Craig & Company

Custom Cabinets & Furniture
911 Lady St.
Columbia, SC 29201

Phone 803-254-5994
FAX 803-252-4907

Machado

Santa Fe Style Furnishings
1302 Cerrillos Rd.
Santa Fe, NM 87501

Mack & Rodel Cabinet Makers

Custom Furniture
Leighton Rd.
RR 1, Box 88
Pownal, ME 04069

Send $4.00 for Catalog/Information
Phone 207-688-4483

Macon Umbrella Corp.

Lawn Furniture, Umbrellas
2 Ingraham St.
Brooklyn, NY 11206

Phone 718-381-4400

Maddison House

Upholstered Furniture
PO Box 414
Bukena Vista, GA 31803

Phone 912-649-2965

Magna Designs Inc.

Furniture
PO Box 1354
Lynnwood, WA 98036

Phone 206-776-2181

Magnokrom Inc.

Door Hardware
171 Nugget Ave.
Scarborough
Ont., CAN M1S 3B1
Canada

Phone 416-265-0000

Furniture

Magnolia Hall

Antique Furniture, Victorian Reproduction Furniture
725 Andover Drive
Atlanta, GA 30327

Send $3.00 for Catalog/Information

Mail Order Available

Credit Cards VISA/MC

Phone 404-237-9725

Mahogany Craft

18th Century Reproduction Furniture
12150 Fingerboard Rd.
Monrovia, MD 21770-9106

Send $5.00 for Catalog/Information

Phone 301-663-4611

Maine Cottage Furniture, Inc.

Handpainted Contemporary Furniture
PO Box 935
Lower Falls Landing
Yarmouth, ME 04096

Mail Order Available

Phone 207-846-1430

FAX 207-846-0602

Majestic Furniture Co.

Upholstered Furniture
574 Boston Ave.
Medford, MA 02155-5534

Phone 617-391-1963

Mallin Co.

Wrought Iron & Tubular Furniture
2665 Leonis Blvd.
Los Angeles, CA 90058

Phone 213-589-6591

Mallory's Fine Furniture

Many Major Brands - Furniture, Carpets, Lamps
PO Box 1150
Jacksonville, NC 28540

Catalog/Information Available Free

Mail Order Available

Credit Cards MC/VISA/Check/Money Order

Phone 910-353-1828

FAX 910-353-3348

Manchester Wood Inc.

Wood Furniture
PO Box 1187
Manchester Center, VT 05255

Phone 802-362-2229

FAX 802-362-3864

Manhattan Cabinetry

Custom Furniture
100 West 72nd St.
New York, NY 10023

Phone 212-721-5151

FAX 212-721-0779

Manheim & Weitz

Custom Reproduction Furniture
13736 Beta Road
Dallas, TX 75244

Phone 214-387-4578

Toll Free 800-327-1624

FAX 214-387-4580

Manivalde Woodworking

Wood Furniture
R.R. 2 Burks Falls
Ont., CAN P0A 1C0
Canada

Phone 705-382-2025

Furniture

Manor House

Reproduction Furniture
200 Lexington Ave.
New York, N.Y. 10016
Mail Order Available
Phone 212-532-1127

Manufactur De Lambton Ltee.

Furniture
199 5E Ave.
Lambton
Que., CAN G0M 1H0
Canada
Phone 418-486-7451
FAX 418-486-7450

Manufacture De Meubles Carol Ann Ltee.

Furniture
11051 Ray Lawson
Ville D'Anjou
Que., CAN H1J 1M6
Canada
Phone 514-363-6072

Maraco Design Inc.

Furniture
134-7 E. Ave.
Daveluyville
Que., CAN G0Z 1C0
Canada
Phone 819-367-2186
FAX 819-367-2259

Marco Fine Furniture

Furniture - Traditional and Contemporary Styles
650 Potrero Ave.
San Francisco, CA 94110
Phone 415-285-3235
FAX 415-285-5440

Marelli International SRL

Italian Furniture
Via Giovanni Da Verrazzano 2
20036 Meda (MI)
Italy
Phone 011-39-362/71779
FAX 011-39-362/340336

Mario Villa Designs

Furniture
3908 Magazine St.
New Orleans, LA 70115
Phone 504-895-8731
FAX 504-895-7431

Marion Travis

Furniture - Ladder Back Chairs, Stools, Tables
PO Box 1041
Statesville, NC 28687
Send $1.00 for Catalog/Information
Mail Order Available
Credit Cards VISA/MC/Check/Money Order
Phone 704-528-4424

Mark & Marjorie Allen

Antique Furniture & Accessories
RD #1 Box 13
Putnam Valley, NY 10579
Mail Order Available
Phone 914-528-8989

Mark Dahlman Wood Products

Oak Tables and Mirrors
PO Box 38
Cromwell, MN 55726
Credit Cards Accepted
Toll Free 800-535-7271

The Complete Sourcebook

6 - 49

Mark Sales Co. Inc.

Wholesale Antique Reproductions - Italian and French Chairs, Tables, Stools
609 East 81st St.
Brooklyn, NY 11236

Send $2.00 for Catalog/Information
Phone 718-763-2591

Mark Wilkinson Furniture Ltd.

USA - 212-308-9674 - Bedroom, Livingroom, Diningroom Furniture
Overton Ho, High St., Bromham
Chippenham, Wiltshire
SN15 2HA
Great Britain
Phone 011-44-380/850004

Marlow Furniture Co. Inc.

Furniture
PO Box 637
Hickory, NC 28601
Phone 704-324-6473

Marsh Furniture Company

Furniture
1001 S. Centennial St.
High Point, NC 27261
Phone 919-884-7363

Martha M. House

Hardcrafted Victorian Furniture
1022 S. Decatur St.
Montgomery, AL 36104

Send $3.00 for Catalog/Information

Credit Cards VISA/MC
Phone 205-264-3558
Toll Free 800-255-4195
FAX 205-262-2610

Martin & Frost Ltd.

Bedroom, Livingroom, Diningroom Furniture
130 McDonald Rd.
Endburgh
EH7 4NN
Great Britain
Phone 011-44-31/5578787

Martin Laque Inc.

Furniture
155-5 Jules Leger
Goucherville
Que., CAN J4B 7K8
Canada
Phone 514-655-1900
FAX 514-655-1900

Martin Timber Co., Inc.

Wood Furniture, Lumber
Hwy. 153 S.
PO Box 99
Castor, LA 71016
Phone 318-544-7205
FAX 318-544-8662

Maryland Classics Inc.

Manufacturer - Furniture
2315 Pennsylvania Ave.
PO Box 2065
Hagerstown, MD 21740
Phone 301-733-7000
FAX 301-791-3732

Mason Art Inc.

Furniture
979 3rd Ave.
New York, NY 10022
Phone 212-371-6868
FAX 212-371-6597

Master Woodcarver

Reproduction Furniture, Moulding, Mantels
103 Corinne Dr.
Pennington, NJ 08534

Send $7.00 for Catalog/Information

Mail Order Available
Phone 609-737-9364

Masterworks

Rockers, Chairs, Beds, Porch Swings, Tables, Chaises

PO Box M
Marietta, GA 30061

Send $2.00 for Catalog/Information

Phone 404-423-9000

Matteograssi SPA

Italian Furniture

Via S. Caterina Da Siena, 26
23066 Mariano Comense (CO)
Italy

Phone 011-39-31/745040
FAX 011-39-31/748388

Maurice Lepine Ltd.

Furniture

1535 Lepine St.
St. Joliette
Que., CAN J6E 4B8
Canada

Phone 514-756-1059
FAX 514-756-4457

Maxalto SPA

Italian Furniture

Strada provinciale
22060 Novedrate (CO)
Italy

Phone 011-39-31/790003
FAX 011-39-31/79-599

Mayan Marble & Onyx Ltd.

Furniture - Marble, Onyx

99 Wyse Rd., Suite 350
Dartmouth
N.S. CAN B3L 1L9
Canada

Phone 902-464-0722
FAX 902-463-0159

Mayhew

Outdoor Furniture

509 Park Ave.
New York, NY 10022

Mail Order Available

Phone 212-759-8120

Maynard House Antiques

Reproduction Country Sofas & Wing Chairs

11 Maynard Street
Westborough, MA 01581

Send $2.00 for Catalog/Information

Mail Order Available

Phone 508-366-2073

McCraig & Company

Furniture

911 Lady Street
Columbia, SC 29201

Phone 803-254-5994

McFlem Furniture Mfg.

Furniture

200 W. 138th St.
Los Angeles, CA 90061

Phone 213-532-3262
FAX 213-532-2685

Meadow Craft

Shaker Furniture

PO Box 100
Rose Hill, NC 28458

Send $2.00 for Catalog/Information

Mail Order Available

Credit Cards VISA/MC

Phone 919-289-3195

Mecklenburg Furniture Shops

Major Brand Furniture

520 Providence Rd.
Charlotte, NC 28207

Catalog/Information Available Free

Mail Order Available

Phone 704-333-5891
Toll Free 800-328-7283

The Complete Sourcebook

Mendes Antiques

Antique American 18th & 19th Century Furniture
Blanding Rd., Rt. 44
Rehoboth, MA 02769

Catalog/Information Available Free

Mail Order Available

Phone 508-336-7381

Menuiserie Joliette Inc.

Furniture
371 Rue Joliette
Sept-Iles
Que., CAN G4R 1B1
Canada

Phone 418-962-2627

FAX 418-962-5637

Mereway Developments Ltd.

Bedroom Furniture
97 Amington Rd.
Yardley, Birmingham
B25 8EP
Great Britain

Phone 011-44-21/7067844

Merritt's Antiques Inc.

Reproduction Furniture
PO Box 277
Douglassville, PA 19518

Send $3.00 for Catalog/Information

Mail Order Available

Phone 215-689-9541

Mersman Waldron Furniture

Furniture
Somers Corp.
500 W. Wayne St.
Celina, OH 45822

Phone 419-586-2351

FAX 419-586-3234

Metalliform Ltd.

Livingroom, Diningroom Furniture
Chambers Rd., Holyland
Barnsley, S Yorkshire
S74 0EZ
Great Britain

Phone 011-44-226/350555

Metropolitan Furniture Corp.

Furniture
1635 Rollins Rd.
Burlingame, CA 94010

Phone 415-697-7900

FAX 415-697-2818

Michael Camp

Handmade Furniture
495 Amerlia
Plymouth, MI 48170

Send $3.00 for Catalog/Information

Mail Order Available

Phone 313-459-1190

Michael M. Reed

Windsor Chairs
132 Morey Rd.
Sharon, CT 06069

Mail Order Available

Phone 203-364-5444

Michael's Classic Wicker

Reproduction Wicker Furniture
620-1/2 Westknoll Dr.
W. Hollywood, CA 90069

Send $5.00 for Catalog/Information

Mail Order Available

Phone 213-854-6035

MidAmerica Furniture

Major Brand Furniture
PO Box 112 , 100 E. Lincoln
Hamburg, AR 71646

Catalog/Information Available Free

Mail Order Available

Credit Cards VISA/MC

Phone 501-853-9093
Toll Free 800-259-7897
FAX 501-853-8854

Minic Custom Woodwork, Inc.

Drape Tables - Ovals, Oblongs, Squares, Octagons
524 East 117th St.
New York, NY 10035

Phone 212-410-5500
FAX 212-410-5533

Minnetonka Woodcraft Co.

Custom Cabinets, Furniture
6022 Culligan Way
Minnetonka, MN 55343

Phone 612-935-9595
FAX 612-935-9493

Minton Co.

Architectural Millwork
599 W. Evelyn Ave.
Mountain View, CA 94040

Phone 415-968-9800

Mirroline Design Ltd.

Furniture, Mirrors & Glass
PO Box 66
Huttonville
Ont., CAN L0J 1B0
Canada

Phone 416-673-8754
FAX 416-455-5709

Modern Classic Furniture Inc.

Furniture
Rte.7, Box 30
Taylorsville, NC 28681

Phone 704-632-7781

Modern Reed & Rattan Co. Inc.

Rattan Furniture
79 Alexander Ave.
Bronx, NY 10454

Phone 212-665-1717

Modern of Marshfield, Inc.

Upholstered Furniture
137 W. 9th St.
Marshfield, WI 54449

Phone 715-387-1181

Mohawk Furniture Inc.

Furniture
5 Mill St.
Broadalbin, NY 12025

Phone 518-883-3424

Molteni & C. SPA

Italian Furniture
Via Rossini, 50
20034 Giussano (MI)
Italy

Phone 011-39-362/851334
FAX 011-39-362852337

Mona Liza Fine Furniture Inc.

Antiques and Antique Reproduction Furniture
23 Meadow Street
Brooklyn, NY 11206

Phone 718-456-8113
FAX 718-417-0494

Mondo

Italian Furniture
Viale Brianza, 16
22060 Carugo (CO)
Italy

Phone 011-39-31/761717
FAX 011-39-31/763322

The Complete Sourcebook

6 - 53

Monzie Joinery Ltd.

Bedroom, Livingroom, Diningroom Furniture
Monzie, Crieff
Perth
PH7 4HE
Great Britain

Phone 011-44-764/4877

Moosehead Mfg. Co.

Furniture
Chapin Ave.
Monson, ME 04464

Phone 207-997-3621

Moultrie Manufacturing Co.

Outdoor Furniture Gates & Fencing
PO Box 1179
Moultrie, GA 31776-1179

Send $3.00 for Catalog/Information

Mail Order Available

Credit Cards MC/VISA/Check/Money Order

Phone 912-985-1312
Toll Free 800-841-8674
FAX 912-985-7245

Murphy Bed Company Inc.

Beds
42 Central Avenue
Farmingdale, NY 11735

Mail Order Available

Phone 516-543-0234
Toll Free 800-845-2337
FAX 516-543-8401

Murphy Furniture Mfg. Co., Inc.

Cedar Chests, Wardrobes
PO Box 1068
Jasper, AL 35502

Phone 205-221-5340

Murrow Furniture Galleries, Inc.

Major Brand Furniture
PO Box 4337
Wilmington, NC 28406

Catalog/Information Available Free

Phone 919-799-4010
Toll Free 800-334-1614
FAX 919-791-2791

Nagykery Imports, Ltd.

Anituqe Furniture - Reproductions and Decorative Accessories
148 39th St.
Brooklyn, NY 11232

Phone 718-499-3511
FAX 718-499-4099

Nathan Furniture Ltd.

Livingroom & Diningroom Furniture
Angel Rd.
London N18 3AD
Great Britain

Phone 011-44-81/8034241

National Furniture Co.

Furniture
PO Box 867
Mount Airy, NC 27030

Phone 919-374-5001
FAX 919-374-6285

Natuzzi Americas Inc.

Italian Furniture
PO Box 2438
High Point, NC 27261

Phone 919-887-8300
FAX 919-887-8500

Neil Rogers Interiors

Bedroom, Livingroom, Diningroom Furniture
Unit 23, Abbeville Mews
88 Clapham Pk Rd., London
SW4 7BX
Great Britain

Phone 011-44-71/4981911

Furniture

New West of Jackson — Northern Rustic Furniture

New West of Jackson

Western Style Home Furnishings
Jackson, WY
Send $3.00 for Catalog/Information
Phone 307-733-5490
Toll Free 800-653-2391

Nichols & Stone

Furniture
232 Sherman St.
Gardner, MA 01440
Phone 508-632-2770

Niedermaier Design Inc.

Furniture, Accessories, Lighting
2828 N. Paulina
Chicago, IL 60657
Phone 312-528-8123
FAX 312-528-0236

Niermann Weeks

Furniture and Accessories
PO Box 6671
Annapolis, MD 21401
Send $25.00 for Catalog/Information
Phone 410-224-0133

Nimetz Woodworking Mfg. Co.

Furniture
56-4742 Pasqua St.
Regina
Sask., CAN S4S 6N8
Canada
Phone 306-757-3811

Nolarec Industries, Inc.

Table Lamps, Planters, Furniture Accessories
N. Pinehurst Rd.
Aberdeen, NC 28315
Phone 919-944-7187

Noritage Inc.

Furniture
220 N. Bellevue
PO Box 125
Embarrass, WI 54933
Phone 715-823-3191
FAX 715-823-1309

Norman's Handmade Reproductions

Pine, Mahogany, Cherry Pencil Post Beds
Rt. 6 Box 695
Dunn, NC 28334
Send $3.00 for Catalog/Information
Credit Cards Accepted
Phone 919-892-4349

North Carolina Furniture Showroom

Major Brand Furniture
3899 Northwest 19th St.
Lauderdale Lakes, FL 33311
Catalog/Information Available Free
Toll Free 800-227-6060

North Hickory Furniture Co.

Furniture
PO Drawer 759
Hickory, NC 28601
Phone 704-328-1841
FAX 704-322-1450

North Woods Chair Shop

Canterbury Rockers, Chairs, Stools
237 Old Tilton Rd.
Canterbury, NH 93224
Send $2.00 for Catalog/Information
Mail Order Available
Credit Cards MC/VISA
Phone 603-783-4595

Northern Rustic Furniture

Willow and Rustic Furniture
Box 11
Harrisville, MI 48740
Send $2.00 for Catalog/Information

The Complete Sourcebook

6 - 55

Northwoods Furniture Co.

Furniture
PO Box 112
St. Michael, MN 55376
Send $2.00 for Catalog/Information
Phone 612-497-3865

Norwalk Furniture Corp.

Furniture
100 Furniture Parkway
Norwalk, OH 44857
Phone 419-668-4461

Nu-Line Industries

Juvenile Furniture
PO Box 217
Suring, WI 54174
Phone 414-842-2141

O'Connor's Cypress Woodworks

Deacon Benches, Porch Swings, Gingerbread
1259 Lions Club Rd.
Scott, LA 70583
Send $2.00 for Catalog/Information
Phone 318-264-9527
Toll Free 800-786-1051
FAX 318-264-9527

O.W. Lee Co., Inc.

Wrought Iron, Outdoor Furniture
930 N. Todd Ave.
Azusa, CA 91702
Phone 818-334-1218
FAX 818-969-5994

Oak Craft Inc.

Early American Reproduction Furniture
26 Jackson St.
Lowell, MA 01852
Phone 508-454-7809

Oak Land Furniture Manufacturing

Furniture
Industrial Park Road
Okolana, MS 38860
Toll Free 800-321-8247

Oakline Chair Co. Inc.

Rockers, Adirondack Lawn Chairs
Hwy. 31 N.
PO Box 1698
Clanton, AL 35045
Phone 205-755-5552

Okla Homer Smith Furniture Mfg. Co.

Juvenile Furniture
PO Box 1148
Fort Smith, AR 72901
Phone 501-783-6191
FAX 501-783-5715

Old Hickory Furniture Co. Inc.

Handcrafted Hickory Furniture - Chairs, Tables, Beds, Rockers, Stools
403 S. Noble St.
Shelbyville, IN 46176
Phone 317-398-3151
Toll Free 800-232-2275
FAX 317-398-2275

Old Road Furniture Co.

Antique Reproductions of Amish Furniture
3457 Old Philadelphia Pike, PO Box 419
Intercourse, PA 17534-0419
Send $5.00 for Catalog/Information
Mail Order Available
Credit Cards MC/VISA
Toll Free 800-762-7171

Old Western Paint Co. Inc.

Paint, Varnish
2001 W. Barberry Pl.
Denver, CO 80204
Phone 303-825-5147
FAX 303-825-2437

Furniture

Olde Mill House Shoppe – Outer Bank Pine Products

Olde Mill House Shoppe

Country Furniture, Braided Rugs, Bath Accessories

105 Strasburg Pike
Lancaster, PA 17602

Send $1.00 for Catalog/Information

Phone 717-299-0678

Ole Timey Furniture Co.

Order Direct - Early American Style Furniture, Post Beds

PO Box 1165
Smithfield, NC 27577

Mail Order Available

Phone 919-965-6555
FAX 919-965-6555

Olympic Custom Furniture, Ltd.

Manufacturer - Custom Furniture

35-01 Queens Blvd.
Long Island City, NY 11101

Phone 718-392-1600
FAX 718-392-2309

Omega Furniture

Custom Sofas

Delamare Road
Chestnut, Herts
EN8 9TF
Great Britain

Phone 011-44-992/626682

Options Bedrooms Ltd.

Bedroom, Livingroom, Diningroom Furniture

Unit B, Roan Ind Est
Mortimer Rd., Mitcham, Surrey
CR4 3HS
Great Britain

Phone 011-44-81/6851525

Original Arts Mfg. Corp.

Furniture

2301 Edgar Rd. E.
Linden, NJ 07036

Phone 201-925-1900

Origines

Fireplace Stone, Marble, Terracotta Tile

14, Porte d'Epernon
Maulette 78550 Houdan
France

Phone 011-33-1-30881515
FAX 011-33-1-30881180

Orleans Carpenters

Reproduction Colonial & Shaker Furniture

PO Box 217
Orleans, MA 02653

Send $3.00 for Catalog/Information

Credit Cards Accepted

Phone 508-255-2646

Osborne Wood Products Inc.

Hardwood Pencil Post Beds - Pine, Oak, Maple, Cherry, Mahogany, Walnut

Hwy. 123, Rt. 3
PO Box 551
Toccoa, GA 30577

Catalog/Information Available Free

Mail Order Available

Credit Cards
MC/VISA/DISCOVER/Check/MO

Phone 706-886-1065
Toll Free 800-849-8876
FAX 706-886-8526

Ottawa Brass Ltd.

Brass Beds & Coffee Tables

20 D Enterprise Ave.
Ottawa
Ont., CAN K2G 0A6
Canada

Phone 613-226-1564

Outer Bank Pine Products

Pine Corner Cabinets

Box 9003
Lester, PA 19113

Send $1.00 for Catalog/Information

Credit Cards Accepted

Phone 215-534-1234

Furniture

The Complete Sourcebook

6 - 57

Oxford Leather

Reproduction Leather Furniture

PO Box 9098
Hickory, NC 28603

Mail Order Available

Phone 704-256-6888

FAX 704-256-4250

Ozark Wood Products

Outdoor Furniture

Hwy. 14 E.,PO Box 41
Mountains View, AR 72560

Phone 501-269-4391

Pacific Design Furniture

Furniture

11037 Lockport Place
Santa Fe Springs, CA 90670

Phone 310-944-0060

FAX 310-941-7831

Palazzetti Inc.

Imported Furniture, Rugs

515 Madison Ave.
New York, NY 10022

Mail Order Available

Phone 212-832-1199

FAX 212-832-1459

Pallavisini Sedersi

Italian Furniture

Via F. Di Manzano 16
33044 Manzano (UD)
Italy

Phone 011-39-432/761030

FAX 011-39-432/750830

Palliser Furniture Corp.

Manufacturer - Furniture

PO Box 2931
Fargo, ND 58102

Phone 701-280-2012

Paramount Mfg. Co.

Furniture

33 Middlesex Ave.
Box 559
Wilmington, MA 01887

Phone 617-729-3200

Park Place

*Victorian Porch Furniture , Casual
Indoor/Outdoor Furniture*

2251 Wisconsin Ave. NW
Washington DC 20007

Send $4.00 for Catalog/Information

Mail Order Available

Phone 202-342-6294

FAX 202-342-9255

Parkway Furniture Galleries

*Name Brand Furniture - Up To %50
Discount - Ship Anywhere*

PO Box 2450, Hwy. 105 South
Boone, NC 28607

Phone 704-264-3993

FAX 704-262-3530

Pashayan

*18th Centry French Reproduction
Furniture*

1137-A 2nd Ave. #314
New York, NY 10022-1465

Patrician Furniture Co.

Furniture

PO Box 2353
High Point, NC 27261

Phone 919-885-6186

Pearson Furniture

Furniture

PO Box 2838
High Point, NC 27261

Phone 910-882-8135

Toll Free 800-243-1822

Furniture

Pecan States Industries, Inc.

Furniture

132 Frances
Alexandria, LA 71301

Phone 318-487-0616

Pegram Contracts Ltd.

*Bedroom, Livingroom, Diningroom
Furniture*

181 Royal College St.
London NW1 0SG
Great Britain

Phone 011-44-71/2671115

Pel Ltd.

*Bedroom, Livingroom, Diningroom
Furniture*

Rood End Rd.
Oldbury, Warley, W Midlands
B69 4HN
Great Britain

Phone 011-44-21/5523377

Pennsylvania House Inc.

Furniture

Old Charlotte Hwy.
PO Box 5010
Monroe, NC 28110

Phone 704-289-8461

Period Furniture Hardware

Reproduction Antique Lighting Fixtures

123 Charles St.
Boston, MA 02114

Send $4.00 for Catalog/Information

Mail Order Available

Phone 617-227-0758

FAX 617-227-2987

Pete Bissonette & Company

Steel Beds

900 E. Wayzatta Blvd.
Wayzatta, MN 55391

Catalog/Information Available Free

Mail Order Available

Phone 612-449-0639

Peter Franklin Cabinetmakers

Cabinetry

1 Cottage St.
Box 1166H
East Hampton, MA 01027

Send $3.00 for Catalog/Information

Mail Order Available

Phone 413-527-4004

Peter Kramer, Cabinetmaker

Furniture

Gay & Jett Sts.
PO Box 232
Washington, VA 22747

Send $5.00 for Catalog/Information

Mail Order Available

Phone 703-675-3625

Peter-Revington Corp.

Furniture

1100 N. Washington
Delphi, IN 46923

Phone 317-564-2586

Pettigrew Associates Inc.

Furniture, Lighting, Fabric, Wallcovering

PO Box 58055
Dallas, TX 75258

Phone 214-745-1351

Pilliod Cabinet Co.

Tables, Bedroom Furniture, Wall Units

302 Church St.
Swanton, OH 43558

Phone 419-826-3565

Pine & Design Imports

Antique Pine Furniture

738 North Highway 17-92
Longwood, FL 32750

Phone 407-332-6800

FAX 407-332-4457

Furniture

The Complete Sourcebook

6 - 59

Pine Tradition Ltd.

Furniture
115 Bowers Rd., Unit 7
Concord
Ont., CAN L4K 1H7
Canada

Phone 416-738-6167

Pioneer Furniture Mfg. Co.

Furniture
Congress Pkwy.
PO Box 705
Athens, TN 37303

Phone 615-745-9127
FAX 615-745-7409

Pipe Casual

PVC Pipe Outdoor Furniture - Factory Direct
2007 S.W. College Rd.
Ocala, FL 32647-3062

Phone 904-867-5822

Pira Ltd.

Livingroom & Diningroom Furniture, Lighting
10 Hoxton Sq.
London N1 6NU
Great Britain

Phone 011-44-71/7397865

Plantation Patterns Inc.

Iron Furniture
PO Box 1357
Birmingham, AL 35201

Phone 205-853-2228

Plaza Furniture Gallery

Furniture - Nationwide Delivery
PO Box 747
241 Timberbrook Lane
Granite Falls, NC 28630

Mail Order Available

Phone 704-396-8150

Pocahontas Furniture Mfg. Co.

Furniture
Hwy. 67 S
Pocahontas, AR 72455

Phone 501-892-5070

Poltronova Design SRL

Italian Furniture
Via Prov Pratese, 23
51037 Montale (PT)
Italy

Phone 011-39-574/718351
FAX 011-39-574/711251

Pompeii

Manufacturer - Indoor/Outdoor Furniture
255 N.W. 25th St.
Miami, FL 33127

Phone 305-576-3600
FAX 305-576-2339

Pottery Barn

Tables, Chairs, Furnishings
Mail Order Department
PO Box 7044
San Francisco, CA 94120-7044

Catalog/Information Available Free

Mail Order Available

Credit Cards VISA/MC/AMEX

Toll Free 800-922-5507

Precision Furniture Corp.

Wrought Iron Furniture
1838 Adee Ave.
Bronx, NY 10469

Phone 212-379-5200

Prestige Mfg. Co.

Manufacturer - Furniture
2384 Vans Ave.
Jacksonville, FL 32207

Phone 904-398-1535

Furniture

Priba Furniture

Order by Phone - Major Brand Furniture
210 Stage Coach Trail
Greensboro, NC 27409

Mail Order Available

Credit Cards VISA/MC

Phone 919-855-9034

FAX 919-855-1370

Primiani Chesterfield Inc.

Furniture
10820 Ave. Racette
Montreal-Nond
Que., CAN H1G 5H6
Canada

Phone 514-323-1033

FAX 514-328-7688

Prince Albert's

Victorian Style Furniture
431 Thames St.
New Port, RI 02840

Phone 401-848-5327

Pulaski Furniture Corp.

Manufacturer - Furniture - Bedroom, Diningroom, Antique Reproductions
PO Box 1371
Pulaski, VA 24301

Phone 703-980-7330

FAX 703-980-4899

Quality Craft Inc.

Furniture
722 Trade St.
PO Box 31814
Morristown, TN 37814

Phone 615-586-8236

Quality Dinettes Incorporated

Country, Contemporary Traditional Dinettes
PO Box 197
Arley, AL 35541

Toll Free 800-223-4041

Quality Furniture Co.

Manufacturer - Bedroom Furniture
79 Alabama Street
Tallapoosa, GA 30176-0025

Phone 404-574-2388

Toll Free 800-448-9888

FAX 404-574-5526

Quality Furniture Market

Furniture - Major Brands - Nationwide Delivery
2034 Hickory Blvd. SW
Lenoir, NC 28645

Mail Order Available

Credit Cards VISA/MC

Phone 704-728-2946

FAX 704-726-0226

Quebeco Furniture Inc.

Furniture
24 Place Sicard, Que, Ste. Therese
De Blainville
CAN J6E 3X6
Canada

Phone 514-437-3670

Queen Ann Furniture Co., Inc.

18th Century Style Furniture
Rt. 2, Box 427
Trinity, NC 27370

Credit Cards VISA/MC/Check/Money Order

Phone 919-431-2562

R. Wagner Company

Painted Furniture
205 NW 10th
Portland, OR 97209

Send $50.00 for Catalog/Information

Mail Order Available

Phone 503-224-7036

Rackstraw Ltd.

Period Wood Furniture - Mahogany, Oak
Droitwich
Worcs WR9 0NX
Great Britain
Phone 011-44-905/795050

Ralston Furniture Reproductions

18th Century Reproduction Furniture
Box 144
Cooperstown, NY 13326
Send $3.00 for Catalog/Information
Phone 607-547-2675

Ranch Wood Products Inc.

Furniture
PO Box 1089
Smithfield, NC 27577
Phone 919-934-3852

Randall Tysinger

Antique and Reproduction Furniture
609 National Highway
PO Box 2066
Thomasville, NC 27361
Phone 919-475-7174
FAX 919-475-5604

Rattan Boricua Mfg. Corp.

Rattan Furniture
Apdo 7977
Caguas, PR 00625
Phone 809-790-9527

Rattan Interiors

Traditional, Contemporary Rattan Furniture
13120 Saticoy St.
North Hollywood, CA 91605
Phone 818-759-0034
FAX 818-759-0035

Rattan Specialties Santa Fe

Furniture
8222 Allport Ave.
Santa Fe Springs, CA 90670
Toll Free 800-826-1808

Rebwood Inc.

Bedroom Furniture
Industrial Park
PO Box 127
Headland, AL 36345
Phone 205-693-3369

Redbridge Furniture

Leather Furniture
Vale Street
Breightmet, Bolton
BL2 6QF
Great Britain

Catalog/Information Available Free
Phone 011-44-204/31875
FAX 011-44-204/31875

Regal Furniture Mfg. Ltd.

Furniture
925 Logan Ave.
Winnipeg
Man., CAN R5E 3L9
Canada
Phone 204-775-0313

Reid Classics

Reproduction Beds
3600 Old Shell Rd.
PO Box 8383
Mobile, AL 36608
Send $3.00 for Catalog/Information
Phone 205-342-1414

Renaissance Furniture and Cabinetry

Reproduction Furniture & Cabinetry
PO Box 207
Chester, CT 06412
Mail Order Available
Phone 203-526-4275

Renray Group Ltd.

*Bedroom, Livingroom, Diningroom
Furniture*
Road Five, Winsford Ind Est
Winsford, Cheshire
CW7 3RB
Great Britain
Phone 011-44-606/593456

Rex Furniture Co. Inc.

Oak Country Dining Room Furniture
3738 Rex Rd.
PO Box 488
Rex, GA 30273
Phone 404-474-8701
FAX 404-474-8337

Rhine-Castle Company

Order by Phone - Name Brand Furniture
PO Box 5165
Hickory, NC 28603
Toll Free 800-934-9699

Rhoney Furniture

Major Brand Furniture
2401 Highway 70 SW
Hickory, NC 28602

Catalog/Information Available Free

Mail Order Available
Phone 704-328-2034
FAX 704-328-2036

Richard B. Zarbin & Associates

Furniture
225 West Hubbard St.
Chicago, IL 60610

Mail Order Available
Phone 312-527-1570

Richard Brooks Company

Custom Cabinets
15 Kensico Dr.
Mt. Kisco, NY 10549
Toll Free 800-244-5432
FAX 914-666-2029

Richard Gervais Collection

Bamboo Furniture & Accessories
1547-B California St.
San Francisco, CA 94109
Phone 415-885-1360

Richardson Bros.

Manufacturer - Furniture - Diningrooms
PO Box 907
Sheboygan Falls, WI 53085
Phone 414-467-4631

River Bend Chair Company

Reproduction Windsor Chairs
PO Box 856
West Chester, OH 45069
Phone 513-554-4900

River East Custom Cabinets

Cabinets
824 Starr Ave.
Toledo, OH 43605-2362
Phone 419-691-4915

Riverside Furniture Corp.

Furniture
PO Drawer 1427
Fort Smith, AR 72902
Phone 501-785-8100

Robert Barrow Furniture Maker

Windsor Chairs
412 Thames Rd.
Bristol, RI 02809

Send $3.00 for Catalog/Information

Mail Order Available
Phone 401-253-4434

Robert M. Albrect Hardwood

Rare Wood for Furniture & Sculpture
18701 Parthenia St.
Northbridge, CA 91324

Send $1.00 for Catalog/Information

Mail Order Available
Phone 213-349-6500

Robert Whitley Studio

Furniture Designer - Custom Reproductions
6677 Laurel Rd., PO Box 69
Solebury, PA 18963
Send $4.00 for Catalog/Information
Phone 215-297-8452

Robert's

Outdoor Furniture
115 East Putnam Avenue
PO Box 433
Greenwich, CT 06836
Send $6.00 for Catalog/Information
Phone 203-869-4610
Toll Free 800-899-4610

Roberts Brass Company

Solid Brass Beds
22118 N.E. 66th Place
Redmond, WA 98053
Send $1.50 for Catalog/Information
Credit Cards VISA/MC
Phone 206-868-4012

Robertson Furniture Mfg. Inc.

Furniture
Box 112
Wilson, MI 49896
Phone 906-639-2151

Robinson Iron

Cast Iron Furniture - Garden Statuary, Lamp Posts (Offered to Architects, Landscape Architects)
Robinson Rd.
PO Box 1119
Alexander City, AL 35010
Catalog/Information Available Free
Phone 205-329-8486
Toll Free 800-824-2157
FAX 205-329-8960

Roche-Bobois

Contemporary Furniture
200 Madison
New York, NY 10016
Send $5.00 for Catalog/Information
Phone 212-725-5513
Toll Free 800-225-2050

Rockford Mills Furniture Co.

Handcrafted Oak Furniture
Rt 1
Box 124
Strasburg, OH 44680-0124
Send $3.00 for Catalog/Information

Roland Park Cabinet Inc.

Cabinets
3500 As St.
Baltimore, MD 21211-2310
Phone 301-889-3535

Room & Board

Handcrafted Comtemporary Style Furniture - Beds, Tables, Chairs
4600 Olson Memorial Hwy.
Minneapolis, MN 55422
Catalog/Information Available Free
Mail Order Available
Credit Cards VISA/MC
Phone 612-588-7525
Toll Free 800-486-6554
FAX 612-588-7971

Rose Hill Furniture

Wood & Laminated Occassional Tables
142 South Main
High Point, NC 27261
Phone 919-889-9927

Roses Wood Products Inc.

Furniture
Box 980 823 1/2 3rd St.
Clinton, IA 52732
Phone 319-242-7673
FAX 319-242-7722

Furniture

Rowal Custom Furniture

Furniture

2900 Vermont
Blue Island, VT 60406-1869

Phone 312-597-3367

Rowe Furniture Corp.

Manufacturer - Furniture

239 Rowan St.
Salem, VA 24153

Toll Free 800-334-7693

Royal Strathclyde Blindcraft Industries

Bedroom, Livingroom, Diningroom Furniture

Atlas Ind Est
Edgefauld Rd, Springburn, Glasgow
G21 1BP
Great Britain

Phone 011-44-41/5581485

Rubbermaid-Allibert Contract

Outdoor Causual Furniture

1200 Hwy 27
South Stanley, NC 28164

Toll Free 800-346-2428

Rubee Furniture Mfg. Corp.

Furniture

2513 W. Cullerton
Chicago, IL 60608

Phone 312-376-8160

Russell Flooring Co.

Furniture

16128 St. Clair Ave.
Cleveland, OH 44110

Phone 216-531-4542

Rustic Furnishings

Hardwood Rustic Furniture

3280 Broadway
New York, NY 10027

Send $3.00 for Catalog/Information

Phone 212-926-3880

Sagga Furnishings Ltd.

Bedroom Furniture

Sagga Ho
Sandwich Ind Est, Sandwich, Kent
CT13 9LU
Great Britain

Phone 011-44-304/614001

Sak Industries Inc.

Wrought Iron Furniture

148 E. Olive St.
PO Box 725
Monrovia, CA 91016

Phone 818-359-5351

Salem Square

Furniture

108 Avondale St.
High Point, NC 27260

Phone 919-887-3416

Sampler Inc.

Cherry Reproduction Furniture

1 Railroad St.
PO Box 68
Homer, IN 46146

Phone 317-663-2233

Sandberg Furniture Mfg. Co.

Furniture

3251 Slauson Ave.
Los Angeles, CA 90058

Phone 213-582-0711
FAX 213-589-5507

Saporiti Italia SPA

Italian Furniture

Via Gallarate, 23
21010 Besnate (VA)
Italy

Phone 011-39-331/274198
FAX 011-39-331/275545

Furniture

The Complete Sourcebook

6 - 65

Saraband Furniture Co.

Bedroom, Livingroom, Diningroom Furniture
Rooksmoor Mills, Bath Rd.
Stroud, Glos
GL5 5ND
Great Britain
Phone 011-44-453/872577

Sarita Furniture

Red Cedar Garden Furniture
314 E. Holly, Box 9754
Bellingham, WA 98227-9754

Send $2.00 for Catalog/Information

Sawtooth Valley Woodcrafts

Log Furniture
4600 Ginzel
Boise, ID 83703

Catalog/Information Available Free
Phone 208-342-5265

Scandecor

English Leather Furniture
20 Castle St.
Brighton
BN1 2HD
Great Britain
Phone 011-44-273/820208

Scandinavian Design

Scandinavian Style Furniture
127 E. 59 St., Room 203
New York, NY 10022
Phone 212-755-6078
FAX 212-888-3928

Scappini Giovanni & C. SAS

Italian Furniture
Via Montello 5
37051 Bovolone (VR)
Italy
Phone 011-39-438/840446
FAX 011-39-4387103637

Schnadig Corp.

Furniture
4820 W. Belmont Ave.
Chicago, IL 60641
Phone 312-545-2300

Schweiger Industries Inc.

Manufacturer - Furniture
116 W. Washington St.
Jefferson, WI 53549
Phone 414-674-2440

Scott's Hardware Inc.

Hardware for Antique Furniture
705 N. 10th Street
Ozark, MO 65721

Send $2.00 for Catalog/Information

Mail Order Available

Credit Cards VISA/MC
Phone 417-581-6525

Scully & Scully

Reproduction Georgian Furniture & Accessories
506 Park Ave.
New York, NY 10022

Send $2.00 for Catalog/Information

Credit Cards VISA/MC/AMEX
Phone 212-755-2590

Sebastian De Lorenzis Custom Furniture

Furniture
505 Hespeler Hwy.
Cambridge
Ont., CAN N1R 6J2
Canada
Phone 519-623-0210

Second Impression Antiques

Antique Wicker Furniture
84 Bay St.
Watch Hill, RI 02891

Send $5.00 for Catalog/Information

Mail Order Available
Phone 401-596-1296

Segal Furniture Co.

Furniture

8211 Sea Island Way
Richmond B.C.
CAN V6X 2W3
Canada

Phone 604-278-9671
FAX 604-278-1233

Selva SPA

Italian Furniture

Via L. Negrelli, 4
39100 Bolzano (BZ)
Italy

Phone 011-39-471/240111
FAX 011-39-471/240112

Selzer Enterprises Inc.

Wood Porch Furniture Kits

PO Box 6324
Charlottesville, VA 22906

Phone 804-293-3114

Seventh Heaven

Restored Antique Beds

Chirk Mill
Chirk, CLWYD, North Wales
LL14 5BU
Great Britain

Phone 011-44-691/777622
FAX 011-44-691/777313

Seybold Industries Inc.

Wood Chairs

PO Box 508
Winter Park, FL 32790

Phone 305-628-5070

Shaffield Industries Inc.

Furniture

390 Sewell Dr.
Sparta, TN 38583

Phone 615-738-3300
FAX 615-738-3300

Shaker Carpenter Shop

Furniture

8267 Oswego Rd.
Liverpool, NY 13090

Send $2.00 for Catalog/Information

Mail Order Available

Phone 315-652-7778

Shaker Shops West

Shaker Furniture

5 Inverness Way
PO Box 487
Inverness, CA 94937

Send $3.00 for Catalog/Information

Mail Order Available

Credit Cards VISA/MC/AMEX

Phone 415-669-7256
Toll Free 800-474-2537
FAX 415-669-7327

Shannon Chair

Chairs

PO Box 589
Houston, MS 38851

Phone 601-456-3056

Shaw Furniture Galleries

Furniture

PO Box 576
Randleman, NC 27317

Catalog/Information Available Free

Mail Order Available

Credit Cards Accepted

Phone 919-498-2628
Toll Free 800-334-6799

Shaw's Custom Cabinets

Custom Cabinets

Rte 3
Washington, MO 63090-9803

Phone 314-239-6506

Furniture

Sheffield Chair Co.

Furniture - Chairs, Rockers, Ottomans, Loveseats, Sectionals

2100 E. 38th St.
PO Box 58812
Los Angeles, CA 90058

Phone 213-232-4161
FAX 213-233-8020

Shelby Williams Industries, Inc.

Wicker and Rattan Furniture

PO Box 1028
5303 E. Tenn Blvd.
Morristown, TN 37816-1028

Phone 615-586-7000
FAX 615-586-2260

Shermag Inc.

Furniture

2171 King W., PO Box 2390
Sherbrooke
Que., CAN J1J 3Y3
Canada

Phone 819-566-1515

Sherrill Furniture Co.

Furniture

Box 189
Hickory, NC 28603

Phone 704-322-2640

Shushan Bentwood Co.

Chairs & Tables

Box E
Shushan, NY 12873

Phone 518-854-7814
FAX 518-854-9205

Sidex Furniture

Furniture

6035D La Grange Blvd. SW
Atlanta, GA 30336-2819

Phone 404-349-4803
Toll Free 800-742-4800

Silhoutte Antiques Inc.

Worldwide Shipping - Mahogany Chippendale Chair, Standard & Custom Size Tables

Mahogany Classics
380 Atlantic Avenue
Brooklyn, NY 11217

Catalog/Information Available Free

Phone 718-522-3114
FAX 718-965-3815

Silik SPA

Italian Furniture

Alan Goldreich, Export Manager
22060 Cantu' (CO)
Via Anglieri, 10
Italy

Phone 011-39-31/730000
FAX 011-39-31/732666

Simmons Juvenile Products Co. Inc.

Juvenile Furniture

613 E. Beacon Ave.
New London, WI 54961

Phone 414-982-2140
FAX 414-982-5052

Simms & Thapper Cabinetmakers

Early American Furniture Reproductions

PO Box 576
North Marshfield, MA 02059

Send $3.00 for Catalog/Information

Mail Order Available

Phone 617-585-8606

Simply Country Furniture

Country Style Furniture

HC 69 Box 147
Rover, AR 72860

Mail Order Available

Credit Cards VISA/MC/DISCOVER/AMEX

Phone 501-272-4794
Toll Free 800-572-1471
FAX 501-272-4140

Furniture

Sittin' Easy

Manufacturer - White Oak Outdoor Furniture

PO Box 180
Eagle Springs Rd.
Eagle Springs, NC 27242

Mail Order Available

Phone 910-673-0033
FAX 910-673-0034

Sklar-Peppler Inc.

Furniture

617 Victoria St. E
Whitby
Ont., CAN L1N 5S7
Canada

Phone 416-668-3315

Sligh Furniture

Home Office Furniture

1201 Industrial Ave.
Holland, MI 49423

Phone 616-392-7101
FAX 616-392-9495

Slumberland PLC

Bedroom, Livingroom, Diningroom Furniture

Salmon Fields Way
Salmon Fields, Royton, Oldham, Lancs
OL2 65B
Great Britain

Phone 011-44-61/6282898

Smed Mfg. Inc.

Furniture

4315 54th Ave. S.W.
Calgary
Alta., CAN T2C 2A2
Canada

Phone 403-279-2575
Toll Free 800-661-9163
FAX 403-236-2858

Smith & Hawken

Outdoor Furniture

117 E. Strawberry Dr.
Mill Valley, CA 94941

Catalog/Information Available Free

Phone 415-383-6399
Toll Free 800-776-3336

Smith & Watson

Fine English Furniture

305 East 63rd St.
New York, NY 10021

Phone 212-355-5615
FAX 212-371-5624

Smith Woodworks and Design

Shaker Furniture

101 Farmersville Rd.
Califon, NJ 07830

Send $2.00 for Catalog/Information

Phone 908-832-2723

Sobol House

Worldwide Delivery - Major Brand Furniture

Richardson Blvd.
Black Mountain, NC 28711

Mail Order Available

Phone 704-669-8031
FAX 704-669-7969

Solway Furniture Inc.

Furniture and Accessories

120 Perimeter Park Dr.
Knoxville, TN 37922

Toll Free 800-422-8011

Sound Wholesale

Cabinets

2102 Abernethy NE
Olympia, WA 98506-3713

Phone 206-459-7986

South Beach Furniture Company

Modern Furniture
180 N.E. 39th St.
Miami, FL 33137
Phone 305-576-4240

South West Joinery Co. Ltd.

Bedroom, Livingroom, Diningroom Furniture
Goodridge Ind Est
Goodridge Ave., Gloucester
GL2 6EB
Great Britain
Phone 011-44-452/306181

Southern Comfort Furniture

Furniture
12925 49th St. N
Clearwater, FL 34622
Phone 813-573-2771
FAX 813-572-4425

Southern Furniture

Furniture
349 Peachtree Hills Ave. NE
Suite C2
Atlanta, GA 30305
Phone 404-266-8557

Southern Kentucky Furniture

Furniture
840 US Hwy 31 W Byp
Bowling Green, KY 42101
Phone 502-842-1343

Southern Manor Furniture Corp.

Furniture
PO Box 1247
Thomasville, GA 31792
Phone 912-226-1281
FAX 912-226-1284

Southern Pine Manufacturing Inc.

Furniture
PO Box 505
Aliceville, AL 35442
Toll Free 800-367-0419

Southhampton Antiques

Video - American Victorian Oak Furniture
172 College Hwy. Rt. 10
Southampton, MA 01073
Catalog/Information Available Free
Send $25.00 for Catalog/Information
Phone 413-527-1022

Southwood Reproductions

Furniture
Box 2245
Hickory, NC 28608
Send $5.00 for Catalog/Information
Phone 704-465-1776

Spaulding Colonial Reproductions

Furniture
118 E. Main St.
Georgetown, MA 01833
Phone 508-352-2921

Spectrum Furniture Co. Inc.

Furniture
PO Box 1682
High Point, NC 27261
Phone 919-434-2111

Splendor in Brass

Brass Beds
123 Market St.
Harve de Grace, MD 21078
Send $6.00 for Catalog/Information
Phone 301-939-1312
FAX 301-939-9433

Spokane Moulding Corp.

Millwork, Moulding
PO Box 4348
Spokane, WA 99202
Phone 509-535-9027

St. Barthelemy Furniture Ltd.

Furniture
1200 Rue Prod'homme, St. Justin Co.
Maskinonge
Que., CAN J0K 2V0
Canada

Phone 819-227-2053

St. Charles Furniture

Order by Phone - Name Brand Furniture
PO Box 2144
High Point, NC 27261

Toll Free 800-545-3287

Stag Meredew Furniture Ltd.

*Bedroom, Livingroom, Diningroom
Furniture*
Haydn Rd.
Nottingham NG5 1DU
Great Britain

Phone 011-44-602/607121

Stanley Chair Co. Inc.

*Manufacturer - Furniture - Chairs, Sofas,
Rockers, Rattan*
5110 W. Hanna Ave.
Tampa, FL 33634

Phone 813-884-1436

Stanley Furniture

Wood Furniture
Route 57 West
Stanleytown, VA 24168

Send $1.00 for Catalog/Information

Phone 703-627-2000

FAX 703-629-4085

Staples & Co. Ltd.

*Bedroom, Livingroom, Diningroom
Furniture*
Windover Rd.
Huntingdon, Cambs
PE18 7EF
Great Britain

Phone 011-44-408/432222

Star Interiors Ltd.

Bedroom Furniture
Unit 59E, Milton Pk
Abingdon, Oxon
OX14 4RX
Great Britain

Phone 011-44-235/861212

Statesville Chair Company

18th Century Reproduction Chairs
PO Box 245
Hiddenite, NC 28636

Send $1.00 for Catalog/Information

Phone 704-632-1800

FAX 704-632-7833

Station West Custom Cabinets & Interiors

Cabinets
Kings Hwy.
Cape Girardeau, MO 63701-4315

Phone 314-335-3231

Statton Furniture Mfg. Co.

Cherry 18th Century Traditional Furniture
PO Box 530
Hagerstown, MD 21741-0530

Phone 301-739-0360

FAX 301-739-8421

Steel Gallery

Iron & Steel Fence Bed
1929 Greenville Avenue
Dallas, TX 75206

Credit Cards Accepted

Toll Free 800-484-9430

Stefanelli

Italian Furniture
Via Livornese Est, 43
56030 Perignano (PS)
Italy

Phone 011-39-587/616022

FAX 011-39-587/617450

Stephen Adams Furniture Makers

Antique Furniture Reproductions
Route 160
PO Box 130
Denmark, ME 04022
Send $4.00 for Catalog/Information
Mail Order Available

Phone 207-452-2444

Sterlingworth Corp.

Furniture
PO Box 610
Jamestwon, NY 14701

Phone 716-665-6115

Steve's Cabinet & Woodworking

Cabinets
3710A 100th SW
Tacoma, WA 98499

Phone 206-581-4311

Steven's Furniture Company, Inc.

Name Brand Furniture
1258 Hickory Blvd.
PO Box 270
Lenoir, NC 28645

Phone 704-728-5511

FAX 704-728-5518

Stone & Phillips co.

Furniture
1625 S. Magnolia Ave.
Monrovia, CA 91016

Phone 213-359-4571

Strafford House

Reproduction Pine Furniture
43 VanSant Rd.
New Hope, PA 18938
Send $2.00 for Catalog/Information

Phone 215-598-0259

Straw Hill Chairs

Windsor Chairs
Roger Scheffer
RFD 1, Straw Hill
West Unity, NH 03743
Send $2.00 for Catalog/Information

Phone 603-542-4367

Stuart Interiors

Bedroom, Livingroom, Diningroom Furniture, Lighting
Barrington Court, Barrington
LIminster, Somerset
TA19 0NQ
Great Britain

Phone 011-44-460/40349

Stuckey Brothers Furniture Co., Inc.

Order by Phone - Indoor and Outdoor Furniture
Rt.1, Box 527
Stuckey, SC 29554
Mail Order Available
Credit Cards Check/Money Order

Phone 803-558-2591

FAX 803-558-9229

Sulak's Cabinet Shop

Cabinets
Hwy 59 & Cemetery Rd.
Ganado, TX 77962

Phone 512-771-2322

Summer Hill Ltd.

Furniture, Fabric, Wallpaper
2682 Middlefield Rd.
Redwood City, CA 94063
Send $5.00 for Catalog/Information

Phone 415-363-2600

FAX 415-363-2680

Furniture

Summit Furniture — Taylor Woodcraft Inc.

Summit Furniture

Manufacturer - Indoor & Outdoor Teak Furniture
5 Harris Court, Bldg. W
Monterey, CA 93940

Phone 408-375-7811
FAX 408-375-0940

Sumter Cabinet Co.

Furniture
PO Box 100
Sumter, SC 29150

Phone 803-778-5444

Suter's Handcrafted Furniture

Furniture
2610 South Main St.
Harrisonburg, VA 22801

Toll Free 800-252-2131

Sutton-Coucil Furniture

Furniture
PO Box 3288
Wilmington, NC 28406

Send $5.00 for Catalog/Information

Phone 919-799-1990
Toll Free 800-334-8493

Swan Brass Bed

Manufacturer - Brass Beds
2417 E. 24th St.
Los Angeles, CA 90058

Send $5.00 for Catalog/Information

Mail Order Available

Phone 213-587-3101
FAX 213-589-2769

Sweet Water Ranch

Western Style Furniture
PO Drawer 398
Cody, WY 82414

Toll Free 800-357-2639

Sylmar Technology Ltd.

Bedroom, Livingroom, Diningroom Furniture
Member of the Jenna Group
10 Aldermans Hill, Palmers, Green London
N13 4PJ
Great Britain

Phone 011-44-81/4478090

Tad Taylor's Fantasy Furniture

Custom Juvenile Furniture
91 Lake Ave.
Greenwich, CT 06830

Catalog/Information Available Free

Phone 203-629-3990

Taos Drums

Drum Tables, Chairs, Pedestals, Lampshades
Box 1916
Taos, NM 87571

Phone 505-758-3796
FAX 505-758-9844

Taos Furniture

Worldwide Shipping - Solid Ponderosa Pine Furniture
PO Box 5555
Santa Fe, NM 87502

Catalog/Information Available Free

Mail Order Available

Phone 505-988-1229
Toll Free 800-443-3448
FAX 505-983-9375

Taylor Woodcraft Inc.

Hardwood Furniture
PO Drawer 245
South River Rd.
Malta, OH 43758

Phone 614-962-3741

The Complete Sourcebook

Telescope Casual Furniture

Outdoor Furniture

85 Church St.
PO Box 299
Granville, NY 12832

Phone 518-642-1100
FAX 518-642-2536

Tennessee Fabricating Co.

Garden Furniture

1822 Lantham St.
Memphis, TN 38106

Send $2.50 for Catalog/Information

Mail Order Available

Phone 901-948-3354

Tennessee Hardwood Co.

Furniture

4111 Dorman Dr.
Nashville, TN 37215

Phone 615-292-1796
FAX 615-292-9944

Texacraft Outdoor Furnishings

Manufacturer - Outdoor Furniture

5610 Parkersburg Dr.
Houston, TX 77036

Phone 713-977-9933
Toll Free 800-231-9790
FAX 713-953-7826

Thayer Coggin Inc.

Furniture

230 South Rd.
PO Box 5867
High Point, NC 27262

Phone 919-883-0111
FAX 919-841-6000

The Antique Catalog

Reproduction Furniture

207 N. Bowman Ave.
Merion Station, PA 19066

Send $3.00 for Catalog/Information

Phone 215-668-1138

The Bartley Collections Ltd.

*Finished & Unfinished Prices - Antique
Reproduction Furniture*

3 Airpark Dr.
Easton, MD 01506

Send $1.00 for Catalog/Information

Credit Cards VISA/MC

Phone 508-820-7722
Toll Free 800-787-2800
FAX 410-820-7059

The Bed Factory

*Order Factory Direct - Nationwide
Shipping - Beds - Wood, Iron, Brass*

PO Box 791
Westerville, OH 43081

Send $1.00 for Catalog/Information

Phone 614-299-4454

The Bedpost

Brass Beds & Accessories

32 South High Street
East Bangor, PA 18013

Send $2.00 for Catalog/Information

Phone 215-588-3824

The Berkline Corp.

Manufacturer - Chairs

1 Berkline Dr.
Morristown, TN 37813

Phone 615-585-1500

The Blacksmiths Shop

Garden Furniture

Stane Street
Halnaker, Chichester, West Sussex
PO18 0NQ
Great Britain

Phone 011-44-243/773431

Furniture

The Bombay Co.

Reproduction English Furniture

560 Bailey Ave.
Fortworth, TX 76161

Catalog/Information Available Free

Credit Cards VISA/MC/AMEX

Phone 817-870-1847

Toll Free 800-535-6876

The Brass Collection

Glass and Brass Tables

Melvin Wolf & Associates Inc.
1500 West Cortland Street
Chicago, IL 60622

Mail Order Available

Phone 312-252-2800

FAX 312-252-5231

The Butcher Company

Butcher Waxes for Antique Furniture and Floors

120 Bartlett St.
Marlborough, MA 01752

Toll Free 800-225-9475

The Caning Shop

Caning Supply

926 Gilman St.
Berkeley, CA 94710

Mail Order Available

Phone 510-527-5010

Toll Free 800-544-3373

The Childrens Furniture Co.

Furniture

PO Box 27157
Baltimore, MD 21230

Phone 410-625-7908

FAX 410-625-7813

The Farmhouse Collection

Custom Furniture

1220 Airport Way
Hailey, ID 83333

Phone 208-788-3187

FAX 208-788-4767

The Furniture Gallery

Furniture

581 Sixth Ave.
New York, NY 10011

Send $3.00 for Catalog/Information

Mail Order Available

Phone 212-675-7562

The Furniture Patch

Indoor & Outdoor Furniture

10283 Beach Drive SW
PO Box 4970
Calabash, NC 28467

Catalog/Information Available Free

Mail Order Available

Phone 910-579-2001

The Furniture Shoppe Inc.

Solid Wood Furniture

PO Box 703
Hudson, NC 28638

Catalog/Information Available Free

Phone 704-396-7850

The Golden Rabbit

Wooden Outdoor Furniture

115 S. Royal Street
Alexandria, VA 22314

Phone 703-276-1495

The Heveningham Collection

Indoor and Outdoor Wrought Iron Furniture

Peacock Cottage, Church Hill
Nether Wallop, Hampshire
SO20 8EY
Great Britain

Phone 011-44-264/781124

The Keeping Room

Furniture - Chairs, Tables, Post Beds, Chests, Armoires, Desks

8405 Richmond Hwy.
Alexandria, VA 22309

Send $6.00 for Catalog/Information

Phone 703-360-6399

The Complete Sourcebook

6 - 75

The Knoll Group

Furniture
105 Wooster St.
New York, NY 10012

Phone 212-343-4000
Toll Free 800-445-5045
FAX 212-343-4180

The Leather Gallery of Kentucky

Furniture & Rugs
228 E. Main
Georgetown, KY 40324

Send $3.00 for Catalog/Information

Mail Order Available

Phone 606-233-9924

The Lenox Shop

Early American Pine Furniture
Rt. 179 Box 64
Lambertville, NJ 08530

Send $1.00 for Catalog/Information

Credit Cards VISA/MC

Phone 609-397-1880

The Odd Chair Company

Nationwide & Overseas Shipping - Antique & Reproduction Upholstered Furniture
66 Derby Road
Longridge, Preston, Lancs
PR3 3FE
Great Britain

Phone 011-44-772/78262
FAX 011-44-772/784290

The Patio

Outdoor Furniture & Accessories
Box 925
San Juan Capistrano, CA 92693

Send $3.00 for Catalog/Information

Credit Cards VISA/MC/AMEX

Phone 714-661-3000
Toll Free 800-817-2846

The Rocker Shop of Marietta

Oak Chairs, Swings, Rockers
1421 White Circle Rd. NW
Marietta, GA 30064

Send $0.50 for Catalog/Information

Phone 404-427-3981

The Schoenheit Co.

Butcher Block Furniture
1600 S. Clinton St.
Chicago, IL 60616

Catalog/Information Available Free

Phone 312-421-1138

The Seraph Country Collection

Nationwide Delivery - Reproduction Furniture, Stencils, Lighting
5606 E. St. Rt. 37
Delaware, OH 43015

Send $10.00 for Catalog/Information

Mail Order Available

Credit Cards VISA/MC

Phone 614-369-1817
Toll Free 800-737-2742

The Shop Woodcrafters, Inc.

Handcrafted Shelves, Tables
PO Box 1450
Quitman, TX 75783

Mail Order Available

Credit Cards VISA/MC

Phone 903-763-5491
FAX 903-763-5766

The Sofa Factory

Furniture - Bedroom, Chairs, Dining, Sofas
Industrial House
Conway Street, Hove, Sussex
BN3 3LW
Great Britain

Phone 011-44-273/736782

Furniture

The Victorian Merchant

Reproduction Victorian Outdoor Furniture
PO Box 124
Wabash, IN 46992
Mail Order Available
Phone 219-563-1584

The Wicker Garden

Antique Wicker Furniture
1318 Madison Ave.
New York, NY 10128
Phone 212-410-7000

The Willow Place Inc.

Twig Furniture
362 S. Atlanta St.
Rosewell, GA 30075
Mail Order Available
Phone 404-587-5541

The Woodlawn Co.

Furniture
PO Box 78
Mt. Vernon, VA 22121
Send $2.00 for Catalog/Information
Mail Order Available

The Workbench

Furniture
470 Park Ave. South
New York, NY 10016
Send $2.00 for Catalog/Information
Mail Order Available
Phone 212-481-5454

Thee Cabinet Shop

Cabinets
2834 Colorado Ave.
Santa Monica, CA 90404-3631
Phone 213-828-8209

This End Up

Pine Handcrafted Furniture
1309 Exchange Alley
Richmond, VA 23219
Toll Free 800-627-5161

Thomas H. Kramer Inc.

Farmhouse Style Furniture
805 Depot Street
Commerce Park
Columbus, IN 47201
Catalog/Information Available Free
Mail Order Available
Credit Cards VISA/MC/Check/Money Order
Phone 812-379-4097
Toll Free 800-258-4097

Thomas Home Furnishings

Furniture
401 S. Hwy 321
Granite Falls, NC 28630
Phone 704-396-2147

Thomasville Furniture

Manufacturer - 1800 Collection Furniture - Bedroom, Livingroom, Diningroom
401 Main St.
PO Box 339
Thomasville, NC 27360
Send $3.00 for Catalog/Information
Phone 919-472-4000
Toll Free 800-833-2052
FAX 919-472-4072

Thos. Moser, Cabinetmakers

Solid Cherry Wood Furniture - Diningroom, Livingroom, Bedroom
415 Cumberland Ave.
Portland, ME 04101
Send $5.00 for Catalog/Information
Mail Order Available
Credit Cards VISA/MC/Check
Phone 207-774-3791

Three Mountaineers, Inc.

Reproduction Furnishings
PO Box 5354
Asheville, NC 28813
Phone 704-253-9851

Furniture

Through The Barn Door Furniture Co.

Rustic Furniture, Crate Furniture
PO Box 927
Henderson, NC 27536
Phone 919-492-9501

Thunderbird Furniture

Furniture
7501 E. Redfield Rd.
Scottsdale, AZ 85260
Phone 602-948-0600

Tidewater Workshop

*Order Direct - Cedar Garden Furniture -
Tables, Chairs, Benches*
PO Box 456
Oceanville, NJ 08231

Catalog/Information Available Free

Mail Order Available

Credit Cards MC/VISA
Phone 609-652-7821
Toll Free 800-666-8433
FAX 609-652-9008

Tiger Mountain Woodworks

Handcrafted Twig Furniture
PO Box 249
Scaly Mountain, SC 28775
Phone 704-526-5577

Tilden Industries (UK) Ltd.

Livingroom, Diningroom Furniture
5 Mead Ct., Cooper Rd.
Thornbury, Bristol
BS12 2UW
Great Britain
Phone 011-44-454/413111

Titan Wood Products Ltd.

Furniture - Finished & Unfinished
615 Orwell St.
Mississauga
Ont., CAN L5A 2W4
Canada
Phone 416-279-0571

Tomlinson Furniture

Furniture
201 E. Holly Hill Rd.
Thomasville, NC 27630
Phone 919-472-5005

Tony's Furniture Factory Outlet

Furniture
117 Albemarle - Troy Rd.
Troy, NC 27371-2903
Phone 919-572-2261

Tools of the Trade Inc.

Hardwood Furniture
PO Box 4533
Burlington, VT 05401
Phone 802-878-7168

Trainor Metal Products Co.

Patio Furniture
171 N.W. 16th St.
PO Box 1176
Boca Raton, FL 33429-1176
Phone 407-395-5520

Treasure Garden Inc.

Outdoor Patio Furniture
13401 Brooks Drive
Baldwin Park, CA 91706
Phone 818-448-7711
FAX 818-448-7790

Treske

Custom Wood Furniture
Station Works
Thirsk, N. Yorkshire
YO7 4NY
Great Britain
Phone 011-44-845/522000

Triad Furniture Discounters

*Order by Phone - Name Brand Furniture
Up To %50 Off*
3930 Hwy. 501
Myrtle Beach, SC 29572

Catalog/Information Available Free
Toll Free 800-323-8469

Furniture

Triangle Pacific Cabinet

Cabinets
800 E. Elm
McKinney, TX 75069-6811
Phone 214-542-0371

Trinity Furniture Inc.

Furniture
State Road 3106
PO Box 150
Trinity, NC 27370
Phone 919-472-6660

Trinity Wood Works

Cabinets
State Rd 46
Nashville, IN 47448
Phone 812-988-0688

Triplett's Furniture Fashions

Furniture
2084 Hickory Blvd.
Lenoir, NC 28645
Catalog/Information Available Free
Phone 704-728-8211

Tropitone

Outdoor Furniture
PO Box 3197
Sarasota, FL 34230
Send $3.00 for Catalog/Information
Phone 813-355-2715
Toll Free 800-876-7288
FAX 813-355-2692

Trott Furniture Co.

Walnut, Cherry, Mahogany Furniture
PO Box 7
Richlands, NC 28574
Send $5.00 for Catalog/Information
Mail Order Available
Phone 919-324-3660
Toll Free 800-682-0095

Turner Tolson, Inc.

Major Brand Furniture
PO Drawer 1507
New Bern, NC 28560
Send $2.00 for Catalog/Information
Credit Cards Accepted
Phone 919-638-2121
Toll Free 800-334-6616

Tysinger Furniture Gallery

Furniture
PO Box 10339
Wilmington, NC 28406
Catalog/Information Available Free
Phone 919-799-8137

Umphreds Inc.

Furniture
354 Preda St.
San Leandro, CA 94577
Phone 415-569-1865

Union City Chair Co.

Manufacturer - Wood Furniture
Market St.
Union City, PA 16438
Phone 814-438-3878
FAX 814-438-7536

Union-National

Furniture
226 Crescent St.
PO Box 1259
Jamestown, NY 14701-1259
Send $2.00 for Catalog/Information
Mail Order Available
Phone 716-487-1165

Unique Furnishings Ltd.

Furniture
12695 59th Way
Clearwater, FL 34620
Phone 813-530-3456

The Complete Sourcebook

Universal Bedroom Furniture Ltd.

Bedroom Furniture
1010 Cherokee Dr.
Morristown, TN 37814

Phone 615-586-7460

Valley Furniture Shop

Manufacturer - Reproduction Furniture
20 Stirling Rd.
Watchung, NJ 07060

Send $5.00 for Catalog/Information

Mail Order Available

Phone 908-756-7623
FAX 908-756-0382

Van Stee Corp.

Solid Wood Bedroom Furniture
200 Crescent St.
Jamestown, NY 14701

Phone 716-664-3900
FAX 716-664-3921

Vargas Furniture Manufacturing

Manufacturer - Unfinished Furniture
8255 Beach
Los Angeles, CA 90001-4014

Phone 213-588-3202

Varner Furniture Sales

Order by Phone - Furniture
2605 Uwharrie Rd.
High Point, NC 27263

Toll Free 800-334-3894

Vaughan Furniture Co. Inc.

Wood Furniture
Railroad Ave.
PO Box 1489
Galax, VA 24333

Phone 804-236-6111

Vermont Furniture Designs

*Solid Cherry - Mission Style Furniture -
Bedroom, Livingroom*
PO Box 4533
Burlington, VT 05406

Mail Order Available

Phone 802-655-6568
FAX 802-655-5979

Vermont Tubbs

*Order Direct - Hardwood Bedroom
Furniture*
PO Box 148
Forest Dale, VT 05745

Mail Order Available

Credit Cards Accepted

Phone 802-247-3414
Toll Free 800-327-7026
FAX 802-247-6395

Victor Stanley

Indoor and Outdoor Furniture
PO Box 144
Dunkirk, MD 20754

Catalog/Information Available Free

Phone 301-855-8300
Toll Free 800-368-2573

Victorian Attic

*Victorian Garden Furniture - Chairs,
Tables, Benches*
PO Box 831, Main Rd.
Mattituc, NY 11952

Send $1.00 for Catalog/Information

Phone 516-298-4789
FAX 516-298-4789

Victorian Brass Works Ltd.

Brass - Beds, Tables, Coat Trees
237 Doney Crescent
Concord
Ont., CAN L4K 1P6
Canada

Phone 416-669-4372

Furniture

Victorian Classics Inc. – Walpole Woodworkers

Victorian Classics Inc.

Manufacturer - Reproduction Furniture
PO Box 60
Montgomery, AL 36101
Toll Free 800-547-5240

Victorian Sampler

Furniture
707 Kautz Rd.
St. Charles, IL 60174

Send $3.50 for Catalog/Information

Mail Order Available
Phone 708-377-8000
FAX 708-377-8194

Victorian Showcase

19th Century Reproduction Furniture, Millwork, Wallcover
1012 Logan St.
McMechen, WV 26040
Toll Free 800-972-3784

Village Furniture

Shaker Furniture
PO Box 1148
Huntersville, NC 28078

Send $5.00 for Catalog/Information

Village Furniture House

Order by Phone - Major Brand Furniture
146 West Ave.
Kannapolis, NC 28081

Mail Order Available
Phone 704-938-9171
Toll Free 800-348-4854
FAX 704-932-2503

Virginia Craftsmen Inc.

Custom Furniture
1157 S. High St.
Harrisonburg, VA 22801-1520
Phone 703-434-4153

Vitra Seating Inc.

Manufacturer - Home Office Furniture
IDCNY 30-20 Thompson Avenue
Long Island City, NY 11101

W. G. Undrill Ltd.

Bedroom, Livingroom, Diningroom Furniture
103-111 Catherine St.
Cambridge CB1 3AP
Great Britain
Phone 011-44-223/247470

Wagner Woodcraft Inc.

Furniture
4627 S. Main St.
High Point, NC 27263
Phone 919-431-1197

Wall Furniture Co.

Karastan
4309 Wiley Davis Rd.
Greensboro, NC 27407

Catalog/Information Available Free
Toll Free 800-877-1955

Wall/Goldfinger Inc.

Furniture, Millwork
7 Belknap St.
Northfield, VT 05663
Phone 802-485-6261

Walpole Woodworkers

Order Direct - Cedar Outdoor Furniture, Mailboxes, Arbors, Planters, Lamps, Posts, Fencing
767 East St.
Walpole, MA 02081

Send $6.00 for Catalog/Information

Credit Cards Accepted
Phone 508-668-2800
Toll Free 800-343-6948

Walters Wicker

Wicker Furniture
12-12 Queens Plaza South
Long Island City, NY 11101
Send $25.00 for Catalog/Information
Phone 718-729-1212
FAX 718-389-1333

Warsaw Furniture Co.

Furniture
308 E. Main St.
PO Box 127
Warsaw, KY 41095
Phone 606-567-7261

Waterford Furniture Makers

Walnut Furniture
PO Box 11888
Lynchburg, VA 24506
Catalog/Information Available Free
Phone 804-847-4468

Waterspring Bed Co. Inc.

Furniture
7430 Pacific Circle
Mississagua
Ont., CAN L5T 2A3
Canada
Phone 416-673-0048
FAX 416-673-9904

Watson Furniture Shop

Wood Furniture
2716 Bond St.
Knoxville, TN 37917
Phone 615-522-8015

Watson Furniture Systems

Furniture
12715 Miller Rd. NE
Bainbridge Island, WA 98110
Phone 206-842-6601
Toll Free 800-426-1202
FAX 206-842-4758

Weatherend Estate Furniture

Manufacturer - Order Direct - Indoor/Outdoor - Mahogany, Teak Furniture
PO Box 648
374 Main St.
Rockland, ME 04841
Catalog/Information Available Free
Mail Order Available
Phone 207-596-6483
Toll Free 800-456-6483
FAX 207-594-4968

Wellington's Furniture

Order by Phone - Up to 50% Savings - Leather Furniture
2301 Blowing Rock Road
PO Box 2178
Boone, NC 28607
Mail Order Available
Credit Cards VISA/MC
Phone 704-264-1049
Toll Free 800-262-1049
FAX 704-265-1049

Wendover's Limited

Furniture - Antique English Pine
6 West 20th Street
New York, NY 10011
Phone 212-924-6066
FAX 212-463-7092

Werco Persian & Oriental Rugs

Persian & Oriental Rugs
3255 Peachtree Rd.
Atlanta, GA 30305
Phone 404-237-2584
Toll Free 800-831-8585

Western Log Furniture

Western Log Furniture
PO Box 1649
Edwards, CO 81632
Toll Free 800-525-6920

Furniture

Western Woodwork Co.

Custom Designed Cabinetry
33 Sheridan Dr.
Naugahuck, CT 06770
Phone 203-723-7451
FAX 203-723-7455

Wheeler Woodworking

Oak Tables
Rte. 1
Douglas Dam Rd.
Strawberry Plains, TN 37871
Phone 615-933-0192

White Furniture Co.

Manufacturer - Furniture
201 E. Center St.
PO Box 367
Mebane, NC 27302
Phone 919-563-1217

White of Mebane

18th Century Furniture
Box 367
Mebane, NC 27302
Phone 919-563-1217

Whitecraft Rattan Inc.

Manufacturer - Rattan Furniture
7350 N.W. Miami Court
Miami, FL 33138
Phone 305-757-3407

Whitson Furniture

Major Brand Furniture
RT 3, Box 157
Highway 64-70W
Newton, NC 28658

Catalog/Information Available Free
Phone 704-464-4596

Whittier Wood Products

Furniture
3787 W. First Ave.
PO Box 2827
Eugene, OR 97402
Phone 503-687-0213
FAX 503-687-2060

Wicker & Rattan

Wicker Furniture
5638 W. Waters Ave.
Tampa, FL 33634

Send $0.25 for Catalog/Information

Mail Order Available
Phone 813-885-4813

Wicker Fixer

Antique Wicker and Restoration
Rt. 1 Box 349
Ozark, MO 65721

Mail Order Available
Phone 417-485-6148

Wicker Gallery

Order by Phone - Wicker and Rattan Furniture
8009 Glenwood Ave.
Raleigh, NC 27612

Catalog/Information Available Free
Phone 919-781-2215

Wicker Ware Inc.

Wicker Products, Bath Accessories
2200 E. Venango St.
Philadelphia, PA 19134
Phone 215-831-8585
FAX 215-288-1212

Furniture

The Complete Sourcebook

Wicker Warehouse Inc.

Order by Phone - Imported Wicker Furniture

195 S. River St.
Hackensack, NJ 07601

Send $2.00 for Catalog/Information

Phone 201-342-6709

Toll Free 800-274-8602

FAX 201-342-1495

Wicker Works

Order by Phone - Wicker Furniture

Furnitureland Station
PO Box 7603
High Point, NC 27264

Catalog/Information Available Free

Mail Order Available

Toll Free 800-745-7455

Wickerworks

Wicker Furniture

267 8th St.
San Francisco, CA 94103

Catalog/Information Available Free

Mail Order Available

Phone 415-626-6730

FAX 415-626-8138

Wild Rose Furniture Mfg. Ltd.

Bedroom Furniture

1605 17 St. S.E.
Calgary, Alta
CAN T2G 3V4
Canada

Phone 403-265-6629

FAX 403-265-6996

Wildwood Furniture House

Furniture

1360 Wildwood Ave. SE
Cleveland, TN 37311-6917

Phone 615-476-5185

Wilkinsons Furniture Ltd.

Bedroom, Livingroom, Diningroom Furniture

Monkhill, Pontefract
W Yorkshire WF8 2NS
Great Britain

Phone 011-44-977/79181

William Ball Ltd.

Bedroom Furniture

Gumley Rd.
Grays, Essex RM16 1XX
Great Britain

Phone 011-44-375/375151

William H. James Co.

Reproduction Antique Wood Furniture

Mill Hill
Denmark, ME 04022

Send $2.00 for Catalog/Information

Mail Order Available

Phone 207-452-2444

William L. Mclean Ltd.

Bedroom, Livingroom, Diningroom Furniture

Wenstrom Ho, Hollingbury Ind Est
Carden Ave, Brighton
BN1 8AF
Great Britain

Phone 011-44-273/565441

William Lawrence & Co. Ltd.

Bedroom, Livingroom, Diningroom Furniture

Vale Rd.
Colwick, Nottingham
NG4 2EH
Great Britain

Phone 011-44-602/616484

Williams Furniture Corp.

Furniture

Fulton St.
Sumter, SC 29150

Phone 803-775-7311

Willsboro Wood Products

Adirondack Cedar Furniture
PO Box 509
South AuSable Street
Keeseville, NY 12944

Catalog/Information Available Free

Mail Order Available

Credit Cards VISA/MC/AMEX

Phone 518-834-5200
Toll Free 800-342-3373
FAX 518-834-5219

Windrift Furniture Gallery

Furniture
PO Box 1507
New Bern, NC 29563-1507

Catalog/Information Available Free

Mail Order Available

Phone 919-273-1886

Windsor Chairmakers

Windsor Furniture
RR2, Box 7
Lincolnville, ME 04849

Catalog/Information Available Free

Phone 207-789-5188

Windspire

Rustic Furniture - Beds, Sofas, Tables, Chairs, Lamps, Benches
PO Box 602
Fallston, MD 21047

Winfield Manor

Factory Direct - Furniture
PO Box 515
Conover, NC 28613

Toll Free 800-548-5894

Winterbrook Inc.

Colonial Reproduction Furniture
Jenifer House
Meredith, NH 03253

Credit Cards Accepted

Phone 413-528-1500

Wofab Custom Cabinets Ltd.

Cabinets & Furniture
Box 7512
Drayton Valley
Alta, CAN T0E 0M0
Canada

Phone 403-542-4103
FAX 403-542-4103

Wood Classics

Outdoor Furniture - Teakwood, Mahogany
Osprey Lane, PO Box 4A
Gardiner, NY 12525

Catalog/Information Available Free

Mail Order Available

Phone 914-225-5599
FAX 914-255-7881

Wood Goods Inc.

Tables & Chairs
220 W. Third Ave.
Box 323
Luck, WI 54853

Phone 715-472-2226

Wood Reproduction Studio

Furniture
55 Taylor Ave.
Bethel, CT 06801

Phone 203-748-1152

Woodcraft Design

Oak Furniture
33 Rayborn Cresent
St. Albert
Alta., CAN T8N 5B5
Canada

Phone 403-458-9044

Woodmasters Furniture Group, Inc.

Furniture
Rt. 6 Box 376
Florence, AL 35633

Toll Free 800-541-0786

The Complete Sourcebook

6 - 85

Woodstock Furniture Ltd.

Manufacturer - Fitted & Free Standing Furniture - Bedroom, Kitchen, Bathroom, Paneling
4 William Street
Knightsbridge, London SW1X 9HL
Great Britain
Phone 011-44-71/2459989

Woolums Mfg. Inc.

Rattan, Bamboo, Wood Portable Lamps
1540 19th St. N
St. Petersburg, FL 33713
Phone 813-822-4685

Worcester Chrome Furniture Mfg. Co.

Furniture
35 New St.
Worcester, MA 01605
Phone 508-753-2654
FAX 508-754-3157

Worcester Parsons/Brass Art

Hardware - Window, Door, Furniture
Lifford Land, Kings Norton
Birmingham, West Midlands
B30 3JR
Great Britain
Phone 011-44-21/4592421
FAX 011-44-21/4596405

Workshop Showcase

Mission & Shaker Style Furniture
PO Box 500107
Austin, TX 78750
Send $2.00 for Catalog/Information
Phone 512-331-5470

Workshops of David T. Smith

Reproduction Chandeliers, Furniture, Lamps, Pottery
3600 Shawhan Rd.
Morrow, OH 45152
Send $5.00 for Catalog/Information
Phone 513-932-2472

Wren House Furniture

Oak Butcher Block Tables & Chairs
3543 West Pine
Mt. Airy, NC 27030
Phone 919-352-3562

Wylder Furniture Manufacturing

Solid Oak Rockers, Ladder Back Chairs
220 Brock Rd.
Westminster, SC 29693
Phone 803-647-2977

Y & J Furniture Co. Inc.

Furniture
PO Box 1361
Durham, NC 27702
Phone 919-682-6131

Yale Mfg. Corp.

Furniture
440 Boston Post Rd.
Orange, CT 06477
Phone 203-795-4757

Yield House

Early American Furniture & Accessories, Wallpaper
Route 16
PO Box 5000
North Conway, NH 03860
Catalog/Information Available Free
Credit Cards VISA/MC/AMEX
Phone 603-356-5338
Toll Free 800-258-4720
FAX 603-447-1717

York Interiors Inc.

Name Brand Carpet & Furniture
2821 East Prospect Rd.
York, PA 17402
Catalog/Information Available Free
Phone 717-755-0200

Furniture

Young-Hindle Corp.

Furniture
PO Box 689
Lexington, NC 27292
Phone 704-249-3101

Younger Furniture

*Bedroom, Livingroom, Diningroom
Furniture*
Monier Rd.
Bow, London
E3 2PD
Great Britain
Phone 011-44-81/9854755

Yungbauer Interiors

Furniture
PO Box 7415
St. Paul, MN 55107-0415
Phone 612-222-5722

Zaldin Sons & Co. Inc.

Furniture
221 McKibbin St.
Brooklyn, NY 11206
Phone 718-386-0048

Zanotta SPA

Italian Furniture
Via A. Veneto 57
20054 Nova Milanese (MI)
Italy
Phone 011-39-362/40453
FAX 011-39-362/451038

Zanotta, S.p.A./Palladio Trading Inc.

Italian Furniture
29 East 64th St., Suite 3C
New York, NY 10021
Phone 212-772-7740
FAX 212-734-0960

Zarbin & Associates, Inc.

Furniture, Bedding, Carpet
401 N. Franklin St.
Chicago, IL 60610
Credit Cards Check/Money Order
Phone 312-527-1570

Zeichman Mfg. Inc.

Furniture
5985 Clay Ave. SW
Grand Rapids, MI 49548
Phone 616-534-8800
FAX 616-534-8955

Zeno Table Co.

Wood Furniture
2001 E. Dyer Rd.
Santa Ana, CA 92705
Phone 714-979-2000

Zest Furniture Industries Ltd.

Furniture
75 Browns Line
Toronto
Ont., CAN M8W 3S5
Canada
Phone 416-255-2324
FAX 416-255-8975

Zimports Collection

European - Iron and Wood Furniture
1532 Hi-Line
Dallas, TX 75207
Phone 214-741-1332
FAX 214-747-1901

The Complete Sourcebook

Garden Supply

A. J. Munzinger & Co.

Reproduction Garden & Housewares - Planters, Brackets
1454 South Devon
Springfield, MO 65809
Phone 417-886-9184

Ameristar

Manufacturer - Fencing
Box 2280
Tulsa, OK 74101
Phone 918-584-5865

Amish Country Gazebos

Manufacturer - Gazebos
739 E. Francis St.
Ontario, CA 91716
Mail Order Available
Phone 909-947-3095
FAX 909-947-2985

Anchor Fence

Manufacturer - Fencing
6500 Eastern Ave.
Baltimore, MD 21224
Phone 301-633-6500

BCS America, Inc.

Shredder/Chipper
PO Box 1739
Matthews, NC 28105
Toll Free 800-438-1242

Basta Sole

Patio Umbrellas
4901 E. 12th St.
Oakland, CA 94601
Phone 415-436-6788

Boswell Roberts Gardens

Patio Umbrellas - Oriental & Italian Style
46 Keyes Road
London NW2 3XA
Great Britain
Phone 011-44-81/2080855
FAX 011-44-81/4500829

BowBends

Garden - Bridges, Gazebos
92 Randal Rd.
PO Box 900
Bolton, MA 01740
Send $3.00 for Catalog/Information
Phone 508-779-2271
FAX 508-779-2272

Bufftech

Vinyl Fencing
2525 Walden Ave.
Buffalo, NY 14225
Phone 716-685-1600
Toll Free 800-333-0569

CanDo Composter

Spinning Barrel Composter
7367 Harmony Grove Church Rd.
Acworth, GA 30101-6128
Phone 404-974-0046
Toll Free 800-432-4312

City Visions Inc. – Gardener's Supply

Garden Supply

Garden Supply

City Visions Inc.

Gazebos
Heritage Garden Houses
311 Seymour Street
Lansing, MI 48933
Send $3.00 for Catalog/Information
Mail Order Available

Phone 517-372-3385

Collier Warehouse Inc.

Solariums, Greenhouses
1485 Bayshore Blvd.
San Francisco, CA 94124

Phone 415-467-9590

Continental Custom Bridge Co.

Garden Bridges
Rt. 5
Alexandria, MN 56308
Catalog/Information Available Free

Phone 612-852-7500
Toll Free 800-328-2047

Custom Ironworks Inc.

Manufacturer - Order Direct - Victorian Iron Fencing
10619 Big Bone Rd., PO Box 180
Union, KY 41091
Send $2.00 for Catalog/Information
Mail Order Available

Phone 604-384-4122
FAX 604-384-4848

Dalton Pavilions Inc.

Manufacturer - Red Cedar Gazebos
20 Commerce Dr.
Telford, PA 18969
Send $5.00 for Catalog/Information
Mail Order Available

Phone 215-721-1492
FAX 215-721-1501

Dolphin Pet Village

Fiberglass Ponds for Water Gardens
1808 W. Campbell Ave.
Campbell, CA 95008
Mail Order Available

Phone 408-379-7600

Farm Wholesale, Inc.

Manufacturer - Greenhouses
2396 Perkins St. NE
Salem, OR 97303
Mail Order Available

Phone 503-393-3973
Toll Free 800-825-1925
FAX 503-393-3119

Florentine Craftsmen Inc.

Garden Furnishings
46-24 28th St.
Long Island City, NY 11101

Phone 718-937-7632

Florian Greenhouse Inc.

Aluminum and Wood Solariums
64 Airport Rd.
West Milford, NJ 07480
Send $5.00 for Catalog/Information

Toll Free 800-356-7426
FAX 201-728-3206

Garden Source Furnishings, Inc.

Outdoor Furniture
45 Bennett St.
Atlanta, GA 30309

Phone 404-351-6446
FAX 404-351-1936

Gardener's Supply

Shredder/Chipper, Composter, Garden Supplies
128 Intervale Rd.
Burlington, VT 05401

Phone 802-863-1700
Toll Free 800-863-1700

7 - 2

The Complete Sourcebook

Garden Supply

Gazebo & Porchworks

Railings, Gingerbread, Porch Swings

728 9th Ave. SW
Puyallup, WA 98371

Send $2.00 for Catalog/Information

Mail Order Available

Phone 206-848-0502

Gazebo Woodcrafters

Order Direct - Cedar Gazebo Kits

PO Box 187
Bellington, WA 98227

Catalog/Information Available Free

Mail Order Available

Credit Cards MC/VISA/Check/Money
Order

Phone 206-734-0463

Haddonstone USA Ltd.

*English Garden Ornaments, Planters,
Columns*

201 Heller Place
Bellmawr, NJ 08031

Send $5.00 for Catalog/Information

Phone 609-931-7011

FAX 609-931-0040

Heritage Fence Company

*Manufacturer - Victorian & Colonial Wood
& Vinyl Fencing*

PO Box 121
Skippack, PA 19464

Phone 610-584-6710

Toll Free 800-286-6710

Hermitage Garden Pools

*Water Garden Pools, Waterfalls,
Waterwheels, Bridges*

PO Box 361
Canastota, NY 13032

Phone 315-697-9093

International Terra Cotta

European Terracotta Planters

690 N. Robertson Blvd.
Los Angeles, CA 90069-5088

Phone 310-657-3752

Toll Free 800-331-5329

FAX 310-659-0865

Ives Weathervanes

Weathervanes

Forget Road
Charlemont, MA 01339

Mail Order Available

Phone 413-339-8534

J. A. Dawley Fine Woodworking

*Manufacturer - Arbors, Benches,
Brackets, Columns, Storm Doors, Posts*

1938 Chase Rd.
Waterloo, NY 13165

Phone 315-539-2555

Janco Greenhouses

Greenhouses

J.A. Nearing Co., Inc.
9390 Davis Ave.
Laurel, MD 20723

Catalog/Information Available Free

Phone 301-323-6933

Toll Free 800-323-6933

Jerith Mfg.

Manufacturer - Fencing

3939 G St.
Philadelphia, PA 19124

Catalog/Information Available Free

Toll Free 800-344-2242

FAX 215-739-4844

Kemp

Compost Tumbler

160 Koser Rd.
Lititz, PA 17543

Garden Supply

The Complete Sourcebook

Kester's Wild Game Food Nurseries

Water Garden - Aquatic Plants
4488 Highway 116 E.
Omro, WI 54963
Mail Order Available
Credit Cards MC/VISA

Phone 414-685-2929
FAX 414-685-6727

Kloter Farms Inc.

Gazebos, Outdoor Furniture, Sheds
216 West Rd.
Ellington, CT 06029
Send $3.00 for Catalog/Information
Mail Order Available
Credit Cards MC/VISA/DISCOVER/AMEX

Phone 203-871-1048
Toll Free 800-289-3463

Landscape Forms Inc.

Manufacturer - Outdoor Furniture
431 Lawndale Ave.
Kalamazoo, MI 49001

Phone 616-381-0396
Toll Free 800-521-2546
FAX 616-381-3455

Lilypons Water Gardens

Water Gardens & Plants
PO Box 10
6800 Lilypons Rd.
Buckeystown, MD 21717-0010
Send $5.00 for Catalog/Information
Mail Order Available
Credit Cards MC/VISA/DISCOVER/AMEX

Phone 301-874-5133
Toll Free 800-999-5459

Lotus Water Garden Products Ltd.

Water Garden Supply
PO Box 36, Junction St. Bumley
Lancs BB12 0NA
Great Britain

Phone 011-44-282/20771

MacKissic Incorporated

Shredder/Chipper for Compost
PO Box 111
Parker Ford, PA 19457

Phone 215-495-7181
FAX 215-495-5951

Machin Conservatories

Conservatories (Greenhouses)
Faverdale
Darlington DL3 0PW
Great Britain

Phone 011-44-800/622446

Maryland Aquatic Nurseries

Water Garden Plants, Pumps, Fish
3427 N. Furnace Road
Jarrettsville, MD 21084
Mail Order Available
Credit Cards VISA/MC

Phone 410-557-7615
FAX 410-692-2837

May's Architectural Detailing

Victorian Garden Arbors
209 South Main
Fairport, NY 14450

Phone 716-223-6795

Musser Forests

Evergreens and Hardwood Seedlings
PO Box 340
Indiana, PA 15701-0340
Catalog/Information Available Free

Phone 412-465-5685
FAX 412-465-9893

Nebraska Plastics Inc.

Manufacturer - Vinyl Fencing
PO Box 45
Cozad, NE 69130

Phone 308-784-3224
Toll Free 800-445-2887
FAX 308-784-3216

Garden Supply

Oryx Trading Ltd.

Patio Umbrellas - Canvas & Hardwood
33 Cornwall Gardens
London
SW7 4AP
Great Britain

> Phone 011-44-71/9382045
> FAX 011-44-71/9379087

Paradise Water Gardens

Water Gardens - Water Lilies, Ponds, Waterfalls
14 May St.
Whitman, MA 02382

Mail Order Available

Credit Cards VISA/MC/Check/Money Order

> Phone 617-447-4711
> FAX 617-442-4591

Peterson Wood Div.

Lawn Furniture, Fences
Gilbert & Bennett Mfg.Co.
101 Fence Factory Rd.
Carney, MI 49812

> Phone 906-639-2132

Plow & Hearth

Porch & Lawn Furniture, Home Furnishings, Fireplace Accessories
PO Box 5000
Madison, VA 22701-1500

Catalog/Information Available Free

Mail Order Available

Credit Cards VISA/MC/AMEX/DISCOVER

> Phone 703-672-1712
> Toll Free 800-627-1712
> FAX 800-843-2509

Prochnow & Prochnow

Garden Furniture - Benches, Chairs, Table, Planters
PO Box 566
Nebraska City, NE 68410

Catalog/Information Available Free

Mail Order Available

Credit Cards Check/Money Order

> Phone 402-873-7622

Prototech Polyvinyl Fencing Systems

Manufacturer - Vinyl Fencing
PO Box 36555
Richmond, VA 23235

> Phone 804-320-5449

Quality Imports

Manufacturer - Hand Made Hammocks
15 Ramsay Rd.
Montclair, NJ 07042

Mail Order Available

> Phone 201-746-0445
> Toll Free 800-735-2918
> FAX 201-783-1471

R & R Crafts

Macrame Lawn Chair Kits
PO Box 1007
Lake Placid, FL 33852

> Phone 813-465-0257

R.P.B. Manufacturing

Tumbling Barrel Composter
727 Thompson Ave.
McKees Rocks, PA 15136

> Phone 412-331-4640

RainDrip Water Systems

Manufacturer - Raindrip Kits - Irrigation Systems
2250 Agate Court
Simi Valley, CA 93065

Mail Order Available

> Toll Free 800-544-3747
> FAX 805-581-9999

Garden Supply

The Complete Sourcebook

S. Scherer & Sons Water Gardens

Water Garden Supplies - Plants, Pools, Pumps

104 Waterside Rd.
Northport, NY 11768

Send $1.00 for Catalog/Information

Mail Order Available

Credit Cards MC/VISA

Phone 516-261-7432

FAX 516-261-9325

Santa Barbara Greenhouse

Greenhouses

721 Richmond Ave.
Oxnard, CA 93030

Mail Order Available

Credit Cards VISA/MC

Phone 805-483-4288

Toll Free 800-544-5276

FAX 805-483-0229

Slocum Water Gardens

Water Garden Plants, Industrial Plastic Ponds

1101 Cypress Gardens Rd.
Winter Haven, FL 33884-1932

Send $3.00 for Catalog/Information

Mail Order Available

Credit Cards MC/VISA

Phone 813-293-7151

FAX 813-299-1896

Solite Solar Greenhouses

Greenhouses, Glass Enclosures, Solariums

1145 Bronx River Rd.
Bronx, NY 10472

Phone 212-842-4441

FAX 212-328-4102

Southeastern Insulated Glass

Manufacturer - Factory Direct Prices - Greenhouses, Sunrooms, Sliding Glass Doors, Skylights

6477 Peachtree Industrial Blvd.
Atlanta, GA 30360

Mail Order Available

Phone 404-455-8838

Toll Free 800-841-9842

Southeastern Wood Products Co.

Fencing

PO Box 113
Griffin, GA 30224

Catalog/Information Available Free

Phone 404-227-7486

Toll Free 800-722-7486

Stewart Iron Works

Manufacturer - Order Direct - Iron Fencing & Gates

20 West 18th Street
PO Box 2612
Covington, KY 41012

Send $3.00 for Catalog/Information

Phone 606-431-1985

FAX 606-431-2035

Stone Forest

Handcarved Granite Garden - Fountains, Birdbaths, Lanterns

Box 2840
Santa Fe, NM 87504

Phone 505-986-8883

FAX 505-982-2712

Stonehaven

Planters and Mailboxes

PO Box 742
Glenview, IL 60025-0742

Send $3.50 for Catalog/Information

Phone 708-635-8014

Submatic Irrigation Systems

Manufacturer - Irrigation Systems

PO Box 246
Lubbock, TX 79048

Toll Free 800-858-4016

Sun Room Company

Greenhouses, Sunrooms, Skylights, Custom Windows

322 E. Main St.
PO Box 301
Leola, PA 17540

Phone 717-656-9391
Toll Free 800-426-2737

Sun-Mar Corp.

Composting Toilets

900 Hertel Ave.
Buffalo, NY 14216

Phone 416-332-1314

Sunglo Solar Greenhouses

Greenhouses

4441 26th Avenue West
Seattle, WA 98199

Catalog/Information Available Free

Credit Cards VISA/MC

Phone 206-284-8900
Toll Free 800-647-0606

TIF Nursery

Trees, Shrubs

Box N
Tifton, GA 31794

Catalog/Information Available Free

TerraCast

Indoor & Outdoor Planters

4700 Mitchell St.
North Las Vegas, NV 89030

Phone 702-643-2644
Toll Free 800-423-8539
FAX 702-643-2641

Texas Standard Picket Company Inc.

Order Factory Direct - Nationwide Shipping - Victorian Fence Pickets

F.H. Morey
606 W. 17th St., Ste. 304
Austin, TX 78701

Catalog/Information Available Free

Phone 512-472-1101

Troy-Bilt Mfg. Co.

Manufacturer - Chipper/Shredder for Mulch & Compost

102nd St. and 9th Ave.
Troy, NY 12180

Toll Free 800-826-6060

Turner Greenhouses

Greenhouses

Highway 117 South
Boldsboro, NC 27530

Toll Free 800-672-4770

Twin Oaks Hammocks

Hammocks, Woven String Furniture

Rt. 4, Box 169
Louisa, VA 23093

Catalog/Information Available Free

Credit Cards VISA/MC/Check/Money Order

Phone 703-894-5126
Toll Free 800-688-8946
FAX 703-894-4112

Urdl's Waterfall Creation Inc.

Water Garden Supplies, Waterfalls

1010 Northwest 1st St.
Del Ray Beach, FL 33444

Phone 305-278-3320

Garden Supply

Van Ness Water Gardens

Water Garden Supplies, Aqatic Plants, Waterfalls

2460 N. Euclid Avenue
Upland, CA 91786-1199

Send $4.00 for Catalog/Information

Mail Order Available

Credit Cards MC/VISA

Phone 909-982-2425
FAX 909-949-7217

Vixen Hill Mfg. Co. Inc.

Manufacturer - Gazebos, Shutters

Main St.
Elverson, PA 19520

Send $3.00 for Catalog/Information

Mail Order Available

Phone 215-286-0909
Toll Free 800-423-2766
FAX 610-286-2099

Water Works

Water Garden Supply, Aquatic Plants, Fish, Pools, Pumps

111 East Fairmount St.
Coopersburg, PA 18036

Phone 215-282-4784

Waterford Gardens

Water Garden Supply, Aquatic Plants, Pools

74 East Allendale Rd.
Saddle River, NJ 07458

Mail Order Available

Phone 201-327-0721

Wicklein's Aquatic Farm & Nursery

Water Garden Plants

1820 Cromwell Bridge Rd.
Baltimore, MD 21234

Phone 301-823-1335

William Tricker, Inc.

Water Garden - Rare and Unusual Water Lilies

7125 Tanglewood Dr.
Independence, OH 44131

Phone 216-524-3491

Wind & Weather

Weathervanes, Garden Ornaments

PO Box 2320
Mendocino, CA 95460

Mail Order Available

Credit Cards MC/VISA/DISCOVER/AMEX

Phone 707-937-0323
Toll Free 800-922-9463
FAX 707-964-1278

Woodnorth

Victorian Garden Benches

2313 WN 65th St.
Seattle, WA 98117

Mail Order Available

Phone 206-782-7607

Worm's Way

Organic Gardening Supplies

Indoor/Outdoor Garden Supply
3151 South Hwy. 446
Bloomington, IN 47401

Catalog/Information Available Free

Mail Order Available

Credit Cards Accepted/Check/Money Order

Phone 812-331-0300
Toll Free 800-274-9676
FAX 812-331-0854

The Complete Sourcebook

Home

Decorating

$5 Wallpaper & Blind Co.

Order by Phone - Wallpaper, Custom Blinds

370 Hall
Pheonixville, PA 19460

Credit Cards Accepted

Toll Free 800-536-5527

1 Day Blinds

Order by Phone - Window Treatments - Blinds, Shades

1925 South Vineyard Ave.
Ontario, CA 91761

Credit Cards Accepted

Toll Free 800-325-4637

3 Day Blinds

Factory Direct - Order by Phone - Mini, Verticals, Wood Blinds

2220 East Cerritos Avenue
Anaheim, CA 92806

Toll Free 800-966-3329

5th Ave Rug Center

Rugs

366 5th Ave.
New York, NY 10001

Phone 212-736-0870

Toll Free 800-642-9108

A & E Blind & Awning Co.

Manufacturer - Blinds, Awnings

2125 Holliday Rd.
Wichita Falls, TX 76301

Phone 817-767-1449

Toll Free 800-777-1221

FAX 817-322-5040

A. Weldon Kent Enterprises

Order by Phone - Blinds & Shades

2641 Esplanade
Chico, CA 95926

Credit Cards VISA/MC/DISCOVER

Toll Free 800-944-5368

A.J. Boyd Industries

Window Treatment - Blinds

275 Market St., Ste 463
Minneapolis, MN 55406

Phone 612-333-9166

Toll Free 800-422-2683

ABC Carpet & Home

Carpet, Rugs, Home Furnishings

888 Broadway
New York, NY 10003

Catalog/Information Available Free

Mail Order Available

Phone 212-473-3000

Toll Free 800-888-7847

FAX 212-995-9474

ABC Decorator Fabrics

Order by Phone - Major Brand Decorative Fabrics
2410 298th Ave. N
Clearwater, FL 34621

Toll Free 800-638-7119

ADO Corp.

Curtains, Draperies
New Cut Rd. & Hwy. I-85
PO Box 3447
Spartanburg, SC 29304

Phone 803-574-2731

FAX 803-574-5835

ALCO Venetian Blind Co. Inc.

Window Treatments - Blinds and Shades
190 E. Hoffman Ave.
PO Box 538
Lindenhurst, NY 11757-0538

Phone 516-226-7000

Toll Free 800-832-5868

FAX 516-226-7268

Aberdeen Mfg. Corp.

Manufacturer - Bedspreads, Curtains, Outdoor Furniture, Umbrellas
1 Park Avenue
New York, NY 10016

Phone 212-951-7800

FAX 212-951-8001

Abrahams Oriental Rugs

Oriental Rugs
5120 Woodway, Suite 6010
Houston, TX 77056

Phone 713-622-4444

FAX 713-622-8928

Access Carpet

Carpet
3068 N. Dug Gap Rd.
Dalton, GA 30722

Toll Free 800-848-7747

Ace Blinds Inc.

Distributor - Window Treatments - Blinds
121 Marketridge Dr.
Jackson, MS 39213

Phone 601-957-1777

Toll Free 800-826-3573

FAX 601-957-0979

Acme Window Coverings Ltd.

Window Treatments - Blinds
3000 Madison St.
Bellwood, IL 60104-2219

Phone 708-544-5000

Toll Free 800-825-2263

FAX 708-544-1634

Acorn Mills Ltd.

Manufacturer - Carpet
Mellor St.
Lees, Oldham OL4 3DA
Great Britain

Phone 011-44-61-6244529

Adac. Rugs & Treasures

Persian and Oriental Rugs
351 Peachtree Hills
Atlanta, GA 30305

Phone 404-237-9435

Adam Carpets Ltd.

Manufacturer - Carpet
Greenhill Wks
Birmingham Rd. Kidderminster, Worcs
DY10 2SH
Great Britain

Phone 011-44-562-829966

Adele-Bishop

Stencils & Supplies
PO Box 3349
Kinston, NC 27591

Send $3.50 for Catalog/Information

Phone 919-527-4186

FAX 919-527-4189

Advance Carpet Decorating Ctr.

Floor Covering, Window Treatments
11022 Manchester Rd.
St. Louis, MO 63122

Phone 314-821-6000

FAX 314-821-1584

Advance Wallcovering

Wallpaper
1300 Stirling Rd.
Dania, FL 33004

Phone 305-925-5141

FAX 305-925-8028

Advanced Consumer Products

Window Treatment - Vertical Blinds
PO Box 95
Garden City, MI 48135

Toll Free 800-677-9090

Age Craft Mfg. Inc.

Window Treatment - Blinds
45 Madison Ave.
Greensburg, PA 15601

Phone 412-838-5580

Toll Free 800-247-5487

FAX 412-838-5594

Alabama Venetian Blinds Co. Inc.

Window Treatment - Blinds
516 Jefferson Blvd.
Birmingham, AL 35217

Phone 205-841-6424

Toll Free 800-663-5894

FAX 205-849-0745

Aladdin Carpet Mills

Manufacturer - Carpet , Rugs
9454 Phillips Hwy.
Jacksonville, FL 32256-1314

Phone 904-260-4122

Alex Cooper Oriental Rugs

Oriental Rugs
908 Norwalk Rd.
Towson, MD 21204

Phone 410-828-4838

Alexander Wallpaper

Handmade Grasscloth Wallpaper
2964 Gallos Rd.
Falls Church, VA 22042

Send $2.50 for Catalog/Information

Phone 301-770-5014

Alexandra's Homespun Textile

Fabrics
PO Box 500
Sturbridge, MA 01566

Send $2.00 for Catalog/Information

Phone 508-347-2241

All Cedar Venetian Blind Mfg. Co.

Window Treatments - Blinds
68 Union
Clifton, NJ 07011

Phone 201-546-0496

All-States Decorating Network

Order by Phone - Window Treatments - Blinds
810 Main Street
Toms River, NJ 08755

Credit Cards Accepted

Toll Free 800-334-8590

Allison T. Seymour, Inc.

Carpet, Rugs, Wallcover
5423 W. Marginal Way SW
Seattle, WA 98106

Phone 206-935-5471

FAX 206-935-6409

Allison Window Fashions

Window Treatments - Blinds
2920 N. Tryon St.
Charlotte, NC 28232

Phone 704-334-8621
FAX 704-375-7078

Ambassador Carpets

Carpets
Duvall Rd.
PO Box 189
Chatsworth, GA 30705

Phone 404-695-7411
Toll Free 800-762-9836
FAX 404-695-0529

American Blind & Wallpaper Factory

Order Kit - Nationwide Shipping - Major Brand Wallpaper & Blinds
28237 Orchard Lake Rd.
Farmington Hills, MI 48334

Credit Cards VISA/MC

Toll Free 800-735-5300
FAX 810-553-6262

American Discount Wallcoverings

Order by Phone - Wallpaper, Blinds, Shades, Fabrics
1411 Fifth Ave.
Pittsburgh, PA 15219

Credit Cards VISA/MC

Toll Free 800-777-2737

American Homes Stencils, Inc.

Stencils
10007 South 76th St.
Franklin, WI 53132

Send $2.50 for Catalog/Information

American Rug

Rugs
PO Box 1481
Dalton GA 30722

Toll Free 800-845-3240

American Rug Craftsmen

Manufacturer - Rugs
PO Box 130
Sugar Valley, GA 30746

Toll Free 800-843-4473
FAX 404-625-3544

American Storage Systems

Closet Organizers
PO Box 3771
Seattle, WA 98124

Credit Cards VISA/MC

Toll Free 800-743-6328

American Treasury Catalog

Giftware, Home Furnishings
Box 1343
Largo, FL 34294

Phone 813-536-2658

American Wallcovering Distributors

Order by Phone - Wallcover
2260 Route 22
Union, NJ 07083

Credit Cards VISA/MC

Toll Free 800-843-6567

American Window Corp.

Manufacturer - Window Treatments - Blinds
8615 NW 54th St.
Miami, FL 33166

Phone 305-558-5000
FAX 305-593-1544

American Window Creation

Manufacturer - Window Treatments - Blinds
291 Grote St.
Buffalo, NY 14207

Phone 716-875-5511
FAX 716-875-5204

Anchor Industries Inc.

Manufacturer - Fabric
1100 Burch Dr.
PO Box 3477
Evansville, IN 47733

Phone 812-867-2421
FAX 812-867-1429

Andreae Designs

Laser Cut Stencils
35673 Ashford Dr.
Sterling Heights, MI 49312

Send $3.50 for Catalog/Information

Credit Cards Accepted/Check/Money Order

Phone 313-826-3404

Angelo's Wallcoverings of Puerto Rico

Major Brand Wallcover & Wallpaper
PO Box 364542
San Juan, PR 00936-4542

Phone 809-766-0610

Archetonic

Manufacturer - Wallcovering, Fabrics
25 Sawmill River Rd.
Yonkers, NY 10701

Phone 914-969-4363
FAX 914-375-1705

Arlin Wallcoverings USA Inc.

Wallpaper & Wallcover
1751 N. Central Park Ave.
Chicago, IL 60647

Phone 312-278-4000

Armstrong-Decorative Accessories

Decorative Home Furnishings
PO Box 3001
Lancaster, PA 17064

Catalog/Information Available Free

Credit Cards VISA/MC/AMEX

Phone 717-291-1544

Around the Window

Order by Phone - Window Treatments - Blinds
326 N. Stonestreet Ave.
Suite 204
Rockville, MD 20850

Credit Cards VISA/MC

Toll Free 800-642-9899

Arrowsmith Trading Company

Victorian Style Ceiling Pot & Pan Rack
PO Box 14
1111 Shearme Rd.
Coombs, B.C. V0R 1M0
Canada

Mail Order Available

Toll Free 800-220-0633

Arthur Gregorian

Oriental Rugs
2284 Washington Street
Newton Lower Falls, MA 02162

Send $2.00 for Catalog/Information

Mail Order Available

Phone 617-244-2553

Artifacteria

Window Treatment - Window Lace Curtains, Tablecloths, Runners
PO Box 22
Skippack, PA 19474

Send $4.00 for Catalog/Information

Mail Order Available

Credit Cards Accepted

Phone 215-584-5507
Toll Free 800-274-5507

Artique Design

Manufacturer - Fabric
PO Box 28863
Philadelphia, PA 19151

Phone 215-878-5312
FAX 215-878-4359

Artisan Handprints Inc.

Manufacturer - Fabric
4234 N. Pulaski Rd.
Chicago, IL 60641

Phone 312-725-8802
FAX 312-725-0316

Artistic Interiors

Stencils
92 Sunset Avenue
Toms River, NJ 08755
Send $3.50 for Catalog/Information

Artistic Surfaces

*Unusual Painted Treatments of Walls,
Floors and Furniture - Murals,
Floorcloths, Decorative Painted Furniture,
Faux Marble Floors*

Heather Whitehouse
13 Summit Street, Studio 304
East Hampton, CT 06424

Phone 203-267-0070

Artloom

Rugs
Div. of Horizon Ind.
PO Box 12069, S. Industrial Blvd.
Calhoun, GA 30701

Phone 404-629-7721
FAX 404-625-3728

Artmark Fabrics Co. Inc.

Fabric
480 Lancaster Ave.
Frazer, PA 19355

Phone 215-647-3220
FAX 215-647-5825

Ashley Wallcoverings

*Manufacturer - Callwood Designer
Wallcoverings, Decor Diary, Highlights,
Pacific Textures & Effects and more*

Private Bag
Porirua, New Zealand
New Zealand

Phone 011-64-4-378029
FAX 011-64-4-378131

Asia Minor Carpets

Handspun Wool, Turkish Carpets
801 Lexington Ave.
New York, NY 10021
Catalog/Information Available Free

Phone 212-223-2288
FAX 212-888-8624

At Home in the Valley

Braided Rugs, Chairpads, Curtains
Box 7303
Van Nuys, CA 91409
Send $1.00 for Catalog/Information

Phone 818-780-4663

Atelier H. Juergen Oellers

*Suppliers of Vinyl Designs for Europa,
Wallcoverings Design and Textile Design
Worldwide*

Minkweg 11 a
Krefeld, W. Germany, D-4150
Germany

Phone 011-49-2151562166
FAX 011-49-2151561662

Atlantic Carpet Corp.

Carpet
Beasley St., PO Box 639
Calhoun, GA 30355-0106

Phone 404-231-9318
Toll Free 800-241-7256
FAX 404-261-5141

Atlantic Venetian Blind & Drapery Co.

Window Treatments - Blinds, Draperies
285 S. Edgewood Ave.
Jacksonville, FL 32205

Phone 904-388-1552
FAX 904-384-3611

Atlas Carpet Mills, Inc.

Manufacturer - Carpet
2200 Saybrook Ave.
City of Commerce, CA 90040

Phone 213-724-9000

Atlas Wallpaper & Paint Co.

Major Brand Wallcover and Wallpaper
975 Route 73 South
PO Box 953
Marlton, NJ 08053

Phone 609-985-5550
FAX 609-596-1130

Atrium Industries/Triumph Designs

Manufacturer - Wallcover
18953 NE 3rd Court
North Miami Beach, FL 33179

Phone 305-652-2352
FAX 305-651-1659

Avena Carpets Ltd.

Manufacturer - Carpet
Bankfield Mill
Haley Hill, W Yorkshire HX3 6ED
Great Britain

Phone 011-44-422/330261

Avondale Distributors Inc.

Manufacturer - Window Treatments - Blinds
2826 Sixth Ave. S
Birmingham, AL 35233

Phone 205-322-0431
FAX 205-324-2368

Axminster Carpets Ltd.

Manufacturer - Carpet - NY Office
212-421-1050
Gamberlake
Woodmede Rd., Axminster, Devon
EX13 5PQ
Great Britain

Phone 011-44-297-32244
FAX 011-44-29735241

Azar's Oriental Rugs

Oriental & Turkish Rugs
670 South Woodward
Birmingham, MI 48012

Phone 810-644-7311

BMI Home Decorating

Order by Phone - Decorator Fabrics, Wallcoverings
PO Box 25905
Lexington, KY 40524

Toll Free 800-999-2091

BMK Ltd.

Manufacturer - Carpet
1144 D-Chelsea Ave.
Santa Monica, CA 90403

Phone 310-829-3389
FAX 310-829-3709

Badger Air Brush Co.

Manufacturer - Stencils & Supply
9128 W. Belmont Ave.
Franklin Park, IL 60131

Phone 708-678-3104
FAX 708-671-4352

Bagindd Prints

Manufacturer - Fabric
2171 Blount Rd.
Pompano Beach, FL 33069

Phone 305-971-9000
Toll Free 800-826-6345
FAX 305-873-1000

Bailey & Griffin Inc.

Fabrics and Wallpapers
1406 E. Mermaid Lane
PO Box 27429
Philadelphia, PA 19118

Phone 215-836-4350
FAX 215-233-3499

Bali Blinds Midwest

Manufacturer - Window Treatments - Blinds
801 Frontenac Rd.
Naperville, IL 60566-1040

Phone 312-983-7800

Bamber Carpets Ltd.

Carpet
Unit 241,Dawson Pl.,Walton Summit Centre
Bamber Bridge, Preston, Lancs
PR5 8AL
Great Britain

Phone 011-44-772-38411

Bamboo & Rattan Works Inc.

Manufacturer - Bamboo Wallcover, Fencing, Caning
470 Oberlin Ave. S
Lakewood, NJ 08701

Mail Order Available

Phone 908-370-0220
FAX 908-905-8386

Bamboo Abbott Florida Corp.

Window Treatments - Blinds
2990 Simms St.
Hollywood, FL 33020

Phone 305-921-4471
Toll Free 800-486-3449
FAX 305-921-5309

Barbara Zinkel Design

Artist/Publisher Silk Screen Prints, Custom Decorative Rugs
333 Pilgrim
Birmingham, MI 48009

Phone 313-642-9789
FAX 313-642-8374

Barker Supply & Window Coverings

Window Treatments - Blinds
819 N. Seventh Ave.
Phoenix, AZ 85007

Phone 602-257-8191

Barra U.S.A. Inc.

Manufacturer - Wallpaper, Wallcover
2150 NW 33rd St., Ste. A
Pompano Beach, FL 33069

Phone 305-968-6958
FAX 305-968-2085

Barrett Carpet Mills

Manufacturer - Rugs, Carpet
Box 2045
Dalton, GA 30722

Phone 404-277-2114
Toll Free 800-241-4064
FAX 404-277-3250

Bassett & Vollum

Reproduction Wallpapers
915 W. Summit St.
Maquoketa, IA 52060

Send $1.00 for Catalog/Information

Phone 319-652-3605

Bayview Wallcoverings

Major Brand Wallcover
PO Box 581
41 E. Sunrise Hwy.
Lindenhurst, NY 11757

Phone 516-884-9000
Toll Free 800-347-9255

Beacon Looms, Inc.

Window Treatments - Curtains, Draperies, Bedspreads
295 5th Ave.
New York, NY 10016

Phone 212-685-5800

Beardon Brothers Carpet

Carpet
4109 S. Dixie Hwy.
Dalton, GA 30721

Catalog/Information Available Free

Credit Cards VISA/MC/AMEX

Toll Free 800-433-0074
FAX 706-277-1754

Beaulieu of America Inc.

Manufacturer - Rugs, Carpet
PO Box 4539
Dalton, GA 30721

Phone 404-278-6666
Toll Free 800-241-4903
FAX 404-278-4961

Beauti-Vue Products Inc.

Manufacturer - Window Treatments - Blinds
8555-194th Ave.
Bristol, WI 53104
Toll Free 800-558-9431
FAX 404-278-4961

Beckler's Carpet Outlet

Carpet
PO Box 9
1-75 At Exit 135
Dalton, GA 30722
Credit Cards Accepted
Toll Free 800-232-5537

Bedroom Secrets

Window Treatments, Wallpaper, Fabric, Comforters
310 E. Military
PO Box 529
Fremont, NE 68025
Send $2.00 for Catalog/Information
Phone 402-727-4004
Toll Free 800-955-2559

Beegun's Galleries of Chicago, Inc.

Distributor - Major Brand Wallcover and Wallpaper
1285 Merchandise Mart
Chicago, IL 60654
Phone 312-828-0393
FAX 312-828-1141

Ben James Ltd.

Manufacturer - Wallcover
PO Box 14006
Ft. Lauderdale, FL 33302
Phone 305-564-0400
FAX 305-565-5917

Benington's

Fabric, Carpet, Rugs, Wallpaper
1271 Manheim Pike
Lancaster, PA 17601
Credit Cards VISA/MC
Toll Free 800-252-5060
FAX 717-299-4889

Bentley Brothers

English Embossed Wallcoverings
2709 South Park Rd.
Louisville, KY 40219
Catalog/Information Available Free
Toll Free 800-824-4777

Bentley Mills, Inc.

Manufacturer - Carpet
14641 E. Don Julian Rd.
City of Industry, CA 91746
Phone 818-333-4585

Bergamo Fabrics Inc.

Upholstery & Drapery Fabrics
Sahco Hesslein Collection
37-20 34th St.
Long Island City, NY 11101
Phone 718-392-5000
FAX 718-784-1214

Berkshire Mfg. Inc.

Window Treatments
230 John Downey Dr.
New Britain, CT 06051
Phone 203-225-9477
Toll Free 800-243-4339
FAX 203-224-6731

Best Blinds

Order by Phone - Blinds
8026 FM 1960 East
Humble, TX 77346
Toll Free 800-548-4840

Best Discount Wallcoverings

Major Brand Wallcovering
417 Jackson St.
St. Charles, MO 63301
Credit Cards Accepted
Toll Free 800-328-5550

Best Wallcoverings Inc.

Order by Phone - Major Brand Wallpaper
2618 Avenue U
Brooklyn, NY 11229
Credit Cards Accepted
Toll Free 800-624-1224

Beverly Stevens Ltd.

Manufacturer - Wallcover, Fabric
182 Earle Ave.
Lynbrook, NY 11563
Phone 516-599-1033
FAX 516-431-5350

Bill Villetto Designs

Manufacturer - Wallcover, Fabric
Division of Alpha Omega H.P.
468 Totowa Ave.
Paterson, NJ 07501
Phone 201-942-7200
FAX 201-595-9390

Birge Wallcoverings

Wallpaper & Wallcover
195 Walker Dr.
Brampton, Ontario L6T 3Z9
Canada
Phone 416-791-8788
FAX 416-791-8078

Biscayne Fabrics Inc.

Decorator Fabric
4000 N. Miami Ave.
Miami, FL 33137
Phone 305-573-1221
Toll Free 800-327-7872

Blautex

Wallcovering and Fabrics for Interior Designers
1400 N.W. 79th Ave.
Miami, FL 33126
Phone 305-593-2000
FAX 305-593-5086

Blind Brite Corp.

Window Treatments - Blinds
1375 Gladys Ave.
Long Beach, CA 90804
Phone 213-434-9202

Blind Busters

Order by Phone - Order Kit - Factory Direct - Window Treatments - Blinds, Shades
10858 Harry Hines Blvd.
Dallas, TX 75220
Credit Cards Accepted
Toll Free 800-883-5000

Blind Center USA, Inc.

Order by Phone - Mini, Micros, Verticals, Wood Blinds, Pleated Shades
30242 Littlecroft
Houston, TX 77386
Toll Free 800-676-5029
FAX 713-298-5835

Blind Design

Manufacturer - Wholesale - Window Treatments - Blinds and Shades
8030 Deering Ave.
Canoga Park, CA 91304-5010
Phone 818-704-5215
FAX 818-704-9879

Blind Design Inc.

Window Treatments
7077 Consolidated Way
San Diego, CA 92121-2633
Phone 619-695-2840
FAX 619-695-2418

Home Decorating

Blinds 'N Things

Window Treatments - Blinds
516 Jefferson Blvd.
Birmingham, AL 35217
Catalog/Information Available Free
Toll Free 800-662-5894

Blue Ridge Carpet Mills

Manufacturer - Carpet
100 Progress Rd.
PO Box 507
Ellijay, GA 30540
Phone 404-276-2001

Bob Mitchell Designs

Wallpaper & Wallcover
Div. of Borden Inc.
PO Box 567
San Gabriel, CA 91778
Phone 213-283-0471
FAX 213-283-0476

Bolta Wallcoverings

Manufacturer - Wallcover, Wallpaper
3 University Plaza
Hackensack, NJ 07601
Phone 201-489-0100
FAX 201-489-4394

Bones Creek Designs

Western Style Mirrors
PO Box 238
Cerrillos, MN 87010
Phone 505-438-0628

Boone Decorative Fabrics

Fabric, Custom Bedspreads
8905 E. Highway 421
Colfax, NC 27235
Toll Free 800-635-3396

Borden Home Wallcoverings

Wallcovering
2925 Courtyards Dr.
Norcross, GA 30071
Phone 404-447-5402

Borg Textile Corp.

Wallpaper, Drapery, Bedspreads
105 Maple St.
Rossville, GA 30741
Phone 404-866-1743

Borges GmbH

Wallpaper & Wallcover
Sanforter Strabe 67
4500 Osnabruck
West Germany
Phone 011-49-54138080

Bradbury & Bradbury Wallpapers

Reproduction 19th Century Wallpaper
PO Box 155
Benicia, CA 94510
Send $10.00 for Catalog/Information
Mail Order Available
Phone 707-746-1900
FAX 707-746-9417

Bradd & Hall Blinds

Window Treatments - Blinds
7234 New Market
Manassas, VA 22110
Catalog/Information Available Free
Credit Cards VISA/MC
Toll Free 800-542-7502

Brandt's

Fabric, Wallpaper
Div. of Color Quest Inc.
4717 N. Seventh St.
Phoenix, AZ 85014
Phone 602-264-4246
FAX 602-264-4270

Brayton Textiles

Fabric
255 Swathmore Ave.
High Point, NC 27264
Phone 919-434-5100
FAX 919-434-5111

The Complete Sourcebook

Bremworth Carpets

Carpet
1776 Arnold Industrial Way
Concord, CA 94520

Phone 415-798-7242
Toll Free 800-227-3408
FAX 415-698-9674

Brentwood Originals

Decorator Pillows
PO Box 6272
Carson, CA 90749

Phone 213-637-6804

Bretlin Carpet

Carpet
Rte 7 Box 7656, Highway 225
Chatsworth, GA 30705

Phone 404-695-6734

Brewster Wallcovering Co.

Major Brand Wallcover and Wallpaper
67 Pacella Park Dr.
Randolph, MA 02368

Phone 617-963-4800
Toll Free 800-366-1700
FAX 617-963-4975

Bridge Wallcoverings

Manufacturer - Major Brand Wallcover
195 Walker Drive
Brampton, Ontario
Canada L6T 3Z9
Canada

Phone 416-791-8788
FAX 416-791-8078

Brintons Carpets USA Ltd.

Manufacturer - Carpet
919 Third Ave.
New York, NY 10022

Phone 212-832-0121

Brockway Carpets Ltd.

Carpet
Hoobrook
Kiddeminster, Worcs DY10 1XW
Great Britain

Phone 011-44-562/824737

Brod Dugan

Distributor - Wallcover, Wallpaper
2145 Schuetz Rd.
St. Louis, MO 63146

Phone 314-567-1111
FAX 314-567-4118

Broward Window Products, Inc.

Window Treatments
1980 Sterling Rd.
Dania, FL 33004

Phone 305-925-1496

Brunschwig & Fils

*English Countryside Style Wallpapers,
Fabrics*
75 Virginia Rd.
North White Plains, NY 10603-0905

Phone 914-684-5800

Burbank Linoleum & Carpet

Carpet
417 Irving Dr.
Burbank, CA 91504

Phone 818-848-9690

Buy Carpet Direct

Custom Carpet and Rugs
3239 S. Dixie Highway
Dalton, GA 30720

Toll Free 800-235-1079
FAX 404-277-9835

C & A Wallcoverings Inc.

Wallpaper & Wallcover
23645 Mercantile Rd.
Cleveland, OH 44122-5917

Phone 216-464-3700

Home Decorating

CS Brooks Corp.

Bedspreads, Comforters, Blankets
7201 Cockrill Bend
PO Box 516
Nashville, TN 37202
Phone 615-350-7400

CSS Decor Inc.

Window Treatments - Blinds
4433 Whitaker Ave.
Philadelphia, PA 19120
Phone 215-455-2440
Toll Free 800-332-6787
FAX 215-457-4210

Cabin Craft Rugs

Carpet & Rugs
Box 1208
Dalton, GA 30722
Phone 404-278-3812
Toll Free 800-275-2415

Cabin Creek Quilts

Order Direct - Custom Quilts, Wallhangings
4208 Malden Drive
Malden, WV 25306-6442
Send $2.00 for Catalog/Information
Mail Order Available
Credit Cards Accepted
Phone 304-925-9499

California Closet Company

Closet Organizers
1130 South Nova Rd.
Ormond Beach, FL 32174-7339
Catalog/Information Available Free
Mail Order Available
Phone 904-673-6969
FAX 904-676-0038

Callaway Carpets & Rugs

Carpets & Rugs
201 Industrial Drive
PO Box 2956
La Grange, GA 30241
Phone 404-883-5814
FAX 404-883-5534

Camelot Carpet Mills

Manufacturer - Carpet
140 S. Manhattan
Fullerton, CA 92631
Phone 714-774-7330

Camelot Design Studio

Manufacturer - Wallcover
61 Willett St.
Passaic, NJ 07055
Phone 201-471-0987

Canada Wallcoverings Corp.

Manufacturer - Wallcover, Wallpaper
49 Underwriters Rd.
Scarborough, ON M1R 3B4,
Canada
Phone 416-752-0000
FAX 416-752-5284

Canner Inc.

Decorative Mirrors, Architectural Moulding
PO Box 198
West Groton, MA 01472
Phone 508-448-6602

Cape Breton Wallcoverings

Manufacturer - Wallpaper, Wallcover
65 Memorial Dr.
North Sydney, NS B2A 3S8
Canada
Phone 902-794-7281
FAX 902-794-2090

Home Decorating

The Complete Sourcebook

Capel Rugs

Manufacturer - Rugs
831 N. Main St., PO Box 826
Troy, NC 27371

Phone 919-576-6211
Toll Free 800-334-3711
FAX 919-576-0718

Capital-Asam, Inc.

*Distributor - Major Brand Wallcover and
Wallpaper*
520 Hampton Park Blvd.
Capitol Heights, MD 20743

Phone 301-350-5400
FAX 301-350-7361

Carol Mead Design

Victorian Wallpaper , Linen
434 Deerfield Road
Pomfret Center, CT 06259

Catalog/Information Available Free
Send $5.00 for Catalog/Information
Mail Order Available

Phone 203-963-1927

Carole Fabrics Inc.

*Manufacturer - Wallpaper, Draperies,
Bedspreds*
Division of Hunter Douglas
PO Box 1436
Augusta, GA 30913

Phone 404-863-4742
FAX 404-863-8186

Caroline Country Ruffles

Curtains
420 W. Franklin Blvd.
Gastona, NC 28052

Send $2.00 for Catalog/Information
Toll Free 800-426-1039

Caroline's Ruffled Curtains, Inc.

Curtains
PO Box 1019
Burgaw, NC 28425

Send $3.50 for Catalog/Information
Phone 919-259-2074
Toll Free 800-282-0082

Carousel Carpet Mills

Manufacturer - Carpet
1 Carousel Lane
Ukiah, CA 95482

Send $10.00 for Catalog/Information
Phone 707-485-0333
FAX 707-485-5911

Carousel Designs Inc.

Manufacturer - Fabric
520 Hampton Park Blvd.
Capital Heights, MD 20743-3801

Carpet Crafts, Inc.

*Manufacturer - Nationwide Shipping &
Worldwide Export - Carpet*
PO Box 667
Dalton, GA 30722

Phone 706-695-0481
Toll Free 800-241-4538
FAX 706-695-0486

Carpet Express

Carpet and Vinyl Flooring
915 Market St.
Dalton, GA 30720

Mail Order Available
Toll Free 800-922-5582

Carpet Outlet

Major Brand - Factory Direct - Carpet
Box 417
Miles City, MT 59301

Mail Order Available
Toll Free 800-225-4351

Home Decorating

Carpetland

Nationwide Delivery - Discounted Prices - Carpet & Rugs

1117 South Wesleyan Blvd.
Rocky Mount, NC 27803-0405

Catalog/Information Available Free

Mail Order Available

Phone 919-446-2311
Toll Free 800-537-7847

Carpeton Mills Inc.

Manufacturer - Carpet

PO Box 57, Hwy. 411
Eton, GA 30724

Phone 404-695-4525
FAX 404-235-6235

Carpets of Georgia

Major Brand - Factory Direct - Carpet

PO Box 29
924 Greenhouse Dr.
Kennesaw, GA 30144

Toll Free 800-444-2259

Carpets of Worth Ltd.

Carpet

Severn Valley Mills
Stouport on Severn, Worcs DY13 9HA
Great Britain

Phone 011-44-299/82722

Carter Canopies

Canopies, Dust Ruffles, Coverlets

PO Box 808
Troutman, NC 28166

Send $1.00 for Catalog/Information

Phone 704-528-4071
FAX 704-528-6437

Carter Carpet

Manufacturer - Rugs, Carpet

617 Excelsior St.
Rome, GA 30161

Phone 404-235-8657
FAX 404-235-6235

Catalano & Sons, Inc.

Mirrors, Glass

301 Stagg St.
Brooklyn, NY 11206

Phone 718-821-6100

Catalina Carpet Mills Inc.

Manufacturer - Carpet

12836 E. Alondra Blvd.
Cerritos, CA 90701

Phone 213-926-5811
FAX 213-404-3925

Cavalier Prints Ltd.

Manufacturer - Wallpaper, Wallcover

44-02 11th St.
Long Island City, NY 11101

Phone 718-786-6657
FAX 718-786-4552

Century Fabrics Inc.

Decorator Fabrics

6435 N. Prosel Ave.
Lincolnwood, IL 60645

Phone 708-673-6435
Toll Free 800-247-4735
FAX 708-673-4333

Century House of Drapes

Window Treatments

2047 E. Palmdale Blvd.
Palmdale, CA 93550-4036

Phone 805-947-7373

Century Wallcoverings Inc.

Wallpaper & Wallcover

86 Finnell Dr.
Weymouth, MA 02188

Phone 617-337-9300
Toll Free 800-225-7828
FAX 617-335-5353

Home Decorating

The Complete Sourcebook

8 - 15

Chambord Prints Inc.

Manufacturer - Wallpaper, Wallcover
38 Jackson St.
Hoboken, NJ 07030

Phone 201-795-2007
FAX 201-792-1713

Charles Graser North America Inc.

Manufacturer - Ashton Gardens, Club Paradise, Corniche, Miki Niki
1055 Clark Blvd.
Bramalea, ON L6T 3W4
Canada

Phone 416-791-2700
FAX 416-791-5281

Charles W. Jacobsen, Inc.

Oriental Rugs
Learbury Centre
401 N. Salina St.
Syracuse, NY 13203

Catalog/Information Available Free
Mail Order Available

Phone 315-422-7832

Charles W. Rice & Co. Inc.

Custom Drapery
PO Box 165
Union City, IN 47390

Phone 317-964-3188
FAX 317-964-6833

Charleston Carpets

Manufacturer - Carpet
PO Box 364
Calhoun, GA 30701

Phone 404-629-7351
Toll Free 800-321-1768

Charleston Linens

Imported Linens
1270 Woodruff Rd.
Suite 109
Greenville, SC 29607

Send $3.00 for Catalog/Information
Credit Cards Accepted

Phone 803-297-5799

Charlton West

Livingroom Furniture
2750 Artesia Blvd.
Redondo Beach, CA 90278

Phone 213-371-7580

Chelsea Enterprises

Wallpaper & Wallcover
180 S. Broadway
White Plains, NY 10605

Toll Free 800-433-4193

Chemrex Inc.

Wallpaper & Wallcover
889 Valley Park Dr., Suite 1001
Shakopee, MN 55379-1854

Chesapeake Bay

Wallpaper & Wallcover
700 Prince Georges Blvd.
Upper Marlboro, MD 20772

Phone 301-249-7900
FAX 301-249-5863

Chesney Carpet Center

Carpet
506 E. Main
Siloam Springs, AK 72761-3212

Phone 501-524-5585

China Seas Inc.

Fabric
152 Maidson Ave.
Suite 1400
New York, NY 10016

Phone 212-725-2002

Churchwell Ltd.

Handpainted Floorcloths
PO Box 37021
Jacksonville, FL 32236

Phone 904-387-4249

Home Decorating

Claremont Rug Company – Colonial Wallcovering

Claremont Rug Company

Oriental Carpets
6087 Claremont Ave.
Oakland, CA 94618
Toll Free 800-441-1332

Clarence House Imports Ltd.

Trade Only - Fabric
211 E. 58th St.
New York, NY 10022
Phone 212-752-2890
FAX 212-755-3314

Classic Revivals, Inc.

*Trade Only - Reproduction Carpet,
Wallpaper, Fabric*
1 Design Center Pl., Suite 545
Boston, MA 02210
Phone 617-574-9030
FAX 617-574-9027

Cleanrite Carpet Sales

Carpet
1200 East Ave. W.
Chico, CA 95926-3034
Phone 916-891-5411

Closet Shop at Home

Closet Organizers
7833 Spring Ave.
Elkins Park, PA 19117
Send $1.00 for Catalog/Information
Phone 215-825-5821

Closet Systems Corp.

Closet Organizers
1175 Broadway
Hewlett, NY 11557
Phone 516-569-1400
Toll Free 800-400-1401
FAX 516-569-1655

Cloth Crafters

Shower Curtain
90 Rhine St.
Elkhart Lake, WI 53020
Catalog/Information Available Free
Credit Cards MC/VISA
Phone 414-876-7250

Codis House S.P.A.

*Manufacturer - Textile Wallcoverings,
Printed Fabrics*
Via Valsesia 44
28061 Biandrate (Novara) Italy
Italy
Phone 011-39-321/838241
FAX 011-39-321/838260

Cole & Son (Wallpapers) Ltd.

Wallpaper & Fabric
142 Offord Rd.
Islington, London N1 1NS
Great Britain
Phone 011-39-71/5802288
FAX 011-44-71/6369083

Collie Carpets Ltd.

Carpet
Causeway Mills (Great Britain)
Express Trading Est, Stonehill Rd.
Farnworth, Bolton BL4 9TP
Great Britain
Phone 011-44-204/71108

Collins & Aikman Corp.

Manufacturer - Wallcover, Wallpaper
23645 Mercantile Rd.
Cleveland, OH 44122
Phone 216-464-3700
Toll Free 800-441-2244
FAX 216-765-8608

Colonial Wallcovering

Wallpaper
707 E. Passyunk Ave.
Philadelphia, PA 19147
Mail Order Available
Phone 215-351-9300

The Complete Sourcebook

8 - 17

Color Your World Inc.

Paint, Varnish, Vinyl Wall Covering
10 Carson St.
Toronto, Ontario
CAN M8W 3R5
Canada

Phone 416-259-3251

Colorel Blinds

Factory Direct - Window Treatments - Blinds
8200 E. Park Meadow
Littleton, CO 80124

Toll Free 800-877-4800

Columbus Mills, Inc.

Carpet
PO Box 1560
Columbus, GA 31902

Phone 404-324-0111

Columbus Wallcovering Co.

Wallpaper & Wallcover
2 Lincoln Ave.
Rockville Centre, NY 11571

Phone 516-764-7100
Toll Free 800-521-5250

Comark Wallcoverings

Wallpaper & Wallcover
1902 Rosanna Ave.
Scranton, PA 18509

Phone 717-961-1622
FAX 717-961-3503

Combeau Industries

Manufacturer - Wallpaper, Wallcover
1400 Welsh Rd.
N. Wales, PA 19454

Phone 215-628-2000
FAX 215-628-8314

Coming Home

Quilts, Rugs, Blinds
Lands' End
1 Lands' End Lane
Dodgeville, WI 53595
Credit Cards VISA/MC/AMEX

Toll Free 800-345-3696

Connecticut Curtain Company

Decorator Drapery Hardware
Commerce Plaza, Rt. 6
Danbury, CT 06810
Mail Order Available
Credit Cards MC/VISA

Phone 203-798-1850
Toll Free 800-732-4549

Conrad Imports

Window Treatments
575 Tenth St.
San Francisco, CA 94103-4884

Phone 415-626-3303
FAX 415-626-6302

Contemporary Interiors, Inc.

Draperies, Drapery Hardware
6113 Benhurst Rd.
Baltimore, MD 21209

Phone 301-358-9111

Contract Wallcoverings

Distributor - Name Brand Wallpaper and Wallcover
2985 W. Twelve Mile Road
Berkley, MI 48072

Phone 313-543-3340
FAX 313-543-4754

Coronet Industries Inc.

Carpet & Rugs
PO Box 1248
Dalton, GA 30720

Phone 404-259-4511

Country Braid House

New England Braided Rugs
R.F.D., #2 Box 29 Clark Rd.
Tilton, NH 03276

Catalog/Information Available Free

Mail Order Available

Credit Cards MC/VISA/DISCOVER

Phone 603-286-4511
FAX 603-286-4155

Country Curtains

Will ship outside USA - Curtains, Comforters, Bedspreads

At The Red Lion Inn
Stockbridge, MA 01262

Catalog/Information Available Free

Mail Order Available

Credit Cards Accepted

Phone 413-243-1300
Toll Free 800-456-0321
FAX 413-243-1067

Country Ruffles & Rods

Window Treatments

3610 Ashley Phosphate Rd.
N. Charleston, SC 29418

Send $1.00 for Catalog/Information

Mail Order Available

Phone 803-760-2095

Couristan

Rugs and Broadloom

Two Executive Drive
Fort Lee, NJ 07024

Send $4.00 for Catalog/Information

Phone 201-585-8500
Toll Free 800-223-6186
FAX 201-585-8582

CoverAge Inc.

Manufacturer - Wallpaper, Wallcover

20 Altieri Way, Unite 3
Warwick, RI 02886

Phone 401-738-1197
Toll Free 800-255-2694
FAX 401-738-1274

Coverwalls, Inc.

Manufacturer - Wallcover

85 Maple St.
Weehawken, NJ 07087

Phone 201-864-1102
FAX 201-864-7265

Covington Fabrics Corp.

Window Lace

267 Fifth Ave.
New York, NY 10016

Mail Order Available

Phone 212-689-2200

Craft King

Craft Supply

252 Leelon Rd.
Lakeland, FL 33809-6106

Send $2.00 for Catalog/Information

Phone 813-686-9600

Craftex Mills, Inc.

Upholstery & Drapery Fabric

450 Sentry Pkwy. East
Blue Bell, PA 19422

Phone 215-941-1212
FAX 215-941-7171

Crane Plumbing

Toilets and Water Closets

1235 Hartrey Ave.
Evanston, IL 60202

Catalog/Information Available Free

Mail Order Available

Phone 708-864-9777

Criterion Mills, Inc.

Manufacturer - Carpet
547 Joe Frank Harris Pkwy.
PO Box 1309
Cartersville, GA 30120

Phone 404-386-2121
Toll Free 800-334-4462

Crown Corp.

Wallcovering, Fabrics, Carpet
1801 Wynkoop St., Ste. 235
Denver, CO 80202

Catalog/Information Available Free

Mail Order Available

Phone 303-292-1313
Toll Free 800-422-2099
FAX 303-292-1933

Crown Wallcovering

Manufacturer - Wallpaper, Wallcover
35 Horizon Blvd.
S. Hackensack, NJ 07606

Phone 201-440-7000
FAX 201-440-7109

Crown Wallpaper Co.

Distributor - Major Brand Wallcover,
Wallpaper, Fabric
88 Ronson Drive
Rexdale, ON M9W 1B9
Canada

Phone 416-245-2900
FAX 416-245-0760

Crutchfield Wallcoverings Inc.

Wallpaper & Wallcover
223 Cumberland Ave.
Memphis, TN 38112

Phone 901-323-4133
FAX 901-327-6661

Curtain Cottage

Custom Country Style Curtains
PO Box 34
Sweet Home, TX 77987

Phone 512-293-7707

Custom Laminations Inc.

Custom Services to the Trade & Pricing -
Window Treatments, Paperbacking
Wallpaper, Vinylized Fabric, Fabric
Backing, Custom Quilts
932 Market St.
PO Box 2066
Paterson, NJ 07509

Send $2.00 for Catalog/Information

Phone 201-279-9174
FAX 201-279-6916

Custom Shades

Custom Lampshades
4434 N.W. 35th Court
Miami, FL 33142

Catalog/Information Available Free

Phone 305-633-1653
FAX 305-635-1037

Custom Windows & Walls

Wallcover, Window Treatments
32525 Stephenson Hwy.
Madison Heights, MI 48071

Catalog/Information Available Free

Mail Order Available

Credit Cards VISA/MC/DISCOVER

Toll Free 800-777-7747

Cynthia Gibson, Inc.

Manufacturer - Cynthia Gibson "Pretty
Rooms" and Romance Wallcoverings and
Fabrics
Box 706 Western Point Rd.
York Harbor, ME 03911

Phone 212-758-8977
FAX 212-758-4961

D & W Carpet & Rug Co.

Carpet, Rugs
PO Box 537
Chatsworth, GA 30705

Phone 404-695-4624
FAX 404-695-6237

D.L. Couch Contract Wallcovering

Distributor - Contract Vinyls, Textiles and Acoustical Wallcoverings
309 Park View Drive
New Castle, IN 47362
Toll Free 800-433-0790

D.S.C. Fabrics Inc.

Custom Draperies, Bedspreads, Blinds
5570 W. 60th Ave.
Arvada, CO 80003
Toll Free 800-873-0000
FAX 303-421-1821

DMI Drapery Mfg.

Wallpaper, Draperies, Bedspreads
8205 SW 29th
Oklahoma City, OK 73179
Phone 405-745-2931
FAX 405-745-2613

Dacor

Manufacturer - Kitchen Cooktops & Ranges
950 South Raymond Ave.
Pasadena, CA 91109
Phone 818-799-1000
Toll Free 800-793-0093

Dae Dong Wallpaper Co. Ltd.

Wallpaper, Wallcover
121 Buam-dong Busanjin-ku
Busan, Korea
Korea
Phone 011-82-51-8081331
FAX 011-82-51-8059511

Daisy Decorative Products

Draperies, Curtains, Bedspreads
108 Brandon Ave.
Toronto
Ont, CAN M6H 2E1
Canada
Phone 416-530-0400
FAX 416-530-1505

Dana Kelly Oriental Rugs

Oriental Rugs
870 East High
Chevy Chase Place
Lexington, KY 40502
Phone 606-266-9274

Dana's Curtains & Draperies

Ruffles, Swags & Jabots
105 Mountain Ave.
Hackettstown, NJ 07840
Send $4.00 for Catalog/Information
Toll Free 800-448-3805

Darren's Decoys & Wooden Ducks

Decoys, Ducks
PO Box 195
Severna Park, MD 21146-0195
Catalog/Information Available Free
Mail Order Available
Phone 410-647-3210
FAX 410-647-3210

David & Dash

Manufacturer - Wallcover, Fabric
Div. of Dash Ind.
2563 N. Miami Ave.
Miami, FL 33137
Phone 305-573-8000
FAX 305-576-4620

David Rothschild Co. Inc.

Upholstery & Drapery Fabrics
512 12th St.
PO Box 2002
Columbus, GA 31902
Phone 404-324-2411
FAX 404-324-3947

David S. Gibson Inc.

Drapery & Upholstery Fabrics
5500 N. Figueroa St.
Los Angeles, CA 90042
Phone 213-256-5415

Davidson-Bishop Corp.

Manufacturer - Window Treatments - Blinds
406 E. Fourth St.
Winston-Salem, NC 27101
Phone 919-722-9450

Davis Braided Rug co.

Rugs, Carpets
PO Box 3333
Cleveland, TN 37311
Phone 615-472-6567

Daycor West Wallcoverings

Distributor - Major Brand Wallpaper and Wallcover
5760 Cedarbridge Way
Richmond, BC V6X 2A7
Canada
Phone 604-273-2296
FAX 604-270-8892

De La West Draperies

Window Treatments - Draperies, Bedspreads
905 Woodrow
Hoston, TX 77006
Phone 713-523-1211

Decor International Wallcovering Inc.

Wallcovering
PO Box 8338
Long Island City, NY 11101
Phone 718-830-8757

Decoral Inc.

Manufacturer - Stencils
165 Marine St.
Farmingdale, NY 11735
Toll Free 800-645-9868
FAX 516-752-1009

Decoy Shop

Decorative Decoys, Lamps
PO Box 270, Main St.
Bowdoinham, ME 04008
Phone 207-666-8461

Dekortex Co.

Manufacturer - Wallcovering & Fabric
6900 Mooradian Dr.
PO Box 282
Niagara Falls, NY 14304
Phone 716-283-7405
FAX 716-283-2126

Del Mar Window Coverings

Manufacturer - Window Treatments
7150 Fenwick Lane
Westminster, CA 92683
Phone 714-891-4311

Dellinger, Inc.

Custom Made Carpet
PO Drawer 273
Rome, GA 30162-0273
Phone 404-291-7402

Design/Craft Fabric Corp.

Decorator Fabric and Vertical Blinds
7227 Oak Park Ave.
Niles, IL 60648
Phone 708-647-0888

Designer Carpets

Carpets
351 Peachtree Hills NE
Atlanta, GA 30305
Phone 404-262-1720
Toll Free 800-241-0456
FAX 404-261-0652

Designer Handprints

Wallpaper & Wallcover
PO Box 28863
Philadelphia, PA 19151
Phone 215-477-6506
FAX 215-878-4359

Designer Home Fabrics

Fabric
PO Box 2650
Cinnaminson, NJ 08077
Toll Free 800-666-4202

Home Decorating

Designer Secrets — Downs Carpet Co., Inc.

Designer Secrets

Wallcoverings, Fabrics, Bedspreads, Furniture, Window Treatments

Box 529
Fremont, NE 68025

Send $2.00 for Catalog/Information

Toll Free 800-955-2559
FAX 402-727-1817

Designer's Edge

Picture Frames

225 Edgeley Blvd., Unit 1
Concord
Ont, CAN 14K 3Y7
Canada

Phone 416-738-7855
FAX 416-738-7815

Diamond Rug & Carpet Mills Inc.

Manufacturer - Rugs & Carpet

PO Box 46
Eton, GA 30724

Phone 404-695-9446

Dianthus Ltd.

Curtains

PO Box 870
Plymounth, MA 02362

Send $4.00 for Catalog/Information

Phone 508-747-4179
Toll Free 800-288-3426

Direct Wallpaper

Wallpaper

374 Hall St.
Phoenixville, PA 19460

Mail Order Available

Credit Cards Accepted

Toll Free 800-336-9255

Distinctive Window Fashions

Blinds

306 Roma Jean Pkwy.
Streamwood, IL 60617

Phone 708-289-4266
FAX 708-289-5125

Domestications

Curtains, Bedspreads, Sheets

PO Box 40
Hanover, PA 17333-0040

Domus Parati S.P.A.

Manufacturer - Capriccio, Mithos and Maxima, Tentazioni Wallcover

Via Valcava 3
Milano, 20155
Italy

Phone 011-39-2/323146
FAX 011-39-2/324209

Dorothy's Ruffled Originals, Inc.

Ready Made Custom Drapes & Curtains

6721 Market St.
Wilmington, NC 28405

Send $4.00 for Catalog/Information

Mail Order Available

Phone 919-791-1296
Toll Free 800-367-6849

Dorsett Carpet Mills Inc.

Manufacturer - Carpet

PO Box 740, Green Rd.
Chatsworth, GA 30705

Toll Free 800-241-4066
FAX 404-695-0797

Downs Carpet Co., Inc.

Carpet

PO Box 475
Willow Grove, PA 19090

Phone 215-672-1100
FAX 215-672-7999

The Complete Sourcebook

Driwood Moulding Co.

Factory Direct - Nationwide Shipping - Architectural Millwork, Moulding, Doors, Curved Stairs, Raised Panel Wall - Poplar Wood, Walnut, Oak, Mahogany, Cherry

PO Box 1729
Florence, SC 29503

Send $6.00 for Catalog/Information

Mail Order Available

Credit Cards Accepted

Phone 803-669-2478
FAX 803-669-4874

Du Pont Stainmaster

Carpet

71 Southgate Blvd.
Southgate Industrial Center
New Castle, DE 19720

Toll Free 800-438-7668

Dunn-Edwards Corp.

Manufacturer - Paints & Wallcoverings

4885 E. 52nd Place
Los Angeles, CA 90040

Phone 213-771-3330
FAX 213-771-2095

Duralee Fabrics

Manufacturer - Fabric

1775 Fifth Ave.
Bayshore, NY 11746

Phone 516-273-8800
FAX 516-273-8996

Duratex Inc.

Blinds

6728 Federal Blvd.
Denver, CO 80221

Phone 303-429-3541

Durkan Patterned Carpet

Manufacturer - Carpet

PO Box 1006
Dalton, GA 30720

Phone 404-278-7037
Toll Free 800-241-4580

Duron Paints & Wallcoverings

Manufacturer - Paints, Wallcover, Wallpaper

10551 Tucker St.
Beltsville, MD 20705

Phone 301-937-4700
Toll Free 800-635-0038
FAX 301-595-0429

E. D. I.

Blinds

PO Box 2177
1515 Leininger Ave.
Elkhart, IN 46515

Phone 219-294-5428
FAX 219-522-1881

East Carolina Wallpaper Market

Order by Phone - Wallpaper

1106 Pink Hill Rd.
Kinston, NC 28501

Credit Cards VISA/MC

Toll Free 800-848-7283

Eddie Bauer Home Collection

Bedding, Furniture, Home Accessories

PO Box 3787
Seattle, WA 98124-3787

Credit Cards Accepted

Toll Free 800-426-8020

Edward Laurence & Co.

Manufacturer - Handprinted Wallcovering and Fabrics

Division of Webster Wallpaper Co. Inc.
2737 Webster Ave.
Bronx, NY 10458

FAX 212-295-7265

Egan-Laing Inc.

Distributor - Wallcover, Wallpaper

204, place d'Youville
Montreal, PQ H2Y 2B4
Canada

Phone 514-288-6122
FAX 514-288-6571

Home Decorating

Einstein Moomjy

Order by Phone - Carpets
150 East 58th St.
New York, NY 10155
Credit Cards VISA/MC/AMEX

Phone 212-758-0900

FAX 212-980-8611

Eisenhart Wallcoverings Co.

Manufacturer - Wallcovering and Fabric for Ashford House, Color Tree Designs and Eisenhart
1649 Broadway, PO Box 464
Hanover, PA 17331

Phone 717-632-5918

Toll Free 800-726-3267

FAX 717-632-3329

Elizabeth Eaton Ltd.

Wallpaper & Co-ordinating Fabric
30 Elizabeth St.
London SW1W 9RB
Great Britain

Phone 011-44-71/5890118

FAX 011-44-71/7307294

Emmet Perry & Co.

Oriental Rugs
5120 Woodway Drive
Houston, TX 77056

Phone 713-961-4665

Emperor Clock Company

Factory Direct - Clocks & Furniture
Emperor Industrial Park
PO Box 1089
Fairhope, AL 36533
Send $1.00 for Catalog/Information

Phone 205-928-2316

Toll Free 800-542-0011

Endisco Supply Co.

Blinds
1315 E. Fifth St.
Tulsa, OK 74120

Phone 918-583-3373

FAX 918-583-3383

Enterprise Wallcoverings, Inc.

Distributor - Major Brand Wallcover, Wallpaper
2320 E. Dominguez St.
Carson, CA 90749-6244

Phone 213-513-0705

FAX 213-513-1593

Epoch Designs

Victorian Stencils
PO Box 4033
Elwyn, PA 19063

Send $3.00 for Catalog/Information

Mail Order Available

Credit Cards MC/VISA/Check/Money Order

Phone 610-565-9180

Especially Lace

Decorative Lace for Windows
202 Fifth St.
West Des Moines, IA 50265

Send $4.00 for Catalog/Information

Mail Order Available

Phone 515-277-8778

Essex Wallcoverings

Manufacturer - Wallpaper, Wallcover
3 University Plaza
Hackensack, NJ 07601

Phone 201-489-0100

FAX 201-489-4394

Eurotex

Carpet, Wallcover
165 West Ontario St.
Philadelphia, PA 19140

Phone 215-739-8844

Toll Free 800-523-0731

FAX 215-423-0940

Home Decorating

The Complete Sourcebook

8 - 25

Exeter Wallcovering

Manufacturer - Wallpaper, Wallcover
79 Madison Ave.
Div. of F. Schumacher & Co.
New York, NY 10016
Phone 212-213-7991

Eyedeal Carpets

Carpet
15705 Condon Ave.
Lawndale, CA 90260-2532
Phone 213-643-9006

Eykis Inc.

Wallpaper & Wallcover
5673 E. Shelby Dr.
Memphis, TN 38141
Phone 901-365-2239

F. Schumacher

Wallpaper & Fabric
79 Madison Ave.
New York, NY 10016
Phone 212-213-7900

FSC Wallcoverings

Distributor - Major Brand Wallcover, Fabric
Division of F. Schumacher & Co.
79 Madison Ave.
New York, NY 10016
Phone 212-213-7900
FAX 212-213-7848

Fabra-Wall Ltd.

Wallcover
PO Box 5117
Sta. E, Edmonton
Alta, CAN T5P 4C5
Canada
Phone 403-987-4444

Fabric Fair

Fabric & Wallpaper
PO Box 143
Orpington, Kent
BR6 0JJ
Great Britain
Credit Cards Accepted
Phone 011-44-689/897183

Fabric Shop

Drapery & Upholstery Fabric
120 North Seneca St.
Shippensburg, PA 17257
Catalog/Information Available Free
Toll Free 800-233-7012

Fabrics By Design

Order by Phone - Decorator Fabrics
343 N.E. Fifth Ave.
Delray Beach, FL 33843
Credit Cards VISA/MC
Phone 407-278-9700
Toll Free 800-527-3776

Fabrics By Phone

Order by Phone - Decorator Fabrics
PO Box 309
Walnut Bottom, PA 17266
Send $3.00 for Catalog/Information
Credit Cards VISA/MC
Toll Free 800-233-7012

Fabrics Plus

Fabric
1981 Moreland Pkwy B-3
Annapolis, MD 21401
Toll Free 800-638-4820

Fabricut

Draperies & Bedspreads
9303 East 46th St.
Tulsa, OK 74145
Phone 918-622-7700
Toll Free 800-888-7171
FAX 918-665-1177

Fairfield Carpets & Fabrics

Carpet, Rugs, Fabrics
3 Market Place Dr.
Hilton Head, SC 29928

Phone 803-689-5404

FAX 803-689-5405

Faith's Lacery

Country & Victorian Window Treatments
89 West Main St.
Dundee, IL 60118

Send $2.00 for Catalog/Information

Family Heir-Loom Weavers

Runners, Carpet, Placemats
485 Meadowview Drive
Red Lion, PA 17356

Send $3.00 for Catalog/Information

Phone 717-246-2431

FAX 717-246-2431

Fara Mfg.Co., Inc.

Draperies, Window Shades, Woven Wood Shades
2754 N.W. North River Dr.
Miami, FL 33142

Phone 305-633-1546

Fashion Tech

Window Treatments - Blinds
PO Box 14160
Portland, OR 97214

Toll Free 800-553-7807

Fashion Wallcoverings

Distributor - Wallcover, Wallpaper
105 West Beaver Creek Rd., Unit 7
Richmond Hill ON L4B 1C6
Canada

Phone 416-882-0313

FAX 416-882-0316

Fashion Wallcoverings, Inc.

Distributor - Wallcover, Wallpaper
2040 W. 110th St.
Cleveland, OH 44102

Phone 216-631-6700

FAX 216-651-0047

Faux Effects Inc.

Manufacturer - Wallcovering - Faux Finishing Products
3435 Aviation Blvd.
Vero Beach, FL 32960

Mail Order Available

Phone 407-778-9044

FAX 407-778-9653

Fibreworks Corp.

Wallpaper & Wallcover
1729 Research Drive
Louisville, KY 40299-2201

Phone 502-499-9944

Toll Free 800-843-0063

FAX 502-499-9880

Fidelity Industries

Manufacturer - Wallcover, Wallpaper
559 Route 23
PO Box 218
Wayne, NJ 07470

Phone 201-696-9120

FAX 201-696-4123

Fieldcrest Cannon, Inc.

Bedspreades, Blankets, Sheets, Towels, Rugs
1271 Avenue of the Americas
New York, NY 10020

Phone 212-536-1200

Toll Free 800-841-3336

Fine Art Wallcovering Ltd.

Wallpaper & Wallcover
224 Buffalo Ave.
Freeport, NY 11520

Phone 516-378-1767

FAX 516-378-1784

Fine Art Wallcoverings, Ltd.

Manufacturer - Wallcover - Doll House, Brush Strokes, Classic Traditions, Floribunda, Co-ordinates, Pastelle, Personal Expressions
Victoria Mill, Macclesfield Rd.
Holmes Chapel, CW4 7PA
Crewe, Chesire, England
Great Britain

Phone 011-44-447-32323

Firth Carpets Ltd.

Carpet
PO Box 17, Clifton Mills
Brighouse, W. Yorkshire
HD6 4EJ
Great Britain

Phone 011-44-484/71371

Flagship Carpet

Carpet & Rugs
Hwy 411 609 S. 3rd Ave.
Chatsworth, GA 30705-1189

Phone 404-695-4055
Toll Free 800-848-4055

Flemington Fabric Decorating Center

Decorator Fabric, Curtains, Window Lace
139 Main St.
Flemington, NJ 08822

Catalog/Information Available Free

Phone 908-782-5111
FAX 908-782-5111

Floorcloths

Reproduction Hand Painted Floorcloths
920 Edgewater
Severna Park, MD 21146

Send $2.00 for Catalog/Information

Mail Order Available

Phone 301-647-3328

Florida Blinds

Window Treatments - Blinds
2377 NW 97th Ave.
Miami, FL 33172

Phone 305-594-3999
FAX 305-477-8887

Florida Shades Inc.

Window Treatments - Blinds & Shades
30798 US Highway 19 N.
Palm Harbor, FL 34684

Phone 813-784-3944
FAX 813-786-3680

Folkheart Rag Rugs

Hand Stenciled Amish Rugs
18 Main St.
Bristol, VT 05443

Mail Order Available

Phone 802-453-4101

Forbo Industries

Flooring - Linoleum
Humboldt Industrial Park
Maplewood Dr., PO Box 667
Hazelton, PA 18201

Phone 717-459-0771
Toll Free 800-842-7839
FAX 717-450-0258

Forbo Wallcoverings Inc.

Wallpaper & Wallcover
3 Killdeer Ct.
Bridgeport, NJ 08014

Phone 609-467-0200
FAX 609-453-3959

Foremost Wallcoverings

Manufacturer - Wallcover, Wallpaper
195 Walker Drive
Brampton, ON L6T 3Z9

Phone 416-791-8788
FAX 416-791-9491

Form III

Custom Area Rugs, Carpeting
108 E. Main St.
PO Box 143
Crothersville, IN 47229
Phone 812-793-3636
FAX 812-793-3637

Four Seasons Wallcoverings

Wallpaper & Wallcover
23645 Mercantile Rd.
Beachwood, OH 44122
Phone 216-464-3700

Frances Lee Jasper Oriental Rugs

Oriental Rugs
1330 Bardstown Rd.
Louisville, KY 40204
Phone 502-459-1044

Frankel Associates, Inc.

Fabric
1948 Troutman Street
Ridgewood, NY 11385
Phone 718-386-2455
Toll Free 800-221-4670
FAX 614-221-5223

Frankford Wallcovering Inc.

Manufacturer - Wallcover, Wallpaper
7120 N. Broad St.
Philadelphia, PA 19126
Phone 215-924-2270

Fred Cole Factory Inc.

Manufacturer - Wallpaper, Wallcover
3505 136th NE
Marysville, WA 98270
Phone 206-659-8471

Fred G. Anderson, Inc.

Distributor - Major Brand Wallcover and Wallpaper
5825 Excelsior Blvd.
Minneapolis, MN 55416
Phone 612-927-1800
FAX 612-927-1851

Fred Moheban Gallery

Oriental and European Carpet and Rugs
730 Fifth Ave at 57th St.
New York, NY 10019
Phone 212-397-9060

Frissell Fabrics, Inc.

Upholstery & Drapery Fabric
PO Box 40
Russville, GA 30741
Phone 404-866-1010

G & L Shades Inc.

Window Treatments - Blinds, Shades
270 S. Milpitas Blvd.
Milpitas, CA 95035
Phone 408-263-8400
FAX 408-263-7474

Gagne Wallcovering Inc.

Wallpaper & Wallcover
2076 Sunnydale Blvd.
Clearwater, FL 34625
Phone 813-461-1812
FAX 813-447-6277

Gail Grisi Stenciling Inc.

Stencils
Box 1263
Haddonfield, NJ 08033
Send $2.00 for Catalog/Information

Galacar & Co.

Available only to Interior Designers & Architects - Handscreened Fabric & Wallpaper
144 Main St.
Essex, MA 01929
Phone 508-768-6118
FAX 508-768-3351

Galaxie Handprints Inc.

Wallpaper & Wallcover
38 William St.
Amityville, NY 11701
Phone 516-789-4224
FAX 516-789-4234

Galaxy Carpet Mills

Manufacturer - Carpet , Rugs
Green Rd.
Chatsworth, GA 30705-8551
Phone 404-695-0531

Gamrod Harman/Shaheen Wallcovering

Distributor - Major Brand Wallcover , Wallpaper
120 LaGrange Ave.
Rochester, NY 14613
Phone 716-254-3030
FAX 716-254-3418

Gamrod-Harman Co.

Window Treatments - Blinds
120 LaGrange Ave.
Rochester, NY 14613
Phone 716-254-4080
FAX 716-254-3418

Gaskell Carpets Ltd.

Carpet
Wheatfield Mill
Rushton, Blackburn, Lancs BB1 4NJ
Great Britain
Phone 011-44-254/885566

Gencorp Polymer Products

Distributor - Major Brand Wallcover, Wallpaper
1722 Indianwood Circle, Ste. A
Maumeeo, OH 43537
Phone 419-891-1500
FAX 419-891-4437

George Wells Rugs

Rug Hooking, Dies, Yarns
565 Cedar Swamp Rd.
Glen Head, NY 11545
Phone 516-676-2056

Georgian Carpets Ltd.

Carpet
Clensmore Mills
Kiddeminster, Worcs
DY10 2LH
Great Britain
Phone 011-44-562/820800

Gilman Wallcoverings

Distributor - Major Brand Wallcover, Wallpaper
325 Fulton Industrial Circle
Atlanta, GA 30336
Phone 404-696-3771
Toll Free 800-222-4894

Glammar Mills Ltd.

Drapery, Curtain, Upholstery Fabric
521 Boul Lebeau
Montreal
Que., CAN H4N 1S2
Canada
Phone 514-334-7002

Glendale Carpet Co.

Carpet
625 1/2 S Brand Blvd.
Glendale, CA 91204
Phone 818-545-7784

Global Blind Express

Name Brand Window Treatments - Blinds
PO Box 39
Arden, NC 28704
Credit Cards Accepted
Toll Free 800-972-3285

Gold Label Carpet Mills

Order Direct- Discounted Prices - Carpet
PO Box 3876
Dalton, GA 30721
Mail Order Available
Toll Free 800-346-4531
FAX 706-673-6390

Homespun Fabrics & Draperies

Fabrics & Draperies
654 McGrath, PO Box 3223
Ventura, CA 93003

Send $2.00 for Catalog/Information

Credit Cards VISA/MC

Phone 805-642-8111

FAX 805-642-0759

Homespun Weavers

Country Style Fabric, Tablecloths, Placements
South Seventh St.
Emmaus, PA 18049

Send $0.50 for Catalog/Information

Mail Order Available

Phone 215-967-4550

Toll Free 800-290-4550

Honani Crafts

Navajo Rugs, Pottery, Basketry
PO Box 317
Second Mesa, AZ 86043

Phone 602-734-2238

Hopi Arts & Crafts

Wicker Baskets, Textiles, Pottery
PO Box 37
Second Mesa, AZ 86043

Phone 602-634-2463

Hornick Industries

Drapery, Curtains, Bedspreads
261 5th Ave.
New York, NY 10016

Phone 212-679-2448

House of Blinds

Blinds
23000 W 8 Mile
Southfield, MI 48034-4394

Phone 313-357-4710

House of Clay

Decorative Indian Pottery
PO Box 80030
Baton Rouge, LA 70808

Catalog/Information Available Free

Credit Cards Accepted

Phone 504-673-8112

House of Persia

Persian and Oriental Rugs
107 West Paces Ferry Rd.
Atlanta, GA 30305

Phone 404-266-8458

Houston Oriental Rug Gallery

Oriental Rugs
2702 Sacket
Houston, TX 77098

Phone 713-528-2666

Hoyne Industries

Mirrors
777 S. Flagler Dr., Ste. 1000E
West Palm Beach, FL 33401-6162

Hudson Venetian Blind Service Inc.

Wood Blinds
2000 Twilight Lane
Richmond, VA 23235

Mail Order Available

Phone 804-276-5700

Hunter & Co., Inc.

Distributor - Major Brand Wallcover , Wallpaper
1945 W. Green Drive
PO Box 2363
High Point, NC 27261

Phone 919-883-4161

FAX 919-889-3270

Golden Wallpaper

Wallpaper & Fabric
1061 Pontiac Rd.
Drexel Hill, PA 19026

Catalog/Information Available Free

Good & Co. Floorclothmakers

Floorcloths
Box 497
Dublin, NH 03444

Mail Order Available

Phone 603-563-8021

Gradus Carpets Ltd.

Carpet
Jack Lee Mill, Knight St.
Macclesfield, Cheshire SK11 7NE
Great Britain

Phone 011-44-625/611969

Graham & Brown Ltd.

Wallpaper & Wallcover
India Mill Harwood St.
Blackburn Lancashire, England
Great Britain

Phone 011-44-25/4661122

FAX 011-44-25/4680849

Gramercy

Art Deco-Style Wallpapers
79 Madison Ave.
New York, NY 10016

Phone 212-213-7900

Toll Free 800-552-9255

Great Carpet Co.

Carpet
207 S. Brand Blvd.
Glendale, CA 91204

Phone 818-247-2990

Greeff Fabrics Inc.

Manufacturer - Period Style Wallpaper, Fabric
210 Madison Ave.
New York, NY 10016

Phone 212-578-1246

Toll Free 800-223-0357

FAX 212-578-1247

Groff's

Wallcover & Wallpaper
1106 Pinkhill Rd.
Kinston, NC 28501

Catalog/Information Available Free

Toll Free 800-848-7283

Groundworks Unlimited

Distributor - Major Brand Wallcover, Wallpaper
800 Central Blvd.
Carlstadt, NJ 07072

Phone 201-438-8444

FAX 201-438-7034

GuildMaster Arts

Decorative Screens
PO Box 10725
Springfield, MO 65808-0725

Gulf Coast Window Covering Inc.

Window Treatments - Blinds
PO Box 25346
Houston, TX 77265-5346

Phone 713-861-8282

Toll Free 800-392-4336

FAX 713-862-9739

Hallie Greer

Fabric and Wallpaper
Cushing Corners Rd.
Freedom, NH 03836

Send $4.00 for Catalog/Information

Credit Cards VISA/MC

Phone 603-539-6007

Hamilton Adams Imports Ltd.

Imported Wallcover, Wallpaper, Fabric
101 County Ave.
Secaucus, NJ 07096-2489

Phone 201-866-3250

FAX 201-866-7213

Hampton Wallcovering

Wallpaper & Wallcover
Div. of Bayview
41 E. Sunrise Hwy.
Lindenhurst, NY 11757

Phone 516-884-9301

Hang-It-Now Wallpaper Stores

Order by Phone - Wallcovering and Decorator Fabrics
10517F N. Main St.
Archdale, NC 27263

Credit Cards Accepted

Toll Free 800-325-9494

FAX 919-431-0449

Hannah Wingate House

19th Century Framed Mirrors
11 Main St.
Rockport MA 01966

Phone 508-546-1008

Harmony Supply Inc.

Wallpaper and Window Treatments
PO Box 313
Medford, MA 02155

Credit Cards VISA/MC

Phone 617-395-2600

FAX 617-396-8218

Harriet's House

Quilts, Cushions
36 The High St.
Royal Tunbridge Wells, Kent
TN1 1XQ
Great Britain

Phone 011-44-892/516105

FAX 011-44-892/516107

Hawthorne Carpet

Carpet & Rugs
414 W. Hawthorne
Dalton, GA 30720

Phone 404-278-8338

FAX 404-278-7994

Hawthorne Prints Inc.

Wallpaper & Wallcover
121-129 Wagaraw Rd.
Hawthorne, NJ 07506

Phone 201-427-4232

FAX 201-423-3303

Helios Carpets

Rugs & Carpet
721 River Street
PO Box 1928
Calhoun, GA 30701

Phone 404-629-5311

Toll Free 800-843-5138

FAX 404-629-1216

Helm Products Ltd.

Wood & Brass Curtain Poles (Rods) - Trade Discounts
Unit 18, Central Trading Est
Staines, Middx
TW18 4XE
Great Britain

Phone 011-44-784/469435

FAX 011-44-784/469436

Henry Calvin Fabrics

Fabric
290 Division St.
San Francisco, CA 94103

Phone 415-863-1944

FAX 415-431-1953

Heritage Floorcloths

Floorcloths
PO Box 10
Sebec Village, ME 04481

Send $2.00 for Catalog/Information

Mail Order Available

Phone 207-564-3941

Heritage Imports, Inc.

Nationwide Shipping - Lace for Windows
PO Box 328
Pella, IA 50219

Catalog/Information Available Free

Credit Cards MC/VISA

Phone 515-628-4949

Toll Free 800-354-0668

FAX 515-628-1689

Heritage Rugs

Handwoven Rag Rugs
964 Almshouse Rd.
Jamison, PA 18929

Mail Order Available

Credit Cards VISA/MC

Phone 215-343-5196

Hickory Wallcovering

Wallpaper & Wallcover
1400 Welsh Rd.
North Wales, PA 19454

Phone 215-628-2000

FAX 215-628-8314

Hinson & Co.

Handscreened Wallpaper and Fabric
27-35 Jackson Ave.
Long Island City, NY 11101

Phone 718-482-1100

FAX 718-937-7566

Hirshfield's, Inc.

Distributor - Major Brand Wallcover & Wallpaper
725 Second Ave. N.
Minneapolis, MN 55405

Phone 612-377-3910

FAX 612-377-2734

Hoffman Mills

Wallpaper & Wallcover
470 Park Ave. S.
New York, NY 10016

Phone 212-684-3700

FAX 212-779-1299

Hollytex Carpet

Carpet
300 N. Baldwin Park
PO Box 1255
City of Industry, CA

Phon

Holvoet NV

Manufacturer - Holvo Wallcovering
Baron De Pelichy Stra
B-8700 Izegem
Belgium

Phone .....

FAX .....

Home Fabric Mills,

Order by Phone - Dec
882 South Main St.
Cheshire, CT 06410

Credit Cards VISA/MC

Phone

Home Fashions, Inc

Vertical Blinds, Pleated
Louverdrape Div.
1100 Colorado Ave.
Santa Monica, CA 9040

Phone ..

FAX ..

Homeland Carpet Mi

Carpet
Div. of Sunrise Ind.
PO Box 1077
Chatsworth, GA 30705

Phone ....

Toll Free ....

FAX ....

Hunter Douglas Window Fashions

Window Treatments - Window Shadings, Pleated Shades, Horizontal and Vertical Blinds

2 Park Way, PO Box 740
Upper Saddle River, NJ 07458

Catalog/Information Available Free

Phone 201-327-8200

Toll Free 800-937-7895

Hunting Valley Prints

Wallcovering & Fabrics

23645 Mercantile Rd.
Cleveland, OH 44122

Phone 216-464-3700

I. Gottlieb & Associates

Distributor - Major Brand Wallcover , Wallpaper

1460 Paddock Drive
Northbrook, IL 60062

Phone 708-273-3636

FAX 708-729-5470

IRM/Queens

Manufacturer - Wallcover

83-59 Smedley St.
Briarwood, NY 11435

Phone 718-523-4323

FAX 718-526-7971

Ideal Glass & Mirror Makers, Ltd.

Mirrors & Glass

80 Millwick Drive
Weston
Ont., CAN M9L 1Y3
Canada

Phone 416-741-6014

FAX 416-740-3124

Images Wallcoverings Ltd.

Distributor - Major Brand Wallcover, Wallpaper

#545 3771 Jacombs Rd.
Richmond, BC V6V 2L9
Canada

Phone 604-279-1944

FAX 604-279-1933

Imperial Mfg. Co.

Wallcovering

23645 Mercantile Rd.
Cleveland, OH 44122

Phone 216-464-3700

Imperial Paper Co.

Wallcovering

Underwood Ave.
Plattsburgh, NY 12901

Phone 518-563-3800

Imperial Stone Ltd.

Decorative Accessories

14-27 27th Ave.
PO Box 2268
Long Island City, NY 11102

Phone 718-728-6093

Imperial Wallcoverings Inc.

Wallcovering

23645 Mercantile Rd.
Cleveland, OH 44122-5917

Phone 216-464-3700

Import Specialists

Imported Rugs

82 Wall St.
New York, NY 10005

Phone 212-709-9633

FAX 212-344-4212

Impressions Handprinters, Inc.

Wallcover

1310 N. Cicero Ave.
Chicago, IL 60651

Phone 312-261-2700

FAX 312-261-4209

Indiana Carpet Distributors

Carpet
5255 Winthrop Ave.
Indianapolis, IN 46220
Phone 317-283-5574
FAX 317-921-0709

Innerlimits Inc.

Wallpaper & Wallcover
6679-A Peachtree Ind. Blvd.
Norcross, GA 30092
Phone 404-449-4290
Toll Free 800-888-2740
FAX 404-449-0078

International Manufacturing Co.

Craft Supply - Silk Flowers, Plants, Trees, Macrame, Potpourri
PO Box 405
Lillian Springs, FL 32351
Send $1.00 for Catalog/Information
Phone 904-875-2918

International Rug Source Ltd.

Oriental Rugs
1141 37th Street
Brooklyn, New York 11218
Phone 718-972-8400
FAX 718-972-4079

International Wallcoverings Ltd.

Wallpaper & Wallcover
151 East Dr.
Brampton
ON L6T 1B5
Canada
Phone 416-791-1547
FAX 416-791-6655

Iron-A-Way Inc.

Built-in Ironing Centers, Toasters, Bathroom Scales, Towel Dispensers
220 West Jackson St.
Morton, IL 61550
Send $1.00 for Catalog/Information
Phone 309-266-7232
FAX 309-266-5088

J & L Floral

Dried Flower Wreaths
399 Bagley Rd.
Berea, OH 44017
Catalog/Information Available Free

J D Fabrics Ltd.

Fabric
5 Dan Road
Canton, MA 02021
Phone 617-828-6750
Toll Free 800-332-2776
FAX 617-828-5055

J. C. Prints

Wallpaper & Wallcover
444 W. Jericho Turnpike
Huntington, NY 11743
Phone 516-692-2900
FAX 516-692-2755

J. Josephson Inc.

Wallpaper & Wallcover
35 Horizon Blvd.
S. Hackensack, NJ 07606
Phone 201-440-7000
FAX 201-440-7190

J. M. Lynne Co., Inc.

Manufacturer - Wallcover , Fabric
59 Gilpin Ave.
PO Box 1010
Smithtown, NY 11788
Phone 516-582-4300
FAX 516-582-4112

J. P. Stevens & Co.

Fabric
1185 Avenue of the Americas
New York, NY 10036
Phone 212-930-2000

Home Decorating

J. R. Burrows & Company – Jeannie Serpa Stencils

J. R. Burrows & Company

Window Lace, Carpet, Wallpaper
PO Box 522
Rockland, MA 02370

Send $5.00 for Catalog/Information

Mail Order Available

Credit Cards MC/VISA

Phone 617-982-1812
FAX 617-982-1636

Jab/Anstoetz

Decorator Fabric
Posdamer Str. 160, PO Box 529
4800 Bielefeld
Germany

Phone 011-49-521/20930
FAX 011-49-5212093388

Jacaranda, Inc.

Distributor - Wood Veneer Wallcover
1590 N.W. 159th St.
Miami, FL 33169

Phone 305-624-0003
FAX 305-621-2022

Jack's Upholstery & Caning Supplies

Upholstery & Caning Supplies
5498 Rt. 34
Oswego, IL 60543

Send $2.00 for Catalog/Information

Mail Order Available

Phone 708-554-1045

Jacpa Ceramic Craftsmen

Decorative Ceramic & Pottery Items
416 S. Clare Ave.
Harrison, MI 48625

Mail Order Available

Phone 517-539-9026

Jacquard Fabrics Co.

Upholstery Fabric
1965 Swarthmore Ave.
Lakewood, NJ 08701

Phone 201-905-4545
FAX 201-905-5334

Jacqueline Vance Oriental Rugs

Oriental Rugs, Tibetan Carpets
3944 Magazine Street
New Orleans, LA 70115

Phone 504-891-3304

Jag Corp.

Window Treatments - Blinds
7020 E. 38th St.
Tulsa, OK 74145

Phone 918-627-1955
FAX 918-622-3726

Jan Dressler Stencils

Stencils
11030 173rd Ave. SE
Renton, WA 98059

Phone 206-226-0306

Jastrac Mfg.

Window Treatments
64 Bridge Rd.
Central Islip, NY 11722-1411

Phone 516-348-1550

Jayson Window Fashions

Name Brand Blinds, Shades,
PO Box 02579
Detroit, MI 48202

Catalog/Information Available Free

Jeannie Serpa Stencils

Victorian, Country, French Stencils
PO Box 672
Jamestown, RI 02835-0672

Send $3.00 for Catalog/Information

Home Decorating

The Complete Sourcebook

8 - 37

Jefferson Industries Inc.

Rugs & Carpet
2100 S. Marshall Blvd.
Chicago, IL 60623

Phone 312-277-6100
FAX 312-277-1547

Jencraft Corp.

Window Treatments - Blinds
1 Taft Rd.
Totowa, NJ 07512

Phone 201-256-6700

Joan Fabrics Corp.

Upholstery Fabric
122 Western Ave.
Lowell, MA 01853

Phone 508-459-7131

Joanne Aviet Stencils

Stencils
36 Chesterfield Crescent, Wing
Leighton Buzzard, Beds
LU7 0TW
Great Britain

John Aga Oriental Rugs

Oriental Rugs
Suite 106 23811 Aliso Creek Rd.
Laguna Niguel, CA 92656

Phone 714-643-2451

John Dixon Inc.

Window Treatments - Blinds
24000 Mercantile Rd.
Beachwood, OH 44122

Phone 216-831-7577
Toll Free 800-321-3296
FAX 216-831-6793

John Perry Wallpapers Ltd.

Wallpaper
142 Offord Rd.
Islington, London
N1 1NS
Great Britain

Phone 011-44-71/6073844
FAX 011-44-71/5802288

Johnson's Carpets

Name Brand Carpet
3239 S.Dixie Highway
Dalton, GA 30720

Credit Cards Accepted

Phone 404-277-2775
Toll Free 800-235-1079
FAX 404-277-9835

Jolie Papier Ltd.

Wallpaper & Wallcover
8000 Cooper Ave., Bldg. #1
Glendale, NY 11385

Phone 718-894-8810
FAX 718-894-9725

Judkins Co.

Window Treatments - Blinds
2550 SW Temple St.
Salt Lake City, UT 84115

Phone 801-486-1085

K & R Custom Interiors

Curtains, Draperies
6161 S. Redwood Rd.
Murray, UT 84107

Phone 801-268-1477

Kaleidoscope Ind. Inc.

Window Treatments - Blinds
1265 Grand Oak Dr.
Howell, MI 48843

Toll Free 800-288-1986
FAX 517-546-5468

Kalkstein Silk Mills, Inc.

Upholstery Fabric
75 Wood St.
Paterson, NJ 07524

Phone 201-278-1600
FAX 201-742-8393

Kamali Oriental Rugs

Oriential Rugs
151 W. 30th St.
3rd Floor
New York, NY 10001

Toll Free 800-222-7010

Kaoud Oriental Rugs

Oriental Rugs
17 S. Main St.
West Hartford, CT 06107

Send $5.00 for Catalog/Information

Credit Cards Accepted

Phone 203-233-6211

Karastan

Manufacturer - Carpet , Rugs
PO Box 129
Elden, NC 27289

Karen Nelson

Tapestries
PO Box 420
80 Franklin St.
New York, NY 10013

Send $5.00 for Catalog/Information

Mail Order Available

Phone 212-925-5582

Karl Mann International

Mirrors
232 E. 59th St.
New York, NY 10022

Phone 212-688-7141
FAX 212-826-2059

Kathleen B. Smith

18th Century Style Fabric
Box 48
W. Chesterfield, MA 01084

Catalog/Information Available Free

Mail Order Available

Credit Cards VISA/MC/DISCOVER/AMEX

Phone 413-296-4437

Katzenbach & Warren Inc.

Fabric Wallcovering
23645 Mercantile Rd.
Cleveland, OH 44122

Phone 216-765-8564
FAX 216-765-8648

Kayser & Allman, Inc.

*Distributor - Name Brand Wallcover ,
Wallpaper*
2511 State Rd.
PO Box 428
Bensalem, PA 19020

Phone 215-638-0676
FAX 215-638-1368

Kelaty International Inc.

Oriental Rugs & Carpet
100 Park Plaza
Secaucus, NJ 07094

Kemp & Beatley, Inc.

Decorative Linens
295 5th Ave.
New York, NY 10016

Phone 212-213-8000
FAX 212-764-2953

Kemp Stuttbacher Designs

Window Treatments
RR 7, Box 214A
Franklin, IN 46131

Mail Order Available

Phone 317-738-2466

Kenney Mfg. Co.

Manufacturer/Importer - Drapery Hardware, Shades, Blinds
1000 Jefferson Blvd.
Warwick, RI 02886-2201

Phone 401-739-2200
FAX 401-821-4240

Kev Don Industries

Distributor - Major Brand Wallcover , Wallpaper
3654 W. Jarvis
Skokie, IL 60076

Phone 708-679-9991
Toll Free 800-458-4925
FAX 708-679-9998

Key Wallcoverings, Inc.

Distributor - Major Brand Wallcover, Wallpaper
4775 Hamilton Blvd.
Theodore, AL 36582

Phone 205-443-6110
FAX 205-443-7461

Kimberly Clark Corp.

Wallpaper & Wallcover
1400 Holcomb Bridge Rd.
Roswell, GA 30076

Phone 404-587-8092

Kinney Wallcoverings

Wallcover & Wallpaper
251 Rhode Island
San Francisco, CA 94103-5131

Phone 415-861-4835

Kirsch

Window Treatments - Blinds
PO Box 0370
309 N. Prospect
Sturgis, MI 49091

Phone 616-651-0309
Toll Free 800-528-1407
FAX 616-651-0212

Kirsch Drapery Hardware

Drapery Hardware
Commerce Plaza
Rt. 6
Danbury, CT 06810

Phone 203-798-1850
Toll Free 800-732-4549

Kiemer & Wiseman

Drapery & Upholstery Fabric
2301 S. Broadway
Los Angeles, CA 90007

Phone 213-747-0307

Knight Distributing Inc.

Carpet
9112 Nieman Rd.
Overland Park, KS 66214

Phone 913-541-9254

Kobe Fabrics Ltd.

Distributor - Major Brand Wallcover , Fabric
5380 S. Service Rd.
Burlington ON L7R 3Y7
Canada

Phone 416-639-2730
FAX 416-634-0992

Kosset Carpets Ltd.

Carpet
PO Box 255
Toftshaw La, Bradford
BD4 6QW
Great Britain

Phone 011-44-274/681881

Kraus Carpet Mills Ltd.

Manufacturer - Carpet
65 Northfield Dr. W.
Waterloo, Ontario
Canada

Phone 519-884-2310
Toll Free 800-265-2787

Home Decorating

Kravet Fabrics – Laurel Mfg. Co. Inc.

Kravet Fabrics

Fabrics, Trimmings, Wallcoverings
225 Central Ave. S.
Bethpage, NY 11714
Phone 516-293-2000
FAX 516-293-2158

Kwal-Howells

*Distributor - Major Brand Wallcover ,
Wallpaper*
4285 S. State St.
Salt Lake City, UT 84107
Phone 801-262-8466
FAX 801-263-1294

La Barge Mirrors, Inc.

Mirrors, Tables, Lamps, Furniture
PO Box 1769
Holland, MI 49422
Send $6.00 for Catalog/Information
Phone 616-392-1473
Toll Free 800-253-3870
FAX 616-392-5001

Lace Country

Window Treatments - Lace for Windows
21 W. 38th St.
New York, NY 10018-5990
Mail Order Available
Phone 212-221-6171

Lacey-Champion Carpets, Inc.

Custom Designed Carpet and Rugs
PO Box 99
Fairmount, GA 30139
Phone 706-337-5365
FAX 706-337-5365

Lafayette Venetian Blind Inc.

Window Treatments - Blinds
820 Roberts St.
PO Box 646
Lafayette, IN 47902-0646
Phone 317-742-8418
Toll Free 800-342-5523
FAX 317-423-2402

Larue Products

Small Wood Decorative Items
Rte. 4, PO Box 143
Menomonie, WI 54751
Phone 715-235-5560

Laue Wallcoverings Inc.

*Distributor - Major Brand Wallcover ,
Wallpaper*
Three E. 28th St.
New York, NY 10016
Phone 212-683-1111
FAX 212-689-7497

Laura Ashley

Fabric, Drapery & Tile
6 St. James Street, #10th
Boston, MA 02116
Mail Order Available
Toll Free 800-367-2000

Laura Copenhaver Industries Inc.

*Canopies, Coverlets, Dust Ruffles,
Curtains*
PO Box 149 , 102 E. Main St.
Marion, VA 24354
Mail Order Available
Credit Cards Accepted
Phone 703-783-4663
Toll Free 800-227-6797

Laurco Fabrics Inc.

Fabric
PO Box 16011
2331 S. Mead
Wichita, KS 67216
Phone 316-262-5022
FAX 316-262-1272

Laurel Mfg. Co. Inc.

Window Treatments - Blinds
64-15 Grand Ave.
Maspeth, NY 11378
Phone 718-894-9228
FAX 718-894-9529

Home Decorating

The Complete Sourcebook

8 - 41

Le Lace Factory, Inc.

English Country and Victorian Lace Curtains
18 West 21st St.
New York, NY 28607
Send $4.00 for Catalog/Information
Phone 212-989-9760

Lee Jofa

Wallcover and Fabric
800 Central Blvd.
Carlstadt, NJ 07072
Phone 201-438-8444
FAX 201-438-7034

Lee's Carpets

Carpet
3330 W. Friendly Ave.
PO Box 27207
Greensboro, NC 27420-7207
Phone 919-379-2407
FAX 919-379-2466

Len-Tex Inc.

Wallpaper & Wallcover
297 Plainfield St.
Springfield, MA 01109
Phone 413-737-9373
FAX 413-731-5995

Lennon Wallpaper Co.

Manufacturer - Wallpaper, Wallcover
7669 National Turnpike
Louisville, KY 40214
Phone 502-368-1234
FAX 502-368-2059

Lenoir Mirror Co.

Mirrors
PO Box 1650
Lenoir, NC 28645
Phone 704-728-3271

Liberty Design Co.

Stencils
611 Province Rd.
Barrington, NH 03825
Toll Free 800-543-0547
FAX 603-664-2705

Limonta USA Inc.

Wallpaper & Wallcover
Div. of Limontaparati SPA Como, Italy
1751 N. Central Park Ave.
Chicago, IL 60647
Phone 312-278-4000

Lin-Gor Wallcovering

Wallpaper & Wallcover
1000 Main Ave.
Clifton, NJ 07011
Toll Free 800-526-7880
FAX 201-473-3968

Linda's Bed & Bath Ltd.

Bath & Bed Accessories
421 Woodstream Dr.
St. Charles, MO 63304-5552
Phone 314-447-2780

Linen & Lace

Lace Curtains
4 Lafayette St.
Washington, MO 63090
Send $2.00 for Catalog/Information
Mail Order Available
Phone 314-239-6499
Toll Free 800-332-5223
FAX 314-239-0070

Linen Lady

Lace Curtains & Linens
5360 H St.
PO Box 19988
Sacramento, CA 95819
Send $3.00 for Catalog/Information
Phone 916-457-6718
FAX 916-736-9383

Lizzie and Charlie's Rag Rugs

Manufacturer - Rag Rugs
210 East Bullion Ave.
Marysvale, UT 84750
Mail Order Available
Phone 801-326-4213

London Lace

Window Treatments - Window Lace
167 Newbury St.
Boston, MA 02116
Send $2.50 for Catalog/Information
Phone 617-267-3506
Toll Free 800-926-5223
FAX 617-267-0770

Long Island Walls

Wallpaper & Wallcover
PO Box 138
W. Sayville, NY 11796
Phone 516-563-9255
FAX 516-563-0468

Long's Carpet Inc.

Order by Phone - Name Brand Carpet
2625 S. Dixie Highway
Dalton, GA 30720
Toll Free 800-545-5664

Lotus Carpets

Carpet
PO Box 1560
Columbus, GA 31993
Phone 404-324-0111
Toll Free 800-627-3768
FAX 205-298-0654

Louis De Poortere

Designer Rugs
240 Peachtree St.
Suite 4 G 2
Atlanta, GA 30303

Lovelia Enterprises

Tapestries
356 East 41st St.
New York, NY 10017
Send $5.00 for Catalog/Information
Phone 212-490-0930
FAX 212-697-8850

Luv Those Rugs

Custom Braided Rugs
103 N. Main St.
Box 236
Elkton, KY 42220
Credit Cards Accepted
Phone 502-265-5550

M. A. Baskind Co.

*Distributor - Major Brand Wallcover ,
Wallpaper, Blinds*
5750 Baum Blvd.
Pittsburgh, PA 15206
Phone 412-665-5055
FAX 412-661-2918

M.A. Bruder & Sons Inc.

*Manufacturer - Paint, Carpeting, Window
Treatments, Wallcover*
600 Reed Road
Broomall, PA 19008
Phone 215-353-5100
FAX 215-353-8189

MDC Direct Inc.

*Order by Phone - Major Brand Blinds,
Bedspreads, Draperies*
PO Box 569
Marrietta,GA 30061
Credit Cards Accepted
Toll Free 800-892-2083

MDC Wallcoverings

Wallcover
1200 Arthur Avenue
Elk Grove, IL 60007
Phone 708-437-4000
Toll Free 800-621-4006
FAX 708-437-4017

Maen Line Fabrics Inc.

Fabric
219 Chestnut St.
Philadelphia, PA 19106

Phone 215-925-5537
FAX 215-923-4491

Mahantango Manor Inc.

Reproduction Telephones
Hickory Corners Rd.
Dalmatia, PA 17017
Mail Order Available

Toll Free 800-642-3966
FAX 717-758-6000

Manorhouse Designs

Stencils
1795 Severn Chapel Rd.
Millersville, MD 21108
Send $4.00 for Catalog/Information
Mail Order Available
Credit Cards MC/VISA/Check/Money Order

Phone 410-721-8945

Mansion Industries, Inc.

Decorative Wood Products, Posts, Shelving
PO Box 2220
Industry, CA 91746

Phone 818-968-9501
FAX 818-330-3084

Marburg Wallcoverings Inc.

Manufacturer - Major Brand Wallpaper , Wallcover
1751 N. Central Park
Chicago, IL 60647

Phone 312-278-4000
FAX 312-278-7041

Marcella Fine Rugs

Rugs
3162 Piedmont Rd. NE
Atlanta, GA 30305
Catalog/Information Available Free

Toll Free 800-786-7847

Marlene's Decorator Fabrics

Order by Phone - Nationwide Shipping - Discounted Major Brand Fabric
301 Beech St.
Hackensack, NJ 07601
Catalog/Information Available Free
Mail Order Available

Toll Free 800-992-7325
FAX 201-843-5688

Mary's Discount Papers

Order by Phone - Wallpaper
1342 West Chester Pike
West Chester, PA 19382
Credit Cards VISA/MC

Toll Free 800-521-3393

Mastercraft

Upholstery Fabrics
Div. of Collins & Aikman Corp.
210 Park St.
Spindale, NC 28160

Masureel International NV

Manufacturer - Masurell International Textile Wallcoverings
B-8750
Harelbeke-Hulste
Belgium

Phone 011-32-56/712316
FAX 011-32-56/705859

Mather's Department Store

Curtains - French & Country Style
31 East Main St.
PO Box 70
Westminster, MD 21157

Phone 301-848-6410

May Silk

Silk Plants
13262 Moore Street
Cerritos, CA 90701
Catalog/Information Available Free
Toll Free 800-282-7455

Mayfair Wallcoverings

*Manufacturer - Britannia 9, Complements,
Style, House & Home, Kitchen & Bath,
Natural Living, Springfields*
Basington Industrial Estate
Northumberland, UK
Great Britain
Catalog/Information Available Free
Phone 011-44-670/736799

Mayfield Leather

Manufacturer - Leather Furniture
340 9th St. SE
Hickory, NC 28603
Toll Free 800-342-7729
FAX 704-324-5127

McInnis Industries

*Order Direct - Window Treatment - Wood
Blinds*
2301 Highway 365
Port Arthur, TX 77640
Catalog/Information Available Free
Mail Order Available
Phone 409-727-0044
FAX 409-729-8811

Meadow Everlasting

Dried Flowers, Potpourri, Wreath Kits
RR 1, 149 Shabbona Rd.
Malta, IL 60150
Send $1.00 for Catalog/Information
Mail Order Available
Credit Cards VISA/MC
Phone 815-825-2539
Toll Free 800-632-3691

Medallion Carpets

Carpet
Division of Sturla Inc.
2434 Polvorosa Ave.
San Leandro, CA 94577
Phone 415-351-8104

Mei Bei International Enterprises Corp.

Wallpaper & Wallcover
6940 Claywood Way
San Jose, CA 95120
Phone 408-268-1146
FAX 408-997-0978

Melded Fabrics North America Inc.

Fabric
292 San Rafael Rd.
Palm Springs, CA 92262
Phone 619-325-8116
FAX 619-325-1037

Mercer Textile Mills, Inc.

Upholstery, Drapery Fabric
PO Box 8235
Trenton, NJ 08650
Phone 609-585-6458

Merida Meridian, Inc.

Manufacturer - Carpet
PO Box 1071
Syracuse, NY 13201-1071
Phone 315-422-4921
Toll Free 800-345-2200

Merit Window Fashions

Window Treatments - Blinds
1585 Draper
Kingsburg, CA 93631-1910
Phone 209-897-2132

Messer Industries, Inc.

Mirrors, Glass Table Tops
PO Box 648-B
Greer, SC 29652
Phone 803-877-0703
FAX 803-877-5816

Metro Blind & Shade

Blinds & Shades
5206 Airport Frwy.
PO Box 14188
Ft. Worth, TX 76117

Phone 817-831-0721
Toll Free 800-825-1001
FAX 817-831-9706

Metro Wallcoverings

Distributor - Major Brand Wallcover ,
Wallpaper
2600 B Steeles Ave.
West Concord, ON L4K 3C8
Canada

Phone 416-738-5177
FAX 416-738-8853

Metropolitan Ceramics

Manufacturer - Ceramic Tile - Indoor and
Outdoor
PO Box 9240
Canton, OH 44711-9240

Phone 216-484-4887
FAX 216-484-4880

Michele Wallpaper

Manufacturer - Wallpaper, Wallcover
PO Box 56
Park Ridge, NJ 07656-0056

Phone 201-307-1586
FAX 201-307-1427

Mike Leary Carpets

Carpet
500 S Lander
Seattle, WA 98134-1931

Phone 206-628-0771

Mike's Carpet Emporium

Carpet
124 E 17th
Costa Mesa, CA 92627

Phone 714-642-0440

Milan Schuster Inc.

Wallpaper & Wallcover
60 McLean Ave.
Yonkers, NY 10705

Phone 914-963-9400

Milbrook Wallcoverings

Manufacturer - Wallcover and Matching
Fabric
23645 Mercantile Rd.
Cleveland, OH 44122

Phone 216-464-3700
FAX 216-765-8648

Miles Carpet

Carpet
PO Box 1403
Chatsworth, GA 30705

Catalog/Information Available Free

Phone 404-695-4551
Toll Free 800-438-6037

Milliken Carpets

Manufacturer - Carpet
201 Lukken Industrial Drive
LaGrange, GA 30240

Phone 706-880-5511
Toll Free 800-241-2327
FAX 706-880-5906

Mills River Industries, Inc.

Rag Rugs, Chairs, Country Style Home
Decorating Accessories
713 Old Orchard Rd.
Hendersonville, NC 28739

Send $2.00 for Catalog/Information

Mail Order Available

Credit Cards VISA/MC/Check/Money
Order

Phone 704-697-9778
Toll Free 800-874-4898
FAX 704-693-1837

Home Decorating

Mills Wallcoverings

*Distributor - Major Brand Wallcover ,
Wallpaper*
8380 River Road
Delta, BC V4G 1B5
Canada

Phone 604-946-7011
FAX 604-946-0352

Minette Mills, Inc.

Upholstery Fabric, Bedspreads
305 Laurel Ave.
Grover, NC 28073

Phone 704-937-7611
FAX 704-937-9951

Mirror Fair

Mirror Frames
1495 Third Ave.
New York, NY 10028-2180

Send $50.00 for Catalog/Information

Mail Order Available

Phone 212-288-5050
FAX 212-772-7936

Mirror-Tech Mfg. Co., Inc.

Mirrors
286 Nepperhan Ave.
Yonkers, NY 10701-3403

Phone 914-423-1600
FAX 914-423-1667

Mission Wallcovering Distributors

*Distributor - Major Brand Wallcover ,
Wallpaper*
5839 Woodson Road
Mission, KS 66202

Phone 913-722-0704
FAX 913-722-0754

Missoni Roubini, Inc.

Decorative Carpets
443 Park Ave. S., 2nd Fl
New York, NY 10016

Phone 212-576-1145
FAX 212-576-1545

Miya Shoji & Interiors Inc.

Japanese Shoji Screens & Tables
109 W. 17th St.
New York, NY 10011

Catalog/Information Available Free

Phone 212-243-6774
FAX 212-243-6780

Moattar Ltd.

Oriental Rugs
351 Peechtree Hills Ave., #314
Atlanta, GA 30305

Phone 404-237-5100

Mohawk Carpet

Carpet
1755 The Exchange
Atlanta, GA 30339

Phone 404-951-6152
Toll Free 800-554-6637

Monterey Carpets

Manufacturer - Carpet
3201 South Susan St.
Santa Ana, CA 92704

Toll Free 800-752-6003

Moon Bear Pottery

Pottery, Sculpture
257 Elizabeth St.
Rockford, MI 49341

Phone 616-866-2519

Morantz Inc.

Curtains
4056 Chestnut St.
Philadelphia, PA 19105

Send $1.50 for Catalog/Information

Phone 215-382-0662

The Complete Sourcebook

8 - 47

Motif Designs

Manufacturer - Wallpaper & Fabric
20 Jones St.
New Rochelle, NY 10801

Phone 914-633-1180
Toll Free 800-431-2424
FAX 914-633-1176

Mountain Craft Carpets

Manufacturer - Carpet
PO Box 667
Dalton, GA 30722-0667

Toll Free 800-241-4055

Mutual Wallpaper & Paint Co., Inc.

Wallpaper, Window Treatments, Paint
3204 Dunlova Ct.
Louisville, KY 40241-2114

Mail Order Available

Credit Cards VISA/MC/DISCOVER

Phone 502-583-0525

Nance Carpet & Rug Co. Inc.

Order Direct - Custom Rugs
PO Box 653
Calhoun, GA 30703-0653

Mail Order Available

Toll Free 800-999-7731

National Assoc. of Mirror Manufacturers

Video - Designing with Light (Mirrors)
Congressional Court
Potomac, MD 20854

Send $2.00 for Catalog/Information

Phone 301-365-2521
FAX 301-365-7705

National Blind & Wallpaper Factory

Order by Phone - Mini Blinds
400 Galleria #400
Southfield, MI 48034

Toll Free 800-477-8000
FAX 800-858-4550

National Carpet

Carpets, Oriental Rugs
1384 Coney Island Ave.
Brooklyn, NY 11230

Send $3.00 for Catalog/Information

Mail Order Available

Credit Cards VISA/MC

Phone 718-253-5700

National Carpet Group Ltd.

Carpet
Castle Ho, Davey Pl.
Norwich
NR2 1PJ
Great Britain

Phone 011-44-603/617541

National Products Inc.

Mirrors
912 Baxter Ave.
Louisville, KY 40204

Phone 502-583-3038
FAX 502-584-1022

National Wallcovering

Distributor - Name Brand Wallcover, Wallpaper
2210 Cantrell Road
Little Rock, AR 72203

Phone 501-378-0039
Toll Free 800-222-1028

Nationwide Wholesalers

Order by Phone - Wallcover, Window Treatments, Fabric
630 Main Street
Hackensack, NJ 07602

Toll Free 800-488-9255

Navajo Arts & Crafts Guild

Navajo Wool Rugs
PO Box 9000/Hwy. 264
Window Rock, AZ 86515

Mail Order Available

Credit Cards VISA/MC/AMEX

Phone 602-871-6673

Home Decorating

Navan Carpets Inc.

Manufacturer - Carpet
200 Lunt
Elk Grove Village, IL 60007

Phone 708-437-6627
Toll Free 800-666-6624

Nels Thybony Co.

Wallpaper & Wallcover
3720 N. Kedzie Ave.
Chicago, IL 60618

Phone 312-463-3005

New Home Window Shade

Blinds
745 N. Keyser Ave.
Scranton, PA 18504

Phone 717-346-2047
FAX 717-346-3213

New Scotland Lace Co.

Victorian Window Lace
PO Box 181
Dartmouth, Nova Scotia
B2Y 3Y3
Canada
Send $3.00 for Catalog/Information

Phone 902-462-4212

New View Blinds Mfg. Ltd.

Blinds & Shades
5727 Burbank Rd. SE
Calgary
Alta., CAN T2H 1Z5
Canada

Phone 403-255-1158
FAX 403-258-3448

Newell Window Furnishings

*Window Treatments - Blinds, Drapery
Accessories*
916 S. Arcade Ave.
Freeport, IL 61032

Phone 815-235-4171
FAX 815-233-8335

Newmarket Limited, Inc.

*Manufacturer - Bridle Path, Classic Suite,
Cotillion, High Sierra, Jodhpurs II,
Provence-The Country Fresh Edition,
Shakertown*
506 Main St.
PO Box 1149
Shelbyville, KY 40065

Phone 502-633-6866
FAX 502-633-6869

North American Decorative Products Inc.

*Manufacturer - Castelton, Innova,
Lennon, Shorewood and Walnut Grove
Wallcover & Wallpaper*
Norwall Group
1055 Clark Blvd.Gramalea, ON L6T 3W4
Canada

Phone 416-791-2700
FAX 416-791-5281

Northern California Imports, Inc.

*Imports and Distributes Wallcover &
Wallpaper*
PO Box 1268
Santa Rosa, CA 95402

Phone 707-544-5452
FAX 707-544-0719

Norton Blumenthal Inc.

Wallcover
42-20 12th St.
Long Island City, NY 11101

Phone 718-361-1234
FAX 718-361-2257

Norwall Group

Wallpaper & Wallcover
7669 National Turnpike
Louisville, KY 40214

Phone 502-368-1234
FAX 502-368-2059

The Complete Sourcebook

Norwick Mills

Rugs
PO Box 949
Dalton, GA 30720

Phone 404-278-5836

Number One Wallpaper

Order by Phone - Wallpaper
2914 Long Beach Rd.
Oceanside, NY 11572

Phone 516-678-4445
Toll Free 800-423-0084

Odegard-Roesner

Original Decorative Carpets
200 Lexington Ave., Suite 1306
New York, NY 10016

Phone 212-545-0069
FAX 212-545-0298

Odyssey Design Products Ltd.

Distributor - Major Brand Wallcover ,
Wallpaper
101-605 W. 8th Ave.
Vancouver, BC V5Z 1C7
Canada

Phone 604-872-7667
FAX 604-872-2477

Old Deerfield Wallpapers

Manufacturer - Old Classics/New Styles
and Scenics by Old Deerfield
30 Canfield Road
Cedar Grove, NJ 07009

Phone 201-239-6600
FAX 201-239-4514

Old Manor House

18th & 19th Century Style Curtains
31 E Main St. Box 70
Westminister, MD 21157

Send $1.50 for Catalog/Information

Mail Order Available

Olde Virginea Trading Co.

Floorcloths, Reproduction Furnishings
PO Box 438
Williamsburg, VA 23185

Send $5.00 for Catalog/Information

Mail Order Available

Phone 804-564-0600

Olney Wallcoverings

Distributor - Major Brand Wallcover ,
Wallpaper
PO Box 1172
Spartanburg, SC 29304

Phone 803-585-2431
FAX 803-583-2577

Omega Carpet Mills Inc.

Carpet
1302 E. Walnut
Dalton, GA 30720

Phone 404-226-2223
Toll Free 800-241-4908
FAX 404-272-7617

Omega Rug Works

Oriental Rugs
1302 E. Walnut Ave.
Dalton, GA 30772

Phone 404-226-2223
Toll Free 800-241-4908
FAX 404-272-7617

Onate's Cupboard

Southwestern Style Cabinet Knobs &
Switch Plates
11516 Palm Springs NE
Albuquerque, NM 87111

Send $2.00 for Catalog/Information

Phone 505-298-6558
FAX 505-298-6558

Ontario Wallcoverings

Distributor - Major Brand Wallcover , Wallpaper
462 Front St. West
Toronto, ON M5V 1B6
Canada

Phone 416-593-4519
Toll Free 800-387-2695

Oriental Rug Outlet Inc.

Oriental Rugs
600 Meadowland Pkwy.
Secaucus, NJ 07094

Phone 201-864-1121
FAX 201-864-0171

Oxford Textile Mills Ltd.

Carpet
Barton Mill, Audlett Dr.
Abingdon, Oxon
OX14 3TS
Great Britain

Phone 011-44-235/528818

Ozite Corporation

Manufacturer - Wallcovering Fabric
1755 Butterfield
Libertyville, IL 60048

Phone 708-362-8210
FAX 708-362-8260

P & M Consumer Products Inc.

Wallpaper & Wallcover
PO Box 7958
Stockton, CA 95267

Phone 209-257-6850
FAX 209-957-6614

Pace-Stone

Major Brand Carpet, Rugs, Oriental Rugs
7304 East Independence Blvd.
Charlotte, NC 28212

Catalog/Information Available Free

Phone 704-535-2786

Pantasote, Inc.

Manufacturer - Wallcovering
Wallcovering Division
1325 E. Drinker Street
Dunmore, PA 18512

Phone 717-348-3770
FAX 717-348-3779

Paradise Mills Inc.

Order by Phone - Factory Direct - Carpet
PO Box 2488
Dalton, GA 30722

Phone 706-226-9064
Toll Free 800-338-7811
FAX 706-226-9061

Paragon Fabrics Co. Inc.

Fabric
441 Broadway
New York, NY 10013

Phone 212-226-8100
FAX 212-226-1249

Paramount Interior Products Corp.

Wallpaper & Wallcover
21717 Republic
Oak Park, MI 48237

Phone 313-542-2570
FAX 313-542-3077

Parisotto

Manufacturer - Italian Metal Home Furnishings
Michael Mesure
166 Prospect Park West
Suite 3R

Mail Order Available

Phone 718-499-4906
FAX 718-499-4906

Parker Window Covering

Blinds, Shades, Draperies, Curtains, Hardware
3101 11th Ave.
Huntsville, AL 35805

Phone 205-536-1821
FAX 205-536-1821

The Complete Sourcebook

Parker's Carpets Inc.

Order Direct - Many Major Brands - Carpet, Vinyl Flooring
3200 Dug Gap Rd.
Dalton, GA 30720

Catalog/Information Available Free

Mail Order Available

Credit Cards VISA/MC

Phone 706-277-3091

Toll Free 800-442-2013

FAX 706-277-2709

Path Of The Sun Images

Sculpture, Crafts
3020 Lowell Blvd.
Denver, CO 80211

Phone 303-477-8442

Patrick J. Mitchell

Manufacturer - Wallcover
18370 Olympic Ave. South
Seattle, WA 98188

Toll Free 800-426-4827

FAX 206-575-4643

Patterncrafts

Quilting, Stencils, Wall Hangings
PO Box 25370
Colorado Springs, CO 80936

Send $2.00 for Catalog/Information

Phone 719-574-2007

Payne's Ristras De Santa Fe

Indian Wall Hangings
PO Box 4817
715th St. Michael's Dr.
Sante Fe, NM 87502

Mail Order Available

Credit Cards VISA/MC

Phone 505-988-9626

Peerless Imported Rugs

Rugs - Oriental, Rag, Navajo, Colonial European Tapestries
3033 N. Lincoln Ave.
Chicago, IL 60657

Send $1.00 for Catalog/Information

Mail Order Available

Credit Cards VISA/MC/AMEX

Phone 312-472-4848

Toll Free 800-621-6573

Peerless Wallpaper

Order by Phone - Wallcover, Window Treatments - Blinds, Verticals, Mini, Aluminum, Vinyl
39500 14 Mile Rd.
Walled Lake, MI 48390

Credit Cards Accepted

Toll Free 800-999-0898

FAX 313-553-8605

Penn Needle Art Co.

Draperies, Curtains
6945 Lynn Way
Pittsburgh, PA 15208

Phone 412-441-7551

Pennsylvania Woven Carpet Mills Inc.

Manufacturer - Carpet
401 E. Allegheny Ave.
Philadelphia, PA 19134

Phone 215-425-5833

FAX 215-634-2543

Perkowitz Window Fashions

Window Blinds, Shutters, Shades
135 Green Bay Road
Wilmette, IL 60091

Send $1.00 for Catalog/Information

Phone 708-251-7700

FAX 708-853-1232

Persian Galleries

Oriental Rugs
3226 Peachtree Blvd.
Atlanta, GA 30305

Phone 404-953-6102

Persian Gallery Company Inc.

Persian Rugs
102 Madison Ave.
New York, NY 10016

Phone 212-683-2699

FAX 212-481-0885

Phifer Wire Products, Inc.

Window Treatment Fabrics, Screens
PO Box 1700
Tuscaloosa, AL 35403-1700

Phone 205-345-2120

Toll Free 800-633-5955

FAX 205-759-4450

Philip Graf Wallpapers

Wallpaper & Wallcover
Div. of Spring Street Designs Inc.
16 Spring St.
Paterson, NJ 07501

Phone 201-684-0166

FAX 201-881-0402

Pickhardt & Seibert (USA) Inc.

Wallpaper & Wallcover
700 Prince George's Blvd.
Upper Marlboro, MD 20772

Phone 301-249-7900

FAX 301-249-5863

Pilgrim House Products

Furniture
Bapist Common Rd.
Templeton, MA 01468

Phone 508-939-5462

Pinnell's Floor Covering

Floorcovering
263 N. Main
Altaville, CA 95222

Phone 209-736-4652

Pintchik Homeworks

Discounts Up To 79% - Major Brand Wallpaper, Window Treatments, Paint
2106 Bath Ave.
Brooklyn, NY 11214

Catalog/Information Available Free

Mail Order Available

Credit Cards VISA/MC

Phone 718-996-5580

Toll Free 800-847-4199

FAX 718-996-1966

Plaid Enterprises Inc.

Wallpaper & Wallcover
1649 International Blvd.
PO Box 7600
Norcorss, GA 30091-7600

Phone 404-923-8200

Planox B.V.

Manufacturer - Vinyl Wallcover
PO Box 12
Helmond, 5700 AA
Holland
Netherlands

Phone 011-31/492070944

FAX 011-31/492070620

Plastic Sun Shade Co. Inc.

Window Treatments - Blinds and Shades, Transparent Sun Shades
PO Box 553
76 Woolsey St.
Irvington, NJ 07111

Phone 201-373-8181

FAX 201-373-9181

Playfield International

Manufacturer - Acoustical Wallcover
Tuftbound Carpet, Box 8
Chatsworth, GA 30705

Phone 706-695-4755
Toll Free 800-237-4068

Porter Wallcoverings

Distributor - Major Brand Wallcover ,
Wallpaper
400 S. 13th St.
Louisville, KY 40203

Phone 502-588-9200
FAX 502-588-9316

Prairie Edge

Indian Art, Crafts and Designs
PO Box 8303
Rapid City, SD 57709-8303

Mail Order Available

Credit Cards Accepted

Phone 605-341-3620
Toll Free 800-541-2388
FAX 605-341-6415

Pride of Paris Fabrics Ltd.

Fabric
140 W. River St.
Paris
ON N3L 3E9
Canada

Phone 519-442-6351
FAX 519-442-7058

Quality Discount Carpets

Major Brand Carpet - Up to 50% savings
1207 W. Walnut Ave., PO Box 1263
Dalton, GA 30720

Catalog/Information Available Free

Mail Order Available

Phone 404-226-7611
Toll Free 800-233-0993

Quality House, Inc.

Importer, Distributor and Manufacturer of
Wallcover
1573 Alvarado St.
San Leandro, CA 94577

Phone 510-483-8400
Toll Free 800-262-9911
FAX 510-483-8536

Quality Wallcovering Inc.

Wallcover & Wallpaper
8 Sutton Pl.
Edison, NJ 08817

Phone 201-985-3349
FAX 201-985-6652

Queen City Glass Ltd.

Antique, Beveled Mirrors, Glass Table
Tops
7634 Woodbine Ave. Unit 5
Markham
Ont., CAN L3R 2N2
Canada

Phone 416-495-5757

Quest Wallcoverings Ltd.

Wallcover
Unit 5, The Benyon Centre
Commercial Rd., Walsall, West Midlands
WS2 7NQ
Great Britain

Phone 011-44-922/473388
FAX 011-44-922/491529

Quix Window Visions & Fabric Works

Nationwide Shipping - Discounted Prices
- Major Brand Upholstery, Drapery Fabric
& Blinds
PO Box 5659
Pittsburgh, PA 15207

Catalog/Information Available Free

Mail Order Available

Credit Cards VISA/AMEX/MC

Toll Free 800-487-6773
FAX 412-521-3597

R. W. Beattie Carpet Industries Inc.

Carpet & Rugs
PO Box 4539
Dalton, GA 30721
>Phone 404-278-3637
>FAX 404-991-2622

Rainbow Creations

Wallpaper & Wallcover
216 Industrial Dr.
Ridgeland, MS 39157
>Phone 601-856-2158
>FAX 601-856-5809

Raintree Designs, Inc.

English Cottage Style Wallpaper and Fabric
979 Third Ave.
Suite 503N
New York, NY 10022
>Phone 212-477-8590

Rastetter Woolen Mill

Rag, Braided, Oriental Rugs
5802 St., Rt. 39
Millersburg, OH 44654
Mail Order Available
>Phone 216-674-2103
>FAX 216-674-2103

Ravenglass Pty. Ltd.

Mirrors & Cabinets
1404 Clark
Box 612
Goodland, KS 67735
Send $2.00 for Catalog/Information
Mail Order Available
>Phone 913-899-2297

Rawson Carpets Ltd.

Carpet
Castle Bank Mills
Portobello Rd. Wakefield, West Yorkshire
WF1 5PS
Great Britain
>Phone 011-44-924/373421

Redona Wallcovering S.P.A.

Manufacturer - Vinyl Wallcover
Via leona XIII
No. 8
Bergamo, 24100
Italy
>Phone 011-39-35/341444
>FAX 011-39-35/347506

Regal Rugs Inc.

Area Rugs, Bath Rugs
819 Buckeye St.
North Vernon, IN 47265
>Phone 812-346-3601
>FAX 812-346-7112

Reservation Creations

Rugs, Pottery, Baskets, Carvings
3333 East Van Buren St.
Phoenix, AZ 85008
>Phone 602-244-8244

Richard E. Thibaut, Inc.

Manufacturer/Distributor - Wallcover, Wallpaper
480 Frelinghuysen Ave.
Newark, NJ 07114
Catalog/Information Available Free
>Phone 201-643-1118
>Toll Free 800-223-0704
>FAX 201-643-3050

Rivalba S.P.A.

Wallcovering
Via Case Sparse N. 16
26040 Vicomoscano di Casalmaggiore (CR)
Italy
>FAX 011-39-375/41765

Robert Allen

Decorator Fabric
One Design Center Place
Boston, MA 02210
>Phone 617-482-6600
>Toll Free 800-773-6601
>FAX 617-737-2087

Robert Allen Fabrics, Inc.

Fabrics
55 Cabot Blvd.
Mansfield, MA 02048

Phone 508-339-9151
Toll Free 800-333-3777
FAX 508-261-9179

Robert Crowder & Co.

Wallcover & Wallpaper
7021 Santa Monica Blvd.
Los Angeles, CA 90038

Phone 213-461-3003
FAX 213-461-1238

Robinson's Wallcovering

Order Direct - Wallpaper, Borders, Fabrics
225 W. Spring St.
Titusville, PA 16354-0427

Send $2.00 for Catalog/Information

Mail Order Available

Credit Cards VISA/MC/AMEX/DISCOVER

Toll Free 800-458-2426
FAX 814-827-1693

Rochester Drapery Inc.

Interior Window Treatments
4450 Lake Ave.
PO Box 12712
Rochester, NY 14612

Phone 716-663-2400

Rodless Decorations Inc.

Bedspreads, Curtains, Comforter Ensembles
184-10 Jamaica Ave.
Hollis, NY 11423

Phone 718-454-8800

Ronnie Draperies

Draperies, Bedspreads
145 Broad Ave.
Fairview, NJ 07022

Send $1.00 for Catalog/Information

Phone 201-945-1900

Rosco Wallcoverings, Inc.

Distributor - Wallcover, Wallpaper
1215 Viceroy Dr.
Dallas, TX 75247

Phone 214-631-4111
FAX 214-637-7707

Rosecore Carpet Co. Inc.

Carpet, Wallcover, Fabric
D & D Building
979 Third Ave.
New York, NY 10022

Phone 212-421-7272
FAX 212-421-7847

Rosedale Wallcoverings Inc.

Wallpaper, Draperies, Bedspreads
8241 Keele St. Unit 9-11
Concord
ON L4K 1Z5
Canada

Phone 416-660-0808
FAX 416-660-0804

Rossville Mills Inc.

Upholstery Fabric
PO Box 40
Rossville, GA 30741

Phone 404-866-1010
FAX 615-867-1382

Royal Crest Inc.

Manufacturer - Custom Window Coverings - Shutters, Shades, Blinds
14851 W. 11 Mile Rd.
Oak Park, MI 48237

Phone 810-399-2476
FAX 810-399-5695

Royalweve Carpet Mills Inc.

Carpet
15125 Marquardt
Santa Fe Springs, CA 90670

Phone 310-404-0048
Toll Free 800-733-7471

Roysons Corp.

Manufacturer - Wallcover, Wallpaper
40 Vanderhoff Ave.
Rockaway, NJ 07866
>Phone 201-625-5570
>FAX 201-625-5917

Rubin & Green Inc.

Order by Phone - Decorator Fabric
290 Grand St.
New York, NY 10002
Credit Cards VISA/MC/AMEX
>Phone 212-226-0313

Rubin Design Studio Inc.

Manufacturer - Wallcover - The Ritz and Passion
PO Box 14006
Ft. Lauderdale, FL 33302
>Phone 305-564-0400
>FAX 305-565-5917

Rue De France Inc.

Lace Curtains, Tablerunners, Drapery Hardware
78 Thames St.
Newport, RI 02840
Send $3.00 for Catalog/Information
Mail Order Available
Credit Cards MC/VISA/AMEX
>Phone 401-846-2084
>Toll Free 800-777-0998

Ruth's Custom Bedspreads

Bedspreads, Dustruffles, Pillows, Shams
1439 N.E. 13th Ave.
Fort Lauderdale, FL 33304
>Phone 305-565-4444

Rutherford Wallcovering

Wallpaper & Wallcover
121 N. Mill
Pontiac, IL 61764
>Phone 815-842-2305

S & S Mills

Order by Phone - Carpet and Padding Samples Carpet - 32 Designer Colors Heatset Nylon - 15 Designer Colors - Berber, Olefin
2650 Lakeland Rd. SE
Dalton, GA 30721
Catalog/Information Available Free
Credit Cards VISA/MC/DISCOVER
>Phone 706-277-3677
>Toll Free 800-241-4013
>FAX 706-277-3922

S R Wood, Inc.

Manufacturer - Acoustic Wallcover, Vinyl Wallcover
1801 Progress Way
Clarksville, IN 47130-9540
>Phone 812-288-9201
>FAX 812-288-5225

S. A. Maxwell Co.

Distributor - Wallcover, Wallpaper
1406 Milwaukee Ave.
Chicago, IL 60622
>Phone 312-276-1520
>Toll Free 800-669-3900
>FAX 312-276-1010

S. M. Hexter & Co.

Wallcovering, Floor Covering, Drapery & Upholstery Fabric
2800 Superior Ave.
Cleveland, OH 44114
>Phone 216-696-0146

S. Morantz Inc.

Blinds
9984 Gantry Rd.
Philadelphia, PA 19115
>Phone 215-969-0266
>FAX 215-969-0566

Safavieh Carpets

Carpet
238 East 59th St.
New York, NY 10022
Phone 212-888-0626

Salem Carpets Inc.

Carpet
Industrial Blvd. 1-75
Ringgold, GA 30736
Phone 404-935-2241
FAX 404-935-6422

Sancar Wallcoverings Inc.

Distributor - Major Brand Wallcover ,
Wallpaper
206 Ditmas Ave.
Brooklyn, NY 11218-4904
Phone 718-438-2860
Toll Free 800-221-0977
FAX 718-436-2868

Sanderson

Trade Only - Wallpaper, Fabric, Tapestry
979 Third Ave.
New York, NY 10022
Phone 212-319-7220
FAX 212-593-6184

Sanderson Carpets Ltd.

Carpet
Union Rd., Bolton
BL2 2HH
Great Britain
Phone 011-44-204/31393

Sandler & Worth

Oriental Rugs
160 Rt. 22
Springfield, NJ 07081
Send $15.00 for Catalog/Information

Sanitas Wallcoverings

Manufacturer - Wallcover
PO Box 3137
Medina, OH 44256
Send $2.00 for Catalog/Information

Santa Fe Oriental Rugs

Oriental Rugs
212 Galestio
Santa Fe, NM 87501
Phone 505-982-5152

Sanz International

Decorator Fabric, Wallpaper
PO Box 1794
1183 E. Lexington Ave.
High Point, NC 27261

Catalog/Information Available Free

Mail Order Available

Credit Cards VISA/MC
Phone 919-882-6212

Satex Textile Mural

Wallpaper & Wallcover
Zone Industrielle 2 Boite 100
Valenciennes Cedex
France
Phone 011-33-27360737
FAX 011-33-27360739

Saxony Carpet Company, Inc.

Carpet
979 Third Ave.
D& D Building
New York, NY 10022
Phone 212-755-7100
FAX 212-223-8130

Scalamandre Inc.

Wallpaper, Wallcover, Fabric
950 Third Ave.
New York, NY 10022

Mail Order Available
Phone 212-980-3888

Scancelli

Wallpaper & Wallcover
190-212 Van Winkle St.
PO Box 416
E. Rutherford, NJ 07073
Phone 201-933-0720
FAX 201-933-8686

Home Decorating

Scandecor Inc.

Wallpaper & Wallcover
430 Pike Rd.
Southampton, PA 18966

Phone 215-355-2410
FAX 215-364-8737

Scher Fabrics Inc.

Fabrics
119 W. 40th St.
New York, NY 10018

Phone 212-382-2266
FAX 212-382-0076

Schoenly's Floral Designs

Indoor, Outdoor Wreaths
5510 Boyertown Pike
Birdsboro, PA 19508

Credit Cards Accepted

Phone 215-689-5230

Schooner Prints

Manufacturer - Wallcover, Wallpaper
8632 115th Ave.
North Largo, FL 33543

Phone 813-397-8572
FAX 813-398-8052

Schumacher & Co. Inc.

Decorative Fabrics, Rugs, Wallpapers
79 Madison Ave.
New York, NY 10016

Phone 212-213-7900
Toll Free 800-552-9255

Scroll Fabrics Inc.

Wallpaper, Drapery, Bedspreads
4500 Highlands Pkwy.
Smyrna, GA 30082

Phone 404-432-7228

Sculpture Studio

Decorative Sculpture
PO Box 297
Lambertville, NJ 08530

Phone 609-397-2896

Seabrook Wallcoverings Inc.

Wallpaper & Wallcover
1325 Farmville Rd., PO Box 22597
Memphis, TN 38122

Phone 901-458-3301
Toll Free 800-238-9152
FAX 901-320-3675

Sebring & Co.

Window Treatments - Blinds
13321 Walnut
Lenexa, KS 66215

Phone 913-888-8141
FAX 913-888-8392

Select Wallcoverings

*Distributor - Major Brand Wallcover ,
Wallpaper*
200 Vinyl Court
Woodbridge, ON L4L 4A3
Canada

Phone 416-856-3444
FAX 416-856-5249

Sellers & Josephson

Vinyl Wallcovering
335 Chestnut St.
Norwood, NJ 07648

Phone 201-767-6977
FAX 201-767-9369

Sentimental Journey

Decorative Pillows
500 Broadway
Santa Monica, CA 90401

Phone 310-319-3441

Seventh Avenue

Home Furnishings
1112 Seventh Ave.
Monroe, WI 53566-1364

Credit Cards Accepted

Phone 608-324-7000

Home Decorating

The Complete Sourcebook

Shades & Verticals & Miniblinds Center

Window Treatments - Shades & Blinds
13816 NW 7th Ave.
Miami, FL 33168
Phone 305-769-0977

Shaheen Wallcoverings

Wallcover & Wallpaper
120 LaGrange Ave.
Rochester, NY 14613
Phone 716-254-4080
FAX 715-254-3418

Shama Imports Inc.

Indian Crewel Fabric
PO Box 2900
Farmington Hills, MI 48333
Catalog/Information Available Free
Credit Cards VISA/MC
Phone 313-478-7740

Sharon Concepts, Inc.

Mirrors - Wall, Screens, Pedestals
1831 Burnet Ave.
Union, NJ 07083
Phone 201-964-1900

Sharp's Pen Wallpapers, Inc.

Wallcoverings
PO Box 237
Bridgeton-Fairton Rd.
Bridgeton, NJ 08302
Catalog/Information Available Free
Mail Order Available
Credit Cards MC/VISA/DISCOVER
Toll Free 800-257-7030
FAX 609-453-0909

Shaw Carpets Ltd.

Carpet
PO Box 4, Darton
Barnsley, S Yorkshire
S75 5NH
Great Britain
Phone 011-44-226/390390

Shaw Industries Inc.

Carpet
616 E. Walnut Ave.
Dalton, GA 30720
Phone 404-278-3812

Shelbourne Wallcoverings

Manufacturer - Wallcover
23645 Mercantile Rd.
Cleveland, OH 44122
Phone 216-464-3700
FAX 216-765-8648

Sherburne Ewing Wallcovering Co.

Manufacturer - Vinyl Wallpaper & Wallcover
2365 Commerce Blvd.
Minneapolis, MN 55364
Phone 612-472-5757
FAX 608-782-3833

Sheridan

Fabric by the Yard
600 Independence Blvd.
Greenville, SC 29615

Sheridan Carpet Mills

Order by Phone - Carpet
1101 Riverbend Rd.
Dalton, GA 30720
Phone 404-278-8243
Toll Free 800-241-4063

Shibui Wallcoverings

Order by Phone - Wallcover & Wallpaper
PO Box 1268
Santa Rosa, CA 95402
Send $4.00 for Catalog/Information
Credit Cards VISA/MC
Phone 707-526-6170
Toll Free 800-824-3030
FAX 707-544-0719

Shriber's

Order by Phone - Wallcover, Wallpaper
3222 Brighton Rd.
Pittsburgh, PA 15212
       Toll Free 800-245-6676

Shutters & Shades

Window Treatments - Shutters & Shades
87 Cresthaven Dr.
West Seneca, NY 14224-1216
       Phone 716-822-4822

Silk Surplus

Decorator Fabrics
235 East 58th St.
New York, NY 10022
Credit Cards VISA/MC
       Phone 212-753-6511

Silver Wallpaper & Paint Co.

Order by Phone - Wallpaper, Blinds, Verticals
3001 Kensington Ave.
Philadelphia, PA 19134
Mail Order Available
Credit Cards VISA/MC
       Toll Free 800-426-6600

Sinclair Wallcovering

Distributor - Major Brand Wallcover , Wallpaper
6100 Garfield
Los Angeles, CA 90040
       Phone 213-724-5000
       FAX 213-721-4107

Singer Wallcoverings

Vinyl Wallcover
PO Box 300
Kings Island, OH 45034
       Toll Free 800-543-0412

Skandia Industries

Window Treatments - Blinds & Shades
270 Crossway Rd.
PO Box 809
Tallahassee, FL 32310
       Phone 904-878-1144
       Toll Free 800-950-1134

Sligh Clocks

Grandfather, Wall & Mantel Clocks
201 Washington Ave.
Zeeland, MI 49464
       Phone 616-392-7101
       FAX 616-772-9632

Smart Wallcoverings

Order by Phone - Major Brand Wallpaper
PO Box 2206
Soutfield, MI 48037
Credit Cards VISA/MC
       Toll Free 800-677-0200

Solartechnic 2000 Ltd.

Blinds, Door & Window Frames and Hardware, Doors, Windows, Screens, Shutters, Solar Controls
Unit 10-11, Power Wks
Slade Green Rd., Slade Green, Erith,Kent
DA8 2HY
Great Britain
       Phone 011-44-322/336676
       FAX 011-44-322/33658

Soletude Inc.

Shoji Screens
4613 Skymont Dr.
Nashville, TN 37215-4205
       Toll Free 800-695-6255

Sommer UK Wall and Floorcoverings

Wall and Floorcoverings
Div. of Sommer Alibert UK Ltd.
Berry Hill ind Est, Droitwich, Worcs
WR9 9AB
Great Britain
       Phone 011-44-905/795004

Sophie's Stencils

Stencils

Le Rapt, Pillac
16390 St. Severin
France

Phone 011-33-1033459864

Southern Comfort Carpets

Order by Phone - Name Brand Carpet

1203 Broadick Drive #210
Dalton, GA 30720-2504

Phone 404-277-3374

Toll Free 800-749-5013

Southern Discount Wallcovering

Name Brand Wallcovering

1583 N. Military Trail
West Palm Beach, FL 33409

Credit Cards Accepted

Toll Free 800-699-9255

Southern Rug

Handcrafted Braided Rugs

2325 Anderson Rd.
Cresent Springs, KY 41017

Send $3.00 for Catalog/Information

Phone 813-381-7847

Toll Free 800-541-7847

Southland Wallcoverings

Manufacturer - Wallcover

4340 NW 10th Ave.
Ft. Lauderdale, FL 33322

Phone 305-771-8747

FAX 305-771-0140

Southwest Florida Blinds Inc.

Window Treatments - Blinds

914 NE 24th Ln. Unit 5
Cape Coral, FL 33909

Phone 813-772-4500

FAX 813-772-5420

Spence Bryson Carpets Ltd.

Carpet

Balloo Ave., Bangor
Co Down   BT19 2RT
Great Britain

Phone 011-44-247/27011

Spring Lace Two

Lace Curtains

221 Morris Ave.
Spring Lake, NJ 07762

Catalog/Information Available Free

Mail Order Available

Toll Free 800-948-4500

Springs Performance Products

Rugs, Bedspreads, Sheets, Comforters

Div. Spring Mills Inc.
PO Box 1328
Dalton, GA 30720

Phone 404-277-1500

Stanwood Drapery Co. Inc.

Curtains & Draperies

27 Drydock Ave.
Marine Industrial Park
Boston, MA 02210

Phone 617-737-1566

FAX 617-737-1569

Stark Carpet

Carpet

979 Third Ave.
New York, NY 10022

Phone 212-752-9000

FAX 212-888-4257

Steeles Carpets Ltd.

Carpets

Subdiv. of Tomkinsons PLC
The Carpet Mill, Barford Rd., Bloxham
Nr Banbury, Oxon OX15 4HA
Great Britain

Phone 011-44-295/720556

Home Decorating

Stenart Inc. – Studio 4 Inc.

Stenart Inc.

Stencils - Country, Victorian, Early American
PO Box 114
Pitman, NJ 08071-0114
Send $2.50 for Catalog/Information
Mail Order Available
Credit Cards VISA/MC
Toll Free 800-677-0033
FAX 609-582-0004

Stencil House of New Hampshire

Stencils
PO Box 16109
Hooksett, NH 03106
Send $2.50 for Catalog/Information
Mail Order Available
Credit Cards MC/VISA
Phone 603-625-1716
Toll Free 800-622-9416

Stencil Outlet

Stencils
PO Box 80
West Nottingham, NH 03291
Send $3.00 for Catalog/Information
Mail Order Available

Stencil World

Decorative Stencils
PO Box 1112
Newport, RI 02840
Send $3.50 for Catalog/Information
Mail Order Available
Phone 401-847-0870

Stencils & Seams Unlimited

Wallpaper & Borders, Stencil Valances
RR2 Box 2377
Raymond, ME 04071
Send $2.50 for Catalog/Information
Phone 207-655-3952

Stephen Leedom Carpets Co. Inc.

Carpet
919 3rd Ave.
New York, NY 10022
Phone 212-758-6000

Steven Linen Associates Inc.

Upholstery Fabric, Wallcovering, Home Furnishings
Louisville Textile Weavers Div.
PO Box 220
Webster, MA 01570
Phone 508-943-0600

Stevens Carpet

Carpet
Div. JPS Textile Group Inc.
PO Box A, Hwy. 5
Aberdeen, NC 28315
Phone 919-944-2371
Toll Free 800-869-2727

Stone Magic Mfg.

Manufacturer - Stone Mantels
5400 Miller
Dallas, TX 75206
Phone 214-826-3606
FAX 214-823-4503

Stroheim & Romann

Fabrics and Wallcover
31-11 Thompson Ave.
Long Island City, NY 11101
Phone 718-706-7000
FAX 718-361-0159

Studio 4 Inc.

Wallpaper & Wallcover
1751 N. Central Park Ave.
Chicago, IL 60647
Toll Free 800-621-7538
FAX 312-278-7041

Home Decorating

The Complete Sourcebook

8 - 63

Style Wallcovering

Order by Phone - Wallpaper
PO Box 865
Southfield, MI 48037
Credit Cards VISA/MC
　　　　Toll Free 800-627-0400

Sue Foster Fabrics

Fabrics
57 High Street, Emsworth
Hampshire PO10 7YA
Great Britain
Credit Cards Accepted
　　　　Phone 011-44-243/378831

Sunflower Studio

Drapery & Upholstery Fabrics
2851 Road B-1/2
Grand Junction, CO 81503
Send $2.50 for Catalog/Information
Credit Cards VISA/MC
　　　　Phone 303-242-3883

Sunnyside Corp.

Wallpaper & Wallcover
225 Carpenter Ave.
Wheeling, IL 60090
　　　　Phone 708-541-5700
　　　　FAX 708-541-9043

Sunnyside Prints

Wallpaper & Wallcover
22-78 35th St.
Long Island City, NY 11105
　　　　Phone 718-274-1460

Sunrise Designs

Wallpaper & Wallcover
Division of Bayview
41 E. Sunrise Hwy.
Lindenhurst, NY 11757
　　　　Phone 516-884-9301

Sunwall Fine Wallcovering

Distributor - Major Brand Wallcover,
Wallpaper
2625 Pine Meadow Court #A
Ouluth, GA 30136-4672
　　　　Phone 404-447-5402
　　　　FAX 404-246-6522

Sunworthy Wallcoverings

Manufacturer - Wallcover - US
800-426-7336
195 Walker Drive
Brampton, ON L6T 3Z9
　　　　Phone 416-791-8788
　　　　FAX 416-791-8078

Surface Materials, Inc.

Distributor - Major Brand Wallcover,
Wallpaper
23775 Commerce Park Rd.
Beachwood, OH 44122
　　　　Phone 216-831-0898
　　　　Toll Free 800-231-3223
　　　　FAX 216-831-3288

Surrey Shoppe Interiors

Shower Curtains
737 Belmont St.
Brockton, MA 02402
Send $1.00 for Catalog/Information
Mail Order Available
　　　　Phone 508-588-2525

Swaim

Upholstery Fabric
1801 South College Drive
PO Box 4189
High Point, NC 27263
　　　　Phone 919-885-6131
　　　　FAX 919-885-6227

Home Decorating

Syracuse Pottery

Pottery, Stoneware, Terracotta Planters
6551 Pottery Rd.
Warners, NY 13164

Phone 315-487-6066
Toll Free 800-448-2313
FAX 315-488-7785

TWG Fabric Outlet

Designer Lace Fabrics for Draperies, Tablecloths
115 Wisner Ave.
Middletown, NY 10940

Send $2.00 for Catalog/Information
Toll Free 800-221-2912

Tandem Fabric Inc.

Fabric
78 Cowansview Road
PO Box 460, Cambridge
Canada

Phone 519-623-9351
FAX 519-623-8589

Tankard Carpets Ltd.

Carpet
York Mills, York St.
Fairweather Green, Bradford, W Yorkshire
BD8 0HR
Great Britain

Phone 011-44-274/495646

Tasso

Manufacturer - Paintable Fiberglass Wallcover
1239 E. Newport Ctr. Dr. #118
Deerfield Beach, FL 33442

Phone 305-429-3883
Toll Free 800-888-2776
FAX 305-429-0208

Taylor Wallcoverings

Manufacturer - Wallcover
2112 W. Jefferson St.
Joliet, IL 60435

Phone 815-744-3366
FAX 815-744-2698

Technique Textiles

Manufacturer - Wallcover
PO Box 4689
Dalton, GA 30721

Phone 706-695-4455
FAX 706-695-1037

Temple Producst of Indiana Inc.

Window Treatments - Blinds
22680 Pine Creek Rd.
Elkhart, IN 46516

Phone 219-294-3621
FAX 219-293-9827

Tentina Window Fashion

Window Treatments - Blinds
1186 Rt. 109
PO Box 615
Lindenhurst, NY 11757

Phone 516-957-3454
FAX 516-957-9588

Texile Wallcoverings International Ltd.

Manufacturer - Wallcover
5100 Highlands Parkway
Smyma, GA 30082

Phone 404-435-9720
FAX 404-432-1415

The 135 Collection Inc.

Carpet & Rugs
135 N.E. 40th St.
Miami, FL 33137

Phone 305-576-5122
FAX 305-576-8968

The Blind Factory

Window Treatments - Blinds
96 N. Beverwyck Rd.
Lake Hiawatha, NJ 07034

Phone 201-263-8888
FAX 201-263-9198

Home Decorating

The Complete Sourcebook

The Blind Maker

Window Treatments - Blinds

2013 Centimeter Circle
Austin, TX 78758

Phone 512-835-5333
Toll Free 800-999-5555

The Blonder Co.

Major Brand Wallcover and Wallpaper

3950 Prospect Ave.
Cleveland, OH 44115

Phone 216-431-3560
FAX 216-391-9608

The Carpetologist

Carpet

596 Berriman St.
Brooklyn, NY 11208

Phone 718-272-9200

The Classic Coverup Inc.

Paintable Wallpaper

2909 Queens Plaza North
Long Island City, NY 11101

Mail Order Available

Phone 718-392-7700
FAX 718-392-7741

The Closet Doctor

Closet Shelving

PO Box 184
Medford, NJ 08055

Catalog/Information Available Free

Toll Free 800-344-4537

The Country House

Colonial Style Home Furnishings

805 E. Main St.
Salisbury, MD 21801

Send $1.00 for Catalog/Information

Phone 301-749-1959

The Curtain Collection

Window Treatments

PO Box 7069
Big Bear Lake, CA 92315

Send $2.00 for Catalog/Information

Toll Free 800-290-6523

The Decorative Center of Houston

Carpeting, Hardwood, Natural Stone, Antique Stone, Granite

5120 Woodway 10th fl.
Houston, TX 77056

Phone 713-961-7402
FAX 713-961-4072

The Decorators Outlet

Order by Phone - Fabric, Window Treatments, Bedspreads

1215 George Washington Memorial Hwy.
Yorktown, VA 23693

Toll Free 800-253-9508

The Fabric Center

Decorator Fabric

485 Electric Ave.
PO Box 8212
Fitchburg, MA 01420-8212

Catalog/Information Available Free

Send $2.00 for Catalog/Information

Credit Cards Accepted

Phone 508-343-4402
FAX 508-343-8139

The Fabric Outlet

Order by Phone - Decorator Fabrics

PO Box 2417
So. Hamilton, MA 01982

Credit Cards VISA/MC

Toll Free 800-635-9715

Home Decorating

The Gazebo of New York — The Stencil Outlet

The Gazebo of New York

Braided Rugs, Curtains, Quilts, Pillows
127 East 57th St.
New York, NY 10022
Send $6.00 for Catalog/Information
Mail Order Available
Phone 212-832-7077
FAX 212-754-0571

The House of Mayfair Ltd.

Wallpaper & Wallcover
Bassington Ind. Estate, Cramlington
Northumberland
Great Britain
Phone 011-44-67/0713333
FAX 011-44-67/0736799

The Hurshtowne Collection

Amish Home Furnishings
PO Box 686
Auburn, IN 46706
Send $3.00 for Catalog/Information
Toll Free 800-824-3473

The Itinerant Stenciler

Stencils
11030 173rd Ave. SE
Renton, WA 98059
Send $4.00 for Catalog/Information
Phone 206-226-0306

The Linen Gallery

Imported Bed, Bath and Table Linens
7001 Preston Rd.
at Lovers Ln.
Dallas, TX 75205
Phone 214-522-6700

The Maya Romanoff Corp.

Wallpaper & Wallcover
1730 W. Greenleaf
Chicago, IL 60626
Phone 312-465-6909
FAX 312-465-7089

The Oriental Rug Co.

Oriental Rugs
PO Box 205
Washington, KY 41096-0205
Catalog/Information Available Free
Phone 419-225-6731

The Persian Carpet

Carpet
5634 Chapel Hill Blvd.
Durham, NC 27707
Toll Free 800-333-1801

The Rug Store

Area Rugs
2201 Crown Point
Executive Drive
Charlotte, NC 28227
Send $5.00 for Catalog/Information
Credit Cards Accepted
Toll Free 800-257-5078

The Rug Warehouse

19th Century Antique Rugs
220 West 80th St.
New York, NY 10024
Phone 212-787-6665

The Stencil Collector

Stencils
1723 Tilghman St.
Allentown, PA 18104
Send $10.00 for Catalog/Information
Mail Order Available
Phone 610-433-2105
FAX 610-433-2105

The Stencil Outlet

Stencils
PO Box 80
West Nottingham, NH 03291
Send $3.00 for Catalog/Information

Home Decorating

The Complete Sourcebook

8 - 67

The Stencil Shoppe, Inc.

Stencils
3634 Silverside Rd.
Wilmington, DE 19810
Send $3.95 for Catalog/Information
Toll Free 800-822-7836

The Twigs Inc.

Fabric
5700 Third St.
San Francisco, CA 94124-2609
Phone 415-822-1626
FAX 415-822-4146

The Walsh Woodworks

Reproduction Colonial & Shaker Furniture
243 Cumings Rd.
Painesville, OH 44077
Send $1.00 for Catalog/Information
Mail Order Available

The Warner Company

Distributor - Major Brand Wallpaper, Fabric
108 S. Desplaines
Chicago, IL 60608
Phone 312-372-3540
Toll Free 800-621-1143
FAX 312-372-9584

The World of Clothing

Decorative Carpet
PO Box 2360
Hendersonville, NC 28793
Toll Free 800-759-9739

Thomas Ray Designs Inc.

Wallpaper & Wallcover
79 Montgomery St.
Paterson, NJ 07501
Phone 201-345-4643
FAX 201-279-6068

Thomas Strahan Co.

Wallpaper & Vinyl Wallcoverings
150 Heard St.
Chelsea, MA 02150
Phone 617-884-7020

Thorndike Mills

Carpets, Rugs
PO Box 350
Palmer, MA 01069
Phone 413-283-9021

Thursday's Child

Stencils
PO Box 221901
Chantilly, VA 22022
Send $5.50 for Catalog/Information
Phone 703-378-9276

Tianjin-Philadelphia Carpet Company

Oriental Rugs
231 W. Mt. Pleasant Ave.
Philadelphia, PA 19119
Phone 215-247-3535
FAX 215-242-8659

Tiara Wallcoverings

Distributor - Major Brand Wallcover, Wallpaper
640 W. 27th St.
Hialeah, FL 33010
Phone 305-887-0687
Toll Free 800-327-0621
FAX 305-883-4692

Tiffany Quilting & Drapery Inc.

Bedspreads, Draperies
206 East Palmetto Ave.
Longwood, FL 32750
Phone 407-834-6386
FAX 407-830-1346

Home Decorating

Tiffany Wholesale Supply Inc.

Window Treatments - Blinds
940 E. Michigan St.
Indianapolis, IN 46202
Phone 317-638-3405

Timeless Design, Inc.

*Wallpaper and Boarders - 17th Century
India & China, Handpainted*
PO Box 20711
Seattle, WA 98102-1711
Phone 206-624-8752
FAX 206-624-1719

Tioga Mill Outlet Stores, Inc.

Upholstery & Drapery Fabric
200 S. Hartman St., PO Box 3171
York, PA 17403

Catalog/Information Available Free

Credit Cards VISA/MC
Phone 717-843-5139
FAX 717-843-5139

Tobin Sporn & Glasser Inc.

Carpets & Rugs
8 W 30th St.
New York, NY 10001
Phone 212-684-1191
FAX 212-779-0249

Touchstone

*18th & 19th Century Decorative
Accessories & Furniture*
Traditional American Living
3589 Broad St.
Atlanta, GA 30341-2203

Credit Cards VISA/MC
Toll Free 800-968-6880

Trafford Carpets Ltd.

Carpet
Mosley Rd., Trafford Pk.
Manchester
M17 1PX
Great Britain
Phone 011-44-61/8721665

Treasured Weavings

Rugs, Pillows, Furniture
3935 Magazine St.
New Orleans, LA 70115
Phone 504-895-6115

Trendsetters by Magden Ltd.

Wallpaper & Wallcover
Route 101, Box 668
Yaphank, NY 11980
Phone 516-924-8471
FAX 516-924-8472

Tretford Carpets Ltd.

Carpet
Lynn La. Shenstone
Lichfield Staffs
WS14 0DU
Great Britain
Phone 011-44-543/480577

Triangle Window Fashions

Window Treatments - Blinds
3025 Sangra Ave. SW
PO Box 65
Grandville, MI 49418
Phone 616-538-9676
FAX 616-538-6051

Triblend Mills

Drapery Fabric
PO Box 548
Tarboro, NC 27610

Mail Order Available
Phone 919-823-1355

Trifles

Curtains, Bedspreads, Furnishings
PO Box 620048
Dallas, TX 75262-0048

Mail Order Available
Toll Free 800-456-7019

The Complete Sourcebook

8 - 69

Triumph Designs Inc. – United Designs Inc.

Home Decorating

Triumph Designs Inc.

Fabric

18953 NE Third Ct.
N. Miami Beach, FL 33179

Phone 305-652-2352
FAX 305-651-1659

Trocadero Textile Art

Oriental Rugs

2313 Calvert
Washington, DC 20008

Phone 202-328-8440

Twil

Wallcover & Wallpaper

5100 Highlands Pkwy.
Smyrna, GA 30082

Phone 404-435-9720
FAX 404-432-1415

U.S. Plush Mills Inc.

Upholstery & Drapery Fabric

181 Conant St.
Pawtucket, RI 02860

Phone 401-722-9000

U.S. Precision Glass

Glass & Mirrors

1920 Holmes Rd.
Elgin, IL 60123

Phone 708-931-1200
FAX 708-931-4144

USA Blind Factory

*Window Treatments - Blinds - Vertical,
Pleated, Mini, Micro, Wood & Area Rugs*

1312 Live Oak
Houston, TX 77003

Toll Free 800-275-3219
FAX 713-227-4011

Ulster Carpet Mills Ltd.

Carpet

Castleisland Factory
Portadown, Craigavon
BT62 1EE
Great Britain

Phone 011-44-762334443

Ultima Wallcoverings

Wallpaper & Wallcover

Divison of Knoll Int'l
15 Akron Rd., Toronto
ON M8W 1T3
Canada

Phone 416-251-1678

Unique Wall Fashions Inc.

Wallpaper & Wallcover

3330 NW 73rd St.
Miami, FL 33147

Phone 305-835-6937
FAX 305-693-4272

Unique Wholesale Distr. Inc.

Blinds

6811 NW 15th Ave.
Fort Lauderdale, FL 33309

Phone 305-975-0227

Unistar Corp.

Carpets

120 N. Industrial Blvd.
PO Box 1992
Dalton, GA 30722

Phone 404-226-8346

United Coated Fabrics Corp.

Manufacturer - Wallcover

245 Wescott Drive
Rahway, NJ 07065

Phone 201-382-7120
FAX 201-381-8313

United Designs Inc.

Blinds, Shades

PO Box 11060
St. Petersburg, FL 33733

Phone 813-327-6434

8 - 70

The Complete Sourcebook

United Supply Co.

Window Treatments - Blinds

PO Box 240198
200 Westinghouse Blvd.
Charlotte, NC 28241

Phone 704-588-3310
Toll Free 800-334-1207
FAX 704-588-1913

United Wallcoverings

Manufacturer - Wallcover , Fabric

23645 Mercantile Rd.
Cleveland, OH 44122

Phone 216-464-3700
FAX 216-765-8648

Upholstery Fabrics

Order by Phone - Major Brand Fabric

Fabcuts
110 E. Highway 13
Brownsville, MN 55337

Credit Cards VISA/MC/AMEX

Toll Free 800-932-2742

V A Wallcoverings

*Wallcoverings, Fabrics - Custom:
Draperies, Bedspreads, Comforters,
Shades, Vertical Blinds*

777 Alness St.
Downsview
ON M3J 2H8
Canada

Phone 416-661-2235
FAX 416-661-5027

V I P Sales Inc.

Carpets

145 Atlantic Dr. SE
PO Box 1776
Dalton, GA 30720

Phone 404-278-3301

Valdese Weavers Inc.

Upholstery Fabric

Box 70
Valdese, NC 28690

Phone 704-874-2181

Valiant Fabrics Corp.

Fabric

55 Walker St.
New York, NY 10013

Phone 212-966-0255
FAX 212-966-1583

Valley Forge Fabrics Inc.

Fabric

6881 NW 16th Terrace
Ft. Lauderdale, FL 33309

Phone 305-971-1776
FAX 305-968-1775

Van Luit Wallcoverings

Manufacturer - Wallcover, Fabrics

23645 Mercantile Rd.
Cleveland, OH 44122

Phone 216-464-3700

Vanderkellen Galleries

Antique Quilts

701 East Second St.
Wichita, KS 67202

Send $9.95 for Catalog/Information

Credit Cards Accepted

Toll Free 800-562-8694

Varsity Rug Co.

Rugs & Carpeting

2000 Hwy. 41 S
PO Box 1392
Dalton, GA 30720

Phone 404-226-7300
FAX 404-226-3537

Versol USA, Inc.

Manufacturer - Window Treatment - Blinds

215 Beecham Drive
PO Box 517
Pittsburgh, PA 15230

Phone 412-922-4300
Toll Free 800-252-2512

Verticals Inc. – Vornhold Wallpaper Inc.

Home Decorating

Verticals Inc.

Window Treatments - Blinds
704 E. 133 St.
Bronx, NY 10454

Phone 718-292-6500
FAX 718-292-6503

Victorian Collectibles

19th Century Style Tile, Victorian Wallpaper
845 East Glenbrook Rd.
Milwaukee, WI 53217

Send $5.00 for Catalog/Information

Phone 414-352-6971
Toll Free 800-783-3829
FAX 414-352-7290

Victorian Interiors

Wallpaper, Moulding
575 Hayes St.
San Francisco, CA 94102

Mail Order Available

Phone 415-431-7191

View Guard

Transparent Shades & Blinds
17200 Foothill Blvd.
Castro Valley, CA 94546

Phone 415-481-1335

Viking Distributors Inc.

Window Treatments - Blinds
202 Hill St.
Rockford, IL 61107

Phone 815-962-3997

Village Carpet

Order by Phone - Major Brand Carpet - Discounted Prices
3203 Highway 70 Southeast
Newton, NC 28685

Phone 704-465-6818

Vintage Valances

Victorian Style Valances
PO Box 43326
Cincinnati, OH 45243

Send $12.00 for Catalog/Information

Phone 513-561-8665
FAX 513-561-8665

Virginia Mirror Co. Inc.

Mirrors & Glass
PO Box 5431
Martinsville, VA 24115

Phone 703-632-9816
FAX 703-632-2488

Vision Wallcoverings Ltd.

Wallpaper & Wallcover
PO Box 97-442
Auckland, New Zealand
New Zealand

Phone 011-64-6492799039
FAX 011-64-6492783205

Vista Products Inc.

Manufacturer - Window Coverings - Blinds & Shades
1788 Barber Rd.
Sarasota, FL 34240

Phone 813-378-3844
FAX 813-378-3514

Vogue Wall Covering Inc.

Wallcover
68 Falulah Rd.
Fitchburg, MA 01420

Phone 508-342-6077

Vornhold Wallpaper Inc.

Wallpaper
501 Main St.
Hulnerville, PA 19047

Phone 215-757-6641

8 - 72

The Complete Sourcebook

Home Decorating

Vorwerk Carpets Ltd.

Carpet
Vorwerk Ho, Toutley Rd.
Wokingham, Berks
RG11 5QN
Great Britain
Phone 011-44-734/343155

W. Hirsch Oriental Rugs

Oriental Rugs
3117 W. Cary St.
Richmond, VA 23220
Phone 804-359-5463

Wakefield Mills

Rugs
S. 7th St.
North Vernon, IN 47265
Phone 812-346-7191

Wall Fabrics Inc.

Fabric
932 Market St.
Paterson, NJ 07509
Phone 201-279-9255
FAX 201-279-6916

Wall Fashions Unlimited

Wallcoverings
549 W. Lake Mary Blvd.
Lake Mary, FL 32746-3419
Phone 407-322-6742

Wall Trends International

Manufacturer - Wallcover
17 Mileed Way Avenue
Avenel, NJ 07001
Phone 908-382-8600
Toll Free 800-524-2609
FAX 908-382-6885

Wall Visions Inc.

Manufacturer - Charleston Way Wallcover
271 Central Ave.
Clark, NJ 07066
Phone 201-815-9700

Wall-Decor, Inc.

Distributor - Major Brand Wallcover, Wallpaper
316 Pinero Ave.
University Gardens Ext.
Rio Piedras, PR 00927
Phone 809-758-8055

Wallcoverings North, Inc.

Distributor - Major Brand Wallcover, Wallpaper
6239 "B" St.
Suite 101
Anchorage, AK 99518
Phone 907-563-2233
FAX 907-563-5670

Walldesigns

Manufacturer/Distributor - Wallcover
2021 N. 63rd St.
PO Box 28863
Philadelphia, PA 19151
Phone 215-878-5312
FAX 215-878-4359

Wallpaper Cottage

Wallcovering
27869 Encanto Dr.
Sun City, CA 92381-3305
Phone 714-679-7708

Wallpaper Imports Inc.

Manufacturer - Wallcover
311 Route 46
Fairfield, NJ 07006
Phone 201-882-8180
FAX 201-882-0168

Wallpaper Outlet

Wallpaper & Blinds
337 Rt. 46
Rockaway, NJ 07866
Phone 800-482-2488
Toll Free 800-291-9255

The Complete Sourcebook

Wallpaper Warehouse Inc.

Order by Phone - Wallcovering
1434 Ellis Ave.
Jackson, MS 39204
Toll Free 800-523-3503

WallpaperXpress

Order by Phone - Fabrics, Wallpaper, Blinds
PO Box 4061
Naperville, IL 60567
Credit Cards VISA/MC/DISCOVER
Toll Free 800-288-9979

Wallquest Inc.

Distributor- Major Brand Wallcover, Wallpaper
465 Devon Park Drive
Wayne, PA 19087-1815
Phone 215-293-1330
Toll Free 800-722-9255
FAX 215-293-9696

Walter L. Brown Ltd.

Importer/Distributor of Wallcoverings and Textiles
17 Vickers Rd.
Toronto, ON M9B 1C2
Canada
Phone 416-231-4499
FAX 416-231-7615

Wamsutta Doblin

Upholstery Fabric
PO Box 2128
Morganton, NC 28655
Phone 704-437-8300

Wamsutta/Pacific

Fabric by the Yard
1285 Avenue of the Americas
New York, NY 10019
Toll Free 800-852-7659

Warehouse Carpets, Inc.

Order by Phone - Major Brand Carpet
PO Box 3233
Dalton, GA 30721
Mail Order Available
Phone 706-226-2229
Toll Free 800-526-2229
FAX 706-278-1008

Warner Co.

Fabric
400 Commercial Ave.
Palisades Park, NJ 07650

Warner Wallpaper Co.

Manufacturer - Wallpaper
6102 Skyline N
Houston, TX 77057
Phone 713-785-6620

Washington Pottery Co.

Pottery & Gardenware
13001 48th Ave.
S. Seattle, WA 98168
Phone 206-243-1191

Washington Wallcoverings

Distributor - Major Brand Wallcover, Wallpaper
4473 1st Ave.
Brooklyn, NY 11232
Mail Order Available
Phone 718-499-3500
FAX 718-499-1991

Waterhouse Wallhangings Inc.

Wallpaper & Wallcover
99 Paul Sullivan Way
Boston, MA 02118
Phone 617-423-7688

Home Decorating

Waverly Fabric — Weymouth Braided Rug Co.

Waverly Fabric

Vinyl Wallcover, Fabric
79 Madison Ave.
New York, NY 10016
Mail Order Available

Phone 212-644-5900
Toll Free 800-955-1550

Waverly Wallcoverings

Guide
PO Box 5114
Farmingdale, NY 11736
Send $2.50 for Catalog/Information

Toll Free 800-423-5881

Wellco Carpet Co.

Carpet & Rugs
PO Box 12281
Calhoun, GA 30701

Phone 404-629-7301
Toll Free 800-241-4357

Wells Interiors

Wholesale Window Treatments - Blinds, Shades
7171 Amandor Valley Plaza Rd.
Dublin, CA 95468
Catalog/Information Available Free
Mail Order Available
Credit Cards VISA/MC

Toll Free 800-547-8982

Wendell Fabrics Corp.

Upholstery Fabric
108 E. Church St.
Blacksburg, SC 29702

Phone 803-839-6341

Wertheimer Sculptures Ltd.

Sculpture
6695 Somerled Ave.
Quebec, Montreal
Que., CAN H4V 1T5
Canada

Phone 514-487-7720

Wesco Fabrics Inc.

Draperies, Bedspreads, Shades
4001 Forest St.
Denver, CO 80216

Phone 303-388-4101
FAX 303-388-3908

West Point Pepperell Inc.

Manufacturer - Carpet, Rugs
120 E. Morris St.
Dalton, GA 30702

Phone 404-272-1400

Western Plaza

Persian and Oriental Rugs
4505 Kingston Pike
Knoxville, TN 37919

Phone 615-558-8777

Westgate Fabrics Inc.

Fabric
1000 Fountain Pkwy.
Grand Prairie, TX 75050

Phone 214-647-2323
Toll Free 800-492-2130
FAX 214-660-7096

Weston of Scandinavia UK Ltd.

Carpet
Fairfax Ho, Causton Rd.
Colchester CO1 1RJ
Great Britain

Phone 011-44-206/42444

Westport Mfg. Co. Inc.

Bedspreads, Draperies
1122 S.W. Marine Dr.
Vancouver
B.C. CAN V6P 5Z3
Canada

Phone 604-261-9326

Weymouth Braided Rug Co.

Manufacturer - Braided Rugs
Box 495
Oxford, MA 01537

Phone 508-987-8525

Home Decorating

The Complete Sourcebook

8 - 75

White Shield of Carolina Inc.

Home Furnishings
PO Box 306
Cherokee, NC 28719

Phone 704-497-2011

Whitecrest Carpet Mills

Carpet
PO Box 740-99 Highland Rd.
Chatsworth, GA 30705

Phone 706-695-9411

Toll Free 800-274-4632

FAX 706-695-5316

Whiting Mfg. Co. Inc.

Bedspreads, Comforters, Drapes
9999 Carver Rd.
Cincinnati, OH 45242

Phone 513-791-9100

Wholesale Carpet

Order by Phone - Carpet
PO Box 3876
Dalton, GA 30721

Phone 404-673-5959

Toll Free 800-346-4531

Wholesale Verticals, Inc.

Order by Phone - Major Brand Blinds
PO Box 305
Baldwin, NY 11510

Credit Cards VISA/MC

Toll Free 800-762-2748

Wild Wings

Retail Home Furnishings, Limited Edition Prints, Collectibles
South Highway 61
PO Box 451
Lake City, MN 55041-0451

Catalog/Information Available Free

Mail Order Available

Credit Cards Accepted

Phone 612-345-5355

Toll Free 800-445-4833

FAX 612-345-2981

Wild Wood Gallery

Home Decorating Accessories
Pratts Falls Rd.
Jamesville, NY 13078

Credit Cards VISA/MC/AMEX

Phone 315-454-8098

Toll Free 800-535-6600

Will Kirkpatrick

Decorative Handcarved - Decoys, Geese, Shorebirds
124 Forest Ave.
Hudson, MA 01749

Send $2.00 for Catalog/Information

Phone 508-562-7841

Wilton Royal Carpet Factory Ltd.

Carpet Tile, Carpets
Ramsey Ind Est, Greatbridge Rd.
Ramsey, Hants SO51 0HR
Great Britain

Phone 011-44-794/515011

FAX 011-44-794/523376

Win-Glo Window Coverings

Window Treatments - Blinds
2390 Zanker Rd.
San Jose, CA 95131

Phone 408-435-8844

Winco Window Coverings

Window Treatments
9 Boyd
Watertown, MA 02172-2534

Phone 617-923-1910

Windo-Shade Distributors Inc.

Window Treatments - Blinds
5700 Brazton #160
PO Box 741738
Houston, TX 77036

Phone 713-978-7900

FAX 713-978-5002

Home Decorating

Window Covering Dist. Inc.

Window Treatments - Blinds
6680 Jones Mill Ct., Ste E
Norcross, GA 30092

Phone 404-446-7258
FAX 404-446-5911

Window Coverings Inc.

Window Treatments - Blinds
2010 SE Eighth Ave.
Portland, OR 97214

Phone 503-238-0666
FAX 503-274-8735

Window Modes

Window Shades & Blinds
979 Third Ave. 16th Fl
New York, NY 10022

Phone 212-752-1140
FAX 718-398-5644

Wisconsin Drapery Supply Inc.

Window Treatments - Blinds, Draperies
24110 W. Bluemound Rd.
Wankesha, WI 51388-1627

Toll Free 800-242-8768
FAX 414-549-5564

Wolf-Gordon, Inc.

Manufacturer - Wallcover and Fabric
33-00 47th Ave.
Long Island City, NY 11101

Phone 718-361-6611
FAX 718-361-1138

Wooden Ewe Farm

Cotton Rugs
PO Box 116
Belmont, VT 05730

Phone 802-259-2282

World Carpets

Carpet
PO Box 1448
Dalton, GA 30722-1448

Phone 404-278-8000
FAX 404-278-6925

Worldwide Wallcoverings & Blinds

Major Brand Wallcoverings and Blinds
333 Skokie Blvd.
Northbrook, IL 60062

Credit Cards Accepted

Toll Free 800-322-5400
FAX 708-559-9000

Wrisco Industries Inc.

Window Treatments - Blinds
12102 Corporate Dr.
Dallas, TX 75228

Phone 214-270-8848
FAX 214-613-7823

Wunda Weve Carpet Co.

Manufacturer - Carpet
PO Box 167
Greenville, SC 29602

Phone 803-298-9120
Toll Free 800-845-2001

Yankee Pride

Braided Rugs
29 Parkside Circle
Braintree, MA 02184

Send $3.00 for Catalog/Information

Mail Order Available

Phone 617-848-7610

Yankee Wallcoverings, Inc.

Order by Phone - Wallpaper
109 Accord Park Drive
Norwell, MA 02061

Credit Cards VISA/MC

Toll Free 800-624-7711

The Complete Sourcebook

York Wallcoverings Inc.

Manufacturer - Wallcovering and Fabric
750 Linden Ave.
York, PA 17404

Phone 717-846-4456
FAX 717-843-5624

Yorktown Wallpaper Outlet

Order by Phone - Wallpaper
2445 S. Queen St.
York, PA 17402

Toll Free 800-847-6142

Yowler & Shepps Stencils

Stencils
3529 Main Street
Conestoga, PA 17516

Send $4.00 for Catalog/Information

Phone 717-872-2820

Zaven A. Kish Oriental Rug Gallery

Oriental Rugs
97 North Tillman
Memphis, TN 38111

Phone 901-327-4422

Zina Studios Inc.

Fabric & Wallcover
45 S. 3rd Avenue
Mt. Vernon, NY 10550

Phone 914-667-6004
FAX 914-667-6004

Home Security

ABCO Supply Company

Burglar Alarm Kits

387 Canal St.
New York, NY 10013

Catalog/Information Available Free

Mail Order Available

Phone 212-431-5066

Toll Free 800-841-8000

Advanced Security

Security Alarm Systems

2964 Peachtree St.
Atlanta, GA 30305

Send$1.00 for Catalog/Information

Mail Order Available

Toll Free 800-241-0267

Alarm Supply Co.

Burglar & Fire Alarms

7294 Glenview
Fort Worth, TX 76118

Send$3.00 for Catalog/Information

Phone 817-284-1731

All Island Security Inc.

Outdoor Security Lighting

662 Franklin Ave.
Garden City, NY 11530

Credit Cards VISA/MC

Toll Free 800-448-6600

Almet Hardware Ltd.

Security Door Lock Hardware

8205 Montreal Toronto Blvd.
Montreal
Que., CAN H4X 1N1
Canada

Phone 514-364-4211

FAX 514-364-4912

Arthur Shaw Manufacturing Ltd.

Manufacturer - Window & Door Security Locks

1 Rose Hill
Willenhall, West Midlands WV13 2AS
Great Britain

Phone 011-44-90-2368638

FAX 011-44-90-2366766

Burdex Security Co.

Burglar & Fire Alarms

1000 West O St., PO Box 82802
Lincoln, NE 68501

Catalog/Information Available Free

Credit Cards VISA/MC

Phone 402-435-3022

Burle Industries, Inc.

Outdoor Security Lighting

1000 New Holland Ave.
Lancaster, PA 17601

Catalog/Information Available Free

Mail Order Available

Phone 717-295-6000

The Complete Sourcebook

Chubb Lock Company

Manufacturer - Window and Door Hardware & Locks, Security Lighting
PO Box 197
Wednesfield Rd., Wolverhampton
Great Britain

Phone 011-44-90-255-111
FAX 011-44-90-2871793

EMEL Electronics

Alarm Equipment
Box 146
Sheffield, MA 01257
Send$1.00 for Catalog/Information

Electronic Sensing Products, Inc.

Sensor Lighting
1050 Colwell Lane Bldg.#3
Conshohocken, PA 19428

Phone 215-825-6600
FAX 215-825-7905

Falcon Eye Inc.

Factory Direct - Outdoor Security Lighting
4511 Ridgehaven Rd.
Fort Worth, TX 76116-7315
Credit Cards VISA/MC

Toll Free 800-541-3507

Gibbons of Willenhall Ltd.

High Security Locks and Latches
Ashmore Lake Way
Willenhall, West Midlands
WV12 4LL
Great Britain

Phone 011-44-90/265253
FAX 011-44-902/602431

Heath Zenith

Manufacturer - Home Security System
Heath Company
Hilltop St.
St. Joseph, MI 49085

Toll Free 800-999-0009

High-Desert Security Systems

Burglar/Fire Alarm
PO Box 902182
Palmdale, CA 93590

Home Automation, Inc.

Manufacturer - Home Security System
2703 Ridgelake Dr.
Metairie, LA 70002-6038

Honeywell Inc.

Manufacturer - Home Security System
Protection Services Division
Honeywell Plaza, PO Box 524
Minneapolis, MN 55440-0524

Imperial Screen Company Inc.

Manufacturer - Door & Window Security Screens
12816 S. Normandie Ave.
Gardena, CA 90249
Mail Order Available

Phone 310-769-0371
FAX 310-769-1707

Maple Chase Co.

Home Security - Smoke Alarms
2820 Thatcher Road
Downer's Grove, IL 60515-4040

Phone 708-963-1550
FAX 708-960-9302

Mountain West Alarm Supply

Burglar & Fire Alarms
Alpha Omega Security Group, Inc.
9420 E. Doubletree Ranch Rd.
Scottsdale, AZ 85258
Send$1.00 for Catalog/Information
Mail Order Available
Credit Cards VISA/MC

Phone 602-971-1200
Toll Free 800-528-6169
FAX 602-860-1411

New England Lock & Hardware Co.

Locks & Hardware
PO Box 544
South Norwalk, CT 06856
           Phone 203-866-9283

Premier Communications Company

Burglar Alarms
1414 Long St.
PO Box 1513
High Point, NC 27261
Catalog/Information Available Free
Mail Order Available
           Toll Free 800-544-8255

Prescolite

Manufacturer - Security Lighting Fixtures
1251 Doolittle Dr.
San Leandro, CA 94577
           Phone 510-562-3500

RAB Electric

Manufacturer - Sensor Lighting, Decorator Switchplates
170 Ludlow Ave.
Northvale, NJ 07647-0970
           Phone 201-784-8600
           FAX 201-784-0077

Rollaway

Manufacturer - Security Shutters
10601 Oak Street NE
St. Petersburg, FL 33716
           Phone 813-576-6044
           Toll Free 800-282-8999

Schlage

Security Systems
5452 Betsy Ross Dr.
Santa Clara, CA 95054
           Phone 408-727-5170
           Toll Free 800-562-1570
           FAX 408-727-6707

Security Link Corporation

Manufacturer - Home Security System
125 Frontage Rd.
PO Box 1249
Orange, CT 06477-7249

The J. Goodman Co.

Security Products, Alarm Systems
29 Arden Rd.
Linvingston, NJ 07039
Catalog/Information Available Free
Credit Cards VISA/MC

Unity System Inc.

Manufacturer - Home Security System
2606 Spring Street
Redwood City, CA 94063
           Phone 415-369-3233
           FAX 415-369-3142

Vision Security Inc.

Outdoor Intrusion Sensors
1762 Technology Dr.
Suite 124
San Jose, CA 95110
           Phone 408-453-1966
           FAX 408-453-1972

Wartian Lock Co.

Window & Door Locks
20525 E. Mile Rd.
St. Clair Shores, MI 48080
           Phone 313-777-2244

Weiser Lock

Indoor Locks
5555 McFadden Ave.
Huntington Beach, CA 92649
           Phone 714-898-0811

Westco Security Systems Inc.

Burglar Alarms
3400 McKnight Rd.
Pittsburgh, PA 15237
           Phone 412-931-5160

The Complete Sourcebook

Yale Security Products Ltd.

Manufacturer - Hardware - Door & Window Locks

Wood Street, Willenhall
West Midlands WV13 1LA
Great Britain

Phone 011-44-90/2366911
FAX 011-44-90/2368535

Kitchen

AGA Cookers

Manufacturer - Call for Distributor - Cast Iron Cooker Stoves

17 Towne Farm Lane
Stowe, VT 05672

Send $2.00 for Catalog/Information

Phone 802-253-9727

FAX 802-253-7815

Allmilmo Corp.

Manufacturer - Kitchen Cabinetry

70 Clinton Road
Fairfield, NJ 07004

Phone 201-227-2502

Alno Network USA

Manufacturer - Kitchen Cabinetry

Boston Design Center
1 Design Center Place, Suite 643
Boston, MA 02210

Phone 617-482-2566

American Brass Mfg.

Manufacturer - Kitchen, Bath, Shower, Faucets, Plumbing Supply

5000 Superior
Cleveland, OH 44103

Phone 216-431-6565

FAX 216-431-9420

American Woodmark Corp.

Manufacturer - Kitchen Cabinetry

3102 Shawnee Drive
PO Box 1980
Winchester, VA 22601

Toll Free 800-388-2483

Aristokraft

Manufacturer - Kitchen Cabinets, Decorative Hardware, Cabinet Organizers

PO Box 420
1 Aristokraft Square
Jasper, IN 47547-0420

Phone 812-482-2527

Artisan Woodworkers

Cabinets

21415 Broadway
Sonoma, CA 95476

Phone 707-938-4796

Barker Cabinets

Manufacturer - Cabinets

Suite J 2221 E. Winston Rd.
Anaheim, CA 92806-5540

Phone 714-991-3601

Barnard Street Woodworks

Manufacturer - Cabinets

2 Barnard
Marblehead, MA 01945-3106

Phone 617-631-7121

Barnstable Stove Shop

Antique Kitchen Ranges & Parlor Stoves

Box 472 Rt. 149
West Barnstable, MA 02668

Send $1.00 for Catalog/Information

Phone 508-362-9913

Beaver Woodworks

Cabinets

20732 Soledad
Canyon Country, CA 91351-2431

Phone 805-251-5270

Blanco

Kitchen Sinks

Oxgate La
Cricklewood, London NW2 7JN
Great Britain

Phone 011-44-81-4509100

Blanco America

*Manufacturer - Distributor List - Sink
Disposal System, Sinks, Cooktops,
Faucets*

1001 Lower Landing Rd.
Suite 607
Blackwood, NJ 08012

Catalog/Information Available Free

Phone 609-228-3500

Toll Free 800-451-5782

FAX 609-228-7956

Blue Jay Fine Woodworker

Cabinets

125 Providence
West Warwick, RI 02893-2504

Phone 401-828-5580

Broan Manufacturing Co. Inc.

Manufacturer - Kitchen Cabinetry

PO Box 140
Hartford, WI 53027

Toll Free 800-548-0790

Brookhaven Cabinetry

Manufacturer - Kitchen Cabinetry

1 Second Street
Kreamer, PA 17833

Phone 717-374-2711

Buckwalter Custom Kitchens

Cabinets

656 White Oak Rd. E.
Christiana, PA 17509-9715

Phone 215-593-2355

Bulthaup Inc.

*Manufacturer - Deal Direct - Nationwide
Shipping - German Kitchen Cabinetry*

153 S. Robertson Blvd.
Los Angeles, CA 90048

Mail Order Available

Phone 310-288-3875

FAX 310-288-3885

C & M Cabinet Co.

Cabinets

400 South Rd.
Fort Myers, FL 33907-2433

Phone 813-936-2424

CECO Products Inc.

Manufacturer - Kitchen Cabinets

2995 Orange Grove Ave.
North Highlands, CA 95660

Phone 916-482-6260

Cabinet Crafters

*Do-it-Yourself Kitchen Cabinets &
Replacement Doors in Oak, Birch, Cherry,
Pine*

3721 South Westnedge
Suite 282
Kalamazoo, MI 49008

Catalog/Information Available Free

Mail Order Available

Toll Free 800-527-5316

Calma's Custom Cabinets

Custom Cabinets

5940 Johnson Pnt. Rd. NE
Olympia, WA 98506-9567

Phone 206-456-1904

Kitchen

Cardell Cabinets

Manufacturer - Kitchen Cabinets - Maple, Cherry, Oak - Raised and Recessed Panel Doors

3215 N. Pan Am Expressway
PO Box 200850
San Antonio, TX 78219-2311

Phone 210-225-0290

FAX 210-223-4439

Carron Phoenix Ltd.

Manufacturer - Granite, Stainless Steel Sinks, Mixers

PO Box 30
Carron, Falkirk FK2 8DW
Great Britain

Phone 011-44-324/38321

FAX 011-44-324/20978

Contemporary Copper

Custom Range Hoods

PO Box 69
Greenfield, MA 01302

Send $4.00 for Catalog/Information

Mail Order Available

Phone 413-773-9242

FAX 413-774-4704

Creda Inc.

Cooktops, Ovens

5700 West Touhy
Chicago, IL 60648

Phone 708-647-8024

Toll Free 800-992-7332

FAX 708-647-8024

Crown Point Cabinetry

Order Direct - Kitchen & Bath Victorian Cabinetry

PO Box 1560
153 Charlestown Rd.
Claremont, NH 03743

Catalog/Information Available Free

Toll Free 800-370-1218

FAX 800-370-1218

Davis & Warshow Inc.

Distributor - American Standard Kitchen & Bath Fixtures

150 East 58th St.
New York, NY 10155

Credit Cards VISA/MC/DISCOVER

Phone 212-688-5990

FAX 212-593-0446

DeWeese Woodworking Company

Bathroom Accessories

Highway 492
PO Box 576
Philadelphia, MS 39350

Catalog/Information Available Free

Mail Order Available

Phone 601-656-4951

Downsview Kitchens

Manufacturer - Kitchen Cabinetry

2635 Rena Road
Mississauga, Ontario L4T 1G6
Canada

Phone 416-677-9354

Eljer

Kitchen & Bath Fixtures, Faucets

17120 Dallas Parkway
Dallas, TX 75248

Phone 214-407-2600

Toll Free 800-423-5537

FAX 214-407-2789

Elkay Mfg. Co.

Manufacturer - Kitchen & Bathroom Fixtures

2222 Camden Ct.
Oak Brook, IL 60521

Phone 708-574-8484

Toll Free 800-635-7500

The Complete Sourcebook

Elmira Stove And Fireplace

Antique Style Electric/Gas Ranges
145 Northfield Dr.
Waterloo, ON N2L 5J3
Canada
Send $5.00 for Catalog/Information
>   Phone 519-725-5500
>   FAX 519-725-5503

Erickson's Antique Stoves

19th & 20th Antique Stoves
2 Taylor St.
Littleton, MA 01460
>   Phone 508-486-3589

Facades Ltd.

Kitchen Cabinet Facades and Worktops
Freepost
Keighley BD20 5BR
Great Britain
>   Phone 011-44-274/511234

Faucet Outlet

Order by Phone - Name Brand Bathroom & Kitchen Faucets
PO Box 565
Monroe, NY 10950
>   Toll Free 800-444-5783

Ferretti Ltd.

Kitchens - Italian Contemporary - Cabinets, Sinks, Cooktops, Countertops
17 Greenhill Parade
Great North Rd., New Bamet, Herts
EN5 1ES
Great Britain
>   Phone 011-44-81/4490614
>   FAX 011-44-81/4409195

Fleurco Industries 1963 Ltd.

Tub & Shower Enclosures, Decorative Mirrors, Medicine Cabinets
PO Box 1200, Lasalle Branch
Ville LaSalle
Que, CAN H8R 3Y4
Canada
>   Phone 514-364-4344

Fox Woodcraft

Victorian Kitchen/Bath Cabinets
PO Box 846
Sutter Creek, CA 95685
Catalog/Information Available Free
>   Phone 209-267-0774
>   FAX 209-267-5051

Frank's Woodwork & Supplies

Cabinets
310 W 1st
Brenham, TX 77833-3606
>   Phone 409-836-9203

Franke Inc.

Manufacturer - Sinks, Faucets, Disposals, Hot Water Dispensers
Kitchen Systems Division
121 Church Rd.
North Wales, PA 19454
Send $3.00 for Catalog/Information
>   Phone 215-699-8761
>   Toll Free 800-626-5771

Fremarc Industries Inc.

Manufacturer - Furniture
18810 E. San Jose Ave.
City of Industry, CA 91748
>   Phone 818-965-0802
>   FAX 818-964-8086

Frigidaire

European Kitchen Refrigerator, (Euroflair From Sweden)
6000 Peremiter Dr.
Dublin, OH 43017
Catalog/Information Available Free
>   Phone 513-489-9210
>   Toll Free 800-272-7992

Gaggenau USA Corporation

Built-in Kitchen Appliances
425 University Ave.
Norwood, MA 02062
Send $5.00 for Catalog/Information
>   Phone 617-255-1766

Garland Commercial Industries, Inc.

Kitchen Range - Restaurant Range for the home

185 East South Street
Freeland, PA 18224

Toll Free 800-257-2643
FAX 717-788-5977

Geba USA, Inc.

Manufacturer - Kitchen Cabinetry

430 Tenth Street
Wilmette, IL 60091

Phone 708-256-4322

Gibson

Cooktops

PO Box 7181
Dublin, OH 43017-7181

Toll Free 800-458-1445

Gracious Home

Kitchen & Bath Faucets, Shower Heads - Chrome, Gold, Nickel

1220 3rd Ave. at 70th St.
New York, NY 10021

Mail Order Available

Phone 212-517-6300
Toll Free 800-338-7809

Grohe America Inc.

Manufacturer - Kitchen and Bath Faucets

241 Covington Drive
Bloomingdale, IL 60108

Send $3.00 for Catalog/Information

Phone 708-582-7711
FAX 708-582-7722

Hansa America

*Kitchen & Bathroom Faucets
Manufactured in Germany*

931 W. 19th St.
Chicago, IL 60608

Phone 312-733-0025
Toll Free 800-343-4431
FAX 312-733-4220

Heritage Custom Kitchens

Custom Kitchen Cabinets

215 Diller Ave.
New Holland, PA 17557

Phone 717-354-4011
FAX 717-354-4487

Home & Cabinet Designs Inc.

Kitchen Cabinets, Raised Panel Doors

149 S. Washington
Box 817
Wichita, KS 67201

Phone 316-262-6281

Homecrest Corporation

Manufacturer - Kitchen & Bath Cabinets

1002 Eisenhower Dr. North
PO Box 595
Goshen, IN 46526

Phone 219-533-9571
FAX 219-534-2550

I. F. M. Co. Ltd.

Eurocave - Wine Storage Cabinet

Great Western Rd.
Martock Business Park, Martock, Somerset
TA12 6HB
Great Britain

Phone 011-44-935/826333
FAX 011-44-935/826310

Indiana Brass

Manufacturer - Plumbers Brass Faucets and Fittings

800 W. Clinton St.
Frankfort, IN 46041

Phone 317-659-3341
Toll Free 800-428-4030
FAX 317-654-4364

J & M Custom Cabinets & Millwork

Kitchen Cabinets, Millwork

2750 North Bauer Rd.
St. Johns, MI 48879

Send $2.00 for Catalog/Information

Mail Order Available

Phone 517-593-2244

J. F. Orr & Sons

Cupboards, Dry Sinks & Tables
135 Plymouth Rd.
Sudbury, MA 01776
Send $2.00 for Catalog/Information
Mail Order Available

Jenn-Air/Maytag

Manufacturer - Custom Designed Cooktops
3035 North Shadeland Ave.
Indianapolis, IN 46226 -0901
Send $5.00 for Catalog/Information

Phone 317-545-2271

Jotul USA

Importer Belgian & Norwegian Stoves
PO Box 1157
Portland, ME 04104

Phone 207-797-5912
Toll Free 800-535-2995
FAX 207-772-0523

Jules D. Becker Wood Products

Cabinets
25250 W. Old Rand Rd.
Wauconda, IL 60084

Phone 708-526-8000

KWC/Rohl Corp.

Faucets
1559 Sunland Way
Costa Mesa, CA 92626

Phone 714-557-1933
Toll Free 800-777-9762
FAX 714-557-8635

Kemper Quality Cabinets

Manufacturer - Custom Kitchen Cabinets
PO Box 1567
Richmond, IN 47374

Phone 317-935-2211

King

Wallpaper, Mini Blinds, Fabrics
Box 304
Albany, GA 31702
Mail Order Available

Phone 912-436-2382

King Refrigerator Corp.

Mini Kitchens - Compact Range - Sink - Refrigerator Combinations
7602 Woodhaven Blvd.
Glendale, NY 11385

Phone 718-897-2200
Toll Free 800-845-5464
FAX 718-830-9440

Kraftmaid Cabinetry

Euro Style Kitchens
16052 Industrial Pkwy.
PO Box 1055
Middlefield, OH 44062

Phone 216-632-5353
Toll Free 800-654-3008

Lakeville Industries, Inc.

Manufacturer - Kitchen Cabinets
PO Box 549
100 South Smith St.
Lindenhurst, NY 11757

Phone 516-957-6800

Marvel Industries

Manufacturer - Under the counter Refrigerators
PO Box 997
Richmond, IN 47375
Catalog/Information Available Free

Phone 317-962-2521
Toll Free 800-428-6644
FAX 317-962-2493

Kitchen

Melbourne Hall Workshop

Custom Hardwood Kitchens, Dressers, Mirror Frames

Melbourne
Derbyshire
DE73 1EN
Great Britain

Phone 011-44-332/862382

Miele

Dishwashers, Cooktops made in Germany

22D World's Fair Drive
Somerset, NJ 08873

Phone 908-560-0899

Toll Free 800-843-7231

FAX 908-560-9649

Millbrook Kitchens Inc.

Kitchen Cabinets

Route 20
Nassau, NY 12123

Phone 518-766-3033

Moen

Manufacturer - Kitchen & Bath Faucets

377 Woodland Ave.
Elyria, OH 44036

Phone 216-323-3341

Toll Free 800-321-8809

Monson's Custom Woodworking

Manufacturer - Custom Cabinets

415 Central Ave.
Faribault, MN 55021-5216

Phone 507-332-2576

Mountain Shadow Mill

Cabinets

390 E. Main
Wellsville, UT 84339

Phone 801-245-4491

Mountaintop Cabinet Manufacturing Corp

Custom Cabinets & Millwork

294 Union Ave.
New Rochelle, NY 10801

Phone 914-636-6613

National Kitchen & Bath Association

Kitchen & Bath Design Guides

Certified Kitchen & Bath Designers
687 Willow Grove Street
Hackettstown, NJ 07840

Catalog/Information Available Free

Phone 908-852-0033

Toll Free 800-367-6522

FAX 908-852-1695

Neff (UK) Ltd.

Kitchen - Built-in Refrigeration

The Quadrangle, Westmount Centre
Uxbridge Rd., Hayes, Middx
UB4 0HD
Great Britain

Phone 011-44-81/8483711

FAX 011-44-81/8481408

Nevamar Corporation

Manufacturer - Kitchen & Bath - Countertop

8339 Telegraph Rd.
Odenton, MD 21113-1397

Phone 301-569-5000

Toll Free 800-638-4380

Northern Refrigerator Company

Manufacturer - Custom Refrigeration

21149 Northland Dr.
PO Box 204
Paris, MI 49338

Mail Order Available

Phone 616-796-8007

The Complete Sourcebook

O'Keefe Cabinet Fixtures

Cabinets

956 Prosperity Ave.
St. Paul, MN 55106

Phone 612-774-5970

Paragon Products

Major Brand Kitchen & Bath Fixtures & Faucets

Faucet Plus Division
PO Box 14914
Scottsdale, AZ 85267

Send $4.50 for Catalog/Information

Mail Order Available

Credit Cards MC/VISA/Check/Money Order

Phone 602-596-9336

Toll Free 800-232-8238

FAX 602-596-9866

Phoenix Lock Co.Inc.

Brass Hardware

321 3rd Ave.
Newark, NJ 07107

Phone 201-483-0976

FAX 201-483-0977

Plain and Fancy Kitchens

Manufacturer - Kitchens - Oak, Birch, Pine and Finishes

PO Box 519
Schaefferstown, PA 17088

Toll Free 800-447-9006

Poggenpohl U.S.A. Corp

Kitchen & Bath Cabinetry

8010 Woodland Center Blvd.
Suite 400
Tampa, FL 33614

Send $7.00 for Catalog/Information

Mail Order Available

Phone 813-882-9292

Practical Homewares

Triple Recycle Center with Newspaper Stacker - Under the Sink Recycle Center

92 Corporate Park, Suite C-215
Irvine, CA 92714

Credit Cards VISA/MC

Toll Free 800-341-1155

RC's Custom Woodwork

Cabinets

1711 Taylor Rd.
Daytona Beach, FL 32014-6733

Phone 904-767-0412

Rayburn

Kitchen Stoves - Gas, Oil, Water Heating

PO Box 30
Ketley, Telford, Shropshire
TF1 4DD
Great Britain

Phone 011-44-952/642000

Regency VSA

Australian Manufacturer - Gas & Electric Cooktops

PO Box 3341
Tustin, CA 92681

Phone 714-544-3530

Rich Craft Custom Kitchens

Kitchen Cabinets

141 West Penn Ave.
Robesonia, PA 19551

Send $1.00 for Catalog/Information

Mail Order Available

Phone 215-693-5871

Running Dog

Home Recycling

PO Box 744
Quincy, MA 02269

Credit Cards VISA/MC

Toll Free 800-765-9007

Kitchen

Russell Range, Inc. — The Hanging Kitchen Co.

Russell Range, Inc.

Manufacturer - Cooktops

229 Ryan Way
S. San Francisco, CA 94080

Catalog/Information Available Free

Phone 415-873-0105

Toll Free 800-878-7877

Rutt Cabinetry

Cabinetry & Woodwork

PO Box 129
1564 Main Street
Goodville, PA 17528

Send $7.00 for Catalog/Information

Phone 215-445-6751

FAX 215-445-9227

Scandia Kitchens Inc.

Manufacturer - Kitchen Cabinetry

38 Maple Street, PO Box 85
Bellingham, MA 02019

Phone 508-966-0300

FAX 508-966-3091

SieMatic Corporation/Smallbone

Kitchens & Bathrooms

886 Town Center Dr.
Langhorne, PA 19044

Send $12.00 for Catalog/Information

Phone 215-496-9945

Toll Free 800-765-5266

FAX 215-750-2911

Smallbone & Co. Ltd.

Kitchens & Bathrooms

Hopton Workshop
Devizes, Wilts
SN10 2EU
Great Britain

Phone 011-44-380/729090

Snaidero

Italian Imported Kitchen Cabinetry

201 W. 132nd St.
Los Angeles, CA 90061

Phone 310-516-8499

Toll Free 800-678-2667

Stephen Huneck Gallery

Kitchen Cupboard & Art Furniture

49 Central St., PO Box 59
Woodstock, VT 05091

Mail Order Available

Credit Cards AMEX/VISA/MC

Phone 802-457-3206

FAX 802-457-3290

Sub Zero Freezer Company, Inc.

Built-in Home Refrigeration

4717 Hammersley, PO Box 44130
Madison, WI 53744-4130

Phone 608-271-2233

Toll Free 800-222-7820

FAX 608-271-1538

Swe Nova Kitchen & Bath

Kitchen & Bath Accessories

300 De Hard
San Francisco, CA 94103-5144

Phone 415-626-8868

The Antique Quit Source

Antique Quilts

385 Springview Road
Carlisle, PA 17013

Send $7.00 for Catalog/Information

Phone 717-245-2054

The Hanging Kitchen Co.

*Pine & Iron Hanging Storage - Pans,
Pots, Utencils*

The Courtyard, Ashengrove Farm
Calbourne, Isle of Wight
PO30 4HU
Great Britain

FAX 011-44-983/78553

The Complete Sourcebook

10 - 9

The Homestead — Wellbilt Kitchen Cabinets

Kitchen

The Homestead

Antique Ranges, Heaters
104 Railroad Ave. W
PO Box 250
Skykomish, WA 98288
Catalog/Information Available Free
Phone 206-677-2840

The House of Webster

Country Cast Iron Electric Range
PO Box 1988
Rogers, AR 72757
Send $1.00 for Catalog/Information
Phone 501-636-4640
FAX 501-636-2974

The Kennebec Company

*Deal Direct USA & Canada - Custom -
Kitchen Cabinetry, Paneling*
One Front St.
Bath, ME 04530
Catalog/Information Available Free
Send $10.00 for Catalog/Information
Mail Order Available
Phone 207-443-2131
FAX 207-443-4380

Thermador

Cooktops
PO Box 22129
Los Angeles, CA 90040
Toll Free 800-735-4328

Traulsen & Co., Inc.

*Manufacturer - Stainless Steel
Refrigerator - 48" Wide*
114-02 15th Ave.
PO Box 560169
College Point, NY 11356
Toll Free 800-542-4022
FAX 718-961-1390

Tricity Bendix Ltd.

Kitchen - Built-in Refrigeration
99 Oakley Rd.
Luton LU4 9QQ
Great Britain
Phone 011-44-582/494000
FAX 011-44-582/588338

Viking Range Corporation

Manufacturer - Cooking Range
PO Drawer 956
111 Front St.
Greenwood, MS 38930
Phone 601-455-1200
FAX 601-453-7939

W. C. Wood Co. Ltd.

*Compact Kitchen, Range Hoods,
Dehumidifiers, Humidifiers*
PO Box 750
Guelph
Ont., CAN N1H 6L9
Canada
Phone 519-821-0900
FAX 519-821-4451

Walker Mfg.

Cabinets
6545 44th St. N
Pinellas Park, FL 34665
Phone 813-522-2195

Watts & Wright

*Manufacturer - Kitchen & Bedroom
Cabinetry and Freestanding Furniture*
114a Wolverhampton Road
West Midlands WS2 8PR
Great Britain
Phone 011-44-922/22247
FAX 011-44-922/22247

Wellbilt Kitchen Cabinets

Cabinets
1193 Montauk Hwy
Mastic, NY 11950-2918
Phone 516-281-9793

Kitchen

10 - 10

The Complete Sourcebook

Kitchen

Weru (UK) Ltd.

Importer & Distributor - Oak Kitchen Corner, Nook Seating
Bruce Grove
Wickford, Essex
SS11 8QN
Great Britain
> Phone 011-44-268/769444

Wood Works by Dan

Cabinets
16939 E. Colony Dr.
Fountain Hills, AZ 85269
> Phone 602-837-1927

Wood-Mode

Custom Built Cabinetry
1 Second St.
Kreamer, PA 17833

Send $5.00 for Catalog/Information

Mail Order Available
> Phone 717-374-2711

Woodburns Custom Cabinets

Cabinets
Box 1018 Rte 2 Bayside Rd.
Leonardtown, MD 20650-9558
> Phone 301-475-5680

Woodworks

Cabinets
124 W. Main
Norman, OK 73069-1307
> Phone 405-329-0407

Woodwrights of Rochester

Custom Cabinetry
1808 SE 3rd Ave.
Rochester, MN 55904-6775
> Phone 507-282-3804

York Cabinet Inc.

Cabinets
12166 York Rd.
Cleveland, OH 44133
> Phone 216-582-1880

Yorktowne Inc.

Built-in Kitchen Cabinets
100 Redco Ave.
PO Box 231
Red Lion, PA 17356
> Phone 717-244-4011

Zanussi Ltd.

Kitchen - Built-in Refrigeration & Range
Zanussi Ho, Hambridge Rd.
Newbury, Berks
RG14 5EP
Great Britain
> Phone 011-44-635/521313
> FAX 011-44-635/52397

The Complete Sourcebook

Lighting

A & A Modern Wire Products

Lighting
633 Union Ave.
Bronx, NY 10455
Phone 212-993-5113

A & M Whitemetal Castings, Inc.

Lighting
47030 No. Division St.
Lancaster, CA 93534
Phone 805-942-1047

A.C. International USA

Lighting
6515 Corporate Dr. Ste. M2
Houston, TX 77036
Phone 713-772-0134
Toll Free 800-772-0135

A.M. Metal Spinning Co.

Lighting
10068 Franklin St.
Franklin Park, IL 60131
Phone 708-678-1590

ABC Lampshades

Lampshades
79 Alexander Ave.
Bronx, NY 10454
Phone 212-292-1378
FAX 212-292-1379

Aagard-Hanley Ltd.

Lighting, Fireplace Surrounds
230 Stanningley Rd.
Bramley, Leeds
LS13 3BA
Great Britain
Phone 011-44-532-568678

Abat Jour Ideal Lampshade Inc.

Lighting, Lampshades
380 Port Royal West
Montreal PQ,CN,H3L 2B8,
Phone 514-384-1518
FAX 514-384-4371

Abbey Roberts Inc.

Lighting Fixtures
3166 Main Avenue
SE Hickory, NC 28602
Phone 704-322-3480

Abe SRL

Italian Lighting
Via Amendola, 47
20037 Paderno Dugnano (MI)
Italy
Phone 011-39-2/99041935
FAX 011-39-2/99041944

Academy

Ceiling Fans
660 Jericho Tpke.
St. James, NY 11780
Credit Cards VISA/MC
Phone 516-265-3577

Accent Lamp & Shade Co. Inc.

Manufacturer - Lighting, Lamps, Lampshades
107 Chapel St.
Newton, MA 02158
Phone 617-527-3900

Accent Lighting

Lighting
5112 Calmview Ave.
Baldwin Park, CA 91706
Phone 818-960-4907
FAX 818-960-0118

Accent Studios

Lighting - Custom Lamps & Shades
805 W. University
Lafayette, LA 70506
Phone 318-233-0186

Aetna Electric Distributing Corp.

Lighting Fixtures, Ceiling Fans
535 Broadway
Hicksville, NY 11801
Phone 516-931-4400
FAX 516-931-2223

Alger Lighting

Lighting
1521 Gardena
Glendale, CA 91204
Phone 818-241-6955
Toll Free 800-223-8523
FAX 818-241-7439

Alkco Lighting

Lighting Fixtures
11500 W. Melrose Ave.
PO Box 1389
Franklin Park, IL 60131
Catalog/Information Available Free
Phone 708-451-0700

All-Lighting

Major Brand Lighting Fixtures
1123 Rt. 100
Trexlertown, PA 18087
Toll Free 800-241-6111

Allied Lighting

Order by Phone - Lighting Fixtures
Drawer E
Trextertown, PA 18087
Toll Free 800-241-6111

Alva Line SRL

Italian Lamps
Via Bassa Dei Sassi, 28
40138 Bologna (BO)
Italy
Phone 011-39-51/538339
FAX 011-39-51/538468

American Heirlooms, Inc.

Lighting Fixtures
Route 2, Box 1120
Bean Station, TN 37708
Phone 615-586-2225

American Lamp Supply

Lighting Fixtures
57 Tyler Town Rd.
Clarksville, TN 37040
Phone 615-647-4949

Antique Street Lamps Inc.

Manufacturer - Reproduction Outdoor Lamps
PO Box 43289
Austin, TX 78745-0289
Mail Order Available
Phone 512-295-3585
FAX 512-295-3330

Lighting

Arlati SRL

Italian Lamps
Via Gramsci, 5
20040 Cornate D'Adda (MI)
Italy

Phone 011-39-692116

FAX 011-39-6826818

Arroyo Craftsman

Lighting Fixtures
4509 Little John St.
Baldwin Park, CA 91706

Send $3.00 for Catalog/Information

Phone 818-960-9411

FAX 818-960-9521

Artcraft

Lighting Fixtures
PO Box 1526 East Service Rd.
Champlain, NY 12919

Toll Free 800-361-4966

Artemide

*National Sales Location - Halogen
Lighting Fixtures - Desk, Floor, Wall,
Table, Ceiling*
1980 New Highway
Farmingdale, NY 11735

Phone 516-694-9292

Toll Free 800-359-7040

FAX 516-694-9275

Artemide GB Ltd.

Lighting
17-19 Neal St.
Convent Garden, London
WC2H 9PU

Phone 011-44-71/2402552

Artistiche Ceramiche Fiorentine

Italian Lamps
Via Bietoletti, 21
50019 Sesto Fiorentino (FI)
Italy

Phone 011-39-55/442600

FAX 011-39-55/4489085

As You Like It Inc.

Lighting
3025 Magazine Street
New Orleans, LA 70115

Send $15.00 for Catalog/Information

Phone 504-897-6915

Toll Free 800-828-2311

Ascot Lamps & Lighting Ltd.

Lamps & Lighting
Unit 4 Pedham Place Est, Wested La
Swanley, Kent BR8 8TE
Great Britain

Phone 011-44-322/66734

Aunt Sylvia's Victorian Collections

*Sell Direct - Victorian Style Lighting,
Lamps*
PO Box 67364
Chestnut Hill, MA 02167-0364

Catalog/Information Available Free

Credit Cards Accepted

Phone 617-327-9220

Toll Free 800-231-6644

Aura Lamp & Lighting, Inc.

Lighting Fixtures
1524 S. Peoria St.
Chicago, IL 60608

Phone 312-666-1661

Toll Free 800-621-1780

FAX 312-666-1792

B & G Antique Lighting

Antique Lighting
28-05 Broadway, Rt. 4W
Fairlawn, NJ 07410

Phone 201-791-6522

FAX 201-791-6545

Lighting

The Complete Sourcebook

B & P Lamp Supply Inc.

Manufacturer - Wholesale Only - Antique Lighting Parts
843 Old Morrison Hwy.
McMinnville, TN 37110
Send $7.00 for Catalog/Information

Phone 615-473-3016
Toll Free 800-822-3450
FAX 615-473-3014

Bala Lighting

Lighting Fixtures
301 W. Washington St.
Riverside, NJ 08075

Phone 608-882-5100

Baldwin Brass Lighting

Brass Lighting Fixtures
841 E. Wyomissing Blvd.
Reading, PA 19612

Phone 215-777-7811

Barbini Alfredo SRL

Italian Lamps
Fondamenta Venier 44/48
30121 Murano (VE)
Italy

Phone 011-39-41/739270
FAX 011-39-41/739265

Barovier & Toso Vetrerie Artistiche

Italian Lamps (Barovier & Toso Vetrerie Artistiche Riunite)
Fondamenta Vetrai 28
30141 Murano (VE)
Italy

Phone 011-39-41/739049
FAX 011-39-41/737385

Bay Shore Light & Elec. Supply

Lighting, Electrical Supply
143 Main St.
Bay Shore, NY 11706

Phone 516-665-5510

Bennett & Fountain Ltd.

Lighting
Maxmoor Ho, 40 Warton Rd.
Stratford, London E15 2ND
Great Britain

Phone 011-44-81-5559999

Best & Lloyd Ltd.

Lighting
William St West
Smethwick, Warley, W Midlands B66 2NX
Great Britain

Phone 011-44-21-5581191

Beverly Hills Fan Co.

Ceiling Fans, Lamps
6033 De Soto Ave.
Woodland Hills, CA 91367-3707

Phone 818-992-3267
Toll Free 800-826-6192

Blanche P. Field Inc.

Custom Lamps, Lighting Fixtures
One Design Center Place, Ste. 647
Boston, MA 02210

Phone 617-423-0715

Blessings

Lamps
Ocean Lights
6915 S.W. Highway 200
Ocala, FL 32674
Send $1.00 for Catalog/Information

Phone 904-237-4610

Boyd Lighting Fixture Co.

Lighting Fixtures, Lamps
56 12th St.
San Francisco, CA 94103

Phone 415-431-4300
FAX 415-431-8603

Lighting

Brandon Industries Inc. — Burwood Lighting Co. Ltd.

Brandon Industries Inc.

Order Direct - Nationwide Delivery -
Aluminum Wall Sconces, Lamp Posts,
Planters

4419 Westgrove Drive
Dallas, TX 75248

Mail Order Available

Phone 214-250-0456
FAX 214-250-0495

Brass Light Gallery

Solid Brass Chandeliers

131 South First St.
Milwaukee, WI 53204

Send $3.00 for Catalog/Information

Phone 414-271-8300
FAX 414-271-7755

Brass Reproductions

Brass Lighting

9711 Canoga Ave.
Chatsworth, CA 91311

Send $8.00 for Catalog/Information

Phone 818-709-7844
FAX 818-709-5918

Brass'n Bounty

Antique Chandeliers, Lamps

68 Front St.
Marblehead, MA 01945

Phone 617-631-3864
FAX 617-631-6204

Brassfinders

Reproduction Victorian Lighting

W. 1918 Clarke
Spokane, WA 99201-1306

Phone 509-747-7412
FAX 509-747-5447

Brasslight

Brass Lamps

90 Main St.
PO Box 695
Nyack, NY 10960

Send $3.00 for Catalog/Information

Mail Order Available

Phone 914-353-0567

Brubaker Metalcrafts

Chandeliers, Lamps

209 N. Franklin
Eaton, OH 45320

Send $2.00 for Catalog/Information

Mail Order Available

Phone 513-456-5834
Toll Free 800-950-5834
FAX 513-456-5786

Buffalo Studios

Lighting & Hardware

1925 E. Deere Ave.
Santa Ana, CA 92705

Mail Order Available

Phone 714-250-7333
FAX 714-250-5893

Burdoch Victorian Lamp Company

Manufacturer - Wholesale Prices -
Reproduction Victorian Lampshades

757 N. Twin Oaks Valley Rd., Ste 2
San Marcos, CA 92069

Send $5.00 for Catalog/Information

Phone 619-591-3911
Toll Free 800-783-8738
FAX 619-591-3837

Burwood Lighting Co. Ltd.

Lighting

Market St.
Exeter EX1 1BW
Great Britain

Phone 011-44-392/59367

The Complete Sourcebook

CSL Lighting Mfg.

Halogen Lighting - Bathroom Collection
27615 Avenue Hopkins
Valencia, CA 91355

Phone 805-257-4155
FAX 805-257-1554

California Lamp Shade Co.

Lampshades
2735 Via Orange Way #104
Spring Valley, CA 91978

Phone 619-670-6811

Campbell Lamp Supply

Reproduction Victorian Lamps and Chandeliers
1108 Pottstown Pike
West Chester, PA 19380

Mail Order Available

Phone 215-696-8070

Capri Lighting

Manufacturer - Lighting Fixtures
6430 East Slauson Avenue
Los Angeles, CA 90040

Phone 213-726-1800

Cardinal Products Inc.

Halogen Floor Lamps
2 South St.
Mt. Vernon, NY 10550

Phone 212-324-0700

Carriage Trade of Tahoe

Brass Lighting
PO Box 7001
Tahoe City, CA 95730

Send $2.00 for Catalog/Information

Mail Order Available

Phone 916-583-2718

Cascade Designs Inc.

Lighting Fixtures
7333 Coldwater Canyon #38
North Hollywood, CA 91605

Phone 818-765-7876
FAX 818-765-2151

Casella Lighting

Lighting, Decorative Hardware
111 Rhode Island
San Francisco, CA 94103

Phone 415-626-9600
FAX 415-626-4539

Catalina Lamp & Shade

Lamps & Shades
9905 Gidley St.
El Monte, CA 91731

Phone 818-448-4774
FAX 818-448-4791

Catalina Lighting, Inc.

Lighting Fixtures and Ceiling Fans
6073 Northwest 167th St.
Miami, FL 33015

Phone 305-558-3024
FAX 305-558-3024

Centel's Lighting

Factory Outlet - Major Brand Lighting
227 Glen Cove Rd.
Carl Place, NY 11542

Credit Cards Accepted

Phone 516-747-4748

Century Studios

Stained Glass Tiffany Style Lamps
200 3rd Ave. North
Minneapolis, MN 55401

Send $10.00 for Catalog/Information

Phone 612-339-0239
FAX 612-339-0239

Lighting

Champion Lamp Shade Co. – Contois Stained Glass Studio

Champion Lamp Shade Co.

Lampshades
PO Box 3005
Quincy, IL 62305

Phone 217-222-0122
Toll Free 800-475-3468
FAX 217-222-7328

Champman Mfg. Co.

Lighting & Antique Reproduction Furniture
481 W. Main St.
Avon, MA 02322

Phone 508-588-3200
FAX 508-587-7592

Charles Co., Inc.

Table Lamps
2700 Maple Ave.
Los Angeles, CA 90011

Phone 213-749-2167

Chatham Brass Co., Inc.

Shower Heads, Tub Spouts
5 Olsen Ave.
Edison, NJ 08820

Phone 201-494-7107
Toll Free 800-526-7553
FAX 201-494-9171

Christopher Wrays Lighting Emporium Ltd.

Decorative Lighting - Lamps, Chandeliers
600 Kings Road
London SW6 2DX
Great Britain
Catalog/Information Available Free

Phone 011-44-71-7368434

City Lights

Antique Lighting Fixtures
2226 Massachusetts Ave.
Cambridge, MA 02140
Send $5.00 for Catalog/Information

Phone 617-547-1490
FAX 617-497-2074

Classic Designs

Lighting Fixtures
130 North Main Street
Spring Valley, NY 10977
Catalog/Information Available Free

Toll Free 800-537-6319

Classic Illumination, Inc.

Manufacturer - Order Direct - Nationwide Delivery - Lighting Fixtures - Period Chandeliers, Sconces, Torchieres in Solid Brass with Blown Glass Shades - Also in Nickel, Brushed Chrome and Copper
2743 Ninth St.
Berkeley, CA 94710
Send $3.00 for Catalog/Information
Mail Order Available

Phone 510-849-1842
FAX 510-849-2328

Conant Custom Brass, Inc.

Antique Brass Lighting Fixtures
270 Pine St.
Burlington, VT 05401
Catalog/Information Available Free
Mail Order Available
Credit Cards MC/VISA/Check/M.O.

Phone 802-658-4482
FAX 802-864-5914

Conservation Technology Ltd.

Ceiling Fans, Track Lighting
3865 Commercial Ave.
Northbrook, IL 60062

Phone 708-559-5500
FAX 708-559-5500

Contois Stained Glass Studio

Stained Glass Lampshades
Box 224-A Rt 2
Hamlin, WV 25523
Send $2.00 for Catalog/Information
Mail Order Available

Phone 304-824-5651

Lighting

The Complete Sourcebook

11 - 7

Copper Lamps by Hutton

Electric Reproduction Lamps & Chandeliers
Rt. 940, Box 418
Pocono Pines, PA 18350
          Phone 717-646-7778

Coran-Sholes Industries

Lighting & Accessories
509 East 2nd St.
South Boston, MA 02127

Send $3.00 for Catalog/Information

Mail Order Available
          Phone 617-268-3780

Cornell Lamp & Shade Co.

Lamps & Shades
PO Box 186
Perth Amboy, NJ 08862
          Phone 201-826-7272

Craig Interiors Ltd.

Lighting
Unit 18, Soho Mills Ind Est
Woodburn Green, High Wycombe, Bucks
HP10 0PF
Great Britain
          Phone 011-44-628/526038

Crescent Lighting Ltd.

Manufacturer - Interior & Exterior Lighting
8 Rivermead, Pipers La
Thatcham, Berks RG13 4NA
Great Britain
          Phone 011-44-635/878888
          FAX 011-44-635873888

Cryselco Ltd.

Manufacturer - Lighting
Cryselco Ho, 274 Ampthill Rd.
Bedford MK42 9QJ
Great Britain
          Phone 011-44-234/273355
          FAX 011-44-234210867

Crystal Creek Lighting

Lighting
Route 8, Box 165
Cullman, AL 35055
          Phone 205-734-1291

Crystal Import Company

Lighting
521 W. Rosecrans Ave.
Gardena, CA 90248
          Phone 213-323-8452
          Toll Free 800-323-8452
          FAX 213-323-8468

Current

Lighting & Furniture
1201 Western Ave.
Seattle, WA 98101
          Phone 206-622-2433

Custom House

Custom Lampshades
6 Kirby Rd.
Cromwell, CT 06416
          Phone 203-828-6885

D'Lights

Lighting Fixtures - Lamps, Chandeliers, Sconces
533 West Windsor Rd.
Glendale, CA 91204

Catalog/Information Available Free
          Phone 818-956-5656
          FAX 818-956-2155

DEMCO Fans

Fans
2256 US Hwy. 19
Holiday, FL 34691
          Phone 813-942-2715
          Toll Free 800-872-4201
          FAX 813-938-9169

Lighting

Dale Tiffany Inc.

Tiffany Lighting Fixtures
6 Willow St.
Moonachie, NJ 07074

Phone 201-473-1900
FAX 201-507-1842

Davey Lighting

Lighting
4 Oak Ind Pk, Chelmsford Rd.
Great Dunmow, Essex
CM6 1XN
Great Britain

Phone 011-44-371/873174

Decorative Dimensions

Deco High Tech Lighting
781 River Street
Paterson, NJ 07524

Phone 201-684-2200
FAX 201-684-0084

Delaware Electric Imports

Antique Ceiling Fans
111 S. Delaware Ave.
Yardley, PA 19067

Catalog/Information Available Free

Mail Order Available

Phone 215-493-1795

Dernier & Hamlyn Ltd.

Lighting
47-48 Burners St.
London W1P 3AD
Great Britain

Phone 011-44-71-5805316

Design Enterprises

Lighting
Box 2343
Rockville, MD 20847

Phone 301-279-0970

Designs for Living Inc.

Lamps - Table and Swag
8265 G Patuxent Range Rd.
Jessup, MD 20794

Phone 301-953-3949

Diane Studios Inc.

Lampshades
34 35th St.
Brooklyn, NY 11232

Phone 718-788-6007
FAX 718-499-7849

Dickson Brothers, Inc.

Lighting Fixtures
PO Box 470245
Tulsa, OK 74147-0245

Phone 918-628-1285
FAX 918-299-8625

Dilor Industries Ltd.

Lighting Fixtures
37749 Second Ave.
Squamish, B.C.
CAN V0N 3G0
Canada

Phone 604-892-9301
FAX 604-892-3052

Dynasty Classics Corp.

Halogen Lighting - Floor, Table, Wall
22333 South Wilmington
Carson, CA 90745

Phone 213-834-3637

Dyno-Electrics

Lighting
Zockoll Ho, 143 Maple Rd.
Surbiton, Surrey KT6 4BJ
Great Britain

Phone 011-44-81-5499711

Lighting

The Complete Sourcebook

E. Molina Lamps & Parts

Lighting - Lamps & Parts
PO Box 1122
Carolina, PR 00628

Phone 809-757-9797
FAX 809-757-9797

ELA Custom & Architectural Co.

Manufacturer - Outdoor Lighting,
Chandeliers
17891 Arenth Ave.
City of Industry, CA 91748

Phone 818-965-0821
Toll Free 800-423-6561
FAX 818-965-9494

ELCO Lamp & Shade Studio, Inc.

Lamps & Shades
2 South St.
Mt. Vernon, NY 10550

Phone 212-324-0700

EMC Tiffany

Tiffany Lamps
45 Paris Rd.
New Hartford, NY 13413

Send $3.00 for Catalog/Information

Phone 315-724-2984

Early American Lighting

Lighting Fixtures
Herald Square
10 Mabel Terrace
Queensbury, NY 12804

Send $3.00 for Catalog/Information

Phone 518-745-1334

Edison Halo Lighting

Lighting
Div. of Libra Trading Ltd.
5 Delaware Dr, Tongwell, Milton, Keynes
MK15 8HG
Great Britain

Phone 011-44-908/617617

Edwards Lamp Shade Co., Inc.

Lampshades
PO Box 4564
Palos Verdes Estates, CA 90274-9607

Phone 213-583-6474
FAX 213-582-1172

Elegante Brass, Inc.

Brass Lighting
1460-65 St.
Brooklyn, NY 11219

Phone 718-256-8988
FAX 718-632-6912

Elsco Lighting Products, Inc.

Lighting Fixtures
PO Box 8946
Stockton, CA 95208

Phone 209-466-0511

Elstead Lighting Ltd.

Traditional Indoor/Outdoor Lighting
Unit 7, Forge Wks, Mill La
Alton, Hants GU34 2QG
Great Britain

Phone 011-44-420/82377
FAX 011-44-420/89261

Emerson Electric Company

Ceiling Fans
8400 Pershall Rd.
Hazelwood, MO 63042

Phone 314-595-1300
FAX 314-595-1356

Emess PLC

Manufacturer - Lighting
20 St James T.
London SW1A 1HA
Great Britain

Phone 011-44-71/3210127
FAX 011-44-719252734

Lighting

Erco Lighting Ltd.

Lighting
38 Dover St.
London W1X 3RB
Great Britain

Phone 011-44-71-4080320

Eurofase Inc.

European Track Lighting
6499 N.W. 12th Ave.
Fort Lauderdale, FL 33309

Phone 305-968-7225

FAX 305-968-7228

European Classics

European Lighting Fixtures
3007 Westchester Ave.
Orlando, FL 32803

Catalog/Information Available Free

Phone 407-898-1453

Exciting Lighting by Pam Morris

Lighting Fixtures
14 E. Sir Francis Drake Blvd.
Larkspur, CA 94939

Phone 415-925-0840

FAX 415-925-1305

Execulamp Inc.

Desk, Table, Wall, Floor, Reading Lamps
601 McDowell Blvd.
San Rafael, CA 94901

Toll Free 800-283-5274

FAX 415-454-0274

Exquisite Lighting and Design, Inc.

Lighting Fixtures Recessed Lighting
7601 Water Ave.
Savannah, GA 31406

Fabby

Ceramic Wall Sconces
450 South La Brea Avenue
Los Angeles, CA 90036

Phone 213-939-1388

FAX 213-939-0206

Fan Fair

Casablanca & Hunter Ceiling Fans - Lamps & Shads
2251 Wisconsin Ave. NW
Washington DC,   20007

Phone 202-342-6290

FAX 202-342-9255

Fantasy Lighting, Inc.

Victorian Style Lampshades
7126 Melrose Ave.
Los Angeles, CA 90046

Send $4.00 for Catalog/Information

Phone 213-933-7244

FAX 213-933-0113

Fasco Industries, Inc.

Manufacturer - Fans - Ceiling & Ventilating - Lighting, Doorbells
PO Box 150
Fayetteville, NC 28302

Toll Free 800-334-4126

FAX 910-483-1547

Fenchel Lamp Shade Co.

Lampshades
612 South Clinton St.
Chicago, IL 60607

Phone 312-922-6454

Toll Free 800-345-1456

FAX 312-922-6468

Fenton Art Glass Company

Lamps
700 Elizabeth St.
Williamstown, WV 26187

Send $10.00 for Catalog/Information

Phone 304-375-6122

Fine Art Lamps

Lamps
7215 West 20th Ave.
Hialeah, FL 33014

Phone 305-821-3850

FAX 305-821-1564

The Complete Sourcebook

Fine Designs Unlimited

Lighting Fixtures
6206 Canadian Trail
Plano, TX 75023

Phone 214-517-0203
FAX 214-669-0179

Fitzgerald Lighting Ltd.

Lighting
Normandy Way
Bodmin, Cornwall PL31 1HH
Great Britain

Phone 011-44-208/75611

Forluce

Imported Lighting - Chandelier and Wall Light (Halogen)
PO Box 19944
New Orleans, LA 70179

Form & Function

Southwestern Style Lighting - Floor Lamps, Sconces, Table Lamps
328 S. Guadalupe St.
Santa Fe, NM 87501

Send $2.00 for Catalog/Information

Phone 505-984-8226

Forma Lighting Ltd.

Lighting
Units 310-311, Business Design Centre
52 Upper St., London N1 0QH
Great Britain

Phone 011-44-71/2886025

Foscarini Murano SPA

Italian Lamps
Fondamenta Manin 1
30141 Murano (VE)
Italy

Phone 011-39-41/739344
FAX 011-39-41/739835

Frederick Cooper Inc.

Hand Painted Lamps
2545 W. Diversey Ave.
Chicago, IL 60647

Fredrick Ramond Inc.

Manufacturer of Original Lighting Fixtures
16121 S. Carmenita Rd.
Cerritos, CA 90701

Phone 213-926-1361
Toll Free 800-421-3517
FAX 213-926-1015

Freedom Lamp Co.

Lighting Fixtures
7648 La Verdura Dr.
Dallas, TX 74248

Phone 214-239-7526

Futimis Ltd.

Lighting
Futimis Ho, 11 Mead Ind Est
River Way, Harlow, Essex CM20 2SE
Great Britain

Phone 011-44-279/411131

G. P. B. Beghelli

Italian Lamps
Via J. Barozzi, 6
40050 Monteveglio (BO)
Italy

Phone 011-39-51/960304
FAX 011-39-51/960551

Garber's Crafted Lighting

Handcrafted Lighting Fixtures, Early American Lighting
Rt. 2
Mammoth Spring, AR 72554

Send $2.00 for Catalog/Information

Phone 501-966-4996

Gardco Lighting

Lighting Fixtures
2661 Alvarado St.
San Leandro, CA 94577

Phone 415-357-6900
FAX 415-357-3088

Lighting

Gaslight Time Antiques – Graham's Lighting Fixtures Inc.

Gaslight Time Antiques

Table & Floor Lamps, Chandeliers
823 President St.
Brooklyn, NY 11215

Send $4.00 for Catalog/Information

Mail Order Available

Phone 718-789-7185
FAX 718-768-2501

Gates Moore

Colonial Lighting
River Road Silvermine
Norwalk, CT 06850

Send $2.00 for Catalog/Information

Mail Order Available

Phone 203-847-3231

Gem Monogram & Cut Glass Corp.

Chandeliers
628 Broadway, 3rd Fl
New York, NY 10012

Mail Order Available

Phone 212-674-8960

Genie House

Lighting Fixtures
PO Box 2478
Red Lion Rd.
Vincentown, NJ 08088

Send $5.00 for Catalog/Information

Mail Order Available

Toll Free 800-634-3643
FAX 609-859-0565

George Kovacs Lighting Inc.

Manufacturer - Lighting Fixtures
67-25 Otto Road
Glendale, NY 11385

Phone 718-628-5201

Georgia Lighting Supply Co.

Lighting Fixtures - French, English, Early American, Victorian
530 14th Street NW
Atlanta, GA 30318

Send $12.00 for Catalog/Information

Phone 404-875-4754
FAX 404-872-4679

Georgian Art Lighting Designs, Inc.

Lighting, Chandeliers, Lamps
PO Box 325
Lawrenceville, GA 30246

Send $5.00 for Catalog/Information

Phone 404-963-6221
FAX 404-963-6225

Gibson Interiors

Major Brand Lighting Fixtures, Furniture
417 S. Wrenn
High Point, NC 27260

Toll Free 800-247-5460

Golden Valley Lighting

Lighting Fixtures & Lamps
274 Eastchester Dr.
High Point, NC 27262

Catalog/Information Available Free

Toll Free 800-735-3377

Grabell of California

Bed Lights
2051 South Garfield Ave.
City of Commerce, CA 90040

Phone 213-685-6720
FAX 213-722-4520

Graham's Lighting Fixtures Inc.

European Imported Lighting
550 S. Cooper
Memphis, TN 38104

Send $3.00 for Catalog/Information

Phone 901-274-6780
FAX 901-725-0147

The Complete Sourcebook

11 - 13

Grand Brass Lamp Parts

Brass Lamp Parts
221 Grand St.
New York, NY 10013-4223
Phone 212-226-2567

Green's Lighting Fixtures

*Manufacturer - Period Style Chandeliers,
Lighting Fixtures - Available through
Designers & Architects*
1059 Third Ave.
New York, NY 10021
Phone 212-753-2507
FAX 212-688-6389

Greg's Antique Lighting

Antique Lighting Fixtures
12005 Wilshire Blvd. W.
Los Angeles, CA 90025
Mail Order Available
Phone 213-478-5475

H. Grabell & Sons

Lampshades, Lamps, Vases
2051 S. Garfield Ave.
City of Commerce, CA 90040
Phone 213-722-5642
FAX 213-722-4520

Halo Lighting Products/Cooper Industries

*Manufacturer - Track Lighting, Recessed
Lighting, Outdoor Lighting*
400 Busse Rd.
Elk Grove Village, IL 60007
Phone 708-956-8400

Halogen Lighting Systems

Halogen Lighting
2033 17th Ave.
Melrose Park, IL 60160
Phone 708-344-3280
FAX 708-344-0723

Hammerworks

Reproduction Lighting Fixtures
6 Fremont St.
Worcester, MA 01603
Send $3.00 for Catalog/Information
Mail Order Available
Phone 508-755-3434

Harris Lamps

Halogen Lighting - Floor Lamps
3757 South Ashland Ave.
Chicago, IL 60609

Harris Marcus Group, Inc.

*Rembrandt Lamps - Ceramic, Wood,
Acrylic*
1548 West 38th St.
Chicago, IL 60609
Phone 312-254-6363

Harry Horn, Inc.

Track and Recess Lighting
622-624 South Street
Philadelphia, PA 19147
Send $2.00 for Catalog/Information
Phone 215-925-6600

Heath Sedgwick

Victorian Lamp, Statuary, Tapestry
PO Box 1305
Stony Brook, NY 11790
Send $3.00 for Catalog/Information
Mail Order Available
Phone 516-751-1129

Heritage Lanterns

*Colonial Reproduction Interior and
Exterior Lighting*
70A Main St.
Yarmouth, ME 04096
Send $3.00 for Catalog/Information
Mail Order Available
Toll Free 800-544-6070

Herwig Lighting Inc.

Art Deco, Modern, Victorian Lighting Fixtures

PO Box 768
Russellville, AR 72811

Mail Order Available

Toll Free 800-643-9523
FAX 501-968-6762

Heter Lighting Enterprises, Inc.

Lighting

230 Fifth Ave.
New York, NY 10001

Phone 212-679-3441
FAX 212-689-2421

Heyward House

Lighting

909 Commerce Circle
Charleston, SC 29411

Hilo Steiner

Lamps

509 Broad St.
Shrewsbury, NJ 07701

Send $2.00 for Catalog/Information

Mail Order Available

Phone 201-741-5862

Hinkley Lighting

Manufacturer - Indoor & Outdoor Lighting Fixtures

12600 Berea Rd.
Cleveland, OH 44111

Phone 216-671-3300
FAX 216-671-4537

Hitech Lighting Ltd.

Lighting

Springwood Dr, Springwood Ind Est
Braintree, Essex
CM7 7YN
Great Britain

Phone 011-44-376/550500

Hobby Hill Inc.

Lamps

2321 N. Keystone
Chicago, IL 60639

Phone 312-342-5700

Hollywood Lamp & Shade Co.

Lighting - Lamps & Shades

2914 Leonis Blvd.
Los Angeles, CA 90058

Phone 213-585-3999
FAX 213-585-4049

Holophane Company Inc.

Lighting Fixtures

250 E. Broad Street, #1400
Columbus, OH 43215

Phone 614-345-9631
FAX 614-349-4426

Holtkotter International, Inc.

Manufacturer - Germany - Lamps, Chandeliers, Spot Lighting, Halogen

261 E. Fifth St.
St. Paul, MN 55101

Phone 612-228-1611
FAX 612-228-0043

Home Decorators Collection

Lamps, Lampshades, Bath, Ceiling, Wall and Outdoor Lighting, Indoor & Outdoor Furniture, Area Rugs

2025 Concourse Dr.
St. Louis, MO 63146

Catalog/Information Available Free

Credit Cards Accepted

Phone 314-993-1516
Toll Free 800-245-2217
FAX 314-993-0502

Home Equipment Mfg.,Co.

Outdoor Lighting, Light Controls, Security Lighting
PO Box 878, 14481 Olive Street
Westminster, CA 92684

Phone 714-892-6681
Toll Free 800-854-6415
FAX 714-898-4502

Howard Ceilings Ltd.

Lighting
45 Mawney Rd.
Ramford, Essex RM7 7HR
Great Britain

Phone 011-44-708/722245

Howard's Antique Lighting

Ship Anywhere - Antique Lighting, Dining Room Tables, Chests, Desks, Rockers, End Tables, Cupboards, Chairs
PO Box 472, Rt. 23 W.
S. Egremont, MA 01258

Mail Order Available

Credit Cards Check/Money Order

Phone 416-528-1232

Hubbardton Forge & Wood Corp.

Lamps, Chandeliers, Pan Racks, Bathroom Accessories
PO Box 827
Castleton Corners, VT 05735

Send $3.00 for Catalog/Information

Phone 802-468-3090

Hubbell Lighting Inc.

Manufacturer - Lighting - Architectural, Indoor/Outdoor
2000 Electric Way
Christansburg, VA 24073-2500

Phone 703-382-6111
FAX 703-382-1526

Hunter Ceiling Fans

Ceiling Fans
2500 Frisco Ave.
Memphis, TN 38114

Send $1.00 for Catalog/Information

Phone 901-745-9286

Hurley Patentee Manor

Reproduction Colonial Lighting Fixtures
464 Old Rt. 209
Kingston, NY 12443

Send $3.00 for Catalog/Information

Mail Order Available

Credit Cards VISA/MC/Check

Phone 914-331-5414
Toll Free 800-247-5414

Hy-Art Lamp Co.

Lamps & Lampshades
PO Box 388
Wilkes Barre, PA 18703

Phone 717-283-6100

Ideal Electric Mfg. Co. Ltd.

Lamps, Lighting Fixtures
372-380 Selkirk Ave.
Winnepeg
Man, CAN R2W 2M2
Canada

Phone 204-582-2388
FAX 204-589-6907

Igmor Crystal Lite Corp.

Lighting
45 W. 25th St.
New York, NY 10010

Phone 212-243-2400
FAX 212-627-9591

Illuma Lighting Ltd.

Lighting
24-32 Riverside Way
Uxbridge UB8 1YF
Great Britain

Phone 011-44-895/272275

Indel UK Ltd.

Lighting
The Airport, Alchome Pl.
Portsmouth, Hants
PO3 5QL
Great Britain
Phone 011-44-705/665331

Insites

Victorian Lighting
PO Box 200
Meriden, CT 06450
Send $5.00 for Catalog/Information
Mail Order Available
Phone 203-269-7333

Irvin's Craft Shop

Reproduction Early American Lighting Fixtures
Rt. 1
Mt. Pleasant Mills, PA 17853
Catalog/Information Available Free
Mail Order Available
Credit Cards VISA/MC
Phone 717-539-8200

J & B Lamp & Shade

Reproduction Lamps & Lampshades
PO Box 549
Talbott, TN 37877
Send $10.00 for Catalog/Information
Credit Cards Accepted
Phone 615-475-9018

J W Lighting Inc.

Lighting
PO Box 45919
Houston, TX 77245
Phone 713-433-4511

J. E. Thorn Lamps Ltd.

Lighting, Lamps
Lincoln Rd.
Enfield, Middx
EN1 1SB
Great Britain
Phone 011-44-81/3361166

Jackson Mfg. Co.

Light Switchplates, Mantels
4445 McEwen, PO Box 801329
Dallas, TX 75380
Phone 214-233-7513
FAX 214-233-7955

Jaegaer USA

Warbird Ceiling Fans
19000 Wyandotte St.
Reseda, CA 91335
Phone 818-708-1500
FAX 818-708-7945

Jamaica Lamp Corp.

Lighting, Lamps
212-26 Jamaica Ave.
Queens Village, NY 11428
Phone 718-776-5039
FAX 718-217-5044

James Crystal Mfg. Co.

Lighting Fixtures, Lamps
1300 Biddle
Wyandotte, MI 48192
Phone 313-285-7900
FAX 313-285-7911

Jardine International Ltd.

Lighting
Rosemount Tower, Wallington Sq.
Wallington, Surrey
SM6 8RR
Great Britain
Phone 011-44-81/6698265

Jimco Lamp & Mfg. Co.

Lamps & Lampshades
Hwy 63 North
Bono, AR 72416
Phone 501-935-6820

Josiah R. Coppersmythe

Handcrafted Early American Lighting Fixtures
80 Stiles Rd.
Boylston, MA 01505

Send $3.00 for Catalog/Information

Mail Order Available

Credit Cards VISA/MC

Phone 508-869-2769

Juno Lighting, Inc.

Indoor and Outdoor Lighting Fixtures
2001 South Mt. Prospect Rd.
PO Box 5065
Des Plaines, IL 60017-5065

Catalog/Information Available Free

Phone 708-827-9880

FAX 708-827-2925

Kalco Lighting Inc.

Lighting
6355 S. Windy St.
Las Vegas, NV 98119

Phone 702-361-4345

FAX 702-361-6487

Keystone Lighting Corp.

Lighting Fixtures
Rt. 13 & Beaver St.
Bristol, PA 19007

Phone 215-788-0811

King's Chandelier

Order Direct - Chandeliers - Silver & Brass
Hwy. 14, PO Box 667
Eden, NC 27288

Send $3.50 for Catalog/Information

Mail Order Available

Credit Cards VISA/MC

Phone 919-623-6188

FAX 919-623-3995

Kiss Lamp Co.

Lighting Fixtures
PO Box 2054
Meriden, CT 06450

Phone 203-634-0282

Kurt Versen Co.

Lighting Fixtures
10 Charles St.
PO Box 677
Westwood, NJ 07675

Phone 201-664-8200

FAX 201-664-4801

L.T. Moses Willard, Inc.

Colonial Reproduction Lighting
1156 U.S. 50
Milford, OH 45150

Send $2.00 for Catalog/Information

Mail Order Available

Credit Cards VISA/MC

Phone 513-831-8956

Ladue Illuminazione

Italian Lighting
Divisione Della Nordlight SPA
Statale Aretine, 29N
50069 Sieci (FI)
Italy

Phone 011-39-55/8309473

FAX 011-39-55/8328369

Lam Lighting Systems

Lighting Fixtures
2200 S. Anne St.
Santa Ana, CA 92704

Phone 714-549-9765

Toll Free 800-732-5213

FAX 714-662-4515

Lighting

Lamp Glass

Glass Lampshades
2230 Massachusetts Ave.
Cambridge, MA 02140
Send $1.00 for Catalog/Information
Mail Order Available
Phone 617-497-0770
FAX 617-497-2074

Lamp Warehouse/New York Ceiling Fan Ctr.

Lamps and Ceiling Fans
1073 39th St.
Brooklyn, NY 11219
Credit Cards VISA/MC/AMEX
Toll Free 800-525-4837
FAX 718-436-8500

Lampshades Inc.

Lampshades
4041 W. Ogden Ave.
PO Box 23199
Chicago, IL 60623
Phone 312-522-2300
FAX 312-522-5589

Lampshades of Antique

Custom Reproduction Lampshades
PO Box 2
Medford, OR 97501
Send $5.00 for Catalog/Information
Mail Order Available
Credit Cards VISA/MC
Phone 503-826-9737

Lampways Ltd.

Lighting
Knowles La, Wakefield Rd.
Bradford
BD 9AB
Great Britain
Phone 011-44-274/686666

Lee's Studio

Lighting Fixtures
1755 Broadway
New York, NY 10019
Phone 212-581-4400
Toll Free 800-544-4801
FAX 212-581-7023

Leiter Lites

Distributor - Lighting Fixtures - Track Lighting, Halogen
202 Bethpage-Sweethollow Rd.
PO Box 188
Old Bethpage, NY 11804
Phone 516-752-1433
Toll Free 800-527-7796
FAX 516-752-9127

Lenox

Lighting - Lamps
Lenox Lighting Collection
Lawrenceville, NJ 08648
Catalog/Information Available Free
Toll Free 800-635-3669

Leonard R. Foss Studios, Inc.

Lampshades
1338-1340 East Twelfth St.
Oakland, CA 94606
Toll Free 800-237-4233
FAX 415-534-7135

Lester H. Berry & Company

Reproduction Lighting Fixtures
PO Box 53377
Philadelphia, PA 19105
Phone 215-923-2603

Leucos Lighting

Lighting
70 Campus Plaza II
Edison, NJ 08837
Toll Free 800-832-3360
FAX 908-225-0250

Leviton Manufacturing Company

Indoor and Outdoor Lighting Fixtures
59-25 Little Neck Parkway
Little Neck, NY 11362
Catalog/Information Available Free
Phone 718-229-4040

Libco Lamp

Lighting
2002 Ave. R.
Grand Prairie, TX 75050
Phone 214-641-3015
Toll Free 800-527-1292
FAX 214-641-8293

Light Ideas

Lighting
PO Box 5776
Rockville, MD 20855-0776
Mail Order Available
Phone 301-424-5483
FAX 301-424-5791

Lighthouse Stained Glass

Lighting - Wholesale - Stained Glass Lamps
1132 West Cox Lane
Santa Maria, CA 93454
Send $3.00 for Catalog/Information
Mail Order Available
Credit Cards Check/COD US ONLY
Phone 805-349-0949

Lighting Source of America

Order by Phone - Lighting - Recessed, Track, Chandelier, Torchier, Lamps, Sconces
29209 Northwestern Hwy. #585
Southfield, MI 48034
Toll Free 800-968-5267

Lightning Bug Ltd.

Lighting
320 W. 202nd St.
Chicago Heights, IL 60411
Phone 708-755-2100
FAX 708-335-3508

Lightolier

Manufacturer - Lighting Fixtures, Chandeliers
100 Lighting Way
Seacaucus, NJ 07084-0508
Send $3.00 for Catalog/Information
Phone 201-864-3000
Toll Free 800-628-8692

Lite Tops

Lampshades
Office & Factory
441 High St., Box 2180
Perth Amboy, NJ 08862
Phone 908-442-0099
FAX 908-442-0208

Luigi Crystal

Lighting Fixtures, Lamps
7332 Frankford Ave.
Philadelphia, PA 19136
Send $2.00 for Catalog/Information
Mail Order Available
Credit Cards VISA/MC/AMEX
Phone 215-338-2978

Luma Lighting Industries, Inc.

Indoor & Outdoor Lighting Fixtures
410 West Fletcher Ave.
Orange, CA 92665
Catalog/Information Available Free
Phone 714-282-1116

Lumax Industries Inc.

Manufacturer - Lighting Fixtures
PO Box 991
Altoona, PA 16603
Phone 814-944-2537
FAX 814-944-6413

Lumea

*Lighting Controls, Dimmers, Fan
Controls, Switches*
7200 Suter Rd.
Coopersberg, PA 10836
Toll Free 800-523-9466

Lumina Italia SRL

Italian Lamps
Via Casorezzo, 63
20010 Arluno (MI)
Italy
Phone 011-39-2/9015498
FAX 011-39-2/9037652

Luminaire

Italian Lamps, Lighting Fixtures, Furniture
301 W. Superior
Chicago, IL 60610
Phone 312-664-8958
FAX 312-664-5045

Lundburg Studios

Reproduced Tiffany & Steuban Lamps
Box C , 131 Old Coast Rd.
Davenport, CA 95017
Send $3.00 for Catalog/Information
Mail Order Available
Credit Cards VISA/MC/AMEX
Phone 408-423-2532
FAX 408-423-0436

Lutron

*Quiet Fan-Speed Controls and Light
Dimmers*
7200 Suter Rd.
Coopersburg, PA 18036-1299
Phone 215-282-3800
Toll Free 800-523-9466
FAX 215-282-6437

Main Street Lighting

Outdoor Lighting - Lamp Posts
1021 Industrial Pkwy.
Medina, OH 44256
Mail Order Available
Phone 216-723-4431
FAX 216-723-2570

Mar-Kel Lighting Inc.

Lamps & Lampshades
Bell Ave. At Hwy. 79
PO Box 190
Paris, TN 38242
Phone 901-642-7190

Marbo Lamp Co.

Lamps, Chandeliers
PO Box 1769
Holland, MI 49422
Send $6.00 for Catalog/Information

Marco Lighting Fixtures

Lighting Fixtures
6100 Wilmington Ave.
Los Angeles, CA 90001
Phone 213-583-6551
FAX 213-583-3155

Mario Industries

Lighting Fixtures
PO Box 3190
Roanoke, VA 24015
Phone 703-342-1111
FAX 703-345-4813

Mark Lighting Fixture Co., Inc.

Lighting Fixtures
25 Knickerbocker Rd.
Moonachie, NJ 07074
Phone 201-939-0880
FAX 201-939-1094

The Complete Sourcebook

Martin's Discount Lighting

Lighting Fixtures, Lamps, Lampshades, Ceiling Fans, Track Lighting
424 Rockaway Turnpike
Cedarhurst, NY 11516
Credit Cards VISA/MC/AMEX
Phone 516-239-5730

Marvel Lighting Corp.

Decorative Lighting
25 E. Spring Valley Ave.
Maywood, NJ 07607
Phone 201-368-8015

Metropolitan Lighting Fixture Co. Inc.

Lighting Fixtures - Chandeliers - Contemporary, Art Deco, Antique Reproductions
315 East 62nd St.
New York, NY 10021-7767
Send $15.00 for Catalog/Information
Phone 212-838-2425
FAX 212-644-2666

Mexico House

Mexican Iron Lamps
PO Box 970
Del Mar, CA 92014
Send $1.00 for Catalog/Information
Mail Order Available
Credit Cards VISA/MC
Phone 619-481-6099

Meyda Stained Glass Studio

Lighting - Stained Glass Floor, Accent, Table, Wall
1123 Stark St.
Utica, NY 13502
Send $5.00 for Catalog/Information
Mail Order Available
Credit Cards MC/VISA/DISCOVER
Phone 315-724-7266
Toll Free 800-222-4009
FAX 315-724-5170

Midwest Chandelier Co.

Lighting Fixtures
100 Funston Rd.
Kansas City, KS 66115
Phone 913-281-1100
FAX 913-281-1967

Minka Lighting Inc.

Lighting
1151 W. Bradford Circle
Corona, CA 91720
Phone 714-735-9220

Mobern Electric Corp.

Lighting Fixtures
Washington Blvd.
PO Box 246
Laurel, MD 20707
Phone 301-725-3030
FAX 301-953-9310

Mooncraft Corp.

Solid Brass Lighting Fixtures
235 55th St.
West New York, NJ 07093
Phone 201-864-7049
FAX 201-866-7221

Morlee Lamp Shade

Lampshades
1785 W. 32nd Place
Hialeah, FL 33012
Catalog/Information Available Free
Phone 305-887-4277
FAX 305-883-5040

Moss Lighting

Home Lighting
271 Main St.
Hackensack, NJ 07601
Phone 201-487-5086

Mowbray Lighting

Lighting
PO Box 4, Old Hawne La
Halesowen, W Midlands
B63 35N
Great Britain
Phone 011-44-21/5501101

Natalie Lamp & Shade Corp.

Lighting - Lamps & Shades
220 Straight St.
Paterson, NJ 07501
Phone 201-278-8800
FAX 201-278-8831

National Industries

Halogen Track & Recessed Lighting
702 Carmony NE
Albuquerque, NM 87107
Toll Free 800-821-6283
FAX 505-344-5801

National Lighting Inc.

Order by Phone - Name Brand Lighting Fixtures
1100 Hooksett Rd.
Suite 410
Hooksett, NH 03106
Credit Cards Accepted
Toll Free 800-728-4642

Natural Light, Inc.

Table Lamps
PO Box 16449
Panama City, FL 32406
Phone 904-265-0800
FAX 904-265-1678

Ner Lighting Inc.

Chandeliers
Chandelier Fashions Inc.
7050 Victoria Ave., Suite 402
Montreal, Quebec H4P 2N5, CN
Canada
Phone 514-733-5321
FAX 514-733-0229

New Brunswick Lampshade Co.Inc.

Lighting, Lampshades
7 Terminal Rd.
PO Box 267
New Brunswick, NJ 08903
Phone 908-545-0377
FAX 908-545-6993

New England Stained Glass Studios

Tiffany Style Stained Glass Lighting
5 Center St.
PO Box 381
West Stockbridge, MA 01266
Phone 413-232-7181

Newman Lighting Co.

Lighting Fixtures
7001 E. 57th Pl.
Commerce City, CO 80022
Phone 303-287-9646

Newstamp Lighting Co.

Lamps & Lighting Fixtures
227 Bay Rd.
PO Box 189
N. Easton, MA 02356
Send $2.00 for Catalog/Information
Mail Order Available
Credit Cards VISA/MC
Phone 508-238-7071
FAX 508-230-8312

Norman Perry

Lighting Fixtures - Table & Floor Lamps
501 West Green Drive
Highpoint, NC 27260
Toll Free 800-841-4951
FAX 910-841-4136

Nova

Tiffany Lamps, Hanging Shades
796 Energy Way
Chula Vista, CA 91911

Catalog/Information Available Free

Phone 619-421-5333

FAX 619-421-5671

Nowells Inc.

Reproduction Brass Lighting Fixtures
490 Gate 5 Rd.
PO Box 295
Sausalito, CA 94966

Send $3.50 for Catalog/Information

Mail Order Available

Phone 415-332-4933

FAX 415-332-4936

NuMerit Electrical Supply

*Electrial Supplies - Imports, Track
Lighting, Chandeliers, Outdoor Lighting*
68 E. Sunrise Hwy.
Freeport, NY 11520

Credit Cards VISA/MC

Phone 516-378-4650

OHM-Rite Electrical

Lamps, Lighting Fixtures
Div. of Danbel Industries
222 Islington Ave., Toronto
Ont., CAN M8V 3W7
Canada

Phone 416-252-9454

Ocean View Lighting

Period Lighting
2743 Ninth St.
Berkeley, CA 94710

Send $5.00 for Catalog/Information

Mail Order Available

Phone 415-841-2937

FAX 510-849-2328

Olde Village Smithery

Traditional Lighting Fixtures
PO Box 1815
61 Finlay Rd.
Orleans, MA 02653

Send $2.50 for Catalog/Information

Mail Order Available

Phone 508-255-4466

Olivers Lighting Company

Period Lighting Switches
6 The Broadway
Crockenhill, Swanley, Kent
BR8 8JH
Great Britain

Phone 011-44-322/614224

Optelma Lighting Ltd.

Lighting
14 Napier Court
The Science Pk, Abingdon, Oxon
OX14 3NB
Great Britain

Phone 011-44-235/553769

Osram Corporation

Lighting
100 Endicott St.
Danvers, MA 01923-3623

Toll Free 800-431-9980

Ozark Shade & Lamp

Lighting - Lamps & Shades
Rt1, Box 65
Morrilton, AR 72110

Phone 501-354-0051

FAX 501-354-2991

Panorama Lighting Ltd.

Lighting
Unit 9, Willersey Ind Est
Willersey, nr Broadway, Worcs
WR12 7PR
Great Britain

Phone 011-44-386/852171

Pass & Seymour

Impressions - Designer Wall Plates, Switches, Dimmers
PO Box 4822
Syracuse, NY 13221

> Phone 315-468-6211
> Toll Free 800-776-4035

Pennsylvania Illuminating Corp.

Lamps
526-528 Ash
Scranton, PA 18509

> Phone 717-346-7357
> FAX 717-346-6075

Period Lighting Fixtures

Early American Lighting Fixtures
167 River Road
Clarksburg, MA 01247

Mail Order Available

Credit Cards VISA/MC

> Phone 413-664-7141
> Toll Free 800-828-6990
> FAX 413-664-7142

Permo Lights Unlimited

Lighting Fixtures
3506 W. Washington Blvd.
Los Angeles, CA 90018

> Phone 213-735-2094

Philadelphia Glass Bending Co.

Lighting Fixtures
2520 Morris St.
Philadelphia, PA 19145

> Phone 215-336-3000

Philip Goldin Associates, Inc.

Lighting - Crisa Glass Shades
2270 Grand Ave.
Baldwin, NY 11510-0365

> Phone 516-868-6666

Philips Lighting Company

Manufacturer - Lighting Fixtures
200 Franklin Square Drive
PO Box 6800
Somerset, NJ 08875-6800

Porter Lighting Sales Inc.

Lighting
16216 E. Arrow Hwy.
Irwindale, CA 91706

> Phone 818-813-1244
> FAX 818-813-1246

Primelite Mfg. Co., Inc.

Lighting
407 S. Main St.
Freeport, NY 11520

> Phone 516-868-4411
> Toll Free 800-327-7583
> FAX 516-868-4609

Primo Lighting

Lighting
114 Washington St.
South Norwalk, CT 06854

> Phone 203-866-4321

Progress Lighting

Manufacturer - Lighting Fixtures
Erie Avenue and G Street
PO Box 12701
Philadelphia, PA 19134

> Phone 215-289-1200

Quip Interior Design & Lighting

Lighting
Div of Bruce & Macintyre Ltd.
71 Tenison Rd., Cambridge
CB1 2DG
Great Britain

> Phone 011-44-223/321277

Quoizel Inc.

Lamps, Lighting Fixtures
325 Kennedy Dr.
Hauppauge, NY 11787

Phone 516-273-2700
FAX 516-231-7102

Rada Lighting Ltd.

Lighting
Hollies Way, High St.
Potters Bar, Herts
EN6 5BH
Great Britain

Phone 011-44-707/43401

Ramco Industries Inc.

Lighting, Lamps
52896 County Rd. 113 N
PO Box 4512
Elkhart, IN 46514

Phone 219-264-2139

Regent Lighting Corp.

Manufacturer - Outdoor Lighting Fixtures
PO Box 2658
Burlington, NC 27216

Phone 910-226-2411
Toll Free 800-334-6871
FAX 910-222-8202

Reggiani Light Gallery

Lighting Fixtures
800A Fifth Ave.
New York, NY 10021

Phone 212-421-0400
FAX 212-838-8517

Reggiani Ltd.

Lighting
Giltland Ho, 12 Chester Rd.
Borehamwood, Herts
WD6 1LT
Great Britain

Phone 011-44-81/9530855

Rejuvenation Lamp & Fixture

Reproduction Victorian Light Fixtures
1100 SE Grand St.
Portland, OR 97214

Catalog/Information Available Free

Mail Order Available

Credit Cards VISA/MC

Phone 503-231-1900
Toll Free 800-526-7329
FAX 800-526-7329

Reliance Lamp & Shade Co. Inc.

Lamps, Lampshades
125 Laser Court
Hauppauge, NY 11788

Phone 516-434-1120

Remcraft Lighting Products

Manufacturer - OutdoorLighting Fixtures
12870 N.W. 45th Ave.
Miami, FL 33054

Phone 305-687-9031
FAX 305-687-5069

Remington

Classic Traditional Lighting
5000 Paschall Ave.
Philadelphia, PA 19143

Phone 215-729-2600
Toll Free 800-234-5267
FAX 215-729-8077

Renaissance Marketing

Reproduction Tiffany Lighting
Box 360
Lake Orion, MI 48362

Send $2.00 for Catalog/Information

Mail Order Available

Credit Cards VISA/MC

Phone 313-693-1109
FAX 313-693-1118

Lighting

Residential Lighting Div. – Russell Electrics Ltd.

Residential Lighting Div.

Lighting Fixtures
Thomas Industries Inc.
950 Breckinridge Lane, Suite G-50
Louisville, KY 40222

Phone 502-894-2400

FAX 502-895-6618

Richard Scofield

Early American Lighting Fixtures
1 W. Main St.
Chester, CT 06412

Send $2.00 for Catalog/Information

Mail Order Available

Credit Cards VISA/MC

Phone 203-526-3690

Robbins & Myers

Ceiling Fans
2500 Frisco Ave.
Memphis, TN 38114

Mail Order Available

Toll Free 800-238-5358

Robelier

Country Style Lamps
1500 South 50th St.
Philadelphia, PA 19143

Catalog/Information Available Free

Phone 215-729-2240

Robert Long Lighting

Lighting Fixtures
PO Box 770
Healdsburg, CA 95448

Phone 707-431-1050

Roff Lighting

Lighting
50 Carnation Ave.
Floral Park, NY 11001

Phone 516-488-6550

Roflan Associates

Lighting Fixtures
66 Lowell Junction Rd.
Andover, MA 01810-5916

Phone 508-475-0100

FAX 508-465-8547

Roseart Lampshades Inc.

Lampshades
225 East 134th St.
Bronx, NY 10451

Catalog/Information Available Free

Phone 212-292-6247

FAX 212-993-7391

Roy Electric Co. Inc.

Victorian Lighting Fixtures
1054 Coney Island Ave.
Brooklyn, NY 11230

Send $5.00 for Catalog/Information

Mail Order Available

Credit Cards MC/VISA/AMEX

Phone 718-434-7002

Toll Free 800-366-3347

FAX 718-421-4678

Royal Haeger Lamp Co.

Ceramic Lamps
PO Box 769
Westport, CT 06881

Phone 203-226-9920

FAX 203-227-5631

Russell Electrics Ltd.

Lighting
43-45 Grays Inn Rd.
London WC1X 8PP
Great Britain

Phone 011-44-71/4051052

Lighting

The Complete Sourcebook

11 - 27

S. Wilder & Co. Inc.

Outdoor Colonial Lighting Fixtures
12 Raybear Road
PO Box 29
South Orleans, MA 02662

Mail Order Available

Phone 508-255-8330

SEC Inc.

Ceiling Fans
406 N. Main St.
Plymouth, MI 48170

Phone 313-455-4500
FAX 313-455-1026

Santa Fe Lights

Indoor & Outdoor Lighting, Southwestern Style Lighting
Rt 10, Box 88-Y
Santa Fe, NM 87501

Send $2.00 for Catalog/Information

Mail Order Available

Credit Cards MC/VISA/Check/Money Order

Phone 505-471-0076

Satco Products Inc.

Lighting
110 Heartland Blvd.
Brentwood, NY 11717

Phone 516-243-2022

Satin and Old Lace Shades

Victorian Style Lampshades
8015 S.E. 13th Ave.
Portland, OR 97202

Send $4.00 for Catalog/Information

Phone 503-234-2650

Saxe Lampshade, Inc.

Lampshades
325 North 13th St.
Philadelphia, PA 19107

Phone 215-627-8328

Schonbek Worldwide Lighting Inc.

Lighting Crystal Chandeliers
61 Industrial Blvd.
Plattsburgh, NY 12901

Phone 518-563-7500
Toll Free 800-443-7358
FAX 518-563-4228

Sea Gull Lighting Products Inc.

Manufacturer - Lighting Fixtures
301 W. Washington St.
Riverside, NJ 08075

Send $6.00 for Catalog/Information

Phone 609-764-0500
FAX 609-764-0813

Securi Style Ltd.

Window and Door Hardware
Kingsmead Industrial Estate
Princess Elizabeth Way, Cheltenham
Glos GL51 7RE
Great Britain

Phone 011-44-24/2221200
FAX 011-44-24/2520828

Sedgefield by Adams

Lighting - Lamps
216 Woodbine St.
High Point, NC 27260

Phone 919-882-0196
Toll Free 800-654-1939

Shades by Sheila

Lampshades
824 North Jackson St.
Kosciusko, MS 39090

Phone 601-289-1609
Toll Free 800-634-8229
FAX 601-289-1622

Lighting

Shades of the Past – St. Louis Antique Lighting Co.

Shades of the Past

Lampshades
PO Box 206
Fairfax, CA 94978

Send $4.00 for Catalog/Information

Mail Order Available

Phone 415-459-6999

ShadyLady

Lampshades
5020 W Eisenhower Blvd.
Loveland, CO 80537-9188

Send $4.50 for Catalog/Information

Mail Order Available

Phone 303-669-1080

Shamrock Lighting Inc.

Lamps & Fixtures
01260 Richmond St.
Montreal
Que., CAN H3K 2H2
Canada

Phone 514-931-4343

FAX 514-931-6926

Shaper Lighting

Architectural Lighting Fixtures
1141 Marina Way S.
Richmond, CA 94804

Phone 415-234-2370

FAX 415-232-1634

Sicotte Lamps Ltd.

Floor & Table Lamps
5972 2nd Ave.
Montreal
Que., CAN H1Y 2Y9
Canada

Phone 514-722-4673

Skipper SPA

Italian Lamps
Via Legnano 28
20122 Milano (MI)
Italy

Phone 011-39-2/76005691

FAX 011-39-427/40077

Southbrooke Shades

Lighting, Lampshades
PO Box 1696
Lexington, NC 27292

Phone 704-246-5710

Toll Free 800-672-5738

FAX 704-249-2648

Southern Shadecrafters

Lampshades
PO Box 5424
2801 Patterson St.
Greensboro, NC 27407

Phone 919-299-8662

Spectrum Shade Co., Inc.

Lampshades
1170 E. 152nd St.
Cleveland, OH 44110

Phone 216-268-0042

FAX 216-268-3915

Speer Collectibles Atlanta

Lighting - Lamps
5315 S. Cobb Dr.
Atlanta, GA 30080

Send $8.00 for Catalog/Information

Phone 404-794-4000

Toll Free 800-241-7515

Spero Electric Corp.

Lighting Fixtures
1705 Noble Rd.
Cleveland, OH 44112-1633

Phone 216-851-3300

FAX 216-851-0300

St. Louis Antique Lighting Co.

Antique & Reproduction Lighting Fixtures
801 N. Skinker Blvd.
St. Louis, MO 63130

Send $3.00 for Catalog/Information

Phone 314-863-1414

FAX 314-863-6702

The Complete Sourcebook

11 - 29

Staff Lighting Corp.

Lighting

300 Route 9W North
Highland, NY 12528

Phone 914-691-6262

Toll Free 800-932-0633

FAX 914-691-6289

Staff Lighting Ltd.

Manufacturer - Indoor & Outdoor Lighting

Hampshire International, Business Pk
Crockford La, Chineham, Basingstoke
Hants RG24 0WH
Great Britain

Phone 011-44-256-707007

Starlowe Lighting & Design Ltd.

Lighting

Starlowe Ho, The Low Energy Centre
32 Broughton St, Cheetham Hill
Manchester M8 8NN
Great Britain

Phone 011-44-61/8317413

Statements In Design

Victorian Lighting

PO Box 177
Hamptonville, NC 27020

Send $2.00 for Catalog/Information

Toll Free 800-433-8014

Sternberg Lanterns Inc.

*Traditional & Colonial Decorative Indoor &
Outdoor Lighting*

5801 N. Tripp Ave.
Chicago, IL 60646

Phone 312-478-4777

FAX 312-267-2055

Studio Design

Tiffany Style Lamps

49 Shark River Rd.
Neptune, NJ 07753

Send $3.00 for Catalog/Information

Mail Order Available

Phone 201-922-1090

Studio Steel

French Country Style Chandeliers

165 New Milford Turnpike
New Preston, CT 06777

Send $2.00 for Catalog/Information

Mail Order Available

Credit Cards VISA/MC/AMEX

Phone 203-868-7305

FAX 203-868-7306

Stylecraft Lamp Shade Co.

Lampshades

934 E. 22nd St., Ste. 1
Brooklyn, NY 11210

Phone 718-768-7508

FAX 718-768-7514

T. A Green Lighting Co.

Lighting Fixtures

1100 S Mateo St.
Los Angeles, CA 90021

Phone 213-627-5378

T. Saveker Ltd.

Window and Door Hardware

Phillips St.
Birmingham, West Midlands
B6 4QL
Great Britain

Phone 011-44-21/3595891

FAX 011-44-21/3598252

Tally-Ho Lighting Ltd.

Lighting

Unit 31, The Cam Centre, Wilbury Way
Hitchin, Herts
SG4 0TW
Great Britain

Phone 011-44-462438336

Lighting

Task Lighting Corporation – The Ceiling Fan Gallery

Task Lighting Corporation

Concealed Lighting Fixtures - Layout & Quotation Service Available

PO Box 1090
Kearney, NE 68848-1090

Catalog/Information Available Free

Phone 308-236-6707
Toll Free 800-445-6404
FAX 308-234-9401

Tempo/Infiniti Lighting

Lighting Fixtures

1051 E. 24th St.
Hialeah, FL 33013

Phone 305-835-2214
Toll Free 800-346-0856
FAX 305-693-7693

Tenby Electrical Ltd.

Lighting

17-21 Wallstone La
Birmingham
B18 9JG
Great Britain

Phone 011-44-21/2001999

Terradek Industries

Order by Phone - Outdoor Lighting

5155 East River Road
Fridley, MN 55421

Credit Cards VISA/MC

Toll Free 800-344-0094

The Basic source Inc.

Lighting Fixtures

93 Utility Court
Rohnert Park, CA 94928

Phone 707-586-5483
Toll Free 800-428-0044
FAX 707-586-5485

The Brass Finial

Architectural Reproduction - Hardware & Plumbing Fixtures

2408 Riverton Rd.
Cinnaminson, NJ 08077

Mail Order Available

Credit Cards VISA/MC/AMEX

Phone 609-786-9337

The Brass Light Gallery

American, Victorian, European Lighting Fixtures

131 S. 1St St.
Milwaukee, WI 53204

Send $3.00 for Catalog/Information

Phone 414-271-8300
FAX 414-271-7755

The Brass Lion

18th Century Reproduction Lighting

5935 South Broadway
Tyler, TX 75703

Send $5.00 for Catalog/Information

Phone 903-561-1111

The C.S. Bell Co.

Outdoor Lighting

PO Box 4-291
Tiffin, OH 44883

Catalog/Information Available Free

Mail Order Available

Phone 419-448-0791

The Ceiling Fan Gallery

Ceiling Fans

1 Indian Neck Lane
Peconic, NY 11958

Send $0.50 for Catalog/Information

Phone 516-734-6545

Lighting

The Complete Sourcebook

11 - 31

The Copper House

Interior & Exterior Lighting
RR1, Box 4
Epsom, NH 03234
Send $3.00 for Catalog/Information
Mail Order Available
Phone 603-736-9798

The Fan Man

Ceiling Fans
2721 NW 109 Terrace
Oklahoma City, OK 73120
Catalog/Information Available Free
Phone 405-751-0933

The Fan Man Inc.

Ceiling Fans
1914 Abrams Parkway
Dallas, TX 75214
Send $2.00 for Catalog/Information
Phone 214-826-7700

The Lamp House

Western Style Lighting
300 E. Market St.
Hallam, PA 17406
Toll Free 800-757-6989
FAX 717-7574408

The London Lighting Co.

Home Lighting - Lamps
135 Fulham Rd.
London SW3 6RT
Great Britain
Phone 011-44-71/5893612

The Marle Company

Indoor & Outdoor Lighting
35 Larkin St.
PO Box 4499
Stamford, CT 06907
Mail Order Available
Phone 203-348-2645

The Saltbox

Reproduction Lighting
American Period Lighting
500-B State Street
Greensboro, NC 27405
Send $4.00 for Catalog/Information
Mail Order Available
Phone 919-273-8758
FAX 919-294-2683

The Tin Bin

18th - 19th Century Interior & Exterior Lighting
20 Valley Rd.
Neffsville, PA 17601
Send $2.00 for Catalog/Information
Mail Order Available
Phone 717-569-6210
FAX 717-560-2979

The Woodworkers Store

Cabinet Lighting and Hardware
21801 Industrial Blvd.
Rogers, MN 55374-9514
Send $2.00 for Catalog/Information
Mail Order Available
Phone 612-428-2199
Toll Free 800-279-4441
FAX 612-428-8668

Thomas Inc.

Lighting
4360 Brownsboro Rd.
Suite 300
Louisville, KY 40232
Phone 502-893-4600

Thousand and One Lamps Ltd.

Lighting, Lamps
4 Barmeston Rd.
London SE6 3BN
Great Britain
Phone 011-44-81/6987238
FAX 011-44-81/6986134

Lighting

Timely Lighting — **Valentine Lamp Co.**

Timely Lighting

Lighting Fixtures
1425 Rockwell Ave.
Cleveland, OH 44114

Phone 216-696-0416
FAX 216-575-1919

Tom Thumb Lighting, Inc.

Lighting, Furniture
12838 Weber Way
Hawthorne, CA 90250

Phone 213-675-6759
Toll Free 800-338-2567
FAX 213-675-0332

Toro Woodlights

Outdoor Lighting
8111 Lyndale Ave. S
Bloomington, MN 55420

Toll Free 800-321-8676

Tower Lighting Center

Lighting - Chandeliers
PO Box 1043
195 Ashland St.
North Adams, MA 01247

Send $3.00 for Catalog/Information

Mail Order Available

Phone 413-663-7681

Track & Plus

Track Lighting and Accessories
9901 NW 79th Ave.
Hialeah Gardens, FL 33016

Phone 305-822-8100
Toll Free 800-633-7844
FAX 305-822-8126

TrimbleHouse Corp.

Lighting
4658 S. Old Peachtree Rd.
Norcross, GA 30071

Phone 404-448-1972
Toll Free 800-241-4317
FAX 404-447-9250

Troy Lighting

Lighting
14625 E. Clark Ave.
City of Industry, CA 91746

Phone 818-336-4511
Toll Free 800-544-8769

Turn Of The Century Lampshades Inc.

Order by Phone - Custom Finished & Kits Victorian Lampshades
PO Box 6599
Bend, OR 97708

Mail Order Available

Credit Cards VISA/MC/DISCOVER

Phone 503-382-1802
Toll Free 800-538-5267

Unique Lampshade Mfg., Co.

Lampshades
5631 Hutchison
Montreal 1
Que., CAN H2V 4B5
Canada

Universal Fixture Manufacturing

Lighting Fixtures
216 W. 18th St., 6th FL
New York, NY 10011

Toll Free 800-225-5260

Unlight Ltd.

Lighting Fixtures, Chandeliers
5530 St. Patrick
Montreal
Que., CAN H4E 1A8
Canada

Phone 514-769-1533
FAX 514-769-8858

Valentine Lamp Co.

Lamps
4415 Union Pacific Ave.
Los Angeles, CA 90023

Phone 213-268-2147

Lighting

The Complete Sourcebook

11 - 33

Versailles Lighting Inc.

Lighting Fixtures
124 W. 30th St.
New York, NY 10001

Phone 212-564-0240

FAX 212-268-7473

Victorian Classics Lampshades

Victorian Style Lampshades
4116 NE Sandy Blvd.
Portland, OR 97212

Send $2.00 for Catalog/Information

Phone 503-233-7055

Victorian Lightcrafters Ltd.

Victorian Style Lighting Fixtures
PO Box 350
Slate Hill, NY 10973

Send $3.00 for Catalog/Information

Credit Cards VISA/MC

Phone 914-355-1300

Victorian Lighting Works

Victorian Style Chandeliers
251 S. Pennsylvania Ave.
PO Box 469
Centre Hall, PA 16828

Send $5.00 for Catalog/Information

Phone 814-364-9577

FAX 814-364-2920

Victorian Reproduction Enterprises

Reproduction Lighting & Glass, Furniture, Brass
1601 Park Ave. So.
Minneapolis, MN 55404

Send $5.00 for Catalog/Information

Mail Order Available

Phone 612-338-3636

Victorian Revival

Antique and Reproduction Accessories, Light Fixtures
48-1755 Pickering Parkway
Pickering, ON L1V 6K5
Canada

Catalog/Information Available Free

Phone 905-686-7557

Victoriana Ltd.

Brass Lighting Fixtures
7998 E. Jefferson
Denver, CO 80205

Phone 303-741-5435

FAX 303-741-5435

Village Lantern

Reproduction Early American Lighting Fixtures
598 Union
N. Marshfield, MA 02059

Send $0.50 for Catalog/Information

Mail Order Available

Phone 617-834-8121

Visioneered Lighting Mfg. Ltd.

Lighting Fixtures, Chandeliers
100 Ossington Ave.
Toronto
Ont., CAN M6J 4A6
Canada

Phone 416-531-1161

Vortek Industries Ltd.

Lamps
1820 Pandora St.
Vancouver
B.C., CAN V5L 1M5
Canada

Phone 604-251-2451

FAX 604-251-3356

WAC Lighting Collection

Track Lighting, Recessed Lighting
18-01 130th St.
College Point, NY 11356

Phone 718-961-0695
Toll Free 800-526-2588
FAX 718-961-0188

Welsbach

Outdoor Lighting -Colonial & Victorian Style Lamp Posts
240 Sargent Dr.
New Haven, CT 06511

Send $2.00 for Catalog/Information

Phone 203-789-1710
FAX 203-776-9644

Wendelighting

Manufacturer - Consultant - Designers - Lighting Fixtures
2445 N. Naomi St.
Burbank, CA 91504

Phone 818-955-8066
Toll Free 800-528-0101
FAX 818-848-0674

Westwood Co.

Lighting Fixtures
8700 Caspner Dr.
El Paso, TX 79907

Phone 915-592-0066
FAX 915-594-5134

Wholesale Fans & Lighting Inc.

Major Brand - Ceiling Fans & Lighting
12928 Dupont Circle
Tampa, FL 33626

Mail Order Available

Credit Cards VISA/MC/DISCOVER

Toll Free 800-521-3267

Wildwood Lamps & Accents

Lighting - Lamps
PO Box 672
Rockymount, NC 27802-0672

Phone 919-446-3266
Toll Free 800-733-1396
FAX 919-977-6669

William Spencer

Reproduction Brass Chandeliers & Scones
Creek Rd.
Rancocas Woods
Mount Holly, NJ 08060

Send $1.00 for Catalog/Information

Mail Order Available

Phone 609-235-1830

Window Creations

Order Direct - Stained Glass Lamps
PO Box 127
Scott, OH 45886

Catalog/Information Available Free

Mail Order Available

Credit Cards VISA/MC/Check/Money Order

Phone 419-622-3210
Toll Free 800-633-4571
FAX 419-622-6691

Wm. Engel Co., Ltd.

Lighting Fixtures, Lamps & Lampshades
777 Richmond St. W
Toronto
Ont., CAN M6J 1C8
Canada

Phone 416-366-2843
FAX 416-367-5666

Wm. Spencer Inc.

Lighting, Chandeliers
Creek Rd.
Rancocas Woods, NJ 08060

Phone 609-235-1830

Yardlighting Systems Inc.

Outdoor Lighting
1039 Charles Ave.
St. Paul, MN 55104

Phone 612-644-8282

Ye Old Lamp Shop

Lighting, Lamps
371 Westport Ave.
Norwalk, CT 06851

Yestershades

Victorian Style Lampshades
4327 SE Hawthorne
Portland, OR 97214

Send $3.50 for Catalog/Information

Phone 503-235-5647

Zalstein Design Works

Lighting Fixtures, Lamps
831 W. Dabvis
Dallas, TX 75208

Phone 214-943-3054

Windows

A & A International

Awnings
544 Central Dr. #110
Virginia Beach, VA 23454-5227

Phone 804-463-1446

A & C Metal Products Co. Inc.

Storm Windows & Doors
PO Box 12727
Winston-Salem, NC 27107

Phone 919-788-6543

A.R. Perry Glass Co.

Storm Windows, Doors, Solariums
Old Epson Rd.
Box 206
Henderson, NC 27536

Phone 919-492-6181

FAX 919-492-2437

A.W.A.

Manufacturer - Windows
Suites 323/324, Golden House
28-31 Great Pulteney Street
London W1R 3DD
Great Britain

Phone 011-44-71-4944560

FAX 011-44-71-2879010

AAA Aluminum Stamping, Inc.

Manufacturer - Windows, Sliding Doors
2 Leonard Blvd.
Lehigh Industrial Park
Lehigh Acres, FL 33936

Phone 813-237-3353

ACRO Extrusion Corp.

Manufacturer - Vinyl Replacement Windows
900 E. 30th St.
PO Box 9410
Wilmington, DE 19809

Phone 302-762-4476

ALCAN Building Products

Manufacturer - Windows and Glass Sliding Doors
390 Griswold Avenue, NE
Warren, OH 44483

Toll Free 800-827-6045

ALCOA Vinyl Windows

Manufacturer - Call for Distributor near you - Windows and Glass Sliding Doors
Division of the Stolle Corp.
725 Pleasant Valley Dr.
Springboro, OH 45066

Phone 513-746-0488

Toll Free 800-323-4289

AMFT

Arbeitsgemeinschaft Der Hersteller Von Metallfenstern,turen Und - Toren (fed. Of European Window Mftr. Assoc.)
Postfach 335
Wiedner Hauptstrasse 63
A-1045 Wien
Austria

Phone 011-43-222/50105

FAX 011-43-2225050928

AMSCO Windows

Manufacturer - Windows and Glass Sliding Doors

1880 S. 1045 W.
PO Box 25368 (84125)
Salt Lake City, UT 84119

Phone 801-972-6444

APC Corporation

Skylights

PO Box 515
Hawthorne, NJ 07507

Catalog/Information Available Free

Phone 201-423-2900

APCA

Associacao Portugue Sa Dos Construtores De Alumino Federation of European Window Manufacturers Association

Rua Veloso Salgado, 37
R/C Esq.
P-1600 Lisboa
Portugal

Phone 011-35-1-7933204

APL Window & Door Company

Manufacturer - Windows and Glass Sliding Doors

6917 Collins Ave.
Miami, FL 33141-3263

Phone 305-971-2000

Abbey Shade & Mfg. Co. Inc.

Window Shades & Blinds

1336 2nd Ave.
New York, NY 10021

Phone 212-879-8500

Acorn Window Systems Inc.

Manufacturer - Windows & Doors

12620 Westwood
Detroit, MI 48223

Phone 313-272-5700

Active Window Products

Manufacturer - Sliding & Swinging Aluminum Screen Doors

5431 San Fernando Rd. West
Los Angeles, CA 90039

Phone 213-245-5185
FAX 818-246-5188

Adams Rite (Europe) Ltd.

Window and Door Hardware, Locks

Unit 6, Moreton Industrial Estate
London Road, Swanley, Kent BR8 8TZ
Great Britain

Phone 011-44-32-268024
FAX 011-44-32-260996

Advanced Aluminum Products

Manufacturer - Window and Door Screens

18 Stonecreek Cir.
Suite 204
Jackson, TN 38362

Phone 901-664-5550
FAX 901-668-8821

Advantage Window Systems Inc.

Manufacturer - Interior Storm Windows

129 Bayview Ave.
Port Washington, NY 11050

Mail Order Available

Phone 516-944-0338

Allied Window Inc.

Aluminum Storm Windows

2724 W. McMicken Ave.
Cincinnati, OH 45214

Catalog/Information Available Free

Phone 513-559-1212
Toll Free 800-445-5411
FAX 513-559-1883

Allmetal, Inc.

Manufacturer - Window and Door Screens

PO Box 850
Bensenville, IL 60106

Phone 708-766-8500
FAX 708-766-1082

Alpine Windows

Manufacturer - Windows and Glass Sliding Doors

19720 Bothell-Everett Hwy., SE
Bothell, WA 98012-8124

Phone 206-481-7101

Alside Window Company

Manufacturer - Windows and Glass Sliding Doors

3800 Farm Gate Road
Kinston, NC 28501

Phone 919-527-5240

Aluma-Craft Corporation

Manufacturer - Window and Door Screens, Frames

7023 Rampart
Houston, TX 77081

Phone 713-666-1828

Aluma-Glass Industries, Inc.

Manufacturer - Windows and Glass Sliding Doors

2715 North Star Road
Nampa, ID 83651

Phone 208-467-4491

Alumaroll Specialty Co., Inc.

Window and Patio Door Screens

2803 S. Taylor Dr.
PO Box 1122
Sheboygan, WI 53082-1122

Phone 414-458-3795
FAX 414-458-9989

Alumax

Manufacturer - Windows & Doors

Magnolia Division
PO Box 40
Magnolia, AR 71753

Toll Free 800-551-0208

Aluminum Products Company

Manufacturer - Windows and Glass Sliding Doors

645 Montroyal Road
Rural Hall, NC 27045

Phone 919-969-6876

Aluminum Specialties Mfg. Co.

Manufacturer - Windows and Glass Sliding Doors

400 South Union Avenue
Pueblo, CO 81003

Phone 719-543-4433

Alwindor Manufacturing, Inc.

Manufacturer - Windows and Glass Sliding Doors

206 North Sierra Place
Upland, CA 91766

Phone 714-946-6726

American Heritage Shutters Inc.

Manufacturer - Interior & Exterior Shutters

2345 Dunn Ave.
Memphis, TN 38114

Catalog/Information Available Free

Phone 901-743-2800
Toll Free 800-541-1186
FAX 901-744-8356

American Screen & Door Co., Inc.

Windows, Screens and Storm Doors

4221 Lamar Ave.
Memphis, TN 38118

Phone 901-365-4951

Amerlite Aluminum Co., Inc.

Replacement Windows, Glass Sliding Doors

122-A W. 25th St.
New York, NY 10001

Phone 212-986-9559
FAX 212-645-6885

Anaconda Aluminum

Replacement & Storm Windows
PO Box 179
Gnadenhutten, OH 44629

Phone 614-254-4381

Andersen Windows Inc.

Manufacturer - Windows
PO Box 3900
Peoria, IL 61614

Toll Free 800-426-4261

Appropriate Technology, Corp.

Heat Saving Window Insulation Shades
PO Box 975
Brattleboro, VT 05302

Phone 802-257-4500

Toll Free 800-257-4501

Architectural Detail In Wood

Wood Interior Storm Windows
41 Parker Road
Shirley, MA 01464

Phone 508-425-9026

Arctic Glass & Window Outlet

Doors, Windows, Skylights
Arctic Supply Inc.
565 Co. Rd. T
Hammond, WI 54015

Send $4.00 for Catalog/Information

Credit Cards
VISA/MC/DISCOVER/Money Order

Phone 715-796-2292

Toll Free 800-428-9276

Arrow Aluminum Ind., Inc.

*Manufacturer - Windows and Glass
Sliding Doors*
113 Neal St.
PO Box 528
Martin, TN 38237

Phone 901-587-9528

Art Glass Unlimited Inc.

*Stained, Leaded, Beveled, Etched
Windows*
412 N. Euclid
St. Louis, MO 63108

Phone 314-361-0474

FAX 314-361-3013

Asefave

*Asociacion Espanola De Fabricantes De
Fachadas Ligeras Y Ventanas Federation
of European Window Manufacturers
Association*
74, Principe de Vergara
6a planta
E-28006 Madrid
Spain

Phone 011-34-1/5614547

FAX 011-34-1/5644290

Astracast PLC

*Manufacturer - Supersinks, Fordham,
Mastersinks, and Sculptura - Sinks, Taps,
Mixers*
PO Box 20 Oakwell Way
Birstall, W Yorksire WF17 9XD
Great Britain

Phone 011-44-924/477466

FAX 011-44-924/475801

Awnings By Jay

Awnings
5107 Australian Ave.
West Palm Beach, FL 33407

Phone 407-844-4444

B & G Custom Window

Windows
6055 Happy Pines Dr.
Foresthill, CA 95631-9634

Phone 916-663-1871

BayForm

Manufacturer - Screens for Windows and Doors

500 Barmac Dr.
Weston, ON M9L 2X8
Canada

Phone 416-746-0662

FAX 416-746-0666

Better Bilt Aluminum Products Co.

Windows, Doors

G-13 St.
Smyrna, TN 37167

Phone 615-459-4161

Better-Bilt Aluminum Products Co.

Manufacturer - Windows and Glass Sliding Doors

7555 Hwy. 69 North
Prescott Valley, AZ 86314

Phone 602-772-7000

BiltBest Windows

Wood Windows and Doors, Frames

175 Tenth St.
Ste. Genevieve, MO 63670

Phone 314-883-3571

FAX 314-883-2858

Binning's Bldg. Products Inc.

Manufacturer - Windows and Glass Sliding Doors

200 Walser Rd.
PO Box 868
Lexington, NC 27292

Phone 704-249-9193

Blaine Window Hardware

Window & Door Hardware

17319 Blaine Drive
Hagerstown, MD 21740

Catalog/Information Available Free

Mail Order Available

Phone 301-797-6500

Toll Free 800-678-1919

FAX 301-797-2510

Blair Joinery Ltd.

Windows

Member of C R Smith Group
9 Baker St., Greenock PA15 4TU
Great Britain

Phone 011-44-475/21256

FAX 011-44-475/87364

Blum Ornamental Glass Co., Inc.

Stained Glass Windows

314 E. Jacobs St.
Louisville, KY 40203

Phone 502-585-3439

Boyd Aluminum Mfg. Company

Manufacturer - Windows and Glass Sliding Doors

3248 E. Division St.
PO Box 1565
Springfield, MO 65801-1565

Phone 417-862-5084

Brammer Mfg. Co.

Manufacturer - Built-in Kitchen Cabinets

PO Box 3547
1701 Rockingham Rd.
Davenport, IA 52808

Phone 319-326-2585

Bristolite Skylights

Manufacturer - Skylights

401 E. Goetz Ave.
PO Box 2515
Santa Ana, CA 92707

Catalog/Information Available Free

Phone 714-540-8950

Toll Free 800-854-8618

Burch Co.

Manufacturer - Aluminum Windows, Doors

1303 Carroll St.
Baltimore, MD 21230

Phone 301-837-8141

C & S Distributors, Inc.

Manufacturer - Windows and Glass Sliding Doors

1640 John Fitch Blvd.
South Windsor, CT 06074

Phone 203-528-9371

C. V. Aluminum, Inc.

Manufacturer - Windows and Glass Sliding Doors

1850 Atlanta Ave.
Riverside, CA 92507

Phone 714-682-2220

Cain Inc.

Beveled Glass Windows

Rt. 1 Box AAA
Bremo Bluff, VA 23022

Phone 804-842-3984

California Glass Bending Corp.

Glass - Victorian Style Windows

320 E. B St.
Wilmington, CA 90744

Toll Free 800-223-6594

FAX 310-549-5398

California Window Corporation

Manufacturer - Windows and Glass Sliding Doors

885 Fairway Dr.
PO Box 1447
Walnut, CA 91788-1447

Phone 714-595-4344

Caradco

Manufacturer - Wood Windows & Patio Doors - Double Hung, Awning Windows, Casement, Bays, Bows

PO Box 920
Rantoul, IL 61866

Phone 217-893-4444

Toll Free 800-238-1866

FAX 217-893-1175

Care Free Aluminum Prod., Inc.

Manufacturer - Windows and Glass Sliding Doors

General Aluminum Products
1023 Reynolds Rd.
Charlotte, MI 48813

Phone 517-543-0430

FAX 517-543-1707

Cego Limited

Window & Door Hardware

Western Road
Silver End, Witham, Essex CM8 3QB
Great Britain

Phone 011-44-37/683241

FAX 011-44-37/683072

Chamberlain Group

Manufacturer - Windows and Glass Sliding Doors

The MayFair Div.
4100 Cameron St.
Lafayette, LA 70506

Phone 318-233-2470

Cheng Design

Kitchens - Custom Designed

1190 Neilson St.
Albany, CA 94706

Classic Designs

Nationwide Delivery - Reproduction Georgian/Victorian Windows, Traditional Casement, Modern Windows

Unit 15, Bilton Industrial Estate
Humber Avenue, Coventry CV3 1JL
Great Britain

Catalog/Information Available Free

Phone 011-44-800-318348

FAX 011-44-203-443104

Coast to Coast Manufacturing Ltd.

Windows & Doors

13643 Fifth St.
Chino, CA 91710

Send $3.00 for Catalog/Information

Phone 714-591-7405

Columbia Glass & Window Company

Manufacturer - Windows and Glass Sliding Doors

1600 North Jackson
Kansas City, MO 64120

Phone 816-241-5800

Columbia Metal Products Co.

Aluminum Windows & Doors

1600 N. Jackson St.
Kansas City, MO 64120

Phone 816-241-5800

Consolidated Aluminum

Manufacturer - Screen Frames, Window Screens, Door Screens

PO Box 129
Jackson, TN 38302

Toll Free 800-238-3953

FAX 901-422-7827

Consolidated American Window Co.

Manufacturer - Windows and Glass Sliding Doors

2301 E. Page Ave.
PO Box 426
Malvern, AR 72104

Phone 501-332-3621

Corn Belt Aluminum Inc.

Manufacturer - Windows and Glass Sliding Doors

109 S.E. 4th Street
PO Box 6097
Des Moines, IA 50309

Phone 515-282-3800

Country Accents

Manufacturer - Order Direct - Worldwide Shipping - Decorative Metal Panels - Copper, Brass, Tin to restyle your Kitchen, and add Country Charm to your Furniture and Cabinets

PO Box 437
Montoursville, PA 17754

Send $5.00 for Catalog/Information

Phone 717-478-4127

FAX 717-478-2007

Courtaulds Performance Films

Manufacturer - Window Sunscreen

PO Box 5068
Martinsvillem, VA 24115

Catalog/Information Available Free

Phone 703-629-1711

Toll Free 800-345-6088

FAX 703-629-8333

Cox Studios

Stained Glass Windows, Door Panels, Lamps, Mirrors

1004 S. 9th St.
Canon City, CO 81212

Send $2.00 for Catalog/Information

Mail Order Available

Credit Cards Certified Check

Phone 719-275-7262

Creative Woodworking Ltd.

Manufacturer - Windows

26 Friendship St.
Westerly, RI 02891

Phone 401-596-4463

FAX 401-596-3418

Crompton Ltd.

Manufacturer - Window & Door Hardware, Locks (Brass and Bronze)

41 Gerard St., Ashton-In-Makerfield
Wilgan, Lancashire WN4 9AN
Great Britain

Phone 011-44-94/2727651

FAX 011-44-94/2271037

Crown Mfg. Corp. of Missouri

*Manufacturer - Windows and Glass
Sliding Doors*
18092 Chesterfield Airport Rd.
PO Box 289
Chesterfield, MO 63017

Phone 314-534-1988

Custom Window Co.

Manufacturer - Custom Windows
PO Box 118
Englewood, CO 80151

Phone 303-761-2909

DAB Studio

Stained Glass Windows, Mirrors
31 North Terrace
PO Box 96
Maplewood, NJ 07040

Catalog/Information Available Free

Phone 201-762-5407

Toll Free 800-682-6151

Decore-Ative Specialties

Cabinets
4414 Azusa Canyon Rd.
Irwindale, CA 91706-2740

Phone 818-960-7731

Delsan Industries, Inc.

*Manufacturer - Windows and Glass
Sliding Doors*
1644 Lotsie Blvd.
St. Louis, MO 63132

Phone 314-423-5900

Devenco Products Inc.

Wood Blinds & Shutters
2688 East Ponce De Leon Ave.
Decatur, GA 30030

Mail Order Available

Phone 404-378-4597

Toll Free 800-888-4597

FAX 404-377-1120

Dilworth Manufacturing Co.

Plexiglass Basement Window Bubbles
PO Box 158
Honey Brook, PA 19344

Mail Order Available

Credit Cards VISA/MC

Phone 717-354-8956

Down River International Inc.

Wood Window and Door Components
738 N. Market Blvd.
PO Box 15290-C
Sacramento, CA 95851

Phone 916-920-0290

Dryad Simplan Limited

Window and Door Hardware & Locks
Frog Island
Leicester LE3 5DP
Great Britain

Phone 011-44-53/3538844

FAX 011-44-53/3513623

Eagle Window & Door

*Manufacturer/Distributor Windows &
Doors - Double Hung, Casement, Circle
Head, Patio, French, Entry, Skylights*
375 East 9th St.
PO Box 1072
Dubuque, IA 52001

Phone 319-556-2270

Toll Free 800-453-3633

FAX 319-556-3825

Empire Pacific Industries

*Manufacturer - Windows and Glass
Sliding Doors*
830 Wilson St.
Eugene, OR 97402

Phone 503-687-8723

Windows

Energy Arsenal — Globe Canvas Products Co.

Energy Arsenal

Window Insulation Systems

107 Industrial Dr.
Ivyland, PA 18974

Catalog/Information Available Free

Credit Cards VISA/MC

Phone 215-322-0363

Toll Free 800-325-2826

Energy Saving Products

*Manufacturer - Windows and Glass
Sliding Doors*

661 Long Hollow Pike
PO Box 1507
Gallatin, TN 37066

Phone 615-452-1240

Englander Millwork Corp.

Wood Windows & Doors

2369 Lorillard Place
Bronx, NY 10458

Mail Order Available

Phone 212-364-4240

First American Resources

*Manufacturer - Screen Frames, Window
Screens, Door Screens*

2030 Riverview Industrial Dr.
Mableton, GA 30059

Phone 404-355-5000

FAX 404-696-9320

Fleetwood Aluminum Products, Inc.

*Manufacturer - Windows and Glass
Sliding Doors*

2485 Railroad St.
Corona, CA 91720

Phone 714-279-1070

Flex Trim

*Architectural Components, Interior
Windows, Partial Walls, Niches*

Box 4227
Rancho Cucamonga, CA 91730

Phone 714-944-6665

G-U Hardware Inc.

Manufacturer - Window & Door Hardware

11761 Rock Landing Dr.
Suite M6
Newport News, VA 23606

Phone 804-873-1097

FAX 804-873-1298

G. L. Downs Designs

*Windowcor Window Tiles - Glass Block
Look*

9401 NW Barry Rd.
Kansas City, MO 64152

Mail Order Available

Phone 816-741-5880

General Aluminum Corporation

*Manufacturer - Windows and Glass
Sliding Doors*

1001 West Crosby Rd.
PO Box 819022
Carrollton, TX 75006

Phone 214-242-5271

Georgia Palm Beach Aluminum Window Corp.

*Manufacturer - Windows and Glass
Sliding Doors*

Jabara Road, Industrial Park
PO Box 819022
Bainbridge, GA 31717

Phone 912-246-2961

Geze UK

Windows

4 Northumberland Court
Dukes Industrial Park
Chelmsford, Essex CM2 6UW
United Kingdom

Phone 011-44-245/451093

FAX 011-44-245/451108

Globe Canvas Products Co.

Awnings

549 Industrial Drive
Yeadon, PA 19050

Phone 215-622-7211

The Complete Sourcebook

12 - 9

Golden Age Glassworks

Stained Glass Windows & Doors
339 Bellvale Rd.
Warwick, NY 10990
Send $2.00 for Catalog/Information
Mail Order Available

Phone 914-986-1487
FAX 914-986-6147

Golden Gate Glass & Mirror Co.,Inc.

Windows, Doors, Mirrors
1031 Valencia St.
San Francisco, CA 94110

Phone 415-282-6663

Goodman Fabrications

Window Treatments - Period Shades & Blinds
PO Box 8164
Prairie Village, KS 66208
Catalog/Information Available Free

Phone 816-942-0832

Gra-Mar Window Treatment

Window Treatments
178 Troy Rd.
East Hanover Township, NJ 07936

Phone 201-887-4751

Graber Industries

Manufacturer - Window Treatments - Blinds
7549 Graber Road
Middleton, WI 53562

Phone 608-836-5383
FAX 608-831-2184

Great Lakes Window

Manufacturer - Windows
30499 Tracy Road
PO Box 1896
Toledo, OH 43603-1896

Phone 419-666-5555

H-R Windows

Manufacturer - Windows and Glass Sliding Doors
2100 East Union Bower
PO Box 226957
Irving, TX 75061

Phone 214-438-9210

Hahn's Woodworking Co.

Manufacturer - Windows, Doors, Shutters
646 W. First Ave.
Roselle, NJ 07205
Mail Order Available

Phone 908-241-8825
FAX 908-241-9293

Hanover Wire Cloth

Manufacturer - Screen Frames, Window Screens, Door Screens
PO Box 473
Hanover, PA 17331

Phone 717-637-3795
FAX 717-637-4766

Hara's Inc.

Manufacturer - Windows and Glass Sliding Doors
1208 Madison Ave.
Nampa, ID 83651

Phone 208-466-4523

Harding's Custom Sheers

Window Treatments - Seamless Sheers
807 S. Auburn
Grass Valley, CA 95945

Toll Free 800-228-0825

Harry G. Barr Company

Manufacturer - Windows and Glass Sliding Doors
6500 S. Zero
PO Box 10226
Ft. Smith, AR 72901

Phone 501-646-7891

Windows

Hayfield Window & Door Co.

*Manufacturer - Windows and Glass
Sliding Doors*

Hayfield Ind. Pk Rd.
PO Box 25
Hayfield, MN 55940

Phone 507-477-3224

Headquarters Window & Walls

*Order by Phone - Window Treatments &
Wallpaper*

8 Clinton Place
Morristown, NJ 07960

Phone 800- 4411288
Toll Free 800-338-4882

Heirwood Shutters

Interior Shutters, Shoji Screens

1977 Placentia
PO Box 703
Costa Mesa, CA 92627

Phone 714-548-6841

Hess Manufacturing Company

*Manufacturer - Order Direct - Windows,
Doors, Glass Enclosures*

Box 127
Quincy, PA 17247

Catalog/Information Available Free

Toll Free 800-541-6666

Historic Window & Door Corp.

Manufacturer - Windows

Glass & Aluminum Construction Svrs. Inc.
PO Box 138
Alstead, NH 03602

Phone 603-835-2918

Historic Windows

Custom Reproduction Shutters

PO Box 1172
Harrisonburg, VA 22801

Send $3.00 for Catalog/Information

Mail Order Available

Phone 703-434-5855

Hogshire Industries Inc.

Awnings

2401 Hampton Blvd.
Norfolk, VA 23517

Phone 804-622-4776

Home Window Systems Ltd.

Windows

Marlowbrook Ho, Cabot La.
Creekmoor, Poole, Dorset
BH17 7BX
Great Britain

Phone 011-44-202/602030

Hope Works Ltd.

Window, Door Hardware & Locks

Pleck Road
Walsall, West Midland
WS2 9HH
Great Britain

Phone 011-44-92/2720072
FAX 011-44-92/2720080

Houston Canvas & Awning

Canvas Awnings

3315 Butter Cup
Houston, TX 77063-5601

Phone 713-789-3774

Howard Industries Inc.

*Manufacturer - Windows and Glass
Sliding Doors*

8130 NW 74th Ave.
Miami, FL 33166-9851

Phone 305-888-1521
FAX 305-884-1445

Hunt Windows and Doors

Windows and Doors

117 Murphy Rd.
Hartford, CT 06114

Phone 203-527-4732

The Complete Sourcebook

IJ Mfg. Ltd.

Wood Frame Windows, Patio Doors, Jambs, Skylights

1255 12th St.
Kamloops, B.C.
CAN V2B 2J6
Canada

Phone 604-376-1021
FAX 604-376-2324

Insulate Industries, Inc.

Manufacturer - Windows and Glass Sliding Doors

7651 South 190th St.
Kent, WA 98032

Phone 206-271-1010

Inter Trade Inc.

Awnings, Patio Covers, Roll Shutters

3175 Fujita St.
Torrance, CA 90505

Phone 310-515-7177
Toll Free 800-452-0452

International Window Corporation

Manufacturer - Windows and Glass Sliding Doors

5625 East Firestone Blvd.
South Gate, CA 90280

Phone 213-928-6411

J. Ring Glass Studio

Beveled Glass Windows

2724 University Ave. SE
Minneapolis, MN 55414

Mail Order Available

Phone 612-379-0920

J. W. Window Components, Inc.

Window and Patio Door Components

1500 N. Oak Mabry
Tampa, FL 33607

Phone 813-871-4053
FAX 813-871-4064

JIL Industries

Factory Direct - Awnings

21 Green St.
Malden, MA 02148

Credit Cards VISA/MC

Toll Free 800-876-2340

James Gibbons Format Ltd.

Window and Door Hardware & Locks, Bathroom Fittings

Colliery Road
Wolverhampton, West Midlands
WV1 2QW
Great Britain

Phone 011-44-90/258585
FAX 011-44-90/250892

Janik Custom Millwork

Custom - Wood Windows, Doors, Mantels, Stairs, Cabinets, Moulding

612 Est Cossitt
La Grange, IL 60525

Phone 708-482-4844
FAX 708-482-4850

Jelco Windows & Doors

Window & Doors

Akers Rd.
Anniston, AL 36202

Phone 205-831-7000

Joe-Keith Industries, Inc.

Manufacturer - Windows and Glass Sliding Doors

4011 E. Columbia
PO Box 27337
Tucson, AZ 85714

Phone 602-748-9033

John Boyle & Co. Inc.

Awnings

PO Box 791
Statesville, NC 28677

Phone 704-872-8151

John Carr Joinery Sales Ltd.

Window & Door Frames, Doors, Kitchen Units, Stairs, Stair Components, Trusses, Windows

Watch House La., Doncaster
5 Yorkshire   DN5 9LR
Great Britain

Phone 011-44-302/783333

FAX 011-44-302/78783

John F. Lavoie Windows

Reproduction Windows

PO Box 15
Springfield, VT 05156

Phone 802-886-8253

JonCo Manufacturing, Inc.

Manufacturer - Windows and Glass Sliding Doors

Hwy. 174
PO Box 287
Joshua, TX 76058

Phone 817-641-7313

Jones Paint & Glass, Inc.

Manufacturer - Windows and Glass Sliding Doors

170 N. 100 W
PO Box 1403
Provo, UT 84601

Phone 801-374-6711

Kansas Aluminum, Inc.

Manufacturer - Windows and Glass Sliding Doors

Oil Hill Ind. Pk.
PO Box 670
El Dorado, KS 67042

Phone 316-321-1970

Kawneer

Windows

555 Guthridge Court
Norcross, GA 30092

Phone 404-449-5555

Keller Aluminum Products

Manufacturer - Windows and Glass Sliding Doors

1800 Grogan Ave.
Merced, CA 95430

Phone 209-383-2221

Ken Jordan Shutters

Window Treatment - Shutters

11362 Kline Dr.
Dallas, TX 75229

Send $1.00 for Catalog/Information

Phone 214-241-7776

FAX 214-247-5765

Kestrel Manufacturing

Shutters & Folding Screens

PO Box 12 , St. Peters Village Gallery
Saint Peters, PA 19470-0012

Mail Order Available

Credit Cards VISA/MC/Check/Money Order

Phone 610-469-6444

Toll Free 800-494-4321

FAX 610-469-6881

Kinco Corporation

Manufacturer - Windows and Glass Sliding Doors

537 Hazel Mill Rd.
PO Box 6279
Asheville, NC 28816

Phone 704-254-2353

Kinco, Ltd.

Manufacturer - Windows and Glass Sliding Doors

5245 Old Kings Road
PO Box 6429
Jacksonville, FL 32205

Phone 904-335-1476

The Complete Sourcebook

Kinro, Inc.

Manufacturer - Windows and Glass Sliding Doors
11700 Industry Ave.
Fontana, CA 92331

Phone 714-681-4236

Kinzee Industries Inc.

Cabinets, Vanities, Cultured Marble Tops
1 Paul Kohner Place
Elmwood Park, NJ 07407

Phone 201-797-4700
FAX 201-797-1360

Koch Originals, Inc.

Lighting - Table Lamps, Occasional Furniture
PO Box 3536
Evansville, IN 47733-3436

Phone 812-421-5600
Toll Free 800-457-3757
FAX 812-421-5608

Kohler Company

Manufacturer - Plumbing Fixtures, Faucets and Bath Accessories
444 Highland Dr.
Kohler, WI 53044

Send $8.00 for Catalog/Information

Phone 414-457-4441
Toll Free 800-456-4537
FAX 414-459-1623

L.F. Pease Co.

Awnings
19 Grosvenor Ave.
PO Box 14205
East Providence, RI 02914

Phone 401-438-2850

Lawrence Canvas Products, Co.

Canvas Awnings
1530 S. Kingshighway
St. Louis, MO 63110

Phone 314-771-4060

Lawson Industries Inc.

Manufacturer - Windows
7030 NW 37th Ct.
Miami, FL 33147

Phone 305-696-8660
FAX 305-696-6006

Lincoln Wood Products, Inc.

Wood Windows and Doors
PO Box 375
Merrill, WI 54452

Phone 715-536-2461
FAX 715-536-9783

Linel, Inc.

Custom Skylights
101 Linel Dr.
Mooresville, IN 46158

Linford Brothers/Utal Glass Co.

Manufacturer - Windows and Glass Sliding Doors
1245 S. 700 W
PO Box 419
Salt lake City, UT 84103

Phone 801-972-6161

Living Windows Corporation

Manufacturer - Windows and Glass Sliding Doors
15022 Old Richmond Rd.
PO Box 36447
Sugar Land, TX 77478

Phone 713-933-3600
FAX 713-933-8103

M F F

Member - Federation of Window Manufacturers Association
Nybrokajen 5
Box 16286
S-103 25 Stockholm
Sweden

Phone 011-46-8/7627600
FAX 011-46-8/6118085

MBS Manufacturing West, Inc.

*Manufacturer - Windows and Glass
Sliding Doors*

7310 Express Road
Temperance, MI 48182

Phone 313-847-3099

MQ Windows of Europe & The Americas

Manufacturer - Windows & Doors

4503, 117 Road
Ste-Agathe-Des-Monts
Quebec J8C 2Z8
Canada

Phone 819-326-0302

FAX 819-326-5321

Made-Rite Aluminum Window Co.

*Windows, Doors, Bath & Shower
Enclosures*

PO Box 3557
Cranston, RI 02910

Phone 401-941-3222

FAX 401-941-9020

Major Industries Inc.

Skylight Systems, Windows

7120 Stewart Ave.
Wausau, WI 54401

Phone 715-842-4616

Malta

*Manufacturer - Wood Replacement
Windows*

PO Box 397
13th Street
Malta, OH 43758

Phone 614-962-3131

Toll Free 800-727-5167

FAX 614-962-3700

Marvin Windows

*Manufacturer & Distributor - Made to
order Windows and Doors*

PO Box 100
Warroad, MN 56763

Catalog/Information Available Free

Toll Free 800-346-5128

Marvin Windows and Doors

Manufacturer - Windows & Doors

PO Box 100
Warroad, MN 56763

Phone 800-346-5128

Mason Corporation

*Manufacturer - Screen Frames, Window
Screens, Door Screens*

PO Box 59226
Birmingham, AL 35259-9226

Phone 205-942-4100

FAX 205-945-4393

Masterview Window Company

*Manufacturer - Windows and Glass
Sliding Doors*

3065 South 43rd Ave.
PO Box 23730
Phoenix, AZ 85009

Phone 602-269-3000

Mercer Industries, Inc.

*Manufacturer - Windows and Glass
Sliding Doors*

10760 SW Denney Road
PO Box 4700
Beaverton, OR 97005

Phone 503-526-3650

Toll Free 800-226-2515

Metal Exchange Corp.

*Manufacturer - Window, Door Screens
and Frames*

111 W. Port Plaza
Suite 704
St. Louis, MO 63146

Phone 314-434-3500

Metal Industries Inc.

Window and Door Screens

1000 Cotter Ave.
PO Box 521
Merrill, WI 54452

Phone 715-536-9541

Metal Industries, Inc.

*Manufacturer - Windows and Glass
Sliding Doors, Screens*
PO Box M, Route 209
Elizabethville, PA 17023
Phone 717-362-8196

Miami Awning

Awnings
282 N.W. 36th St.
Miami, FL 33127
Phone 305-576-2029
FAX 305-576-0514

Midwest Wood Products

Windows, Doors, Screens
1051 S. Rolff St.
Davenport, IA 52802
Send $2.00 for Catalog/Information
Phone 319-323-4757
FAX 319-323-1483

Milgard Manufacturing, Inc.

*Manufacturer - Windows and Glass
Sliding Doors*
1010-54th Ave. E
PO Box 11368
Tacoma, WA 98411-0368
Phone 206-922-6030

Miller Industries, Inc.

*Manufacturer - Windows and Glass
Sliding Doors*
16295 N.W. 13th Ave.
Miami, FL 33169-0910
Phone 305-621-0501

Milwaukee Faucets

Manufacturer - Faucets & Fixtures
Div. of Universal-Rundle Corp.
N. 124th St.
Milwaukee, WI 53222
Phone 414-461-8700
FAX 414-461-8721

Modu-Line Windows

Manufacturer - Windows
930 Single Ave.
Wausau, WI 54401
Phone 715-845-9666
Toll Free 800-521-8742

Moeller-Reimer Company

*Manufacturer - Windows and Glass
Sliding Doors*
9245 Dielman Industrial Dr.
St. Louis, MO 63132
Phone 314-997-5310

Mon-Ray Windows, Inc.

*Storm Windows & Doors, Porch
Enclosures, Replacement Windows &
Doors*
8224 Hwy. 55
Golden Valley, MN 55427
Phone 612-544-3646
FAX 612-546-8977

Moran Canvas Products Inc.

Canvas Awnings
393 Wilmington St.
Jackson, MS 39204-0271
Phone 601-373-4051

Morgan Industries

Awnings
28 Blanchard Rd.
Burlington, MA 01803
Phone 617-273-9964

Moss Supply Company, Inc.

*Manufacturer - Windows and Glass
Sliding Doors*
5001 N. Graham St.
PO Box 26338
Charlotte, NC 28221
Phone 704-596-8717

Mt. Lebanon Awning & Tent Co.

Awnings
Box 27
Presto, PA 15142
Phone 412-221-2233

NT Jenkins Manufacturing Co.

Manufacturer - Windows and Glass Sliding Doors
Monarch Windows & Doors
PO Box 249, Frank Akers Rd.
Anniston, AL 36202

Phone 205-831-7000
Toll Free 800-633-2323
FAX 800-261-6116

Nana Windows & Doors Inc.

Call for Local Representative - French Doors - Opening Glass Wall
707 Redwood Highway
Mill Valley, CA 94941

Catalog/Information Available Free

Phone 415-383-3148
Toll Free 800-873-5673
FAX 415-383-0312

Nanik

Window Treatments - Wood Blinds, Optix Suncontrol Blinds
7200 Stewart Ave., PO Box 1766
Wausau, WI 54402-1766

Catalog/Information Available Free

Phone 715-843-4653
Toll Free 800-422-4544
FAX 715-842-3510

Napco

Insulated Windows
10425 Hampshire Ave. S.
Bloomington, MN 55438

Catalog/Information Available Free

Phone 612-944-5120

Naturay Systems Corp.

Skylights
501 E. 16th
Kansas City, MO 64108

Phone 816-471-1326

Nelson A. Taylor Co., Inc.

Awnings
PO Box 1190
10 W. 9th Ave.
Gloversville, NY 12079

Phone 518-725-0681

New Haven Awning Co.

Awnings
11-13 Edwards St.
New Haven, CT 06511

Phone 203-562-7232

New Morning Windows, Inc.

Manufacturer - Wood Windows and Doors, Frames
11921 Portland Ave. S.
Burnsville, MN 55337

Phone 612-895-6175
FAX 612-895-6180

New Panes Creations

Manufacturer - Windows
24659 Las Patranas
Yorba Linda, CA 92687

Phone 303-482-6971

New York Replacement Parts Corp.

Plumbing Supplies
1464 Lexington Ave.
New York, NY 10028

Phone 212-534-0818

New York Wire Company

Manufacturer - Screen Frames, Window Screens, Door Screens
PO Box 310
Mt. Wolf, PA 17347

Phone 717-266-5626
FAX 717-266-5871

Newpro

Windows, Patio Rooms, Doors
26 Cedar Street
Woburn, MA 01808

Mail Order Available

Phone 617-933-4100

Nichols-Homeshield, Inc.

Manufacturer - Screen Frames, Window Screens, Door Screens

PO Box 3038
Naperville, IL 60566-7038

Phone 708-355-5400
FAX 708-355-5490

Norandex, Inc.

Manufacturer - Windows and Glass Sliding Doors

8450 S. Bedford Rd.
Macedonia, OH 44056-2033

Phone 216-468-2200
FAX 216-468-8116

Norco Windows Inc.

Manufacturer - Windows & Patio Doors

PO Box 140
811 Factory St.
Hawkins, WI 54530-0140

Phone 715-585-6311
FAX 715-585-6357

North Star Company

Manufacturer - Window, Door Screens & Frames

14912 S. Broadway
Gardena, CA 90248

Phone 213-770-8000
FAX 213-516-2138

Northwest Aluminum Products

Manufacturer - Windows and Glass Sliding Doors

East 5414 Broadway Ave.
Spokane, WA 99212-0908

Phone 509-535-3015

O'Neals Tarpaulin & Awning Co.

Awnings

549 W. Indianola Ave.
Youngstown, OH 44511

Phone 216-788-6504

O.K. McCloy Awnings

Awnings

2029 Noble St.
Pittsburgh, PA 15218

Phone 412-271-4044

ODL Inc.

Skylights, Door Lights, Side Lights

215 E. Roosevelt Ave.
Zeeland, MI 49464

Phone 616-772-9111
FAX 616-772-9110

Ohline Corp.

Manufacturer - Wooden Shutters

1930 W. 139th St.
Gardena, CA 90249

Phone 213-327-4630
FAX 310-538-5742

Optimum Window Mfg. Corp.

Windows, Doors, Entrances

311A Casanova St.
Bronx, NY 10474

Toll Free 800-617-4937
FAX 212-617-6608

Oxford Sash Window Company

Sliding Sash Windows

Middleway
Summertown, Oxford
OX2 7LG
Great Britain

Phone 011-44-865/513113
FAX 011-44-865/58668

P. C. Henderson Ltd.

Window, Door Hardware and Locks

Romford
Essex RM3 8UL
Great Britain

Phone 011-44-40/2345555
FAX 011-44-40/2372000

Windows

P. J. McBride Inc.

Awnings
410 Eastern Parkway
Farmingdale, NY 11735

Phone 516-694-1939

Pacesetter Building Systems

Windows, Doors, Awnings, Patio Covers
4343 S. 96th St.
Omaha, NE 68127

Phone 402-331-9400

Pacific Industries/PI. Inc.

Manufacturer - Windows and Glass Sliding Doors
3511 Finch Rd.
PO Box 577097
Modesto, CA 95357-7097

Phone 209-527-8020

Paulson's Stained Glass Studio

Stained Glass Windows & Lampshades
67 Ridge Rd.
Upton, MA 01568

Phone 508-529-6950

Peerless Products Inc.

Aluminum Window Systems, Sliding Glass Doors
PO Box 2469
Shawnee Mission, KS 66201

Phone 913-432-2232
Toll Free 800-279-9999
FAX 913-432-3004

Pella Corporation

Manufacturer - Windows, Doors, Skylights, Sunrooms
102 Main St.
Pella, IA 50219
Catalog/Information Available Free

Phone 515-628-1000
Toll Free 800-524-3700
FAX 515-628-6070

Pennco, Inc.

Manufacturer - Windows and Glass Sliding Doors
5601 Roberts Drive
Ashland, KY 41101-9047

Phone 606-928-6476

Perkins Manufacturing & Distributing

Wood Window Frames, Doors, Wood Specialties
1712 Cass Ave.
Bay City, MI 48708

Phone 517-895-8591

Perma Window & Door Service

Window & Door Glass
271 E. Northampton St.
Wilkes Barre, PA 18702-5813

Toll Free 800-227-3762

Peterson Window Corp.

Manufacturer - Aluminum Rolling Windows & Doors
700 Livernois Ave.
Ferndale, MI 48220

Phone 313-548-9700
Toll Free 800-521-7932
FAX 313-548-4693

Petit Industries Inc.

Interior Storm Windows
PO Box 1156
Saco, ME 04072-1156

Phone 207-283-1900
FAX 207-283-1905

Pike Tent & Awning Co., Inc.

Awnings
605 N.E. 21st Ave.
Portland, OR 97232

Phone 503-232-7070

The Complete Sourcebook

Pioneer Roll Shutter Co.

Shutters
155 Glendale Ave. #8
Sparks, NV 89431
Catalog/Information Available Free
Phone 702-355-8686

Plains Plastics Inc.

Manufacturer - Windows
1132 W. 1st St.
McPherson, KS 67460
Phone 316-241-5119

Plunkett - Webster Inc.

Manufacturer - Windows
2400 Hamilton Blvd.
South Plainfield, NJ 07080
Phone 201-754-1644
FAX 201-754-2814

Point-Five Windows

Manufacturer - Windows
1314 Duff Dr.
Fort Collins, CO 80524
Phone 303-482-6971

Pompei & Company Art Glass

Windows, Doors, Mirrors
454 High St.
Medford, MA 02155
Send $5.00 for Catalog/Information
Mail Order Available
Phone 617-395-8867

Portal Inc.

Windows
Avon Industrial Park
Avon, MA 02322
Phone 508-588-3030
Toll Free 800-966-3030
FAX 508-580-9943

Pozzi Wood Windows

Manufacturer - Wood Windows & Doors
PO Box 5249
Bend, OR 97708
Phone 503-382-4411
Toll Free 800-547-6880
FAX 503-382-1292

Pro-Glass Technology/Vinyl Tech Inc.

Manufacturer - Windows and Glass Sliding Doors
247 James Street
PO Box 749
Venice, FL 34292
Phone 813-493-4858

Public Supply Company

Manufacturer - Windows and Glass Sliding Doors
1236 NW 4th St.
PO Box 60486
Oklahoma City, OK 73146

Pueblo Truss Co.

Roof Trusses
1982 Aspen Circle
Pueblo, CO 81006
Phone 719-546-1422

Puget Sound Tent & Awning

Awnings
620 Industrial Way S.
Seattle, WA 98108
Phone 206-622-8219

Quaker Window Products Co.

Manufacturer - Windows and Glass Sliding Doors
Hwy. 63 South
PO Box 128
Freeburg, MO 65035
Phone 314-744-5211

Quantum Wood Windows

Windows and Doors
2720 34th St.
Everett, WA 98201
Phone 206-783-9115

R. Cartwright & Co., Ltd.

Window, Door Hardware and Locks
Fleet Works, Straight Rd.
Short Heath, Willenhall, West Midlands
W12 5QY
Great Britain
Phone 011-44-92/2401606
FAX 011-44-92/2495344

R. Lang Co.

*Window & Door Hardware, Windows,
Doors, Skylights*
637 Ohio Ave.
Richmond, CA 94804
Phone 415-237-5055
FAX 415-232-4341

REM Industries

Manufacturer - Interior & Exterior Shutters
PO Box 504
Northborough, MA 01532
Mail Order Available
Phone 508-393-8424

Ralston Regulux Inc.

Windows
926 Bransten Rd.
San Carlos, CA 94070
Phone 415-595-8585

Rasmussen Millwork Inc./Colonial Craft

Wood Window & Door Grilles, Door Decors
2772 Fairview Ave.
St. Paul, MN 55113
Phone 612-631-3110
Toll Free 800-289-6653
FAX 612-631-2925

Rem Industries

Custom Made Wood Interior and Exterior Shutters
PO Box 504
Northborough, MA 01532
Send $2.00 for Catalog/Information
Mail Order Available
Phone 508-393-8424

Remington/Div. of Metal Ind., Inc.

Manufacturer - Windows and Glass Sliding Doors
Magnolia Ind. Pk.
PO Box 1038
Millen, GA 30442
Phone 912-982-4330

Republic Aluminum Inc.

Manufacturer - Windows and Glass Sliding Doors
1725 West Diversey Parkway
Chicago, IL 60614-1009
Phone 312-525-6000

Republic Midwest Inc.

Distributor - Major Brand Wallcover , Wallpaper
500 W. Florida St.
PO Box 04279
Milwaukee, WI 53204
Phone 414-277-1171
FAX 414-277-1405

Reynolds Aluminum Building

Windows
901 Idlewilde Blvd.
Columbia, SC 29201-4827
Phone 803-252-6966
FAX 803-779-1858

Reynolds Metals Company

Manufacturer - Vinyl Siding, Windows
PO Box 27003
Richmond, VA 23261
Phone 804-281-2000

Reynolds Mfg. Company, Inc.

*Manufacturer - Windows and Glass
Sliding Doors*
105 East 6th St.
PO Box 1637
Cisco, TX 76437
Phone 817-442-1380

Rockwell Window Co. Inc.

Wood Windows & Doors
1001 W. Culver Rd.
PO Box 130
Knox, IN 46534
Phone 219-772-2955
FAX 219-772-3824

Roddiscraft Inc.

Manufacturer - Windows & Patio Doors
5112 N. 37th St.
Milwaukee, WI 53209
Phone 414-466-1468

Rogow Window/Ideal Aluminum

*Manufacturer - Windows and Glass
Sliding Doors*
100 West 7th St.
PO Box 48
Bayonne, NJ 07002-0048
Phone 201-437-4300

Rolladen Inc.

Shutters & Windows
1328 Bennett Dr.
Longwood, FL 32750
Phone 305-834-7577

Rollamatic Roofs Incorporated

Skylights
1441 Yosemite Ave.
San Francisco, CA 94124
Catalog/Information Available Free
Phone 415-822-5655
Toll Free 800-345-7392

Rollyson Aluminum Products

*Manufacturer - Windows and Glass
Sliding Doors*
County Roade One, Box 578
South Point, OH 45680
Phone 614-377-4351

Roto-Frank of America, Inc.

Roof Windows and Skylights
PO Box 599
Research Park
Chester, CT 06412
Phone 203-526-4996
FAX 203-526-3785

Royal Plastics, Inc.

*Manufacturer - Window, Door Screens
and Frames*
Box 418 - 1523 Western Ave.
Brookings, SD 57006
Phone 605-692-2171
FAX 605-692-5977

S. D. Davis, Inc.

*Manufacturer - Windows and Glass
Sliding Doors*
2228 East Tioga St.
Philadelphia, PA 19134
Phone 215-535-5400

S.N.F.A.

*Member - Federation of European
Window Manufacturers Association*
9, rue La Perouse
F-75784 Paris
France
Phone 011-33-1/40695218
FAX 011-33-1/47320231

S.Z.F.F./C.S.F.F.

*Member - Federation of European
Window Manufacturers Association*
Seestrasse 105
CH-8027 Zurich
Switzerland
Phone 011-41-1/2017376
FAX 011-41-1/2010482

Windows

Seal-O-Matic Industries Inc.

Windows and Doors
900 Passaic Ave.
E. Newark, NJ 07029

Phone 201-918-8100

FAX 201-918-9737

SealRite Windows, Inc.

Wood Windows and Doors, Frames
3500 N. 44th St.
PO Box 4468
Lincoln, NE 68504

Phone 402-464-0202

FAX 402-467-4101

Season-All Industries Inc.

Manufacturer - Windows & Doors
1480 Wayne Ave.
Indiana, PA 15701

Phone 412-349-4600

Toll Free 800-999-1847

Seaway Manufacturing Corp.

Manufacturer - Windows and Glass Sliding Doors
2250 East 33rd St.
Erie, PA 16510

Phone 814-898-2255

Sebastapol Wood Windows

Custom Doors and Windows
9775 Mill Station Rd.
Sebastopol, CA 95472

Phone 707-823-8796

Shuttercraft

Exterior Shutters and Hardware, In many Styles and Sizes, Finished or Unfinished
282 Stepstone Hill Rd.
Guilford, CT 06437

Catalog/Information Available Free

Mail Order Available

Credit Cards VISA/MC/Check/Money Order

Phone 203-453-1973

FAX 203-245-5969

Simonton Building Products, Inc.

Manufacturer - Windows and Glass Sliding Doors
PO Box 457
Industrial Park
Pennsboro, WV 26415

Phone 304-659-2851

Skotty Aluminum Prod. Co.

Manufacturer - Windows and Glass Sliding Doors
2101 E. Union Bower Rd.
PO Box 226957
Irving, TX 75061

Phone 214-438-4787

Skytech Systems

Manufacturer - Skylights, Sunspaces, Pool Enclosures, Insulated Glass Doors
Columbia County Industrial Park
PO Box 763
Bloomsburg, PA 17815

Send $3.00 for Catalog/Information

Phone 717-752-1111

Toll Free 800-437-5795

FAX 717-752-3535

Solaroll Shade & Shutter Corp.

Manufacturer - Shutters
915 South Dixie Hgwy. E.
Pompano Beach, FL 33060

Phone 305-782-7211

FAX 305-943-3675

Somfy Systems Inc.

Manufacturer - Rolling Shutters, Doors, Awnings, Shades
2 Sutton Place
Edison, NJ 08817

Phone 201-287-3600

Toll Free 800-227-6639

FAX 201-248-0818

Windows

The Complete Sourcebook

South Jersey Awning Co.

Awnings
1125 Oak Ave.
PO Box 925
Pleasantville, NJ 08232
Phone 609-646-2002

Stained Glass Associates

Skylights, Cupboard Panels, Sidelights
PO Box 1531
Raleigh, NC 27602
Phone 919-266-2493

Stanfield Shutter Co. Inc.

Manufacturer - Shutters
3214 South 300 West
Salt Lake City, UT 84115
Mail Order Available
Phone 801-467-8823
FAX 801-467-8871

Sun Control Center Of Indiana

Window Film
1214 Charles Street
Huntington, IN 46750
Catalog/Information Available Free
Phone 219-356-2907
Toll Free 800-662-8468

Sun Window Company, Inc.

Manufacturer - Windows and Glass Sliding Doors
1400 S. Main St.
Troy, MO 63379
Phone 314-528-5887

Sunburst Shutters Inc.

Manufacturer - Custom Shutters
3637 E. Maricopa Freeway
Phoenix, AZ 85040
Phone 602-275-0400

Sunglo Skylights

Skylights
3124 Gillham Plaza
Kansas City, MO 64109
Phone 816-561-1155

Superior Metal Products Co.

Manufacturer - Window, Door Screens and Frames
116 Citation Ct.
Birmingham, AL 35209-6307
Phone 205-945-1200

Tent City Canvas House

Canvas Awnings
3328 N. Duke Ave.
Fresno, CA 93727
Phone 209-292-1221

Teskey Enterprises Inc.

Window and Door Hardware
32 Hammond
Irvine, CA 92718-1637
Phone 714-842-2378

The Alternative Window Co.

Interior Storm Windows
11 Herman Drive
Simsbury, CT 06070
Phone 203-651-3951
Toll Free 800-743-6207

The Astrup Company

Awnings
2937 W. 25th St.
Cleveland, OH 44113
Phone 216-696-2820
FAX 216-696-0977

The Blount Lumber Company

Wood Windows and Doors, Frames
8320 DeMott St.
PO Box 220
Lacona, NY 13083
Phone 315-387-3451
FAX 315-387-6358

The Canvas Smith

Canvas Awnings
165 N. Morgan St.
Chicago, IL 60607
Phone 312-666-0400

Windows

The Gerkin Company

*Manufacturer - Windows and Glass
Sliding Doors*

1501 Zenith Dr.
PO Box 3203
Sioux City, IA 51102

Phone 712-255-5061

The Jordan Companies

*Manufacturer - Windows and Glass
Sliding Doors*

4661 Burbank Rd.
PO Box 29001
Phoenix, AZ 85283

Phone 602-437-3035

The Loxcreen Company, Inc.

*Manufacturer - Window and Door
Screens, Frames*

1630 Old Dunbar Road
PO Box 4004
West Columbia, SC 29171

Phone 803-822-8200

FAX 803-822-8547

The Shutter Depot

*Interior & Exterior Wood Shutters, Heart
Pine Flooring*

Rt. 2, Box 157
Greenville, GA 30222

Mail Order Available

Credit Cards VISA/MC/Check/Money
Order

Phone 706-672-1214

FAX 706-672-1122

Therma-Tru Corporation

Manufacturer - Windows & Doors

1684 Woodlands Drive
PO Box 8780
Maumee, OH 43537

Phone 419-891-7400

Thermal Windows, Inc.

*Manufacturer - Windows and Glass
Sliding Doors*

7003 East 38th St.
Tulsa, OK 74145

Phone 918-665-8998

Thermo-Press Corp.

Manufacturer - Interior Storm Windows

5406 Distributor Drive
Richmond, VA 23225

Mail Order Available

Phone 804-231-2964

FAX 804-232-0454

Thermo-Vu-Sun Lite Industries Inc.

Skylights

51 Rodeo Dr.
Edgewood, NY 11717

Phone 516-243-1000

Thomas Awnings

Awnings

3470 N.W. 7th St.
Miami, FL 33125

Thomas Canopies

Awnings

12067 Tech Rd.
Silver Springs, MD 20904

Phone 301-680-2500

Thorp Awnings Inc.

Awnings

1101 E. 54th St.
Indianapolis, IN 46220

Phone 317-251-9439

Torrance Steel Window Co. Inc.

*Manufacturer - Steel Casement Windows
and Doors*

1819 Abalone Ave.
Torrance, CA 90501

Phone 213-328-9181

FAX 213-328-7485

The Complete Sourcebook

Traco

Manufacturer - Windows and Glass Sliding Doors

Cranberry Ind. Pk.
PO Box 805
Warrendale, PA 15095

Phone 412-335-4450

Trico Mfg./Div. of Tri-State

Manufacturer - Windows and Glass Sliding Doors

Wholesale Building Supplies Inc.
1550 Central Ave.
Cincinnati, OH 45214

Phone 513-381-1231

Twin City Tent & Awning

Awnings - Call for local awning firm

308 East Anthony Dr.
PO Box 638
Urbana, IL 61801

Phone 217-328-5749

Toll Free 800-252-1355

FAX 217-328-5759

U.T.M.M./T.U.M.S.

Member - Federation of European Window Manufacturers Association

C/O Fabrimetal
21, Rue des Drapiers
B-1050 Bruxelles
Belgium

Phone 011-32-2/5102311

FAX 011-32-2/5102301

Uncsaal

Member - Federation of European Window Manufacturers Association

Via Sidoli 11
I-20129 Milano
Italy

Phone 011-39-2/70101530

FAX 011-39-2/76110502

Unique Art Glass Co.

Stained Glass Windows & Lamps

5201 Pattison
St. Louis, MO 63110

Mail Order Available

Phone 314-771-4840

Unitex

Awnings

5175 Commerce Dr. Bldg. L
Baldwin Park, CA 91706

Toll Free 800-456-6282

Universal Components

Manufacturer - Windows and Glass Sliding Doors

1401 Dunn Dr. #106
PO Box 226957
Carrollton, TX 75006

Phone 214-323-9355

VMRG

Member - Federation of European Window Manufacturers Association

Einsteinbaan 1
Postbus 1496
3430 BL Nieuwegein
Netherlands

Phone 011-31-3402/53644

FAX 011-31-3402/53260

Van Liew's

Outdoor Furniture

7343 Prospect Ave.
Kansas City, MO 64132

Phone 816-523-1760

Van Nuys Awnings Co., Inc.

Awnings

5661 Sepulveda Blvd.
Van Nuys, CA 91411

Phone 818-782-8607

Vent Vue

Manufacturer - Redwood Windows

2424 Glover Place
Los Angeles, CA 90031

Phone 213-225-2288

Ventarama Skylight Corp.

Skylights
303 Sunnyside Blvd.
Plainview, NY 11803

Catalog/Information Available Free

Mail Order Available

Phone 516-349-8855
Toll Free 800-237-8096
FAX 516-576-3445

Verband der Fenster

*Member - Federation of European
Window Manufacturers Association*

Bockenheimer
Anlage 13, D-6000 Frankfurt 1
Germany

Phone 011-49-69/550068
FAX 011-49-69/5973644

Vetter Mfg. Co.

Windows & Doors
730 Third Street
Wausau, WI 54402-8007

Phone 715-344-4780
FAX 715-847-6603

Victorian Stained Glass Illusions

Stained Glass Window Applique
PO Box 931
Marinette, WI 54143

Phone 715-735-7425
FAX 715-735-0303

Viking Industries, Inc.

*Manufacturer - Windows and Glass
Sliding Doors*

18600 NE Wilkes Rd.
PO Box 20518
Portland, OR 97218

Phone 503-667-6030

Vinyl Building Products Inc.

Manufacturer - Windows & Doors
One Raritan Rd.
Oakland, NJ 07436

Toll Free 800-468-4695

Vinyl Therm Inc.

Vinyl Windows
321 W. 83rd St.
Bloomington, MN 55420

Phone 612-884-4329

W & F Mfg. Inc.

Window & Door Hardware
600 Paula Ave.
PO Box 30
Glendale, CA 91209

Phone 213-245-7441
FAX 818-502-1847

Walsh Screen & Window Inc.

Screens, Windows
554 East Third St.
Mount Vernon, NY 10553

Mail Order Available

Phone 914-668-7811
FAX 914-668-7872

Weather Shield Mfg., Inc.

*Manufacturer - Wood & Steel Windows,
Doors*
PO Box 309
Medford, WI 54451

Phone 715-748-2100
Toll Free 800-477-6808

Weathervane Window Company

*Windows - Insulated Glass and
Ponderosa Pine Contruction*
PO Box 2424
Kirkland, WA 98033-2424

Catalog/Information Available Free

Phone 206-827-9669
FAX 206-822-9797

Weblon Inc.

Awnings
Fox Island Rd.
PO Box 190
Port Chester, NY 10573

Phone 914-937-3900

The Complete Sourcebook

Wells Aluminum, Inc.

Manufacturer - Windows and Glass Sliding Doors
Rt. 8, PO Box 1470
Moultrie, GA 31768
Phone 912-985-9889

Wenco Windows

Manufacturer - Doors & Windows
Box 1248
Mount Vernon, OH 43050
Catalog/Information Available Free
Phone 614-397-1144
Toll Free 800-458-9128
FAX 614-397-4277

West Coast Windows Inc.

Window Treatments - Blinds
3773 Arnold Ave.
Naples, FL 33942
Phone 813-643-1551
FAX 813-643-7058

Western Insulated Glass co.

Windows & Doors
5621 S. 25th St.
Phoenix, AZ 85040-3628
Phone 602-258-7084

Wilcox Canvas Awnings

Canvas Awnings
622 East Woodruff Ave.
Toledo, OH 43264
Phone 419-241-9181

Willard Shutter Co. Inc.

Manufacturer - Shutters
4420 NW 35th Ct.
Miami, FL 33142
Phone 305-633-0162
Toll Free 800-826-4530
FAX 305-638-8634

Williams Art Glass Studios

Beveled, Etched, Stained Glass - Windows, Doors, Sidelights
22 N. Washington (M-24)
Oxford, MI 48371
Catalog/Information Available Free
Phone 810-628-1111

Williams Shade & Awning

Awnings
3332 Commercial Parkway
Memphis, TN 38116
Phone 901-396-2290

Window Grille Specialists

Decorative Grilles for Windows and Doors
2772 Fairview Ave.
St. Paul, MN 55113
Catalog/Information Available Free
Mail Order Available
Phone 612-645-5736
Toll Free 800-328-5187

Wizard Windows

Leaded and Stained Glass Windows
1200 Kerron St.
Winlock, WA 98596
Catalog/Information Available Free
Phone 206-785-3501
Toll Free 800-233-3847

Yale Ogron Mfg. Co. Inc.

Windows & Doors
671 W. 18th
Hialeah, FL 33010
Phone 305-887-2646
FAX 305-883-1309

Index

Accessory – Aluminum

Index

Accessory

(Bathroom, Decorative, Fireplace, etc.)

Absolute Accessories, 2 - 1
An Affair of the Hearth, 3 - 7
Antique Emporium, 1 - 4
Art Marble and Stone, 1 - 7
Barclay Products Co., 2 - 2
Bathroom Machineries, 2 - 3
Black Country Heritage Ltd., 2 - 3
Blackhawk Marble Mfg., 2 - 3
Brass Tacks Hardware Ltd., 3 - 16
Butler Specialty Co., 6 - 13
Century Fireplace Furnishings Inc., 3 - 21
Coran-Sholes Industries, 11 - 8
DeWeese Woodworking Company, 10 - 3
Decorative Crafts Inc., 6 - 22
Dina Division, 2 - 4
Eddie Bauer Home Collection, 8 - 24
Emsworth Fireplaces Ltd., 1 - 15
Energy Etcetera, 3 - 34
Ethan Allen, Inc., 6 - 27
FV America Corporation, 2 - 4
Feature Fires Ltd., 1 - 16
Franklin Brass Mfg. Co., 2 - 4
Frizelle Enos Co., 3 - 38
Furniture Craft, 6 - 30
Gilmer Potteries, Inc., 2 - 5
Global Mid-South Mfg. Co., 2 - 5
H & M Marble, 2 - 5
Hans Grohe Ltd., 2 - 5
Hart Fireplace Furnishings, 3 - 44
Hewi, Inc., 3 - 45
Hodkin & Jones (Sheffield, etc.) Ltd., 3 - 46
Horchow Home Collection, 6 - 36
Hubbardton Forge & Wood Corp., 11 - 16
Hutch Mfg. Co., 3 - 48
Ideal-Standard Ltd., 2 - 6
Imperial Marble, Inc., 3 - 49
Imperial Stone Ltd., 8 - 35
Kayne & Son Custom Forged Hardware, 3-51
Kemp & George, 3 - 52
Kohler Company, 12 - 14
Larue Products, 8 - 41
Linda's Bed & Bath Ltd., 8 - 42
Mark & Marjorie Allen, 6 - 49
Mills River Industries, Inc., 8 - 46
Minuteman International Co., 3 - 61
Nagykery Imports, Ltd., 6 - 54
Newell Window Furnishings, 8 - 49
Niedermaier Design Inc., 6 - 55
Niermann Weeks, 6 - 55
Nolarec Industries, Inc., 6 - 55
Olde Mill House Shoppe, 6 - 57
P. E. Guerin Inc., 3 - 67

Parisotto, 8 - 51
Perkins & Powell, 2 - 8
Peter Goldberger, 2 - 8
Plow & Hearth, 7 - 5
Richard Burbidge Ltd., 3 - 75
Rustic Home Hardware, 3 - 77
Solway Furniture Inc., 6 - 69
Stone Mfg. Co., 3 - 83
Swe Nova Kitchen & Bath, 10 - 9
The Adams Company, 3 - 87
The Sink Factory, 2 - 11
Tile Emporium International, 3 - 90
Touchstone, 8 - 69
TradeCom International Inc., 3 - 91
Trevi Showers, 2 - 11
Triton PLC, 2 - 12
Wicker Ware Inc., 6 - 83
Wild Wood Gallery, 8 - 76
Yankee Hearth, 3 - 101
Yield House, 6 - 86

Acrylic

(Furniture, Lamps, etc.)

Acrylic Innovations Inc., 6 - 2
Harris Marcus Group, Inc., 11 - 14

Air

(Central Air Grilles, etc.)

Deco-Trol, 3 - 30

Alarm

(Burglar, Fire, etc.)

ABCO Supply Company, 9 - 1
Advanced Security, 9 - 1
Alarm Supply Co., 9 - 1
Burdex Security Co., 9 - 1
EMEL Electronics, 9 - 2
High-Desert Security Systems, 9 - 2
Maple Chase Co., 9 - 2
Mountain West Alarm Supply, 9 - 2
Premier Communications Company, 9 - 3
The J. Goodman Co., 9 - 3
Westco Security Systems Inc., 9 - 3

Aluminum

(Doors, Windows, Downspouts, Gutters, etc.)

A K Exteriors, 6 - 1
A-J Industries Inc., 4 - 1
AAA Aluminum Products Ltd., 3 - 2
AAA Aluminum Stamping, Inc., 12 - 1
Academy Mfg. Co. Inc., 4 - 1
Accurate Aluminum Products, Inc., 3 - 3
Active Window Products, 12 - 2

The Complete Sourcebook

Index - 1

Amish – Antique

Allied Window Inc., 12 - 2
Aluminum Industries of Arkansas, 3 - 6
Amerlite Aluminum Co., Inc., 12 - 3
Anaconda Aluminum, 12 - 4
Arcadia Mfg. Inc., 1 - 5
Arrow Aluminum Ind., Inc., 12 - 4
Burch Co., 12 - 5
Cline Aluminum Doors Inc., 4 - 3
Columbia Metal Products Co., 12 - 7
Dunbarton Corp., 4 - 6
Fleetwood Aluminum Products, Inc.,12 - 9
Florian Greenhouse Inc., 7 - 2
Kinsman Company, 3 - 52
Northwest Aluminum Products, 12 - 18
Peerless Products Inc., 12 - 19
Peerless Wallpaper, 8 - 52
Peterson Window Corp., 12 - 19
Register & Grille Manufacturing Co. 1 - 29
Stairways Inc., 1 - 32

Amish

Amish Furniture Collection, 6 - 4
Folkheart Rag Rugs, 8 - 28
Old Road Furniture Co., 6 - 56

Antique

(Bathroom & Lighting Fixtures, Furniture, Hardware, etc.)

18th Century Hardware Co. Inc., 3 - 1
A-Ball Plumbing Supply, 2 - 1
Acorn Antique Doors, 4 - 1
Adam A. Weschler & Sons, 6 - 2
Adkins Architectural Antiques, 1 - 2
Aged Woods, 5 - 1
Albany Woodworks Inc., 3 - 5
American Furniture Galleries, 6 - 4
American Home Supply, 3 - 6
Angel House Designs, 6 - 4
Anglo-American Brass Co., 3 - 8
Anthropologie, 6 - 4
Antiquarian Traders, 6 - 5
Antique Builders Hardware, 3 - 8
Antique Emporium, 1 - 4
Antique Furniture Copies, 6 - 5
Antique Furniture Workroom, 6 - 5
Antique Hardware Store, 3 - 8
Antique Pine Co., 5 - 1
Architectural Antique Warehouse, 3 - 9
Architectural Antiques Exchange, 1 - 5
Architectural Antiques, 1 - 5
Architectural Antiquities, 1 - 5
Architectural Salvage Company, 1 - 6
Architectural Timber & Millwork, 1 - 6
Arden Forge, 3 - 9
Arkitektura Inc., 6 - 5
Artefact-Architectural Antiques, 1 - 7
Artefacts Architectural Antiques, 1 - 7
Authentic Designs, 3 - 10
B & G Antique Lighting, 11 - 3
B & P Lamp Supply Inc., 11 - 4
Ball and Ball, 6 - 7
Barclay Products Co., 2 - 2
Bargain John's Antiques, 6 - 7
Barnstable Stove Shop, 10 - 1
Bartley Collection, 6 - 8
Bassett & Vollum, 8 - 8
Bathroom Machineries, 2 - 3
Bevan Funnel Limited, 6 - 9
Big Country, 6 - 9
Blue Ox Millworks, 3 - 15
Bombay Company, 6 - 10

Boyles Furniture, 6 - 11
Bradbury & Bradbury Wallpapers, 8 - 11
Brassfinders, 11 - 5
Brass'n Bounty, 11 - 5
British Antique Replicas, 6 - 12
Bryant Stove Works, 3 - 17
By-Gone Days Antiques Inc., 1 - 9
C. H. Southwell, 6 - 13
C. Neri, Antiques, 6 - 13
Caldwell Chair Company, 6 - 13
Campbell Lamp Supply, 11 - 6
Campbellsville Industries, 3 - 19
Castle Burlingame, 5 - 2
Centre Mills Antique Floors & Beams, 5 - 2
Champman Mfg. Co., 11 - 7
Chapin Townsend Furniture, 6 - 15
Chelsea Decorative Metal Co., 1 - 10
City Lights, 11 - 7
Cleveland Wrecking, 1 - 11
Coastal Millworks Inc., 1 - 11
Collection Reproductions, 6 - 17
Colonial Antiques, 1 - 11
Colonial Designs Furniture, 6 - 18
Colonial Williamsburg, 6 - 18
Conant Custom Brass, Inc., 11 - 7
Conklin's Authentic Antique Barnwood, 3-26
Copper Lamps by Hutton, 11 - 8
Country Bed Shop, 6 - 19
Country Furniture Shop, 6 - 19
Country Pine Furniture, 6 - 19
Country Plumbing, 3 - 27
Craft House, 6 - 20
Crawford's Old House Store, 3 - 27
Cricket on the Hearth, Inc., 6 - 20
Crossland Studio, 1 - 12
Crown City Hardware, 3 - 28
Cumberland Woodcraft Co., 1 - 13
DS Locksmithing Company, 3 - 29
Dana Robes Wood Craftsmen, 6 - 21
Danny Alessandro Ltd./Edwin Jackson ,1-14
David W. Lamb Cabinetmaker, 6 - 21
Decker Antique Reproductions, 6 - 22
Decorum Inc., 1 - 14
Deep River Trading Company, 6 - 22
Delaware Electric Imports, 11 - 9
Derby Desk Company, 6 - 23
Dickinsons Architectural Antiques, 1 - 14
Dovetail Antiques, 1 - 15
DuraGlaze Service Corp., 2 - 4
Dutch Products & Supply Co., 3 - 32
Edward P. Schmidt Cabinetmaker, 6 - 25
Eldrid Wheeler, 6 - 25
Elmira Stove And Fireplace, 10 - 4
Ephraim Marsh, 6 - 26
Erickson's Antique Stoves, 10 - 4
Eugenia's Place, 4 - 6
Fellenz Antiques, 3 - 35
Florida Victorian Arch. Antiques, 1 - 17
Gaslight Time Antiques, 11 - 13
Georgian Reproduction, 6 - 31
Gerald Curry-Cabinetmaker, 6 - 31
Goodman Fabrications, 12 - 10
Governor's Antiques & Arch. Materials,1-18
Grandpa Snazzy's Hardware, 3 - 41
Great Gatsby's Auction Galley, 1 - 18
Great Meadows Joinery, 6 - 32
Greeff Fabrics Inc., 8 - 31
Green's Lighting Fixtures, 11 - 14
Greg's Antique Lighting, 11 - 14
Habersham Plantation Corp., 6 - 33
Hammerworks, 11 - 14

Index - 2

The Complete Sourcebook

Index

Appliance – Architectural Details

Hannah Wingate House, 8 - 32
Hearthstone Hardware Co., 3 - 44
Heating Research Co., 3 - 45
Heirloom Reproductions, 6 - 35
Hekman Furniture, 6 - 35
Helen Williams - Delft Tiles, 3 - 45
Henkel-Harris, 6 - 35
Heritage Lanterns, 11 - 14
Historic Charleston Reproductions, 6 - 35
Historic Housefitters, 3 - 46
Hollingsworth, 6 - 36
Homestead Furniture, 6 - 36
Horesfeathers Architectural Antiques, 1 - 20
Howard's Antique Lighting, 11 - 16
Howerton Antique Reproductions, 6 - 37
Hyde Park Antiques, Ltd., 6 - 38
Investment Antiques & Collectibles, 1 - 20
Iron Intentions Forge, 3 - 49
Irvin's Craft Shop, 11 - 17
JMW Gallery, 6 - 39
James Lea-Cabinetmaker, 6 - 39
Janis Aldridge, Inc., 6 - 40
Jeffrey P. Greene, Furniture Maker, 6 - 40
John Congdon, Cabinetmaker, 6 - 40
John F. Lavoie Windows, 12 - 13
Karges Furniture Co., Inc., 6 - 41
Kathleen B. Smith, 8 - 39
Keokuk Stove Works, 3 - 52
Lampshades of Antique, 11 - 19
LeFort, 6 - 44
Leonard's Reproductions & Antiques, 6 - 45
Lester H. Berry & Company, 11 - 19
Lewis Mittman, Inc., 6 - 45
Lexington Furniture Industries, 6 - 46
Lion House Antique (Copies, etc.), 6 - 46
Liz's Antique Hardware, 3 - 55
M. Wolchonok & Son Inc., 3 - 56
Mac The Antique Plumber, 3 - 56
Magnolia Hall, 6 - 48
Mahantango Manor Inc., 8 - 44
Mahogany Craft, 6 - 48
Manor House, 6 - 49
Marion H. Campbell, 1 - 23
Mark & Marjorie Allen, 6 - 49
Mark Sales Co. Inc., 6 - 50
Marshall Galleries, Inc., 1 - 23
Mendes Antiques, 6 - 52
Merritt's Antiques Inc., 6 - 52
Metropolitan Artifacts, Inc., 1 - 23
Miracle Method Bathroom Restoration, 2-7
Mona Liza Fine Furniture Inc., 6 - 53
Monroe Coldren & Sons, 3 - 62
Mountain Lumber Co., 5 - 7
Nagykery Imports, Ltd., 6 - 54
Norman's Handmade Reproductions, 6 -55
North Fields Restorations, 3 - 65
Nostalgia, 1 - 25
Nottingham Gallery, 4 - 12
Oak Craft Inc., 6 - 56
Old Fashioned Milk Paint Co., 3 - 66
Old Home Building & Restoration, 3 - 66
Old Road Furniture Co., 6 - 56
Olde Theatre Architectural Salvage, 1 - 26
Ole Fashion Things, 2 - 8
Omega Too, 2 - 8
Paxton Hardware Ltd., 3 - 68
Pelnick Wrecking Company, Inc., 3 - 69
Period Furniture Hardware, 6 - 59
Period Lighting Fixtures, 11 - 25
Phyllis Kennedy Restoration Hardware, 3 - 70
Pine & Design Imports, 6 - 59

Pulaski Furniture Corp., 6 - 61
Queen Ann Furniture Co., Inc., 6 - 61
Queen City Architectural Salvage, 1 - 28
Queen City Glass Ltd., 8 - 54
Ralston Furniture Reproductions, 6 - 62
Randall Tysinger, 6 - 62
Rare Wood, 4 - 14
Restoration Resource, 3 - 74
Richard Blaschke Cabinet Glass, 3 - 75
River City Woodworks, 5 - 8
Rufkahr's, 3 - 77
Scott's Hardware Inc., 6 - 66
Seventh Heaven, 6 - 67
Southern Accents Architectural Antique, 1 - 31
St. Louis Antique Lighting Co., 11 - 29
Stamford Wrecking, 3 - 82
Statesville Chair Company, 6 - 71
Stephen Adams Furniture Makers, 6 - 72
Strafford House, 6 - 72
Sylvan Brandt Inc., 5 - 9
The Antique Catalog, 6 - 74
The Antique Plumber, 3 - 87
The Bank Architectural Antiques, 1 - 34
The Bartley Collections Ltd., 6 - 74
The Brass Knob, 3 - 87
The Brass Lion, 11 - 31
The Butcher Company, 6 - 75
The Coldren Company, 3 - 88
The Emporium, 1 - 34
The Homestead, 10 - 10
The Odd Chair Company, 6 - 76
The Rug Warehouse, 8 - 67
The Tin Bin, 11 - 32
The Wicker Garden, 6 - 77
The Woods Company, 5 - 10
Timeless Design, Inc., 8 - 69
United House Wrecking, Inc., 3 - 93
Urban Archaeology, 1 - 35
Urban Artifacts, 1 - 35
Vanderkellen Galleries, 8 - 71
Victorian Revival, 11 - 34
Victorian Showcase, 6 - 81
Vintage Lumber & Construction Co., 5 - 11
Vitistor's Catalog, 2 - 12
Wendover's Limited, 6 - 82
Westlake Architectural Antiques, 1 - 37
White of Mebane, 6 - 83
Wicker Fixer, 6 - 83
William H. James Co., 6 - 84
Wooden Nickel Architectural Antique, 1 - 38
Woodhouse, 5 - 11

Appliance

(Built In, etc.)

Gaggenau USA Corporation, 10 - 4
Iron-A-Way Inc., 8 - 36

Arch

Grand Era Reproductions, 4 - 8
May's Architectural Detailing, 7 - 4
NMC Focal Point, 1 - 24
Raymond Enkeboll Designs, 1 - 28
Walpole Woodworkers, 6 - 81
Western Archrib, 3 - 97

Architectural Details

A.F. Schwerd Manufacturing Co., 1 - 1
ACCRA Wood Products Ltd., 1 - 1
AFG Industries, Inc., 1 - 2
Abaroot Manufacturing Company, 1 - 2
Ability Woodwork Co. Inc., 1 - 2

The Complete Sourcebook

Index - 3

Architectural Details — Architectural Details

Index

Accent Millwork Inc., 1 - 2
Accurate Lock & Hardware Co., 1 - 2
Acorn Structures Inc., 1 - 2
Acrylic Innovations Inc., 6 - 2
Adkins Architectural Antiques, 1 - 2
Adornments for Architecture, 1 - 2
Algoma Hardwoods, Inc., 1 - 2
Allied Bronze Corp., 1 - 3
American Architectural Art Company, 1 - 3
American Custom Millwork Inc., 1 - 3
Anderson-McQuaid Company Inc., 1 - 4
Andreas Lehman Fine Glasswork, 1 - 4
Antiquarian Traders, 6 - 5
Antique Emporium, 1 - 4
Anything Fiberglass, 1 - 4
Arcadia Mfg. Inc., 1 - 5
Architectural Antique Warehouse, 3 - 9
Architectural Antiques Exchange, 1 - 5
Architectural Antiques, 1 - 5
Architectural Antiquities, 1 - 5
Architectural Artifacts, 1 - 5
Architectural Cataloguer, USA, 1 - 5
Architectural Elements, 1 - 5
Architectural Grille, 1 - 5
Architectural Iron Company, 1 - 6
Architectural Lathe & Mill, 1 - 6
Architectural Paneling, 1 - 6
Architectural Salvage Company, 1 - 6
Architectural Systems, Inc., 1 - 6
Aristocrat Products Inc., 1 - 6
Armstrong World Industries Inc., 1 - 6
Art Directions, 1 - 7
Artefact-Architectural Antiques, 1 - 7
Artefacts Architectural Antiques, 1 - 7
Artistry in Veneers Inc., 1 - 7
Baldinger Architectural Lighting, Inc., 1 - 7
Blenko Glass Company Inc., 3 - 15
Blue Ox Millworks, 3 - 15
Boston Turning Works, 1 - 8
Bow House, 1 - 8
Boyertown Planing Mill Co., 1 - 8
Brill & Walker Associates Inc., 1 - 9
By-Gone Days Antiques Inc., 1 - 9
C. G. Girolami & Sons, 1 - 9
Canner Inc., 8 - 13
Cape Cod Cupola Co., Inc., 1 - 9
Cascade Wood Products Inc., 1 - 10
Center Lumber Company, 1 - 10
Chadsworth, Inc., 1 - 10
Cheyenne Company, 1 - 10
Cider Hill Woodworks, 1 - 10
CinderWhit & Company, 1 - 10
Classic Architectural Specialties, 1 - 10
Classic Mouldings Inc., 1 - 11
Cleveland Wrecking, 1 - 11
Coastal Millworks Inc., 1 - 11
Colonial Cupolas Inc., 1 - 11
Constantine's, 1 - 12
Continental Woodworking Co., 1 - 12
Crossland Studio, 1 - 12
Crown Plastering, 1 - 12
Curvoflite Inc., 1 - 13
Custom & Historic Millwork, 1 - 13
Custom Hardwood Productions, 1 - 13
Customwood Mfg. Co., 1 - 13
Deck House, 1 - 14
Decorative Plaster Supply Co., 1 - 14
Decorators Supply Corp., 1 - 14
Decorum Inc., 1 - 14
Dimitrios Klitsas, 1 - 14
Driwood Moulding Co., 8 - 24

Drums Sash & Dove Co., 1 - 15
Entol Industries, 1 - 16
Felber Ornamental Plastering Corp., 1 - 16
Fibertech Corporation, 1 - 16
Fine Woodworking by Living Tree, 6 - 28
Fischer & Jirouch Company, 1 - 16
Flex Trim, 12 - 9
Florida Victorian Arch. Antiques, 1 - 17
Florida Wood Moulding & Trim, 1 - 17
Frederick Wilbur, Carver, 1 - 17
Fritz V. Sterbak Antiques, 1 - 17
Fypon Molded Millwork, 1 - 17
Garland Woodcraft Co. Inc., 1 - 18
Glostal Systems Ltd., 1 - 18
Gotham Inc., 1 - 18
Governor's Antiques & Arch. Materials, 1 - 18
Great Gatsby's Auction Galley, 1 - 18
H.I.C. Millwork Inc., 1 - 19
Hallidays America Inc., 1 - 19
Hampton Decor, 1 - 19
Hartman-Sanders Co., 1 - 19
Heritage Woodcraft, 1 - 20
Horesfeathers Architectural Antiques, 1 - 20
Hubbell Lighting Inc., 11 - 16
Investment Antiques & Collectibles, 1 - 20
J. A. du Lac Company, 1 - 20
J. P. Weaver Co., 1 - 21
J. Zeluck Inc., 1 - 21
K & G, 1 - 21
Kentucky Millwork Inc., 1 - 21
Kneeshaw Woodworking Installations 1 - 21
Kolson, 1 - 21
Konceptual Design, 1 - 21
Lynn Lumber Company, 1 - 22
MacBeath Hardwood Co., 1 - 22
Mad River Woodworks, 1 - 22
Maine Architectural Millwork, Inc., 1 - 22
Materials Unlimited, 1 - 23
Metropolitan Artifacts, Inc., 1 - 23
Minton Co., 6 - 53
NMC Focal Point, 1 - 24
New England Tool Company, 3 - 64
Newman Brothers Inc., 1 - 25
Nostalgia, 1 - 25
Olde Theatre Architectural Salvage, 1 - 26
Ole Fashion Things, 2 - 8
Outwater Plastic Industries, 1 - 26
Palmer Creek Hewn Wood Products, 1 - 27
Partelow Custom Wood Turnings, 1 - 27
Pilkington Glass Ltd., 1 - 27
Pridgen Cabinet Works, Inc., 1 - 28
Queen City Architectural Salvage, 1 - 28
Ralph H. Simpson Co., 1 - 28
Randall Bros. Inc., 1 - 28
Raymond Enkeboll Designs, 1 - 28
Register & Grille Manufacturing Co. , 1 - 29
Rennovator's Supply, 1 - 29
Riverview Millworks Inc., 1 - 29
S. A. Bendheim Co. Inc., 1 - 30
Saco Manufacturing & Woodworking, 1 - 30
Salas & Co., 1 - 30
San Francisco Victoriana, 1 - 30
Seneca Millwork Inc., 1 - 31
Shaper Lighting, 11 - 29
Shatterproof Glass Corp., 1 - 31
Southern Accents Architectural Antiqs,1-31
Sporthill Inc., 1 - 32
Stamford Wrecking, 3 - 82
States Industries Inc., 1 - 32
Style-Mark, Inc., 1 - 33
Taco, 1 - 33

Index - 4

The Complete Sourcebook

Index

Armoire – Bath

Taconic Architectural Woodworking,   1 - 33
Tallahassee Mouldings & Millwork,   1 - 33
The Balmer Studios Inc.,   1 - 34
The Bank Architectural Antiques,   1 - 34
The Brass Knob, 3 - 87
The Emporium,   1 - 34
The Fixture Exchange,   2 - 11
The Salamander and the Web,   1 - 34
The Woods Company,   5 - 10
United States Woodworking, Inc.,   1 - 35
Urban Archaeology,   1 - 35
Urban Artifacts,   1 - 35
Uroboros Glass Studios Inc.,   1 - 36
Vetter Stone Co.,   1 - 36
Vicor Corp.,   1 - 36
Vintage Pine Company,   5 - 11
Vintage Wood Works,   1 - 36
W. F. Norman Corporation,   1 - 36
Walker & Zanger,   3 - 95
Westlake Architectural Antiques,   1 - 37
Windham Millwork Inc.,   1 - 37
Wohners Inc.,   1 - 37
Woodcraft Architectural Millwork Inc., 1 - 37
Wooden Nickel Architectural Antique,   1 - 38
Woodstone Company,   1 - 38
Worthington Group, Ltd.,   1 - 38
Wright's Stained Glass,   1 - 38

Armoire

The Keeping Room,   6 - 75

Ash

BRE Lumber,   3 - 11
Bangkok International, 5 - 2
Boen Hardwood Flooring, 5 - 2
EDLCO, 3 - 33
Livermore Wood Floors, 5 - 6
River Bend Turnings,   1 - 29
Treework Services Ltd., 5 - 10

Atrium

Atrium Door and Window Co.,   4 - 2
Four Seasons,   3 - 38

Awning

A & A International,   12 - 1
A & E Blind & Awning Co.,   8 - 1
AAA Aluminum Products Ltd.,   3 - 2
AWNCO Inc.,   3 - 2
Awnings By Jay, 12 - 4
Awnings by Shuster,   3 - 10
Baraboo Tent & Awning, 3 - 12
Benton Harbor Awning & Tent,   3 - 14
Bower's Awning & Shade,   3 - 16
Capital City Awning,   3 - 20
Carroll Awning Co. Inc.,   3 - 20
Chesterfield Awning Co.,   3 - 24
City Awning of South Bend,   3 - 24
Coastal Canvas & Awning,   3 - 25
Custom Canvas Awning, Inc.,   3 - 28
Dean Custom Awnings,   3 - 30
Delray Awnings, Inc.,   3 - 30
Dickson Elbertson Mills, Inc.,   3 - 31
Dize Company,   3 - 31
Durking Awning Corp.,   3 - 32
Enduro Fabric Awnings, 3 - 34
Glen Raven Mills Inc., 3 - 40
Globe Canvas Products Co.,   12 - 9
Hogshire Industries Inc.,   12 - 11
Houston Canvas & Awning,   12 - 11
Inter Trade Inc.,   12 - 12

JIL Industries, 12 - 12
John Boyle & Co. Inc., 12 - 12
Kohler Awning, Inc.,   2 - 6
L.F. Pease Co., 12 - 14
Lawrence Canvas Products, Co., 12 - 14
Miami Awning,   12 - 16
Moran Canvas Products Inc.,   12 - 16
Morgan Industries,   12 - 16
Mt. Lebanon Awning & Tent Co.,   12 - 16
Nelson A. Taylor Co., Inc.,   12 - 17
New Haven Awning Co.,   12 - 17
O.K. McCloy Awnings,   12 - 18
O'Neals Tarpaulin & Awning Co.,   12 - 18
P. J. McBride Inc.,   12 - 19
Pike Tent & Awning Co., Inc.,   12 - 19
Puget Sound Tent & Awning,   12 - 20
Somfy Systems Inc.,   12 - 23
South Jersey Awning Co.,   12 - 24
Tent City Canvas House, 12 - 24
The Astrup Company,   12 - 24
The Canvas Smith,   12 - 24
Thomas Awnings, 12 - 25
Thomas Canopies,   12 - 25
Thorp Awnings Inc.,   12 - 25
Twin City Tent & Awning,   12 - 26
Unitex, 12 - 26
Van Nuys Awnings Co., Inc.,   12 - 26
Weblon Inc.,   12 - 27
Wilcox Canvas Awnings, 12 - 28
Williams Shade & Awning,   12 - 28

Azteca

(Clay Roofing, etc.)
Cal-Shake, Inc.,   3 - 19

Bamboo

(Bannister, Furniture, etc.)
Richard Gervais Collection,   6 - 63
W. R. Outhwaite & Son, 3 - 95
Woolums Mfg. Inc.,   6 - 86

Baseboard

(Heating, etc.)
Axeman-Anderson Co.,   3 - 11
Burnham,   3 - 18
Cadet Mfg. Co., 3 - 19
Crown Boiler,   3 - 28
Edwards Engineering,   3 - 33
Radiant Technology,   3 - 73
Weil-McLain,   3 - 97

Basement

(Doors, Toilets, etc.)
Combination Door Company,   4 - 4
Dilworth Manufacturing Co.,   12 - 8
McPherson Inc., 2 - 7
The Bilco Co.,   4 - 17

Basin

A-Ball Plumbing Supply, 2 - 1
Angelo Amaru Tile & Bath Collection,   3 - 8
Ideal-Standard Ltd.,   2 - 6
Perkins & Powell,   2 - 8

Bath

(Fixtures, Tile, Showers, Vanities, etc.)
ACIF Ceramiche S.R.L.,   3 - 2
Absolute Accessories,   2 - 1
Ace Shower Door Co. Inc.,   2 - 1
Alfa Ceramiche, 3 - 5

The Complete Sourcebook

Index - 5

Bath – Bath

Index

Amaru Tile, 3 - 6
American Brass Mfg., 10 - 1
American International, 3 - 6
American Shower Door Corp., 2 - 2
American Standard, 2 - 2
Ann Sacks Tile & Stone, 3 - 8
Antiche Ceramiche D'Talia (ACIT) S.R.L.3 - 8
Antique Baths & Kitchens, 2 - 2
Antique Hardware Store, 3 - 8
Aqua Glass Corporation, 2 - 2
Aston Matthews, 2 - 2
Barclay Products Co., 2 - 2
Basco, 2 - 2
BathEase, 2 - 2
Bathroom Jewlery, 2 - 2
Bathroom Machineries, 2 - 3
Baths From The Past Inc., 2 - 3
Beach Craft, Inc., 2 - 3
Black Country Heritage Ltd., 2 - 3
Blackhawk Marble Mfg., 2 - 3
Brass & Traditional Sinks Ltd., 2 - 3
Brass Tacks Hardware Ltd., 3 - 16
Broadway Industries, 2 - 3
CSL Lighting Mfg., 11 - 6
California Tile Supply, 3 - 19
Cancos Tile Corporation, 3 - 19
Carlos Shower Doors Inc., 2 - 3
Century Shower Door, Inc., 2 - 3
Ceramica Candia S.P.A., 3 - 22
Ceramica Colli Di Sassuolo S.P.A., 3 - 22
Ceramica Del Conca S.P.A., 3 - 22
Ceramica Ilsa S.P.A., 3 - 22
Ceramica Panaria S.P.A., 3 - 22
Ceramiche Atlas Concorde S.P.A., 3 - 22
Ceramiche Brunelleschi S.P.A., 3 - 22
Ceramiche Cuoghitalia S.P.A., 3 - 22
Ceramiche Edilcuoghi S.P.A., 3 - 23
Ceramiche Edilgres-Sirio S.P.A., 3 - 23
Ceramografia Artigiana S.P.A., 3 - 23
Cerdomus Ceramiche S.P.A., 3 - 23
Cerim Ceramiche S.P.A., 3 - 23
Chatham Brass Co., Inc., 11 - 7
Cheviot Products Inc., 2 - 3
Cisa-Cerdisa-Smov, 3 - 24
Clivus Multrum, Inc., 2 - 4
Coastal Industries, Inc., 2 - 4
Conservation Building Products Ltd., 3 - 26
Cooperativa Ceramica D'Imola A.R.L., 3 - 27
Crane Plumbing, 8 - 19
Crest Distributors, 3 - 28
Crown Point Cabinetry, 10 - 3
Custom Hardware Mfg., Inc., 3 - 29
D & B Tile Distributors, 3 - 29
D & D Natural Stone and Marble, 3 - 29
Dado Ceramica S.R.L., 3 - 29
Davis & Warshow Inc., 10 - 3
De Best Mfg. Co., Inc., 3 - 30
DeWeese Woodworking Company, 10 - 3
Decorum Inc., 1 - 14
Dickinsons Architectural Antiques, 1 - 14
Dina Division, 2 - 4
EFRON America, 2 - 4
East Coast Tile Imports Inc., 3 - 33
Eljer, 10 - 3
Elkay Mfg. Co., 10 - 3
F & M Plumbing Supply, 2 - 4
FV America Corporation, 2 - 4
Faneuil Furniture Hardware Co. Inc., 6 - 28
Faucet Outlet, 10 - 4
Fellenz Antiques, 3 - 35
Fleurco Industries 1963 Ltd., 10 - 4

Florida Ceramic Tile Center, 3 - 37
Fox Woodcraft, 10 - 4
Franklin Brass Mfg. Co., 2 - 4
G.M. Ketcham Co., Inc., 2 - 5
Gabbianelli S.R.L., 3 - 39
Garofalo Studio, 2 - 5
Gemini Bath & Kitchen, 2 - 5
Gibraltar, 3 - 40
Gilmer Potteries, Inc., 2 - 5
Global Mid-South Mfg. Co., 2 - 5
Gracious Home, 10 - 5
Granite Lake Pottery, 2 - 5
Grohe America Inc., 10 - 5
H & M Marble, 2 - 5
H & W Plastics Inc., 2 - 5
Hans Grohe Ltd., 2 - 5
Hansa America, 10 - 5
Harden Industries, 2 - 5
Hastings Tile & Il Bagno Collection, 3 - 44
Hewi, Inc., 3 - 45
Hiawatha, Inc., 2 - 5
Home Decorators Collection, 11 - 15
Homecrest Corporation, 10 - 5
Hubbardton Forge & Wood Corp., 11 - 16
Huntington/Pacific Ceramics, Inc., 3 - 48
Hutcherson Tile, 3 - 48
I. C. R. S.P.A. (Appiani, etc.), 3 - 48
Ideal-Standard Ltd., 2 - 6
Imperial Marble, Inc., 3 - 49
Imperial Shower Door Co., 2 - 6
Interbath Inc., 2 - 6
International Supply Co., 2 - 6
Jacuzzi Inc., 2 - 6
Jado Bathroom & Hardware Mfg. Co., 2 - 6
James Gibbons Format Ltd., 12 - 12
KWC/Rohl Corp., 10 - 6
Kallista, 2 - 6
Kemp & George, 3 - 52
Kimstock Inc., 2 - 6
Kohler Company, 12 - 14
Kraft, 2 - 6
LaFaenza America Inc., 3 - 53
LaMont Ltd., 2 - 6
Lasco Bathware, 2 - 7
Latco Ceramic Tile, 3 - 54
Lenape Products, Inc., 2 - 7
Linda's Bed & Bath Ltd., 8 - 42
Lippert Corp., 2 - 7
L'esperance Tile Works, 3 - 53
M & H Design & Home Center, 2 - 7
MDM Marble Co. Inc., 2 - 7
Made-Rite Aluminum Window Co., 12 - 15
Marcello Marble & Tile PLS, 2 - 7
McPherson Inc., 2 - 7
Merit Cabinet Distributors, 2 - 7
Metco Tile Distributors, 3 - 60
Midland Manufacturing Corp., 2 - 7
Mission Pipe & Supply, 2 - 7
Moen, 10 - 7
Monarch Metal Products Corp., 2 - 8
Mosaic Supplies Inc., 3 - 62
National Ceramics of Florida, 3 - 63
National Kitchen & Bath Association, 10 - 7
Nemo Tile Company, Inc., 3 - 63
Nevamar Corporation, 10 - 7
Nicola Ceramics & Marble, 3 - 64
Nope, 2 - 8
Nordic Showers, 2 - 8
Old Country Ceramic Tile, 3 - 66
Old World Hardware Co., 3 - 66
Olde Mill House Shoppe, 6 - 57

Index - 6

The Complete Sourcebook

Index

Beam – Bed

Ole Fashion Things,   2 - 8
P. E. Guerin Inc.,   3 - 67
PE O'Hair & Co.,   2 - 8
Pacific Faucets,   2 - 8
Paragon Products,   10 - 8
Perkins & Powell,   2 - 8
Peter Goldberger,   2 - 8
Peter Josef Korzilius Soehne GmbH, 3 - 69
Phoenix Products Inc., 3 - 70
Pipe Dreams,   2 - 9
Plastic Creations Inc., 2 - 9
Poggenpohl U.S.A. Corp, 10 - 8
Porcher Ltd.,   2 - 9
Praire Marketing,   3 - 71
Price Pfister Inc.,   2 - 9
Puccio Marble & Onyx,   3 - 72
Quintessentials,   2 - 9
Rams Imports,   3 - 73
Rapetti Faucets,   2 - 9
Raphael Ltd.,   2 - 9
Reflections USA,   2 - 9
Regal Rugs Inc.,   8 - 55
Rockingham Plumbing Supply,   2 - 9
Roman Limited,   2 - 9
Santa Catalina, 3 - 77
Sherle Wagner,   2 - 10
Sherwood Shower Door Co.,   2 - 10
Shower-Rite Corp.,   2 - 10
Showerlux U.S.A.,   2 - 10
Showerlux UK Ltd.,   2 - 10
SieMatic Corporation/Smallbone, 10 - 9
Smallbone & Co. Ltd.,   10 - 9
Solid Surface Products Inc.,   2 - 10
St. Thomas Creations Inc.,   2 - 10
Sterling Plumbing Group,   2 - 10
Sun-Mar Corp.,   7 - 7
Sunrise Specialty,   2 - 10
Surrey Shoppe Interiors,   8 - 64
Swe Nova Kitchen & Bath,   10 - 9
The Antique Hardware Store,   3 - 87
The Antique Plumber,   3 - 87
The Broadway Collection,   2 - 11
The Chicago Faucet Company,   2 - 11
The Faucet Factory,   2 - 11
The Linen Gallery,   8 - 67
The Shop,   3 - 89
The Sink Factory,   2 - 11
Thermo Spas Inc.,   2 - 11
Tile Emporium International,   3 - 90
Tile West Distributors, 3 - 91
Tomlin Industries Inc., 2 - 11
TradeCom International Inc.,   3 - 91
Triton PLC,   2 - 12
Tub-Master Corp.,   2 - 12
Universal Bath Systems, 2 - 12
Urban Archaeology,   1 - 35
Valley Fibrebath Ltd., 2 - 12
Villeroy & Boch (USA, etc.) Inc.,   2 - 12
Villeroy & Boch AG,   2 - 12
Villeroy & Boch Ltd.,   2 - 12
Vintage Plumbing,   2 - 12
Vitistor's Catalog,   2 - 12
W. T. Weaver & Sons,   2 - 12
Walker Industries,   3 - 96
Water Faucets, 2 - 13
Water Saver Faucet Co., 2 - 13
Watercolors Inc.,   2 - 13
Wayne Tile Company,   3 - 96
Western Pottery Co. Inc.,   2 - 13
Wicker Ware Inc.,   6 - 83
Woodstock Furniture Ltd.,   6 - 86

Beam

Albany Woodworks Inc.,   3 - 5
Alpine Engineer Products Inc.,   3 - 5
Anthony Forest Product Co.,   3 - 8
Architectural Timber & Millwork,   1 - 6
Bear Creek Lumber,   3 - 13
Broad-Axe Beam Co.,   5 - 2
Browne Winther & Co. Ltd.,   1 - 9
Centre Mills Antique Floors & Beams,   5 - 2
Conklin's Authentic Antique Barnwood, 3 - 26
E. F. Bufton & Son Builders,   1 - 15
Goodwin Lumber, 3 - 41
Guyon, 5 - 4
Kaatskill Post & Beam, 1 - 21
M & H Truss Co. Inc.,   3 - 56
Pacific Post & Beam,   3 - 68
River City Woodworks,   5 - 8
The Joinery Company,   5 - 10
The Woods Company,   5 - 10
Timberpeg,   1 - 35
Vermont Frames, 1 - 36
Western Archrib,   3 - 97
Willamette Industries Inc.,   3 - 99

Bed

American Starbuck,   6 - 4
Amish Country Collection,   6 - 4
Art In Iron,   6 - 5
Bales Furniture Mfg.,   6 - 7
Bedlam Brass,   6 - 8
Bedquarters,   6 - 8
Beds By Benzcian, Inc., 6 - 9
Big Table Furniture,   6 - 9
Boudoir Furniture Mfg. Corp.,   6 - 10
Brass Bed Factory,   6 - 11
Brass Bed Shoppe,   6 - 11
Brass Beds Direct,   6 - 11
Charles P. Rogers,   6 - 16
Charleston Iron Works, 6 - 16
Cohasset Colonials,   6 - 17
Comoexport-Divisione Di Cantu, 6 - 18
Country Bed Shop,   6 - 19
Designer Repros,   6 - 23
Elmo Guernsey, 6 - 26
Flexform,   6 - 28
Flexform,   6 - 28
Gallery of H B, 6 - 31
Good Tables Inc.,   6 - 32
Grabell of California, 11 - 13
Grange Furniture, Inc., 6 - 32
Hollingsworth, 6 - 36
Hunt Galleries, Inc., 6 - 38
Isabel Brass Furniture, 6 - 39
J.A.G. International Inc.,   6 - 39
Kenneth Winslow Furniture,   6 - 41
Kopil & Associates Timeless Furniture, 6 - 43
Kraemer Furniture Designs,   6 - 43
Lisa Victoria Beds,   6 - 46
Masterworks,   6 - 51
Murphy Bed Company Inc.,   6 - 54
Northwoods Furniture Co.,   6 - 56
Old Hickory Furniture Co. Inc., 6 - 56
Ole Timey Furniture Co.,   6 - 57
Osborne Wood Products Inc.,   6 - 57
Ottawa Brass Ltd.,   6 - 57
Pete Bissonette & Company,   6 - 59
Reid Classics, 6 - 62
Roberts Brass Company, 6 - 64
Room & Board,   6 - 64
Seventh Heaven, 6 - 67

The Complete Sourcebook

Bedding – Beech

Splendor in Brass, 6 - 70
Steel Gallery, 6 - 71
The Bed Factory, 6 - 74
The Bedpost, 6 - 74
The Keeping Room, 6 - 75
Victorian Brass Works Ltd., 6 - 80
Windspire, 6 - 85

Bedding

Eddie Bauer Home Collection, 8 - 24
Zarbin & Associates, Inc., 6 - 87

Bedroom

AEL Furniture Group, 6 - 1
Acmetrack Ltd., 6 - 2
Allied Manufacturing Co. (London) Ltd., 6 - 3
Anglo Nordic Marketing (UK) Ltd., 6 - 4
Aram Designs Ltd., 6 - 5
Ashby & Horner Joinery Ltd., 6 - 6
Athens Furniture, 6 - 6
Bedroom Secrets, 8 - 9
Bevan Funnell Ltd., 6 - 9
Boyles Furniture, 6 - 11
CS Brooks Corp., 8 - 13
Cabin Creek Furniture, 6 - 13
Carleton Furniture Group Ltd., 6 - 14
Carter Canopies, 8 - 15
Cochrane Furniture Co., 6 - 17
Coming Home, 8 - 18
Davis Cabinet Company, 6 - 22
Dean & Brook Ltd., 6 - 22
Del Tongo (UK, etc.) Ltd., 6 - 22
Design Furniture Mfg. Ltd., 6 - 23
E.C. Hodge Ltd., 6 - 25
Evertidy Furniture Ltd., 6 - 27
Fieldcrest Cannon, Inc., 8 - 27
Griffon Furniture Ltd., 6 - 33
Hamlet Furniture Ltd., 6 - 34
Harts Mfg. Co., Inc., 6 - 34
Holder Pearce, 6 - 36
Hostess Furniture Ltd., 6 - 37
House of Brougham Collection, 6 - 37
Hyperion Wall Furniture Ltd., 6 - 38
Hyphen Fitted Furniture, 6 - 38
J. T. Ellis & Co. Ltd., 6 - 39
John Pulsford Associates Ltd., 6 - 40
Kesterport Ltd., 6 - 42
L & J.G. Stickley, Inc., 6 - 43
Lanzet (UK, etc.) Ltd., 6 - 44
Lehigh Furniture, 6 - 45
Leverwood Ltd., 6 - 45
Lexterten Ltd., 6 - 46
Limelight Bedrooms, 6 - 46
Linda's Bed & Bath Ltd., 8 - 42
Mark Wilkinson Furniture Ltd., 6 - 50
Martin & Frost Ltd., 6 - 50
Mereway Developments Ltd., 6 - 52
Monzie Joinery Ltd., 6 - 54
Neil Rogers Interiors, 6 - 54
Options Bedrooms Ltd., 6 - 57
Pegram Contracts Ltd., 6 - 59
Pel Ltd., 6 - 59
Plaza Furniture Gallery, 6 - 60
Pulaski Furniture Corp., 6 - 61
Quality Furniture Co., 6 - 61
Quality Furniture Market, 6 - 61
Rebwood Inc., 6 - 62
Renray Group Ltd., 6 - 63
Royal Strathclyde Blindcraft Ind., 6 - 65
Ruth's Custom Bedspreads, 8 - 57
Sagga Furnishings Ltd., 6 - 65

Saraband Furniture Co., 6 - 66
Slumberland PLC, 6 - 69
South West Joinery Co. Ltd., 6 - 70
Stag Meredew Furniture Ltd., 6 - 71
Staples & Co. Ltd., 6 - 71
Star Interiors Ltd., 6 - 71
Stuart Interiors, 6 - 72
Swan Brass Bed, 6 - 73
Sylmar Technology Ltd., 6 - 73
The Antique Quit Source, 10 - 9
The Linen Gallery, 8 - 67
The Sofa Factory, 6 - 76
The Yorkshire Door Company Ltd., 4 - 17
Thomasville Furniture, 6 - 77
Thos. Moser, Cabinetmakers, 6 - 77
Universal Bedroom Furniture Ltd., 6 - 80
Van Stee Corp., 6 - 80
Vermont Furniture Designs, 6 - 80
Vermont Tubbs, 6 - 80
W. G. Undrill Ltd., 6 - 81
Watts & Wright, 10 - 10
Wesco Fabrics Inc., 8 - 75
Westport Mfg. Co. Inc., 8 - 75
Whiting Mfg. Co. Inc., 8 - 76
Wild Rose Furniture Mfg. Ltd., 6 - 84
Wilkinsons Furniture Ltd., 6 - 84
William Ball Ltd., 6 - 84
William L. Mclean Ltd., 6 - 84
William Lawrence & Co. Ltd., 6 - 84
Woodstock Furniture Ltd., 6 - 86
Younger Furniture, 6 - 87

Bedspread

Aberdeen Mfg. Corp., 8 - 2
Beacon Looms, Inc., 8 - 8
Bedspreads By Thomas, 6 - 9
Boone Decorative Fabrics, 8 - 11
Borg Textile Corp., 8 - 11
CS Brooks Corp., 8 - 13
Carole Fabrics Inc., 8 - 14
D.S.C. Fabrics Inc., 8 - 21
DMI Drapery Mfg., 8 - 21
Daisy Decorative Products, 8 - 21
De La West Draperies, 8 - 22
Domestications, 8 - 23
Fabricut, 8 - 26
Fieldcrest Cannon, Inc., 8 - 27
Hornick Industries, 8 - 34
MDC Direct Inc., 8 - 43
Minette Mills, Inc., 8 - 47
Rodless Decorations Inc., 8 - 56
Ronnie Draperies, 8 - 56
Rosedale Wallcoverings Inc., 8 - 56
Ruth's Custom Bedspreads, 8 - 57
Scroll Fabrics Inc., 8 - 59
Springs Performance Products, 8 - 62
The Decorators Outlet, 8 - 66
Tiffany Quilting & Drapery Inc., 8 - 68
Trifles, 8 - 69
V A Wallcoverings, 8 - 71
Wesco Fabrics Inc., 8 - 75
Westport Mfg. Co. Inc., 8 - 75
Whiting Mfg. Co. Inc., 8 - 76

Beech

ACCRA Wood Products Ltd., 1 - 1
Boen Hardwood Flooring, 5 - 2
River Bend Turnings, 1 - 29
The Natural Woodflooring Company, 5 - 10

Index

Bench – Blind

Bench

Adirondack Designs, 6 - 3
Candlertown Chairworks, 6 - 14
Frederick Duckloe & Bros., 6 - 30
Hunt Galleries, Inc., 6 - 38
Kings River Casting, 6 - 42
O'Connor's Cypress Woodworks, 6 - 56
Prochnow & Prochnow, 7 - 5
The Old Wagon Factory, 4 - 17
Tidewater Workshop, 6 - 78
Victorian Attic, 6 - 80
Woodnorth, 7 - 8

Beveled

(Glass, Mirrors, etc.)

AMCOA Inc., 6 - 1
Alter Design Inc., 3 - 5
Art Glass Unlimited Inc., 12 - 4
Bevel Glass & Mirror, 4 - 2
Cain Inc., 12 - 6
Cherry Creek Enterprises Inc., 4 - 3
Curran Glass & Mirror Co., 3 - 28
Delphi Stained Glass, 3 - 30
Electric Glass Co., 3 - 33
Glass Craft Specialties, Inc., 4 - 8
Huntington/Pacific Ceramics, Inc., 3 - 48
Ideal-Standard Ltd., 2 - 6
J. Ring Glass Studio, 12 - 12
Manufacturers Glass, 4 - 11
Materials Unlimited, 1 - 23
Morgan-Bockius Studios Inc., 4 - 12
Path Enterprises, Inc., 3 - 68
Queen City Glass Ltd., 8 - 54
Sunburst Stained Glass Co. Inc., 3 - 84
Visador Co., 1 - 36
Williams Art Glass Studios, 12 - 28

Birch

ACCRA Wood Products Ltd., 1 - 1
Bangkok International, 5 - 2
Boen Hardwood Flooring, 5 - 2
Cabinet Crafters, 10 - 2
EDLCO, 3 - 33
Maurice L. Condon Co., 3 - 59
Plain and Fancy Kitchens, 10 - 8
Rural Hall Inc., 4 - 14

Blind

(Mini, Wood, Vinyl, Vertical, etc.)

$5 Wallpaper & Blind Co., 8 - 1
3 Day Blinds, 8 - 1
A & E Blind & Awning Co., 8 - 1
A. Weldon Kent Emterprises, 8 - 1
A.J. Boyd Industries, 8 - 1
ALCO Venetian Blind Co. Inc., 8 - 2
Abbey Shade & Mfg. Co. Inc., 12 - 2
Ace Blinds Inc., 8 - 2
Acme Window Coverings Ltd., 8 - 2
Advanced Consumer Products, 8 - 3
Age Craft Mfg. Inc., 8 - 3
Alabama Venetian Blinds Co. Inc., 8 - 3
All Cedar Venetian Blind Mfg. Co., 8 - 3
All-States Decorating Network, 8 - 3
Allison Window Fashions, 8 - 4
American Blind & Wallpaper Factory, 8 - 4
American Discount Wallcoverings, 8 - 4
American Window Corp., 8 - 4
American Window Creation, 8 - 4
Around the Window, 8 - 5

Atlantic Venetian Blind & Drapery Co., 8 - 6
Avondale Distributors Inc., 8 - 7
Aye Attracting Awnings, 3 - 11
Bali Blinds Midwest, 8 - 7
Bamboo Abbott Florida Corp., 8 - 8
Barker Supply & Window Coverings, 8 - 8
Beauti-Vue Products Inc., 8 - 9
Best Blinds, 8 - 9
Blind Brite Corp., 8 - 10
Blind Busters, 8 - 10
Blind Center USA, Inc., 8 - 10
Blind Design Inc., 8 - 10
Blind Design, 8 - 10
Blinds 'N Things, 8 - 11
Bradd & Hall Blinds, 8 - 11
CSS Decor Inc., 8 - 13
Colorel Blinds, 8 - 18
D.S.C. Fabrics Inc., 8 - 21
Davidson-Bishop Corp., 8 - 22
Design/Craft Fabric Corp., 8 - 22
Designer Window Decor/Truview, 6 - 23
Devenco Products Inc., 12 - 8
Distinctive Window Fashions, 8 - 23
Duratex Inc., 8 - 24
E. D. I., 8 - 24
Endisco Supply Co., 8 - 25
Fashion Tech, 8 - 27
Florida Blinds, 8 - 28
Florida Shades Inc., 8 - 28
G & L Shades Inc., 8 - 29
Gamrod-Harman Co., 8 - 30
Global Blind Express, 8 - 30
Goodman Fabrications, 12 - 10
Graber Industries, 12 - 10
Gulf Coast Window Covering Inc., 8 - 31
Home Fashions, Inc., 8 - 33
House of Blinds, 8 - 34
Hudson Venetian Blind Service Inc., 8 - 34
Hunter Douglas Window Fashions, 8 - 35
Jag Corp., 8 - 37
Jayson Window Fashions, 8 - 37
Jencraft Corp., 8 - 38
John Dixon Inc., 8 - 38
Judkins Co., 8 - 38
Kaleidoscope Ind. Inc., 8 - 38
Kenney Mfg. Co., 8 - 40
King, 10 - 6
Kirsch, 8 - 40
Lafayette Venetian Blind Inc., 8 - 41
Laurel Mfg. Co. Inc., 8 - 41
MDC Direct Inc., 8 - 43
McInnis Industries, 8 - 45
Merit Window Fashions, 8 - 45
Metro Blind & Shade, 8 - 46
Nanik, 12 - 17
National Blind & Wallpaper Factory, 8 - 48
New Home Window Shade, 8 - 49
New View Blinds Mfg. Ltd., 8 - 49
Newell Window Furnishings, 8 - 49
Parker Window Covering, 8 - 51
Peerless Wallpaper, 8 - 52
Perkowitz Window Fashions, 8 - 52
Plastic Sun Shade Co. Inc., 8 - 53
Quix Window Visions & Fabric Works, 8 - 54
Qwik Blinds, 8 - 1
S. Morantz Inc., 8 - 57
Sebring & Co., 8 - 59
Shades & Verticals & Miniblinds Ctr, 8 - 60
Silver Wallcovering Co., 8 - 61
Skandia Industries, 8 - 61
Solartechnic 2000 Ltd., 8 - 61

The Complete Sourcebook

Index - 9

Block – Brass

Index

Southwest Florida Blinds Inc., 8 - 62
Temple Producst of Indiana Inc., 8 - 65
Tentina Window Fashion, 8 - 65
The Blind Factory, 8 - 65
The Blind Maker, 8 - 66
Tiffany Wholesale Supply Inc., 8 - 69
Triangle Window Fashions, 8 - 69
USA Blind Factory, 8 - 70
Unique Wholesale Distr. Inc., 8 - 70
United Designs Inc., 8 - 70
United Supply Co., 8 - 71
V A Wallcoverings, 8 - 71
Versol USA, Inc., 8 - 71
Verticals Inc., 8 - 72
View Guard, 8 - 72
Viking Distributors Inc., 8 - 72
WallpaperXpress, 8 - 74
Wells Interiors, 8 - 75
West Coast Windows Inc., 12 - 28
Wholesale Verticals, Inc., 8 - 76
Win-Glo window Coverings, 8 - 76
Windo-Shade Distributors Inc., 8 - 76
Window Covering Dist. Inc., 8 - 77
Window Coverings Inc., 8 - 77
Window Modes, 8 - 77
Wisconsin Drapery Supply Inc., 8 - 77
Worldwide Wallcoverings & Blinds, 8 - 77
Wrisco Industries Inc., 8 - 77

Block

(Foundation, Glass, etc.)

ABC Glass Block Company, 3 - 2
Acme Brick Co., 3 - 3
Acrymet Industires Inc., 1 - 2
Circle Redmont Inc., 3 - 24
Fred Beyer Co., 3 - 38
G. L. Downs Designs, 12 - 9
Glashaus Inc., 3 - 40
Glass Block Co., 3 - 40
Glass Blocks Unlimited Inc., 1 - 18
Italian Glass Block Designs Ltd., 1 - 20
National Concrete Masonry Assoc., 3 - 63
Pittsburgh Corning, 3 - 70
Sholton Assoc., 3 - 79
Supro Building Products Corp., 3 - 85
Tafco Corp., 3 - 86
The Schoenheit Co., 6 - 76
Wren House Furniture, 6 - 86

Boiler

A.A. Used Boiler Supply Co., 3 - 1
TARM USA, Inc., 3 - 86

Bookcase

Amherst Woodworking & Supply Inc., 1 - 4
Bales Furniture Mfg., 6 - 7
Brill & Walker Associates Inc., 1 - 9
F. E. Hale Mfg., 6 - 34
Grand Era Reproductions, 4 - 8
Hallidays America Inc., 1 - 19
Style-Mark, Inc., 1 - 33

Braided

At Home in the Valley, 8 - 6
Cornucopia, Inc., 6 - 19
Country Braid House, 8 - 19
Kimberly Black, 3 - 52
Luv Those Rugs, 8 - 43
Olde Mill House Shoppe, 6 - 57
Rastetter Woolen Mill, 8 - 55
Southern Rug, 8 - 62

The Gazebo of New York, 8 - 67
Weymouth Braided Rug Co., 8 - 75
Yankee Pride, 8 - 77

Brass

(Accents, Beds, Hardware, Lighting, etc.)

A & B Industries Inc., 3 - 1
A Touch of Brass, 3 - 1
ARMAC Brassfounders Group Ltd., 3 - 2
American Home Supply, 3 - 6
Anglo-American Brass Co., 3 - 8
Artistic Brass, 3 - 9
Baldwin Brass Lighting, 11 - 4
Bedlam Brass, 6 - 8
Brass & Traditional Sinks Ltd., 2 - 3
Brass Accents, 3 - 16
Brass Bed Factory, 6 - 11
Brass Bed Shoppe, 6 - 11
Brass Beds Direct, 6 - 11
Brass Light Gallery, 11 - 5
Brass Reproductions, 11 - 5
Brasslight, 11 - 5
Builders Brass Works Corp., 3 - 17
CMF Colonial Moulding, 1 - 9
Carriage Trade of Tahoe, 11 - 6
Central Brass Mfg. Co., 3 - 21
Charles P. Rogers, 6 - 16
Classic Accents, 3 - 25
Classic Illumination, Inc., 11 - 7
Conant Custom Brass, Inc., 11 - 7
Country Accents, 12 - 7
Crompton Ltd., 12 - 7
D.C. Mitchell Reproductions, 3 - 29
Deco-Trol, 3 - 30
Designer Repros, 6 - 23
Dutch Products & Supply Co., 3 - 32
Elegante Brass, Inc., 11 - 10
Faneuil Furniture Hardware Co. Inc., 6 - 28
Frank Allart & Co., Ltd., 4 - 7
Garbe Industries Inc., 3 - 39
Grand Brass Lamp Parts, 11 - 14
Horton Brasses, 3 - 47
Indiana Brass, 10 - 5
Isabel Brass Furniture, 6 - 39
Konceptual Design, 1 - 21
Lisa Victoria Beds, 6 - 46
Merit Metal Products Corp., 3 - 60
Midwest Custom Brass, 3 - 60
Mooncraft Corp., 11 - 22
New England Brassworks, 3 - 64
Nowells Inc., 11 - 24
Oregon Wooden Screen Door Co., 4 - 13
Ottawa Brass Ltd., 6 - 57
Pfanstiel Hardware Co., 3 - 69
Phoenix Lock Co.Inc., 10 - 8
Price Pfister Inc., 2 - 9
Register & Grille Manufacturing Co., 1 - 29
Renaissance Decorative Hardware Co.,3 - 74
Restoration Works, 3 - 74
Ritter & Son Hardware, 3 - 76
Roberts Brass Company, 6 - 64
Rockford-Eclipse, 3 - 76
Royal Brass Mfg. Co., 3 - 76
Salter Industries, 1 - 30
Schoenherr Iron Work, 1 - 30
Shower-Rite Corp., 2 - 10
Splendor in Brass, 6 - 70
Stairways Inc., 1 - 32
Swan Brass Bed, 6 - 73
The Bed Factory, 6 - 74

Index - 10

The Complete Sourcebook

Index

Brick – Building

The Bedpost, 6 - 74
The Brass Collection, 6 - 75
The Brass Knob, 3 - 87
The Wise Company, 3 - 90
U.S. Brass Turning Co. Inc., 3 - 92
Van Dyke's Restorers, 3 - 94
Victorian Brass Works Ltd., 6 - 80
Victoriana Ltd., 11 - 34
WSI Distributors, 3 - 95
Whitechapel Ltd., 3 - 98
William Spencer, 11 - 35

Brick

Association of Greek Heavy Clay Mftrs., 3 - 10
Associazione Nazionale degli Industriali, 3 - 10
Baltarbo Tegelbruk AB, 3 - 12
Boral Bricks, Inc., 3 - 16
Bundesverband der Deutschen, 3 - 18
Conservation Building Products Ltd., 3 - 26
Continental Clay Company, 3 - 27
Endicott Clay Products Co., 3 - 34
Groupement National de l'Industrie, 3 - 42
Kalk-og Teglvaerksforeningen af 1893, 3 - 51
Koninkijk Verbond van Nederlandse, 3 - 53
Nailite International Inc., 3 - 63
Norges Teglindustrieforening, 3 - 64
Old Carolina Brick Company, 3 - 66
Optiroc AB, 3 - 67
Stone Products Corporation, 3 - 83
Strabruken AB, 3 - 83
Suomen Tiiliteollisuusliitto r.y., 3 - 85
The Brick Development Association, 3 - 87
The Brickyard Inc., 3 - 88
Verband Schweiz. Ziegel, 3 - 95
Yxhult AB, 3 - 101

Bridge

BowBends, 7 - 1
Continental Custom Bridge Co., 7 - 2
Hermitage Garden Pools, 7 - 3

Bronze

Crompton Ltd., 12 - 7
Pfanstiel Hardware Co., 3 - 69

Building

A.F. Schwerd Manufacturing Co., 1 - 1
Abatron Inc., 3 - 3
Acorn Structures Inc., 1 - 2
Addington-Beamon Lumber, 6 - 2
Albany Woodworks Inc., 3 - 5
Albeni Falls Building Supply, 3 - 5
American Building Components, 3 - 6
American Building Restoration, 3 - 6
Antioch Building Materials, 3 - 8
Architectural Antiques Exchange, 1 - 5
Architectural Antiques, 1 - 5
Architectural Cataloguer, USA, 1 - 5
Architectural Elements, 1 - 5
Architectural Lathe & Mill, 1 - 6
Architectural Systems, Inc., 1 - 6
Artefacts Architectural Antiques, 1 - 7
Aylward Products Co., 3 - 11
BMC West Building Materials, 3 - 11
Badgerland Building Material, 3 - 11
Boston Turning Works, 1 - 8
Bow House, 1 - 8
Briar Hill Stone Co., 3 - 17
Brown Moulding Company, 1 - 9
Builders Bargains, 3 - 17
Builders Square, 3 - 17

Building Products of America Corp., 3 - 17
CBS Home Express, 3 - 18
CGM Inc., 3 - 18
CPN Inc., 3 - 18
Chadsworth, Inc., 1 - 10
Cleveland Wrecking, 1 - 11
Coker's Wholesale Building Supply, 3 - 25
Colonial Antiques, 1 - 11
Colonial Building Supply, 3 - 25
Complete Carpentry Inc., 3 - 26
Conservation Building Products Ltd., 3 - 26
Continental Clay Company, 3 - 27
Crockett Log & Timber Frame Homes, 1 - 12
Dale Incor, Inc., 3 - 29
Daniels-Olsen Building Products, 3 - 29
Deck House, 1 - 14
Delaware Quarries, Inc., 3 - 30
Deltacrafts Mfg. Ltd., 6 - 23
Devine Lumber Do-It-Center, 3 - 31
Donald Durham Co., 3 - 31
Dundee Manufacturing Co., 3 - 32
E. F. Bufton & Son Builders, 1 - 15
E.L. Hilts & Company, 3 - 32
Endicott Clay Products Co., 3 - 34
Fastenation, 1 - 16
Florida Victorian Arch. Antiques, 1 - 17
Forest Siding Supply Inc., 3 - 38
General Building Products Corp., 3 - 39
Gold Bond Building Products, 3 - 41
Granville Manufacturing Co. Inc., 3 - 42
Greeter Building Center, 3 - 42
H. H. Robertson Co., 3 - 43
H. M. Stauffer & Sons Inc., 3 - 43
Hartman-Sanders Co., 1 - 19
Home Improvement Supply, 3 - 47
Home Quarters Warehouse, 3 - 47
Home Warehouse Inc., 3 - 47
Housecraft Associates, 3 - 47
ITT Rayonier Inc., 3 - 49
Island Lumber Co., Inc., 3 - 50
Lakeland Builders Supply, 3 - 53
M & S Systems, 3 - 56
Marion Plywood Corp., 3 - 58
Marjam Supply Company, 3 - 58
Maryland Lumber Co., 3 - 59
Midwest Lumber & Supply, 3 - 60
Moller's Building & Home Centers, 3 - 61
Mount Baker Plywood Inc., 3 - 62
Nashville Sash & Door Co., 3 - 63
National Concrete Masonry Assoc., 3 - 63
National Home Products, 3 - 63
Nevada County Building Supply, 3 - 63
Old Home Building & Restoration, 3 - 66
PDC Home Supply, 3 - 67
PGL Building Products, 3 - 68
Payless Cashways, 3 - 68
Pecora Corporation, 3 - 69
Pelnick Wrecking Company, Inc., 3 - 69
Pioneer Roofing Tile Inc., 3 - 70
Porter-Cable Corp., 3 - 71
PriceKing Building Supply Inc., 3 - 71
Pukall Lumber Co., 3 - 72
Restoration Resource, 3 - 74
Sanders Building Supply Inc., 3 - 77
Sav On Discount Material, 3 - 77
Schmitt Builders Supply, 3 - 78
South & Jones Lumber Co., 3 - 80
Southland Building Inc., 3 - 81
Specification Chemicals Inc., 3 - 81
Stamford Wrecking, 3 - 82
Supply Line, 3 - 85

Index

The Complete Sourcebook

Index - 11

Built-in – Cabinet

Index

TJ International Inc., 3 - 86
Texas Standard Picket Company Inc., 7 - 7
The 18th Century Company, 3 - 87
The Stone & Marble Supermarket, 3 - 89
Thompson Lumber Co., 3 - 90
Thorn Lumber Co., 3 - 90
Timber Truss Housing Systems Inc., 3 - 91
Tri-City Lumber/Building Supplies, 3 - 92
Trimall Interior Products Inc., 3 - 92
Trus Joist Corporation, 3 - 92
Tuff-Kote Company, 3 - 92
United House Wrecking, Inc., 3 - 93
United States Gypsum Company, 3 - 93
Valley Builders Supply, 3 - 94
Valley Lumber & Hardware, 3 - 94
Vaughan & Sons Inc., 3 - 94
Vermont Frames, 1 - 36
Vestal Mfg., 3 - 95
Vetter Stone Co., 1 - 36
Wallace Supply& Wholesale Distributor 3 - 96
West Michigan Nail Co., 3 - 97
Western Red Cedar Lumber Assoc.,3 - 98
Wiggins & Son Inc., 3 - 98
Wilco Building Material Distributors, 3 - 98
Wolohan Lumber & Improvement, 3 - 100
Worthington Group, Ltd., 1 - 38
Wyoming Lumber & Supply Co., 3 - 101

Built-in

(Household Appliances, etc.)

Gaggenau USA Corporation, 10 - 4
Iron-A-Way Inc., 8 - 36
Neff (UK, etc.) Ltd., 10 - 7
Omar's Built-In Vacuum Systems, 3 - 66
Sub Zero Freezer Company, Inc., 10 - 9
Tricity Bendix Ltd., 10 - 10
Wanda Mfg. Co. Inc., 3 - 96
Zanussi Ltd., 10 - 11

Burglar

Alarm Supply Co., 9 - 1
Beckett, R.W. Corp., 3 - 13
Burdex Security Co., 3 - 13
High-Desert Security Systems, 9 - 2
Mountain West Alarm Supply, 9 - 2
Westco Security Systems Inc., 9 - 3

Butcher

The Schoenheit Co., 6 - 76
Wren House Furniture, 6 - 86

Cabinet

(Furniture, Kitchen, etc.)

Acorn Manufacturing Co. Inc., 3 - 3
Addkison Hardware Co. Inc., 3 - 4
Architectural Paneling, 1 - 6
Aristokraft, 10 - 1
Artisan Woodworkers, 10 - 1
Athens Furniture, 6 - 6
Baldwin Hardware, 3 - 12
Barker Cabinets, 10 - 1
Barnard Street Woodworks, 10 - 1
Basco, 2 - 2
Beaver Woodworks, 10 - 2
Berbaum Millwork Inc., 3 - 14
Bjorndal Woodworks, 1 - 8
Blue Canyon Woodworks, 6 - 10
Blue Jay Fine Woodworker, 10 - 2
Boulton & Paul PLC, 3 - 16
Brammer Mfg. Co., 12 - 5
Brill & Walker Associates Inc., 1 - 9

Bruce Hardwood Floors, 5 - 2
Buckwalter Custom Kitchens, 10 - 2
C & M Cabinet Co., 10 - 2
CECO Products Inc., 10 - 2
Cabinet Crafters, 10 - 2
Calma's Custom Cabinets, 10 - 2
Cardell Cabinets, 10 - 3
Cherry Creek Enterprises Inc., 4 - 3
Cheyenne Company, 1 - 10
Creative Designs, 6 - 20
Curvoflite Inc., 1 - 13
Decore-Ative Specialties, 12 - 8
Deltacrafts Mfg. Ltd., 6 - 23
Elk Valley Woodworking Inc., 6 - 26
Eudy Cabinet Shop Inc., 6 - 27
Facades Ltd., 10 - 4
Ferretti Ltd., 10 - 4
Fleurco Industries 1963 Ltd., 10 - 4
Fox Woodcraft, 10 - 4
Frank's Woodwork & Supplies, 10 - 4
G.M. Ketcham Co., Inc., 2 - 5
Glass Craft Specialties, Inc., 4 - 8
Hallidays America Inc., 1 - 19
Heritage Custom Kitchens, 10 - 5
Hewi, Inc., 3 - 45
Home & Cabinet Designs Inc., 10 - 5
Homecrest Corporation, 10 - 5
I. F. M. Co. Ltd., 10 - 5
J & C Crafts, 6 - 39
J & M Custom Cabinets & Millwork, 10 - 5
Janik Custom Millwork, 12 - 12
Jasper Cabinet Co., 6 - 40
Johnny's Cabinet Shop, 6 - 41
Jules D. Becker Wood Products, 10 - 6
Kemper Quality Cabinets, 10 - 6
King Brothers Woodworking Inc., 6 - 42
Kinzee Industries Inc., 12 - 14
Kraftmaid Cabinetry, 10 - 6
Lakeville Industries, Inc., 10 - 6
M. Craig & Company, 6 - 47
Merit Cabinet Distributors, 2 - 7
Merit Metal Products Corp., 3 - 60
Millbrook Kitchens Inc., 10 - 7
Minnetonka Woodcraft Co., 6 - 53
Monson's Custom Woodworking, 10 - 7
Mountain Shadow Mill, 10 - 7
Mountaintop Cabinet Manufacturing, 10 - 7
National Kitchen & Bath Association, 10 - 7
Outer Bank Pine Products, 6 - 57
O'Keefe Cabinet Fixtures, 10 - 8
Perkins & Powell, 2 - 8
Plain and Fancy Kitchens, 10 - 8
Poggenpohl U.S.A. Corp, 10 - 8
Pridgen Cabinet Works, Inc., 1 - 28
RC's Custom Woodwork, 10 - 8
Ravenglass Pty. Ltd., 8 - 55
Rich Craft Custom Kitchens, 10 - 8
Richard Blaschke Cabinet Glass, 3 - 75
Richard Brooks Company, 6 - 63
River East Custom Cabinets, 6 - 63
Roland Park Cabinet Inc., 6 - 64
Scherr's Cabinets, 4 - 15
Shaw's Custom Cabinets, 6 - 67
Sound Wholesale, 6 - 69
Specialty Woodworks Co., 4 - 16
Station West Custom Cabinet & Int., 6 - 71
Steve's Cabinet & Woodworking, 6 - 72
Sulak's Cabinet Shop, 6 - 72
Taconic Architectural Woodworking, 1 - 33
The Woodworkers Store, 11 - 32
Thee Cabinet Shop, 6 - 77

Index

Cabinetry – Carpet

TradeCom International Inc., 3 - 91
Triangle Pacific Cabinet, 6 - 79
Trimall Interior Products Inc., 3 - 92
Trinity Wood Works, 6 - 79
Walker Mfg., 10 - 10
Wellbilt Kitchen Cabinets, 10 - 10
Western Woodwork Co., 6 - 83
Wofab Custom Cabinets Ltd., 6 - 85
Wood Works by Dan, 10 - 11
Wood-Mode, 10 - 11
Woodburns Custom Cabinets, 10 - 11
Woodworking Specialties, 3 - 100
Woodworks, 10 - 11
Woodwrights of Rochester, 10 - 11
York Cabinet Inc., 10 - 11
Yorktowne Inc., 10 - 11
Zimmerman's Millwork & Cabinet, 1 - 38

Cabinetry

Albany Woodworks Inc., 3 - 5
Allmilmo Corp., 10 - 1
Alno Network USA, 10 - 1
American Woodmark Corp., 10 - 1
Antique Emporium, 1 - 4
Boise Moulding & Lumber, 3 - 15
Broan Manufacturing Co. Inc., 10 - 2
Brookhaven Cabinetry, 10 - 2
Bulthaup Inc., 10 - 2
Crown Point Cabinetry, 10 - 3
Downsview Kitchens, 10 - 3
Federal Millwork Corp., 1 - 16
Fine Woodworking by Living Tree, 6 - 28
Garland Woodcraft Co. Inc., 1 - 18
Geba USA, Inc., 10 - 5
James M. Taylor & Co., 6 - 40
Kneeshaw Woodworking Installations , 1 - 21
Old World Moulding & Finishing Co., 1 - 26
Peter Franklin Cabinetmakers, 6 - 59
Reeves Design Workshop Ltd., 1 - 28
Renaissance Furniture and Cabinetry, 6 - 62
Rutt Cabinetry, 10 - 9
Scandia Kitchens Inc., 10 - 9
Snaidero, 10 - 9
Southern Millwork, Inc., 1 - 31
The Joinery Company, 5 - 10
The Kennebec Company, 10 - 10
Watts & Wright, 10 - 10
Wood-Mode, 10 - 11
Woodstock Furniture Ltd., 6 - 86
Woodwrights of Rochester, 10 - 11

Caning

Bamboo & Rattan Works Inc., 8 - 8
Cane & Basket Supply Company, 6 - 14
Jack's Upholstery & Caning Supplies, 8 - 37
The Caning Shop, 6 - 75

Canopy

Carter Canopies, 8 - 15
Laura Copenhaver Industries Inc., 8 - 41

Canvas

Baraboo Tent & Awning, 3 - 12
Coastal Canvas & Awning, 3 - 25
Custom Canvas Awning, Inc., 3 - 28
Houston Canvas & Awning, 12 - 11
Lawrence Canvas Products, Co., 12 - 14
Moran Canvas Products Inc., 12 - 16
Tent City Canvas House, 12 - 24
The Canvas Smith, 12 - 24
Wilcox Canvas Awnings, 12 - 28

Carpet

ABC Carpet & Home, 8 - 1
Access Carpet, 8 - 2
Acorn Mills Ltd., 8 - 2
Adam Carpets Ltd., 8 - 2
Aladdin Carpet Mills, 8 - 3
Allison T. Seymour, Inc., 8 - 3
Ambassador Carpets, 8 - 4
Asia Minor Carpets, 8 - 6
Atlantic Carpet Corp., 8 - 6
Atlas Carpet Mills, Inc., 8 - 6
Avena Carpets Ltd., 8 - 7
Axminster Carpets Ltd., 8 - 7
BMK Ltd., 8 - 7
Bamber Carpets Ltd., 8 - 8
Barrett Carpet Mills, 8 - 8
Beardon Brothers Carpet, 8 - 8
Beaulieu of America Inc., 8 - 8
Beckler's Carpet Outlet, 8 - 9
Benington's, 8 - 9
Bentley Mills, Inc., 8 - 9
Blue Ridge Carpet Mills, 8 - 11
Bremworth Carpets, 8 - 12
Bretlin Carpet, 8 - 12
Brintons Carpets USA Ltd., 8 - 12
Brockway Carpets Ltd., 8 - 12
Burbank Linoleum & Carpet, 8 - 12
Buy Carpet Direct, 8 - 12
Cabin Craft Rugs, 8 - 13
Callaway Carpets & Rugs, 8 - 13
Camelot Carpet Mills, 8 - 13
Carousel Carpet Mills, 8 - 14
Carpet Crafts, Inc., 8 - 14
Carpet Express, 8 - 14
Carpet Outlet, 8 - 14
Carpetland, 8 - 15
Carpeton Mills Inc., 8 - 15
Carpets of Georgia, 8 - 15
Carpets of Worth Ltd., 8 - 15
Carter Carpet, 8 - 15
Catalina Carpet Mills Inc., 8 - 15
Charleston Carpets, 8 - 16
Cherry Hill Furniture,Carpet & Interiors, 6 - 16
Chesney Carpet Center, 8 - 16
Claremont Rug Company, 8 - 17
Classic Revivals, Inc., 8 - 17
Cleanrite Carpet Sales, 8 - 17
Collie Carpets Ltd., 8 - 17
Columbus Mills, Inc., 8 - 18
Coronet Industries Inc., 8 - 18
Couristan, 8 - 19
Criterion Mills, Inc., 8 - 20
Crown Corp. D/B/A Mile Hi Crown, 8 - 20
D & W Carpet & Rug Co., 8 - 20
Davis Braided Rug co., 8 - 22
Dellinger, Inc., 8 - 22
Designer Carpets, 8 - 22
Diamond Rug & Carpet Mills Inc., 8 - 23
Dorsett Carpet Mills Inc., 8 - 23
Downs Carpet Co., Inc., 8 - 23
Du Pont Stainmaster, 8 - 24
Durkan Patterned Carpet, 8 - 24
Einstein Moomjy, 8 - 25
Eurotex, 8 - 25
Eyedeal Carpets, 8 - 26
Fairfield Carpets & Fabrics, 8 - 27
Family Heir-Loom Weavers, 8 - 27
Firth Carpets Ltd., 8 - 28
Flagship Carpet, 8 - 28
Floortown, 5 - 4

The Complete Sourcebook

Index - 13

Casement – Cedar

Form III, 8 - 29
Fred Moheban Gallery, 8 - 29
Galaxy Carpet Mills, 8 - 30
Gaskell Carpets Ltd., 8 - 30
Georgian Carpets Ltd., 8 - 30
Glendale Carpet Co., 8 - 30
Gold Label Carpet Mills, 8 - 30
Gradus Carpets Ltd., 8 - 31
Great Carpet Co., 8 - 31
Hawthorne Carpet, 8 - 32
Helios Carpets, 8 - 32
Hollytex Carpet Mills, Inc., 8 - 33
Homeland Carpet Mills, 8 - 33
Indiana Carpet Distributors, 8 - 36
J. R. Burrows & Company, 8 - 37
Jacqueline Vance Oriental Rugs, 8 - 37
Jefferson Industries Inc., 8 - 38
Johnson's Carpets, 8 - 38
Karastan, 8 - 39
Kelaty International Inc., 8 - 39
Knight Distributing Inc., 8 - 40
Kosset Carpets Ltd., 8 - 40
Kraus Carpet Mills Ltd., 8 - 40
Lacey-Champion Carpets, Inc., 8 - 41
Lee's Carpets, 8 - 42
Long's Carpet Inc., 8 - 43
Lotus Carpets, 8 - 43
M.A. Bruder & Sons Inc., 8 - 43
Mallory's Fine Furniture, 6 - 48
Medallion Carpets, 8 - 45
Merida Meridian, Inc., 8 - 45
Mike Leary Carpets, 8 - 46
Mike's Carpet Emporium, 8 - 46
Miles Carpet, 8 - 46
Milliken Carpets, 8 - 46
Missoni Roubini, Inc., 8 - 47
Mohawk Carpet, 8 - 47
Monterey Carpets, 8 - 47
Mountain Craft Carpets, 8 - 48
Nance Carpet & Rug Co. Inc., 8 - 48
National Carpet Group Ltd., 8 - 48
National Carpet, 8 - 48
Navan Carpets Inc., 8 - 49
Odegard-Roesner, 8 - 50
Omega Carpet Mills Inc., 8 - 50
Oxford Textile Mills Ltd., 8 - 51
Pace-Stone, 8 - 51
Paradise Mills Inc., 8 - 51
Parker's Carpets Inc., 8 - 52
Pennsylvania Woven Carpet Mills , 8 - 52
Quality Discount Carpets, 8 - 54
R. W. Beattie Carpet Industries Inc., 8 - 55
Rawson Carpets Ltd., 8 - 55
Rosecore Carpet Co. Inc., 8 - 56
Royalweve Carpet Mills Inc., 8 - 56
S & S Mills, 8 - 57
Safavieh Carpets, 8 - 58
Salem Carpets Inc., 8 - 58
Sanderson Carpets Ltd., 8 - 58
Saxony Carpet Company, Inc., 8 - 58
Shaw Carpets Ltd., 8 - 60
Shaw Industries Inc., 8 - 60
Sheridan Carpet Mills, 8 - 60
Southern Comfort Carpets, 8 - 62
Spence Bryson Carpets Ltd., 8 - 62
Stark Carpet, 8 - 62
Steeles Carpets Ltd., 8 - 62
Stephen Leedom Carpets Co. Inc., 8 - 63
Stevens Carpet, 8 - 63
Tankard Carpets Ltd., 8 - 65
The 135 Collection Inc., 8 - 65

The Carpetologist, 8 - 66
The Decorative Center of Houston, 8 - 66
The Persian Carpet, 8 - 67
The World of Clothing, 8 - 68
Thorndike Mills, 8 - 68
Tobin Sporn & Glasser Inc., 8 - 69
Trafford Carpets Ltd., 8 - 69
Tretford Carpets Ltd., 8 - 69
Ulster Carpet Mills Ltd., 8 - 70
Unistar Corp., 8 - 70
V I P Sales Inc., 8 - 71
Varsity Rug Co., 8 - 71
Village Carpet, 8 - 72
Vorwerk Carpets Ltd., 8 - 73
Warehouse Carpets, Inc., 8 - 74
Wellco Carpet Co., 8 - 75
West Point Pepperell Inc., 8 - 75
Weston of Scandinavia UK Ltd., 8 - 75
Whitecrest Carpet Mills, 8 - 76
Wholesale Carpet, 8 - 76
Wilton Royal Carpet Factory Ltd., 8 - 76
World Carpets, 8 - 77
Wunda Weve Carpet Co., 8 - 77
York Interiors Inc., 6 - 86
Zarbin & Associates, Inc., 6 - 87

Casement

Caradco, 12 - 6
Classic Designs, 12 - 6
Eagle Window & Door, 12 - 8
Peachtree Doors, Inc., 4 - 13
Torrance Steel Window Co. Inc., 12 - 25

Cast

A.A. Used Boiler Supply Co., 3 - 1
AGA Cookers, 10 - 1
Cirecast, 3 - 24
Dovre, 3 - 32
Good Time Stove Co., 3 - 41
Heating Research Co., 3 - 45
Robinson Iron, 6 - 64
Sheppard Millwork, Inc., 4 - 15
Silverton Victorian Millworks, 1 - 31
The House of Webster, 10 - 10
The Iron Shop, 1 - 34

Caulking

Pecora Corporation, 3 - 69

Cedar

(Furniture, Lumber, Shake, Shingle, etc.)
C & H Roofing Inc., 3 - 18
Cedar Plus, 3 - 20
Cedar Shake & Shingle Bureau, 3 - 21
Corning Moulding Corporation, 1 - 12
Creative Structures, 3 - 27
Dalton Pavilions Inc., 7 - 2
Elk Valley Woodworking Inc., 6 - 26
Gazebo Woodcrafters, 7 - 3
Green River, 3 - 42
Hamilton Cedar Products Inc., 3 - 43
International Woodworking, 6 - 39
Julius Seidel & Company, 3 - 51
Lindal Cedar Sunrooms, 3 - 55
Mill & Timber Products, Ltd., 3 - 60
Murphy Furniture Mfg. Co., Inc., 6 - 54
Nailite International Inc., 3 - 63
North Hoquiam Cedar Products Inc., 3 - 65
Ostermann & Scheiwe, USA, Inc., 1 - 26
Red Rose Millwork, 1 - 28
Sacramento Valley Moulding Co., 1 - 30

Index

Ceiling – Ceramic

Sarita Furniture, 6 - 66
Sky Lodge Farm, 3 - 79
Tidewater Workshop, 6 - 78
Walpole Woodworkers, 6 - 81
Wesco Cedar Inc., 3 - 97
West Forest Wood Products, 3 - 97
Western Red Cedar Lumber Association,3 - 98
Willsboro Wood Products, 6 - 85

Ceiling
(Buttons, Fans, Medallions, Panel, etc.)

A A Abbingdon Affilliates, Inc., 1 - 1
Academy, 11 - 1
Aetna Electric Distributing Corp., 11 - 2
Apache Building Products, 1 - 4
Architectural Antique Warehouse, 3 - 9
Architectural Paneling, 1 - 6
Armstrong World Industries Inc., 1 - 6
Arrowsmith Trading Company, 8 - 5
Artemide, 11 - 3
Beverly Hills Fan Co., 11 - 4
Booth-Muirie Ltd., 1 - 8
Catalina Lighting, Inc., 11 - 6
Charles Street Supply Co., 3 - 24
Chelsea Decorative Metal Co., 1 - 10
Classic Ceilings, 1 - 11
Conservation Technology Ltd., 11 - 7
Delaware Electric Imports, 11 - 9
Eaton-Gaze Ltd., 1 - 15
Emerson Electric Company, 11 - 10
Fan Fair, 11 - 11
Fastenation, 1 - 16
Felber Ornamental Plastering Corp., 1 - 16
Guyon, 5 - 4
Hunter Ceiling Fans, 11 - 16
Hyde Park Fine Art of Mouldings, 1 - 20
Jaegaer USA, 11 - 17
Jali Ltd., 3 - 50
Lamp Warehouse/New York Ceiling Fan,11-19
Martin's Discount Lighting, 11 - 22
Midwestern Wood Products, 1 - 24
Outwater Plastic Industries, 1 - 26
Robbins & Myers, 11 - 27
SEC Inc., 11 - 28
Snelling's Thermo-Vac, Inc., 3 - 79
The Balmer Studios Inc., 1 - 34
The Ceiling Fan Gallery, 11 - 31
The Fan Man Inc., 11 - 32
The Fan Man, 11 - 32
United Plastics Corp., 1 - 35
W. F. Norman Corporation, 1 - 36
Wholesale Fans & Lighting Inc., 11 - 35

Central
(Air, Vacumn, etc.)

Deco-Trol, 3 - 30
Wal-Vac Inc., 3 - 95
Wanda Mfg. Co. Inc., 3 - 96

Ceramic

ACIF Ceramiche S.R.L., 3 - 2
Actiengesellschaft, 3 - 3
Agrob-Wessel-Servais AG, 3 - 4
Amaru Tile, 3 - 6
American International, 3 - 6
American Marazzi Tile, 3 - 7
American Olean Tile Co., 3 - 7
Andrews & Sons (Marbles & Tiles, etc.), 3 - 7
Angelo Amaru Tile & Bath Collection, 3 - 8
Ann Sacks Tile & Stone, 3 - 8

Antiche Ceramiche D'Talia (ACIT) S.R.L., 3 - 8
Arius Tile Co., 3 - 9
Arnold-Missouri Corp., 3 - 9
Art on Tiles, 3 - 9
Badger Tiles, 3 - 11
Baukeramik U., 3 - 12
Bellegrove Ceramics Ltd., 3 - 13
Bertin Studio Tiles, 3 - 14
Brooklyn Tile Supply Co., 3 - 17
Calendar Tiles Ltd., 3 - 19
California Tile Supply, 3 - 19
California Wholesale Tile, 3 - 19
Cambridge Tile Mfg. Co., 3 - 19
Cancos Tile Corporation, 3 - 19
Candy Tiles Ltd., 3 - 20
Cedir S.P.A., 3 - 21
Cedit S.P.A., 3 - 21
Cemar International S.P.A., 3 - 21
Central Distributors Inc., 3 - 21
Century Floors Inc., 5 - 3
Ceramica Candia S.P.A., 3 - 22
Ceramica Colli Di Sassuolo S.P.A., 3 - 22
Ceramica Del Conca S.P.A., 3 - 22
Ceramica Ilsa S.P.A., 3 - 22
Ceramica Panaria S.P.A., 3 - 22
Ceramiche Atlas Concorde S.P.A., 3 - 22
Ceramiche Brunelleschi S.P.A., 3 - 22
Ceramiche Cuoghitalia S.P.A., 3 - 22
Ceramiche Edilcuoghi S.P.A., 3 - 23
Ceramiche Edilgres-Sirio S.P.A., 3 - 23
Ceramografia Artigiana S.P.A., 3 - 23
Cerdomus Ceramiche S.P.A., 3 - 23
Cerim Ceramiche S.P.A., 3 - 23
Cisa-Cerdisa-Smov, 3 - 24
Co-Em S.R.L., 3 - 25
Color Tile Ceramic Mfr. Co., 3 - 26
Color Tile Inc., 3 - 26
Continental Ceramic Tile, 3 - 27
Cooperativa Ceramica D'Imola Soc.ARL,3-27
Country Floors, 5 - 3
Crest Distributors, 3 - 28
Croonen KG, 3 - 28
Crossville Ceramics, 3 - 28
D & B Tile Distributors, 3 - 29
Dado Ceramica S.R.L., 3 - 29
Dal-Tile, 3 - 29
Designer Ceramics, 3 - 30
Designs in Tile, 3 - 31
D'Mundo Tile, 3 - 29
East Coast Tile Imports Inc., 3 - 33
Elon Inc., 3 - 33
Endicott Tile Ltd., 3 - 34
Fierst Distributing Co., 3 - 36
Fired Earth Tiles PLC, 5 - 4
Flooring Distributors, 5 - 4
Florano Ceramic Tile Design Center, 3 - 37
Florian Tiles, 3 - 37
Florida Brick & Clay Co.,Inc., 3 - 37
Florida Ceramic Tile Center, 3 - 37
Florida Tile Industries, Inc., 3 - 37
Focus Ceramics Ltd., 3 - 37
GMT Floor Tile, Inc., 3 - 38
GTE Products Corp., 3 - 39
Gabbianelli S.R.L., 3 - 39
Gilmer Potteries, Inc., 2 - 5
Gruppo Elba S.P.A., 3 - 42
H & R Johnson Tiles, 3 - 42
Harris Marcus Group, Inc., 11 - 14
Hastings Tile & Il Bagno Collection, 3 - 44
Hutcherson Tile, 3 - 48
I. C. R. S.P.A. (Appiani, etc.), 3 - 48

The Complete Sourcebook

Index - 15

Chair – Chair

Index

IMPO Glaztile, 3 - 48
Impronta S.P.A., 3 - 49
Jacpa Ceramic Craftsmen, 8 - 37
KPT, Incorporated, 3 - 51
Klingenberg Dekoramik GmbH, 3 - 53
Kris Elosvolo, 3 - 53
La Luz Canyon Studio, 3 - 53
LaFaenza America Inc., 3 - 53
Latco Ceramic Tile, 3 - 54
Laticrete International Inc., 3 - 54
Laufen International, Inc., 3 - 54
Leonardo 1502 Ceramica S.p. A., 3 - 54
Lone Star Ceramics Company, 3 - 55
Mannington Ceramic Tile, 3 - 57
Marlborough Ceramic Tiles, 3 - 58
McIntyre Tile Co. Inc., 3 - 59
Meissen-Keramik GmbH, 3 - 60
Metco Tile Distributors, 3 - 60
Metropolitan Ceramics, 8 - 46
Mission Tile West, 3 - 61
Monarch Tile Inc., 3 - 61
Motawi Tileworks, 3 - 62
National Ceramics of Florida, 3 - 63
National Ceramics, 3 - 63
Nemo Tile Company, Inc., 3 - 63
Novatile Ltd., 3 - 65
Nuove Ceramiche Ricchetti, S.r.l., 3 - 65
Old Country Ceramic Tile, 3 - 66
Onyx Enterprises of America, 3 - 67
Orignial Style, 3 - 67
Ostara-Fliesen Gmbh & Co. KG, 3 - 67
Paris Ceramics, 3 - 68
Peter Josef Korzilius Soehne GmbH, 3 - 69
Pewabic Pottery Co., 3 - 69
Plain and Fancy Ceramic Tile, 3 - 70
Porcelanosa, 3 - 71
Praire Marketing, 3 - 71
Quarry Tile Company, 3 - 73
Rams Imports, 3 - 73
Richmond Ceramic Tile Distributors , 3 - 75
Ro-Tile Inc., 3 - 76
Royal Haeger Lamp Co., 11 - 27
San Do Designs, 3 - 77
Santa Catalina, 3 - 77
Sherle Wagner, 2 - 10
Sikes Corp, 3 - 79
Simpson Tile Co., 3 - 79
Southampton Brick & Tile Co., 3 - 81
Spiegelwerk Wilsdruff GmbH, 3 - 81
Staloton - Die keramiker H.H., 3 - 82
Standard Tile Distributors Inc., 3 - 82
Starbuck Goldner Tile, 3 - 82
Stonelight Tile Co., 3 - 83
Stoneware Tile Company, 3 - 83
Structural Stoneware Inc., 3 - 83
Swedecor Ltd., 3 - 85
Tarkett Ceramic Inc., 3 - 86
Tarkett Inc., 5 - 9
The Decorative Tile Works, 3 - 88
The Tile Collection, 3 - 89
The Tileworks, 3 - 89
The Willette Corporation, 3 - 90
Tile & Marble Designs, 3 - 90
Tile Creations, 3 - 90
Tile Mart International, 3 - 91
Tile Promotion Board, 3 - 91
Tile West Distributors, 3 - 91
Tile with Style, 3 - 91
Tilepak America Inc., 3 - 91
U.S. Ceramic Tile Co., 3 - 92
United Ceramic Tile Corp., 3 - 93

United States Ceramic Tile Co., 3 - 93
Villeroy & Boch AG, 2 - 12
Villeroy & Boch Ltd., 2 - 12
Walker & Zanger, 3 - 95
Wandplattenfabrik Engers GmbH, 3 - 96
Wayne Tile Company, 3 - 96
Western Oregon Tile Supplies, 3 - 97
Western Tile, 3 - 98
Wilh. Gail'sche Tonwerke KG a.A., 3 - 99
Winburn Tile Manufacturing Co., 3 - 99
Wirth-Salander Studios, 2 - 13
World's End Tiles, 3 - 101
Yulix Inc., 3 - 101

Chair

Acme Furniture Mfg. Inc., 6 - 2
Action Industries Inc., 6 - 2
Adirondack Designs, 6 - 3
Alfresco Porch Swing Company, 6 - 3
Arrben Di O. Benvenuto, 6 - 5
At Home in the Valley, 8 - 6
Baker Chair Co., 6 - 7
Barnes & Barnes, 6 - 8
Barnett Products Co., 6 - 8
Boyd R. Smith, 6 - 10
Builtright Chair Co. Inc., 6 - 12
Candlertown Chairworks, 6 - 14
Chaircraft Inc., 6 - 15
Ciro Coppa, 6 - 16
Classic Choice, 6 - 17
Cohasset Colonials, 6 - 17
Comoexport-Divisione Di Cantu, 6 - 18
Continental Chair Co., 6 - 18
Coppa Woodworking, 6 - 18
Cornucopia, Inc., 6 - 19
Country Bed Shop, 6 - 19 , 6 - 24
Country Bed Shop, 6 - 19
Door Store, 6 - 24
Fairfield Chair Co., 6 - 27
Fancher Chair Co. Inc., 6 - 27
Flexform, 6 - 28
Flexform, 6 - 28
Flexsteel Industries, 6 - 28
Fong Brothers Company, 6 - 29
Frederick Duckloe & Bros., 6 - 30
Georgia Chair Co., 6 - 31
Grand Manor Furniture Inc., 6 - 32
Grange Furniture, Inc., 6 - 32
Hickory Chair Co., 6 - 35
Howard's Antique Lighting, 11 - 16
Hunt Galleries, Inc., 6 - 38
Kenneth Winslow Furniture, 6 - 41
Kings River Casting, 6 - 42
Klein Design Inc., 6 - 43
Larkspur Furniture Co., 6 - 44
Marion Travis, 6 - 49
Mark Sales Co. Inc., 6 - 50
Masterworks, 6 - 51
Maynard House Antiques, 6 - 51
Michael M. Reed, 6 - 52
Mills River Industries, Inc., 8 - 46
Minton Corley Collection, 3 - 61
North Woods Chair Shop, 6 - 55
Oakline Chair Co. Inc., 6 - 56
Old Hickory Furniture Co. Inc., 6 - 56
Pottery Barn, 6 - 60
Prochnow & Prochnow, 7 - 5
R & R Crafts, 7 - 5
River Bend Chair Company, 6 - 63
Robert Barrow Furniture Maker, 6 - 63
Room & Board, 6 - 64

Index - 16

The Complete Sourcebook

Index

Chandelier — Coal

Seybold Industries Inc., 6 - 67
Shaker Shops West, 6 - 67
Shaker Workshops, 3 - 78
Shannon Chair, 6 - 67
Sheffield Chair Co., 6 - 68
Shushan Bentwood Co., 6 - 68
Silhoutte Antiques Inc., 6 - 68
Stanley Chair Co. Inc., 6 - 71
Statesville Chair Company, 6 - 71
Straw Hill Chairs, 6 - 72
Taos Drums, 6 - 73
The Berkline Corp., 6 - 74
The Keeping Room, 6 - 75
The Rocker Shop of Marietta, 6 - 76
The Sofa Factory, 6 - 76
Tidewater Workshop, 6 - 78
Victorian Attic, 6 - 80
Vitra Seating Inc., 6 - 81
Wellington's Furniture, 6 - 82
Windspire, 6 - 85
Wood Goods Inc., 6 - 85
Wylder Furniture Manufacturing, 6 - 86
Zanotta, S.p.A./Palladio Trading Inc., 6 - 87

Chandelier

All-Lighting, 11 - 2
Architectural Crystal Ltd., 1 - 5
Brass Light Gallery, 11 - 5
Brass'n Bounty, 11 - 5
Brubaker Metalcrafts, 11 - 5
Campbell Lamp Supply, 11 - 6
Chartwell Group Ltd., 3 - 24
Christopher Wrays Lighting Emporium , 11 - 7
Classic Illumination, Inc., 11 - 7
Copper Lamps by Hutton, 11 - 8
D'Lights, 11 - 8
ELA Custom & Architectural Co., 11 - 10
Forluce, 11 - 12
Gaslight Time Antiques, 11 - 13
Gem Monogram & Cut Glass Corp., 11 - 13
Georgian Art Lighting Designs, Inc., 11 - 13
Great Gatsby's Auction Galley, 1 - 18
Green's Lighting Fixtures, 11 - 14
Holtkotter International, Inc., 11 - 15
Hubbardton Forge & Wood Corp., 11 - 16
King's Chandelier, 11 - 18
Lighting Source of America, 11 - 20
Lightolier, 11 - 20
Luigi Crystal, 11 - 20
Marbo Lamp Co., 11 - 21
Metropolitan Lighting Fixture Co. Inc., 11 - 22
Ner Lighting Inc., 11 - 23
NuMerit Electrical Supply, 11 - 24
Schonbek Worldwide Lighting Inc., 11 - 28
Studio Steel, 11 - 30
Tower Lighting Center, 11 - 33
Unlight Ltd., 11 - 33
Victorian Lighting Works, 11 - 34
Visioneered Lighting Mfg. Ltd., 11 - 34
William Spencer, 11 - 35
Wm. Spencer Inc., 11 - 35
Workshops of David T. Smith, 6 - 86

Cherry

(Cabinets, Flooring, Furniture, etc.)
BRE Lumber, 3 - 11
Blackwelder's Industries, Inc., 6 - 9
Cabinet Crafters, 10 - 2
Cardell Cabinets, 10 - 3
DeSoto Hardwood Flooring Company, 5 - 3
Driwood Moulding Co., 8 - 24

EDLCO, 3 - 33
Grange Furniture, Inc., 6 - 32
Kopil & Associates Timeless Furniture, 6 - 43
L & J.G. Stickley, Inc., 6 - 43
Larkin Company, 1 - 22
Livermore Wood Floors, 5 - 6
Maple Grove Restorations, 1 - 22
Maurice L. Condon Co., 3 - 59
Midwest Dowel Works, Inc., 3 - 60
Osborne Wood Products Inc., 6 - 57
P. W. Plumly Lumber Corporation, 1 - 26
River Bend Turnings, 1 - 29
Rural Hall Inc., 4 - 14
Sampler Inc., 6 - 65
Statton Furniture Mfg. Co., 6 - 71
The Burruss Company, 5 - 10
Thomas H. Kramer Inc., 6 - 77
Thos. Moser, Cabinetmakers, 6 - 77
Trott Furniture Co., 6 - 79
Vermont Furniture Designs, 6 - 80

Chest

Country Bed Shop, 6 - 19
Dimitrios Klitsas, 1 - 14
Murphy Furniture Mfg. Co., Inc., 6 - 54
The Keeping Room, 6 - 75

Chimney

Beldes, Inc., 3 - 13
Heat-Fab Inc., 3 - 44
Heatilator Inc., 3 - 45

Chipper

BCS America, Inc., 7 - 1
Gardener's Supply, 7 - 3
MacKissic Incorporated, 7 - 4
Troy-Bilt Mfg. Co., 7 - 7

Chrome

(Grilles, Moulding, etc.)
CMF Colonial Moulding, 1 - 9
Deco-Trol, 3 - 30
Shower-Rite Corp., 2 - 10

Clay

Brass & Traditional Sinks Ltd., 2 - 3
Cal-Shake, Inc., 3 - 19
Elon Inc., 3 - 33
Kraftile Company, 3 - 53

Clock

Emperor Clock Company, 8 - 25
Howard Miller Clock Company, 6 - 37
Sligh Clocks, 8 - 61

Closet

(Doors, Organizers, etc.)
American Storage Systems, 8 - 4
California Closet Company, 8 - 13
Closet Shop at Home, 8 - 17
Closet Systems Corp., 8 - 17
Crane Plumbing, 8 - 19
Diston Industries Inc., 2 - 4
Dunbarton Corp., 4 - 6
Paniflex Corp., 1 - 27
The Closet Doctor, 8 - 66
Wing Industries Inc., 4 - 18

Coal

Ceramic Radiant Heat, 3 - 22
Keokuk Stove Works, 3 - 52
Thermal Control Co., 3 - 90

The Complete Sourcebook

Colonial – Cooktop

Index

Colonial

A.J.P. Coppersmith,   1 - 1
American Furniture Co., 6 - 4
Authentic Designs,   3 - 10
Cohasset Colonials,   6 - 17
Colonial Furniture Shops, Inc., 6 - 18
Creative Openings,   4 - 4
DS Locksmithing Company,   3 - 29
Dutch Products & Supply Co.,   3 - 32
Foreign Traders,   6 - 29
Gates Moore,   11 - 13
Heritage Fence Company, 7 - 3
Heritage Lanterns,   11 - 14
Hurley Patentee Manor, 11 - 16
L.T. Moses Willard, Inc.,   11 - 18
Ole Country Barn,   3 - 66
Orleans Carpenters,   6 - 57
Peerless Imported Rugs, 8 - 52
S. Wilder & Co. Inc.,   11 - 28
The Country House,   8 - 66
The Walsh Woodworks,   8 - 68
Welsbach,   11 - 35
Winterbrook Inc.,   6 - 85

Column

A.F. Schwerd Manufacturing Co., 1 - 1
Abaroot Manufacturing Company, 1 - 2
Allen Iron Works & Supply,   1 - 3
American Wood Column Corp.,   1 - 4
Architectural Antique Warehouse,   3 - 9
Architectural Lathe & Mill,   1 - 6
Architectural Salvage Company, 1 - 6
Aristocrat Products Inc.,   1 - 6
Boston Turning Works,   1 - 8
Brown Moulding Company, 1 - 9
Campbellsville Industries,   3 - 19
Cascade Wood Products Inc.,   1 - 10
Chadsworth, Inc.,   1 - 10
CinderWhit & Company,   1 - 10
Classic Mouldings Inc., 1 - 11
Crown Plastering,   1 - 12
Custom Wood Turnings,   1 - 13
Elk Valley Woodworking Inc.,   6 - 26
Florida Wood Moulding & Trim,   1 - 17
Haas Woodworking Company Inc., 1 - 19
Haddonstone USA Ltd.,   7 - 3
Hartman-Sanders Co.,   1 - 19
J. A. Dawley Fine Woodworking,   7 - 3
Jeffries Wood Works Inc.,   1 - 21
Leslie-Locke Inc.,   3 - 55
M. L. Condon Company Inc.,   3 - 56
NMC Focal Point,   1 - 24
Nord Company,   4 - 12
Outwater Plastic Industries,   1 - 26
Pagliacco Turning & Milling,   1 - 26
Partelow Custom Wood Turnings, 1 - 27
R & R Lumber & Building Supply Corp.,1 - 28
Raymond Enkeboll Designs,   1 - 28
Replico Products Inc., 1 - 29
Rich Woodturning Inc., 1 - 29
Rogue River Millwork, 1 - 30
Saco Manufacturing & Woodworking, 1 - 30
Somerset Door & Column Co.,   4 - 15
Starling Inc., 1 - 32
The Fixture Exchange, 2 - 11
Visador Co.,   1 - 36
Worthington Group, Ltd.,   1 - 38

Comforter

Bedroom Secrets,   8 - 9

CS Brooks Corp.,   8 - 13
Rodless Decorations Inc.,   8 - 56
Springs Performance Products, 8 - 62
Whiting Mfg. Co. Inc.,   8 - 76

Component

(Architectural, Building, etc.)

A.F. Schwerd Manufacturing Co., 1 - 1
Albany Woodworks Inc., 3 - 5
American Building Components, 3 - 6
American Building Restoration, 3 - 6
Antiquarian Traders,   6 - 5
Architectural Antiques Exchange,   1 - 5
Architectural Antiques, 1 - 5
Architectural Antiquities,   1 - 5
Architectural Cataloguer, USA, 1 - 5
Architectural Elements, 1 - 5
Architectural Lathe & Mill,   1 - 6
Architectural Systems, Inc.,   1 - 6
Artefact-Architectural Antiques,   1 - 7
Artefacts Architectural Antiques,   1 - 7
Bassett & Findley Ltd., 4 - 2
Boston Turning Works,   1 - 8
Botrea Stairs, 1 - 8
Brill & Walker Associates Inc., 1 - 9
Brown Moulding Company, 1 - 9
Browne Winther & Co. Ltd.,   1 - 9
Chadsworth, Inc.,   1 - 10
Cleveland Wrecking,   1 - 11
Clivus Multrum, Inc.,   2 - 4
Colonial Antiques,   1 - 11
Conservation Building Products Ltd.,   3 - 26
Contact Lumber Company, 3 - 27
Dale Incor, Inc.,   3 - 29
Down River Intl. Inc., 12 - 8
E. F. Bufton & Son Builders, 1 - 15
Flex Trim,   12 - 9
Florida Victorian Arch. Antiques,   1 - 17
Hartman-Sanders Co.,   1 - 19
J. W. Window Components, Inc., 12 - 12
Jali Ltd.,   3 - 50
John Carr Joinery Sales Ltd.,   12 - 13
Kemp,   7 - 4
MacKissic Incorporated, 7 - 4
Palmer Creek Hand-Hewn Wood Prod.,1 - 27
Pelnick Wrecking Company, 3 - 69
Restoration Resource,   3 - 74
Richard Burbidge Ltd.,   3 - 75
Stamford Wrecking,   3 - 82
Sun-Mar Corp.,   7 - 7
Taco, 1 - 33
Timber Truss Housing Systems Inc., 3 - 91
United House Wrecking, Inc.,   3 - 93
Vintage Pine Company,   5 - 11
Worthington Group, Ltd.,   1 - 38

Composter

CanDo Composter,   7 - 2
Gardener's Supply, 7 - 3
R.P.B. Manufacturing,   7 - 5

Compound

(Restoration, etc.)

Abatron Inc.,   3 - 3
Specification Chemicals Inc.,   3 - 81

Cooktop

Allister Door Control Systems Inc.,   4 - 1
Blanco America, 10 - 2 ,   10 - 5
Creda Inc.,   10 - 3
Ferretti Ltd.,   10 - 4

Index

Copper – Curtain

Gaggenau USA Corporation, 10 - 4
Jenn-Air, 10 - 6
Lumea, 11 - 21
Lutron, 11 - 21
Miele, 10 - 7
Precision Multiple Controls, Inc., 3 - 71
RAB Electric, 9 - 3
Russell Range, Inc., 10 - 9
Thermador, 10 - 10

Copper
(Panel, Roofing, etc.)
Conklin Metal Industries, 3 - 26
Country Accents, 12 - 7

Cornice
Aristocrat Products Inc., 1 - 6
Felber Ornamental Plastering Corp., 1 - 16
Fischer & Jirouch Company, 1 - 16
Replico Products Inc., 1 - 29

Countertop
ADI Corporation, 1 - 1
Abet Laminati, 3 - 3
Accents In Stone, 3 - 3
Ashfield Stone Quarry, 3 - 9
Avonite, 3 - 10
Ferretti Ltd., 10 - 4
Gawet Marble & Granite Inc., 3 - 39
Gibraltar, 3 - 40
Granite Design, 3 - 41
Huntington/Pacific Ceramics, Inc., 3 - 48
Ideal-Standard Ltd., 2 - 6
Kinzee Industries Inc., 12 - 14
Marble & Tile Imports, 3 - 57
Merit Cabinet Distributors, 2 - 7
Nevamar Corporation, 10 - 7
The Decorative Center of Houston, 8 - 66
Trimall Interior Products Inc., 3 - 92
V-T Industries Inc., 4 - 17
Vermont Soapstone Co., 3 - 95

Country
Boyles Furniture, 6 - 11
Brunschwig & Fils, 8 - 12
Country Crossroads Furniture, 6 - 19
Country Pine Furniture, 6 - 19
Curtain Cottage, 8 - 20
Deacon & Sandys, 6 - 22
Deep River Trading Company, 6 - 22
Faith's Lacery, 8 - 27
Franklin Custom Furniture, 6 - 30
French Country Living, 6 - 30
Grand Era Reproductions, 4 - 8
Homestead Furniture, 6 - 36
Jeannie Serpa Stencils, 8 - 37
Le Lace Factory, Inc., 8 - 42
Mather's Department Store, 8 - 44
Maynard House Antiques, 6 - 51
Mills River Industries, Inc., 8 - 46
Olde Mill House Shoppe, 6 - 57
Quality Dinettes Incorporated, 6 - 61
Rex Furniture Co. Inc., 6 - 63
Robelier, 11 - 27
Simply Country Furniture, 6 - 68
Stenart Inc., 6 - 63
Studio Steel, 11 - 30
The Seraph Country Collection, 6 - 76
Thomas H. Kramer Inc., 6 - 77
Vintage Wood Works, 1 - 36

Cover
(Bed, Patio, etc.)
AAA Aluminum Products Ltd., 3 - 2
Accurate Aluminum Products, Inc., 3 - 3
Barker Metalcraft, 3 - 12
Carter Canopies, 8 - 15
Glen Raven Mills Inc., 3 - 40
Jali Ltd., 3 - 50
Pacesetter Building Systems, 12 - 19
Winther Browne, 3 - 99

Craft
Anthropologie, 6 - 4
Craft King, 8 - 19
Dried Flower Creations, 6 - 24
George Wells Rugs, 8 - 30
Honani Crafts, 8 - 34
Hopi Arts & Crafts, 8 - 34
International Manufacturing Co., 8 - 36
J & L Floral, 8 - 36
Meadow Everlasting, 8 - 45
Path Of The Sun Images, 8 - 52
Patterncrafts, 8 - 52
Prairie Edge, 8 - 54
R & R Crafts, 7 - 5
Reservation Creations, 8 - 55
Schoenly's Floral Designs, 8 - 59

Cupola
Adornments for Architecture, 1 - 2
Campbellsville Industries, 3 - 19
Cape Cod Cupola Co., Inc., 1 - 9
Colonial Cupolas Inc., 1 - 11
Country Cupolas, 1 - 12
Crosswinds Gallery, 1 - 12
J. A. du Lac Company, 1 - 20
J. F. Orr & Sons, 10 - 6

Curtain
ADO Corp., 8 - 2
Aberdeen Mfg. Corp., 8 - 2
Artifacteria, 8 - 5
At Home in the Valley, 8 - 6
Beacon Looms, Inc., 8 - 8
Caroline Country Ruffles, 8 - 14
Caroline's Ruffled Curtains, Inc., 8 - 14
Century House of Drapes, 8 - 15
Cloth Crafters, 8 - 17
Country Curtains, 8 - 19
Daisy Decorative Products, 8 - 21
Dana's Curtains & Draperies, 8 - 21
Dianthus Ltd., 8 - 23
Domestications, 8 - 23
Dorothy's Ruffled Originals, Inc., 8 - 23
Flemington Fabric Decorating Center, 8 - 28
Harding's Custom Sheers, 12 - 10
Helm Products Ltd., 8 - 32
Hornick Industries, 8 - 34
J. M Mills, 2 - 6
J. R. Burrows & Company, 8 - 37
K & R Custom Interiors, 8 - 38
Laura Copenhaver Industries Inc., 8 - 41
Le Lace Factory, Inc., 8 - 42
Linen & Lace, 8 - 42
Linen Lady, 8 - 42
Mather's Department Store, 8 - 44
Morantz Inc., 8 - 47
Nope, 2 - 8
Old Manor House, 8 - 50
Parker Window Covering, 8 - 51

The Complete Sourcebook

Index - 19

Cushion – Decorative

Index

Penn Needle Art Co., 8 - 52
Rodless Decorations Inc., 8 - 56
Rue De France Inc., 8 - 57
Spring Lace Two, 8 - 62
Stanwood Drapery Co. Inc., 8 - 62
Surrey Shoppe Interiors, 8 - 64
The Curtain Collection, 8 - 66
The Gazebo of New York, 8 - 67
Trifles, 8 - 69

Cushion

Barnett Products Co., 6 - 8
Harriet's House, 8 - 32
Hines of Oxford, 3 - 46

Custom

(Cabinets, Doors, Drapery, Furniture, Stained Glass, Woodwork, etc.)

Andreas Lehman Fine Glasswork, 1 - 4
Antiquity, 6 - 5
Barbara Zinkel Design, 8 - 8
Bevis Custom Furniture, 6 - 9
Boone Decorative Fabrics, 8 - 11
Boulder Art Glass Co., 3 - 16
Buy Carpet Direct, 8 - 12
Calma's Custom Cabinets, 10 - 2
Cassidy Brothers Forge, Inc., 1 - 10
Charles W. Rice & Co. Inc., 8 - 16
Cheng Design, 12 - 6
Cheyenne Company, 1 - 10
Cole Sewell Corp., 4 - 4
Contemporary Copper, 10 - 3
Continental Custom Made Furniture, 6 - 18
Creative Designs, 6 - 20
Curtain Cottage, 8 - 20
Custom Canvas Awning, Inc., 3 - 28
Custom Furniture Corp., 6 - 20
Custom House, 11 - 8
Custom Shades, 8 - 20
Custom Window Co., 12 - 8
D.S.C. Fabrics Inc., 8 - 21
Dean Custom Awnings, 3 - 30
Dellinger, Inc., 8 - 22
Elk Valley Woodworking Inc., 6 - 26
Essential Items, 6 - 27
Expressions Custom Furniture, 6 - 27
Form III, 8 - 29
Gunther Mills Inc., 1 - 19
Heritage Custom Kitchens, 10 - 5
Historic Windows, 12 - 11
Iberia Millwork, 4 - 9
Janik Custom Millwork, 12 - 12
Jenn-Air/Maytag, 10 - 6
John Alan Designs, 6 - 40
Kemper Quality Cabinets, 10 - 6
Knipp & Co. Inc., 6 - 43
Lacey-Champion Carpets, Inc., 8 - 41
Lamson-Taylor Custom Doors, 4 - 11
Linel, Inc., 12 - 14
Luv Those Rugs, 8 - 43
M. Craig & Company, 6 - 47
Mack & Rodel Cabinet Makers, 6 - 47
Mad River Woodworks, 1 - 22
Manhattan Cabinetry, 6 - 48
Manheim & Weitz, 6 - 48
Mar-Flo, Inc., 4 - 12
Maui Trading Co., 3 - 59
Michael's Fine Colonial Products, 1 - 24
Minnetonka Woodcraft Co., 6 - 53
Monson's Custom Woodworking, 10 - 7
Northern Refrigerator Company, 10 - 7

Old Kentucky Wood Products, 1 - 26
Olympic Custom Furniture, Ltd., 6 - 57
Peachtree Doors, Inc., 4 - 13
Port-O-Lite Corporation, 1 - 28
PriceKing Building Supply Inc., 3 - 71
Putnam Rolling Ladder Company Inc., 3 - 72
Richard Brooks Company, 6 - 63
River East Custom Cabinets, 6 - 63
Robert Whitley Studio, 6 - 64
Robillard, 1 - 29
Ruth's Custom Bedspreads, 8 - 57
Sebastapol Wood Windows, 12 - 23
Shaw's Custom Cabinets, 6 - 67
Sunburst Shutters Inc., 12 - 24
Tad Taylor's Fantasy Furniture, 6 - 73
Tatem Mfg. Co. Inc., 1 - 33
The Farmhouse Collection, 6 - 75
The Kennebec Company, 10 - 10
The Wood Factory, 1 - 35
Treske, 6 - 78
Virginia Craftsmen Inc., 6 - 81
Westbury Conservatories, 3 - 97
Western Woodwork Co., 6 - 83
Wood-Mode, 10 - 11
Woodburns Custom Cabinets, 10 - 11
Woodwrights of Rochester, 10 - 11

Danish

E. J. Evans, 6 - 25
Genada Imports, 6 - 31

Decking

Western Red Cedar Lumber Assoc., 3 - 98

Decorative

(Accessories, Fabric, Glass, Hardware, Moulding, Screens, Tile, etc.)

American Tack & Decorative Hardware, 3 - 7
Amerock Corporation, 3 - 7
Aristokraft, 10 - 1
Armstrong World Industries Inc., 1 - 6
Armstrong-Decorative Accessories, 8 - 5
Art-Line Design, 3 - 9
Artistic Surfaces, 8 - 6
Baldwin Hardware Corp., 3 - 12
Barbara Zinkel Design, 8 - 8
Barnett Products Co., 6 - 8
Bel Vasaio Ltd., 3 - 13
Belwith International, 3 - 14
Bona Decorative Hardware, 3 - 16
Brass Accents, 3 - 16
Buesche Inc., 3 - 17
Canner Inc., 8 - 13
Casella Lighting, 11 - 6
Chelsea Decorative Metal Co., 1 - 10
Country Accents, 12 - 7
Country Cupolas, 1 - 12
Cross Industries, 3 - 28
Crown City Hardware, 3 - 28
De Best Mfg. Co., Inc., 3 - 30
Decorative Hardware Studio, 3 - 30
Decoy Shop, 8 - 22
Design/Craft Fabric Corp., 8 - 22
Distepro USA Inc., 3 - 31
Fleurco Industries 1963 Ltd., 10 - 4
Flora & Fauna, 3 - 37
Gentron Corp., 3 - 39
Great Paines Glassworks, 4 - 8
GuildMaster Arts, 8 - 31
High Point Glass & Decorative Co., 3 - 45
Horchow Home Collection, 6 - 36

Index - 20

The Complete Sourcebook

Index

Decorator – Door

House of Clay, 8 - 34
House of Fara Inc., 3 - 47
Hy-Ko Products Co., 3 - 48
Imperial Stone Ltd., 8 - 35
Jacpa Ceramic Craftsmen, 8 - 37
Kebring Hardware, 3 - 52
Kemp & Beatley, Inc., 8 - 39
Kolson, 1 - 21
Larue Products, 8 - 41
Merit Metal Products Corp., 3 - 60
Miya Shoji & Interiors Inc., 8 - 47
Mystica & Company Inc., 3 - 62
Nagykery Imports, Ltd., 6 - 54
Nexton Industries Inc., 3 - 64
Ornamental Mouldings, Ltd., 1 - 26
P. E. Guerin Inc., 3 - 67
Parisotto, 8 - 51
Pfanstiel Hardware Co., 3 - 69
Port-O-Lite Corporation, 1 - 28
Quality Marble Inc., 3 - 72
RAB Electric, 9 - 3
Sculpture Studio, 8 - 59
Sentimental Journey, 8 - 59
Sequence USA Co. Ltd., 3 - 78
Snelling's Thermo-Vac, Inc., 3 - 79
Soletude Inc., 8 - 61
Southeast Hardware Mfg. Co., 3 - 81
Summitville Tiles Inc., 3 - 84
The Decorative Tile Works, 3 - 88
The Dize Co., 3 - 88
V-T Industries Inc., 4 - 17
Visador Co., 1 - 36
Window Grille Specialists, 12 - 28
Woodstock Soapstone Co., Inc., 3 - 100
Worthy Works Inc., 3 - 101

Decorator

(Fabric, etc.)

Brentwood Originals, 8 - 12
Century Fabrics Inc., 8 - 15
Fabrics By Design, 8 - 26
Fabrics By Phone, 8 - 26
Home Fabric Mills, Inc., 8 - 33
Jab/Anstoetz, 8 - 37
Robert Allen, 8 - 55
The Fabric Center, 8 - 66

Decoy

Darren's Decoys & Wooden Ducks, 8 - 21
Decoy Shop, 8 - 22
Will Kirkpatrick, 8 - 76

Delft

Dutch Products & Supply Co., 3 - 32
Helen Williams - Delft Tiles, 3 - 45

Desk

Artemide, 11 - 3
Derby Desk Company, 6 - 23
Door Store, 6 - 24
Grand River Workshop, 6 - 32
Kopil & Associates Timeless Furniture, 6 - 43
Lazy Lawyer Co. Inc., 6 - 44
The Keeping Room, 6 - 75
Vitra Seating Inc., 6 - 81

Dining Room

Allmilmo Ltd., 6 - 3
Anglo Nordic Marketing (UK) Ltd., 6 - 4
Aram Designs Ltd., 6 - 5
Artistic Upholstery Ltd., 6 - 6

Ashby & Horner Joinery Ltd., 6 - 6
Bevan Funnell Ltd., 6 - 9
Boyles Furniture, 6 - 11
Caldwell Chair Company, 6 - 13
Carleton Furniture Group Ltd., 6 - 14
Castle Mount, 6 - 15
Cochrane Furniture Co., 6 - 17
D & L Mfg., Co., 6 - 21
Dean & Brook Ltd., 6 - 22
Del Tongo (UK, etc.) Ltd., 6 - 22
E.C. Hodge Ltd., 6 - 25
Griffon Furniture Ltd., 6 - 33
H. Morris & Co. Ltd., 6 - 33
Hale Co., 6 - 33
Hamlet Furniture Ltd., 6 - 34
Holder Pearce, 6 - 36
Homeway Furniture Co., 6 - 36
Hostess Furniture Ltd., 6 - 37
Hyperion Wall Furniture Ltd., 6 - 38
J. T. Ellis & Co. Ltd., 6 - 39
John Pulsford Associates Ltd., 6 - 40
Kesterport Ltd., 6 - 42
Leboff International Ltd., 6 - 45
Leverwood Ltd., 6 - 45
Lexterten Ltd., 6 - 46
Marble & Tile Imports, 3 - 57
Mark Wilkinson Furniture Ltd., 6 - 50
Martin & Frost Ltd., 6 - 50
Metalliform Ltd., 6 - 52
Monzie Joinery Ltd., 6 - 54
Nathan Furniture Ltd., 6 - 54
Neil Rogers Interiors, 6 - 54
Options Bedrooms Ltd., 6 - 57
Pass & Seymour, 11 - 25
Pegram Contracts Ltd., 6 - 59
Pel Ltd., 6 - 59
Pira Ltd., 6 - 60
Plaza Furniture Gallery, 6 - 60
Pulaski Furniture Corp., 6 - 61
Quality Dinettes Incorporated, 6 - 61
Quality Furniture Market, 6 - 61
Renray Group Ltd., 6 - 63
Rex Furniture Co. Inc., 6 - 63
Richardson Bros., 6 - 63
Royal Strathclyde Blindcraft Ind., 6 - 65
Saraband Furniture Co., 6 - 66
Slumberland PLC, 6 - 69
South West Joinery Co. Ltd., 6 - 70
Stag Meredew Furniture Ltd., 6 - 71
Staples & Co. Ltd., 6 - 71
Stuart Interiors, 6 - 72
Sylmar Technology Ltd., 6 - 73
The Sofa Factory, 6 - 76
Thomasville Furniture, 6 - 77
Thos. Moser, Cabinetmakers, 6 - 77
Tilden Industries (UK, etc.) Ltd., 6 - 78
W. G. Undrill Ltd., 6 - 81
Wilkinsons Furniture Ltd., 6 - 84
William L. Mclean Ltd., 6 - 84
William Lawrence & Co. Ltd., 6 - 84
Younger Furniture, 6 - 87

Dishwasher

Miele, 10 - 7

Disposal

Blanco America, 10 - 2
Franke Inc., 10 - 4

Door

A & C Metal Products Co. Inc., 12 - 1

The Complete Sourcebook

Index - 21

Door – Door

Index

A & S Window Associates, Inc., 3 - 1
A-J Industries Inc., 4 - 1
A.J.P. Weslock Industries Co., 3 - 2
A.R. Perry Glass Co., 12 - 1
AAA Aluminum Stamping, Inc., 12 - 1
ALCAN Building Products, 12 - 1
ALCOA Vinyl Windows, 12 - 1
AMSCO Windows, 12 - 2
APL Window & Door Company, 12 - 2
ARMAC Brassfounders Group Ltd., 3 - 2
Academy Mfg. Co. Inc., 4 - 1
Ace Shower Door Co. Inc., 2 - 1
Acorn Antique Doors, 4 - 1
Acorn Manufacturing Co. Inc., 3 - 3
Acorn Window Systems Inc., 12 - 2
Active Window Products, 12 - 2
Adams Rite (Europe, etc.) Ltd., 12 - 2
Addkison Hardware Co. Inc., 3 - 4
Adkins Architectural Antiques, 1 - 2
Advanced Aluminum Products, 12 - 2
Albany Hardware Specialty Mfg. Co. , 3 - 4
Albany Woodworks Inc., 3 - 5
Albert Marston & Co. Ltd., 4 - 1
Alexander Moulding Mill Co., Inc., 4 - 1
Algoma Hardwoods, Inc., 1 - 2
Allgood Shower Door Corp., 2 - 1
Allister Door Control Systems Inc., 4 - 1
Allmetal, Inc., 12 - 2
Almet Hardware Ltd., 9 - 1
Alpine Windows, 12 - 3
Alside Window Company, 12 - 3
Aluma-Craft Corporation, 12 - 3
Aluma-Glass Industries, Inc., 12 - 3
Alumaroll Specialty Co., Inc., 12 - 3
Alumax, 12 - 3
Aluminum Products Company, 12 - 3
Aluminum Specialties Mfg. Co., 12 - 3
Alwindor Manufacturing, Inc., 12 - 3
American Door Co. Inc., 4 - 1
American Door Co. of Michigan Inc., 4 - 1
American Home Supply, 3 - 6
American Home Supply, 3 - 6
American Screen & Door Co., Inc., 12 - 3
American Shower Door Corp., 2 - 2
American Wood Column Corp., 1 - 4
Amerlite Aluminum Co., Inc., 12 - 3
Apex Doors Ltd., 4 - 1
Aqua Glass Corporation, 2 - 2
Arcadia Mfg. Inc., 1 - 5
Architectural Antiques West, 1 - 5
Architectural Antiquities, 1 - 5
Architectural Components, 1 - 5
Architectural Salvage Company, 1 - 6
Arctic Glass & Window Outlet, 12 - 4
Arrow Aluminum Ind., Inc., 12 - 4
Art Marble and Stone, 1 - 7
Arthur Shaw Manufacturing Ltd., 9 - 1
Artistic Doors and Windows, 4 - 1
Arvid's Historic Woods, 1 - 7
Atlas Roll-lite Door Co., 4 - 2
Atrium Door and Window Co., 4 - 2
B & B Products, 1 - 7
B. Lilly & Sons Ltd., 3 - 11
Baldwin Hardware Corp., 3 - 12
Baldwin Hardware, 3 - 12
Barnett Millworks, Inc., 1 - 8
Basco, 2 - 2
Bassett & Findley Ltd., 4 - 2
BayForm, 12 - 5
Baydale Architectural Metalwork Ltd., 1 - 8
Beech River Mill Company, 3 - 13

Bel-Air Door Co., 4 - 2
Benchmark, 4 - 2
Bend Millwork Systems Inc., 4 - 2
Bennett Industries Inc., 4 - 2
Berbaum Millwork Inc., 3 - 14
Berea Prehung Door, Inc., 4 - 2
Berke Door & Hardware, Inc., 3 - 14
Besam Ltd., 4 - 2
Better Bilt Aluminum Products Co., 12 - 5
Better-Bilt Aluminum Products Co., 12 - 5
Bevel Glass & Mirror, 4 - 2
Billings Sash & Door Co., 4 - 2
BiltBest Windows, 12 - 5
Binning's Bldg. Products Inc., 12 - 5
Bison Manufacturing, 4 - 2
Bjorndal Woodworks, 1 - 8
Black Millwork Co. Inc., 4 - 3
Blaine Window Hardware, 12 - 5
Blue Canyon Woodworks, 6 - 10
Boise Moulding & Lumber, 3 - 15
Bostwick Doors UK Ltd., 4 - 3
Boulton & Paul PLC, 3 - 16
Boyd Aluminum Mfg. Company, 12 - 5
Brass Tacks Hardware Ltd., 3 - 16
Bright Star Woodworking, 4 - 3
Browne Winther & Co. Ltd., 1 - 9
Buell Door Company, 4 - 3
Builders Brass Works Corp., 3 - 17
Burch Co., 12 - 5
Burt Millwork Corp., 1 - 9
C & S Distributors, Inc., 12 - 6
C. V. Aluminum, Inc., 12 - 6
CECO Corp., 4 - 3
Cabinet Crafters, 10 - 2
Cal-Wood Door Inc., 4 - 3
California Window Corporation, 12 - 6
Cape May Millworks, 1 - 10
Caradco, 12 - 6
Cardell Cabinets, 10 - 3
Care Free Aluminum Prod., Inc., 12 - 6
Carlos Shower Doors Inc., 2 - 3
Carolina Components Corp., 3 - 20
Cascade Mill & Glass Works, 4 - 3
Castlegate, Inc., 4 - 3
Catnic Ltd., 4 - 3
Cego Limited, 12 - 6
Century Shower Door, Inc., 2 - 3
Century Wood Door Limited, 4 - 3
CertainTeed Corp., 3 - 23
Chamberlain Group, 12 - 6
Cherry Creek Enterprises Inc., 4 - 3
Chubb Lock Company, 9 - 2
Ciro Coppa, 6 - 16
Cline Aluminum Doors Inc., 4 - 3
Clopay Corporation, 4 - 4
Coast to Coast Manufacturing Ltd., 12 - 6
Coastal Industries, Inc., 2 - 4
Cole Sewell Corp., 4 - 4
Collingdale Millwork Co., 1 - 11
Columbia Glass & window Company, 12 - 7
Columbia Metal Products Co., 12 - 7
Combination Door Company, 4 - 4
Conner's Architectural Antiques, 1 - 11
Conservation Building Products Ltd., 3 - 26
Consolidated Aluminum, 12 - 7
Consolidated American Window Co., 12 - 7
Contact Lumber Company, 3 - 27
Coppa Woodworking, 6 - 18
Corn Belt Aluminum Inc., 12 - 7
Corning Moulding Corporation, 1 - 12
Cotswold Architectural Products Ltd., 1 - 12

Index - 22

The Complete Sourcebook

Index

Door – Door

Cotswood Door Specialists Ltd., 4 - 4
Country Cupolas,   1 - 12
Cox Studios,   12 - 7
Craftline,   4 - 4
Crawford Door Ltd.,   4 - 4
Creative Openings,   4 - 4
Crestline,   4 - 4
Crompton Ltd., 12 - 7
Crown Door Corp.,   4 - 4
Crown Mfg. Corp. of Missouri,   12 - 8
Cumberland Woodcraft Co.,   1 - 13
Curriers Co.,   4 - 4
Customwood Mfg. Co.,   1 - 13
D.C. Mitchell Reproductions,   3 - 29
Deacon & Sandys,   6 - 22
Defiance Forest Products,   4 - 4
Delmar Hardware Mfg. Ltd.,   4 - 5
Delsan Industries, Inc.,   12 - 8
Delta Door Co., Inc.,   4 - 5
Dexter Lock,   4 - 5
Dickinsons Architectural Antiques,   1 - 14
Diston Industries Inc., 2 - 4
Donat Flamand, Inc.,   4 - 5
Door Systems Inc.,   4 - 5
DoorCraft Manufacturing Co.,   4 - 5
Doorcraft Mfg. Ltd.,   4 - 5
Doorland 2000 Inc.,   4 - 5
Doorman Hardware,   4 - 5
Doormen,   4 - 5
Doors, Incorporated,   4 - 5
Dor-Win Manufacturing, 4 - 5
Down River Intl. Inc.,   12 - 8
Driwood Moulding Co.,   8 - 24
Dryad Simplan Limited,   12 - 8
Dunbarton Corp.,   4 - 6
Duraflex Systems Ltd., 4 - 6
EMCO,   4 - 6
ENJO Doors and Windows, 4 - 6
Eagle Plywood & Door Mftrs. Inc.,   4 - 6
Eagle Window & Door,   12 - 8
Edward P. Schmidt Cabinetmaker, 6 - 25
Eggers Industries,   4 - 6
Elegant Entries,   4 - 6
Elite Interior Doors,   4 - 6
Energy Saving Products, 12 - 9
Englander Millwork Corp.,   12 - 9
Entrances Inc., 4 - 6
Erebus Limited, 4 - 6
Ernest Thompson Furniture,   6 - 26
Eugenia's Place,   4 - 6
F. E. Schumacher Co., Inc.,   4 - 7
Fancy Front Brassiere Co.,   1 - 16
Faneuil Furniture Hardware Co. Inc.,   6 - 28
Fayston Iron & Steel Works,   3 - 35
Feather River Wood & Glass Co., 4 - 7
Fenebee Inc.,   4 - 7
Fenestra Corp., 4 - 7
Fenestra Wood Door Div.,   4 - 7
Fiberlux, Inc., 4 - 7
Filmore Thomas & Co., Inc.,   4 - 7
Fine Woodworking by Living Tree,   6 - 28
Fineman Doors Inc.,   4 - 7
First American Resources,   12 - 9
Fleetwood Aluminum Products, Inc., 12 - 9
Frank Allart & Co., Ltd.,   4 - 7
Fraser Woods Inc.,   4 - 7
Fuji Hardware Co., Ltd.,   2 - 4
G & T Woodworking Ltd., 4 - 7
G-U Hardware Inc.,   12 - 9
G. R. Theriault Ltd.,   4 - 7
GT Doors & Locks,   4 - 8

Garofalo Studio,   2 - 5
Garran Mfg. Ltd.,   4 - 8
General Aluminum Corporation,   12 - 9
General Products Co. Inc.,   4 - 8
Georgia Palm Beach Aluminum Window,12-9
Gibbons of Willenhall Ltd.,   9 - 2
Glass Craft Specialties, Inc.,   4 - 8
Golden Age Glassworks,   12 - 10
Golden Gate Glass & Mirror Co.,Inc., 12 - 10
Graham Mfg. Corp.,   4 - 8
Grand Era Reproductions,   4 - 8
Grande Entrance Door Company,   4 - 8
Great Paines Glassworks,   4 - 8
H-R Windows,   12 - 10
Hahn's Woodworking Co.,   12 - 10
Haley Bros.,Inc.,   4 - 8
Hanover Wire Cloth,   12 - 10
Hara's Inc.,   12 - 10
Harry G. Barr Company, 12 - 10
Hayfield Window & Door Co.,   12 - 11
Hazelmere Industries Ltd.,   4 - 8
Hendricks Woodworking, 4 - 9
Hess Manufacturing Company,   12 - 11
Hewi, Inc.,   3 - 45
Hiawatha, Inc., 2 - 5
Hicksville Woodworks Co.,   1 - 20
Hillaldam Coburn Topdor Ltd.,   4 - 9
Hipkiss & Co. Ltd.,   3 - 46
Hoff Forest Products, Inc.,   3 - 46
Home & Cabinet Designs Inc.,   10 - 5
Hope Works Ltd.,   12 - 11
Horesfeathers Architectural Antiques,   1 - 20
Howard Industries Inc., 12 - 11
Hunt Windows and Doors, 12 - 11
Hurd Millwork Company, 3 - 48
IJ Mfg. Ltd.,   12 - 12
Iberia Millwork,   4 - 9
Ideal Door Co., 4 - 9
Ideal Wood Products,   4 - 9
Imperial Screen Company Inc.,   9 - 2
Imperial Shower Door Co.,   2 - 6
Insulate Industries, Inc.,   12 - 12
International Window Corporation,   12 - 12
International Wood Products,   4 - 9
Iowa Des Moines Door & Hardware,   4 - 9
Irreplaceable Artifacts,   1 - 20
J. A. Dawley Fine Woodworking, 7 - 3
J. Legge & Co. Ltd.,   4 - 9
J. W. Window Components, Inc.,   12 - 12
J. Zeluck Inc., 1 - 21
JJJ Specialty Co.,   4 - 9
Jack Wallis Doors,   4 - 9
James Gibbons Format Ltd.,   12 - 12
Janik Custom Millwork, 12 - 12
Jelco Windows & Doors, 12 - 12
Jeld-Wen,   4 - 10
Jessup Door Company,   4 - 10
Joe-Keith Industries, Inc.,   12 - 12
John Carr Joinery Sales Ltd.,   12 - 13
Johnson Metal Products, 4 - 10
JonCo Manufacturing, Inc.,   12 - 13
Jones & Barclay Ltd., 3 - 51
Jones Paint & Glass, Inc.,   12 - 13
Josiah Parkes and Sons Ltd.,   4 - 10
Kansas Aluminum, Inc., 12 - 13
Karona Inc.,   4 - 10
Kaylien,   4 - 10
Keller Aluminum Products,   12 - 13
Keller Industries Inc., 4 - 10
Kenmore Industries,   4 - 10
Kinco Corporation,   12 - 13

The Complete Sourcebook

Index - 23

Door – Door

Kinco, Ltd., 12 - 13
King Brothers Woodworking Inc., 6 - 42
Kinro, Inc., 12 - 14
Kirby Millworks, 4 - 10
Klamath Doors, 4 - 10
Kolbe & Kolbe Millwork Co. Inc., 1 - 21
Korona, 4 - 10
Kwikset Corp., 4 - 11
Laflamme & Frere, Inc., 4 - 11
Lamson-Taylor Custom Doors, 4 - 11
Landmark Doors, 4 - 11
Landquist & Son, Inc., 4 - 11
Leicester Joinery Co., 4 - 11
Lincoln Wood Products, Inc., 12 - 14
Linford Brothers/Utal Glass Co., 12 - 14
Living Windows Corporation, 12 - 14
Louisiana-Pacific Corporation, 3 - 56
Lynden Door, Inc., 4 - 11
M. L. Condon Company Inc., 3 - 56
MBS Manufacturing West, Inc., 12 - 15
MQ Windows of Europe&TheAmericas,12-15
Mad River Woodworks, 1 - 22
Madawaska Doors Inc., 4 - 11
Made-Rite Aluminum Window Co., 12 - 15
Magnet Trade, 4 - 11
Magnokrom Inc., 6 - 47
Manufacturers Glass, 4 - 11
Mar-Flo, Inc., 4 - 12
Marvin Windows and Doors, 12 - 15
Marvin Windows, 12 - 15
Marwin Co., 3 - 59
Mason Corporation, 12 - 15
Masonite Corp., 4 - 12
Masterview Window Company, 12 - 15
Maurer & Shepherd Joyners Inc., 1 - 23
Maywood Inc., 4 - 12
McDan Woodworking, 1 - 23
Mercer Industries, Inc., 12 - 15
Merit Metal Products Corp., 3 - 60
Metal Exchange Corp., 12 - 15
Metal Industries Inc., 12 - 15
Metal Industries, Inc., 12 - 16
Michael Farr Custom Woodworking, 1 - 24
Michael's Fine Colonial Products, 1 - 24
Midland Manufacturing Corp., 2 - 7
Midwest Dowel Works, Inc., 3 - 60
Midwest Wood Products, 12 - 16
Milgard Manufacturing, Inc., 12 - 16
Miller Industries, Inc., 12 - 16
Millwork Supply Company, 4 - 12
Minuteman International Co., 3 - 61
Moeller-Reimer Company, 12 - 16
Mohawk Flush Doors, Inc., 4 - 12
Mon-Ray Windows, Inc., 12 - 16
Monroe Coldren & Sons, 3 - 62
Morgan Distribution, 4 - 12
Morgan Manufacturing, 4 - 12
Morgan-Bockius Studios Inc., 4 - 12
Moss Supply Company, Inc., 12 - 16
Mystica & Company Inc., 3 - 62
NT Jenkins Manufacturing Co., 12 - 17
Nana Windows & Doors Inc., 12 - 17
National Screen Company, Inc., 4 - 12
National Woodworks, Inc., 1 - 25
New Morning Windows, Inc., 12 - 17
New York Wire Company, 12 - 17
Newpro, 12 - 17
Nichols-Homeshield, Inc., 12 - 18
Norandex, Inc., 12 - 18
Norco Windows Inc., 12 - 18
Nord Company, 4 - 12

North Central Door Co., 4 - 12
North Star Company, 12 - 18
Northwest Aluminum Products, 12 - 18
Nose Creek Forest Products, Ltd., 1 - 25
Nottingham Gallery, 4 - 12
Nu-Air Mfg. Co., 4 - 13
Oak Leaves Studio, 1 - 25
Oakwood Classic & Custom Woodwork,1 -25
Olde South Door, 4 - 13
Omega Garage Door, 4 - 13
Omnia Industries, 3 - 67
Optimum Window Mfg. Corp., 12 - 18
Oregon Wooden Screen Door Co., 4 - 13
Overhead Door Corp., 4 - 13
P. C. Henderson Ltd., 12 - 18
Pacesetter Building Systems, 12 - 19
Pacific Industries/Pl. Inc., 12 - 19
Palmer Creek Hand-Hewn Wood Prod.,1 - 27
Paniflex Corp., 1 - 27
Peachtree Doors, Inc., 4 - 13
Pease Industries, Inc., 4 - 13
Peerless Products Inc., 12 - 19
Pella Corporation, 12 - 19
Pennco, Inc., 12 - 19
Perfection Metal & Supply Co., 3 - 69
Perkins & Powell, 2 - 8
Perkins Architectural Millwork, 1 - 27
Perkins Manufacturing & Distributing, 12 - 19
Perma Window & Door Service, 12 - 19
Perma-Door, 4 - 13
Peter Goldberger, 2 - 8
Peterson Window Corp., 12 - 19
Philips Home Products, 4 - 13
Phillips Industries Inc., 3 - 70
Pinecrest, 1 - 27
Pixley Lumber Co., 4 - 13
Pompei & Company Art Glass, 12 - 20
Portes Belhumeur Inc., 4 - 14
Pozzi Wood Windows, 12 - 20
Premdor Inc., 4 - 14
Pro-Glass Technology/Vinyl Tech Inc., 12 - 20
Public Supply Company, 12 - 20
Quaker Window Products Co., 12 - 20
Quality Door & Millwork, 4 - 14
Quantum Wood Windows, 12 - 21
Queen City Architectural Salvage, 1 - 28
R & R Lumber & Building Supply Corp.,1 - 28
R. Cartwright & Co., Ltd., 12 - 21
R. Lang Co., 12 - 21
Rare Wood, 4 - 14
Rasmussen Millwork /Colonial Craft,12 - 21
Ray Tenebruso, 4 - 14
Raynor Garage Doors, 4 - 14
Red-E-Built Products, 4 - 14
Regal Manufacturing Co., 3 - 74
Remington/Div. of Metal Ind., Inc., 12 - 21
Republic Aluminum Inc., 12 - 21
Restorer's Supply, 4 - 14
Reynolds Mfg. Company, Inc., 12 - 22
Ridge Doors, 4 - 14
River City Woodworks, 5 - 8
Riverside Millwork Co. Inc., 1 - 29
Riverview Millworks Inc., 1 - 29
Rockwell Window Co. Inc., 12 - 22
Roddiscraft Inc., 12 - 22
Rogow Window/Ideal Aluminum, 12 - 22
Rollyson Aluminum Products, 12 - 22
Royal Plastics, Inc., 12 - 22
Rural Hall Inc., 4 - 14
S. D. Davis, Inc., 12 - 22
SNE Enterprises, Inc., 4 - 14

Index

Downspout – Drapery

Samuel B. Sadtler & Co., 1 - 30
Sauder Door Corporation, 4 - 14
Scherr's Cabinets, 4 - 15
Schuco International, 4 - 15
Seal-O-Matic Industries Inc., 12 - 23
SealRite Windows, Inc., 12 - 23
Season-All Industries Inc., 12 - 23
Seaway Manufacturing Corp., 12 - 23
Sebastapol Wood Windows, 12 - 23
Securi Style Ltd., 11 - 28
Semling-Menke Company, Inc., 4 - 15
Setzer Forest Products, 3 - 78
Sheppard Millwork, Inc., 4 - 15
Sherwood Shower Door Co., 2 - 10
Shower-Rite Corp., 2 - 10
Silverton Victorian Millworks, 1 - 31
Simonton Building Products, Inc., 12 - 23
Simpson Door Company, 4 - 15
Skotty Aluminum Prod. Co., 12 - 23
Skytech Systems, 12 - 23
Solartechnic 2000 Ltd., 8 - 61
Somerset Door & Column Co., 4 - 15
Somfy Systems Inc., 12 - 23
Southeastern Aluminum Products Inc., 4 - 15
Southeastern Insulated Glass, 7 - 6
Southern Millwork, Inc., 1 - 31
Southwest Door Company Inc., 4 - 15
Southwood Door Company, 4 - 15
Sovereign Group Ltd., 4 - 15
Sovereign Wright, 4 - 16
Spanish Pueblo Doors Inc., 4 - 16
Specialty Woodworks Co., 4 - 16
Stanley Door Systems, 4 - 16
Steldor Ltd., 4 - 16
Sterling Plumbing Group, 2 - 10
Steves & Sons, 4 - 16
Stone Door & Truss, 3 - 83
Stripling-Blake Lumber Co. Inc., 4 - 16
Sun Window Company, Inc., 12 - 24
Sunburst Stained Glass Co. Inc., 3 - 84
Superior Metal Products Co., 12 - 24
Swan Mfg. Co., 2 - 10
Swish Products Ltd., 4 - 16
Sylvan Brandt Inc., 5 - 9
T. Saveker Ltd., 11 - 30
Taylor Brothers Inc., 4 - 16
Taylor Building Products, 4 - 16
Temple Products, Inc., 4 - 16
Teskey Enterprises Inc., 12 - 24
The Bank Architectural Antiques, 1 - 34
The Bilco Co., 4 - 17
The Blount Lumber Company, 12 - 24
The Fixture Exchange, 2 - 11
The Gerkin Company, 12 - 25
The Joinery Company, 5 - 10
The Jordan Companies, 12 - 25
The London Door Company, 4 - 17
The Loxcreen Company, Inc., 12 - 25
The Old Wagon Factory, 4 - 17
The Smoot Lumber Co., 4 - 17
The Wood Factory, 1 - 35
The Yorkshire Door Company Ltd., 4 - 17
Therma-Tru Corporation, 12 - 25
Thermal Profiles, Inc., 4 - 17
Thermal Windows, Inc., 12 - 25
Torrance Steel Window Co. Inc., 12 - 25
Touchstone Woodworks, 4 - 17
Traco, 12 - 26
Triangle Brass Mfg. Co. Inc., 3 - 92
Trico Mfg./Div. of Tri-State, 12 - 26
Trimall Interior Products Inc., 3 - 92

United States Woodworking, Inc., 1 - 35
Universal Components, 12 - 26
Urban Artifacts, 1 - 35
Urban Ore, 4 - 17
V-T Industries Inc., 4 - 17
Valley Planing Mill Inc., 1 - 36
Vancouver Door Co. Inc., 4 - 17
Vaughan & Sons Inc., 3 - 94
Velux America Inc., 4 - 17
Vetter Mfg. Co., 12 - 27
Viking Industries, Inc., 12 - 27
Vintage Wood Works, 1 - 36
Vinyl Building Products Inc., 12 - 27
W & F Mfg. Inc., 12 - 27
Wallace-Crossly Corp., 4 - 17
Wartian Lock Co., 9 - 3
Wayne-Dalton Corporation, 4 - 18
Weather Shield Mfg., Inc., 12 - 27
Wells Aluminum, Inc., 12 - 28
Wenco Windows, 12 - 28
Weslock National, 4 - 18
Western Insulated Glass co., 12 - 28
Western Oregon Doors, Inc., 4 - 18
Westlake Architectural Antiques, 1 - 37
Wholesale Door Company, 4 - 18
Wilkening Fireplace Co., 3 - 99
Williams Art Glass Studios, 12 - 28
Willis Lumber Company Inc., 1 - 37
Windsor Door, 4 - 18
Windsor Mill, Inc., 1 - 37
Wing Industries Inc., 4 - 18
Winter Seal of Flint, Inc., 1 - 37
Wohners Inc., 1 - 37
Woodgrain Millwork, Inc., 4 - 18
Woodland Industries, Inc., 4 - 18
Woodpecker Products Inc., 4 - 18
Woodstone Company, 1 - 38
Yale Ogron Mfg. Co. Inc., 12 - 28
Young Manufacturing Co., 4 - 18
Yuba River Moulding & Millwork, Inc., 1 - 38

Downspout

Accurate Aluminum Products, Inc., 3 - 3
Alumax Aluminum Corp., 3 - 6
Beaver Industries, 3 - 13
Genova Products, 3 - 39
Royal-Apex Mfg. Co. Inc., 3 - 76

Drapery

ADO Corp., 8 - 2
Atlantic Venetian Blind & Drapery Co., 8 - 6
Aye Attracting Awnings, 3 - 11
Beacon Looms, Inc., 8 - 8
Borg Textile Corp., 8 - 11
Brentwood Manor Furnishings, 6 - 11
Carole Fabrics Inc., 8 - 14
Charles W. Rice & Co. Inc., 8 - 16
Connecticut Curtain Company, 8 - 18
Contemporary Interiors, Inc., 8 - 18
D.S.C. Fabrics Inc., 8 - 21
DMI Drapery Mfg., 8 - 21
Daisy Decorative Products, 8 - 21
De La West Draperies, 8 - 22
Dorothy's Ruffled Originals, Inc., 8 - 23
Fabric Shop, 8 - 26
Fabricut, 8 - 26
Fara Mfg.Co., Inc., 8 - 27
Frissell Fabrics, Inc., 8 - 29
Glammar Mills Ltd., 8 - 30
Homespun Fabrics & Draperies, 8 - 34
Hornick Industries, 8 - 34

The Complete Sourcebook

Index - 25

Dresser – English

Index

K & R Custom Interiors, 8 - 38
Kenney Mfg. Co., 8 - 40
Kirsch Drapery Hardware, 8 - 40
Klemer & Wiseman, 8 - 40
Laura Ashley, 8 - 41
MDC Direct Inc., 8 - 43
Mercer Textile Mills, Inc., 8 - 45
Newell Window Furnishings, 8 - 49
Parker Window Covering, 8 - 51
Penn Needle Art Co., 8 - 52
Quix Window Visions & Fabric Works, 8 - 54
Ronnie Draperies, 8 - 56
Rosedale Wallcoverings Inc., 8 - 56
Rue De France Inc., 8 - 57
Scroll Fabrics Inc., 8 - 59
Stanwood Drapery Co. Inc., 8 - 62
Tiffany Quilting & Drapery Inc., 8 - 68
V A Wallcoverings, 8 - 71
Wesco Fabrics Inc., 8 - 75
Westport Mfg. Co. Inc., 8 - 75
Whiting Mfg. Co. Inc., 8 - 76
Wisconsin Drapery Supply Inc., 8 - 77

Dresser

Bales Furniture Mfg., 6 - 7
Melbourne Hall Workshop, 10 - 7

Driveway

North American Stone Co. Ltd., 3 - 64

Dryer

National Home Products, 3 - 63

Drywall

Bridge Lumber Co., 3 - 17
Pittcon Industries Inc., 1 - 27

Electronic

Amsterdam Corporation, 3 - 7
Leslie-Locke Inc., 3 - 55

Electric

Solar Depot, 3 - 80

Electrical

All-Phase Electric Supplies, 3 - 5
Bay Shore Light & Elec. Supply, 11 - 4
Consolidated Electrical Distributor, 3 - 27
Electrical Wholesale, 3 - 33
Home Electric Supply, 3 - 47
Kelly & Hayes Electrical Supply Inc., 3 - 52
Kennedy Electrical Supply, 3 - 52
Precision Multiple Controls, Inc., 3 - 71
Westinghouse Electric Supply, 3 - 98

Elm

Jameson Home Products, 3 - 50
Treework Services Ltd., 5 - 10

Enclosure

ARDCO, Inc., 2 - 1
Ace Shower Door Co. Inc., 2 - 1
Allgood Shower Door Corp., 2 - 1
American Shower Door Corp., 2 - 2
Aqata Limited, 2 - 2
Arsco Manufacturing Co., 3 - 9
Basco, 2 - 2
Berjen Metal Industries, 3 - 14
Burnham Corp., 3 - 18
Carlos Shower Doors Inc., 2 - 3
Coastal Industries, Inc., 2 - 4
EFRON America, 2 - 4

Fleurco Industries 1963 Ltd., 10 - 4
Fuji Hardware Co., Ltd., 2 - 4
Garofalo Studio, 2 - 5
Hans Grohe Ltd., 2 - 5
Hess Manufacturing Company, 12 - 11
Ideal-Standard Ltd., 2 - 6
Imperial Shower Door Co., 2 - 6
Keller Industries Inc., 4 - 10
Ketcham, G.M. Co., Inc., 2 - 5
Kimstock Inc., 2 - 6
Made-Rite Aluminum Window Co., 12 - 15
Mon-Ray Windows, Inc., 12 - 16
Monarch, 3 - 61
Nordic Showers, 2 - 8
Reflections, 2 - 9
Roman Limited, 2 - 9
Sherwood Shower Door Co., 2 - 10
Showerlux U.S.A., 2 - 10
Showerlux UK Ltd., 2 - 10
Skytech Systems, 12 - 23
Solite Solar Greenhouses, 7 - 6
Sterling, 2 - 10
Thermo-Rite Mfg. Co., 3 - 90
Universal Bath Systems, 2 - 12

Energy

American Energy Technologies Inc., 3 - 6
American Solar Network, 3 - 7
Barrel Builders, 3 - 12
Bonus Books, 3 - 16
Fafco Inc., 3 - 35
G S Energy Industries Inc., 3 - 38
HCP Solar Div., 3 - 43
Kallwall's Solar Components Center, 3 - 51
Livingston Systems Inc., 3 - 55
National Solar Supply, 3 - 63
Real Goods Trading Corp., 3 - 73
Rho Sigma Inc., 3 - 75
Samson Industries Inc., 3 - 77
Seelye Equipment Specialists, 3 - 78
Solar Development Inc., 3 - 80
Solar Heating & Air Conditioning Corp., 3 - 80
Solar Innovations Inc., 3 - 80
Solar Oriented Environmental Systems, 3 - 80
Solarmetrics Inc., 3 - 80
Sun Ray Solar Heaters, 3 - 84
SunEarth Inc., 3 - 84
Sunelco, 3 - 84
Sunheating Mfg. Co., 3 - 84
The Sun Electric Co., 3 - 89
Thermomax USA Ltd., 3 - 90
U.S. Electricar Co., 3 - 92
United Solar Technology Inc., 3 - 93
Vaughn Mfg. Corp., 3 - 94
Yellow Jacket Solar, 3 - 101

English

(Furniture, Panel, Lighting, etc.)

Architectural Paneling, 1 - 6
Bevan Funnel Limited, 6 - 9
Blakeson Inc., 3 - 15
Boyles Furniture, 6 - 11
Brunschwig & Fils, 8 - 12
Cricket on the Hearth, Inc., 6 - 20
Deacon & Sandys, 6 - 22
Georgia Lighting Supply Co., 11 - 13
Haddonstone USA Ltd., 7 - 3
Harriet's House, 8 - 32
Holloways, 6 - 36
Hyde Park Antiques, Ltd., 6 - 38
John Minter Furniture Ltd., 6 - 40

Index - 26

The Complete Sourcebook

Index

Entryway – Fabric

Le Lace Factory, Inc., 8 - 42
Raintree Designs, Inc., 8 - 55
Scandecor, 6 - 66
Smith & Watson, 6 - 69
The Bombay Co., 6 - 75
Wendover's Limited, 6 - 82
White of Mebane, 6 - 83
Whitechapel Ltd., 3 - 98

Entryway

Bend Millwork Systems Inc., 4 - 2
Castlegate, Inc., 4 - 3
Eagle Window & Door, 12 - 8
Great Gatsby's Auction Galley, 1 - 18
Hartman-Sanders Co., 1 - 19
Jack Wallis Doors, 4 - 9
Jeld-Wen, 4 - 10
Kenmore Industries, 4 - 10
Manufacturers Glass, 4 - 11
Maurer & Shepherd Joyners Inc., 1 - 23
Oak Leaves Studio, 1 - 25
Optimum Window Mfg. Corp., 12 - 18
Style-Mark, Inc., 1 - 33
Visador Co., 1 - 36
Wooden Nickel Architectural Antique, 1 - 38

Epoxy

Housecraft Associates, 3 - 47

Equipment

(Fireplace, Ventilation, etc.)
Pilgram Fireplace Equipment Co., 3 - 70
Superior Clay Corp., 3 - 85
Vestal Mfg., 3 - 95
York International Corp., 3 - 101

Etched

Art Glass Unlimited Inc., 12 - 4
Curran Glass & Mirror Co., 3 - 28
Morgan-Bockius Studios Inc., 4 - 12
Sunburst Stained Glass Co. Inc., 3 - 84
Williams Art Glass Studios, 12 - 28

European

(Bathroom Fixtures, Furniture, Hardware, Lighting, etc.)
A-Ball Plumbing Supply, 2 - 1
Collection Reproductions, 6 - 17
Eurofase Inc., 11 - 11
European Classics, 11 - 11
European Furniture Importers, 6 - 27
Fine Paints of Europe, 3 - 36
Fred Moheban Gallery, 8 - 29
Frigidaire, 10 - 4
Graham's Lighting Fixtures Inc., 11 - 13
Heating Research Co., 3 - 45
Imported European Hardware, 3 - 49
International Terra Cotta, 7 - 3
Peerless Imported Rugs, 8 - 52
Seventh Heaven, 6 - 67
The Brass Light Gallery, 11 - 31
Zimports Collection, 6 - 87

Exterior

(Doors, Lighting, Paint, Shutters, Tile, etc.)
American Heritage Shutters Inc., 12 - 3
Beech River Mill Company, 3 - 13
Bennett Industries Inc., 4 - 2
Berea Prehung Door, Inc., 4 - 2
Champion International Corp., 3 - 23

Crescent Lighting Ltd., 11 - 8
Dow Chemical USA, 3 - 32
Elegant Entries, 4 - 6
Fine Paints of Europe, 3 - 36
Florida Wood Moulding & Trim, 1 - 17
Fuller O'Brien Paints, 3 - 38
H. B. Fuller Co./TEC Incorporated, 3 - 43
Heritage Lanterns, 11 - 14
Iberia Millwork, 4 - 9
Illahe Tileworks, 3 - 49
Jeld-Wen, 4 - 10
Jessup Door Company, 4 - 10
Korona, 4 - 10
Mar-Flo, Inc., 4 - 12
McDan Woodworking, 1 - 23
Morgan Manufacturing, 4 - 12
National Woodworks, Inc., 1 - 25
Nord Company, 4 - 12
Ole Country Barn, 3 - 66
Pixley Lumber Co., 4 - 13
Primrose Distributing, 3 - 71
REM Industries, 12 - 21
Rem Industries, 12 - 21
Shutter Shop, 3 - 79
Shuttercraft, 12 - 23
Stuc-O-Flex International Inc., 3 - 83
Stulb's Old Village Paints, 3 - 83
The Color People, 1 - 34
The Copper House, 11 - 32
The Muralo Company Inc., 3 - 88
The Natural Choice Catalog, 3-88
The Porch Factory, 1 - 34
The Shutter Depot, 12 - 25
The Tin Bin, 11 - 32
Trimall Interior Products Inc., 3 - 92
Vermont Marble Co., 3 - 95
Vetter Stone Co., 1 - 36

Fabric

ABC Decorator Fabrics, 8 - 2
Alexandra's Homespun Textile, 8 - 3
American Discount Wallcoverings, 8 - 4
Anchor Industries Inc., 8 - 5
Archetonic, 8 - 5
Artique Design, 8 - 5
Artisan Handprints Inc., 8 - 6
Artmark Fabrics Co. Inc., 8 - 6
BMI Home Decorating, 8 - 7
Bagindd Prints, 8 - 7
Bailey & Griffin Inc., 8 - 7
Bedroom Secrets, 8 - 9
Bedspreads By Thomas, 6 - 9
Benington's, 8 - 9
Bergamo Fabrics Inc., 8 - 9
Beverly Stevens Ltd., 8 - 10
Bill Villetto Designs, 8 - 10
Biscayne Fabrics Inc., 8 - 10
Blautex, 8 - 10
Boone Decorative Fabrics, 8 - 11
Brandt's, 8 - 11
Brayton Textiles, 8 - 11
Brentwood Manor Furnishings, 6 - 11
Brunschwig & Fils, 8 - 12
Carousel Designs Inc., 8 - 14
Century Fabrics Inc., 8 - 15
China Seas Inc., 8 - 16
Clarence House Imports Ltd., 8 - 17
Classic Revivals, Inc., 8 - 17
Codis House S.P.A., 8 - 17
Cole & Son (Wallpapers, etc.) Ltd., 8 - 17
Craftex Mills, Inc., 8 - 19

The Complete Sourcebook

Index - 27

Facing – Fan

Crown Corp. D/B/A Mile Hi Crown, 8 - 20
Crown Wallpaper Co., 8 - 20
Custom Laminations Inc., 8 - 20
Cynthia Gibson, Inc., 8 - 20
David & Dash, 8 - 21
David Rothschild Co. Inc., 8 - 21
David S. Gibson Inc., 8 - 21
Dekortex Co., 8 - 22
Design/Craft Fabric Corp., 8 - 22
Designer Home Fabrics, 8 - 22
Designer Secrets, 8 - 23
Duralee Fabrics, 8 - 24
Edward Laurence & Co., 8 - 24
Eisenhart Wallcoverings Co., 8 - 25
Elizabeth Eaton Ltd., 8 - 25
Enduro Fabric Awnings, 3 - 34
F. Schumacher, 8 - 26
FSC Wallcoverings, 8 - 26
Fabric Fair, 8 - 26
Fabric Shop, 8 - 26
Fabrics By Design, 8 - 26
Fabrics By Phone, 8 - 26
Fabrics Plus, 8 - 26
Fairfield Carpets & Fabrics, 8 - 27
Flemington Fabric Decorating Center, 8 - 28
Frankel Associates, Inc., 8 - 29
Frissell Fabrics, Inc., 8 - 29
Galacar & Co., 8 - 29
Glammar Mills Ltd., 8 - 30
Golden Wallpaper, 8 - 31
Greeff Fabrics Inc., 8 - 31
Hallie Greer, 8 - 31
Hamilton Adams Imports Ltd., 8 - 32
Hang-It-Now Wallpaper Stores, 8 - 32
Henry Calvin Fabrics, 8 - 32
Hinson & Co., 8 - 33
Home Fabric Mills, Inc., 8 - 33
Homespun Fabrics & Draperies, 8 - 34
Homespun Weavers, 8 - 34
Hunting Valley Prints, 8 - 35
J D Fabrics Ltd., 8 - 36
J. M. Lynne Co., Inc., 8 - 36
J. P. Stevens & Co., 8 - 36
Jab/Anstoetz, 8 - 37
Jacquard Fabrics Co., 8 - 37
Joan Fabrics Corp., 8 - 38
Kalkstein Silk Mills, Inc., 8 - 39
Kathleen B. Smith, 8 - 39
King, 10 - 6
Klemer & Wiseman, 8 - 40
Kobe Fabrics Ltd., 8 - 40
Kravet Fabrics, 8 - 41
Laura Ashley, 8 - 41
Laurco Fabrics Inc., 8 - 41
Lee Jofa, 8 - 42
Maen Line Fabrics Inc., 8 - 44
Marlene's Decorator Fabrics, 8 - 44
Mastercraft, 8 - 44
Melded Fabrics North America Inc., 8 - 45
Mercer Textile Mills, Inc., 8 - 45
Milbrook Wallcoverings, 8 - 46
Minette Mills, Inc., 8 - 47
Motif Designs, 8 - 48
Nationwide Wholesalers, 8 - 48
Old Deerfield Wallpapers, 8 - 50
Paragon Fabrics Co. Inc., 8 - 51
Pettigrew Associates Inc., 6 - 59
Phifer Wire Products, Inc., 8 - 53
Pride of Paris Fabrics Ltd., 8 - 54
Quix Window Visions & Fabric Works, 8 - 54
Raintree Designs, Inc., 8 - 55

Robert Allen Fabrics, Inc., 8 - 56
Robert Allen, 8 - 55
Robinson's Wallcovering, 8 - 56
Rosecore Carpet Co. Inc., 8 - 56
Rossville Mills Inc., 8 - 56
Rubin & Green Inc., 8 - 57
S. M. Hexter & Co., 8 - 57
Sanderson, 8 - 58
Sanz International, 8 - 58
Scalamandre Inc., 8 - 58
Scher Fabrics Inc., 8 - 59
Schumacher & Co. Inc., 8 - 59
Shama Imports Inc., 8 - 60
Sheridan, 8 - 60
Silk Surplus, 8 - 61
Steven Linen Associates Inc., 8 - 63
Stroheim & Romann, 8 - 63
Sue Foster Fabrics, 8 - 64
Summer Hill Ltd., 6 - 72
Sunflower Studio, 8 - 64
Swaim, 8 - 64
TWG Fabric Outlet, 8 - 65
Tandem Fabric Inc., 8 - 65
The Decorators Outlet, 8 - 66
The Fabric Center, 8 - 66
The Fabric Outlet, 8 - 66
The Twigs Inc., 8 - 68
The Warner Company, 8 - 68
Tioga Mill Outlet Stores, Inc., 8 - 69
Triblend Mills, 8 - 69
Triumph Designs Inc., 8 - 70
U.S. Plush Mills Inc., 8 - 70
United Wallcoverings, 8 - 71
Upholstery Fabrics, 8 - 71
V A Wallcoverings, 8 - 71
Valdese Weavers Inc., 8 - 71
Valiant Fabrics Corp., 8 - 71
Valley Forge Fabrics Inc., 8 - 71
Van Luit Wallcoverings, 8 - 71
Wall Fabrics Inc., 8 - 73
WallpaperXpress, 8 - 74
Walter L. Brown Ltd., 8 - 74
Wamsutta Doblin, 8 - 74
Wamsutta/Pacific, 8 - 74
Warner Co., 8 - 74
Waverly Fabric, 8 - 75
Wendell Fabrics Corp., 8 - 75
Westgate Fabrics Inc., 8 - 75
Wolf-Gordon, Inc., 8 - 77
York Wallcoverings Inc., 8 - 78
Zina Studios Inc., 8 - 78

Facing

(Door, Fireplace, etc.)

American Wood Column Corp., 1 - 4
Browne Winther & Co. Ltd., 1 - 9
Elite Fireplace Facings Inc., 3 - 33
Marble & Tile Imports, 3 - 57
Masonite Corp., 4 - 12

Fan

Academy, 11 - 1
Aetna Electric Distributing Corp., 11 - 2
Beverly Hills Fan Co., 11 - 4
Catalina Lighting, Inc., 11 - 6
Conservation Technology Ltd., 11 - 7
DEMCO Fans, 11 - 8
Delaware Electric Imports, 11 - 9
Emerson Electric Company, 11 - 10
Fan Fair, 11 - 11
Fasco Industries, Inc., 11 - 11

Index

Faucet – Fireplace

Hunter Ceiling Fans, 11 - 16
Jaegaer USA, 11 - 17
Lamp Warehouse/NYCeiling Fan,11-19
Martin's Discount Lighting, 11 - 22
Robbins & Myers, 11 - 27
SEC Inc., 11 - 28
The Ceiling Fan Gallery, 11 - 31
The Fan Man Inc., 11 - 32
The Fan Man, 11 - 32
Wholesale Fans & Lighting Inc., 11 - 35

Faucet

A-Ball Plumbing Supply, 2 - 1
American Brass Mfg., 10 - 1
Aston Matthews, 2 - 2
Astracast PLC, 12 - 4
Barber Wilsons & Co. Ltd., 2 - 2
Baths From The Past Inc., 2 - 3
Blanco America, 10 - 2
Carron Phoenix Ltd., 10 - 3
Chatham Brass Co., Inc., 11 - 7
Eljer, 10 - 3
FV America Corporation, 2 - 4
Faucet Outlet, 10 - 4
Franke Inc., 10 - 4
Gemini Bath & Kitchen, 2 - 5
Gracious Home, 10 - 5
Grohe America Inc., 10 - 5
Hans Grohe Ltd., 2 - 5
Hansa America, 10 - 5
Harden Industries, 2 - 5
Ideal-Standard Ltd., 2 - 6
Indiana Brass, 10 - 5
Jado Bathroom & Hardware Mfg. Co., 2 - 6
KWC/Rohl Corp., 10 - 6
Kallista, 2 - 6
Kohler Company, 12 - 14
Magnet Trade, 4 - 11
Milwaukee Faucets, 12 - 16
Miracle Method Bathroom Restoration, 2 - 7
Moen, 10 - 7
Ohmega Salvage, 2 - 8
Old & Elegant Distributing, 2 - 8
Pacific Faucets, 2 - 8
Paragon Products, 10 - 8
Peter Goldberger, 2 - 8
Phoenix Products Inc., 3 - 70
Porcher Ltd., 2 - 9
Price Pfister Inc., 2 - 9
Rapetti Faucets, 2 - 9
Raphael Ltd., 2 - 9
SEPCO Industries Inc., 2 - 9
T & S Brass & Bronze Works Inc., 2 - 11
The Chicago Faucet Company, 2 - 11
The Faucet Factory, 2 - 11
The Sink Factory, 2 - 11
Trevi Showers, 2 - 11
Water Faucets, 2 - 13
Water Saver Faucet Co., 2 - 13

Fencing

Ameristar, 7 - 1
Anchor Fence, 7 - 1
Bamboo & Rattan Works Inc., 8 - 8
Beaver Industries, 3 - 13
Bufftech, 7 - 1
Conner's Architectural Antiques, 1 - 11
Custom Ironworks Inc., 7 - 2
Dutch Products & Supply Co., 3 - 32
Heritage Fence Company, 7 - 3
Jerith Mfg., 7 - 3

Leslie-Locke Inc., 3 - 55
Moultrie Manufacturing Co., 6 - 54
Nebraska Plastics Inc., 7 - 5
Peterson Wood Div., 7 - 5
Prototech Polyvinyl Fencing Systems, 7 - 5
Queen City Architectural Salvage, 1 - 28
Southeastern Wood Products Co., 7 - 6
Stewart Iron Works, 7 - 6
Texas Standard Picket Company Inc., 7 - 7
Walpole Woodworkers, 6 - 81

Fiberglass

(Architectural, Ponds, Roofing, Showers, etc.)

Beach Craft, Inc., 2 - 3
Castlegate, Inc., 4 - 3
Dolphin Pet Village, 7 - 2
Fibertech Corporation, 1 - 16
GAF Building Materials Corp., 3 - 38
Kimstock Inc., 2 - 6

Fieldstone

Stone Products Corporation, 3 - 83

Film

Sun Control Center Of Indiana, 12 - 24

Finish

Absolute Coatings Inc., 3 - 3
Aexcel Corp., 3 - 4
Basic Coatings, 3 - 12
Bonakemi USA, Inc., 5 - 2
Boston Turning Works, 1 - 8
Carver Tripp, 5 - 2
Cider Hill Woodworks, 1 - 10
Daly's Wood Finishing Products, 3 - 29
Deft, Inc., 5 - 3
Dura Seal, 5 - 4
Epifanes USA, 3 - 34
Fabulon Products, 3 - 35
Faux Effects Inc., 8 - 27
Finishing Products, 3 - 36
Flood Company, 3 - 37
Gaston's Wood Finishes & Antiques, 3 - 39
Glidden Co., 3 - 40
Harco Chemical Coatings, 3 - 43
Homestead Paint & Finishes, 3 - 47
Livos PlanChemistry, 3 - 55
McCloskey Corp., 3 - 59
Partelow Custom Wood Turnings, 1 - 27
Star Bronze Co., 3 - 82
The Natural Choice Catalog, 3 - 88
Tru-Test General Paint & Chemical, 3 - 92
United Coatings Co., 3 - 93
Wilsonart, 3 - 99
Wood Kote, 3 - 100

Fire

Alarm Supply Co., 9 - 1
Burdex Security Co., 9 - 1
High-Desert Security Systems, 9 - 2
Mountain West Alarm Supply, 9 - 2

Fireplace

Aagard-Hanley Ltd., 11 - 1
An Affair of the Hearth, 3 - 7
Appalachian Stove & Fab, 3 - 8
Architectural Heritage, 1 - 6
Art Marble and Stone, 1 - 7
Axon Products, 1 - 7
BD Mantels Ltd., 1 - 7

The Complete Sourcebook

Beldes, Inc., 3 - 13
Blakeson Inc., 3 - 15
Browne Winther & Co. Ltd., 1 - 9
Butler Stove Co., 3 - 18
Century Fireplace Furnishings Inc., 3 - 21
Condar Company, 3 - 26
Conservation Building Products Ltd., 3 - 26
Crate Fires, 3 - 27
Diamond K. Co., Inc., 5 - 3
Dickinsons Architectural Antiques, 1 - 14
Dovre, 3 - 32
Draper & Draper, 1 - 15
Elite Fireplace Facings Inc., 3 - 33
Emsworth Fireplaces Ltd., 1 - 15
Energy Etcetera, 3 - 34
Fayston Iron & Steel Works, 3 - 35
Feature Fires Ltd., 1 - 16
Fergene Studio, 3 - 35
Flame & Hearth Fireplaces, 3 - 36
Florida Mantel Shoppe, 1 - 17
Fritz V. Sterbak Antiques, 1 - 17
Gawet Marble & Granite Inc., 3 - 39
Grate Fires Inc., 3 - 42
Hart Fireplace Furnishings, 3 - 44
Heat-Fab Inc., 3 - 44
Heat-N-Glo Fireplace Products Inc., 3 - 45
Heatilator Inc., 3 - 45
Heritage Energy Systems, 3 - 45
Hodkin & Jones (Sheffield) Ltd., 3 - 46
Hutch Mfg. Co., 3 - 48
Kayne & Son Custom Forged Hardware,3-51
Lemee's Fireplace Equipment, 3 - 54
Majestic Co., 3 - 56
Malm Fireplaces Inc., 3 - 57
Maple Grove Restorations, 1 - 22
Marble & Tile Imports, 3 - 57
Martin Industries Inc., 3 - 58
Meeco Mfg. Co., 3 - 59
Minuteman International Co., 3 - 61
New-Aire Mfg. Co., Inc., 3 - 64
Nicola Ceramics & Marble, 3 - 64
Origines, 6 - 57
Pilgram Fireplace Equipment Co., 3 - 70
Plow & Hearth, 7 - 5
Ranchwood Mfg., 1 - 28
Readybuilt Products Co., 1 - 28
Richard Burbidge Ltd., 3 - 75
Roger Pearson, 1 - 30
Rustic Home Hardware, 3 - 77
Stone Mfg. Co., 3 - 83
Structural Slate Co., 3 - 83
Sun House Tiles, 3 - 84
Sundance II Fireplace Distributors, 3 - 84
Sunshine Architectural Woodworks, 1 - 33
Superior Clay Corp., 3 - 85
Superior Fireplace Co., 3 - 85
T. G. Schmeiser Co. Inc., 3 - 85
TEMCO, 3 - 86
Technical Glass Products, 3 - 86
The Adams Company, 3 - 87
The Country Iron Foundry, 3 - 88
The Country Iron Foundry, 3 - 88
The Shop, 3 - 89
The Structural Slate Co., 3 - 89
The Woodbury Blacksmith & Forge, 3 - 90
Thermo-Rite Mfg. Co., 3 - 90
Vermont Castings, 3 - 95
Vermont Soapstone Co., 3 - 95
Vestal Mfg., 3 - 95
Wilkening Fireplace Co., 3 - 99
William Jackson Co., 1 - 37

Wm. H. Jackson Co., 1 - 37
Yankee Hearth, 3 - 101

Fixture

(Bathroom, Lighting, Plumbing, etc.)

A K Exteriors, 6 - 1
A-Ball Plumbing Supply, 2 - 1
A.J.P. Coppersmith, 1 - 1
AAA Plumbing Pottery Corp., 2 - 1
Abbey Roberts Inc., 11 - 1
Aetna Electric Distributing Corp., 11 - 2
Alkco Lighting, 11 - 2
Allied Lighting, 11 - 2
American Heirlooms, Inc., 11 - 2
American Lamp Supply, 11 - 2
American Standard, 2 - 2
Antique Baths & Kitchens, 2 - 2
Antique Emporium, 1 - 4
Antique Hardware Store, 3 - 8
Architectural Antique Warehouse, 3 - 9
Architectural Crystal Ltd., 1 - 5
Architectural Rarities Ltd., 1 - 6
Arroyo Craftsman, 11 - 3
Art Directions, 1 - 7
Artcraft, 11 - 3
Aston Matthews, 2 - 2
Aura Lamp & Lighting, Inc., 11 - 3
Authentic Designs, 3 - 10
B & G Antique Lighting, 11 - 3
Bala Lighting, 11 - 4
Baldwin Brass Lighting, 11 - 4
Bathroom Jewelry, 2 - 2
Bathroom Machineries, 2 - 3
Baths From The Past Inc., 2 - 3
Blackhawk Marble Mfg., 2 - 3
Blanche P. Field Inc., 11 - 4
Boyd Lighting Fixture Co., 11 - 4
Broadway Industries, 2 - 3
Carriage Trade of Tahoe, 11 - 6
Cascade Designs Inc., 11 - 6
Catalina Lighting, Inc., 11 - 6
Centel's Lighting, 11 - 6
Central Brass Mfg. Co., 3 - 21
Champion Irrigation Products, 3 - 23
Cisco, 3 - 24
City Lights, 11 - 7
Classic Illumination, Inc., 11 - 7
Conant Custom Brass, Inc., 11 - 7
Crane Plumbing, 8 - 19
Crawford's Old House Store, 3 - 27
Dale Tiffany Inc., 11 - 9
Davis & Warshow Inc., 10 - 3
Decorative Dimensions, 11 - 9
Decorum, 1 - 14
Dickson Brothers, Inc., 11 - 9
Dilor Industries Ltd., 11 - 9
Dutch Products & Supply Co., 3 - 32
Early American Lighting, 11 - 10
Eljer, 10 - 3
Elkay Mfg. Co., 10 - 3
Elsco Lighting Products, Inc., 11 - 10
European Classics, 11 - 11
Exciting Lighting by Pam Morris, 11 - 11
Exquisite Lighting and Design, Inc., 11 - 11
F & M Plumbing Supply, 2 - 4
Fellenz Antiques, 3 - 35
Fine Designs Unlimited, 11 - 12
Fredrick Ramond Inc., 11 - 12
Frombruche', 11 - 7
Garber's Crafted Lighting, 11 - 12

Index

Fixture — Fixture

Gates Moore, 11 - 13
Genie House, 11 - 13
Georgian Art Lighting Designs, Inc., 11 - 13
Gerber Plumbing Fixtures Corp, 3 - 40
Gibson Interiors, 11 - 13
Global Mid-South Mfg. Co., 2 - 5
Golden Valley Lighting, 11 - 13
Grabell of California, 11 - 13
Green's Lighting Fixtures, 11 - 14
Greg's Antique Lighting, 11 - 14
Halo Lighting Products, 11 - 14
Hammerworks, 11 - 14
Hinkley Lighting, 11 - 15
Historic Housefitters, 3 - 46
Holophane Company Inc., 11 - 15
Holtkotter International, Inc., 11 - 15
Hurley Patentee Manor, 11 - 16
Ideal Electric Mfg. Co. Ltd., 11 - 16
Indiana Brass, 10 - 5
Insites, 11 - 17
International Supply Co., 2 - 6
Irvin's Craft Shop, 11 - 17
James Crystal Mfg. Co., 11 - 17
Josiah R. Coppersmythe, 11 - 18
Juno Lighting, Inc., 11 - 18
Keystone Lighting Corp., 11 - 18
King's Chandelier, 11 - 18
Kiss Lamp Co., 11 - 18
Kohler Company, 12 - 14
Kraft, 2 - 6
Kurt Versen Co., 11 - 18
L.T. Moses Willard, Inc., 11 - 18
Lam Lighting Systems, 11 - 18
Lasco Bathware, 2 - 7
Lee's Studio, 11 - 19
Leiter Lites, 11 - 19
Lenape Products, Inc., 2 - 7
Lester H. Berry & Company, 11 - 19
Leviton Manufacturing Company, 11 - 20
Luigi Crystal, 11 - 20
Luma Lighting Industries, Inc., 11 - 20
Lumax Industries Inc., 11 - 20
Luminaire, 11 - 21
Marcello Marble & Tile PLS, 2 - 7
Marco Lighting Fixtures, 11 - 21
Mario Industries, 11 - 21
Mark Lighting Fixture Co., Inc., 11 - 21
Martin's Discount Lighting, 11 - 22
McPherson Inc., 2 - 7
Metropolitan Lighting Fixture Co. Inc., 11 - 22
Midwest Chandelier Co., 11 - 22
Midwest Custom Brass, 3 - 60
Milwaukee Faucets, 12 - 16
Minnco Inc., 3 - 61
Mission Pipe & Supply, 2 - 7
Mobern Electric Corp., 11 - 22
Monarch Metal Products Corp., 2 - 8
Mooncraft Corp., 11 - 22
National Industries, 11 - 23
National Lighting Inc., 11 - 23
Newman Lighting Co., 11 - 23
Newstamp Lighting Co., 11 - 23
Nowells, 11 - 24
NuMerit Electrical Supply, 11 - 24
OHM-Rite Electrical, 11 - 24
Ocean View Lighting, 11 - 24
Olde Village Smithery, 11 - 24
Ole Fashion Things, 2 - 8
O'Keefe Cabinet Fixtures, 10 - 8
PE O'Hair & Co., 2 - 8
Paragon Products, 10 - 8

Peerless Pottery, 3 - 69
Period Furniture Hardware, 6 - 59
Period Lighting Fixtures, 11 - 25
Permo Lights Unlimited, 11 - 25
Philadelphia Glass Bending Co., 11 - 25
Phylrich International, 2 - 8
Plumb-Craft Mfg., 3 - 70
Porcher Ltd., 2 - 9
Prescolite, 9 - 3
Progress Lighting, 11 - 25
Quintessentials, 2 - 9
Quoizel Inc., 11 - 26
Reggiani Light Gallery, 11 - 26
Rejuvenation Lamp & Fixture, 11 - 26
Remcraft Lighting Products, 11 - 26
Remington, 11 - 26
Remodeler's Supply Co., 3 - 74
Residential Lighting Div., 11 - 27
Restoration Works, 3 - 74
Richard Scofield, 11 - 27
Robert Long Lighting, 11 - 27
Rockingham Plumbing Supply, 2 - 9
Roflan Associates, 11 - 27
Roy Electric Co. Inc., 11 - 27
S. Wilder & Co. Inc., 11 - 28
Sea Gull Lighting Products Inc., 11 - 28
Shamrock Lighting Inc., 11 - 29
Shaper Lighting, 11 - 29
Sherle Wagner, 2 - 10
Sink Factory, 2 - 11
Spero Electric Corp., 11 - 29
St. Louis Antique Lighting Co., 11 - 29
St. Thomas Creations Inc., 2 - 10
Stern-Williams Co. Inc., 3 - 82
Sun-Mar Corp., 7 - 7
Sunrise Specialty, 2 - 10
T. A Green Lighting Co., 11 - 30
Task Lighting Corporation, 11 - 31
Tempo/Infiniti Lighting, 11 - 31
The Antique Hardware Store, 3 - 87
The Antique Plumber, 3 - 87
The Basic source Inc., 11 - 31
The Brass Finial, 11 - 31
The Brass Light Gallery, 11 - 31
The Brass Lion, 11 - 31
The Fixture Exchange, 2 - 11
The Saltbox, 11 - 32
The Tin Bin, 11 - 32
The Wise Company, 3 - 90
Timely Lighting, 11 - 33
Ultraflo Corp., 3 - 93
Universal Fixture Manufacturing, 11 - 33
Universal Rundle Corp., 3 - 94
Unlight Ltd., 11 - 33
Urban Archaeology, 1 - 35
Versailles Lighting Inc., 11 - 34
Victorian Lightcrafters Ltd., 11 - 34
Victorian Revival, 11 - 34
Victoriana Ltd., 11 - 34
Village Lantern, 11 - 34
Villeroy & Boch (USA, etc.) Inc., 2 - 12
Villeroy & Boch AG, 2 - 12
Vintage Plumbing, 2 - 12
Visioneered Lighting Mfg. Ltd., 11 - 34
Vitistor's Catalog, 2 - 12
W. T. Weaver & Sons, 2 - 12
Walker Industries, 3 - 96
Watercolors Inc., 2 - 13
Wendelighting, 11 - 35
Western Pottery Co. Inc., 2 - 13
Westwood Co., 11 - 35

The Complete Sourcebook

Index - 31

Flagstone – Flooring

Index

Wm. Engel Co., Ltd., 11 - 35
Zalstein Design Works, 11 - 36

Flagstone

Conklin's Authentic Antique Barnwood, 3 - 26

Flashing

Cannon Rainwater Systems Ltd., 3 - 20

Floor

(Lamps, Tile, Trusses, etc.)

Agrob-Wessel-Servais AG, 3 - 4
Ailene Lumber Inc., 3 - 4
Albert Gunther, 3 - 5
Alfa Ceramiche, 3 - 5
Alpine Engineer Products Inc., 3 - 5
Amaru Tile, 3 - 6
American Building Component, 3 - 6
American International, 3 - 6
Angelo Amaru Tile & Bath Collection, 3 - 8
Ann Sacks Tile & Stone, 3 - 8
Antiche Ceramiche D'Talia (ACIT) SRL, 3 - 8
Arius Tile Co., 3 - 9
Armstar, 3 - 9
Artemide, 11 - 3
Artistic Surfaces, 8 - 6
Ashfield Stone Quarry, 3 - 9
Basic Coatings, 3 - 12
Baukeramik U., 3 - 12
Bisazza Mosaico S.P.A., 3 - 15
Bonakemi USA, Inc., 5 - 2
CPN Inc., 3 - 18
Caberboard Ltd., 3 - 18
California Tile Supply, 3 - 19
Cambridge Tile Mfg. Co., 3 - 19
Cancos Tile Corporation, 3 - 19
Carolina Truss Mfg. Co., Inc., 3 - 20
Carver Tripp, 5 - 2
Ceramica Candia S.P.A., 3 - 22
Ceramica Ilsa S.P.A., 3 - 22
Ceramica Panaria S.P.A., 3 - 22
Ceramiche Brunelleschi S.P.A., 3 - 22
Cerim Ceramiche S.P.A., 3 - 23
Cisa-Cerdisa-Smov, 3 - 24
Colonial Marble Products Ltd., 3 - 25
Crest Distributors, 3 - 28
Croonen KG, 3 - 28
D & B Tile Distributors, 3 - 29
Daly's Wood Finishing Products, 3 - 29
Deft, Inc., 5 - 3
Dura Seal, 5 - 4
Dynasty Classics Corp., 11 - 9
East Coast Tile Imports Inc., 3 - 33
Execulamp Inc., 11 - 11
Fabricated Wood Products, 3 - 35
Fabulon Products, 3 - 35
Florida Ceramic Tile Center, 3 - 37
Gaslight Time Antiques, 11 - 13
Glidden Co., 3 - 40
H & R Johnson Tiles, 3 - 42
Harco Chemical Coatings, 3 - 43
Harris Lamps, 11 - 14
Hastings Tile & Il Bagno Collection, 3 - 44
Hjelmeland Truss Corp., 3 - 46
Hutcherson Tile, 3 - 48
Keen Building Components Inc., 3 - 52
Kent Trusses Ltd., 3 - 52
Kilian Industries Ltd., 3 - 52
Klingenberg Dekoramik GmbH, 3 - 53
Kunico Truss & Prefab Ltd., 3 - 53
Latco Ceramic Tile, 3 - 54

Leduc Truss, 3 - 54
Livos PlanChemistry, 3 - 55
Lumber Specialties, 3 - 56
McCloskey Corp., 3 - 59
Metco Tile Distributors, 3 - 60
National Ceramics of Florida, 3 - 63
Nemo Tile Company, Inc., 3 - 63
New England Slate Company, 3 - 64
Norman Perry, 11 - 23
Northern Michigan Truss Co., 3 - 65
Olympic Structures Inc., 3 - 66
Ostara-Fliesen Gmbh & Co. KG, 3 - 67
Perfection Truss Co. Inc., 3 - 69
Puccio Marble & Onyx, 3 - 72
Ridgway Roof Truss Co. Inc., 3 - 75
SRI, 3 - 77
Santa Catalina, 3 - 77
Schubert Lumber Co., 3 - 78
Silver State Components, 3 - 79
Southern Components Inc., 3 - 81
Staloton - Die keramiker H.H., 3 - 82
Summitville Tiles Inc., 3 - 84
Thorn Lumber Co., 3 - 90
Tile West Distributors, 3 - 91
Timber Top Truss Ltd., 3 - 91
Tri State Truss Co., 3 - 92
Tru-Test General Paint & Chemical, 3 - 92
Trusses Inc., 3 - 92
Uniflor, 3 - 93
United Coatings Co., 3 - 93
Universal Forest Products, 3 - 94
Villaume Industries Inc., 3 - 95
Warren Truss Co. Inc., 3 - 96
Wascana Wood Components Ltd., 3 - 96
Wayne Tile Company, 3 - 96
Wm. D. Bowers Lumber Co., 3 - 100
Wood Kote, 3 - 100
Wood Structures Inc., 3 - 100

Floorcloth

Artistic Surfaces, 8 - 6
Churchwell Ltd., 8 - 16
Floorcloths, 8 - 28
Good & Co. Floorclothmakers, 8 - 31
Heritage Floorcloths, 8 - 32
Olde Virginea Trading Co., 8 - 50

Floorcover

Advance Carpet Decorating Ctr., 8 - 3
Cherry Hill Furniture,Carpet & Interiors, 6 - 16
Fired Earth Tiles PLC, 5 - 4
Pinnell's Floor Covering, 8 - 53
S. M. Hexter & Co., 8 - 57
Sommer UK Wall and Floorcoverings, 8 - 61

Flooring

(Wood, Tile, Vinyl, etc.)

A.E. Gombert Lumber Co., 3 - 1
ACCRA Wood Products Ltd., 1 - 1
AGA Corporation, 5 - 1
Abet Laminati, 3 - 3
Accents In Stone, 3 - 3
Aged Woods, 5 - 1
Albany Woodworks Inc., 3 - 5
Anderson Hardwood Flooring, 5 - 1
Anthony Forest Product Co., 3 - 8
Antique Pine Co., 5 - 1
Architectural Timber & Millwork, 1 - 6
Arizona Tile, 5 - 1
Arkansas Oak Flooring Co., 5 - 1
Authentic Pine Floors Inc., 5 - 1

Index - 32

The Complete Sourcebook

Index

Flooring – Flooring

B.A. Mullican Lumber & Manufacturing, 5 - 1
BRE Lumber, 3 - 11
Bangkok International, 5 - 2
Biwood Flooring, 5 - 2
Boen Hardwood Flooring, 5 - 2
Boise Moulding & Lumber, 3 - 15
Broad-Axe Beam Co., 5 - 2
Bruce Hardwood Floors, 5 - 2
Carlisle Restoration Lumber, 5 - 2
Carpet Express, 8 - 14
Castle Burlingame, 5 - 2
Centre Mills Antique Floors & Beams, 5 - 2
Coastal Millworks Inc., 1 - 11
Color Tile Inc., 3 - 26
Concrete Technology Inc., 3 - 26
Conklin's Authentic Antique Barnwood, 3 - 26
Continental Woodworking Co., 1 - 12
Craftsman Lumber Co., 5 - 3
Cumberland Lumber & Manufacturing, 5 - 3
DeSoto Hardwood Flooring Company, 5 - 3
Diamond K. Co., Inc., 5 - 3
Diamond "W" Floor Covering, 5 - 3
Dixon Lumber Company, 5 - 3
Domco Floors, 5 - 3
E. T. Moore Company, 5 - 4
Erie Flooring & Wood Products, 5 - 4
Felix Huard Inc., 5 - 4
Flexicore Co., Inc., 3 - 36
Floors By Juell, 5 - 4
Floortown, 5 - 4
Forbo Industries, 8 - 28
Fraser Woods Inc., 4 - 7
Galleher Hardwood Co., 5 - 4
Gibco Services Inc., 1 - 18
Goodwin Lumber, 3 - 41
Governor's Antiques & Arch. Materials, 1 - 18
Guyon, 5 - 4
H. B. Fuller Co./TEC Incorporated, 3 - 43
Handcraft Tile Inc., 3 - 43
Hardwood Flooring & Paneling Inc., 5 - 4
Harmony Exchange, 5 - 5
Harris-Tarkett, Inc., 5 - 5
Hartco/Tibbals Flooring Company, 5 - 5
Hayes Forest Products, Inc., 5 - 5
Historic Floors of Oshkosh, 5 - 5
Hoboken Floors Inc., 5 - 5
Hunt County Hardwoods, Inc., 5 - 5
Imperial Black Marble Co., 5 - 5
J. L. Powell & Company Inc., 5 - 5
Johnsonius Precision Millwork, 3 - 50
Kakabeka Timber Ltd., 3 - 51
Kentucky Wood Floors, 5 - 5
L.D. Brinkman & Co. Inc., 5 - 5
Lamb Flooring & Trim Co., 5 - 6
Launstein Hardwood, 5 - 6
Lebanon Oak Flooring, 5 - 6
Leslie Brothers Lumber Company, 5 - 6
Lindal Cedar Sunrooms, 3 - 55
Linden Lumber Company, 5 - 6
Linoleum City, 5 - 6
Livermore Wood Floors, 5 - 6
Louisiana-Pacific Corporation, 3 - 56
Madison Flooring Company, 5 - 6
Mannington Wood Floors, 5 - 6
Marjam Supply Company, 3 - 58
McMinnville Manufacturing Co., 5 - 6
Memphis Hardwood Flooring Co., 5 - 7
Midwestern Terrazzo corp., 5 - 7
Miller & Company, Inc., 5 - 7
Missouri Floor Co., 5 - 7
Missouri Hardwood Flooring Co., 5 - 7

Monticello Flooring & Lumber Co., 5 - 7
Mountain Lumber Co., 5 - 7
National Floor Products Co., Inc., 5 - 7
National Hardwood Floors, 5 - 7
New England Hardwood Supply Co., 5 - 7
Nora Flooring, 5 - 7
North Country Lumber Co. Inc., 3 - 64
Oakwood Classic & Custom Woodwork,1-25
Overseas Hardwoods Co. Inc., 5 - 7
P. W. Plumly Lumber Corporation, 1 - 26
Paris Ceramics, 3 - 68
Parker's Carpets Inc., 8 - 52
Partee Flooring Mill, 5 - 8
Peace Flooring Co. Inc., 5 - 8
Penn Big Bed Slate Co. Inc., 3 - 69
Pine Floors Inc., 5 - 8
Pine Plains Woodworking Inc., 5 - 8
Plancher Beauceville Inc., 5 - 8
Plaza Hardwood Inc., 5 - 8
Potlatch Corporation, 5 - 8
Pukall Lumber Co., 3 - 72
Quality Woods Ltd., 5 - 8
Razorback Hardwood, Inc., 5 - 8
River City Woodworks, 5 - 8
Riverside Millwork Co. Inc., 1 - 29
Robbins Hardwood Flooring, 5 - 8
Robbins Inc., 5 - 8
Sandy Pond Hardwoods, 3 - 77
Searcy Flooring, Inc., 5 - 9
Shaw Marble Works, 5 - 9
Smith Flooring, Inc., 5 - 9 , 12 - 25
Somerset Wood Products, Inc., 5 - 9
Stanley Knight, 5 - 9
Structural Slate Co., 3 - 83
Stuart Flooring Corp., 5 - 9
Stuart Lerman Inc., 5 - 9
Sykes Flooring Products, 5 - 9
Sylvan Brandt Inc., 5 - 9
Tarkett Inc., 5 - 9
Tatko Brothers Slate Company, 3 - 86
The Amtico Co., Ltd., 5 - 9
The Bank Architectural Antiques, 1 - 34
The Burruss Company, 5 - 10
The Butcher Company, 6 - 75
The Decorative Center of Houston, 8 - 66
The Floor Shop, 5 - 10
The Joinery Company, 5 - 10
The Natural Woodflooring Company, 5 - 10
The Roane Co., 5 - 10
The Roof, Tile & Slate Co., 3 - 89
The Structural Slate Co., 3 - 89
The Woods Company, 5 - 10
Thompson Oak Flooring Co., 5 - 10
Toli International, 5 - 10
Tools of the Trade Inc., 6 - 78
Treework Services Ltd., 5 - 10
Trus Joist Corporation, 3 - 92
Valley Flooring Distributors, 5 - 10
Vassallo Precast Mfg. Corp., 2 - 12
Vermont Antique Lumber Co., 3 - 95
Vintage Lumber & Construction Co., 5 - 11
Vintage Pine Company, 5 - 11
White River, 5 - 11
Willis Lumber Company Inc., 1 - 37
Woodhouse, 5 - 11
Woods American, 5 - 11
Yawkey-Bissell Hardwood Flooring, 5 - 11
Zickgraf Hardwood Company, 5 - 11

The Complete Sourcebook

Index - 33

Frame

(Door, Window, etc.)

Aluma-Craft Corporation, 12 - 3
Anger Mfg. Co., Inc., 6 - 4
Architectural Components, 1 - 5
Bear Creek Lumber, 3 - 13
Bend Millwork Systems Inc., 4 - 2
BiltBest Windows, 12 - 5
Boulton & Paul PLC, 3 - 16
Cal-Wood Door Inc., 4 - 3
Century Wood Door Limited, 4 - 3
Cline Aluminum Doors Inc., 4 - 3
Consolidated Aluminum, 12 - 7
Contact Lumber Company, 3 - 27
Creative Structures, 3 - 27
Curriers Co., 4 - 4
Defiance Forest Products, 4 - 4
Designer's Edge, 8 - 23
Dimitrios Klitsas, 1 - 14
Diversified Millwork, 1 - 14
Donat Flamand, Inc., 4 - 5
Dunbarton Corp., 4 - 6
Eggers Industries, 4 - 6
F. E. Schumacher Co., Inc., 4 - 7
Fenestra Corp., 4 - 7
First American Resources, 12 - 9
Haley Bros.,Inc., 4 - 8
Hanover Wire Cloth, 12 - 10
Hoff Forest Products, Inc., 3 - 46
Iowa Des Moines Door & Hardware, 4 - 9
JJJ Specialty Co., 4 - 9
John Carr Joinery Sales Ltd., 12 - 13
Kaatskill Post & Beam, 1 - 21
Landquist & Son, Inc., 4 - 11
Leicester Joinery Co., 4 - 11
Lynden Door, Inc., 4 - 11
Mason Corporation, 12 - 15
Melbourne Hall Workshop, 10 - 7
Metal Exchange Corp., 12 - 15
Mirror Fair, 8 - 47
Mohawk Flush Doors, Inc., 4 - 12
New Morning Windows, Inc., 12 - 17
New York Wire Company, 12 - 17
Nichols-Homeshield, Inc., 12 - 18
North Star Company, 12 - 18
Nose Creek Forest Products, Ltd., 1 - 25
Pacific Post & Beam, 3 - 68
Perfection Metal & Supply Co., 3 - 69
Perkins Manufacturing & Distributing, 12 - 19
Phillips Industries, Inc., 3 - 70
Royal Plastics, Inc., 12 - 22
Sauder Door Corporation, 4 - 14
Schlesser Co., Inc., 1 - 30
SealRite Windows, Inc., 12 - 23
Semling-Menke Company, Inc., 4 - 15
Setzer Forest Products, 3 - 78
Solartechnic 2000 Ltd., 8 - 61
Southern Millwork, Inc., 1 - 31
Sovereign Wright, 4 - 16
Steldor Ltd., 4 - 16
Steves & Sons, 4 - 16
Superior Metal Products Co., 12 - 24
The Blount Lumber Company, 12 - 24
The Loxscreen Company, Inc., 12 - 25
Trimcraft Inc., 1 - 35
Vermont Frames, 1 - 36
Western Oregon Doors, Inc., 4 - 18
Wholesale Door Company, 4 - 18
Woodgrain Millwork, Inc., 4 - 18

Young Manufacturing Co., 4 - 18
Yuba River Moulding & Millwork, Inc., 1 - 38

French

(Doors, Furniture, Stencils, etc.)

Albert Gunther, 3 - 5
American Furniture Galleries, 6 - 4
Architectural Antiques West, 1 - 5
Architectural Paneling, 1 - 6
Bennett Industries Inc., 4 - 2
Bison Manufacturing, 4 - 2
Bright Star Woodworking, 4 - 3
Crestline, 4 - 4
Deep River Trading Company, 6 - 22
Eagle Window & Door, 12 - 8
French Country Living, 6 - 30
General Products Co. Inc., 4 - 8
Georgia Lighting Supply Co., 11 - 13
Heirloom Reproductions, 6 - 35
Iberia Millwork, 4 - 9
Jeannie Serpa Stencils, 8 - 37
Jessup Door Company, 4 - 10
Mark Sales Co. Inc., 6 - 50
Mather's Department Store, 8 - 44
Morgan Distribution, 4 - 12
Morgan Manufacturing, 4 - 12
Nana Windows & Doors Inc., 12 - 17
Pashayan, 6 - 58
Peachtree Doors, Inc., 4 - 13
Studio Steel, 11 - 30
Wing Industries Inc., 4 - 18

Furnace

Charmaster, 6 - 16
Daniels Co., Inc., 3 - 29
Eagle, 3 - 33
Rinnai America Corp., 3 - 75
TARM USA, Inc., 3 - 86
York International Corp., 3 - 101

Furnishing

ABC Carpet & Home, 8 - 1
American Treasury Catalog, 8 - 4
Armstrong-Decorative Accessories, 8 - 5
Craft House, 6 - 20
Florentine Craftsmen Inc., 7 - 2
Fraser Woods Inc., 4 - 7
Jackelope Furniture, 6 - 39
New West of Jackson, 6 - 55
Olde Virginea Trading Co., 8 - 50
Seventh Avenue, 8 - 59
Sporthill Inc., 1 - 32
Steven Linen Associates Inc., 8 - 63
The Country House, 8 - 66
The Hurshtowne Collection, 8 - 67
Trifles, 8 - 69
White Shield of Carolina Inc., 8 - 76
Wild Wings, 8 - 76
Wild Wood Gallery, 8 - 76
Wm. H. Jackson Co., 1 - 37

Furniture

A K Exteriors, 6 - 1
A-1 Mfg. Co. Inc., 6 - 1
A. Brandt Co., Inc., 6 - 1
A. Liss & Co., 6 - 1
A.L.F. Uno Spa, 6 - 1
AEL Furniture Group, 6 - 1
ARM Industries Inc., 6 - 1
Abacus Mfg. Ltd., 6 - 2
Aberdeen Mfg. Corp., 8 - 2

Index

Furniture – Furniture

Accademia, 6 - 2
Acerbis International Spa, 6 - 2
Acme Furniture Mfg. Inc., 6 - 2
Acmetrack Ltd., 6 - 2
Acrylic Innovations Inc., 6 - 2
Action Industries Inc., 6 - 2
Adam A. Weschler & Sons, 6 - 2
Adams Wood Products, Inc., 6 - 2
Adden Furniture Inc., 6 - 2
Adirondack Designs, 6 - 3
Adirondacks Store & Gallery, 6 - 3
Advance Modular Concepts, 6 - 3
Airon SRL, 6 - 3
Albert M. Lock & Son, 6 - 3
Alfresco Porch Swing Company, 6 - 3
Alivar SRL, 6 - 3
Allibert, 6 - 3
Allied Manufacturing Co. (London) Ltd., 6 - 3
Allmilmo Ltd., 6 - 3
American Drew, 6 - 3
American Furniture Co., 6 - 4
American Furniture Galleries, 6 - 4
American Liberty Furniture, 6 - 4
American Moulding & Millwork Co., 1 - 3
America's Finest Furniture, 6 - 3
Amish Country Collection, 6 - 4
Amish Furniture Collection, 6 - 4
Anderson Furniture, 6 - 4
Anderson Furniture, 6 - 4
Andrews Custom Woodworking, 1 - 4
Angel House Designs, 6 - 4
Anglo Nordic Marketing (UK) Ltd., 6 - 4
Anthropologie, 6 - 4
Antiquaria, 6 - 5
Antiquarian Traders, 6 - 5
Antique Furniture Copies, 6 - 5
Antique Furniture Workroom, 6 - 5
Antiquity, 6 - 5
Aram Designs Ltd., 6 - 5
Arc Linea Arredamenti SPA, 6 - 5
Archbold Furniture Co., 6 - 5
Arflex, 6 - 5
Arkitektura Inc., 6 - 5
Arrben Di O. Benvenuto, 6 - 5
Art In Iron, 6 - 5
Arte de Mexico, 6 - 6
Artesanos Imports, Inc., 6 - 6
Artistic Upholstery Ltd., 6 - 6
Ashby & Horner Joinery Ltd., 6 - 6
Ashely Manor, 6 - 6
Ashley Furniture Industries, 6 - 6
Atelier SRL, 6 - 6
Athens Furniture, 6 - 6
Atlanta Furniture Craftsmen, 6 - 6
Atlantic Furniture Sytems, 6 - 6
Avanti Furniture Corp., 6 - 6
B & B Italia Spa, 6 - 7
B & I Furniture, 6 - 7
Backwoods Furnishings, 6 - 7
Baker Chair Co., 6 - 7
Baker Furniture, 6 - 7
Baleri Italia, 6 - 7
Bales Furniture Mfg., 6 - 7
Ball and Ball, 6 - 7
Banana River Open Air Furniture, 6 - 7
Barbary Coast Furniture Co., 6 - 7
Barclay Furniture Associates Inc., 6 - 7
Bargain John's Antiques, 6 - 7
Barlow Tyrie, 6 - 8
Barnes & Barnes, 6 - 8
Barnett Products Co., 6 - 8

Bartley Collection, 6 - 8
Bassett Furniture Industries Inc., 6 - 8
Bausman & Company, Inc., 6 - 8
Bazzani Alberto di F. Bazzani & C. SAS, 6 - 8
Beachley Furniture Co., Inc., 6 - 8
Bedquarters, 6 - 8
Beds By Benzcian, Inc., 6 - 9
Bernhardt Furniture Co., 6 - 9
Best Furniture Distributors, Inc., 6 - 9
Bevan Funnel Limited, 6 - 9
Bevan Funnell Ltd., 6 - 9
Bevis Custom Furniture, 6 - 9
Bielecky Brothers, Inc., 6 - 9
Big Country, 6 - 9
Big Table Furniture, 6 - 9
Billing Croft of Salem, 6 - 9
Bjorndal Woodworks, 1 - 8
Blackwelder's Industries, Inc., 6 - 9
Blake Industries, 6 - 10
Blanton & Moore Co., 6 - 10
Blue Canyon Woodworks, 6 - 10
Bograd's, 6 - 10
Bombay Company, 6 - 10
Bonaldo SPA, 6 - 10
Bonaventure Furniture Ind., 6 - 10
Boston & Winthrop, 6 - 10
Boudoir Furniture Mfg. Corp., 6 - 10
Boyd R. Smith, 6 - 10
Boyles Furniture, 6 - 11
Bracewell Furniture Co., 6 - 11
Bradington Young, 6 - 11
Brady Furniture Co., 6 - 11
Braman Furniture Mfg., 6 - 11
Brayton International Inc., 6 - 11
Brentwood Manor Furnishings, 6 - 11
Bridgewater, 6 - 12
Bristol House, 6 - 12
British Antique Replicas, 6 - 12
British-American Marketing Services, 6 - 12
Brooks Furniture Mfg. Inc., 6 - 12
Bros's SRL, 6 - 12
Brown Jordon Furniture, 6 - 12
Broyhill Furniture Ind. Inc., 6 - 12
Brunati SRL, 6 - 12
Budoff Outdoor Furniture, 6 - 12
Builtright Chair Co. Inc., 6 - 12
Burcham Furniture Manufacturing, 6 - 13
Butcher Block & More Furniture, 6 - 13
Butler Specialty Co., 6 - 13
C. H. Southwell, 6 - 13
C. Neri, Antiques, 6 - 13
CM Comini Modonutti SRL, 6 - 13
Cabin Creek Furniture, 6 - 13
Caldwell Chair Company, 6 - 13
California Marble Co., 6 - 13
Calligaris SPA, 6 - 13
Camel International SRL, 6 - 13
Cameo Mica Furniture Manufacturer, 6 - 13
Candlertown Chairworks, 6 - 14
Cappellini International Interiors SPA, 6 - 14
Carl Forslund, 6 - 14
Carleton Furniture Group Ltd., 6 - 14
Carlton Mfg. Inc., 6 - 14
Carolina Furniture Works, Inc., 6 - 14
Carolina Interiors, 6 - 14
Carolina Strand Co., Inc., 6 - 14
Carrier Furniture Inc., 6 - 14
Carson's Furniture, 6 - 14
Casa Stradivari, 6 - 15
Cassina SPA, 6 - 15
Cassina USA Inc., 6 - 15

The Complete Sourcebook

Furniture – Furniture

Index

Castle Mount, 6 - 15
Catherine Ann Furnishings, 6 - 15
Cattelan Italia SPA, 6 - 15
Cedar Design Ltd., 6 - 15
Cedar Rock Home Furnishings, 6 - 15
Century Furniture, 6 - 15
Chaircraft Inc., 6 - 15
Champman Mfg. Co., 11 - 7
Channel Hall, 6 - 15
Chapin Townsend Furniture, 6 - 15
Charles Webb Furniture, 6 - 16
Charleston Iron Works, 6 - 16
Charlton West, 8 - 16
Chatsworth Interiors, 6 - 16
Cherry & Deen Furniture, 6 - 16
Cherry Hill Furniture,Carpet & Interiors, 6 - 16
Cidue, 6 - 16
Ciro Coppa, 6 - 16
Clapper's, 6 - 16
Clark Casual Furniture Inc., 6 - 17
Classic Choice, 6 - 17
Classic Gallery Inc., 6 - 17
Classic Leather, 6 - 17
Clayton Marcus Co., Inc., 6 - 17
Clear Lake Furniture, 6 - 17
Cochrane Furniture Co., 6 - 17
Coffey Discount Furniture, 6 - 17
Cohasset Colonials, 6 - 17
Collection Reproductions, 6 - 17
Colombo Mobili SNC, 6 - 18
Colonial Designs Furniture, 6 - 18
Colonial Furniture Shops, Inc., 6 - 18
Colonial Williamsburg, 6 - 18
Color-Tex Distributors, 6 - 18
Comoexport-Divisione Di Cantu, 6 - 18
Concepts International, 6 - 18
Concepts in Comfort, 6 - 18
Conexport, 6 - 18
Continental Chair Co., 6 - 18
Continental Custom Made Furniture, 6 - 18
Continental Woodworking Co., 1 - 12
Coppa Woodworking, 6 - 18
Cornucopia, Inc., 6 - 19
Corsican, 6 - 19
Country Bed Shop, 6 - 19
Country Casual, 6 - 19
Country Crossroads Furniture, 6 - 19
Country Furniture Shop, 6 - 19
Country Pine Furniture, 6 - 19
Country Store, 6 - 19
Country Workshop, 6 - 19
Craft House, 6 - 20
Crate & Barrel Furniture, 6 - 20
Crawford Furniture Mfg. Corp., 6 - 20
Creative Furniture Systems, 6 - 20
Cricket on the Hearth, Inc., 6 - 20
Crossland Studio, 1 - 12
Cumberland Furniture, 6 - 20
Curran Upholstered Furniture, 6 - 20
Current, 11 - 8
Custom Furniture Corp., 6 - 20
Customcraft, 6 - 20
Cymann Designs, 6 - 20
Cypress Street Center, 6 - 20
D & L Mfg., Co., 6 - 21
DHM Cabinetmakers Inc., 6 - 21
DHU Designs, Inc., 6 - 21
DMI Furniture, Inc., 6 - 21
Dan Wilson & Company, 6 - 21
Dana Robes Wood Craftsmen, 6 - 21
Dancan Mfg. Ltd., 6 - 21

Dapha Limited, 6 - 21
David Edward Ltd., 6 - 21
David W. Lamb Cabinetmaker, 6 - 21
Davis Cabinet Company, 6 - 22
Davis Furniture Industries, Inc., 6 - 22
Deacon & Sandys, 6 - 22
Dean & Brook Ltd., 6 - 22
Decker Antique Reproductions, 6 - 22
Decor-Rest Furniture Ltd., 6 - 22
Decorative Crafts Inc., 6 - 22
Deep River Trading Company, 6 - 22
Del Tongo (UK, etc.) Ltd., 6 - 22
Delta Furniture Inc., 6 - 22
Deltacrafts Mfg. Ltd., 6 - 23
Dependable Furniture Mfg. Co., 6 - 23
Derby Desk Company, 6 - 23
Design Furniture Mfg. Ltd., 6 - 23
Design Gallery Milano, 6 - 23
Design Systems International, 6 - 23
Designer Gallery Ltd., 6 - 23
Designer Secrets, 8 - 23
Deutsch, 6 - 23
Dimas Manufacturing Inc., 6 - 23
Dimitrios Klitsas, 1 - 14
Direct Furniture, 6 - 23
Directional of North Carolina Inc., 6 - 23
Directions Inc., 6 - 24
Distinction Furniture Corp., 6 - 24
Dixie Furniture Co., 6 - 24
Dominion Chair, Ltd., 6 - 24
Don Ruseau Inc., 6 - 24
Doolings of Santa Fe, 6 - 24
Door Store, 6 - 24
Dor-Val Mfg. Ltd., 6 - 24
Dovetail Antiques, 1 - 15
Drexel Heritage, 6 - 24
Driade SPA, 6 - 24
Dunhill Furniture Corp., 6 - 25
Dutailer Inc., 6 - 25
Dynasty Wood Products Inc., 6 - 25
E. J. Evans, 6 - 25
E. T. Moore Company, 5 - 4
E.C. Hodge Ltd., 6 - 25
ETA Wood Concepts, 6 - 25
Eddie Bauer Home Collection, 8 - 24
Edgar B Furniture, 6 - 25
Edra SPA, 6 - 25
Edward P. Schmidt Cabinetmaker, 6 - 25
Eldrid Wheeler, 6 - 25
Ellenburg's Furniture, 6 - 26
Elm Industries, 6 - 26
Elmo Guernsey, 6 - 26
Emerson Leather Co., 6 - 26
Emperor Clock Company, 8 - 25
Empire State Chair Co., Inc., 6 - 26
Ephraim Marsh, 6 - 26
Ercol Furniture Ltd., 6 - 26
Ernest Thompson Furniture, 6 - 26
Erwin-Lambeth, Inc., 6 - 26
Esse SRL, 6 - 26
Essential Items, 6 - 27
Ethan Allen, Inc., 6 - 27
Eudy Cabinet Shop Inc., 6 - 27
European Furniture Importers, 6 - 27
Evertidy Furniture Ltd., 6 - 27
Expressions Custom Furniture, 6 - 27
FDY Furniture Mfg. Ltd., 6 - 27
Fabian Furniture Mfg. Co. Ltd., 6 - 27
Fairchild of Calfornia, 6 - 27
Fairfield Chair Co., 6 - 27
Fama SPA, 6 - 27

Index - 36

The Complete Sourcebook

Index

Furniture – Furniture

Fancher Chair Co. Inc., 6 - 27
Fancher Furniture Co., 6 - 28
Faneuil Furniture Hardware Co. Inc., 6 - 28
Felice rossi SRL, 6 - 28
Ferretti F.LLi Di Ferretto SPA, 6 - 28
Ficks Reed Co., 6 - 28
Fine Arts Furniture Co., 6 - 28
Fine Woodworking by Living Tree, 6 - 28
Finkel Outdoors Products Inc., 6 - 28
Flanders Industries Inc., 6 - 28
Flexform, 6 - 28
Flexsteel Industries, 6 - 28
Florida Furniture Industries, 6 - 29
Florida Headboard & Furniture Mfg., 6 - 29
Fly By Nite Futons, 6 - 29
Fly Line, 6 - 29
Fong Brothers Company, 6 - 29
Fontaine Bros. Inc., 6 - 29
Fontana Arte SPA, 6 - 29
Foreign Traders, 6 - 29
Foremost Furniture, 6 - 29
Foster Bros. Mfg. Co., 6 - 29
Foster Manufacturing, 6 - 29
Founders Furniture Co., 6 - 29
Frank & Son Inc., 6 - 29
Franklin Custom Furniture, 6 - 30
Fran's Basket House, 6 - 29
Frederick Duckloe & Bros., 6 - 30
Frederick Wilbur, Carver, 1 - 17
Fremarc Industries Inc., 10 - 4
French Country Living, 6 - 30
Frisco Mfg. Co., 6 - 30
Fulgini Orilio & F.LLI SPA, 6 - 30
Furnitrad Inc., 6 - 30
Furniture Collections of Carolina, 6 - 30
Furniture Craft, 6 - 30
Furniture Design Imports, 6 - 30
Furniture Forge, 6 - 30
Furniture Mart Design Center, 6 - 30
Furniture That Exceeds Your Expectation,6-30
Futon Furnishings, 6 - 31
G & G Furniture, 6 - 31
Gaby's Shoppe, 6 - 31
Galeria San Ysidro, Inc., 6 - 31
Gallery of H B, 6 - 31
Garcia Imports, 6 - 31
Garden Source Furnishings, Inc., 7 - 2
Gaston's Wood Finishes & Antiques, 3 - 39
Genada Imports, 6 - 31
General Mica Corp., 6 - 31
Georgia Chair Co., 6 - 31
Georgian Furnishings Co., Ltd., 6 - 31
Georgian Reproduction, 6 - 31
Gerald Curry-Cabinetmaker, 6 - 31
Gibson Interiors, 11 - 13
Gilliam Furniture Inc., 6 - 32
Giovanni Erba & C. SNC, 6 - 32
Glober Mfg. Co., 6 - 32
Gold Medal Inc., 6 - 32
Good Tables Inc., 6 - 32
Gordon's Inc., 6 - 32
Grand Manor Furniture Inc., 6 - 32
Grand River Workshop, 6 - 32
Grange Furniture, Inc., 6 - 32
Great American Log Furniture, 6 - 32
Great Gatsby's Auction Galley, 1 - 18
Great Meadows Joinery, 6 - 32
Great Western Furniture Mfg. Co., 6 - 33
Green Brothers Furniture Co., 6 - 33
Green Country Furniture Mfg. Co., 6 - 33
Green Enterprises, 6 - 33

Greystone Victorian Furniture, 6 - 33
Griffon Furniture Ltd., 6 - 33
Grindstaff's Interiors, 6 - 33
Guy Vincent Custom Furniture& Crafts, 6 - 33
H. Morris & Co. Ltd., 6 - 33
H.U.D.D.L.E., 6 - 33
Habersham Plantation Corp., 6 - 33
Hale Co., 6 - 33
Haliburton & White Ltee., 6 - 34
Hamilton Furniture, 6 - 34
Hamlet Furniture Ltd., 6 - 34
Hammary Furniture Co., 6 - 34
Harden Furniture Inc., 6 - 34
Harden Mfg. Co., 6 - 34
Hart Furniture, 6 - 34
Harts Mfg. Co., Inc., 6 - 34
Harvest House Furniture, 6 - 34
Heath Craft Wood Works, 6 - 34
Hedstrom Corp., 6 - 34
Heirloom Reproductions, 6 - 35
Hekman Furniture, 6 - 35
Henkel-Harris, 6 - 35
Henredon, 6 - 35
Heron-Parigi, 6 - 35
Hickory Chair Co., 6 - 35
Hickory Furniture Co., 6 - 35
Hickory Furniture Mart, 6 - 35
Hickory White, 6 - 35
Highland House of Hickory Inc., 6 - 35
Historic Charleston Reproductions, 6 - 35
Hitchcock Chair Co., 6 - 36
Holder Pearce, 6 - 36
Holiday Pool & Patio, 6 - 36
Hollingsworth, 6 - 36
Holloways, 6 - 36
Holton Furniture Co., 6 - 36
Home Decorators Collection, 11 - 15
Homecrest Industries, Inc., 6 - 36
Homestead Furniture, 6 - 36
Homeway Furniture Co., 6 - 36
Horchow Home Collection, 6 - 36
Horm SRL, 6 - 36
Hostess Furniture Ltd., 6 - 37
House Dressing Furniture, 6 - 37
House of Brougham Collection, 6 - 37
Howard Miller Clock Company, 6 - 37
Howe Furniture Corp., 6 - 37
Howerton Antique Reproductions, 6 - 37
Hudson's Discount Furniture, 6 - 37
Hughes Furniture Industries, Inc., 6 - 37
Hunt Country Furniture, 6 - 37
Hunt Galleries, Inc., 6 - 38
Huntingburg Wood Products co., 6 - 38
Hyde Park Antiques, Ltd., 6 - 38
Hyperion Wall Furniture Ltd., 6 - 38
Hyphen Fitted Furniture, 6 - 38
I. P. E. SPA, 6 - 38
Images of America Inc., 6 - 38
Imperial of Morristown, 6 - 38
Indian Ocean Trading Co., 6 - 38
Interior Furnishings, Ltd., 6 - 38
Interna Furniture Design Ltd., 6 - 38
International Woodworking, 6 - 39
Irving & Jones Fine Garden Furnishings,6-39
Isabel Brass Furniture, 6 - 39
J D Furniture Mfg. Ltd., 6 - 39
J. T. Ellis & Co. Ltd., 6 - 39
J.A.G. International Inc., 6 - 39
JMW Gallery, 6 - 39
Jackson Sales, Inc., 6 - 39
James Lea-Cabinetmaker, 6 - 39

The Complete Sourcebook

Index - 37

Furniture – Furniture

James M. Taylor & Co., 6 - 40
Janis Aldridge, Inc., 6 - 40
Jarabosky, 6 - 40
Jasper Cabinet Co., 6 - 40
Jeffco, 6 - 40
Jeffrey P. Greene, Furniture Maker, 6 - 40
Jesper Furniture USA, 6 - 40
John Alan Designs, 6 - 40
John Congdon, Cabinetmaker, 6 - 40
John Michael Furniture, 6 - 40
John Minter Furniture Ltd., 6 - 40
John Pulsford Associates Ltd., 6 - 40
John Widdicomb Co., 6 - 41
Jones Brothers, 6 - 41
Jones' Oak Furniture, 6 - 41
K & C Southwest Interiors, 6 - 41
Kane Masterbuilt Furniture Co., 6 - 41
Karges Furniture Co., Inc., 6 - 41
Kartell SPA, 6 - 41
Keller Manufacturing Co., 6 - 41
Kenneth D. Lynch & Sons, Inc., 6 - 41
Kenneth Winslow Furniture, 6 - 41
Kesterport Ltd., 6 - 42
Key City Furniture Co., Inc., 6 - 42
Kimball Furniture Reproductions, 6 - 42
Kincaid Galleries, 6 - 42
King Hickory Furniture Co. Inc., 6 - 42
Kingsdown Inc., 6 - 42
Kingsley Furniture Co. Inc., 6 - 42
Kingsley-Bate, Ltd., 6 - 42
Kirby Mfg. Co. Inc., 6 - 42
Kisabeth Furniture, 6 - 42
Kittinger Co., 6 - 43
Klein Design Inc., 6 - 43
Kloter Farms Inc., 7 - 4
Knight Galleries, 6 - 43
Knipp & Co. Inc., 6 - 43
Koch Originals, Inc., 12 - 14
Kopil & Associates Timeless Furniture, 6 - 43
Kraemer Furniture Designs, 6 - 43
Kramer Brothers, 6 - 43
Kroehler Furniture Co., 6 - 43
L & J.G. Stickley, Inc., 6 - 43
La Barge Mirrors, Inc., 8 - 41
La Lune Collection, 6 - 43
La-Z-Boy Furniture, 6 - 44
Ladd Furniture Industries, Inc., 6 - 44
Lanark Furniture Corp., 6 - 44
Landscape Forms Inc., 7 - 4
Lane Company, Inc., 6 - 44
Lanier Furniture Company, 6 - 44
Lanzet (UK, etc.) Ltd., 6 - 44
Larkspur Furniture Co., 6 - 44
Larry & Alley, Inc., 6 - 44
Lawing's, 6 - 44
Lazy Lawyer Co. Inc., 6 - 44
LeFort, 6 - 44
Leather Furniture Sales, Inc., 6 - 45
Leather Interiors, 6 - 45
Leboff International Ltd., 6 - 45
Lee Industries Inc., 6 - 45
Lee L. Woodard Sons Inc., 6 - 45
Legendary Furniture of Ezra G., 6 - 45
Lehigh Furniture, 6 - 45
Lenore Mulligan Designs, Inc., 6 - 45
Leonard's Reproductions & Antiques, 6 - 45
Leverwood Ltd., 6 - 45
Lewis Mittman, Inc., 6 - 45
Lewittes Furniture Enterprises Inc., 6 - 45
Lexington Furniture Industries, 6 - 46
Lexterten Ltd., 6 - 46

Liberty Hall, 6 - 46
Limelight Bedrooms, 6 - 46
Lincoln House Furniture, 6 - 46
Lineas Sas Di Asgnaghi Giannarturo, 6 - 46
Link-Taylor Corp., 6 - 46
Lion House Antique (Copies, etc.), 6 - 46
Lisa Victoria Beds, 6 - 46
Lister Teak, Inc., 6 - 46
Little Colorado Inc., 6 - 46
Lloyd Loom Catalogue, 6 - 46
Lloyd/Flanders, 6 - 47
Loftin-Black Furniture Co., 6 - 47
Louis Interiors Inc., 6 - 47
Louisiana Cypress Ltd., 6 - 47
Lyon-Shaw, 6 - 47
L'Image Design, 6 - 43
M. Craig & Company, 6 - 47
Machado, 6 - 47
Mack & Rodel Cabinet Makers, 6 - 47
Macon Umbrella Corp., 6 - 47
Maddison House, 6 - 47
Magna Designs Inc., 6 - 47
Magnolia Hall, 6 - 48
Mahogany Craft, 6 - 48
Maine Cottage Furniture, Inc., 6 - 48
Majestic Furniture Co., 6 - 48
Mallin Co., 6 - 48
Mallory's Fine Furniture, 6 - 48
Manchester Wood Inc., 6 - 48
Manhattan Cabinetry, 6 - 48
Manheim & Weitz, 6 - 48
Manivalde Woodworking, 6 - 48
Manor House, 6 - 49
Manufactur De Lambton Ltee., 6 - 49
Manufacture De Meubles Carol Ann Ltee., 6-49
Maraco Design Inc., 6 - 49
Marco Fine Furniture, 6 - 49
Marelli International SRL, 6 - 49
Mario Villa Designs, 6 - 49
Marion H. Campbell, 1 - 23
Marion Travis, 6 - 49
Mark & Marjorie Allen, 6 - 49
Mark Dahlman Wood Products, 6 - 49
Mark Sales Co. Inc., 6 - 50
Mark Wilkinson Furniture Ltd., 6 - 50
Marlow Furniture Co. Inc., 6 - 50
Marsh Furniture Company, 6 - 50
Martha M. House, 6 - 50
Martin & Frost Ltd., 6 - 50
Martin Laque Inc., 6 - 50
Martin Timber Co., Inc., 6 - 50
Maryland Classics Inc., 6 - 50
Mason Art Inc., 6 - 50
Master Woodcarver, 6 - 50
Masterworks, 6 - 51
Materials Unlimited, 1 - 23
Matteograssi SPA, 6 - 51
Maui Trading Co., 3 - 59
Maurice Lepine Ltd., 6 - 51
Maxalto SPA, 6 - 51
Mayan Marble & Onyx Ltd., 6 - 51
Mayfield Leather, 8 - 45
Mayhew, 6 - 51
Maynard House Antiques, 6 - 51
McCraig & Company, 6 - 51
McFlem Furniture Mfg., 6 - 51
Meadow Craft, 6 - 51
Mecklenburg Furniture Shops, 6 - 51
Mendes Antiques, 6 - 52
Menuiserie Joliette Inc., 6 - 52

Index

Furniture – Furniture

Mereway Developments Ltd., 6 - 52
Merit Metal Products Corp., 3 - 60
Merritt's Antiques Inc., 6 - 52
Mersman Waldron Furniture, 6 - 52
Metalliform Ltd., 6 - 52
Metropolitan Furniture Corp., 6 - 52
Michael Camp, 6 - 52
Michael M. Reed, 6 - 52
Michael's Classic Wicker, 6 - 52
MidAmerica Furniture, 6 - 53
Minic Custom Woodwork, Inc., 6 - 53
Minnetonka Woodcraft Co., 6 - 53
Minton Corley Collection, 3 - 61
Mirroline Design Ltd., 6 - 53
Modern Classic Furniture Inc., 6 - 53
Modern Reed & Rattan Co. Inc., 6 - 53
Modern of Marshfield, Inc., 6 - 53
Mohawk Furniture Inc., 6 - 53
Molteni & C. SPA, 6 - 53
Mona Liza Fine Furniture Inc., 6 - 53
Mondo, 6 - 53
Monzie Joinery Ltd., 6 - 54
Moosehead Mfg. Co., 6 - 54
Moultrie Manufacturing Co., 6 - 54
Murphy Bed Company Inc., 6 - 54
Murphy Furniture Mfg. Co., Inc., 6 - 54
Murrow Furniture Galleries, Inc., 6 - 54
Nagykery Imports, Ltd., 6 - 54
Nathan Furniture Ltd., 6 - 54
National Furniture Co., 6 - 54
Natuzzi Americas Inc., 6 - 54
Neil Rogers Interiors, 6 - 54
New West of Jackson, 6 - 55
Nichols & Stone, 6 - 55
Niedermaier Design Inc., 6 - 55
Niermann Weeks, 6 - 55
Nimetz Woodworking Mfg. Co., 6 - 55
Nolarec Industries, Inc., 6 - 55
Noritage Inc., 6 - 55
Norman's Handmade Reproductions, 6 - 55
North Carolina Furniture Showroom, 6 - 55
North Hickory Furniture Co., 6 - 55
North Woods Chair Shop, 6 - 55
Northern Rustic Furniture, 6 - 55
Northwoods Furniture Co., 6 - 56
Norwalk Furniture Corp., 6 - 56
Nu-Line Industries, 6 - 56
O.W. Lee Co., Inc., 6 - 56
Oak Craft Inc., 6 - 56
Oak Land Furniture Manufacturing, 6 - 56
Oakline Chair Co. Inc., 6 - 56
Okla Homer Smith Furniture Mfg. Co., 6 - 56
Old Hickory Furniture Co. Inc., 6 - 56
Old Road Furniture Co., 6 - 56
Olde Mill House Shoppe, 6 - 57
Ole Timey Furniture Co., 6 - 57
Olympic Custom Furniture, Ltd., 6 - 57
Omega Furniture, 6 - 57
Options Bedrooms Ltd., 6 - 57
Original Arts Mfg. Corp., 6 - 57
Orleans Carpenters, 6 - 57
Osborne Wood Products Inc., 6 - 57
Ottawa Brass Ltd., 6 - 57
Oxford Leather, 6 - 58
Ozark Wood Products, 6 - 58
Pacific Design Furniture, 6 - 58
Palazzetti Inc., 6 - 58
Pallavisini Sedersi, 6 - 58
Palliser Furniture Corp., 6 - 58
Paramount Mfg. Co., 6 - 58
Parisotto, 8 - 51

Park Place, 6 - 58
Parkway Furniture Galleries, 6 - 58
Pashayan, 6 - 58
Patrician Furniture Co., 6 - 58
Pearson Furniture, 6 - 58
Pecan States Industries, Inc., 6 - 59
Pegram Contracts Ltd., 6 - 59
Pel Ltd., 6 - 59
Pennsylvania House Inc., 6 - 59
Pete Bissonette & Company, 6 - 59
Peter Kramer, Cabinetmaker, 6 - 59
Peter-Revington Corp., 6 - 59
Peterson Wood Div., 7 - 5
Pettigrew Associates Inc., 6 - 59
Pilgrim House Products, 8 - 53
Pilliod Cabinet Co., 6 - 59
Pine & Design Imports, 6 - 59
Pine Tradition Ltd., 6 - 60
Pioneer Furniture Mfg. Co., 6 - 60
Pipe Casual, 6 - 60
Pira Ltd., 6 - 60
Plantation Patterns Inc., 6 - 60
Plaza Furniture Gallery, 6 - 60
Plow & Hearth, 7 - 5
Pocahontas Furniture Mfg. Co., 6 - 60
Poltronova Design SRL, 6 - 60
Pompeii, 6 - 60
Pottery Barn, 6 - 60
Precision Furniture Corp., 6 - 60
Prestige Mfg. Co., 6 - 60
Priba Furniture, 6 - 61
Primiani Chesterfield Inc., 6 - 61
Prince Albert's, 6 - 61
Prochnow & Prochnow, 7 - 5
Pulaski Furniture Corp., 6 - 61
Quality Craft Inc., 6 - 61
Quality Dinettes Incorporated, 6 - 61
Quality Furniture Co., 6 - 61
Quality Furniture Market, 6 - 61
Quality Imports, 7 - 5
Quebeco Furniture Inc., 6 - 61
Queen Ann Furniture Co., Inc., 6 - 61
R. Wagner Company, 6 - 61
Rackstraw Ltd., 6 - 62
Ralston Furniture Reproductions, 6 - 62
Ranch Wood Products Inc., 6 - 62
Randall Tysinger, 6 - 62
Rattan Boricua Mfg. Corp., 6 - 62
Rattan Interiors, 6 - 62
Rattan Specialties Santa Fe, 6 - 62
Rebwood Inc., 6 - 62
Redbridge Furniture, 6 - 62
Reed Bros., 3 - 74
Regal Furniture Mfg. Ltd., 6 - 62
Reid Classics, 6 - 62
Renaissance Furniture and Cabinetry, 6 - 62
Renray Group Ltd., 6 - 63
Rex Furniture Co. Inc., 6 - 63
Rhine-Castle Company, 6 - 63
Rhoney Furniture, 6 - 63
Richard B. Zarbin & Associates, 6 - 63
Richard Gervais Collection, 6 - 63
Richardson Bros., 6 - 63
River Bend Chair Company, 6 - 63
Riverside Furniture Corp., 6 - 63
Robert Barrow Furniture Maker, 6 - 63
Robert Whitley Studio, 6 - 64
Roberts Brass Company, 6 - 64
Robertson Furniture Mfg. Inc., 6 - 64
Robert's, 6 - 64
Robinson Iron, 6 - 64

The Complete Sourcebook

Index - 39

Furniture – Furniture

Index

Roche-Bobois, 6 - 64
Rockford Mills Furniture Co., 6 - 64
Room & Board, 6 - 64
Rose Hill Furniture, 6 - 64
Roses Wood Products Inc., 6 - 64
Rowal Custom Furniture, 6 - 65
Rowe Furniture Corp., 6 - 65
Royal Strathclyde Blindcraft Ind., 6 - 65
Rubbermaid-Allibert Contract, 6 - 65
Rubee Furniture Mfg. Corp., 6 - 65
Russell Flooring Co., 6 - 65
Rustic Furnishings, 6 - 65
Sagga Furnishings Ltd., 6 - 65
Sak Industries Inc., 6 - 65
Salem Square, 6 - 65
Sampler Inc., 6 - 65
Sandberg Furniture Mfg. Co., 6 - 65
Saporiti Italia SPA, 6 - 65
Saraband Furniture Co., 6 - 66
Sarita Furniture, 6 - 66
Sawtooth Valley Woodcrafts, 6 - 66
Scandecor, 6 - 66
Scandinavian Design, 6 - 66
Scappini Giovanni & C. SAS, 6 - 66
Schnadig Corp., 6 - 66
Schweiger Industries Inc., 6 - 66
Scully & Scully, 6 - 66
Sebastian DeLorenzis Custom Furniture,6-66
Second Impression Antiques, 6 - 66
Segal Furniture Co., 6 - 67
Selva SPA, 6 - 67
Selzer Enterprises Inc., 6 - 67
Seventh Avenue, 8 - 59
Seventh Heaven, 6 - 67
Seybold Industries Inc., 6 - 67
Shaffield Industries Inc., 6 - 67
Shaker Carpenter Shop, 6 - 67
Shaker Shops West, 6 - 67
Shaker Workshops, 3 - 78
Shannon Chair, 6 - 67
Shaw Furniture Galleries, 6 - 67
Sheffield Chair Co., 6 - 68
Shelby Williams Industries, Inc., 6 - 68
Shermag Inc., 6 - 68
Sherrill Furniture Co., 6 - 68
Shushan Bentwood Co., 6 - 68
Sidex Furniture, 6 - 68
Silhoutte Antiques Inc., 6 - 68
Silik SPA, 6 - 68
Simmons Juvenile Products Co. , 6 - 68
Simms & Thapper Cabinetmakers, 6 - 68
Simply Country Furniture, 6 - 68
Sittin' Easy, 6 - 69
Sklar-Peppler Inc., 6 - 69
Sligh Furniture, 6 - 69
Slumberland PLC, 6 - 69
Smed Mfg. Inc., 6 - 69
Smith & Hawken, 6 - 69
Smith & Watson, 6 - 69
Smith Woodworks and Design, 6 - 69
Sobol House, 6 - 69
Solway Furniture Inc., 6 - 69
South Beach Furniture Company, 6 - 70
South West Joinery Co. Ltd., 6 - 70
Southern Comfort Furniture, 6 - 70
Southern Furniture, 6 - 70
Southern Kentucky Furniture, 6 - 70
Southern Manor Furniture Corp., 6 - 70
Southern Pine Manufacturing Inc., 6 - 70
Southhampton Antiques, 6 - 70
Southwood Reproductions, 6 - 70

Spaulding Colonial Reproductions, 6 - 70
Spectrum Furniture Co. Inc., 6 - 70
Splendor in Brass, 6 - 70
St. Barthelemy Furniture Ltd., 6 - 71
St. Charles Furniture, 6 - 71
Stag Meredew Furniture Ltd., 6 - 71
Stanley Chair Co. Inc., 6 - 71
Stanley Furniture, 6 - 71
Staples & Co. Ltd., 6 - 71
Star Interiors Ltd., 6 - 71
Statesville Chair Company, 6 - 71
Statton Furniture Mfg. Co., 6 - 71
Stefanelli, 6 - 71
Stephen Adams Furniture Makers, 6 - 72
Stephen Huneck Gallery, 10 - 9
Sterlingworth Corp., 6 - 72
Steven's Furniture Company, Inc., 6 - 72
Stone & Phillips co., 6 - 72
Strafford House, 6 - 72
Straw Hill Chairs, 6 - 72
Stuart Interiors, 6 - 72
Stuckey Brothers Furniture Co., Inc., 6 - 72
Summer Hill Ltd., 6 - 72
Summit Furniture, 6 - 73
Sumter Cabinet Co., 6 - 73
Suter's Handcrafted Furniture, 6 - 73
Sutton-Coucil Furniture, 6 - 73
Sweet Water Ranch, 6 - 73
Sylmar Technology Ltd., 6 - 73
Tad Taylor's Fantasy Furniture, 6 - 73
Taos Furniture, 6 - 73
Taylor Woodcraft Inc., 6 - 73
Telescope Casual Furniture, 6 - 74
Tennessee Fabricating Co., 6 - 74
Tennessee Hardwood Co., 6 - 74
Texacraft Outdoor Furnishings, 6 - 74
Thayer Coggin Inc., 6 - 74
The Antique Catalog, 6 - 74
The Bartley Collections Ltd., 6 - 74
The Bed Factory, 6 - 74
The Bedpost, 6 - 74
The Berkline Corp., 6 - 74
The Blacksmiths Shop, 6 - 74
The Bombay Co., 6 - 75
The Brass Collection, 6 - 75
The Butcher Company, 6 - 75
The Childrens Furniture Co., 6 - 75
The Farmhouse Collection, 6 - 75
The Furniture Gallery, 6 - 75
The Furniture Patch, 6 - 75
The Furniture Shoppe Inc., 6 - 75
The Golden Rabbit, 6 - 75
The Heveningham Collection, 6 - 75
The Keeping Room, 6 - 75
The Knoll Group, 6 - 76
The Leather Gallery of Kentucky, 6 - 76
The Lenox Shop, 6 - 76
The Odd Chair Company, 6 - 76
The Patio, 6 - 76
The Rocker Shop of Marietta, 6 - 76
The Schoenheit Co., 6 - 76
The Seraph Country Collection, 6 - 76
The Sofa Factory, 6 - 76
The Victorian Merchant, 6 - 77
The Walsh Woodworks, 8 - 68
The Wicker Garden, 6 - 77
The Willow Place Inc., 6 - 77
The Woodlawn Co., 6 - 77
The Workbench, 6 - 77
The Yorkshire Door Company Ltd., 4 - 17
This End Up, 6 - 77

Index - 40

The Complete Sourcebook

Index

Garage – Garden

Thomas H. Kramer Inc., 6 - 77
Thomas Home Furnishings, 6 - 77
Thomasville Furniture, 6 - 77
Thos. Moser, Cabinetmakers, 6 - 77
Three Mountaineers, Inc., 6 - 77
Through The Barn Door Furniture Co., 6 - 78
Thunderbird Furniture, 6 - 78
Tidewater Workshop, 6 - 78
Tiger Mountain Woodworks, 6 - 78
Tilden Industries (UK, etc.) Ltd., 6 - 78
Titan Wood Products Ltd., 6 - 78
Tom Thumb Lighting, Inc., 11 - 33
Tomlinson Furniture, 6 - 78
Tony's Furniture Factory Outlet, 6 - 78
Touchstone, 8 - 69
Trainor Metal Products Co., 6 - 78
Treasure Garden Inc., 6 - 78
Treasured Weavings, 8 - 69
Treske, 6 - 78 , 10 - 9
Triad Furniture Discounters, 6 - 78
Trinity Furniture Inc., 6 - 79
Triplett's Furniture Fashions, 6 - 79
Tropitone, 6 - 79
Trott Furniture Co., 6 - 79
Turner Tolson, Inc., 6 - 79
Twin Oaks Hammocks, 7 - 7
Tysinger Furniture Gallery, 6 - 79
Umphreds Inc., 6 - 79
Union City Chair Co., 6 - 79
Union-National, 6 - 79
Unique Furnishings Ltd., 6 - 79
Universal Bedroom Furniture Ltd., 6 - 80
Urban Artifacts, 1 - 35
Urban Glassworks, 3 - 94
Valley Furniture Shop, 6 - 80
Van Liew's, 12 - 26
Van Stee Corp., 6 - 80
Vargas Furniture Manufacturing, 6 - 80
Varner Furniture Sales, 6 - 80
Vaughan Furniture Co. Inc., 6 - 80
Vermont Furniture Designs, 6 - 80
Vermont Tubbs, 6 - 80
Victor Stanley, 6 - 80
Victorian Attic, 6 - 80
Victorian Classics Inc., 6 - 81
Victorian Reproduction Enterprises, 11 - 34
Victorian Sampler, 6 - 81
Victorian Showcase, 6 - 81
Village Furniture House, 6 - 81
Village Furniture, 6 - 81
Virginia Craftsmen Inc., 6 - 81
Vitra Seating Inc., 6 - 81
W. G. Undrill Ltd., 6 - 81
Wagner Woodcraft Inc., 6 - 81
Wall/Goldfinger Inc., 6 - 81
Walpole Woodworkers, 6 - 81
Walters Wicker, 6 - 82
Warsaw Furniture Co., 6 - 82
Waterford Furniture Makers, 6 - 82
Waterspring Bed Co. Inc., 6 - 82
Watson Furniture Shop, 6 - 82
Watson Furniture Systems, 6 - 82
Watts & Wright, 10 - 10
Weatherend Estate Furniture, 6 - 82
Wellington's Furniture, 6 - 82
Wendover's Limited, 6 - 82
Weru (UK, etc.) Ltd., 10 - 11
Western Log Furniture, 6 - 82
Wheeler Woodworking, 6 - 83
White Furniture Co., 6 - 83
White of Mebane, 6 - 83

Whitecraft Rattan Inc., 6 - 83
Whitson Furniture, 6 - 83
Whittier Wood Products, 6 - 83
Wicker & Rattan, 6 - 83
Wicker Gallery, 6 - 83
Wicker Warehouse Inc., 6 - 84
Wicker Works, 6 - 84
Wickerworks, 6 - 84
Wild Rose Furniture Mfg. Ltd., 6 - 84
Wildwood Furniture House, 6 - 84
Wilkinsons Furniture Ltd., 6 - 84
William Ball Ltd., 6 - 84
William H. James Co., 6 - 84
William L. Mclean Ltd., 6 - 84
William Lawrence & Co. Ltd., 6 - 84
Williams Furniture Corp., 6 - 84
Willsboro Wood Products, 6 - 85
Windrift Furniture Gallery, 6 - 85
Windsor Chairmakers, 6 - 85
Windspire, 6 - 85
Winfield Manor, 6 - 85
Winterbrook Inc., 6 - 85
Wofab Custom Cabinets Ltd., 6 - 85
Wood Classics, 6 - 85
Wood Goods Inc., 6 - 85
Wood Reproduction Studio, 6 - 85
Woodcraft Design, 6 - 85
Wooden Nickel Architectural Antique, 1 - 38
Woodmasters Furniture Group, Inc., 6 - 85
Woodnorth, 7 - 8
Woodstock Furniture Ltd., 6 - 86
Worcester Chrome Furniture Mfg. , 6 - 86
Workshop Showcase, 6 - 86
Workshops of David T. Smith, 6 - 86
Wren House Furniture, 6 - 86
Wylder Furniture Manufacturing, 6 - 86
Y & J Furniture Co. Inc., 6 - 86
Yale Mfg. Corp., 6 - 86
Yield House, 6 - 86
York Interiors Inc., 6 - 86
Young-Hindle Corp., 6 - 87
Younger Furniture, 6 - 87
Yungbauer Interiors, 6 - 87
Zaldin Sons & Co. Inc., 6 - 87
Zanotta SPA, 6 - 87
Zarbin & Associates, Inc., 6 - 87
Zeichman Mfg. Inc., 6 - 87
Zeno Table Co., 6 - 87
Zest Furniture Industries Ltd., 6 - 87
Zimports Collection, 6 - 87

Garage

Apex Doors Ltd., 4 - 1
Atlas Roll-lite Door Co., 4 - 2
Clopay Corporation, 4 - 4
Combination Door Company, 4 - 4
Doorcraft Mfg. Ltd., 4 - 5
Hazelmere Industries Ltd., 4 - 8
Ideal Door Co., 4 - 9
North Central Door Co., 4 - 12
Omega Garage Door, 4 - 13
Philips Home Products, 4 - 13
Raynor Garage Doors, 4 - 14
Ridge Doors, 4 - 14
Stone Door & Truss, 3 - 83
Wayne-Dalton Corporation, 4 - 18
Windsor Door, 4 - 18

Garden

A. J. Munzinger & Co., 7 - 1
Amish Country Gazebos, 7 - 1

Gate – Glass

Index

BCS America, Inc., 7 - 1
Boswell Roberts Gardens, 7 - 1
BowBends, 7 - 1
Champion Irrigation Products, 3 - 23
City Visions Inc., 7 - 2
Clapper's, 6 - 16
Continental Custom Bridge Co., 7 - 2
Dalton Pavilions Inc., 7 - 2
Dolphin Pet Village, 7 - 2
Farm Wholesale, Inc., 7 - 2
Flanders Industries Inc., 6 - 28
Florentine Craftsmen Inc., 7 - 2
Gardener's Supply, 7 - 3
Gazebo Woodcrafters, 7 - 3
Haddonstone USA Ltd., 7 - 3
Hermitage Garden Pools, 7 - 3
Kester's Wild Game Food Nurseries, 7 - 4
Kloter Farms Inc., 7 - 4
Kramer Brothers, 6 - 43
Lilypons Water Gardens, 7 - 4
Lotus Water Garden Products Ltd., 7 - 4
Maryland Aquatic Nurseries, 7 - 4
May's Architectural Detailing, 7 - 4
Musser Forests, 7 - 4
Paradise Water Gardens, 7 - 5
Prochnow & Prochnow, 7 - 5
Quality Imports, 7 - 5
R.P.B. Manufacturing, 7 - 5
RainDrip Water Systems, 7 - 5
Robinson Iron, 6 - 64
S. Scherer & Sons Water Gardens, 7 - 6
Sarita Furniture, 6 - 66
Slocum Water Gardens, 7 - 6
Staloton - Die keramiker H.H., 3 - 82
Stone Forest, 7 - 6
Stonehaven, 7 - 6
Submatic Irrigation Systems, 7 - 7
Syracuse Pottery, 8 - 65
TerraCast, 7 - 7
Tidewater Workshop, 6 - 78
Twin Oaks Hammocks, 7 - 7
Urdl's Waterfall Creation Inc., 7 - 7
Van Ness Water Gardens, 7 - 8
Victorian Attic, 6 - 80
Walpole Woodworkers, 6 - 81
Washington Pottery Co., 8 - 74
Water Works, 7 - 8
Waterford Gardens, 7 - 8
Westbury Conservatories, 3 - 97
Wicklein's Aquatic Farm & Nursery, 7 - 8
William Tricker, Inc., 7 - 8
Wind & Weather, 7 - 8
Worm's Way, 7 - 8

Gate

Blue Canyon Woodworks, 6 - 10
Stewart Iron Works, 7 - 6
Grand Era Reproductions, 4 - 8

Gazebo

Amish Country Gazebos, 7 - 1
BowBends, 7 - 1
Campbellsville Industries, 3 - 19
City Visions Inc., 7 - 2
Dalton Pavilions Inc., 7 - 2
Gazebo Woodcrafters, 7 - 3
Great Gatsby's Auction Galley, 1 - 18
Jali Ltd., 3 - 50
Kloter Farms Inc., 7 - 4
Vixen Hill Mfg. Co. Inc., 7 - 8

Georgian

(Doors, Furniture, Windows, etc.)

Acorn Antique Doors, 4 - 1
Classic Designs, 12 - 6
Scully & Scully, 6 - 66

German

(Appliances, Bathroom Fixtures, Tile, etc.)

Actiengesellschaft, 3 - 3
Agrob-Wessel-Servais AG, 3 - 4
Baukeramik U., 3 - 12
Bulthaup Inc., 10 - 2
Croonen KG, 3 - 28
Klingenberg Dekoramik GmbH, 3 - 53
Meissen-Keramik GmbH, 3 - 60
Ostara-Fliesen Gmbh & Co. KG, 3 - 67
Peter Josef Korzilius Soehne GmbH, 3 - 69
Spiegelwerk Wilsdruff GmbH, 3 - 81
Villeroy & Boch AG, 2 - 12
Wandplattenfabrik Engers GmbH, 3 - 96
Wilh. Gail'sche Tonwerke KG a.A., 3 - 99

Glass

(Architectural, Block, Beveled, Etched, Stained, etc.)

ABC Glass Block Company, 3 - 2
AFG Industries, Inc., 1 - 2
AMCOA Inc., 6 - 1
ARDCO, Inc., 2 - 1
Acme Brick Co., 3 - 3
Acrymet Industires Inc., 1 - 2
Alpine Windows, 12 - 3
Alside Window Company, 12 - 3
Alter Design Inc., 3 - 5
Aluma-Glass Industries, Inc., 12 - 3
Aluminum Products Company, 12 - 3
Aluminum Specialties Mfg. Co., 12 - 3
Alwindor Manufacturing, Inc., 12 - 3
American Glass & Mirror Corp., 3 - 6
Amerlite Aluminum Co., Inc., 12 - 3
Andreas Lehman Fine Glasswork, 1 - 4
Arcadia Mfg. Inc., 1 - 5
Architectural Artifacts, 1 - 5
Architectural Salvage Company, 1 - 6
Arrow Aluminum Ind., Inc., 12 - 4
Art Marble and Stone, 1 - 7
Artglass By Misci, 3 - 9
Bennett Industries Inc., 4 - 2
Better-Bilt Aluminum Products Co., 12 - 5
Binning's Bldg. Products Inc., 12 - 5
Blenko Glass Company Inc., 3 - 15
Blum Ornamental Glass Co., Inc., 12 - 5
Boulder Art Glass Co., 3 - 16
Boyd Aluminum Mfg. Company, 12 - 5
C & S Distributors, Inc., 12 - 6
C. V. Aluminum, Inc., 12 - 6
CW Design Inc., 3 - 18
Cain Inc., 12 - 6
California Window Corporation, 12 - 6
Care Free Aluminum Prod., Inc., 12 - 6
Catalano & Sons, Inc., 8 - 15
Century Studios, 11 - 6
CertainTeed Corp., 3 - 23
Chamberlain Group, 12 - 6
Cherry Creek Enterprises Inc., 4 - 3
Circle Redmont Inc., 3 - 24
Cline Glass Company, 3 - 25
Columbia Glass & Window Company, 12 - 7
Conner's Architectural Antiques, 1 - 11

Index - 42

The Complete Sourcebook

Index

Granite – Granite

Consolidated American Window Co., 12 - 7
Contois Stained Glass Studio, 11 - 7
Corn Belt Aluminum Inc., 12 - 7
Cox Studios, 12 - 7
Crown Mfg. Corp. of Missouri, 12 - 8
Cummings Stained Glass Studios Inc., 3 - 28
Curran Glass & Mirror Co., 3 - 28
DAB Studio, 12 - 8
Delphi Stained Glass, 3 - 30
Delsan Industries, Inc., 12 - 8
Electric Glass Co., 3 - 33
Empire Pacific Industries, 12 - 8
Energy Saving Products, 12 - 9
Enhanced Glass Corp., 3 - 34
Feather River Wood & Glass Co., 4 - 7
Fiberlux, Inc., 4 - 7
Fleetwood Aluminum Products, Inc., 12 - 9
Floral Glass & Mirror, Inc., 1 - 17
Franklin Art Glass Studios, 3 - 38
Fred Beyer Co., 3 - 38
Fritz V. Sterbak Antiques, 1 - 17
Fuji Hardware Co., Ltd., 2 - 4
G. L. Downs Designs, 12 - 9
General Aluminum Corporation, 12 - 9
Gentron Corp., 3 - 39
Georgia Palm Beach Aluminum Window, 12-9
Gercomi Corp., 3 - 40
Glashaus Inc., 3 - 40
Glass Block Co., 3 - 40
Glass Blocks Unlimited Inc., 1 - 18
Glass Craft Specialties, Inc., 4 - 8
Glostal Systems Ltd., 1 - 18
Golden Age Glassworks, 12 - 10
Great Gatsby's Auction Galley, 1 - 18
Great Paines Glassworks, 4 - 8
H-R Windows, 12 - 10
Hara's Inc., 12 - 10
Harry G. Barr Company, 12 - 10
Hayfield Window & Door Co., 12 - 11
Hess Manufacturing Company, 12 - 11
High Point Glass & Decorative Co., 3 - 45
Howard Industries Inc., 12 - 11
Ideal Glass & Mirror Makers, Ltd., 8 - 35
Insulate Industries, Inc., 12 - 12
International Window Corporation, 12 - 12
Investment Antiques & Collectibles, 1 - 20
Italian Glass Block Designs Ltd., 1 - 20
J. Ring Glass Studio, 12 - 12
Joe-Keith Industries, Inc., 12 - 12
JonCo Manufacturing, Inc., 12 - 13
Jones Paint & Glass, Inc., 12 - 13
Kansas Aluminum, Inc., 12 - 13
Kaylien, 4 - 10
Keller Aluminum Products, 12 - 13
Kinco Corporation, 12 - 13
Kinco, Ltd., 12 - 13
Kinro, Inc., 12 - 14
Lamp Glass, 11 - 19
Lighthouse Stained Glass, 11 - 20
Linford Brothers/Utal Glass Co., 12 - 14
Living Windows Corporation, 12 - 14
MBS Manufacturing West, Inc., 12 - 15
MacDonald Stained Glass, 3 - 56
Manufacturers Glass, 4 - 11
Masterview Window Company, 12 - 15
Materials Unlimited, 1 - 23
Mercer Industries, Inc., 12 - 15
Messer Industries, Inc., 8 - 45
Metal Industries, Inc., 12 - 16
Meyda Stained Glass Studio, 11 - 22
Milgard Manufacturing, Inc., 12 - 16

Miller Industries, Inc., 12 - 16
Mirroline Design Ltd., 6 - 53
Moeller-Reimer Company, 12 - 16
Morgan-Bockius Studios Inc., 4 - 12
Moss Supply Company, Inc., 12 - 16
NT Jenkins Manufacturing Co., 12 - 17
New England Stained Glass Studios, 11 - 23
Norandex, Inc., 12 - 18
Northwest Aluminum Products, 12 - 18
Nouveau Glass Art, 3 - 65
Path Enterprises, Inc., 3 - 68
Paulson's Stained Glass Studio, 12 - 19
Peachtree Doors, Inc., 4 - 13
Perma Window & Door Service, 12 - 19
Philip Goldin Associates, Inc., 11 - 25
Pilkington Glass Ltd., 1 - 27
Pittsburgh Corning, 3 - 70
Queen City Glass Ltd., 8 - 54
Richard Blaschke Cabinet Glass, 3 - 75
S. A. Bendheim Co. Inc., 1 - 30
Shatterproof Glass Corp., 1 - 31
Sholton Assoc., 3 - 79
Skytech Systems, 12 - 23
Southeastern Insulated Glass, 7 - 6
Stained Glass Overlay Inc., 3 - 81
Sunburst Stained Glass Co. Inc., 3 - 84
Sunrise Stained Glass, 3 - 84
Supro Building Products Corp., 3 - 85
Swan Mfg. Co., 2 - 10
Sylvan Brandt Inc., 5 - 9
Taco, 1 - 33
Tafco Corp., 3 - 86
Technical Glass Products, 3 - 86
The Brass Collection, 6 - 75
Thermal Profiles, Inc., 4 - 17
U.S. Precision Glass, 8 - 70
Unique Art Glass Co., 12 - 26
Urban Glassworks, 3 - 94
Uroboros Glass Studios Inc., 1 - 36
Victorian Stained Glass Illusions, 12 - 27
Virginia Mirror Co. Inc., 8 - 72
Visador Co., 1 - 36
Wallace-Crossly Corp., 4 - 17
Westlake Architectural Antiques, 1 - 37
Willet Stained Glass Studios, 3 - 99
Williams Art Glass Studios, 12 - 28
Window Creations, 11 - 35
Wizard Windows, 12 - 28
Wooden Nickel Architectural Antique, 1 - 38
Wright's Stained Glass, 1 - 38

Granite

ADI Corporation, 1 - 1
Accents In Stone, 3 - 3
Andrews & Sons (Marbles & Tiles), 3 - 7
Bergen Bluestone Co. Inc., 3 - 14
Cangelosi Marble & Granite, 3 - 20
Carron Phoenix Ltd., 10 - 3
Chester Granite Co., 3 - 24
Cold Spring Granite Co., 3 - 25
Colonial Marble Products Ltd., 3 - 25
D & D Natural Stone and Marble, 3 - 29
Dal-Tile, 3 - 29
Delaware Quarries, Inc., 3 - 30
Fired Earth Tiles PLC, 5 - 4
Gawet Marble & Granite Inc., 3 - 39
Globe Marble & Tile, 3 - 41
Granite Creations Inc., 3 - 41
Granite Design, 3 - 41
Granitech Corp., 3 - 41
International Granite & Marble, 3 - 49

The Complete Sourcebook

Index - 43

Grasscloth – Hardware

Marble Institute of America, 3 - 57
Marble Modes Inc., 3 - 57
Mojave Granite Co., 3 - 61
Nicola Ceramics & Marble, 3 - 64
Quality Marble Ltd., 3 - 72
Stenindustriens Landssammenslutning,3 - 82
Stone Products Corporation, 3 - 83
Sveriges Stenindustriforbund, 3 - 85
The Decorative Center of Houston, 8 - 66
Walker & Zanger, 3 - 95

Grasscloth

Alexander Wallpaper, 8 - 3

Greenhouse

Amdega Ltd., 3 - 6
Burnham Corp., 3 - 18
Collier Warehouse Inc., 7 - 2
Farm Wholesale, Inc., 7 - 2
Glass Houses, 3 - 40
Janco Greenhouses, 7 - 3
Machin Conservatories, 7 - 4
Progressive Building Products, 3 - 72
Santa Barbara Greenhouse, 7 - 6
Solite Solar Greenhouses, 7 - 6
Southeastern Insulated Glass, 7 - 6
Sun Room Company, 7 - 7
Sunglo Solar Greenhouses, 7 - 7
Troy-Bilt Mfg. Co., 7 - 7
Turner Greenhouses, 7 - 7
Westbury Conservatories, 3 - 97

Grille

Architectural Grille, 1 - 5
Barker Metalcraft, 3 - 12
Brass Tacks Hardware Ltd., 3 - 16
Customwood Mfg. Co., 1 - 13
Deco-Trol, 3 - 30
Federal Millwork Corp., 1 - 16
Fischer & Jirouch Company, 1 - 16
Holden Register, Inc., 3 - 47
Rasmussen Millwork Inc., 12 - 21
Register & Grille Manufacturing Co., 1 - 29
The Reggio Register Co. Inc., 3 - 89
Window Grille Specialists, 12 - 28

Guard

(Gutter, Window, etc.)
Beldes, Inc., 3 - 13
Leslie-Locke Inc., 3 - 55

Gutter

Accurate Aluminum Products, Inc., 3 - 3
Alumax Aluminum Corp., 3 - 6
Apex Gutter Systems Ltd., 3 - 8
Bay Cities Metal Products, 3 - 12
Berger Building Products Corp., 3 - 14
Cannon Rainwater Systems Ltd., 3 - 20
Coast Trim Company, 3 - 25
Genova Products, 3 - 39
GutterCrest Ltd., 3 - 42
Gutterfast Ltd., 3 - 42
Kinsman Company, 3 - 52
Rainhandler, 3 - 73
Royal-Apex Mfg. Co. Inc., 3 - 76
Southern Maryland Aluminum Prod., 3 - 81
Yost Mfg. & Supply Inc., 3 - 101

Halogen

Artemide, 11 - 3
CSL Lighting Mfg., 11 - 6

Cardinal Products Inc., 11 - 6
Dynasty Classics Corp., 11 - 9
Forluce, 11 - 12
Halogen Lighting Systems, 11 - 14
Harris Lamps, 11 - 14
Holtkotter International, Inc., 11 - 15
National Industries, 11 - 23

Hammock

Twin Oaks Hammocks, 7 - 7
Quality Imports, 7 - 5

Handwoven

Lamont Ltd., 2 - 6
Heritage Rugs, 8 - 33

Hanging

Hines of Oxford, 3 - 46
Payne's Ristras De Santa Fe, 8 - 52

Hardboard

Aetna Plywood, Inc., 3 - 4
Bill Koehler Co., 3 - 15
Champion International Corp., 3 - 23
Ply-Gem Mfg., 3 - 70

Hardware

*(Antique, Reproduction, Brass, Cabinet,
Decorative, Door, Furniture, Window, etc.)*
18th Century Hardware Co. Inc., 3 - 1
A & B Industries Inc., 3 - 1
A Touch of Brass, 3 - 1
A.J.P. Weslock Industries Co., 3 - 2
ARMAC Brassfounders Group Ltd., 3 - 2
Accurate Lock & Hardware Co., 1 - 2
Acorn Manufacturing Co. Inc., 3 - 3
Adams Rite (Europe, etc.) Ltd., 12 - 2
Addkison Hardware Co. Inc., 3 - 4
Albany Hardware Specialty Mfg. Co., 3 - 4
Albert Marston & Co. Ltd., 4 - 1
Almet Hardware Ltd., 9 - 1
Alpine Engineer Products Inc., 3 - 5
American Home Supply, 3 - 6
American Tack & Decorative Hardware, 3 - 7
Amerock Corporation, 3 - 7
Androck Hardware Corp., 3 - 7
Anglo-American Brass Co., 3 - 8
Antique Builders Hardware, 3 - 8
Antique Hardware Store, 3 - 8
Architectural Antiquities, 1 - 5
Architectural Elements, 1 - 5
Architectural Salvage Company, 1 - 6
Arden Forge, 3 - 9
Aristokraft, 10 - 1
Art-Line Design, 3 - 9
Artefact-Architectural Antiques, 1 - 7
Artefacts Architectural Antiques, 1 - 7
Artistic Brass, 3 - 9
Austin Hardware West, 3 - 10
B & B Products, 1 - 7
B. F. Gilmour Co., 3 - 11
B. Lilly & Sons Ltd., 3 - 11
Baldwin Hardware Corp., 3 - 12
Baldwin Hardware, 3 - 12
Barrett Hardware Co., 3 - 12
Belwith International, 3 - 14
Berke Door & Hardware, Inc., 3 - 14
Blaine Window Hardware, 12 - 5
Bona Decorative Hardware, 3 - 16
Brass Accents, 3 - 16
Brass Tacks Hardware Ltd., 3 - 16

Index - 44

The Complete Sourcebook

Index

Hardware – Hardware

Broadway Industries, 2 - 3
Buesche Inc., 3 - 17
Buffalo Studios, 11 - 5
Builders Brass Works Corp., 3 - 17
Bulldog Home Hardware, 3 - 17
By-Gone Days Antiques Inc., 1 - 9
California Builders Hardware, 3 - 19
Cambridge Smithy, 3 - 19
Casella Lighting, 11 - 6
Castle Wholesalers Inc., 3 - 20
Cego Limited, 12 - 6
Chubb Lock Company, 9 - 2
Cirecast, 3 - 24
Connecticut Curtain Company, 8 - 18
Conner's Architectural Antiques, 1 - 11
Constantine's, 1 - 12
Contemporary Interiors, Inc., 8 - 18
Cotswold Architectural Products Ltd., 1 - 12
Country Cupolas, 1 - 12
Crawford's Old House Store, 3 - 27
Crompton Ltd., 12 - 7
Crown City Hardware, 3 - 28
Custom Hardware Mfg., Inc., 3 - 29
D.C. Mitchell Reproductions, 3 - 29
DS Locksmithing Company, 3 - 29
Decorative Hardware Studio, 3 - 30
Decorum Inc., 1 - 14
Delmar Hardware Mfg. Ltd., 4 - 5
Deutscher & Sons, Inc., 3 - 31
Dexter Lock, 4 - 5
Distepro USA Inc., 3 - 31
Doorman Hardware, 4 - 5
Dryad Simplan Limited, 12 - 8
E B Bradley Co., 3 - 32
EK Hardware Co., Inc., 3 - 33
Erebus Limited, 4 - 6
Eugenia's Place, 4 - 6
Faneuil Furniture Hardware Co. Inc., 6 - 28
Fayston Iron & Steel Works, 3 - 35
Fellenz Antiques, 3 - 35
Flora & Fauna, 3 - 37
Foothill Hardware & Lumber, 3 - 37
Frank Allart & Co., Ltd., 4 - 7
Frazier Park Lumber & Hardware, 3 - 38
Freundlich Supply Co., 3 - 38
G-U Hardware Inc., 12 - 9
Garbe Industries Inc., 3 - 39
Gaston's Wood Finishes & Antiques, 3 - 39
Grandpa Snazzy's Hardware, 3 - 41
Hager Hinge Co., 3 - 43
Hall Hardware Co., 3 - 43
Hardware + Plus Inc., 3 - 44
Hearthstone Hardware Co., 3 - 44
Henssgen Hardware Corp., 3 - 45
Hewi, Inc., 3 - 45
Hiawatha, Inc., 2 - 5
Hipkiss & Co. Ltd., 3 - 46
Hippo Hardware & Trading Co., 3 - 46
Historic Housefitters, 3 - 46
Hope Works Ltd., 12 - 11
Horton Brasses, 3 - 47
Hy-Ko Products Co., 3 - 48
Imported European Hardware, 3 - 49
Iron Intentions Forge, 3 - 49
J. Legge & Co. Ltd., 4 - 9
James Gibbons Format Ltd., 12 - 12
Jones & Barclay Ltd., 3 - 51
Josiah Parkes and Sons Ltd., 4 - 10
Kanebridge Corp., 3 - 51
Kayne& Son Custom Forged Hardware, 3-51
Kebring Hardware, 3 - 52

Kemp & George, 3 - 52
Kenney Mfg. Co., 8 - 40
King Brothers Woodworking Inc., 6 - 42
Kirsch Drapery Hardware, 8 - 40
Kolson, 1 - 21
Konceptual Design, 1 - 21
Kraft, 2 - 6
Kwikset Corp., 4 - 11
Leicester Joinery Co., 4 - 11
Liz's Antique Hardware, 3 - 55
M. Wolchonok & Son Inc., 3 - 56
Magnet Trade, 4 - 11
Magnokrom Inc., 6 - 47
Marsak Cohen, Cohen Corp., 3 - 58
Merit Metal Products Corp., 3 - 60
Miracle Method Bathroom Restoration, 2 - 7
Monroe Coldren & Sons, 3 - 62
Mutual Screw & Supply, 3 - 62
Mystica & Company Inc., 3 - 62
New England Brassworks, 3 - 64
New England Lock & Hardware, 9 - 3
Nexton Industries Inc., 3 - 64
Northwest Builders Hardware, 3 - 65
Old & Elegant Distributing, 2 - 8
Old World Hardware Co., 3 - 66
Ole Fashion Things, 2 - 8
Omnia Industries, 3 - 67
Oregon Wooden Screen Door Co., 4 - 13
P. C. Henderson Ltd., 12 - 18
P. E. Guerin Inc., 3 - 67
Parker Window Covering, 8 - 51
Paxton Hardware Ltd., 3 - 68
Perkins & Powell, 2 - 8
Peter Goldberger, 2 - 8
Pfanstiel Hardware Co., 3 - 69
Phoenix Lock Co.Inc., 10 - 8
Phyllis Kennedy Restoration Hardware, 3-70
Precision Hardware Inc., 3 - 71
Queen City Architectural Salvage, 1 - 28
R. Cartwright & Co., Ltd., 12 - 21
R. Lang Co., 12 - 21
Rare Wood, 4 - 14
Remodeler's Supply Co., 3 - 74
Renaissance Decorative Hardware, 3 - 74
Restoration Hardware, 3 - 74
Restoration Works, 3 - 74
Ritter & Son Hardware, 3 - 76
Rue De France Inc., 8 - 57
Rufkahr's, 3 - 77
Rustic Home Hardware, 3 - 77
Samuel B. Sadtler & Co., 1 - 30
Sayville Plumbing Go., 3 - 77
Scott's Hardware Inc., 6 - 66
Securi Style Ltd., 11 - 28
Sequence USA Co. Ltd., 3 - 78
Solartechnic 2000 Ltd., 8 - 61
Southeast Hardware Mfg. Co., 3 - 81
Sylvan Brandt Inc., 5 - 9
T. Saveker Ltd., 11 - 30
Teskey Enterprises Inc., 12 - 24
The 18th Century Company, 3 - 87
The Antique Hardware Store, 3 - 87
The Antique Plumber, 3 - 87
The Brass Finial, 11 - 31
The Broadway Collection, 2 - 11
The Coldren Company, 3 - 88
The Dize Co., 3 - 88
The Fixture Exchange, 2 - 11
The Wise Company, 3 - 90
The Woodbury Blacksmith & Forge, 3 - 90
The Woodworkers Store, 11 - 32

The Complete Sourcebook

Index - 45

Hardwood – Heater

Triangle Brass Mfg. Co. Inc., 3 - 92
Triton PLC, 2 - 12
Van Dyke's Restorers, 3 - 94
W & F Mfg. Inc., 12 - 27
W. T. Weaver & Sons, 2 - 12
WSI Distributors, 3 - 95
Wartian Lock Co., 9 - 3
Weiser Lock, 9 - 3
Weslock National, 4 - 18
Whitechapel Ltd., 3 - 98
Wiggins & Son Inc., 3 - 98
Williams Lumber & Hardware, 3 - 99
Williamsburg Blacksmiths Inc., 3 - 99
Worcester Parsons/Brass Art, 6 - 86
World Innovations Ltd., 3 - 101
Worthy Works Inc., 3 - 101
Yale Security Products Ltd., 9 - 4

Hardwood

(Flooring, Furniture, Moulding, Paneling, etc.)

A & M Wood Specialty Inc., 3 - 1
Abitibi-Price, 1 - 2
Adelmann & Clark Inc., 3 - 4
Adonis Forest Products, Inc., 3 - 4
Anderson Hardwood Flooring, 5 - 1
Bangkok International, 5 - 2
Biwood Flooring, 5 - 2
Boen Hardwood Flooring, 5 - 2
Bruce Hardwood Floors, 5 - 2
Country Workshop, 6 - 19
Croy-Marietta Hardwoods Inc., 3 - 28
Diamond Wood Products, Inc., 3 - 31
Dimension Lumber & Milling, 1 - 14
EDLCO, 3 - 33
Erie Flooring & Wood Products, 5 - 4
Fineman Doors Inc., 4 - 7
Fraser Woods Inc., 4 - 7
Furniture That Exceeds Your
Expectation, 6-30
Galleher Hardwood Co., 5 - 4
Hardwood Flooring & Paneling Inc., 5 - 4
Harris-Tarkett, Inc., 5 - 5
Harrison Hardwood Mfg. Inc., 3 - 44
Hayes Forest Products, Inc., 5 - 5
Henegan's Wood Shed, 3 - 45
House of Fara Inc., 3 - 47
House of Moulding, 1 - 20
Hunt County Hardwoods, Inc., 5 - 5
Hyde Park Raised Panel, 1 - 20
International Wood Products, 4 - 9
Jasper Wood Products Co., Inc., 3 - 50
Kawartha Wood Products Ltd., 3 - 51
Kountry Kraft Hardwoods, 3 - 53
Larkspur Furniture Co., 6 - 44
Launstein Hardwood, 5 - 6
Lemire Lumber Co. Inc., 3 - 54
Leslie Brothers Lumber Company, 5 - 6
Lewis Brothers Lumber Co. Inc., 1 - 22
Melbourne Hall Workshop, 10 - 7
Memphis Hardwood Flooring Co., 5 - 7
Midwestern Wood Products, 1 - 24
Monadnock Forest Products, Inc., 3 - 61
National Forest Products, Inc., 1 - 25
National Hardwood Floors, 5 - 7
New England Hardwood Supply Co., 5 - 7
Northland Hardwood Lumber Co., 3 - 65
Northwest Hardwoods Inc., 3 - 65
Ohio Hardwood Lumber Co., 3 - 66
Old Kentucky Wood Products, 1 - 26

Old World Moulding & Finishing Co., 1 - 26
Ontario Hardwood Products Ltd., 3 - 67
Ornamental Mouldings, 1 - 26
Overseas Hardwoods Co. Inc., 5 - 7
Peace Flooring Co. Inc., 5 - 8
Perkins Architectural Millwork, 1 - 27
Pickens Hardwoods, 3 - 70
Plancher Beauceville Inc., 5 - 8
Plaza Hardwood Inc., 5 - 8
Port-O-Lite Corporation, 1 - 28
Pukall Lumber Co., 3 - 72
Robbins Hardwood Flooring, 5 - 8
Rustic Furnishings, 6 - 65
Stanley Knight, 5 - 9
States Industries Inc., 1 - 32
Sykes Flooring Products, 5 - 9
Taylor Woodcraft Inc., 6 - 73
The Floor Shop, 5 - 10
Tools of the Trade Inc., 6 - 78
Treework Services Ltd., 5 - 10
United States Mahogany Corp., 3 - 94
Vermont Tubbs, 6 - 80
White River, 5 - 11
Woodworkers, 3 - 100
Yawkey-Bissell Hardwood Flooring, 5 - 11
Zickgraf Hardwood Company, 5 - 11

Heater

Alpine Engineer Products Inc., 3 - 5
American Energy Technologies Inc., 3 - 6
American Solar Network, 3 - 7
Axeman-Anderson Co., 3 - 11
Cadet Mfg. Co., 3 - 19
Carrier Corp., 3 - 20
Charmaster, 6 - 16
Crown Boiler, 3 - 28
Edwards Engineering, 3 - 33
G S Energy Industries Inc., 3 - 38
Gas Appliance Manufacturers, 3 - 39
Heatway, 3 - 45
Hydrotherm Inc., 3 - 48
Jameson Home Products, 3 - 50
Lennox International Inc., 3 - 54
Lochinvar Water Heater Corp., 3 - 55
Martin Industries Inc., 3 - 58
Monitor products, 3 - 62 , 3 - 65
Nepco, Inc., 3 - 63
Nutone, 3 - 65
Orbit Mfg. Co., 3 - 67
Radco Products Inc., 3 - 73
Radiant Technology, 3 - 73
Rheem Mfg Co., 3 - 75
Rho Sigma Inc., 3 - 75
Rinnai America Corp., 3 - 75
Riteway Mfg. Co. Inc., 3 - 75
Snyder General Corp., 3 - 79
Solar Depot, 3 - 80
Solar Development Inc., 3 - 80
Solar Oriented Environmental Systems,3 - 80
Solar Water Heater, 3 - 80
State Industries Inc., 3 - 82
Sun Ray Solar Heaters, 3 - 84
SunEarth Inc., 3 - 84
Sunheating Mfg. Co., 3 - 84
TARM USA, Inc., 3 - 86
Taylor Manufacturing, Inc., 3 - 86
Tetco, 3 - 87
The Homestead, 10 - 10
Thermal Energy Systems Inc., 3 - 90
Thermomax USA Ltd., 3 - 90
Vaughn Mfg. Corp., 3 - 94

Index

Heating — Indoor

Vermont Castings, 3 - 95
Weil-McLain, 3 - 97

Heating
Andrews Distributing Co., 3 - 7
Aquatek Systems, Inc., 3 - 9
Axeman-Anderson Co., 3 - 11
B. F. Gilmour Co., 3 - 11
Backwoods Solar Electric Systems, 3 - 11
Bard Manufacturing Company, 3 - 12
Beckett, R.W. Corp., 3 - 13
Bohemia Plumbing Supply Co. Inc., 3 - 15
Burnham, 3 - 18
Cadet Mfg. Co., 3 - 19
Carrier Corp., 3 - 20
Celsisus Energy Company, 3 - 21
Charmaster, 6 - 16
Climate Master Inc., 3 - 25
Command-Aire Corporation, 3 - 26
Crispaire, 3 - 28
Crown Boiler, 3 - 28
Daniels Co., Inc., 3 - 29
Deutscher & Sons, Inc., 3 - 31
Eagle, 3 - 33
Energy Pioneers, 3 - 34
Enerjee International, 2 - 4
FHP Manufacturing, 3 - 35
Fahrenheat Heating Products, 3 - 35
Freundlich Supply Co., 3 - 38
Gas Appliance Manufacturers, 3 - 39
Gyp-Crete Corporation, 3 - 42
HCP Solar Div., 3 - 43
Heat Controller, Inc., 3 - 44
Heckler Brothers, 3 - 45
Holden Register, Inc., 3 - 47
Hudevad Britain, 3 - 47
Hydrotherm Inc., 3 - 48
Jacobsen Energy Industries, Inc., 3 - 50
Jameson Home Products, 3 - 50
Kallwall's Solar Components Center, 3 - 51
Kanebridge Corp., 3 - 51
Lennox International Inc., 3 - 54
Livingston Systems Inc., 3 - 55
Mammoth, 3 - 57
Marsak Cohen, Cohen Corp., 3 - 58
Meeco Mfg. Co., 3 - 59
Meyer Furnace Co., 3 - 60
Mutual Screw & Supply, 3 - 62
Nepco, Inc., 3 - 63
Radiant Technology, 3 - 73
Sayville Plumbing Go., 3 - 77
Snyder General Corp., 3 - 79
Suburban Manufacturing Company, 3 - 84
Tetco, 3 - 87
Thermal Energy Systems Inc., 3 - 90
Weil-McLain, 3 - 97
York International Corp., 3 - 101

Hemlock
(Staircases, etc.)
Cascade Wood Products Inc., 1 - 10

Home
(Furnishings, etc.)
American Treasury Catalog, 8 - 4
Armstrong-Decorative Accessories, 8 - 5
Jackelope Furniture, 6 - 39
Stanley Door Systems, 4 - 16
Steven Linen Associates Inc., 8 - 63
The Country House, 8 - 66

The Hurshtowne Collection, 8 - 67
White Shield of Carolina Inc., 8 - 76
Wild Wings, 8 - 76
Wild Wood Gallery, 8 - 76

Hot Tub
Almost Heaven Hot Tubs, 2 - 1
Barrel Builders, 3 - 12
Contemporary Copper, 10 - 3
Sequoia Industries Inc., 3 - 78
W. C. Wood Co. Ltd., 10 - 10

Imported
(Furniture, Lighting, Tile, etc.)
ACIF Ceramiche S.R.L., 3 - 2
Alfa Ceramiche, 3 - 5
Century Floors Inc., 5 - 3
Charleston Linens, 8 - 16
Country Floors, 5 - 3
Crest Distributors, 3 - 28
Elon Inc., 3 - 33
Forluce, 11 - 12
Furniture Design Imports, 6 - 30
Graham's Lighting Fixtures Inc., 11 - 13
Hamilton Adams Imports Ltd., 8 - 32
Helen Williams - Delft Tiles, 3 - 45
Hines of Oxford, 3 - 46
Import Specialists, 8 - 35
Imported European Hardware, 3 - 49
Impronta S.P.A., 3 - 49
Jotul USA, 10 - 6
Mosaic Supplies Inc., 3 - 62
Northern California Imports, 8 - 49
Palazzetti Inc., 6 - 58
Pickens Hardwoods, 3 - 70
Snaidero, 10 - 9
Tarkett Ceramic Inc., 3 - 86
The Linen Gallery, 8 - 67
Wicker Warehouse Inc., 6 - 84

Indian
(Crafts, Pottery, etc.)
House of Clay, 8 - 34
Prairie Edge, 8 - 54

Indoor
(Furniture, Lighting, etc.)
All-Lighting, 11 - 2
Blake Industries, 6 - 10
Catherine Ann Furnishings, 6 - 15
Corsican, 6 - 19
Halo Lighting Products/Cooper Ind., 11 - 14
Hedstrom Corp., 6 - 34
Hinkley Lighting, 11 - 15
Home Decorators Collection, 11 - 15
Horchow Home Collection, 6 - 36
Hubbell Lighting Inc., 11 - 16
Juno Lighting, Inc., 11 - 18
Leviton Manufacturing Company, 11 - 20
Lloyd/Flanders, 6 - 47
Luma Lighting Industries, Inc., 11 - 20
Metropolitan Ceramics, 8 - 46
Pompeii, 6 - 60
Reed Bros., 3 - 74
Santa Fe Lights, 11 - 28
Sternberg Lanterns Inc., 11 - 30
Stuckey Brothers Furniture Co., Inc., 6 - 72
Summit Furniture, 6 - 73
Task Lighting Corporation, 11 - 31
TerraCast, 7 - 7

The Complete Sourcebook

Insert – Iron

Index

The Furniture Patch, 6 - 75
The Heveningham Collection, 6 - 75
The Marle Company, 11 - 32
Victor Stanley, 6 - 80
Weatherend Estate Furniture, 6 - 82

Insert

(Fireplace, etc.)

New-Aire Mfg. Co., Inc., 3 - 64

Insulated

(Siding, Windows, etc.)

Mastic Corp., 3 - 59
Skytech Systems, 12 - 23

Insulation

AMOCO Foam Products Co., 3 - 2
American Thermal Products Inc., 3 - 7
Apache Products Company, 3 - 8
Appropriate Technology, Corp., 12 - 4
Associated Foam Manufacturers, 3 - 10
Atlas Roofing Corporation, 3 - 10
Celotex Corp., 3 - 21
Century Insulation Mfg., 3 - 22
CertainTeed Corp., 3 - 23
Dorning Roofing & Insulation Co., 3 - 32
Dow Chemical USA, 3 - 32
Energy Arsenal, 12 - 9
Fiberfine of Memphis Inc., 3 - 36
Firestone Building Products Co., 3 - 36
Foil-Sulate Div., 3 - 37
Georgia Pacific Corp., 3 - 40
H. B. Fuller Co./TEC Incorporated, 3 - 43
Homasote Company, 3 - 47
Louisiana-Pacific Corporation, 3 - 56
NRG Barriers, Inc., 3 - 63
Pilkington Glass Ltd., 1 - 27
Raven Industries Inc., 3 - 73
Romet Inc., 3 - 76
Simplex Products Division, 3 - 79
South & Sons Panels Inc., 3 - 80
U.S. Fiber Corp., 3 - 93

Interior

(Doors, Lighting, Paint, Shutters, Tile, Windows, etc.)

Advantage Window Systems Inc., 12 - 2
American Heritage Shutters Inc., 12 - 3
Architectural Detail In Wood, 12 - 4
Beech River Mill Company, 3 - 13
Bennett Industries Inc., 4 - 2
Berea Prehung Door, Inc., 4 - 2
Champion International Corp., 3 - 23
Crescent Lighting Ltd., 11 - 8
Elegant Entries, 4 - 6
Elite Interior Doors, 4 - 6
Fine Paints of Europe, 3 - 36
Fineman Doors Inc., 4 - 7
Flex Trim, 12 - 9
Fuller O'Brien Paints, 3 - 38
Heirwood Shutters, 12 - 11
Heritage Lanterns, 11 - 14
Iberia Millwork, 4 - 9
Illahe Tileworks, 3 - 49
Jeld-Wen, 4 - 10
Jessup Door Company, 4 - 10
Korona, 4 - 10
Mar-Flo, Inc., 4 - 12
McDan Woodworking, 1 - 23
Miya Shoji & Interiors Inc., 8 - 47

Morgan Manufacturing, 4 - 12
Nord Company, 4 - 12
Ole Country Barn, 3 - 66
Perkins Architectural Millwork, 1 - 27
Petit Industries Inc., 12 - 19
Pixley Lumber Co., 4 - 13
Premdor Inc., 4 - 14
Primrose Distributing, 3 - 71
REM Industries, 12 - 21
Rem Industries, 12 - 21
Shutter Shop, 3 - 79
Stulb's Old Village Paints, 3 - 83
The Alternative Window Co., 12 - 24
The Copper House, 11 - 32
The Muralo Company Inc., 3 - 88
The Natural Choice Catalog, 3 - 88
The Porch Factory, 1 - 34
The Shutter Depot, 12 - 25
The Stulb Company, 3 - 89
The Tin Bin, 11 - 32
The Woodworkers Store, 11 - 32
Thermo-Press Corp., 12 - 25
Trimall Interior Products Inc., 3 - 92
Vermont Marble Co., 3 - 95
Vetter Stone Co., 1 - 36
Wing Industries Inc., 4 - 18

Iron

(Fencing, Furniture, Stairs, Stoves, etc.)

A.A. Used Boiler Supply Co., 3 - 1
AGA Cookers, 10 - 1
Allen Iron Works & Supply, 1 - 3
Architectural Iron Company, 1 - 6
Art In Iron, 6 - 5
Arte de Mexico, 6 - 6
Brass Bed Shoppe, 6 - 11
Cambridge Smithy, 3 - 19
Charleston Iron Works, 6 - 16
Cirecast, 3 - 24
Conner's Architectural Antiques, 1 - 11
Designer Repros, 6 - 23
Dovre, 3 - 32
Gaby's Shoppe, 6 - 31
Goddard Manufacturing, 1 - 18
Good Time Stove Co., 3 - 41
Hearthstone Hardware Co., 3 - 44
Heating Research Co., 3 - 45
Kenneth D. Lynch & Sons, Inc., 6 - 41
Kramer Brothers, 6 - 43
Lee L. Woodard Sons Inc., 6 - 45
Leslie-Locke Inc., 3 - 55
Lyon-Shaw, 6 - 47
Mallin Co., 6 - 48
Mexico House, 11 - 22
O.W. Lee Co., Inc., 6 - 56
Plantation Patterns Inc., 6 - 60
Precision Furniture Corp., 6 - 60
Robinson Iron, 6 - 64
Sak Industries Inc., 6 - 65
Schoenherr Iron Work, 1 - 30
Spiral Stairs of America, 1 - 32
Steel Gallery, 6 - 71
Stewart Iron Works, 7 - 6
The Bed Factory, 6 - 74
The Heveningham Collection, 6 - 75
The House of Webster, 10 - 10
The Iron Shop, 1 - 34
Thermal Control Co., 3 - 90
Williamsburg Blacksmiths Inc., 3 - 99
Zimports Collection, 6 - 87

Index - 48

The Complete Sourcebook

Index

Irrigation — Jamb

Irrigation
RainDrip Water Systems, 7 - 5
Submatic Irrigation Systems, 7 - 7

Italian
(Furniture, Lighting, Tile, etc.)
A.L.F. Uno Spa, 6 - 1
Abe SRL, 11 - 1
Accademia, 6 - 2
Acerbis International Spa, 6 - 2
Airon SRL, 6 - 3
Alivar SRL, 6 - 3
Alva Line SRL, 11 - 2
Amaru Tile, 3 - 6
American International, 3 - 6
Arc Linea Arredamenti SPA, 6 - 5
Arflex, 6 - 5
Arlati SRL, 11 - 3
Arrben Di O. Benvenuto, 6 - 5
Artistiche Ceramiche Fiorentine, 11 - 3
Atelier SRL, 6 - 6
B & B Italia Spa, 6 - 7
Baleri Italia, 6 - 7
Barbini Alfredo SRL, 11 - 4
Bazzani Alberto di F. Bazzani & C. SAS, 6 - 8
Bonaldo SPA, 6 - 10
Boswell Roberts Gardens, 7 - 1
Bros's SRL, 6 - 12
Brunati SRL, 6 - 12
CM Comini Modonutti SRL, 6 - 13
Calligaris SPA, 6 - 13
Camel International SRL, 6 - 13
Cancos Tile Corporation, 3 - 19
Cappellini International Interiors SPA, 6 - 14
Cassina SPA, 6 - 15
Cassina USA Inc., 6 - 15
Cattelan Italia SPA, 6 - 15
Ceramica Candia S.P.A., 3 - 22
Cidue, 6 - 16
Colombo Mobili SNC, 6 - 18
Comoexport-Divisione Di Cantu, 6 - 18
Conexport, 6 - 18
Continental Ceramic Tile, 3 - 27
D & B Tile Distributors, 3 - 29
Design Gallery Milano, 6 - 23
Driade SPA, 6 - 24
Edra SPA, 6 - 25
Esse SRL, 6 - 26
Fama SPA, 6 - 27
Felice rossi SRL, 6 - 28
Ferretti F.LLi Di Ferretto SPA, 6 - 28
Ferretti Ltd., 10 - 4
Flexform, 6 - 28
Florano Ceramic Tile Design Center, 3 - 37
Fly Line, 6 - 29
Fontana Arte SPA, 6 - 29
Foscarini Murano SPA, 11 - 12
Fulgini Orilio & F.LLI SPA, 6 - 30
G. P. B. Beghelli, 11 - 12
Giovanni Erba & C. SNC, 6 - 32
Hastings Tile & Il Bagno Collection, 3 - 44
Heron-Parigi, 6 - 35
Horm SRL, 6 - 36
Hutcherson Tile, 3 - 48
I. P. E. SPA, 6 - 38
Ideal tile of Manhatttan Inc., 3 - 49
Italian Tile Center, 3 - 50
Kartell SPA, 6 - 41
Kris Elosvolo, 3 - 53
LaFaenza America Inc., 3 - 53
Ladue Illuminazione, 11 - 18
Leonardo 1502 Ceramica S.p. A., 3 - 54
Lineas Sas Di Asgnaghi Giannarturo, 6 - 46
Lumina Italia SRL, 11 - 21
Marelli International SRL, 6 - 49
Mark Sales Co. Inc., 6 - 50
Matteograssi SPA, 6 - 51
Maxalto SPA, 6 - 51
Molteni & C. SPA, 6 - 53
Mondo, 6 - 53
Mosaic Supplies Inc., 3 - 62
National Ceramics of Florida, 3 - 63
Natuzzi Americas Inc., 6 - 54
Nemo Tile Company, Inc., 3 - 63
Nuove Ceramiche Ricchetti, S.r.l., 3 - 65
Old Country Ceramic Tile, 3 - 66
Pallavisini Sedersi, 6 - 58
Parisotto, 8 - 51
Poltronova Design SRL, 6 - 60
Praire Marketing, 3 - 71
Richmond Ceramic Tile Distributors, 3 - 75
Saporiti Italia SPA, 6 - 65
Scappini Giovanni & C. SAS, 6 - 66
Selva SPA, 6 - 67
Silik SPA, 6 - 68
Skipper SPA, 11 - 29
Snaidero, 10 - 9
Southampton Brick & Tile Co., 3 - 81
Standard Tile Distributors Inc., 3 - 82
Stefanelli, 6 - 71
Tarkett Ceramic Inc., 3 - 86
The Tile Collection, 3 - 89
Tile West Distributors, 3 - 91
Tile and Designs Inc., 3 - 91
Zanotta SPA, 6 - 87

Jabot
Dana's Curtains & Draperies, 8 - 21

Jamb
American Millwork Inc., 1 - 3
Corning Moulding Corporation, 1 - 12
Defiance Forest Products, 4 - 4
Diversified Millwork, 1 - 14
Double D Mouldings Inc., 1 - 15
Foreign & Domestic Woods, Inc., 1 - 17
Heritage Hardwoods, 1 - 19
Hoff Forest Products, Inc., 3 - 46
IJ Mfg. Ltd., 12 - 12
Lianga Pacific, Inc., 1 - 22
Medallion Millwork, Inc., 1 - 23
Medford Moulding Company, 1 - 23
Mt. Taylor Millwork, Inc., 1 - 24
National Forest Products, Inc., 1 - 25
Navajo Forest Products Ind., 1 - 25
Oregon Fir Millwork, Inc., 1 - 26
Ostermann & Scheiwe, USA, Inc., 1 - 26
Ponderosa Mouldings, 1 - 27
Rogue River Millwork, 1 - 30
Sacramento Valley Moulding Co., 1 - 30
Schlesser Co., Inc., 1 - 30
Sierra Pacific Industries Millwork Div., 1 - 31
Trimcraft Inc., 1 - 35
Walter H. Weaber Sons, Inc., 1 - 36
Western Moulding Company, Inc., 1 - 37
Windsor Mill, Inc., 1 - 37
Yakima Manufacturing Co., 1 - 38
Yellowstone Woodworks, 1 - 38
Yuba River Moulding & Millwork, Inc., 1 - 38

The Complete Sourcebook

Juvenile — Kitchen

Juvenile

Boston & Winthrop,   6 - 10
H.U.D.D.L.E.,   6 - 33
Little Colorado Inc.,   6 - 46
Nu-Line Industries,   6 - 56
Okla Homer Smith Furniture Mfg., 6 - 56
Simmons Juvenile Products Co.,   6 - 68
Tad Taylor's Fantasy Furniture,   6 - 73
The Childrens Furniture Co.,   6 - 75

Kitchen

(Appliances, Cabinets, Fixtures, Tile, etc.)
ACIF Ceramiche S.R.L., 3 - 2
Alfa Ceramiche, 3 - 5
Allmilmo Corp., 10 - 1
Alno Network USA,   10 - 1
Amaru Tile,   3 - 6
American Brass Mfg.,   10 - 1
American International, 3 - 6
American Woodmark Corp.,   10 - 1
Angelo Amaru Tile & Bath Collection,   3 - 8
Ann Sacks Tile & Stone, 3 - 8
Antiche Ceramiche D'Talia (ACIT) SRL, 3 - 8
Antique Baths & Kitchens,   2 - 2
Aristokraft,   10 - 1
Arrowsmith Trading Company,   8 - 5
Astracast PLC, 12 - 4
Avonite,   3 - 10
Barnstable Stove Shop, 10 - 1
Blanco America, 10 - 2
Blanco, 10 - 2
Brammer Mfg. Co.,   12 - 5
Brass & Traditional Sinks Ltd., 2 - 3
Broan Manufacturing Co. Inc.,   10 - 2
Brookhaven Cabinetry,   10 - 2
Brown Stove Works Inc., 3 - 17
Bryant Stove Works,   3 - 17
Buckwalter Custom Kitchens,   10 - 2
Bulthaup Inc., 10 - 2
CECO Products Inc.,   10 - 2
Cabinet Crafters,   10 - 2
California Tile Supply, 3 - 19
Cancos Tile Corporation,   3 - 19
Cardell Cabinets,   10 - 3
Carron Phoenix Ltd.,   10 - 3
Ceramica Candia S.P.A., 3 - 22
Ceramica Colli Di Sassuolo S.P.A., 3 - 22
Ceramica Ilsa S.P.A., 3 - 22
Ceramica Panaria S.P.A.,   3 - 22
Ceramiche Atlas Concorde S.P.A., 3 - 22
Ceramiche Brunelleschi S.P.A., 3 - 22
Cerim Ceramiche S.P.A., 3 - 23
Cheng Design, 12 - 6
Cisa-Cerdisa-Smov,   3 - 24
Contemporary Copper,   10 - 3
Creda Inc.,   10 - 3
Crest Distributors,   3 - 28
Crown Point Cabinetry, 10 - 3
D & B Tile Distributors,   3 - 29
D & D Natural Stone and Marble, 3 - 29
Dacor, 8 - 21
Davis & Warshow Inc.,   10 - 3
Decorum Inc.,   1 - 14
Downsview Kitchens,   10 - 3
East Coast Tile Imports Inc.,   3 - 33
Eljer, 10 - 3
Elkay Mfg. Co., 10 - 3
Facades Ltd.,   10 - 4
Faucet Outlet, 10 - 4

Ferretti Ltd., 10 - 4
Florida Ceramic Tile Center,   3 - 37
Fox Woodcraft, 10 - 4
Franke Inc.,   10 - 4
Frigidaire,   10 - 4
Gabbianelli S.R.L.,   3 - 39
Gaggenau USA Corporation,   10 - 4
Garland Commercial Industries, Inc., 10 - 5
Geba USA, Inc., 10 - 5
Gemini Bath & Kitchen, 2 - 5
Gibson, 10 - 5
Gracious Home, 10 - 5
Grohe America Inc.,   10 - 5
Hansa America, 10 - 5
Harden Industries,   2 - 5
Hastings Tile & Il Bagno Collection,   3 - 44
Heritage Custom Kitchens,   10 - 5
Home & Cabinet Designs Inc.,   10 - 5
Homecrest Corporation, 10 - 5
Hubbardton Forge & Wood Corp., 11 - 16
Huntington/Pacific Ceramics, Inc.,   3 - 48
Hutcherson Tile,   3 - 48
I. C. R. S.P.A. (Appiani, etc.),   3 - 48
I. F. M. Co. Ltd.,   10 - 5
J & M Custom Cabinets & Millwork, 10 - 5
Jenn-Air/Maytag,   10 - 6
John Carr Joinery Sales Ltd.,   12 - 13
KWC/Rohl Corp., 10 - 6
Kemper Quality Cabinets,   10 - 6
Keokuk Stove Works,   3 - 52
King Refrigerator Corp.,   10 - 6
Kraftmaid Cabinetry,   10 - 6
Lakeville Industries, Inc.,   10 - 6
Latco Ceramic Tile,   3 - 54
L'esperance Tile Works,   3 - 53
Marble & Tile Imports, 3 - 57
Marvel Industries,   10 - 6
Melbourne Hall Workshop,   10 - 7
Merit Cabinet Distributors,   2 - 7
Metco Tile Distributors,   3 - 60
Miele, 10 - 7
Millbrook Kitchens Inc.,   10 - 7
Moen,   10 - 7
National Ceramics of Florida,   3 - 63
National Kitchen & Bath Association, 10 - 7
Neff (UK, etc.) Ltd., 10 - 7
Nemo Tile Company, Inc.,   3 - 63
Nevamar Corporation,   10 - 7
Nicola Ceramics & Marble,   3 - 64
Northern Refrigerator Company, 10 - 7
Old Country Ceramic Tile,   3 - 66
Pacific Faucets,   2 - 8
Paragon Products,   10 - 8
Peter Josef Korzilius Soehne GmbH, 3 - 69
Phoenix Products Inc., 3 - 70
Plain and Fancy Kitchens,   10 - 8
Poggenpohl U.S.A. Corp, 10 - 8
Porcher Ltd.,   2 - 9
Practical Homewares,   10 - 8
Price Pfister Inc.,   2 - 9
Rapetti Faucets,   2 - 9
Rayburn,   10 - 8
Regency VSA,   10 - 8
Rich Craft Custom Kitchens,   10 - 8
Running Dog,   10 - 8
Russell Range, Inc.,   10 - 9
Scandia Kitchens Inc.,   10 - 9
SieMatic Corporation/Smallbone, 10 - 9
Smallbone & Co. Ltd.,   10 - 9
Snaidero,   10 - 9
Stephen Huneck Gallery, 10 - 9

Index - 50   *The Complete Sourcebook*

Index

Knocker – Lamp

Sub Zero Freezer Company, Inc., 10 - 9
Swe Nova Kitchen & Bath,   10 - 9
The Chicago Faucet Company,   2 - 11
The Hanging Kitchen Co.,   10 - 9
The House of Webster,   10 - 10
The Kennebec Company,   10 - 10
The Shop,   3 - 89
The Yorkshire Door Company Ltd.,   4 - 17
Thermador,   10 - 10
Tile West Distributors, 3 - 91
Traulsen & Co., Inc.,   10 - 10
Tricity Bendix Ltd.,   10 - 10
Viking Range Corporation,   10 - 10
W. C. Wood Co. Ltd.,   10 - 10
Water Faucets, 2 - 13
Watts & Wright, 10 - 10
Wayne Tile Company,   3 - 96
Weru (UK, etc.) Ltd., 10 - 11
Wood-Mode,   10 - 11
Woodstock Furniture Ltd.,   6 - 86
Yorktowne Inc.,   10 - 11
Zanussi Ltd.,   10 - 11

Knocker

D.C. Mitchell Reproductions,   3 - 29

Lace

Artifacteria, 8 - 5
Covington Fabrics Corp.,   8 - 19
Especially Lace,   8 - 25
Faith's Lacery,   8 - 27
Flemington Fabric Decorating Center, 8 - 28
Heritage Imports, Inc., 8 - 33
J. R. Burrows & Company,   8 - 37
Lace Country, 8 - 41
Le Lace Factory, Inc., 8 - 42
Linen & Lace, 8 - 42
London Lace,   8 - 43
New Scotland Lace Co., 8 - 49
Rue De France Inc.,   8 - 57
Spring Lace Two,   8 - 62
TWG Fabric Outlet,   8 - 65

Ladder

Putnam Rolling Ladder Company, 3 - 72

Laminate

Abet Laminati, 3 - 3
V-T Industries Inc.,   4 - 17
Wilsonart,   3 - 99

Lamp

ABC Lampshades, 11 - 1
Abat Jour Ideal Lampshade Inc., 11 - 1
Abe SRL,   11 - 1
Accent Lamp & Shade Co. Inc.,   11 - 2
Accent Studios, 11 - 2
All-Lighting, 11 - 2
Alva Line SRL, 11 - 2
Antique Street Lamps Inc.,   11 - 2
Architectural Crystal Ltd.,   1 - 5
Arlati SRL,   11 - 3
Artistiche Ceramiche Fiorentine,   11 - 3
Ascot Lamps & Lighting Ltd.,   11 - 3
Aunt Sylvia's Victorian Collections,   11 - 3
Baldwin Hardware Corp., 3 - 12
Barbini Alfredo SRL,   11 - 4
Barovier & Toso Vetrerie Artistiche,   11 - 4
Beverly Hills Fan Co., 11 - 4
Blanche P. Field Inc., 11 - 4
Blessings,   11 - 4

Boyd Lighting Fixture Co.,   11 - 4
Brandon Industries Inc.,   11 - 5
Brasslight,   11 - 5
Brass'n Bounty,   11 - 5
Brubaker Metalcrafts,   11 - 5
Bulluck Furniture Co., 6 - 12
Campbell Lamp Supply, 11 - 6
Cardinal Products Inc., 11 - 6
Catalina Lamp & Shade, 11 - 6
Century Studios,   11 - 6
Charles Co., Inc.,   11 - 7
Christopher Wrays Lighting Emporium, 11 - 7
City'Lights,   11 - 8
Copper Lamps by Hutton, 11 - 8
Cornell Lamp & Shade Co.,   11 - 8
Cox Studios,   12 - 7
Custom Shades, 8 - 20
Decoy Shop,   8 - 22
Designs for Living Inc.,   11 - 9
Dynasty Classics Corp., 11 - 9
E. Molina Lamps & Parts,   11 - 10
ELCO Lamp & Shade Studio, Inc., 11 - 10
EMC Tiffany,   11 - 10
Ethan Allen, Inc.,   6 - 27
Execulamp Inc., 11 - 11
Fan Fair,   11 - 11
Fenton Art Glass Company,   11 - 11
Fine Art Lamps, 11 - 11
Flexform,   6 - 28
Flexform,   6 - 28
Form & Function,   11 - 12
Foscarini Murano SPA, 11 - 12
Frederick Cooper Inc., 11 - 12
Freedom Lamp Co.,   11 - 12
G. P. B. Beghelli,   11 - 12
Gaslight Time Antiques, 11 - 13
Georgian Art Lighting Designs, Inc.,   11 - 13
Golden Valley Lighting, 11 - 13
Harris Lamps,   11 - 14
Harris Marcus Group, Inc.,   11 - 14
Heath Sedgwick, 11 - 14
Hilo Steiner, 11 - 15
Hobby Hill Inc.,   11 - 15
Hollywood Lamp & Shade Co.,   11 - 15
Home Decorators Collection,   11 - 15
Hubbardton Forge & Wood Corp., 11 - 16
Hy-Art Lamp Co.,   11 - 16
Ideal Electric Mfg. Co. Ltd., 11 - 16
J & B Lamp & Shade,   11 - 17
J. E. Thorn Lamps Ltd., 11 - 17
Jamaica Lamp Corp.,   11 - 17
James Crystal Mfg. Co., 11 - 17
Jimco Lamp & Mfg. Co., 11 - 17
La Barge Mirrors, Inc., 8 - 41
Ladue Illuminazione,   11 - 18
Lamp Glass,   11 - 19
Lehman Hardware,   3 - 54
Lenox, 11 - 19
Lighthouse Stained Glass,   11 - 20
Lighting Source of America,   11 - 20
Luigi Crystal, 11 - 20
Lumina Italia SRL,   11 - 21
Luminaire,   11 - 21
Lundburg Studios,   11 - 21
MacDonald Stained Glass,   3 - 56
Main Street Lighting, 11 - 21
Mallory's Fine Furniture, 6 - 48
Mar-Kel Lighting Inc., 11 - 21
Marbo Lamp Co., 11 - 21
Martin's Discount Lighting,   11 - 22
Mexico House, 11 - 22

The Complete Sourcebook

Index - 51

Lampshade – Lighting

Index

Meyda Stained Glass Studio, 11 - 22
Natalie Lamp & Shade Corp., 11 - 23
Natural Light, Inc., 11 - 23
Newstamp Lighting Co., 11 - 23
Nolarec Industries, Inc., 6 - 55
Norman Perry, 11 - 23
Nova, 11 - 24
OHM-Rite Electrical, 11 - 24
Ozark Shade & Lamp, 11 - 24
Pennsylvania Illuminating Corp., 11 - 25
Quoizel Inc., 11 - 26
Ramco Industries Inc., 11 - 26
Reliance Lamp & Shade Co. Inc., 11 - 26
Robelier, 11 - 27
Royal Haeger Lamp Co., 11 - 27
Sedgefield by Adams, 11 - 28
Shamrock Lighting Inc., 11 - 29
Sicotte Lamps Ltd., 11 - 29
Skipper SPA, 11 - 29
Speer Collectibles Atlanta, 11 - 29
Statements In Design, 11 - 30
Studio Design, 11 - 30
The London Lighting Co., 11 - 32
Thousand and One Lamps Ltd., 11 - 32
Unique Art Glass Co., 12 - 26
Valentine Lamp Co., 11 - 33
Van Dyke's Restorers, 3 - 94
Victorian Classics Lampshades, 11 - 34
Vortek Industries Ltd., 11 - 34
Walpole Woodworkers, 6 - 81
Welsbach, 11 - 35
Wildwood Lamps & Accents, 11 - 35
Window Creations, 11 - 35
Windspire, 6 - 85
Wm. Engel Co., Ltd., 11 - 35
Woolums Mfg. Inc., 6 - 86
Workshops of David T. Smith, 6 - 86
Ye Old Lamp Shop, 11 - 36
Yestershades, 11 - 36
Zalstein Design Works, 11 - 36

Lampshade

Accent Lamp & Shade Co. Inc., 11 - 2
Burdoch Victorian Lamp Company, 11 - 5
California Lamp Shade Co., 11 - 6
Catalina Lamp & Shade, 11 - 6
Champion Lamp Shade Co., 11 - 7
Contois Stained Glass Studio, 11 - 7
Cornell Lamp & Shade Co., 11 - 8
Custom House, 11 - 8
Diane Studios Inc., 11 - 9
ELCO Lamp & Shade Studio, Inc., 11 - 10
Edwards Lamp Shade Co., Inc., 11 - 10
Electric Glass Co., 3 - 33
Fan Fair, 11 - 11
Fantasy Lighting, Inc., 11 - 11
Fenchel Lamp Shade Co., 11 - 11
Gibbons of Willenhall Ltd., 9 - 2
H. Grabell & Sons, 11 - 14
Home Decorators Collection, 11 - 15
Hy-Art Lamp Co., 11 - 16
J & B Lamp & Shade, 11 - 17
Jimco Lamp & Mfg. Co., 11 - 17
Lampshades Inc., 11 - 19
Lampshades of Antique, 11 - 19
Leonard R. Foss Studios, Inc., 11 - 19
Lite Tops, 11 - 20
Mar-Kel Lighting Inc., 11 - 21
Martin's Discount Lighting, 11 - 22
Morlee Lamp Shade, 11 - 22
Natalie Lamp & Shade Corp., 11 - 23

New Brunswick Lampshade Co., 11 - 23
Nova, 11 - 24
Paulson's Stained Glass Studio, 12 - 19
Philip Goldin Associates, Inc., 11 - 25
Reliance Lamp & Shade Co. Inc., 11 - 26
Roseart Lampshades Inc., 11 - 27
Satin and Old Lace Shades, 11 - 28
Saxe Lampshade, Inc., 11 - 28
Shades by Sheila, 11 - 28
Shades of the Past, 11 - 29
ShadyLady, 11 - 29
Southbrooke Shades, 11 - 29
Southern Shadecrafters, 11 - 29
Spectrum Shade Co., Inc., 11 - 29
Stylecraft Lamp Shade Co., 11 - 30
Taos Drums, 6 - 73
Turn Of The Century Lampshades, 11 - 33
Unique Lampshade Mfg., Co., 11 - 33
Victorian Classics Lampshades, 11 - 34
Wm. Engel Co., Ltd., 11 - 35
Yestershades, 11 - 36

Lattice

Cross Industries, 3 - 28

Lawn

Champion Irrigation Products, 3 - 23

Leader

Yost Mfg. & Supply Inc., 3 - 101

Leather

Classic Leather, 6 - 17
Emerson Leather Co., 6 - 26
Leather Furniture Sales, Inc., 6 - 45
Leather Interiors, 6 - 45
Lincoln House Furniture, 6 - 46
Mayfield Leather, 8 - 45
Oxford Leather, 6 - 58
Redbridge Furniture, 6 - 62
Scandecor, 6 - 66
The Leather Gallery of Kentucky, 6 - 76
Wellington's Furniture, 6 - 82

Lighting

A & A Modern Wire Products, 11 - 1
A & M Whitemetal Castings, Inc., 11 - 1
A.C. International USA, 11 - 1
A.J.P. Coppersmith, 1 - 1
A.M. Metal Spinning Co., 11 - 1
ABC Lampshades, 11 - 1
Aagard-Hanley Ltd., 11 - 1
Abat Jour Ideal Lampshade Inc., 11 - 1
Abbey Roberts Inc., 11 - 1
Abe SRL, 11 - 1
Accent Lamp & Shade Co. Inc., 11 - 2
Accent Lighting, 11 - 2
Accent Studios, 11 - 2
Adkins Architectural Antiques, 1 - 2
Aetna Electric Distributing Corp., 11 - 2
Alger Lighting, 11 - 2
Alkco Lighting, 11 - 2
All Island Security Inc., 9 - 1
All-Lighting, 11 - 2
Allied Lighting, 11 - 2
Alva Line SRL, 11 - 2
American Heirlooms, Inc., 11 - 2
American Lamp Supply, 11 - 2
Antique Hardware Store, 3 - 8
Antique Street Lamps Inc., 11 - 2
Aram Designs Ltd., 6 - 5

Index - 52

The Complete Sourcebook

Index

Lighting – Lighting

Architectural Antique Warehouse, 3 - 9
Architectural Antiquities, 1 - 5
Architectural Artifacts, 1 - 5
Architectural Crystal Ltd., 1 - 5
Architectural Rarities Ltd., 1 - 6
Arlati SRL, 11 - 3
Arroyo Craftsman, 11 - 3
Art Directions, 1 - 7
Artcraft, 11 - 3
Arte de Mexico, 6 - 6
Artemide GB Ltd., 11 - 3
Artemide, 11 - 3
Artesanos Imports, Inc., 6 - 6
Artistiche Ceramiche Fiorentine, 11 - 3
As You Like It Inc., 11 - 3
Ascot Lamps & Lighting Ltd., 11 - 3
Aunt Sylvia's Victorian Collections, 11 - 3
Aura Lamp & Lighting, Inc., 11 - 3
Authentic Designs, 3 - 10
B & G Antique Lighting, 11 - 3
B & P Lamp Supply Inc., 11 - 4
Backwoods Solar Electric Systems, 3 - 11
Bala Lighting, 11 - 4
Baldinger Architectural Lighting, Inc., 1 - 7
Baldwin Brass Lighting, 11 - 4
Baldwin Hardware Corp., 3 - 12
Ball and Ball, 6 - 7
Barbini Alfredo SRL, 11 - 4
Barovier & Toso Vetrerie Artistiche, 11 - 4
Bay Shore Light & Elec. Supply, 11 - 4
Bennett & Fountain Ltd., 11 - 4
Best & Lloyd Ltd., 11 - 4
Blanche P. Field Inc., 11 - 4
Blessings, 11 - 4
Boyd Lighting Fixture Co., 11 - 4
Brass Light Gallery, 11 - 5
Brass Reproductions, 11 - 5
Brassfinders, 11 - 5
Brasslight, 11 - 5
Brass'n Bounty, 11 - 5
Brubaker Metalcrafts, 11 - 5
Buffalo Studios, 11 - 5
Bulluck Furniture Co., 6 - 12
Burdoch Victorian Lamp Company, 11 - 5
Burle Industries, Inc., 9 - 1
Burwood Lighting Co. Ltd., 11 - 5
C. Neri, Antiques, 6 - 13
CSL Lighting Mfg., 11 - 6
California Lamp Shade Co., 11 - 6
Campbell Lamp Supply, 11 - 6
Capri Lighting, 11 - 6
Cardinal Products Inc., 11 - 6
Carriage Trade of Tahoe, 11 - 6
Cascade Designs Inc., 11 - 6
Casella Lighting, 11 - 6
Catalina Lamp & Shade, 11 - 6
Catalina Lighting, Inc., 11 - 6
Centel's Lighting, 11 - 6
Century Studios, 11 - 6
Champion Lamp Shade Co., 11 - 7
Champman Mfg. Co., 11 - 7
Charles Co., Inc., 11 - 7
Chartwell Group Ltd., 3 - 24
Christopher Wrays Lighting Emporium, 11 - 7
Chubb Lock Company, 9 - 2
City Lights, 11 - 7
Classic Accents, 3 - 25
Classic Designs, 11 - 7
Classic Illumination, Inc., 11 - 7
Conant Custom Brass, Inc., 11 - 7
Conner's Architectural Antiques, 1 - 11

Conservation Technology Ltd., 11 - 7
Contois Stained Glass Studio, 11 - 7
Copper Lamps by Hutton, 11 - 8
Coran-Sholes Industries, 11 - 8
Cornell Lamp & Shade Co., 11 - 8
Craig Interiors Ltd., 11 - 8
Crawford's Old House Store, 3 - 27
Crescent Lighting Ltd., 11 - 8
Cryselco Ltd., 11 - 8
Crystal Creek Lighting, 11 - 8
Crystal Import Company, 11 - 8
Current, 11 - 8
Custom House, 11 - 8
Custom Shades, 8 - 20
Dale Tiffany Inc., 11 - 9
Davey Lighting, 11 - 9
Decorative Dimensions, 11 - 9
Decorum Inc., 1 - 14
Dernier & Hamlyn Ltd., 11 - 9
Design Enterprises, 11 - 9
Designs for Living Inc., 11 - 9
Diane Studios Inc., 11 - 9
Dickinsons Architectural Antiques, 1 - 14
Dickson Brothers, Inc., 11 - 9
Dilor Industries Ltd., 11 - 9
Dutch Products & Supply Co., 3 - 32
Dynasty Classics Corp., 11 - 9
Dyno-Electrics, 11 - 9
D'Lights, 11 - 8
E. Molina Lamps & Parts, 11 - 10
ELA Custom & Architectural Co., 11 - 10
ELCO Lamp & Shade Studio, Inc., 11 - 10
EMC Tiffany, 11 - 10
Early American Lighting, 11 - 10
Edison Halo Lighting, 11 - 10
Edwards Lamp Shade Co., Inc., 11 - 10
Electronic Sensing Products, Inc., 9 - 2
Elegante Brass, Inc., 11 - 10
Elsco Lighting Products, Inc., 11 - 10
Elstead Lighting Ltd., 11 - 10
Emess PLC, 11 - 10
Erco Lighting Ltd., 11 - 11
Eurofase Inc., 11 - 11
European Classics, 11 - 11
Exciting Lighting by Pam Morris, 11 - 11
Execulamp Inc., 11 - 11
Exquisite Lighting and Design, Inc., 11 - 11
Fabby, 11 - 11
Falcon Eye Inc., 9 - 2
Fantasy Lighting, Inc., 11 - 11
Fasco Industries, Inc., 11 - 11
Fellenz Antiques, 3 - 35
Fenchel Lamp Shade Co., 11 - 11
Fenton Art Glass Company, 11 - 11
Fine Art Lamps, 11 - 11
Fine Designs Unlimited, 11 - 12
Fitzgerald Lighting Ltd., 11 - 12
Fontana Arte SPA, 6 - 29
Forluce, 11 - 12
Form & Function, 11 - 12
Forma Lighting Ltd., 11 - 12
Foscarini Murano SPA, 11 - 12
Frederick Cooper Inc., 11 - 12
Fredrick Ramond Inc., 11 - 12
Freedom Lamp Co., 11 - 12
Futimis Ltd., 11 - 12
G. P. B. Beghelli, 11 - 12
Garber's Crafted Lighting, 11 - 12
Gardco Lighting, 11 - 12
Gaslight Time Antiques, 11 - 13
Gates Moore, 11 - 13

Index

The Complete Sourcebook

Index - 53

Lighting – Lighting

Gem Monogram & Cut Glass Corp., 11 - 13
Genie House, 11 - 13
George Kovacs Lighting Inc., 11 - 13
Georgia Lighting Supply Co., 11 - 13
Georgian Art Lighting Designs, Inc., 11 - 13
Gibson Interiors, 11 - 13
Golden Valley Lighting, 11 - 13
Grabell of California, 11 - 13
Graham's Lighting Fixtures Inc., 11 - 13
Grand Brass Lamp Parts, 11 - 14
Green's Lighting Fixtures, 11 - 14
Greg's Antique Lighting, 11 - 14
H. Grabell & Sons, 11 - 14
Halo Lighting Products/Cooper Ind., 11 - 14
Halogen Lighting Systems, 11 - 14
Hammerworks, 11 - 14
Hardware + Plus Inc., 3 - 44
Harris Lamps, 11 - 14
Harris Marcus Group, Inc., 11 - 14
Harry Horn, Inc., 11 - 14
Heath Sedgwick, 11 - 14
Heritage Lanterns, 11 - 14
Herwig Lighting Inc., 11 - 15
Heter Lighting Enterprises, Inc., 11 - 15
Heyward House, 11 - 15
Hilo Steiner, 11 - 15
Hinkley Lighting, 11 - 15
Hippo Hardware & Trading Co., 3 - 46
Historic Housefitters, 3 - 46
Hitech Lighting Ltd., 11 - 15
Hobby Hill Inc., 11 - 15
Hollywood Lamp & Shade Co., 11 - 15
Holophane Company Inc., 11 - 15
Holtkotter International, Inc., 11 - 15
Home Decorators Collection, 11 - 15
Home Equipment Mfg.,Co., 11 - 16
Horesfeathers Architectural Antiques, 1 - 20
Howard Ceilings Ltd., 11 - 16
Howard's Antique Lighting, 11 - 16
Hubbardton Forge & Wood Corp., 11 - 16
Hubbell Lighting Inc., 11 - 16
Hurley Patentee Manor, 11 - 16
Hy-Art Lamp Co., 11 - 16
Ideal Electric Mfg. Co. Ltd., 11 - 16
Igmor Crystal Lite Corp., 11 - 16
Illuma Lighting Ltd., 11 - 16
Indel UK Ltd., 11 - 17
Insites, 11 - 17
Irvin's Craft Shop, 11 - 17
J & B Lamp & Shade, 11 - 17
J W Lighting Inc., 11 - 17
J. E. Thorn Lamps Ltd., 11 - 17
Jackson Mfg. Co., 11 - 17
Jamaica Lamp Corp., 11 - 17
James Crystal Mfg. Co., 11 - 17
Jardine International Ltd., 11 - 17
Jimco Lamp & Mfg. Co., 11 - 17
Josiah R. Coppersmythe, 11 - 18
Juno Lighting, Inc., 11 - 18
Kalco Lighting Inc., 11 - 18
Kemp & George, 3 - 52
Keystone Lighting Corp., 11 - 18
King's Chandelier, 11 - 18
Kiss Lamp Co., 11 - 18
Koch Originals, Inc., 12 - 14
Kurt Versen Co., 11 - 18
L.T. Moses Willard, Inc., 11 - 18
Ladue Illuminazione, 11 - 18
Lam Lighting Systems, 11 - 18
Lamp Glass, 11 - 19
Lamp Warehouse/N.Y. Ceiling Fan, 11 - 19

Lampshades Inc., 11 - 19
Lampshades of Antique, 11 - 19
Lampways Ltd., 11 - 19
Lee's Studio, 11 - 19
Lehman Hardware, 3 - 54
Leiter Lites, 11 - 19
Lenox, 11 - 19
Leonard R. Foss Studios, Inc., 11 - 19
Lester H. Berry & Company, 11 - 19
Leucos Lighting, 11 - 19
Leviton Manufacturing Company, 11 - 20
Libco Lamp, 11 - 20
Light Ideas, 11 - 20
Lighthouse Stained Glass, 11 - 20
Lighting Source of America, 11 - 20
Lightning Bug Ltd., 11 - 20
Lightolier, 11 - 20
Lite Tops, 11 - 20
Luigi Crystal, 11 - 20
Luma Lighting Industries, Inc., 11 - 20
Lumax Industries Inc., 11 - 20
Lumea, 11 - 21
Lumina Italia SRL, 11 - 21
Luminaire, 11 - 21
Lundburg Studios, 11 - 21
Lutron, 11 - 21
Main Street Lighting, 11 - 21
Mar-Kel Lighting Inc., 11 - 21
Marbo Lamp Co., 11 - 21
Marco Lighting Fixtures, 11 - 21
Mario Industries, 11 - 21
Mark Lighting Fixture Co., Inc., 11 - 21
Martin's Discount Lighting, 11 - 22
Marvel Lighting Corp., 11 - 22
Metropolitan Lighting Fixture Co. Inc., 11 - 22
Mexico House, 11 - 22
Meyda Stained Glass Studio, 11 - 22
Midwest Chandelier Co., 11 - 22
Minka Lighting Inc., 11 - 22
Mobern Electric Corp., 11 - 22
Monarch Metal Products Corp., 2 - 8
Mooncraft Corp., 11 - 22
Morlee Lamp Shade, 11 - 22
Moss Lighting, 11 - 22
Mowbray Lighting, 11 - 23
Natalie Lamp & Shade Corp., 11 - 23
National Industries, 11 - 23
National Lighting Inc., 11 - 23
Natural Light, Inc., 11 - 23
Ner Lighting Inc., 11 - 23
New Brunswick Lampshade Co.Inc., 11 - 23
New England Stained Glass Studios, 11 - 23
Newman Lighting Co., 11 - 23
Newstamp Lighting Co., 11 - 23
Niedermaier Design Inc., 6 - 55
Norman Perry, 11 - 23
Nova, 11 - 24
Nowells Inc., 11 - 24
NuMerit Electrical Supply, 11 - 24
OHM-Rite Electrical, 11 - 24
Ocean View Lighting, 11 - 24
Olde Village Smithery, 11 - 24
Olivers Lighting Company, 11 - 24
Omega Too, 2 - 8
Onate's Cupboard, 8 - 50
Optelma Lighting Ltd., 11 - 24
Osram Corporation, 11 - 24
Ozark Shade & Lamp, 11 - 24
Panorama Lighting Ltd., 11 - 24
Pass & Seymour, 11 - 25
Pennsylvania Illuminating Corp., 11 - 25

Index

Limestone – Liner

Period Furniture Hardware, 6 - 59
Period Lighting Fixtures, 11 - 25
Permo Lights Unlimited, 11 - 25
Pettigrew Associates Inc., 6 - 59
Philadelphia Glass Bending Co., 11 - 25
Philip Goldin Associates, Inc., 11 - 25
Philips Lighting Company, 11 - 25
Pira Ltd., 6 - 60
Porter Lighting Sales Inc., 11 - 25
Prescolite, 9 - 3
Primelite Mfg. Co., Inc., 11 - 25
Primo Lighting, 11 - 25
Progress Lighting, 11 - 25
Queen City Architectural Salvage, 1 - 28
Quip Interior Design & Lighting, 11 - 25
Quoizel Inc., 11 - 26
RAB Electric, 9 - 3
Rada Lighting Ltd., 11 - 26
Ramco Industries Inc., 11 - 26
Regent Lighting Corp., 11 - 26
Reggiani Light Gallery, 11 - 26
Reggiani Ltd., 11 - 26
Rejuvenation Lamp & Fixture, 11 - 26
Reliance Lamp & Shade Co. Inc., 11 - 26
Remcraft Lighting Products, 11 - 26
Remington, 11 - 26
Renaissance Marketing, 11 - 26
Residential Lighting Div., 11 - 27
Richard Scofield, 11 - 27
Robelier, 11 - 27
Robert Long Lighting, 11 - 27
Roff Lighting, 11 - 27
Roflan Associates, 11 - 27
Roseart Lampshades Inc., 11 - 27
Roy Electric Co. Inc., 11 - 27
Royal Haeger Lamp Co., 11 - 27
Russell Electrics Ltd., 11 - 27
S. Wilder & Co. Inc., 11 - 28
Santa Fe Lights, 11 - 28
Satco Products Inc., 11 - 28
Satin and Old Lace Shades, 11 - 28
Saxe Lampshade, Inc., 11 - 28
Schonbek Worldwide Lighting Inc., 11 - 28
Sea Gull Lighting Products Inc., 11 - 28
Sedgefield by Adams, 11 - 28
Shades by Sheila, 11 - 28
Shades of the Past, 11 - 29
ShadyLady, 11 - 29
Shamrock Lighting Inc., 11 - 29
Shaper Lighting, 11 - 29
Sicotte Lamps Ltd., 11 - 29
Skipper SPA, 11 - 29
Southbrooke Shades, 11 - 29
Southern Shadecrafters, 11 - 29
Spectrum Shade Co., Inc., 11 - 29
Speer Collectibles Atlanta, 11 - 29
Spero Electric Corp., 11 - 29
St. Louis Antique Lighting Co., 11 - 29
Staff Lighting Corp., 11 - 30
Staff Lighting Ltd., 11 - 30
Starlowe Lighting & Design Ltd., 11 - 30
Statements In Design, 11 - 30
Sternberg Lanterns Inc., 11 - 30
Stuart Interiors, 6 - 72
Studio Design, 11 - 30
Studio Steel, 11 - 30
Stylecraft Lamp Shade Co., 11 - 30
Sunelco, 3 - 84
T. A Green Lighting Co., 11 - 30
Tally-Ho Lighting Ltd., 11 - 30
Task Lighting Corporation, 11 - 31

Tempo/Infiniti Lighting, 11 - 31
Tenby Electrical Ltd., 11 - 31
Terradek Industries, 11 - 31
The Basic source Inc., 11 - 31
The Brass Light Gallery, 11 - 31
The Brass Lion, 11 - 31
The C.S. Bell Co., 11 - 31
The Copper House, 11 - 32
The Lamp House, 11 - 32
The London Lighting Co., 11 - 32
The Marle Company, 11 - 32
The Saltbox, 11 - 32
The Seraph Country Collection, 6 - 76
The Tin Bin, 11 - 32
The Woodworkers Store, 11 - 32
Thomas Inc., 11 - 32
Thousand and One Lamps Ltd., 11 - 32
Timely Lighting, 11 - 33
Tom Thumb Lighting, Inc., 11 - 33
Toro Woodlights, 11 - 33
Tower Lighting Center, 11 - 33
Track & Plus, 11 - 33
TrimbleHouse Corp., 11 - 33
Troy Lighting, 11 - 33
Turn Of The Century Lampshades Inc.11 - 33
Unique Lampshade Mfg., Co., 11 - 33
United Plastics Corp., 1 - 35
Universal Fixture Manufacturing, 11 - 33
Unlight Ltd., 11 - 33
Urban Archaeology, 1 - 35
Valentine Lamp Co., 11 - 33
Versailles Lighting Inc., 11 - 34
Victorian Classics Lampshades, 11 - 34
Victorian Lightcrafters Ltd., 11 - 34
Victorian Lighting Works, 11 - 34
Victorian Reproduction Enterprises, 11 - 34
Victorian Revival, 11 - 34
Victoriana Ltd., 11 - 34
Village Lantern, 11 - 34
Visioneered Lighting Mfg. Ltd., 11 - 34
Vortek Industries Ltd., 11 - 34
WAC Lighting Collection, 11 - 35
Welsbach, 11 - 35
Wendelighting, 11 - 35
Westwood Co., 11 - 35
Wholesale Fans & Lighting Inc., 11 - 35
Wildwood Lamps & Accents, 11 - 35
William Spencer, 11 - 35
Window Creations, 11 - 35
Wm. Engel Co., Ltd., 11 - 35
Wm. Spencer Inc., 11 - 35
Woolums Mfg. Inc., 6 - 86
Workshops of David T. Smith, 6 - 86
Yardlighting Systems Inc., 11 - 36
Ye Old Lamp Shop, 11 - 36
Yestershades, 11 - 36
Zalstein Design Works, 11 - 36

Limestone

Delaware Quarries, Inc., 3 - 30
Paris Ceramics, 3 - 68

Linen

Carol Mead Design, 8 - 14
Charleston Linens, 8 - 16
Kemp & Beatley, Inc., 8 - 39
Linen Lady, 8 - 42
The Linen Gallery, 8 - 67

Liner

Heat-Fab Inc., 3 - 44

The Complete Sourcebook

Index - 55

Linoleum – Lumber

Linoleum
Forbo Industries, 8 - 28
Linoleum City, 5 - 6

Lintel
Briar Hill Stone Co., 3 - 17

Living Room
Allmilmo Ltd., 6 - 3
Anglo Nordic Marketing (UK, etc.) Ltd., 6 - 4
Aram Designs Ltd., 6 - 5
Artistic Upholstery Ltd., 6 - 6
Ashby & Horner Joinery Ltd., 6 - 6
Bevan Funnell Ltd., 6 - 9
Boyles Furniture, 6 - 11
Carleton Furniture Group Ltd., 6 - 14
Castle Mount, 6 - 15
Dean & Brook Ltd., 6 - 22
Del Tongo (UK, etc.) Ltd., 6 - 22
E.C. Hodge Ltd., 6 - 25
Griffon Furniture Ltd., 6 - 33
H. Morris & Co. Ltd., 6 - 33
Hamlet Furniture Ltd., 6 - 34
Holder Pearce, 6 - 36
Hostess Furniture Ltd., 6 - 37
Hyperion Wall Furniture Ltd., 6 - 38
J. T. Ellis & Co. Ltd., 6 - 39
John Pulsford Associates Ltd., 6 - 40
Kesterport Ltd., 6 - 42
L & J.G. Stickley, Inc., 6 - 43
Leboff International Ltd., 6 - 45
Leverwood Ltd., 6 - 45
Lexterten Ltd., 6 - 46
Mark Wilkinson Furniture Ltd., 6 - 50
Martin & Frost Ltd., 6 - 50
Metalliform Ltd., 6 - 52
Monzie Joinery Ltd., 6 - 54
Nathan Furniture Ltd., 6 - 54
Neil Rogers Interiors, 6 - 54
Options Bedrooms Ltd., 6 - 57
Pegram Contracts Ltd., 6 - 59
Pel Ltd., 6 - 59
Pira Ltd., 6 - 60
Plaza Furniture Gallery, 6 - 60
Quality Furniture Market, 6 - 61
Renray Group Ltd., 6 - 63
Royal Strathclyde Blindcraft Industries, 6 - 65
Saraband Furniture Co., 6 - 66
Slumberland PLC, 6 - 69
South West Joinery Co. Ltd., 6 - 70
Stag Meredew Furniture Ltd., 6 - 71
Staples & Co. Ltd., 6 - 71
Stuart Interiors, 6 - 72
Sylmar Technology Ltd., 6 - 73
Thomasville Furniture, 6 - 77
Thos. Moser, Cabinetmakers, 6 - 77
Tilden Industries (UK) Ltd., 6 - 78
Vermont Furniture Designs, 6 - 80
W. G. Undrill Ltd., 6 - 81
Wilkinsons Furniture Ltd., 6 - 84
William L. Mclean Ltd., 6 - 84
William Lawrence & Co. Ltd., 6 - 84
Younger Furniture, 6 - 87

Locks
Accurate Lock & Hardware Co., 1 - 2
Adams Rite (Europe, etc.) Ltd., 12 - 2
Albany Hardware Specialty Mfg.,3 - 4
Almet Hardware Ltd., 9 - 1
American Home Supply, 3 - 6
Arthur Shaw Manufacturing Ltd., 9 - 1

Besam Ltd., 4 - 2
Brass Tacks Hardware Ltd., 3 - 16
Catnic Ltd., 4 - 3
Chubb Lock Company, 9 - 2
Cotswold Architectural Products Ltd., 1 - 12
Crompton Ltd., 12 - 7
D.C. Mitchell Reproductions, 3 - 29
DS Locksmithing Company, 3 - 29
Dexter Lock, 4 - 5
Dryad Simplan Limited, 12 - 8
Erebus Limited, 4 - 6
GT Doors & Locks, 4 - 8
Gibbons of Willenhall Ltd., 9 - 2
Hope Works Ltd., 12 - 11
J. Legge & Co. Ltd., 4 - 9
James Gibbons Format Ltd., 12 - 12
Jones & Barclay Ltd., 3 - 51
Josiah Parkes and Sons Ltd., 4 - 10
Magnet Trade, 4 - 11
New England Lock & Hardware Co., 9 - 3
P. C. Henderson Ltd., 12 - 18
R. Cartwright & Co., Ltd., 12 - 21
Weiser Lock, 9 - 3
Weslock National, 4 - 18
Yale Security Products Ltd., 9 - 4

Log
(Furniture, Homes, etc.)

Barnes & Barnes, 6 - 8
Ciro Coppa, 6 - 16
Cline Aluminum Doors Inc., 4 - 3
Coppa Woodworking, 6 - 18
Crockett Log & Timber Frame Homes, 1 - 12
Great American Log Furniture, 6 - 32
Klein Design Inc., 6 - 43
La-Z-Boy Furniture, 6 - 44
Pukall Lumber Co., 3 - 72
Sawtooth Valley Woodcrafts, 6 - 66
Sheffield Chair Co., 6 - 68
Western Log Furniture, 6 - 82

Lumber
A. Johnson Co., 3 - 1
Adelmann & Clark Inc., 3 - 4
Adonis Forest Products, Inc., 3 - 4
Allied Building Products Corp., 3 - 5
Anthony Forest Product Co., 3 - 8
BRE Lumber, 3 - 11
Bear Creek Lumber, 3 - 13
Bergen Brick & Tile Co., 3 - 14
Berkheiser Lumber Co. Inc., 3 - 14
Better Trees, 3 - 15
Blount Lumber Co., 3 - 15
Brent Materials Co., 3 - 17
Bridge Lumber Co., 3 - 17
Center Lumber Company, 1 - 10
Cersosimo Lumber Co., 3 - 23
Champion International Corp., 3 - 23
Coastal Lumber Co., 3 - 25
Conrolled Acoustics Corp., 3 - 26
Constantine's, 1 - 12
Croy-Marietta Hardwoods Inc., 3 - 28
Diamond Wood Products, Inc., 3 - 31
Dwight Lewis Lumber Co., Inc., 3 - 32
EDLCO, 3 - 33
Elof Hansson, Inc., 3 - 33
Enterprise Lumber Co., 3 - 34
Felix Huard Inc., 5 - 4
Fibreboard Box & Millwork Corp., 3 - 36
Finlay Forest Industries Ltd., 3 - 36
Florence Corp., 3 - 37

Index - 56

The Complete Sourcebook

Index

Mantel – Mantel

Foothill Hardware & Lumber, 3 - 37
Frampton Industries Inc., 3 - 38
Frazier Park Lumber & Hardware, 3 - 38
General Building Products Corp., 3 - 39
Georgia Pacific Corp., 3 - 40
Gilchrist Timber Co., 3 - 40
Gilmer Wood Co., 3 - 40
Goodwin Lumber, 3 - 41
Groff & Hearne Lumber, 3 - 42
H. M. Stauffer & Sons Inc., 3 - 43
H. Verby Co. Inc., 3 - 43
Harrison Hardwood Mfg. Inc., 3 - 44
Hartwood Ltd., 3 - 44
Henegan's Wood Shed, 3 - 45
Herbert H. Sabbeth Corp., 3 - 45
Hill & Lumber & Hardware Co., 1 - 20
Hiskson Corporation, 3 - 46
Hoff Forest Products, Inc., 3 - 46
Hurd Lumber Co., 3 - 48
ITT Rayonier Inc., 3 - 49
Independent Lumber Co., 3 - 49
Indiana Wood Products, Inc., 3 - 49
J. H. Hamlen & Son, 3 - 50
Johnston & Rhodes Bluestone Co., 3 - 51
Kawartha Wood Products Ltd., 3 - 51
Lawrence R. McCoy & Co. Inc., 3 - 54
Lemire Lumber Co. Inc., 3 - 54
Lewis Brothers Lumber Co. Inc., 1 - 22
M. L. Condon Company Inc., 3 - 56
Manufacturers Lumber & Millwork, Inc., 3 - 57
Marjam Supply Company, 3 - 58
Marquette Lumber Co. Inc., 3 - 58
Martin Timber Co., Inc., 6 - 50
Maryland Lumber Co., 3 - 59
McMillen Lumber Co., 3 - 59
Midwest Lumber & Supply, 3 - 60
Mill & Timber Products, Ltd., 3 - 60
Monadnock Forest Products, Inc., 3 - 61
Mongold Lumber Co., Inc., 3 - 61
Murray Bros. Lumber Co. Ltd., 3 - 62
Native American Hardwoods, 3 - 63
North Country Lumber Co. Inc., 3 - 64
North Fields Restorations, 3 - 65
Northland Hardwood Lumber Co., 3 - 65
Northwest Hardwoods Inc., 3 - 65
Ohio Hardwood Lumber Co., 3 - 66
Old Kentucky Wood Products, 1 - 26
Ontario Hardwood Products Ltd., 3 - 67
Oregon Fir Millwork, Inc., 1 - 26
Pacific Burl and Hardwood, 3 - 68
Penrod Co., 3 - 69
Pine Products Corp., 3 - 70
Pine River Lumber Co. Ltd., 3 - 70
Pukall Lumber Co., 3 - 72
Randall Bros. Inc., 1 - 28
Razorback Hardwood, Inc., 5 - 8
River City Woodworks, 5 - 8
Robbins Inc., 5 - 8
Sandy Pond Hardwoods, 3 - 77
Scotch Lumber Co., 3 - 78
Setzer Forest Products, 3 - 78
South Coast Lumber Co., 3 - 80
Stuart Post & Lumber Co., 1 - 32
Talarico Hardwoods, 3 - 86
The Berea Hardwoods Co., 3 - 87
The Dorris Lumber & Moulding Co., 3 - 88
Thompson Lumber Co., 3 - 90
Tri-City Lumber/Building Supplies, 3 - 92
Trimall Interior Products Inc., 3 - 92
Valley Planing Mill Inc., 1 - 36
Vaughan & Sons Inc., 3 - 94

Vermont Antique Lumber Co., 3 - 95
Welawood Inc., 3 - 97
Westar Timber Ltd., 3 - 97
White Brothers, 3 - 98
Whitson Lumber Co. Inc., 3 - 98
Wilcox Lumber Inc., 3 - 99
Willard Brothers Woodcutters, 3 - 99
Williams Lumber & Hardware, 3 - 99
Wolohan Lumber & Improvement, 3 - 100
Wood World, 3 - 100
Woodcrafters Supply, 3 - 100
Zeidler Forest Industries Ltd., 3 - 102

Mantel

ACCRA Wood Products Ltd., 1 - 1
ADI Corporation, 1 - 1
Adkins Architectural Antiques, 1 - 2
Amherst Woodworking & Supply Inc., 1 - 4
Architectural Antique Warehouse, 3 - 9
Architectural Antiquities, 1 - 5
Architectural Artifacts, 1 - 5
Architectural Salvage Company, 1 - 6
Art Marble and Stone, 1 - 7
Arvid's Historic Woods, 1 - 7
Ashfield Stone Quarry, 3 - 9
Axon Products, 1 - 7
BD Mantels Ltd., 1 - 7
BRE Lumber, 3 - 11
Ballard Designs, 1 - 8
Bangkok International, 5 - 2
Bradley Custom Mantels & Woodworking,1-9
Brill & Walker Associates Inc., 1 - 9
By-Gone Days Antiques Inc., 1 - 9
Cider Hill Woodworks, 1 - 10
Classic Mouldings Inc., 1 - 11
Colonial Marble Products Ltd., 3 - 25
Continental Woodworking Co., 1 - 12
Cotswood Door Specialists Ltd., 4 - 4
Country Casual, 6 - 19
Danny Alessandro Ltd./Edwin Jackson, 1- 14
Draper & Draper, 1 - 15
Driwood Moulding Co., 8 - 24
Drummond Woodworks, 1 - 15
EDLCO, 3 - 33
Elk Valley Woodworking Inc., 6 - 26
Emsworth Fireplaces Ltd., 1 - 15
Executive Woodsmiths Inc., 1 - 16
Feature Fires Ltd., 1 - 16
Florida Mantel Shoppe, 1 - 17
Foster Mantels, 1 - 17
Frederick Wilbur, Carver, 1 - 17
Gregor's Studios, 1 - 19
Hallidays America Inc., 1 - 19
Hazelmere Industries Ltd., 4 - 8
Heritage Mantels Inc., 1 - 19
Horesfeathers Architectural Antiques, 1 - 20
I. F. M. Co. Ltd., 10 - 5
Irreplaceable Artifacts, 1 - 20
Jackson Mfg. Co., 11 - 17
Janik Custom Millwork, 12 - 12
Kingsley-Bate, Ltd., 6 - 42
Larkin Company, 1 - 22
Larkin Company, 1 - 22
Maizefeld Mantels, 1 - 22
Mantels of Yesteryear Inc., 1 - 22
Marion H. Campbell, 1 - 23
Marshall Galleries, Inc., 1 - 23
Master Woodcarver, 6 - 50
Midwest Dowel Works, Inc., 3 - 60
Millwork Supply Company, 4 - 12
Monroe Coldren & Sons, 3 - 62

The Complete Sourcebook

Index - 57

Maple – Metal

Index

Mountain Lumber Co., 5 - 7
Nevers Oak Fireplace Mantels, 1 - 25
Norman's Handmade Reproductions, 6 - 55
Oak Leaves Studio, 1 - 25
Oakwood Classic & Custom Woodwork,1- 25
Olde South Door, 4 - 13
Osborne Wood Products Inc., 6 - 57
Palmer Creek Hewn Wood Products, 1 - 27
Partelow Custom Wood Turnings, 1 - 27
Perkins Architectural Millwork, 1 - 27
Piedmont Mantel & Millwork, 1 - 27
Pinecrest, 1 - 27
R & R Lumber & Building Supply, 1 - 28
Rackstraw Ltd., 6 - 62
Ranchwood Mfg., 1 - 28
Raymond Enkeboll Designs, 1 - 28
Readybuilt Products Co., 1 - 28
Replico Products Inc., 1 - 29
Restorer's Supply, 4 - 14
Samuel B. Sadtler & Co., 1 - 30
Silhoutte Antiques Inc., 6 - 68
Sligh Clocks, 8 - 61
Stone Magic Mfg., 8 - 63
Stonehaven, 7 - 6
Sunshine Architectural Woodworks, 1 - 33
Sunshine Woodworks, 1 - 33
Tallahassee Mouldings & Millwork, 1 - 33
The Bank Architectural Antiques, 1 - 34
The London Door Company, 4 - 17
The Natural Woodflooring Company, 5 - 10
Trott Furniture Co., 6 - 79
Valley Planing Mill Inc., 1 - 36
Weatherend Estate Furniture, 6 - 82
Westlake Architectural Antiques, 1 - 37
William Jackson Co., 1 - 37
Wm. H. Jackson Co., 1 - 37
Wohners Inc., 1 - 37
Wood Classics, 6 - 85
Wooden Nickel Architectural Antique, 1 - 38
York Spiral Stairs, 1 - 38

Maple

(Cabinets, Flooring, Furniture, etc.)
ACCRA Wood Products Ltd., 1 - 1
Adirondacks Store & Gallery, 6 - 3
B.A. Mullican Lumber & Manufacturing, 5 - 1
BRE Lumber, 3 - 11
Boen Hardwood Flooring, 5 - 2
Cardell Cabinets, 10 - 3
DeSoto Hardwood Flooring Company, 5 - 3
Dixon Lumber Company, 5 - 3
EDLCO, 3 - 33
Habersham Plantation Corp., 6 - 33
Livermore Wood Floors, 5 - 6
Maurice L. Condon Co., 3 - 59
Midwest Dowel Works, Inc., 3 - 60
Monticello Flooring & Lumber Co., 5 - 7
Pacific Burl and Hardwood, 3 - 68
River Bend Turnings, 1 - 29
Robbins Inc., 5 - 8
Room & Board, 6 - 64
Rural Hall Inc., 4 - 14
Searcy Flooring, Inc., 5 - 9
The Burruss Company, 5 - 10
The Natural Woodflooring Company, 5 - 10
Zickgraf Hardwood Company, 5 - 11

Marble

ADI Corporation, 1 - 1
Accents In Stone, 3 - 3
American Marble Co., Inc., 3 - 7

Andrews & Sons (Marbles & Tiles), 3 - 7
Arizona Tile, 5 - 1
Armstar, 3 - 9
Art Marble and Stone, 1 - 7
Belfi Bros. & Co., Inc., 3 - 13
Bergen Bluestone Co. Inc., 3 - 14
California Marble Co., 6 - 13
Cangelosi Marble & Granite, 3 - 20
Chester Granite Co., 3 - 24
Colonial Marble Products Ltd., 3 - 25
D & D Natural Stone and Marble, 3 - 29
Dal-Tile, 3 - 29
Designer Ceramics, 3 - 30
Dina Division, 2 - 4
Fired Earth Tiles PLC, 5 - 4
Frank Scolaro Mrable Co. Inc., 3 - 38
Fritz V. Sterbak Antiques, 1 - 17
Gawet Marble & Granite Inc., 3 - 39
Georgia Marble Company, 3 - 39
Globe Marble & Tile, 3 - 41
Granite Design, 3 - 41
H & M Marble, 2 - 5
Imperial Black Marble Co., 5 - 5
Imperial Marble, Inc., 3 - 49
International Granite & Marble, 3 - 49
Kinzee Industries Inc., 12 - 14
MDM Marble Co. Inc., 2 - 7
Marble Concepts, 3 - 57
Marble Institute of America, 3 - 57
Marble Modes Inc., 3 - 57
Marble Technics Ltd., 3 - 58
Marble Unlimited, 3 - 58
Marcello Marble & Tile PLS, 2 - 7
Mayan Marble & Onyx Ltd., 6 - 51
Milano Marble Co., Inc., 2 - 7
Moretti-Harrah Marble Co., 3 - 62
Nicola Ceramics & Marble, 3 - 64
Origines, 6 - 57
Pasvalco, 3 - 68
Ply-Gem Mfg., 3 - 70
Puccio Marble & Onyx, 3 - 72
Quality Marble Inc., 3 - 72
Quality Marble Ltd., 3 - 72
Roger Pearson, 1 - 30
Samuel B. Sadtler & Co., 1 - 30
Shaw Marble Works, 5 - 9
Shelly Tile Inc., 3 - 78
Stenindustriens Landssammenslutning,3 - 82
Sveriges Stenindustriforbund, 3 - 85
Swedecor Ltd., 3 - 85
The Stone & Marble Supermarket, 3 - 89
Tile & Marble Designs, 3 - 90
Tile Emporium International, 3 - 90
Tile with Style, 3 - 91
Valley Marble & Slate Corp., 3 - 94
Vermont Marble Co., 3 - 95
Vetter Stone Co., 1 - 36
Victory Tile & Marble, 3 - 95
Walker & Zanger, 3 - 95

Medallion

Classic Ceilings, 1 - 11
Drummond Woodworks, 1 - 15
Entol Industries, 1 - 16

Metal

ASC Pacific Inc., 3 - 2
Berea Prehung Door, Inc., 4 - 2
Berke Door & Hardware, 3 - 14
Berridge Manufacturing Co., 3 - 14
Chelsea Decorative Metal Co., 1 - 10

Index

Metalwork – Mirror

Conklin Metal Industries, 3 - 26
Corsican, 6 - 19
Country Accents, 12 - 7
Country Cupolas, 1 - 12
Kaylien, 4 - 10
Readybuilt Products Co., 1 - 28
Reinke Shakes, 3 - 74
Tegola USA, 3 - 87

Metalwork

Allied Bronze Corp., 1 - 3
New England Tool Company, 3 - 64
Newman Brothers Inc., 1 - 25

Mexican

(Furniture, Lighting, Tile, etc.)
Artesanos Imports, Inc., 6 - 6
Elon Inc., 3 - 33
Mexico House, 11 - 22

Millwork

Adelmann & Clark Inc., 3 - 4
American Custom Millwork Inc., 1 - 3
American Millwork Inc., 1 - 3
American Moulding & Millwork Co., 1 - 3
Anderson-McQuaid Company Inc., 1 - 4
Barnett Millworks, Inc., 1 - 8
Berbaum Millwork Inc., 3 - 14
Billings Sash & Door Co., 4 - 2
Bjorndal Woodworks, 1 - 8
Blanton & Moore Co., 6 - 10
Blount Lumber Co., 3 - 15
Blue Ox Millworks, 3 - 15
Boise Moulding & Lumber, 3 - 15
Boyertown Planing Mill Co., 1 - 8
Bright Wood Corp., 1 - 9
Burt Millwork Corp., 1 - 9
Center Lumber Company, 1 - 10
Coastal Millworks Inc., 1 - 11
Curvoflite Inc., 1 - 13
Custom & Historic Millwork, 1 - 13
Custom Hardwood Productions, 1 - 13
Customwood Mfg. Co., 1 - 13
DHM Cabinetmakers Inc., 6 - 21
Driwood Moulding Co., 8 - 24
Empire Woodworks, 1 - 15
Fancy Front Brassiere Co., 1 - 16
Federal Millwork Corp., 1 - 16
Fibreboard Box & Millwork Corp., 3 - 36
Fine Woodworking by Living Tree, 6 - 28
Frank E. Wilson Lumber Co. Inc., 1 - 17
Fypon Molded Millwork, 1 - 17
Garland Woodcraft Co. Inc., 1 - 18
Gazebo & Porchworks, 7 - 3
Georgia Pacific Corp., 3 - 40
Gunther Mills Inc., 1 - 19
H. M. Stauffer & Sons Inc., 3 - 43
H.I.C. Millwork Inc., 1 - 19
Haas Woodworking Company Inc., 1 - 19
Hicksville Woodworks Co., 1 - 20
Hill & Lumber & Hardware Co., 1 - 20
Iberia Millwork, 4 - 9
J & M Custom Cabinets & Millwork, 10 - 5
Johnsonius Precision Millwork, 3 - 50
K & G, 1 - 21
Kentucky Millwork Inc., 1 - 21
King Brothers Woodworking Inc., 6 - 42
Knipp & Co. Inc., 6 - 43
Lewis Brothers Lumber Co. Inc., 1 - 22
M. L. Condon Company Inc., 3 - 56
MacBeath Hardwood Co., 1 - 22

Mad River Woodworks, 1 - 22
Maine Architectural Millwork, Inc., 1 - 22
Manufacturers Lumber & Millwork, 3 - 57
Materials Unlimited, 1 - 23
Minton Co., 6 - 53
Mongold Lumber Co., Inc., 3 - 61
Mountaintop Cabinet Manufacturing, 10 - 7
National Woodworks, Inc., 1 - 25
Old Kentucky Wood Products, 1 - 26
Ornamental Mouldings, Ltd., 1 - 26
O'Connor's Cypress Woodworks, 6 - 56
Paniflex Corp., 1 - 27
Port-O-Lite Corporation, 1 - 28
PriceKing Building Supply Inc., 3 - 71
Quality Door & Millwork, 4 - 14
Randall Bros. Inc., 1 - 28
Red Rose Millwork, 1 - 28
Riverside Millwork Co. Inc., 1 - 29
Robillard, 1 - 29
Salas & Co., 1 - 30
Seneca Millwork Inc., 1 - 31
Silverton Victorian Millworks, 1 - 31
Smith Millwork, Inc., 1 - 31
Southern Millwork, Inc., 1 - 31
Spokane Moulding Corp., 6 - 70
Sunset Moulding Co., 1 - 33
Tafcor Inc., 1 - 33
The James Wood Company, 1 - 34
The Joinery Company, 5 - 10
The Porch Factory, 1 - 34
The Smoot Lumber Co., 4 - 17
Unique Spiral Stairs & Millwork Inc., 1 - 35
Universal Window Corp., 1 - 35
Valley Planing Mill Inc., 1 - 36
Victorian Showcase, 6 - 81
Wall/Goldfinger Inc., 6 - 81
Windham Millwork Inc., 1 - 37
Windsor Mill, Inc., 1 - 37
Woodcraft Architectural Millwork Inc., 1 - 37
Zimmerman's Millwork & Cabinet, 1 - 38

Mirror

Ace Shower Door Co. Inc., 2 - 1
American Glass & Mirror Corp., 3 - 6
Architectural Antique Warehouse, 3 - 9
Artesanos Imports, Inc., 6 - 6
Basco, 2 - 2
Bevel Glass & Mirror, 4 - 2
Bones Creek Designs, 8 - 11
CW Design Inc., 3 - 18
Canner Inc., 8 - 13
Carlos Shower Doors Inc., 2 - 3
Catalano & Sons, Inc., 8 - 15
Cox Studios, 12 - 7
Curran Glass & Mirror Co., 3 - 28
DAB Studio, 12 - 8
DeAurora Showrooms Inc., 1 - 14
Doors, Inc., 6 - 24
Fleurco Industries 1963 Ltd., 10 - 4
Golden Gate Glass & Mirror Co.,Inc., 12 - 10
Hannah Wingate House, 8 - 32
Hoyne Industries, 8 - 34
Ideal Glass & Mirror Makers, Ltd., 8 - 35
Karl Mann International, 8 - 39
La Barge Mirrors, Inc., 8 - 41
Lenoir Mirror Co., 8 - 42
Mark Dahlman Wood Products, 6 - 49
Melbourne Hall Workshop, 10 - 7
Messer Industries, Inc., 8 - 45
Minton Corley Collection, 3 - 61
Mirroline Design Ltd., 6 - 53

The Complete Sourcebook

Mixer – Moulding

Index

Mirror Fair, 8 - 47
Mirror-Tech Mfg. Co., Inc., 8 - 47
National Assoc. of Mirror Manufacturers,8- 48
National Products Inc., 8 - 48
Pompei & Company Art Glass, 12 - 20
Queen City Glass Ltd., 8 - 54
Ravenglass Pty. Ltd., 8 - 55
Sharon Concepts, Inc., 8 - 60
Spiegelwerk Wilsdruff GmbH, 3 - 81
U.S. Precision Glass, 8 - 70
Virginia Mirror Co. Inc., 8 - 72
Wing Industries Inc., 4 - 18

Mixer

(Bathroom, etc.)

Astracast Products PLC, 12 - 4
Barber Wilsons & Co. Ltd., 2 - 2
Carron Phoenix Ltd., 10 - 3
Hans Grohe Ltd., 2 - 5
Meynell Valves Ltd., 2 - 7
Trevi Showers, 2 - 11

Modern

Classic Designs, 12 - 6
Genada Imports, 6 - 31
Herwig Lighting Inc., 11 - 15
South Beach Furniture Company, 6 - 70

Mosaic

Bellegrove Ceramics Ltd., 3 - 13
Bisazza Mosaico S.P.A., 3 - 15
Ceramica Del Conca S.P.A., 3 - 22
Ceramica Panaria S.P.A., 3 - 22
Ceramiche Atlas Concorde S.P.A., 3 - 22
Ceramografia Artigiana S.P.A., 3 - 23
Designer Ceramics, 3 - 30
Focus Ceramics Ltd., 3 - 37
National Ceramics, 3 - 63
Swedecor Ltd., 3 - 85
Tile with Style, 3 - 91

Moulding

A.E. Gombert Lumber Co., 3 - 1
ACCRA Wood Products Ltd., 1 - 1
Abitibi-Price, 1 - 2
Accents In Stone, 3 - 3
Alpine Moulding, 1 - 3
Aluma Trim, 1 - 3
American Architectural Art Company, 1 - 3
American Custom Millwork Inc., 1 - 3
American Millwork Inc., 1 - 3
American Moulding & Millwork Co., 1 - 3
American Wood Column Corp., 1 - 4
Amherst Woodworking & Supply Inc., 1 - 4
Andrews Custom Woodworking, 1 - 4
Apex Gutter Systems Ltd., 3 - 8
Architectural Components, 1 - 5
Architectural Timber & Millwork, 1 - 6
Armstrong World Industries Inc., 1 - 6
Arvid's Historic Woods, 1 - 7
Ballard Designs, 1 - 8
Barnett Millworks, Inc., 1 - 8
Bassett & Findley Ltd., 4 - 2
Bendix Mouldings, 1 - 8
Best Moulding Corporation, 1 - 8
Bill Koehler Co., 3 - 15
Boise Moulding & Lumber, 3 - 15
Booth-Muirie Ltd., 1 - 8
Bright Wood Corp., 1 - 9
Brill & Walker Associates Inc., 1 - 9
Browne Winther & Co. Ltd., 1 - 9

Burt Millwork Corp., 1 - 9
C. G. Girolami & Sons, 1 - 9
CMF Colonial Moulding, 1 - 9
Canner Inc., 8 - 13
Cape May Millworks, 1 - 10
Center Lumber Company, 1 - 10
Classic Ceilings, 1 - 11
Classic Mouldings Inc., 1 - 11
Clifton Moulding Corporation, 1 - 11
Coastal Millworks Inc., 1 - 11
Collingdale Millwork Co., 1 - 11
Consolidated Pine, Inc., 1 - 11
Contact Lumber Company, 3 - 27
Country Wood Products Inc., 1 - 12
Crown Plastering, 1 - 12
Cumberland Lumber & Manufacturing, 5 - 3
Cumberland Woodcraft Co., 1 - 13
Curvoflite Inc., 1 - 13
Custom Decorative Mouldings, 1 - 13
Custom Wood Turnings, 1 - 13
DeAurora Showrooms Inc., 1 - 14
Defiance Forest Products, 4 - 4
Dimension Lumber & Milling, 1 - 14
Diversified Millwork, 1 - 14
Double D Mouldings Inc., 1 - 15
Driwood Moulding Co., 8 - 24
Drummond Woodworks, 1 - 15
Duke City Moulding Company, 1 - 15
Eaton-Gaze Ltd., 1 - 15
Empire Moulding Co., 1 - 15
Entol Industries, 1 - 16
Eric Schuster Corp., 1 - 16
Evergreen Lumber and Molding, 3 - 34
Executive Woodsmiths Inc., 1 - 16
Federal Millwork Corp., 1 - 16
Fibreboard Box & Millwork Corp., 3 - 36
Fischer & Jirouch Company, 1 - 16
Florida Wood Moulding & Trim, 1 - 17
Foreign & Domestic Woods, Inc., 1 - 17
Forester Moulding & Lumber, 1 - 17
Frederick Wilbur, Carver, 1 - 17
Fypon Molded Millwork, 1 - 17
Geneva Designs, 1 - 18
Gibco Services Inc., 1 - 18
Glazing Products Corp., 1 - 18
Gossen Corp., 1 - 18
Haas Woodworking Company Inc., 1 - 19
Hallidays America Inc., 1 - 19
Hampton Decor, 1 - 19
Hardware + Plus Inc., 3 - 44
Hendricks Woodworking, 4 - 9
Heritage Hardwoods, 1 - 19
Hodkin & Jones (Sheffield) Ltd., 3 - 46
Hoff Forest Products, Inc., 3 - 46
House of Fara Inc., 3 - 47
House of Moulding, 1 - 20
Hyde Park Fine Art of Mouldings, 1 - 20
Irreplaceable Artifacts, 1 - 20
Janik Custom Millwork, 12 - 12
Kirby Millworks, 4 - 10
Lamb Flooring & Trim Co., 5 - 6
Larkin Company, 1 - 22
Lianga Pacific, Inc., 1 - 22
Lynn Lumber Company, 1 - 22
M. L. Condon Company Inc., 3 - 56
MacBeath Hardwood Co., 1 - 22
Mad River Woodworks, 1 - 22
Madison Flooring Company, 5 - 6
Magnet Trade, 4 - 11
Marjam Supply Company, 3 - 58
Marley Mouldings, 1 - 23

Index - 60

The Complete Sourcebook

Index

Mural – Niche

Master Woodcarver, 6 - 50
Maurer & Shepherd Joyners Inc., 1 - 23
McDan Woodworking, 1 - 23
Medallion Millwork, Inc., 1 - 23
Medford Moulding Company, 1 - 23
Mercer Products Co., 1 - 23
Michael Farr Custom Woodworking,1 - 24
Michael's Fine Colonial Products, 1 - 24
Miller & Company, Inc., 5 - 7
Millwork Supply Company, 4 - 12
Mitchell Moulding Co., 1 - 24
Moorwood, 1 - 24
Mountain Lumber Co., 5 - 7
Mt. Taylor Millwork, Inc., 1 - 24
Myro Inc., 1 - 24
NMC Focal Point, 1 - 24
Nashotah Moulding Co., Inc., 1 - 24
National Forest Products, 1 - 25
Navajo Forest Products Ind., 1 - 25
New England Hardwood Supply Co., 5 - 7
Nor-Cal Moulding Company, 1 - 25
Nord Company, 4 - 12
Northern Moulding Co., 1 - 25
Nose Creek Forest Products, Ltd., 1 - 25
Oakwood Classic & Custom Woodwork,1- 25
Old World Moulding & Finishing Co., 1 - 26
Oregon Fir Millwork, Inc., 1 - 26
Ornamental Mouldings, 1 - 26
Ornamental Mouldings, Ltd., 1 - 26
Ostermann & Scheiwe, USA, Inc., 1 - 26
Outwater Plastic Industries, 1 - 26
P. W. Plumly Lumber Corporation, 1 - 26
Partelow Custom Wood Turnings, 1 - 27
Perkins Architectural Millwork, 1 - 27
Pine Plains Woodworking Inc., 5 - 8
Pittcon Industries Inc., 1 - 27
Ponderosa Mouldings, 1 - 27
Port-O-Lite Corporation, 1 - 28
R & R Lumber & Building Supply Corp.,1 - 28
Raymond Enkeboll Designs, 1 - 28
Reliance Industries Inc., 1 - 29
Replico Products Inc., 1 - 29
Richard Burbidge Ltd., 3 - 75
River City Woodworks, 5 - 8
Riverview Millworks Inc., 1 - 29
Roberts Consolidated, 1 - 29
Robillard, 1 - 29
Rocky Mountain Forest Products, 1 - 29
Rogue River Millwork, 1 - 30
Sacramento Valley Moulding Co., 1 - 30
San Francisco Victoriana, 1 - 30
Schlesser Co., Inc., 1 - 30
Seneca Millwork Inc., 1 - 31
Setzer Forest Products, 3 - 78
Sheppard Millwork, Inc., 4 - 15
Sierra Pacific Industries Millwork Div., 1 - 31
Silverton Victorian Millworks, 1 - 31
Smith Millwork, Inc., 1 - 31
Southern Millwork, Inc., 1 - 31
Sovereign Group Ltd., 4 - 15
Spokane Moulding Corp., 6 - 70
Style-Mark, Inc., 1 - 33
Sunset Moulding Co., 1 - 33
Sunshine Woodworks, 1 - 33
Superior Architectural Cornices, 1 - 33
Swish Products Ltd., 4 - 16
Tafcor Inc., 1 - 33
Tallahassee Mouldings & Millwork, 1 - 33
Tennessee Moulding & Frame Inc., 1 - 33
Tewa Moulding Corporation, 1 - 34
The Balmer Studios Inc., 1 - 34

The Dorris Lumber & Moulding Co., 3 - 88
The James Wood Company, 1 - 34
The Joinery Company, 5 - 10
The Smoot Lumber Co., 4 - 17
The Wood Factory, 1 - 35
The Woods Company, 5 - 10
Thunderbird Moulding Company, 1 - 35
Trimcraft Inc., 1 - 35 , 3 - 91
Valley Mouldings Inc., 1 - 36
Van Dyke's Restorers, 3 - 94
Victorian Interiors, 8 - 72
Vintage Wood Works, 1 - 36
Visador Co., 1 - 36
Walter H. Weaber Sons, Inc., 1 - 36
Western Moulding Company, Inc., 1 - 37
Williams & Hussey Machine Co. Inc., 1 - 37
Willis Lumber Company Inc., 1 - 37
Windham Millwork Inc., 1 - 37
Windsor Mill, Inc., 1 - 37
Winther Browne, 3 - 99
Wood World, 3 - 100
Woodcrafters Supply, 3 - 100
Woods American, 5 - 11
Worthington Group, Ltd., 1 - 38
Yakima Manufacturing Co., 1 - 38
Yellowstone Woodworks, 1 - 38
Yuba River Moulding & Millwork, Inc., 1 - 38

Mural

Arius Tile Co., 3 - 9
Artistic Surfaces, 8 - 6
La Luz Canyon Studio, 3 - 53

Natural

(Granite, Marble, Stone, etc.)

A/S Johs. Gronseth & Co., 3 - 2
ABN, 1 - 1
Ashfield Stone Quarry, 3 - 9
Assimagra, 3 - 10
Assomarmi, 3 - 10
Carl Schilling Stoneworks, 3 - 20
Deutscher Naturwerstein, 3 - 31
FBAMTP, 3 - 35
FFPM, 3 - 35
FNMMB, 3 - 35
Idaho Quartzite Corp., 3 - 49
Johnston & Rhodes Bluestone Co., 3 - 51
National Association of Master Masons,3 - 63
Panhellenic Marble Association, 3 - 68
Pasvalco, 3 - 68
Stenindustriens Landssammenslutning,3 - 82
Stone Federation, 3 - 83
Stone Products Corporation, 3 - 83
Sveriges Stenindustriforbund, 3 - 85
UCSMB, 3 - 93
UGIMA, 3 - 93

Navajo

Honani Crafts, 8 - 34
Navajo Arts & Crafts Guild, 8 - 48
Peerless Imported Rugs, 8 - 52

Niche

Flex Trim, 12 - 9
Felber Ornamental Plaster Corp., 1 - 16
Fischer & Jirouch Company, 1 - 16
Outwater Plastic Industries, 1 - 26

The Complete Sourcebook

Oak – Oriental

Oak

(Cabinets, Doors, Flooring, Furniture, Moulding, etc.)

ACCRA Wood Products Ltd., 1 - 1
Acorn Antique Doors, 4 - 1
Adirondacks Store & Gallery, 6 - 3
American Starbuck, 6 - 4
Anger Mfg. Co., Inc., 6 - 4
Arkansas Oak Flooring Co., 5 - 1
B.A. Mullican Lumber & Manufacturing, 5 - 1
BRE Lumber, 3 - 11
Bangkok International, 5 - 2
Bennett Industries Inc., 4 - 2
Best Moulding Corporation, 1 - 8
Blackwelder's Industries, Inc., 6 - 9
Boen Hardwood Flooring, 5 - 2
Burcham Furniture Manufacturing, 6 - 13
Butcher Block & More Furniture, 6 - 13
Cabinet Crafters, 10 - 2
Caldwell Chair Company, 6 - 13
Cardell Cabinets, 10 - 3
Cascade Wood Products Inc., 1 - 10
Centre Mills Antique Floors & Beams, 5 - 2
Craftsman Lumber Co., 5 - 3
Creative Structures, 3 - 27
DeSoto Hardwood Flooring Company, 5 - 3
Deacon & Sandys, 6 - 22
Dixon Lumber Company, 5 - 3
Doors, Inc., 6 - 24
Driwood Moulding Co., 8 - 24
E. F. Bufton & Son Builders, 1 - 15
EDLCO, 3 - 33
Elk Valley Woodworking Inc., 6 - 26
Evergreen Lumber and Molding, 3 - 34
Guy Vincent Custom Furniture & Crafts, 6 - 33
Habersham Plantation Corp., 6 - 33
Heritage Hardwoods, 1 - 19
I. F. M. Co. Ltd., 10 - 5
Jones' Oak Furniture, 6 - 41
Kirby Millworks, 4 - 10
L & J.G. Stickley, Inc., 6 - 43
Lebanon Oak Flooring, 5 - 6
Lianga Pacific, Inc., 1 - 22
Linden Lumber Company, 5 - 6
Livermore Wood Floors, 5 - 6
Maple Grove Restorations, 1 - 22
Mark Dahlman Wood Products, 6 - 49
Maurice L. Condon Co., 3 - 59
McMinnville Manufacturing Co., 5 - 6
Memphis Hardwood Flooring Co., 5 - 7
Midwest Dowel Works, Inc., 3 - 60
Miller & Company, Inc., 5 - 7
Missouri Floor Co., 5 - 7
Missouri Hardwood Flooring Co., 5 - 7
Monticello Flooring & Lumber Co., 5 - 7
Mt. Taylor Millwork, Inc., 1 - 24
Mylen, 1 - 24
North Fields Restorations, 3 - 65
Oak Craft Inc., 6 - 56
Olde South Door, 4 - 13
Osborne Wood Products Inc., 6 - 57
P. W. Plumly Lumber Corporation, 1 - 26
Partee Flooring Mill, 5 - 8
Plain and Fancy Kitchens, 10 - 8
Potlatch Corporation, 5 - 8
Rackstraw Ltd., 6 - 62
Rex Furniture Co. Inc., 6 - 63
River Bend Turnings, 1 - 29
Robbins Inc., 5 - 8

Rockford Mills Furniture Co., 6 - 64
Rural Hall Inc., 4 - 14
Salter Industries, 1 - 30
Searcy Flooring, Inc., 5 - 9
Shamokin Trail Shingle Co., 3 - 78
Sittin' Easy, 6 - 69
Smith Flooring, Inc., 5 - 9
Somerset Wood Products, Inc., 5 - 9
Southhampton Antiques, 6 - 70
Stair-Pak Products Co. Inc., 1 - 32
Tewa Moulding Corporation, 1 - 34
The Burruss Company, 5 - 10
The Iron Shop, 1 - 34
The London Door Company, 4 - 17
The Natural Woodflooring Company, 5 - 10
Thomas H. Kramer Inc., 6 - 77
Thompson Oak Flooring Co., 5 - 10
Treework Services Ltd., 5 - 10
Vintage Lumber & Construction Co., 5 - 11
Walter H. Weaber Sons, Inc., 1 - 36
Wheeler Woodworking, 6 - 83
Woodcraft Design, 6 - 85
Woodhouse, 5 - 11
Wren House Furniture, 6 - 86
Wylder Furniture Manufacturing, 6 - 86
York Spiral Stairs, 1 - 38
Zickgraf Hardwood Company, 5 - 11

Occasional

(Furniture, etc.)

Butler Specialty Co., 6 - 13

Oil

Beckett, R.W. Corp., 3 - 13

Onyx

Colonial Marble Products Ltd., 3 - 25
Marble Institute of America, 3 - 57
Mayan Marble & Onyx Ltd., 6 - 51
Puccio Marble & Onyx, 3 - 72

Organizer

American Storage Systems, 8 - 4
Aristokraft, 10 - 1
California Closet Company, 8 - 13
Closet Shop at Home, 8 - 17
Closet Systems Corp., 8 - 17
The Hanging Kitchen Co., 10 - 9

Oriental

A Candle In The Night, 5 - 1
Abrahams Oriental Rugs, 8 - 2
Adac. Rugs & Treasures, 8 - 2
Alex Cooper Oriental Rugs, 8 - 3
Arthur Gregorian, 8 - 5
Azar's Oriental Rugs, 8 - 7
Boswell Roberts Gardens, 7 - 1
Charles W. Jacobsen, Inc., 8 - 16
Claremont Rug Company, 8 - 17
Dana Kelly Oriental Rugs, 8 - 21
Emmet Perry & Co., 8 - 25
Frances Lee Jasper Oriental Rugs, 8 - 29
Fred Moheban Gallery, 8 - 29
House of Persia, 8 - 34
Houston Oriental Rug Gallery, 8 - 34
International Rug Source Ltd., 8 - 36
Jacqueline Vance Oriental Rugs, 8 - 37
John Aga Oriental Rugs, 8 - 38
Kamali Oriental Rugs, 8 - 39
Kaoud Oriental Rugs, 8 - 39
Kelaty International Inc., 8 - 39

Index - 62

The Complete Sourcebook

Index

Ornament — Outdoor

Moattar Ltd., 8 - 47
National Carpet, 8 - 48
Omega Rug Works, 8 - 50
Oriental Rug Outlet Inc., 8 - 51
Pace-Stone, 8 - 51
Peerless Imported Rugs, 8 - 52
Persian Galleries, 8 - 53
Rastetter Woolen Mill, 8 - 55
Sandler & Worth, 8 - 58
Santa Fe Oriental Rugs, 8 - 58
Talebloo Oriental Rugs, 3 - 86
The Oriental Rug Co., 8 - 67
Tianjin-Philadelphia Carpet Co., 8 - 68
Trocadero Textile Art, 8 - 70
W. Hirsch Oriental Rugs, 8 - 73
Werco Persian & Oriental Rugs, 6 - 82
Western Plaza, 8 - 75
Zaven A. Kish Oriental Rug Gallery, 8 - 78

Ornament

Acrylic Innovations Inc., 6 - 2
Adornments for Architecture, 1 - 2
Allied Bronze Corp., 1 - 3
American Architectural Art Company, 1 - 3
Anything Fiberglass, 1 - 4
C. G. Girolami & Sons, 1 - 9
Classic Architectural Specialties, 1 - 10
Classic Mouldings Inc., 1 - 11
Constantine's, 1 - 12
Crown Plastering, 1 - 12
Decorative Plaster Supply Co., 1 - 14
Decorators Supply Corp., 1 - 14
Dimitrios Klitsas, 1 - 14
Entol Industries, 1 - 16
Felber Ornamental Plastering Corp., 1 - 16
Fischer & Jirouch Company, 1 - 16
Gotham Inc., 1 - 18
Haddonstone USA Ltd., 7 - 3
Hampton Decor, 1 - 19
Heritage Woodcraft, 1 - 20
Ives Weathervanes, 7 - 3
J. A. du Lac Company, 1 - 20
J. P. Weaver Co., 1 - 21
Mad River Woodworks, 1 - 22
Maine Architectural Millwork, Inc., 1 - 22
New England Tool Company, 3 - 64
Newman Brothers Inc., 1 - 25
Ole Fashion Things, 2 - 8
Omega Too, 2 - 8
Ornamental Mouldings, Ltd., 1 - 26
Outwater Plastic Industries, 1 - 26
Ralph H. Simpson Co., 1 - 28
Raymond Enkeboll Designs, 1 - 28
Replico Products Inc., 1 - 29
Ritter & Son Hardware, 3 - 76
San Francisco Victoriana, 1 - 30
Staloton - Die keramiker H.H., 3 - 82
Stone Forest, 7 - 6
The Balmer Studios Inc., 1 - 34
W. F. Norman Corporation, 1 - 36
Wind & Weather, 7 - 8
Wohners Inc., 1 - 37

Ornamental

Leslie-Locke Inc., 3 - 55
Schoenherr Iron Work, 1 - 30

Ottoman

Acme Furniture Mfg. Inc., 6 - 2
Barnes & Barnes, 6 - 8
Essential Items, 6 - 27

Hunt Galleries, Inc., 6 - 38
Larkspur Furniture Co., 6 - 44
Sheffield Chair Co., 6 - 68

Outdoor

(Furniture, Lighting, etc.)

A K Exteriors, 6 - 1
ARM Industries Inc., 6 - 1
Aberdeen Mfg. Corp., 8 - 2
Adirondack Designs, 6 - 3
Adirondacks Store & Gallery, 6 - 3
Alfresco Porch Swing Company, 6 - 3
All Island Security Inc., 9 - 1
All-Lighting, 11 - 2
Allibert, 6 - 3
Antique Street Lamps Inc., 11 - 2
Banana River Open Air Furniture, 6 - 7
Barlow Tyrie, 6 - 8
Basta Sole, 7 - 1
Blake Industries, 6 - 10
Boswell Roberts Gardens, 7 - 1
British-American Marketing Services, 6 - 12
Brown Jordon Furniture, 6 - 12
Budoff Outdoor Furniture, 6 - 12
Burle Industries, Inc., 9 - 1
Catherine Ann Furnishings, 6 - 15
Cedar Design Ltd., 6 - 15
Ciro Coppa, 6 - 16
Clapper's, 6 - 16
Coppa Woodworking, 6 - 18
Country Casual, 6 - 19
Cypress Street Center, 6 - 20
Dan Wilson & Company, 6 - 21
ELA Custom & Architectural Co., 11 - 10
Elm Industries, 6 - 26
Falcon Eye Inc., 9 - 2
Finkel Outdoors Products Inc., 6 - 28
Flanders Industries Inc., 6 - 28
Garden Source Furnishings, Inc., 7 - 2
Green Enterprises, 6 - 33
Halo Lighting Products/Cooper Ind., 11 - 14
Hedstrom Corp., 6 - 34
Hinkley Lighting, 11 - 15
Holiday Pool & Patio, 6 - 36
Home Decorators Collection, 11 - 15
Home Equipment Mfg.,Co., 11 - 16
Homecrest Industries, Inc., 6 - 36
Horchow Home Collection, 6 - 36
Hubbell Lighting Inc., 11 - 16
Indian Ocean Trading Co., 6 - 38
Irving & Jones Fine Gardeb Furnishings,6-39
Ives Weathervanes, 7 - 3
Juno Lighting, Inc., 11 - 18
Kenneth D. Lynch & Sons, Inc., 6 - 41
Kingsley-Bate, Ltd., 6 - 42
Kloter Farms Inc., 7 - 4
Landscape Forms Inc., 7 - 4
Larkspur Furniture Co., 6 - 44
Leviton Manufacturing Company, 11 - 20
Lister Teak, Inc., 6 - 46
Lloyd/Flanders, 6 - 47
Luma Lighting Industries, Inc., 11 - 20
Macon Umbrella Corp., 6 - 47
Main Street Lighting, 11 - 21
Mayhew, 6 - 51
Metropolitan Ceramics, 8 - 46
Moultrie Manufacturing Co., 6 - 54
NuMerit Electrical Supply, 11 - 24
O.W. Lee Co., Inc., 6 - 56
Oakline Chair Co. Inc., 6 - 56

The Complete Sourcebook

Index - 63

Overhead – Panel

Index

Oryx Trading Ltd., 7 - 5
Ozark Wood Products, 6 - 58
O'Connor's Cypress Woodworks, 6 - 56
Park Place, 6 - 58
Peterson Wood Div., 7 - 5
Pipe Casual, 6 - 60
Plow & Hearth, 7 - 5
Pompeii, 6 - 60
Quality Imports, 7 - 5
R & R Crafts, 7 - 5
Reed Bros., 3 - 74
Regent Lighting Corp., 11 - 26
Remcraft Lighting Products, 11 - 26
Ritter & Son Hardware, 3 - 76
Robert's, 6 - 64
Rubbermaid-Allibert Contract, 6 - 65
Santa Fe Lights, 11 - 28
Sarita Furniture, 6 - 66
Selzer Enterprises Inc., 6 - 67
Sittin' Easy, 6 - 69
Smith & Hawken, 6 - 69
Sternberg Lanterns Inc., 11 - 30
Stone Forest, 7 - 6
Stonehaven, 7 - 6
Stuckey Brothers Furniture Co., Inc., 6 - 72
Summit Furniture, 6 - 73
Sunelco, 3 - 84
Syracuse Pottery, 8 - 65
Telescope Casual Furniture, 6 - 74
Tennessee Fabricating Co., 6 - 74
TerraCast, 7 - 7
Terradek Industries, 11 - 31
Texacraft Outdoor Furnishings, 6 - 74
The Blacksmiths Shop, 6 - 74
The C.S. Bell Co., 11 - 31
The Furniture Patch, 6 - 75
The Golden Rabbit, 6 - 75
The Heveningham Collection, 6 - 75
The Marle Company, 11 - 32
The Patio, 6 - 76
The Victorian Merchant, 6 - 77
Tidewater Workshop, 6 - 78
Toro Woodlights, 11 - 33
Trainor Metal Products Co., 6 - 78
Treasure Garden Inc., 6 - 78
Tropitone, 6 - 79
Twin Oaks Hammocks, 7 - 7
Van Liew's, 12 - 26
Victor Stanley, 6 - 80
Victorian Attic, 6 - 80
Vision Security Inc., 9 - 3
Walpole Woodworkers, 6 - 81
Weatherend Estate Furniture, 6 - 82
Welsbach, 11 - 35
Wood Classics, 6 - 85
Woodnorth, 7 - 8
Yardlighting Systems Inc., 11 - 36

Overhead

(Garage Doors, etc.)

Hazelmere Industries Ltd., 4 - 8
Ideal Door Co., 4 - 9

Paint

Aexcel Corp., 3 - 4
Allentown Paint Division, 3 - 5
Bay City Paint Company, 3 - 12
Behr Process Corp., 3 - 13
Bel-Mar Paint Corp., 3 - 13
Color Your World Inc., 8 - 18
Cook & Dunn Paint Corp., 3 - 27

Duncan Enterprises, 3 - 32
Dunn-Edwards Corp., 8 - 24
Duron Paints & Wallcoverings, 8 - 24
Fine Paints of Europe, 3 - 36
Fuller O'Brien Paints, 3 - 38
Historic Paints Ltd., 3 - 46
Homestead Paint & Finishes, 3 - 47
Johnson Paint Co. Inc., 3 - 50
M.A. Bruder & Sons Inc., 8 - 43
Martin-Senour Paints, 3 - 58
Morris Paint & Varnish Co., 3 - 62
Murmac Paint Mfg. Co., 3 - 62
Mutual Wallpaper & Paint Co., Inc., 8 - 48
Nonweiler Co., 3 - 64
Old Fashioned Milk Paint Co., 3 - 66
Old Western Paint Co. Inc., 6 - 56
Ole Country Barn, 3 - 66
Parks Corporation, 3 - 68
Pintchik Homeworks, 8 - 53
Porter Paints, 3 - 71
Pratt & Lambert, 3 - 71
Primrose Distributing, 3 - 71
Standard Brands Paint Co., 3 - 82
Standard Paint Co., 3 - 82
Stulb's Old Village Paints, 3 - 83
The 3E Group Inc., 3 - 87
The Color People, 1 - 34
The Muralo Company Inc., 3 - 88
The Natural Choice Catalog, 3-88
The Stulb Company, 3 - 89
Waterlox Chemical & Coating Corp., 3 - 96
Wm. Zinsser & Co. Inc., 3 - 100

Painted

(Floorcloths, Furniture, Tile, etc.)

Amsterdam Corporation, 3 - 7
Artistic Surfaces, 8 - 6
Blackland Moravian Tile Works, 3 - 15
Firebird Inc., 3 - 36
Floorcloths, 8 - 28
Frederick Cooper Inc., 11 - 12
John Minter Furniture Ltd., 6 - 40
R. Wagner Company, 6 - 61
San Do Designs, 3 - 77
Terra Designs, Inc., 3 - 87
Timeless Design, Inc., 8 - 69
Wirth-Salander Studios, 2 - 13

Panel

American Moulding & Millwork Co., 1 - 3
Apache Building Products, 1 - 4
Armstar, 3 - 9
Armstrong World Industries Inc., 1 - 6
Barrel Builders, 3 - 12
Booth-Muirie Ltd., 1 - 8
Cardell Cabinets, 10 - 3
Country Accents, 12 - 7
Cox Studios, 12 - 7
Crockett Log & Timber Frame Homes, 1 - 12
Cross Industries, 3 - 28
Cumberland Woodcraft Co., 1 - 13
Customwood Mfg. Co., 1 - 13
Dimitrios Klitsas, 1 - 14
Driwood Moulding Co., 8 - 24
Electric Glass Co., 3 - 33
Feather River Wood & Glass Co., 4 - 7
Garofalo Studio, 2 - 5
Granitech Corp., 3 - 41
Hyde Park Raised Panel, 1 - 20
Jali Ltd., 3 - 50
Kaylien, 4 - 10

Index - 64

The Complete Sourcebook

Index

Paneled – Pine

Maple Grove Restorations, 1 - 22
Maurer & Shepherd Joyners Inc., 1 - 23
McDan Woodworking, 1 - 23
Michael Farr Custom Woodworking,Inc., 1 - 24
Midwestern Wood Products, 1 - 24
Milano Marble Co., Inc., 2 - 7
Nailite International Inc., 3 - 63
Pittcon Industries Inc., 1 - 27
South & Sons Panels Inc., 3 - 80
Stained Glass Associates, 12 - 24
States Industries Inc., 1 - 32
Sunburst Stained Glass Co. Inc., 3 - 84
Urban Glassworks, 3 - 94

Paneled

Bennett Industries Inc., 4 - 2
Temple Products, Inc., 4 - 16

Paneling

A.E. Gombert Lumber Co., 3 - 1
Adelmann & Clark Inc., 3 - 4
Albany Woodworks Inc., 3 - 5
Amherst Woodworking & Supply Inc., 1 - 4
Anthony Forest Product Co., 3 - 8
Architectural Heritage, 1 - 6
Architectural Paneling, 1 - 6
California Redwood Association, 3 - 19
Conservation Building Products Ltd., 3 - 26
Craftsman Lumber Co., 5 - 3
Curvoflite Inc., 1 - 13
Deacon & Sandys, 6 - 22
Georgia Pacific Corp., 3 - 40
Goodwin Lumber, 3 - 41
Hardwood Flooring & Paneling Inc., 5 - 4
Harmony Exchange, 5 - 5
Kakabeka Timber Ltd., 3 - 51
Marble Technics Ltd., 3 - 58
Mill & Timber Products, Ltd., 3 - 60
Northern Moulding Co., 1 - 25
Old World Moulding & Finishing Co., 1 - 26
Ply-Gem Mfg., 3 - 70
Potlatch Corporation, 5 - 8
Pukall Lumber Co., 3 - 72
Sunshine Woodworks, 1 - 33
The James Wood Company, 1 - 34
The Kennebec Company, 10 - 10
Willis Lumber Company Inc., 1 - 37
Woods American, 5 - 11
Woodstock Furniture Ltd., 6 - 86

Parts

(Stairs, etc.)

Adams Stair Works Carpentry Inc., 3 - 4
Custom Woodturnings, 1 - 13
Perkins Architectural Millwork, 1 - 27
River City Woodworks, 5 - 8

Patio

(Covers, Doors, Furniture, etc.)

AAA Aluminum Products Ltd., 3 - 2
Accurate Aluminum Products, Inc., 3 - 3
Alumaroll Specialty Co., Inc., 12 - 3
Ashfield Stone Quarry, 3 - 9
Basta Sole, 7 - 1
Boswell Roberts Gardens, 7 - 1
Caradco, 12 - 6
Cedar Design Ltd., 6 - 15
Concrete Technology Inc., 3 - 26
Crestline, 4 - 4

Eagle Window & Door, 12 - 8
Flanders Industries Inc., 6 - 28
Four Seasons, 3 - 38
Glen Raven Mills Inc., 3 - 40
Hurd Millwork Company, 3 - 48
Inter Trade Inc., 12 - 12
J. W. Window Components, Inc., 12 - 12
Louisiana-Pacific Corporation, 3 - 56
Newpro, 12 - 17
Norco Windows Inc., 12 - 18
North American Stone Co. Ltd., 3 - 64
Nu-Air Mfg. Co., 4 - 13
Oryx Trading Ltd., 7 - 5
Pacesetter Building Systems, 12 - 19
Roddiscraft Inc., 12 - 22
Taylor Building Products, 4 - 16
Trainor Metal Products Co., 6 - 78
Treasure Garden Inc., 6 - 78

Pencil Post Beds

American Starbuck, 6 - 4
Hollingsworth, 6 - 36
Kopil & Associates Timeless Furniture, 6 - 43
Norman's Handmade Reproductions, 6 - 55
Osborne Wood Products Inc., 6 - 57
The Bed Factory, 6 - 74

Persian

Adac. Rugs & Treasures, 8 - 2
House of Persia, 8 - 34
Persian Gallery Company Inc., 8 - 53
Werco Persian & Oriental Rugs, 6 - 82
Western Plaza, 8 - 75

Picture Frame

Designer's Edge, 8 - 23

Pillow

Barnett Products Co., 6 - 8
Brentwood Originals, 8 - 12
Ruth's Custom Bedspreads, 8 - 57
Sentimental Journey, 8 - 59
The Gazebo of New York, 8 - 67
Treasured Weavings, 8 - 69

Pine

(Cabinets, Doors, Flooring, Furniture, Moulding, etc.)

A.E. Gombert Lumber Co., 3 - 1
Acorn Antique Doors, 4 - 1
Aged Woods, 5 - 1
Albany Woodworks Inc., 3 - 5
American Moulding & Millwork Co., 1 - 3
American Starbuck, 6 - 4
Antique Pine Co., 5 - 1
Arkansas Oak Flooring Co., 5 - 1
Authentic Pine Floors Inc., 5 - 1
Best Moulding Corporation, 1 - 8
Big Table Furniture, 6 - 9
Blackwelder's Industries, Inc., 6 - 9
Boen Hardwood Flooring, 5 - 2
Bright Wood Corp., 1 - 9
Broad-Axe Beam Co., 5 - 2
Burcham Furniture Manufacturing, Inc., 6 - 13
Cabin Creek Furniture, 6 - 13
Cabinet Crafters, 10 - 2
Carlisle Restoration Lumber, 5 - 2
Centre Mills Antique Floors & Beams, 5 - 2
Consolidated Pine, Inc., 1 - 11
Contact Lumber Company, 3 - 27
Corning Moulding Corporation, 1 - 12

Country Pine Furniture, 6 - 19
Craftsman Lumber Co., 5 - 3
Duke City Moulding Company, 1 - 15
E. T. Moore Company, 5 - 4
Elk Valley Woodworking Inc., 6 - 26
Evergreen Lumber and Molding, 3 - 34
Gilchrist Timber Co., 3 - 40
Goodwin Lumber, 3 - 41
Habersham Plantation Corp., 6 - 33
J. L. Powell & Company Inc., 5 - 5
Liberty Hall, 6 - 46
Linden Lumber Company, 5 - 6
Livermore Wood Floors, 5 - 6
Maple Grove Restorations, 1 - 22
Medallion Millwork, Inc., 1 - 23
Medford Moulding Company, 1 - 23
Mountain Lumber Co., 5 - 7
Mt. Taylor Millwork, Inc., 1 - 24
Navajo Forest Products Ind., 1 - 25
Nor-Cal Moulding Company, 1 - 25
Norman's Handmade Reproductions, 6 - 55
North Fields Restorations, 3 - 65
Osborne Wood Products Inc., 6 - 57
Outer Bank Pine Products, 6 - 57
Pine & Design Imports, 6 - 59
Pine Floors Inc., 5 - 8
Pine Products Corp., 3 - 70
Plain and Fancy Kitchens, 10 - 8
Ponderosa Mouldings, 1 - 27
River City Woodworks, 5 - 8
Rocky Mountain Forest Products, 1 - 29
Rogue River Millwork, 1 - 30
Sacramento Valley Moulding Co., 1 - 30
Strafford House, 6 - 72
Taos Furniture, 6 - 73
Tewa Moulding Corporation, 1 - 34
The Burruss Company, 5 - 10
The Joinery Company, 5 - 10
The Lenox Shop, 6 - 76 , 12 - 25
The London Door Company, 4 - 17
The Natural Woodflooring Company, 5 - 10
This End Up, 6 - 77
Thomas H. Kramer Inc., 6 - 77
Thunderbird Moulding Company, 1 - 35
Vintage Lumber & Construction Co., 5 - 11
Vintage Pine Company, 5 - 11
Wendover's Limited, 6 - 82
Western Moulding Company, Inc., 1 - 37
Woodhouse, 5 - 11

Pipe

Heat-Fab Inc., 3 - 44

Placemat

Family Heir-Loom Weavers, 8 - 27

Planter

A. J. Munzinger & Co., 7 - 1
Adirondack Designs, 6 - 3
Brandon Industries Inc., 11 - 5
International Terra Cotta, 7 - 3
May Silk, 8 - 45
Nolarec Industries, Inc., 6 - 55
Prochnow & Prochnow, 7 - 5
Stonehaven, 7 - 6
Syracuse Pottery, 8 - 65
TerraCast, 7 - 7
The Old Wagon Factory, 4 - 17
Walpole Woodworkers, 6 - 81

Plaster

Charles Street Supply Co., 3 - 24
Classic Mouldings Inc., 1 - 11
Eaton-Gaze Ltd., 1 - 15
Fastenation, 1 - 16
Felber Ornamental Plastering Corp., 1 - 16
Fischer & Jirouch Company, 1 - 16
Superior Architectural Cornices, 1 - 33

Plate

(Switch, etc.)
Jackson Mfg. Co., 11 - 17
Pass & Seymour, 11 - 25
Classic Accents, 3 - 25

Plumbing

A-Ball Plumbing Supply, 2 - 1
AAA Plumbing Pottery Corp., 2 - 1
Absolute Bathroom Boutique, 3 - 3
Acme Plumbing Specialties, 3 - 3
Adkins Architectural Antiques, 1 - 2
Alro Plumbing Specialty Co. Inc., 3 - 5
American Brass Mfg., 10 - 1
American China, 3 - 6
Architectural Antique Warehouse, 3 - 9
Architectural Antiquities, 1 - 5
B. F. Gilmour Co., 3 - 11
Baja Products Ltd., 3 - 11
BathEase, 2 - 2
Beautyware Plumbing Products, 3 - 13
Bohemia Plumbing Supply Co. Inc., 3 - 15
Bootz Plumbingware, 3 - 16
Central Brass Mfg. Co., 3 - 21
Champion Irrigation Products, 3 - 23
Cisco, 3 - 24
Country Plumbing, 3 - 27
Crawford's Old House Store, 3 - 27
Crest/Good Mfg. Co., Inc., 3 - 28
De Best Mfg. Co., Inc., 3 - 30
Deutscher & Sons, Inc., 3 - 31
DuraGlaze Service Corp., 2 - 4
Freundlich Supply Co., 3 - 38
Genova Products, 3 - 39
Gerber Plumbing Fixtures Corp., 3 - 40
Hancock Gross Inc., 3 - 43
Hardware + Plus Inc., 3 - 44
Hippo Hardware & Trading Co., 3 - 46
Indiana Brass, 10 - 5
Jameco Industries Inc., 3 - 50
Kanebridge Corp., 3 - 51
Kohler Company, 12 - 14
Mac The Antique Plumber, 3 - 56
Mansfield Plumbing Products, 3 - 57
Manville Manufacturing Corporation, 3 - 57
Marque Enterprises, 3 - 58
Marsak Cohen, Cohen Corp., 3 - 58
Masco Corporation, 3 - 59
Minnco Inc., 3 - 61
Mutual Screw & Supply, 3 - 62
New York replacement Parts Corp., 12 - 17
Olderman Mfg. Corp., 3 - 66
Peerless Pottery, 3 - 69
Phylrich International, 2 - 8
Plumb-Craft Mfg., 3 - 70
Price Pfister Inc., 2 - 9
Re-Bath Corporation, 3 - 73
Restoration Works, 3 - 74
Richmond Foundry & Mfg. Co., 3 - 75
Rockford-Eclipse, 3 - 76

Index

Plywood – Pump

Royal Brass Mfg. Co., 3 - 76
Rubens & Locke, 3 - 76
SEPCO Industries Inc., 2 - 9
Santile International Corp., 3 - 77
Sayville Plumbing Go., 3 - 77
Sign of the Crab, 3 - 79
Sioux Chief Mfg. Co. Inc., 3 - 79
Stern-Williams Co. Inc., 3 - 82
Supply Line, 3 - 85
T & S Brass & Bronze Works Inc., 2 - 11
The Brass Finial, 11 - 31
The Fixture Exchange, 2 - 11
The Soft Bathtub Co., 2 - 11
Tub-Master Corp., 2 - 12
Ultraflo Corp., 3 - 93
Universal Rundle Corp., 3 - 94
Watco Mfg. Co., 3 - 96
Woodward-Wanger Co., 3 - 100
Wrightway Mfg. Co., 3 - 101

Plywood

A & M Wood Specialty Inc., 3 - 1
Aetna Plywood, Inc., 3 - 4
Bill Koehler Co., 3 - 15
Bridge Lumber Co., 3 - 17
Certainly Wood, 3 - 23
Champion International Corp., 3 - 23
EDLCO, 3 - 33
Florida Plywoods, Inc., 3 - 37
Georgia Pacific Corp., 3 - 40
Grant Plywood & Dimension Co., 3 - 42
Hartwood Ltd., 3 - 44
Hill & Lumber & Hardware Co., 1 - 20
Jasper Wood Products Co., Inc., 3 - 50
Levesque Plywood Ltd., 3 - 55
MacBeath Hardwood Co., 1 - 22
Marion Plywood Corp., 3 - 58
Maurice L. Condon Co., 3 - 59
Mount Baker Plywood Inc., 3 - 62
Ply-Gem Mfg., 3 - 70
Plywood Mfg. Of California Inc., 3 - 71
Richmond Plywood Corp., 3 - 75
The Plywood Depot, 3 - 89
United States Mahogany Corp., 3 - 94
Valley Planing Mill Inc., 1 - 36
White City Plywood Co., 3 - 98
Willamette Industries Inc., 3 - 99
Wood World, 3 - 100
Zeidler Forest Industries Ltd., 3 - 102

Ponds

(Plants, Water Gardens, etc.)

Dolphin Outdoors, 7 - 2
Kester's Wild Game Food Nurseries, 7 - 4
Lilypons Water Gardens, 7 - 4
Maryland Aquatic Nurseries, 7 - 4
Musser Forests, 7 - 4
Paradise Water Gardens, 7 - 5
S. Scherer & Sons, 7 - 6
Slocum Water Gardens, 7 - 6
Van Ness Water Gardens, 7 - 8
Water Works, 7 - 8
Waterford Gardens, 7 - 8
Wicklein's Aquatic Farm & Nursery, 7 - 8
William Tricker, Inc., 7 - 8

Porcelain

Cerim Ceramiche S.P.A., 3 - 23
Cisa-Cerdisa-Smov, 3 - 24
Cooperativa Ceramica D'Imola A.R.L., 3 - 27
Praire Marketing, 3 - 71

Rams Imports, 3 - 73
Santa Catalina, 3 - 77

Post

(Architectural, Beds, etc.)

A.F. Schwerd Manufacturing Co., 1 - 1
Abaroot Manufacturing Company, 1 - 2
American Starbuck, 6 - 4
Architectural Lathe & Mill, 1 - 6
Boston Turning Works, 1 - 8
Brandon Industries Inc., 11 - 5
Brown Moulding Company, 1 - 9
Bruce Post Company Inc., 3 - 17
Cider Hill Woodworks, 1 - 10
CinderWhit & Company, 1 - 10
Custom Wood Turnings, 1 - 13
Custom Woodturnings, 1 - 13
E. F. Bufton & Son Builders, 1 - 15
Haas Woodworking Company Inc., 1 - 19
Hollingsworth, 6 - 36
J. A. Dawley Fine Woodworking, 7 - 3
Jeffries Wood Works Inc., 1 - 21
Kaatskill Post & Beam, 1 - 21
Kings River Casting, 6 - 42
Kopil & Associates Timeless Furniture, 6 - 43
Main Street Lighting, 11 - 21
Mansion Industries, Inc., 8 - 44
Nord Company, 4 - 12
Norman's Handmade Reproductions, 6 - 55
Osborne Wood Products Inc., 6 - 57
Pacific Post & Beam, 3 - 68
Pagliacco Turning & Milling, 1 - 26
Partelow Custom Wood Turnings, 1 - 27
Raymond Enkeboll Designs, 1 - 28
Rich Woodturning Inc., 1 - 29
River Bend Turnings, 1 - 29
Rogue River Millwork, 1 - 30
Starling Inc., 1 - 32
Stuart Post & Lumber Co., 1 - 32
The Bed Factory, 6 - 74
Timberpeg, 1 - 35
Vintage Wood Works, 1 - 36
Walpole Woodworkers, 6 - 81
Welsbach, 11 - 35

Pottery

(Bathroom Fixtures, Indian, etc.)

Hopani Crafts, 8 - 34
Hopi Arts & Crafts, 8 - 34
House of Clay, 8 - 34
JMW Gallery, 6 - 39
Jackelope Furniture, 6 - 39
Jacpa Ceramic Craftsmen, 8 - 37
Moon Bear Pottery, 8 - 47
Phylrich International, 2 - 8
Reservation Creations, 8 - 55
Syracuse Pottery, 8 - 65
Washington Pottery Co., 8 - 74
Workshops of David T. Smith, 6 - 86

Pump

Andrews Distributing Co., 3 - 7
Aquatek Systems, Inc., 3 - 9
Bard Manufacturing Company, 3 - 12
Celsisus Energy Company, 3 - 21
Climate Master Inc., 3 - 25
Command-Aire Corporation, 3 - 26
Crispaire, 3 - 28
FHP Manufacturing, 3 - 35
Heat Controller, Inc., 3 - 44
Jacobsen Energy Industries, Inc., 3 - 50

The Complete Sourcebook

Index - 67

Quilt – Reproduction

Mammoth, 3 - 57
Martin Industries Inc., 3 - 58
Nepco, Inc., 3 - 63
Pumphouse, 3 - 72
S. Scherer & Sons, 7 - 6
Snyder General Corp., 3 - 79
Solar Oriented Environmental Systems,3 - 80
Tetco, 3 - 87
Water Works, 7 - 8

Quilt

Cabin Creek Quilts, 8 - 13
Coming Home, 8 - 18
Harriet's House, 8 - 32
Vanderkellen Galleries, 8 - 71

Radiator

Arsco Manufacturing Co., 3 - 9
Axeman-Anderson Co., 3 - 11
Barker Metalcraft, 3 - 12
Berjen Metal Industries, 3 - 14
Burnham, 3 - 18
Crown Boiler, 3 - 28
Edwards Engineering, 3 - 33
Jali Ltd., 3 - 50
Monarch Radiator Enclosures, 3 - 61
Walter Norman & Co., 3 - 96
Weil-McLain, 3 - 97
Winther Browne, 3 - 99

Rag

Peerless Imported Rugs, 8 - 52
Rastetter Woolen Mill, 8 - 55

Railing

Allen Iron Works & Supply, 1 - 3
B & B Products, 1 - 7
Cassidy Brothers Forge, Inc., 1 - 10
Danbury Stairs Corp., 1 - 13
Gazebo & Porchworks, 7 - 3
House of Moulding, 1 - 20
Leslie-Locke Inc., 3 - 55
M. L. Condon Company Inc., 3 - 56
Rogue River Millwork, 1 - 30
Schoenherr Iron Work, 1 - 30
Stair Building & Millwork Co. Inc., 1 - 32
Taco, 1 - 33
Vintage Wood Works, 1 - 36

Raised

Cardell Cabinets, 10 - 3
Hyde Park Raised Panel, 1 - 20

Range

Barnstable Stove Shop, 10 - 1
Brown Stove Works Inc., 3 - 17
Bryant Stove Works, 3 - 17
Contemporary Copper, 10 - 3
Dacor, 8 - 21
Elmira Stove And Fireplace, 10 - 4
Garland Commercial Industries, Inc., 10 - 5
King Refrigerator Corp., 10 - 6
Russell Range, Inc., 10 - 9
The Homestead, 10 - 10
The House of Webster, 10 - 10
Viking Range Corporation, 10 - 10
W. C. Wood Co. Ltd., 10 - 10
Zanussi Ltd., 10 - 11

Rattan

Bielecky Brothers, Inc., 6 - 9
Clark Casual Furniture Inc., 6 - 17

Deutsch, 6 - 23
Ellenburg's Furniture, 6 - 26
Ficks Reed Co., 6 - 28
Grange Furniture, Inc., 6 - 32
Modern Reed & Rattan Co. Inc., 6 - 53
Rattan Boricua Mfg. Corp., 6 - 62
Rattan Interiors, 6 - 62
Rattan Specialties Santa Fe, 6 - 62
Shelby Williams Industries, Inc., 6 - 68
Stanley Chair Co. Inc., 6 - 71
Whitecraft Rattan Inc., 6 - 83
Wicker & Rattan, 6 - 83
Wicker Gallery, 6 - 83
Woolums Mfg. Inc., 6 - 86

Recessed Lighting

All-Lighting, 11 - 2
Cardell Cabinets, 10 - 3
Exquisite Lighting and Design, Inc., 11 - 11
Halo Lighting Products/Cooper Ind., 11 - 14
Harry Horn, Inc., 11 - 14
Lighting Source of America, 11 - 20
National Industries, 11 - 23
WAC Lighting Collection, 11 - 35

Recycling

Practical Homewares, 10 - 8
Running Dog, 10 - 8

Redwood

(Decking, Furniture, Windows, Wood, etc.)

Adirondack Designs, 6 - 3
Bruce Post Company Inc., 3 - 17
California Redwood Association, 3 - 19
Elk Valley Woodworking Inc., 6 - 26
Pacific Burl and Hardwood, 3 - 68
Vent Vue, 12 - 26
Windsor Mill, Inc., 1 - 37

Refrigerator

Frigidaire, 10 - 4
King Refrigerator Corp., 10 - 6
Marvel Industries, 10 - 6
Neff (UK, etc.) Ltd., 10 - 7
Northern Refrigerator Company, 10 - 7
Sub Zero Freezer Company, Inc., 10 - 9
Traulsen & Co., Inc., 10 - 10
Tricity Bendix Ltd., 10 - 10
Zanussi Ltd., 10 - 11

Register

(Decorative, etc.)

A Touch of Brass, 3 - 1
All American Wood Register Co., 3 - 5
Hart & Cooley, 3 - 44
Merit Metal Products Corp., 3 - 60
The Reggio Register Co. Inc., 3 - 89

Reproduction

(Bathroom Fixtures, Furniture, Hardware, Lighting, Mantels, Stoves, Wallpaper, etc.)

Antique Furniture Copies, 6 - 5
Antique Street Lamps Inc., 11 - 2
Bassett & Vollum, 8 - 8
Bradbury & Bradbury Wallpapers, 8 - 11
Brassfinders, 11 - 5
British Antique Replicas, 6 - 12
Burdoch Victorian Lamp Company, 11 - 5

Index

Rocker – Rolling

C. H. Southwell, 6 - 13
Caldwell Chair Company, 6 - 13
Campbell Lamp Supply, 11 - 6
Campbellsville Industries, 3 - 19
Charles Rupert Designs, 3 - 23
Classic Designs, 12 - 6
Classic Revivals, Inc., 8 - 17
Collection Reproductions, 6 - 17
Colonial Designs Furniture, 6 - 18
Colonial Williamsburg, 6 - 18
Country Furniture Shop, 6 - 19
Crawford's Old House Store, 3 - 27
Cricket on the Hearth, Inc., 6 - 20
Cumberland Woodcraft Co., 1 - 13
DS Locksmithing Company, 3 - 29
Dana Robes Wood Craftsmen, 6 - 21
Danny Alessandro Ltd./Edwin Jackson,1 - 14
David W. Lamb Cabinetmaker, 6 - 21
Decker Antique Reproductions, 6 - 22
Deep River Trading Company, 6 - 22
Deer Creek Pottery, 3 - 30
Detail Millwork Inc., 1 - 14
Drummond Woodworks, 1 - 15
Dutch Products & Supply Co., 3 - 32
Edward P. Schmidt Cabinetmaker, 6 - 25
Eldrid Wheeler, 6 - 25
Ephraim Marsh, 6 - 26
Georgian Reproduction, 6 - 31
Gerald Curry-Cabinetmaker, 6 - 31
Great Meadows Joinery, 6 - 32
Greystone Victorian Furniture, 6 - 33
Hearthstone Hardware Co., 3 - 44
Heirloom Reproductions, 6 - 35
Hekman Furniture, 6 - 35
Henkel-Harris, 6 - 35
Heritage Mantels Inc., 1 - 19
Historic Charleston Reproductions, 6 - 35
Historic Windows, 12 - 11
Homestead Furniture, 6 - 36
Howerton Antique Reproductions, 6 - 37
Hurley Patentee Manor, 11 - 16
Iron Intentions Forge, 3 - 49
Irvin's Craft Shop, 11 - 17
J & B Lamp & Shade, 11 - 17
James Lea-Cabinetmaker, 6 - 39
John Congdon, Cabinetmaker, 6 - 40
John F. Lavoie Windows, 12 - 13
Karges Furniture Co., Inc., 6 - 41
Kimball Furniture Reproductions, 6 - 42
L.T. Moses Willard, Inc., 11 - 18
LeFort, 6 - 44
Leonard's Reproductions & Antiques, 6 - 45
Lester H. Berry & Company, 11 - 19
Lewis Mittman, Inc., 6 - 45
Lexington Furniture Industries, 6 - 46
Liberty Hall, 6 - 46
Lion House Antique (Copies, etc.), 6 - 46
M. Wolchonok & Son Inc., 3 - 56
Magnolia Hall, 6 - 48
Mahantango Manor Inc., 8 - 44
Mahogany Craft, 6 - 48
Manheim & Weitz, 6 - 48
Manor House, 6 - 49
Maynard House Antiques, 6 - 51
Merritt's Antiques Inc., 6 - 52
Michael's Classic Wicker, 6 - 52
Miracle Method Bathroom Restoration, 2 - 7
Mona Liza Fine Furniture Inc., 6 - 53
Nagykery Imports, Ltd., 6 - 54
Nowells Inc., 11 - 24
Oak Craft Inc., 6 - 56

Old Road Furniture Co., 6 - 56
Old World Hardware Co., 3 - 66
Olde Virginea Trading Co., 8 - 50
Orleans Carpenters, 6 - 57
Oxford Leather, 6 - 58
Pashayan, 6 - 58
Period Furniture Hardware, 6 - 59
Pulaski Furniture Corp., 6 - 61
Ralston Furniture Reproductions, 6 - 62
Randall Tysinger, 6 - 62
Reid Classics, 6 - 62
Renaissance Furniture and Cabinetry, 6 - 62
Renaissance Marketing, 11 - 26
River Bend Chair Company, 6 - 63
Robert Whitley Studio, 6 - 64 , 11 - 26
Robert Whitley Studio, 6 - 64
Rufkahr's, 3 - 77
Rustic Home Hardware, 3 - 77
Sampler Inc., 6 - 65
Samuel B. Sadtler & Co., 1 - 30
Scully & Scully, 6 - 66
Simms & Thapper Cabinetmakers, 6 - 68
St. Louis Antique Lighting Co., 11 - 29
Statesville Chair Company, 6 - 71
Stephen Adams Furniture Makers, 6 - 72
Strafford House, 6 - 72
The Antique Hardware Store, 3 - 87
The Antique Plumber, 3 - 87
The Bartley Collections Ltd., 6 - 74
The Bombay Co., 6 - 75
The Brass Lion, 11 - 31
The Coldren Company, 3 - 88
The Odd Chair Company, 6 - 76
The Saltbox, 11 - 32
The Seraph Country Collection, 6 - 76
The Victorian Merchant, 6 - 77
The Walsh Woodworks, 8 - 68
The Wise Company, 3 - 90
The Woodbury Blacksmith & Forge Co.,3 - 90
Three Mountaineers, Inc., 6 - 77
Urban Archaeology, 1 - 35
Valley Furniture Shop, 6 - 80
Victorian Classics Inc., 6 - 81
Victorian Reproduction Enterprises, 11 - 34
Victorian Revival, 11 - 34
Victorian Showcase, 6 - 81
Village Lantern, 11 - 34
Vitistor's Catalog, 2 - 12
William H. James Co., 6 - 84
William Spencer, 11 - 35
Williamsburg Blacksmiths Inc., 3 - 99
Winterbrook Inc., 6 - 85
Workshops of David T. Smith, 6 - 86

Rocker

Acme Furniture Mfg. Inc., 6 - 2
Burcham Furniture Manufacturing, Inc., 6 - 13
Cornucopia, Inc., 6 - 19
Dominion Chair, Ltd., 6 - 24
Frederick Duckloe & Bros., 6 - 30
Klein Design Inc., 6 - 43
Masterworks, 6 - 51
North Woods Chair Shop, 6 - 55
Oakline Chair Co. Inc., 6 - 56
Shaker Workshops, 3 - 78
Sheffield Chair Co., 6 - 68
Stanley Chair Co. Inc., 6 - 71
The Rocker Shop of Marietta, 6 - 76
Wylder Furniture Manufacturing, 6 - 86

Rolling

Windsor Door, 4 - 18

The Complete Sourcebook

Index - 69

Roof, Roofing

A. Moorhouse Co.,   3 - 1
ALCOA Building Products,   3 - 2
ASC Pacific Inc.,   3 - 2
Able Fabricators Inc., 3 - 3
AcuTruss Industries Ltd.,   3 - 4
Adam Lumber Inc.,   3 - 4
Ailene Lumber Inc.,   3 - 4
Allied Building Products Corp., 3 - 5
Alpine Engineer Products Inc., 3 - 5
American Building Component,   3 - 6
Apex Gutter Systems Ltd.,   3 - 8
Atas International Corp.,   3 - 10
Bay Cities Metal Products,   3 - 12
Beachwood Lumber & Mfg.,   3 - 13
Bender Roof Tile Ind.Inc.,   3 - 14
Berridge Manufacturing Co.,   3 - 14
Bird, Inc.,   3 - 15
Boston Valley Pottery, 3 - 16
Bradco Supply Corp.,   3 - 16
C & H Roofing Inc.,   3 - 18
Cal-Shake, Inc.,   3 - 19
Campbellsville Industries,   3 - 19
Carolina Truss Mfg. Co., Inc., 3 - 20
Causeway Lumber Co.,   3 - 20
Celadon Ceramic Slate, 3 - 21
Celotex Corp., 3 - 21
CertainTeed Corp.,   3 - 23
Classic Products,   3 - 25
Conklin Metal Industries,   3 - 26
Dibiten USA,   3 - 31
Dorning Roofing & Insulation Co.,   3 - 32
E.L. Hilts & Company,   3 - 32
Evergreen Slate Co.,   3 - 34
Fabricated Wood Products,   3 - 35
FibreCem Corporation,   3 - 36
Fields Corporation,   3 - 36
Flexicore Co., Inc.,   3 - 36
GAF Building Materials Corp., 3 - 38
GS Roofing Products Co., Inc., 3 - 39
Gate Roofing Manufacturing Inc.,   3 - 39
Georgia Pacific Corp., 3 - 40
Gerard Roofing Technologies,   3 - 40
Globe Building Materials Inc.,   3 - 41
Heart Truss & Engineering,   3 - 44
Hilltop Slate Co.,   3 - 46
Hjelmeland Truss Corp., 3 - 46
Hughes Roof Truss Co. Ltd.,   3 - 48
Humes, 3 - 48
IKO Manufacturing Inc., 3 - 48
Idowa Timber,   3 - 49
Julius Seidel & Company,   3 - 51
Keen Building Components Inc., 3 - 52
Kent Trusses Ltd.,   3 - 52
Kunico Truss & Prefab Ltd.,   3 - 53
Lampe Lumber Co.,   3 - 53
Landmark Truss, Inc.,   3 - 53
Leatherback Industries, 3 - 54
Leduc Truss,   3 - 54
Liberty Cedar, 3 - 55
Lifetile,   3 - 55
Lifetime Rooftile Co., 3 - 55
Louisiana-Pacific Corporation, 3 - 56
Ludowici Celadon Co. Inc.,   3 - 56
Lumber Specialties,   3 - 56
M & H Truss Co. Inc.,   3 - 56
Manufacturers Wholesale,   3 - 57
Manville/Schuller,   3 - 57
Marley Roof Tiles, Canada Ltd., 3 - 58

Maruhachi Ceramics of America Inc.,   3 - 58
Mays Lumber Co.,   3 - 59
McLaughlin Roof Trusses Ltd.,   3 - 59
Met-Tile, Inc., 3 - 60
Mid-State Truss Co., Inc.,   3 - 60
Millen Roofing Company, 3 - 60
Monier Roof Tile Inc.,   3 - 61
New England Slate Company,   3 - 64
Northern Michigan Truss Co.,   3 - 65
OK Truss Co. Inc.,   3 - 66
Olympic Structures Inc.,   3 - 66
Owens Corning Fiberglass Corp., 3 - 67
O'Brien Bros. Slate Company,   3 - 65
P. B. Trusses Ltd.,   3 - 67
Pabco Roofing Products, 3 - 68
Paulis Co.,   3 - 68
Penn Big Bed Slate Co. Inc.,   3 - 69
Penna Supply & Mfg. Co.,   3 - 69
Perfection Truss Co. Inc.,   3 - 69
Pioneer Roofing Tile Inc.,   3 - 70
Pueblo Truss Co.,   12 - 20
Quality Truss, 3 - 72
Quarry Slate Industries Inc.,   3 - 72
Raleigh Inc., 3 - 73
Read Bros. Building Supply,   3 - 73
Red Deer Truss Systems, 3 - 74
Reinke Shakes, 3 - 74
Renaissance Roofing Inc.,   3 - 74
Ridgway Roof Truss Co. Inc.,   3 - 75
Rimbey Truss Systems Inc.,   3 - 75
Rising & Nelson Slate Company, 3 - 75
Riverside Roof Truss Inc.,   3 - 76
Roofage,   3 - 76
Roofmaster Products Company,   3 - 76
SRI,   3 - 77
Schubert Lumber Co.,   3 - 78
Shakertown Corp.,   3 - 78
Shamokin Trail Shingle Co.,   3 - 78
Shingle Mill Inc.,   3 - 78
Shoffner Industries Inc.,   3 - 79
Silver State Components,   3 - 79
Sky Lodge Farm, 3 - 79
South Side Roofing Co. Inc.,   3 - 80
Southern Components Inc.,   3 - 81
Southern Maryland Aluminum Prod.Co.3 - 81
Staco Roof Tile Manufacturing, 3 - 81
Stark Truss Co. Inc.,   3 - 82
Stone Door & Truss,   3 - 83
Structural Slate Co.,   3 - 83
Superior Truss & Components Inc.,   3 - 85
Supradur Manufacturing Corp.,   3 - 85
Tarmac Roofing Systems Inc.,   3 - 86
Tatko Brothers Slate Company,   3 - 86
Tegola USA,   3 - 87
The Durable Slate Company,   3 - 88
The Northern Roof Tile Sales Co.,   3 - 89
The Roof, Tile & Slate Co.,   3 - 89
The Structural Slate Co.,   3 - 89
Thorn Lumber Co.,   3 - 90
Tilton Truss Mfrs. Inc.,   3 - 91
Timber Tech Truss Systems Ltd., 3 - 91
Timber Top Truss Ltd.,   3 - 91
Tri State Truss Co.,   3 - 92
Tru-Truss Inc., 3 - 92
Trusses Inc.,   3 - 92
Uniflor,   3 - 93
United Wholesale Distributors, 3 - 94
Universal Forest Products,   3 - 94
Valley Truss Co.,   3 - 94
Vande Hey-Raleigh Manufacturing Inc.,3 - 94
Villaume Industries Inc.,   3 - 95

Index

Rosewood – Rustic

W. F. Norman Corporation, 1 - 36
Warren Truss Co. Inc., 3 - 96
Wascana Wood Components Ltd., 3 - 96
Weems Roof Truss Co., 3 - 97
Wendricks Roof Trusses, 3 - 97
Western Wood Fabricators Inc., 3 - 98
Wm. D. Bowers Lumber Co., 3 - 100
Wood Structures Inc., 3 - 100
Youngstown Roof Truss Co., 3 - 101
Zappone Manufacturing, 3 - 102

Rosewood

Black Millwork Co. Inc., 4 - 3
Entol Industries, 1 - 16
Quality Woods Ltd., 5 - 8

Ruffle

Carter Canopies, 8 - 15
Dana's Curtains & Draperies, 8 - 21
Ruth's Custom Bedspreads, 8 - 57

Rug, Runner

5th Ave Rug Center, 8 - 1
A Candle In The Night, 5 - 1
ABC Carpet & Home, 8 - 1
Abrahams Oriental Rugs, 8 - 2
Adac. Rugs & Treasures, 8 - 2
Aladdin Carpet Mills, 8 - 3
Alex Cooper Oriental Rugs, 8 - 3
Allison T. Seymour, Inc., 8 - 3
American Rug Craftsmen, 8 - 4
American Rug, 8 - 4
Arthur Gregorian, 8 - 5
Artloom, 8 - 6
At Home in the Valley, 8 - 6
Azar's Oriental Rugs, 8 - 7
Barbara Zinkel Design, 8 - 8
Barrett Carpet Mills, 8 - 8
Beaulieu of America Inc., 8 - 8
Benington's, 8 - 9
Buy Carpet Direct, 8 - 12
Cabin Craft Rugs, 8 - 13
Callaway Carpets & Rugs, 8 - 13
Capel Rugs, 8 - 14
Carpetland, 8 - 15
Carter Carpet, 8 - 15
Charles W. Jacobsen, Inc., 8 - 16
Cherry Hill Furniture,Carpet & Interiors, 6 - 16
Coming Home, 8 - 18
Cornucopia, Inc., 6 - 19
Coronet Industries Inc., 8 - 18
Country Braid House, 8 - 19
Couristan, 8 - 19
D & W Carpet & Rug Co., 8 - 20
Dana Kelly Oriental Rugs, 8 - 21
Davis Braided Rug co., 8 - 22
Diamond Rug & Carpet Mills Inc., 8 - 23
Emmet Perry & Co., 8 - 25
Ethan Allen, Inc., 6 - 27
Fairfield Carpets & Fabrics, 8 - 27
Family Heir-Loom Weavers, 8 - 27
Fieldcrest Cannon, Inc., 8 - 27
Flagship Carpet, 8 - 28
Folkheart Rag Rugs, 8 - 28
Form III, 8 - 29
Frances Lee Jasper Oriental Rugs, 8 - 29
Fred Moheban Gallery, 8 - 29
Galaxy Carpet Mills, 8 - 30
Hawthorne Carpet, 8 - 32
Helios Carpets, 8 - 32
Heritage Rugs, 8 - 33

Home Decorators Collection, 11 - 15
Honani Crafts, 8 - 34
House of Persia, 8 - 34
Houston Oriental Rug Gallery, 8 - 34
Import Specialists, 8 - 35
International Rug Source Ltd., 8 - 36
Jacqueline Vance Oriental Rugs, 8 - 37
Jefferson Industries Inc., 8 - 38
John Aga Oriental Rugs, 8 - 38
Kamali Oriental Rugs, 8 - 39
Kaoud Oriental Rugs, 8 - 39
Karastan, 8 - 39
Kelaty International Inc., 8 - 39
Kimberly Black, 3 - 52
Lacey-Champion Carpets, Inc., 8 - 41
Lizzie and Charlie's Rag Rugs, 8 - 43
Louis De Poortere, 8 - 43
Luv Those Rugs, 8 - 43
Marcella Fine Rugs, 8 - 44
Mills River Industries, Inc., 8 - 46
Moattar Ltd., 8 - 47
Nance Carpet & Rug Co. Inc., 8 - 48
National Carpet, 8 - 48
Navajo Arts & Crafts Guild, 8 - 48
Norwick Mills, 8 - 50
Olde Mill House Shoppe, 6 - 57
Omega Rug Works, 8 - 50
Oriental Rug Outlet Inc., 8 - 51
Pace-Stone, 8 - 51
Palazzetti Inc., 6 - 58
Peerless Imported Rugs, 8 - 52
Persian Galleries, 8 - 53
Persian Gallery Company Inc., 8 - 53
R. W. Beattie Carpet Industries Inc., 8 - 55
Rastetter Woolen Mill, 8 - 55
Regal Rugs Inc., 8 - 55
Reservation Creations, 8 - 55
Sandler & Worth, 8 - 58
Santa Fe Oriental Rugs, 8 - 58
Schumacher & Co. Inc., 8 - 59
Southern Rug, 8 - 62
Springs Performance Products, 8 - 62
Talebloo Oriental Rugs, 3 - 86
The 135 Collection Inc., 8 - 65
The Gazebo of New York, 8 - 67
The Leather Gallery of Kentucky, 6 - 76
The Oriental Rug Co., 8 - 67
The Rug Store, 8 - 67
The Rug Warehouse, 8 - 67
Thorndike Mills, 8 - 68
Tianjin-Philadelphia Carpet Company, 8 - 68
Tobin Sporn & Glasser Inc., 8 - 69
Treasured Weavings, 8 - 69
Trocadero Textile Art, 8 - 70
USA Blind Factory, 8 - 70
Varsity Rug Co., 8 - 71
W. Hirsch Oriental Rugs, 8 - 73
Wakefield Mills, 8 - 73
Wall Furniture Co., 6 - 81
Wellco Carpet Co., 8 - 75
Werco Persian & Oriental Rugs, 6 - 82
West Point Pepperell Inc., 8 - 75
Western Plaza, 8 - 75
Weymouth Braided Rug Co., 8 - 75
Wooden Ewe Farm, 8 - 77
Yankee Pride, 8 - 77
Zaven A. Kish Oriental Rug Gallery, 8 - 78

Rustic

Backwoods Furnishings, 6 - 7
Classic Products, 3 - 25

The Complete Sourcebook

Index - 71

Sandstone – Settee

Index

Elmo Guernsey, 6 - 26
Northern Rustic Furniture, 6 - 55
Rustic Furnishings, 6 - 65
Through The Barn Door Furniture Co., 6 - 78
Windspire, 6 - 85

Sandstone

EPRO, Inc., 3 - 33
Sveriges Steninindustriforbund, 3 - 85

Sash

Architectural Components, 1 - 5
Hoff Forest Products, Inc., 3 - 46

Sauna

Almost Heaven Hot Tubs, 2 - 1
Cecil Ellis Sauna Corp., 3 - 20
Nordic Showers, 2 - 8
Sequoia Industries Inc., 3 - 78
Thermo Spas Inc., 2 - 11

Sconce

Brandon Industries Inc., 11 - 5
Classic Illumination, Inc., 11 - 7
Fabby, 11 - 11
Form & Function, 11 - 12
Lighting Source of America, 11 - 20
MacDonald Stained Glass, 3 - 56

Screen

(Decorative, Door, Window, etc.)

Academy Mfg. Co. Inc., 4 - 1
Active Window Products, 12 - 2
Advanced Aluminum Products, 12 - 2
Allmetal, Inc., 12 - 2
Aluma-Craft Corporation, 12 - 3
Alumaroll Specialty Co., Inc., 12 - 3
American Screen & Door Co., Inc., 12 - 3
BayForm, 12 - 5
Black Millwork Co. Inc., 4 - 3
Cascade Mill & Glass Works, 4 - 3
Ciro Coppa, 6 - 16
Combination Door Company, 4 - 4
Consolidated Aluminum, 12 - 7
Coppa Woodworking, 6 - 18
Creative Openings, 4 - 4
Fancy Front Brassiere Co., 1 - 16
First American Resources, 12 - 9
Grand Era Reproductions, 4 - 8
GuildMaster Arts, 8 - 31
Hanover Wire Cloth, 12 - 10
Heirwood Shutters, 12 - 11
Hicksville Woodworks Co., 1 - 20
Imperial Screen Company Inc., 9 - 2
Kestrel Manufacturing, 12 - 13
Mad River Woodworks, 1 - 22
Mason Corporation, 12 - 15
Metal Exchange Corp., 12 - 15
Metal Industries Inc., 12 - 15
Metal Industries, Inc., 12 - 16
Midwest Wood Products, 12 - 16
Miya Shoji & Interiors Inc., 8 - 47
National Screen Company, Inc., 4 - 12
New York Wire Company, 12 - 17
Nichols-Homeshield, Inc., 12 - 18
North Star Company, 12 - 18
Oregon Wooden Screen Door Co., 4 - 13
Perfection Metal & Supply Co., 3 - 69
Phifer Wire Products, Inc., 8 - 53
Phillips Industries Inc., 3 - 70
Roman Limited, 2 - 9

Royal Plastics, Inc., 12 - 22
Solartechnic 2000 Ltd., 8 - 61
Solartechnic 2000 Ltd., 8 - 61
Superior Metal Products Co., 12 - 24
The Loxcreen Company, Inc., 12 - 25
The Wood Factory, 1 - 35
Thermo-Rite Mfg. Co., 3 - 90
Vintage Wood Works, 1 - 36
Walsh Screen & Window Inc., 12 - 27

Sculpture

Felber Ornamental Plastering Corp., 1 - 16
Moon Bear Pottery, 8 - 47
Oak Leaves Studio, 1 - 25
Path Of The Sun Images, 8 - 52
Sculpture Studio, 8 - 59
Wertheimer Sculptures Ltd., 8 - 75

Sealant

Pecora Corporation, 3 - 69
The 3E Group Inc., 3 - 87

Seat

(Love Seats, etc.)

Acme Furniture Mfg. Inc., 6 - 2
Hunt Galleries, Inc., 6 - 38
Sheffield Chair Co., 6 - 68

Security

(Alarms, Lighting, etc.)

ABCO Supply Company, 9 - 1
Advanced Security, 9 - 1
Alarm Supply Co., 9 - 1
All Island Security Inc., 9 - 1
Almet Hardware Ltd., 9 - 1
Arthur Shaw Manufacturing Ltd., 9 - 1
Burdex Security Co., 9 - 1
Burle Industries, Inc., 9 - 1
Chubb Lock Company, 9 - 2
EMEL Electronics, 9 - 2
Electronic Sensing Products, Inc., 9 - 2
Falcon Eye Inc., 9 - 2
Gibbons of Willenhall Ltd., 9 - 2
Heath Zenith, 9 - 2
High-Desert Security Systems, 9 - 2
Home Automation, Inc., 9 - 2
Home Equipment Mfg.,Co., 11 - 16
Honeywell Inc., 9 - 2
Imperial Screen Company Inc., 9 - 2
Maple Chase Co., 9 - 2
Mountain West Alarm Supply, 9 - 2
Nutone, 3 - 65
Premier Communications Company, 9 - 3
Prescolite, 9 - 3
Rollaway, 9 - 3
Schlage, 9 - 3
Security Link Corporation, 9 - 3
Stanley Door Systems, 4 - 16
The J. Goodman Co., 9 - 3
Unity System Inc., 9 - 3
Vision Security Inc., 9 - 3
Westco Security Systems Inc., 9 - 3

Sensor

Electronic Sensing Products, Inc., 9 - 2
RAB Electric, 9 - 3

Settee

John Alan Designs, 6 - 40

Index - 72

The Complete Sourcebook

Index

Shade

A. Weldon Kent Emterprises,   8 - 1
ALCO Venetian Blind Co. Inc.,   8 - 2
Abbey Shade & Mfg. Co. Inc.,   12 - 2
American Discount Wallcoverings,   8 - 4
Appropriate Technology, Corp., 12 - 4
Aye Attracting Awnings, 3 - 11
Blind Busters,   8 - 10
Blind Center USA, Inc., 8 - 10
Blind Design,   8 - 10
Fara Mfg.Co., Inc.,   8 - 27
Florida Shades Inc.,   8 - 28
G & L Shades Inc.,   8 - 29
Goodman Fabrications,   12 - 10
Home Fashions, Inc.,   8 - 33
Hunter Douglas Window Fashions, 8 - 35
Jayson Window Fashions, 8 - 37
Kenney Mfg. Co.,   8 - 40
Metro Blind & Shade,   8 - 46
New View Blinds Mfg. Ltd.,   8 - 49
Parker Window Covering, 8 - 51
Perkowitz Window Fashions,   8 - 52
Plastic Sun Shade Co. Inc.,   8 - 53
Qwik Blinds,   8 - 1
Shades & Verticals & Miniblinds Cnter, 8 - 60
Shutters & Shades,   8 - 61
Skandia Industries,   8 - 61
Somfy Systems Inc.,   12 - 23
United Designs Inc.,   8 - 70
View Guard,   8 - 72
Wells Interiors,   8 - 75
Wesco Fabrics Inc.,   8 - 75
Window Modes,   8 - 77

Shake

Cedar Plus,   3 - 20
Cedar Shake & Shingle Bureau,   3 - 21
Green River,   3 - 42
Hamilton Cedar Products Inc.,   3 - 43
Humes, 3 - 48
J. H. Wood Shake Inc.,   3 - 50
Julius Seidel & Company,   3 - 51
Nailite International Inc.,   3 - 63
North Coast Shake Co., 3 - 64
North Hoquiam Cedar Products Inc.,   3 - 65
Pioneer Roofing Tile Inc.,   3 - 70
Shakertown Corp.,   3 - 78
Wesco Cedar Inc.,   3 - 97
West Forest Wood Products,   3 - 97

Shaker

Billing Croft of Salem, 6 - 9
C. H. Southwell,   6 - 13
Cabin Creek Furniture, 6 - 13
Dana Robes Wood Craftsmen,   6 - 21
David W. Lamb Cabinetmaker,   6 - 21
Ellenburg's Furniture,   6 - 26
Great Meadows Joinery, 6 - 32
James M. Taylor & Co., 6 - 40
Lane Company, Inc.,   6 - 44
Lanier Furniture Company,   6 - 44
Meadow Craft,   6 - 51
Orleans Carpenters,   6 - 57
Shaker Shops West,   6 - 67
Smith Woodworks and Design,   6 - 69
The Walsh Woodworks,   8 - 68
Village Furniture,   6 - 81
Workshop Showcase,   6 - 86

Shelving

A. Liss & Co.,   6 - 1
Art In Iron,   6 - 5
LaMont Ltd.,   2 - 6
Mansion Industries, Inc.,   8 - 44
The Closet Doctor,   8 - 66
The Shop Woodcrafters, Inc.,   6 - 76
Wohners Inc.,   1 - 37

Shingle

Bird, Inc.,   3 - 15
C & H Roofing Inc.,   3 - 18
Cedar Plus,   3 - 20
Cedar Shake & Shingle Bureau,   3 - 21
Cedar Valley Shingle Systems,   3 - 21
Celotex Corp.,   3 - 21
CertainTeed Corp.,   3 - 23
Classic Products,   3 - 25
FibreCem Corporation,   3 - 36
GAF Building Materials Corp.,   3 - 38
Green River,   3 - 42
J. H. Wood Shake Inc.,   3 - 50
Julius Seidel & Company,   3 - 51
Mad River Woodworks,   1 - 22
Manville/Schuller,   3 - 57
Miller Shingle Co., Inc.,   3 - 61
North Coast Shake Co., 3 - 64
North Hoquiam Cedar Products Inc.,   3 - 65
Shakertown Corp.,   3 - 78
Shamokin Trail Shingle Co.,   3 - 78
Shingle Mill Inc.,   3 - 78
Sky Lodge Farm, 3 - 79
South Coast Shingle Company Inc.,   3 - 80
Supradur Manufacturing Corp.,   3 - 85
Tegola USA,   3 - 87
W. F. Norman Corporation,   1 - 36
Wesco Cedar Inc.,   3 - 97
Zappone Manufacturing, 3 - 102

Shower

(Doors, Enclosures, Faucets, Glass Block, etc.)

A-Ball Plumbing Supply, 2 - 1
ARDCO, Inc.,   2 - 1
Accents In Stone,   3 - 3
Ace Shower Door Co. Inc.,   2 - 1
Acrymet Industires Inc.,   1 - 2
Allgood Shower Door Corp.,   2 - 1
American Shower Door Corp.,   2 - 2
Aqata Limited, 2 - 2
Aqua Glass Corporation, 2 - 2
Aston Matthews, 2 - 2
Barber Wilsons & Co. Ltd.,   2 - 2
Basco, 2 - 2
Beach Craft, Inc.,   2 - 3
Carlos Shower Doors Inc.,   2 - 3
Century Shower Door, Inc.,   2 - 3
Chatham Brass Co., Inc.,   11 - 7
Cloth Crafters, 8 - 17
Coastal Industries, Inc.,   2 - 4
Diston Industries Inc., 2 - 4
EFRON America, 2 - 4
Fleurco Industries 1963 Ltd.,   10 - 4
Fuji Hardware Co., Ltd.,   2 - 4
G.M. Ketcham Co., Inc., 2 - 5
Garofalo Studio,   2 - 5
Glashaus Inc., 3 - 40
Glass Block Co.,   3 - 40
Glass Blocks Unlimited Inc.,   1 - 18

The Complete Sourcebook

Shredder – Siding

Gracious Home, 10 - 5
Great Paines Glassworks, 4 - 8
H & W Plastics Inc., 2 - 5
Hans Grohe Ltd., 2 - 5
Hiawatha, Inc., 2 - 5
Huntington/Pacific Ceramics, Inc., 3 - 48
Ideal-Standard Ltd., 2 - 6
Imperial Shower Door Co., 2 - 6
Interbath Inc., 2 - 6
Italian Glass Block Designs Ltd., 1 - 20
J. M Mills, 2 - 6
Jacuzzi Inc., 2 - 6
Kallista, 2 - 6
Kimstock Inc., 2 - 6
Lippert Corp., 2 - 7
Made-Rite Aluminum Window Co., 12 - 15
Meynell Valves Ltd., 2 - 7
Midland Manufacturing Corp., 2 - 7
Nope, 2 - 8
Nordic Showers, 2 - 8
Pipe Dreams, 2 - 9
Pittsburgh Corning, 3 - 70
Raphael Ltd., 2 - 9
Reflections USA, 2 - 9
Roman Limited, 2 - 9
SEPCO Industries Inc., 2 - 9
Sherwood Shower Door Co., 2 - 10
Sholton Assoc., 3 - 79
Shower-Rite Corp., 2 - 10
Showerlux U.S.A., 2 - 10
Showerlux UK Ltd., 2 - 10
Sterling Plumbing Group, 2 - 10
Sunflower Shower Company, 2 - 10
Supro Building Products Corp., 3 - 85
Surrey Shoppe Interiors, 8 - 64
Swan Mfg. Co., 2 - 10
Tafco Corp., 3 - 86
Tomlin Industries Inc., 2 - 11
Trevi Showers, 2 - 11
Universal Bath Systems, 2 - 12
Valley Fibrebath Ltd., 2 - 12
Vassallo Precast Mfg. Corp., 2 - 12
Water Saver Faucet Co., 2 - 13

Shredder

BCS America, Inc., 7 - 1
Gardener's Supply, 7 - 3
MacKissic Incorporated, 7 - 4
Troy-Bilt Mfg. Co., 7 - 7

Shrub

TIF Nursery, 7 - 7

Shutter

(Interior, Exterior, Rolling, Window, Wood, etc.)

Alside, 3 - 5
American Heritage Shutters Inc., 12 - 3
Aye Attracting Awnings, 3 - 11
Beech River Mill Company, 3 - 13
Devenco Products Inc., 12 - 8
Entrances Inc., 4 - 6
Florida Wood Moulding & Trim, 1 - 17
Hahn's Woodworking Co., 12 - 10
Heirwood Shutters, 12 - 11
Historic Windows, 12 - 11
Iberia Millwork, 4 - 9
Inter Trade Inc., 12 - 12
Jali Ltd., 3 - 50
Ken Jordan Shutters, 12 - 13
Kestrel Manufacturing, 12 - 13

Maple Grove Restorations, 1 - 22
Michael's Fine Colonial Products, 1 - 24
Monroe Coldren & Sons, 3 - 62
Ohline Corp., 12 - 18
Perkins Architectural Millwork, 1 - 27
Perkowitz Window Fashions, 8 - 52
Pinecrest, 1 - 27
Pioneer Roll Shutter Co., 12 - 20
REM Industries, 12 - 21
Rare Wood, 4 - 14
Ray Tenebruso, 4 - 14
Rem Industries, 12 - 21
Replico Products Inc., 1 - 29
Rolladen Inc., 12 - 22
Rollaway, 9 - 3
Royal Crest Inc., 8 - 56
Shutter Shop, 3 - 79
Shuttercraft, 12 - 23
Shutters & Shades, 8 - 61
Solaroll Shade & Shutter Corp., 12 - 23
Solartechnic 2000 Ltd., 8 - 61
Somfy Systems Inc., 12 - 23
Sovereign Group Ltd., 4 - 15
Stanfield Shutter Co. Inc., 12 - 24
Sunburst Shutters Inc., 12 - 24
Sunshine Woodworks, 1 - 33
The Bank Architectural Antiques, 1 - 34
The Coldren Company, 3 - 88
The Old Wagon Factory, 4 - 17
The Shutter Depot, 12 - 25
Vixen Hill Mfg. Co. Inc., 7 - 8
Willard Shutter Co. Inc., 12 - 28
Windsor Door, 4 - 18
Woodpecker Products Inc., 4 - 18

Sidelight

Solartechnic 2000 Ltd., 8 - 61
Stained Glass Associates, 12 - 24

Siding

ALCOA Building Products, 3 - 2
Abitibi-Price, 1 - 2
Allied Building Products Corp., 3 - 5
Alside, 3 - 5
Aluminum Industries of Arkansas, 3 - 6
Anthony Forest Product Co., 3 - 8
Berger Building Products Corp., 3 - 14
Cedar Valley Shingle Systems, 3 - 21
Dryvit Systems, Inc., 3 - 32
Elixer Vinyl Siding, 3 - 33
Forest Siding Supply Inc., 3 - 38
Georgia Pacific Corp., 3 - 40
Louisiana-Pacific Corporation, 3 - 56
Masonite Corp., 4 - 12
Master Shield, 3 - 59
Mastic Corp., 3 - 59
Mill & Timber Products, Ltd., 3 - 60
Nailite International Inc., 3 - 63
Pukall Lumber Co., 3 - 72, 12 - 19
Reynolds Metals Company, 12 - 21
Southern Maryland Aluminum Co., 3 - 81
Supradur Manufacturing Corp., 3 - 85
USG Corporation, 3 - 93
W. F. Norman Corporation, 1 - 36
Ward Clapboard Mill Inc., 3 - 96
Western Red Cedar Lumber Assoc., 3 - 98
Weyerhaeuser Company, 3 - 98
Wolverine Technologies Inc., 3 - 100
Woods American, 5 - 11

Index - 74   *The Complete Sourcebook*

Silk – Sliding

Silk
(Plants, etc.)
May Silk, 8 - 45

Sill
Briar Hill Stone Co., 3 - 17
Imperial Marble, Inc., 3 - 49
MacBeath Hardwood Co., 1 - 22
Structural Slate Co., 3 - 83

Sink
A-Ball Plumbing Supply, 2 - 1
Astracast PLC, 12 - 4
Blanco America, 10 - 2
Blanco, 10 - 2
Brass & Traditional Sinks Ltd., 2 - 3
Carron Phoenix Ltd., 10 - 3
Conservation Building Products Ltd., 3 - 26
DuraGlaze Service Corp., 2 - 4
Ferretti Ltd., 10 - 4
Franke Inc., 10 - 4
Granite Lake Pottery, 2 - 5
J. F. Orr & Sons, 10 - 6
Old & Elegant Distributing, 2 - 8
Omega Too, 2 - 8
Pipe Dreams, 2 - 9
The Fixture Exchange, 2 - 11

Skylight
APC Corporation, 12 - 2
Allied Building Products Corp., 3 - 5
Arctic Glass & Window Outlet, 12 - 4
Black Millwork Co. Inc., 4 - 3
Bristolite Skylights, 12 - 5
Burnham Corp., 3 - 18
Circle Redmont Inc., 3 - 24
Fuji Hardware Co., Ltd., 2 - 4
IJ Mfg. Ltd., 12 - 12
Leslie-Locke Inc., 3 - 55
Linel, Inc., 12 - 14
Major Industries Inc., 12 - 15
Naturay Systems Corp., 12 - 17
ODL Inc., 12 - 18
Pella Corporation, 12 - 19
Progressive Building Products, 3 - 72
R. Lang Co., 12 - 21
Regal Manufacturing Co., 3 - 74
Rollamatic Roofs Incorporated, 12 - 22
Roto-Frank of America, Inc., 12 - 22
Skytech Systems, 12 - 23
Southeastern Insulated Glass, 7 - 6
Stained Glass Associates, 12 - 24
Sun Room Company, 7 - 7
Sunglo Skylights, 12 - 24
Sunshine Rooms Inc., 3 - 85
Thermo-Vu-Sun Lite Industries Inc., 12 - 25
Ventarama Skylight Corp., 12 - 27
Wasatch Solar Engineering, 3 - 96

Slate
Bergen Bluestone Co. Inc., 3 - 14
Delaware Quarries, Inc., 3 - 30
Evergreen Slate Co., 3 - 34
FibreCem Corporation, 3 - 36
Marble Institute of America, 3 - 57
Millen Roofing Company, 3 - 60
New England Slate Company, 3 - 64
O'Brien Bros. Slate Company, 3 - 65

Penn Big Bed Slate Co. Inc., 3 - 69
Quarry Slate Industries Inc., 3 - 72
Rising & Nelson Slate Company, 3 - 75
South Side Roofing Co. Inc., 3 - 80
Stenindustriens Landssammenslutning, 3 - 82
Structural Slate Co., 3 - 83
Tatko Brothers Slate Company, 3 - 86
The Durable Slate Company, 3 - 88
The Merchant Tiler, 3 - 88
The Roof, Tile & Slate Co., 3 - 89
Valley Marble & Slate Corp., 3 - 94
Williams & Sons Slate & Tile Inc., 3 - 99

Sliding
AAA Aluminum Stamping, Inc., 12 - 1
ALCAN Building Products, 12 - 1
ALCOA Vinyl Windows, 12 - 1
AMSCO Windows, 12 - 2
APL Window & Door Company, 12 - 2
Ace Shower Door Co. Inc., 2 - 1
Active Window Products, 12 - 2
Alpine Windows, 12 - 3
Alside Window Company, 12 - 3
Aluma-Glass Industries, Inc., 12 - 3
Aluminum Products Company, 12 - 3
Aluminum Specialties Mfg. Co., 12 - 3
Alwindor Manufacturing, Inc., 12 - 3
Amerlite Aluminum Co., Inc., 12 - 3
Arcadia Mfg. Inc., 1 - 5
Arrow Aluminum Ind., Inc., 12 - 4
Better-Bilt Aluminum Products Co., 12 - 5
Binning's Bldg. Products Inc., 12 - 5
Boyd Aluminum Mfg. Company, 12 - 5
C & S Distributors, Inc., 12 - 6
C. V. Aluminum, Inc., 12 - 6
California Window Corporation, 12 - 6
Care Free Aluminum Prod., Inc., 12 - 6
CertainTeed Corp., 3 - 23
Chamberlain Group, 12 - 6
Columbia Glass & Window Company, 12 - 7
Consolidated American Window Co., 12 - 7
Corn Belt Aluminum Inc., 12 - 7
Crown Mfg. Corp. of Missouri, 12 - 8
Delsan Industries, Inc., 12 - 8
Dunbarton Corp., 4 - 6
Empire Pacific Industries, 12 - 8
Energy Saving Products, 12 - 9
Fiberlux, Inc., 4 - 7
Fleetwood Aluminum Products, Inc., 12 - 9
General Aluminum Corporation, 12 - 9
Georgia Palm Beach Aluminum Window, 2 - 9
H-R Windows, 12 - 10
Hara's Inc., 12 - 10
Harry G. Barr Company, 12 - 10
Hayfield Window & Door Co., 12 - 11
Hillaldam Coburn Topdor Ltd., 4 - 9
Howard Industries Inc., 12 - 11
Hurd Millwork Company, 3 - 48
Insulate Industries, Inc., 12 - 12
International Window Corporation, 12 - 12
Jeld-Wen, 4 - 10
Joe-Keith Industries, Inc., 12 - 12
JonCo Manufacturing, Inc., 12 - 13
Jones Paint & Glass, Inc., 12 - 13
Kansas Aluminum, Inc., 12 - 13
Keller Aluminum Products, 12 - 13
Kinco Corporation, 12 - 13
Kinco, Ltd., 12 - 13
Kinro, Inc., 12 - 14
Linford Brothers/Utal Glass Co., 12 - 14
Living Windows Corporation, 12 - 14

The Complete Sourcebook

Sofa – Spindle

Index

MBS Manufacturing West, Inc., 12 - 15
Masterview Window Company,   12 - 15
Mercer Industries, Inc.,   12 - 15
Metal Industries, Inc., 12 - 16
Midland Manufacturing Corp., 2 - 7
Milgard Manufacturing, Inc., 12 - 16
Miller Industries, Inc.,   12 - 16
Moeller-Reimer Company, 12 - 16
Moss Supply Company, Inc.,   12 - 16
NT Jenkins Manufacturing Co., 12 - 17
Norandex, Inc., 12 - 18
Northwest Aluminum Products, 12 - 18
Oxford Sash Window Company,   12 - 18
Pacific Industries/Pl. Inc.,   12 - 19
Peachtree Doors, Inc., 4 - 13
Peerless Products Inc., 12 - 19
Pennco, Inc., 12 - 19
Pro-Glass Technology/Vinyl Tech Inc., 12 - 20
Public Supply Company, 12 - 20
Quaker Window Products Co.,   12 - 20
Remington/Div. of Metal Ind., Inc.,   12 - 21
Republic Aluminum Inc., 12 - 21
Reynolds Mfg. Company, Inc.,   12 - 22
Rogow Window/Ideal Aluminum,   12 - 22
Rollyson Aluminum Products,   12 - 22
S. D. Davis, Inc.,   12 - 22
Seaway Manufacturing Corp.,   12 - 23
Simonton Building Products, Inc.,   12 - 23
Skotty Aluminum Prod. Co.,   12 - 23
Southeastern Insulated Glass, 7 - 6
Sun Window Company, Inc.,   12 - 24
The Gerkin Company,   12 - 25
The Jordan Companies, 12 - 25
Thermal Profiles, Inc., 4 - 17
Thermal Windows, Inc., 12 - 25
Traco, 12 - 26
Trico Mfg./Div. of Tri-State, 12 - 26
Universal Components, 12 - 26
Viking Industries, Inc.,   12 - 27
Wallace-Crossly Corp., 4 - 17
Wells Aluminum, Inc., 12 - 28
Winter Seal of Flint, Inc.,   1 - 37

Sofa

Baker Chair Co.,   6 - 7
Barnes & Barnes,   6 - 8
Classic Choice, 6 - 17
Comoexport-Divisione Di Cantu, 6 - 18
Grand Manor Furniture Inc.,   6 - 32
John Alan Designs,   6 - 40
Klein Design Inc.,   6 - 43
La-Z-Boy Furniture,   6 - 44
Maynard House Antiques, 6 - 51
Northwoods Furniture Co.,   6 - 56
Omega Furniture,   6 - 57
Stanley Chair Co. Inc., 6 - 71
The Sofa Factory,   6 - 76
Windspire,   6 - 85

Softwood

Dimension Lumber & Milling,   1 - 14
EDLCO, 3 - 33
Henegan's Wood Shed,   3 - 45
House of Moulding,   1 - 20

Solar

American Energy Technologies Inc.,   3 - 6
American Solar Network, 3 - 7
Backwoods Solar Electric Systems,   3 - 11
Barrel Builders,   3 - 12
Bonus Books,   3 - 16

Fafco Inc.,   3 - 35
G S Energy Industries Inc.,   3 - 38
HCP Solar Div., 3 - 43
Kallwall's Solar Components Center,   3 - 51
Livingston Systems Inc.,   3 - 55
National Home Products, 3 - 63
National Solar Supply, 3 - 63
Radco Products Inc., 3 - 73
Real Goods Trading Corp.,   3 - 73
Rho Sigma Inc., 3 - 75
Samson Industries Inc., 3 - 77
Seelye Equipment Specialists, 3 - 78
Solar Additions Inc., 3 - 79
Solar Depot,   3 - 80
Solar Development Inc., 3 - 80
Solar Heating & Air Conditioning Corp., 3 - 80
Solar Innovations Inc., 3 - 80
Solar Oriented Environmental Systems,3 - 80
Solar Water Heater,   3 - 80
Solarmetrics Inc.,   3 - 80
State Industries Inc., 3 - 82
Sun Ray Solar Heaters, 3 - 84
SunEarth Inc., 3 - 84
Sunelco,   3 - 84
Sunheating Mfg. Co.,   3 - 84
The Sun Electric Co., 3 - 89
Thermomax USA Ltd.,   3 - 90
U.S. Electricar Co.,   3 - 92
United Solar Technology Inc., 3 - 93
Vaughn Mfg. Corp.,   3 - 94
Wasatch Solar Engineering,   3 - 96
Yellow Jacket Solar, 3 - 101

Solarium

A.R. Perry Glass Co.,   12 - 1
Abundant Energy, Inc., 2 - 1
Advance Technologies, Inc.,   3 - 4
Brady & Sun,   3 - 16
Burnham Corp., 3 - 18
Collier Warehouse Inc., 7 - 2
Creative Structures,   3 - 27
Florian Greenhouse Inc.,   7 - 2
Progressive Building Products, 3 - 72
Solar Additions Inc., 3 - 79
Solite Solar Greenhouses,   7 - 6
Sunbilt Solar Products, 3 - 84
Sunshine Rooms Inc.,   3 - 85

Southwestern

Lenore Mulligan Designs, Inc., 6 - 45
Onate's Cupboard, 8 - 50
Blue Canyon Woodworks, 6 - 10
Doolings of Santa Fe,   6 - 24
Ernest Thompson Furniture,   6 - 26
Form & Function,   11 - 12

Spa

Almost Heaven Hot Tubs, 2 - 1
Jacuzzi Inc.,   2 - 6
Softub Inc.,   1 - 31
Sonoma Spas,   3 - 80
Thermo Spas Inc.,   2 - 11

Spanish

Deer Creek Pottery,   3 - 30
Foreign Traders,   6 - 29
Met-Tile, Inc., 3 - 60
Spanish Pueblo Doors Inc.,   4 - 16

Spindle

CinderWhit & Company, 1 - 10

Index - 76

The Complete Sourcebook

Spiral – Staircase

Custom Woodturnings, 1 - 13
Mark A. Knudsen, 1 - 23

Spiral

Albion Design, 1 - 2
American General Products, 1 - 3
American Ornamental Corporation, 1 - 4
Aqualand Manufacturing Inc., 1 - 5
Atlantic Stairworks, 1 - 7
H & Brothers, 1 - 19
Logan Co., 1 - 22
Mylen, 1 - 24
Piedmont Home Products Inc., 1 - 27
Rich Woodturning Inc., 1 - 29
Salter Industries, 1 - 30
Spiral Manufacturing, 1 - 31
Spurwink Spiral Stairs, 1 - 32
Stair Building & Millwork Co. Inc., 1 - 32
Stair-Pak Products Co. Inc., 1 - 32
Stairways Inc., 1 - 32
Steptoe & Wife Antiques Ltd., 1 - 32
The Iron Shop, 1 - 34
Unique Spiral Stairs & Millwork Inc., 1 - 35
Visador Co., 1 - 36
York Spiral Stairs, 1 - 38

Sprinkler

Cassidy Brothers Forge, Inc., 1 - 10
Champion Irrigation Products, 3 - 23
Curvoflite Inc., 1 - 13
Duvinage Corporation, 1 - 15
Goddard Manufacturing, 1 - 18

Stain

Absolute Coatings Inc., 3 - 3
Behr Process Corp., 3 - 13
Bel-Mar Paint Corp., 3 - 13
Cabot Stains, 3 - 19
Cook & Dunn Paint Corp., 3 - 27
Star Bronze Co., 3 - 82
The Natural Choice Catalog, 3 - 88

Stained

Architectural Artifacts, 1 - 5
Architectural Salvage Company, 1 - 6
Art Glass Unlimited Inc., 12 - 4
Artglass By Misci, 3 - 9
Blenko Glass Company Inc., 3 - 15
Blum Ornamental Glass Co., Inc., 12 - 5
Boulder Art Glass Co., 3 - 16
Century Studios, 11 - 6
Cline Glass Company, 3 - 25
Conner's Architectural Antiques, 1 - 11
Contois Stained Glass Studio, 11 - 7
Cox Studios, 12 - 7
Cummings Stained Glass Studios Inc., 3 - 28
DAB Studio, 12 - 8
Delphi Stained Glass, 3 - 30
Electric Glass Co., 3 - 33
Franklin Art Glass Studios, 3 - 38
Fritz V. Sterbak Antiques, 1 - 17
Golden Age Glassworks, 12 - 10
Great Gatsby's Auction Galley, 1 - 18
Investment Antiques & Collectibles, 1 - 20
Lighthouse Stained Glass, 11 - 20
MacDonald Stained Glass, 3 - 56
Materials Unlimited, 1 - 23
Meyda Stained Glass Studio, 11 - 22
Morgan-Bockius Studios Inc., 4 - 12
New England Stained Glass Studios, 11 - 23
Nouveau Glass Art, 3 - 65

Path Enterprises, Inc., 3 - 68
Paulson's Stained Glass Studio, 12 - 19
Stained Glass Overlay Inc., 3 - 81
Sunburst Stained Glass Co. Inc., 3 - 84
Sunrise Stained Glass, 3 - 84
Unique Art Glass Co., 12 - 26
Victorian Stained Glass Illusions, 12 - 27
Westlake Architectural Antiques, 1 - 37
Willet Stained Glass Studios, 3 - 99
Williams Art Glass Studios, 12 - 28
Window Creations, 11 - 35
Wizard Windows, 12 - 28
Wooden Nickel Architectural Antique, 1 - 38
Wright's Stained Glass, 1 - 38

Stainless

(Sinks, etc.)

Carron Phoenix Ltd., 10 - 3

Stair

Adams Stair Works Carpentry Inc., 3 - 4
Allen Iron Works & Supply, 1 - 3
Aqualand Manufacturing Inc., 1 - 5
Bassett & Findley Ltd., 4 - 2
Bessler Stairway Co., 3 - 14
Botrea Stairs, 1 - 8
Brown Moulding Company, 1 - 9
Browne Winther & Co. Ltd., 1 - 9
Carolina Components Corp., 3 - 20
Collingdale Millwork Co., 1 - 11
Colonial Stair & Woodwork Co., 3 - 26
Cooper Stair Co., 3 - 27
Custom Woodturnings, 1 - 13
Danbury Stairs Corp., 1 - 13
Driwood Moulding Co., 8 - 24
Hollywood Disappearing Attic Stair Co.,3 - 47
Janik Custom Millwork, 12 - 12
John Carr Joinery Sales Ltd., 12 - 13
M. L. Condon Company Inc., 3 - 56
Magnet Trade, 4 - 11
Marwin Co., 3 - 59
Millwork Specialties, 1 - 24
Perkins Architectural Millwork, 1 - 27
Piedmont Home Products Inc., 1 - 27
Rich Woodturning Inc., 1 - 29
Richard Burbidge Ltd., 3 - 75
River City Woodworks, 5 - 8
Salter Industries, 1 - 30
Sheppard Millwork, Inc., 4 - 15
Stair Building & Millwork Co. Inc., 1 - 32
Stair Parts Ltd., 3 - 81
Stair Specialist Inc., 3 - 81
Stair-Pak Products Co. Inc., 1 - 32
Taney Stair Products Inc., 3 - 86
The Iron Shop, 1 - 34
Unique Spiral Stairs & Millwork Inc., 1 - 35
Visador Co., 1 - 36
W. R. Outhwaite & Son, 3 - 95

Staircase

Albion Design, 1 - 2
American General Products, 1 - 3
American Ornamental Corporation, 1 - 4
Aqualand Manufacturing Inc., 1 - 5
Atlantic Stairworks, 1 - 7
Cascade Wood Products Inc., 1 - 10
Cassidy Brothers Forge, Inc., 1 - 10
Colonial Stair & Woodwork Co., 3 - 26
Curvoflite Inc., 1 - 13
Dahlke Stair Co., 1 - 13
Duvinage Corporation, 1 - 15

The Complete Sourcebook

Stairway – Stool

Fayston Iron & Steel Works, 3 - 35
Goddard Manufacturing, 1 - 18
H & Brothers, 1 - 19
Logan Co., 1 - 22
Mark A. Knudsen, 1 - 23
Mylen, 1 - 24
Piedmont Home Products Inc., 1 - 27
Southern Staircase Co., 1 - 31
Spiral Manufacturing, 1 - 31
Spiral Stairs of America, 1 - 32
Spurwink Spiral Stairs, 1 - 32
Stair-Pak Products Co. Inc., 1 - 32
Stairways Inc., 1 - 32
Steptoe & Wife Antiques Ltd., 1 - 32
The Iron Shop, 1 - 34
United Stair Corp., 1 - 35
York Spiral Stairs, 1 - 38

Stairway

Albion Design, 1 - 2
American General Products, 1 - 3
American Ornamental Corporation, 1 - 4
Atlantic Stairworks, 1 - 7
Bessler Stairway Co., 3 - 14
Cassidy Brothers Forge, Inc., 1 - 10
Dahlke Stair Co., 1 - 13
Duvinage Corporation, 1 - 15
Goddard Manufacturing, 1 - 18
H & Brothers, 1 - 19
Mylen, 1 - 24
Stairways Inc., 1 - 32
Tomlin Industries Inc., 2 - 11
United Stair Corp., 1 - 35
York Spiral Stairs, 1 - 38

Steel

(Staircases, Trusses, etc.)
A & S Window Associates, Inc., 3 - 1
American Ornamental Corporation, 1 - 4
Atlas Roll-lite Door Co., 4 - 2
CECO Corp., 4 - 3
Carron Phoenix Ltd., 10 - 3
Castlegate, Inc., 4 - 3
Cirecast, 3 - 24
Conklin Metal Industries, 3 - 26
Curriers Co., 4 - 4
Dale Incor, Inc., 3 - 29
Dunbarton Corp., 4 - 6
Enterprise Industries, Inc., 3 - 34
Fenestra Corp., 4 - 7
General Products Co. Inc., 4 - 8
Heart Truss & Engineering, 3 - 44
Iowa Des Moines Door & Hardware, 4 - 9
Johnson Metal Products, 4 - 10
Met-Tile, Inc., 3 - 60
Monarch Radiator Enclosures, 3 - 61
Mylen, 1 - 24
North Central Door Co., 4 - 12
Overhead Door Corp., 4 - 13
Pease Industries, Inc., 4 - 13
Perma-Door, 4 - 13
Register & Grille Manufacturing Co. ,1 - 29
Reid Building & Truss Co., 3 - 74
Room & Board, 6 - 64
Spiral Stairs of America, 1 - 32
Stairways Inc., 1 - 32
Steldor Ltd., 4 - 16
Taylor Building Products, 4 - 16
Torrance Steel Window Co. Inc., 12 - 25
Traulsen & Co., Inc., 10 - 10
Wayne-Dalton Corporation, 4 - 18

Stencil

Adele-Bishop, 8 - 2
American Homes Stencils, Inc., 8 - 4
Andreae Designs, 8 - 5
Artistic Interiors, 8 - 6
Badger Air Brush Co., 8 - 7
Decoral Inc., 8 - 22
Epoch Designs, 8 - 25
Gail Grisi Stenciling Inc., 8 - 29
Jan Dressler Stencils, 8 - 37
Jeannie Serpa Stencils, 8 - 37
Joanne Aviet Stencils, 8 - 38
Liberty Design Co., 8 - 42
Manorhouse Designs, 8 - 44
Sophie's Stencils, 8 - 62
Stenart Inc., 8 - 63
Stencil House of New Hampshire, 8 - 63
Stencil Outlet, 8 - 63
Stencil World, 8 - 63
The Itinerant Stenciler, 8 - 67
The Seraph Country Collection, 6 - 76
The Stencil Collector, 8 - 67
The Stencil Outlet, 8 - 67
The Stencil Shoppe, Inc., 8 - 68
Thursday's Child, 8 - 68
Yowler & Shepps Stencils, 8 - 78

Stone

(Granite, Marble, Flagstone, Sandstone, etc.)
A/S Johs. Gronseth & Co., 3 - 2
ABN, 1 - 1
Ashfield Stone Quarry, 3 - 9
Assimagra, 3 - 10
Assomarmi, 3 - 10
Briar Hill Stone Co., 3 - 17
Carl Schilling Stoneworks, 3 - 20
Delaware Quarries, Inc., 3 - 30
Deutscher Naturwerstein, 3 - 31
Diamond K. Co., Inc., 5 - 3
Eurocobble, 3 - 34
FBAMTP, 3 - 35
FFPM, 3 - 35
FNMMB, 3 - 35
Georgia Marble Company, 3 - 39
Idaho Quartzite Corp., 3 - 49
Johnston & Rhodes Bluestone Co., 3 - 51
Marble Institute of America, 3 - 57
Nailite International Inc., 3 - 63
National Association of Master Masons, 3 - 63
North American Stone Co. Ltd., 3 - 64
Origines, 6 - 57
Panhellenic Marble Association, 3 - 68
Pasvalco, 3 - 68
Rocktile Specialty Products Inc., 3 - 76
Steninindustriens Landssammenslutning, 3 - 82
Stone Federation, 3 - 83
Stone Magic Mfg., 8 - 63
Stone Products Corporation, 3 - 83
Sveriges Stenindustriforbund, 3 - 85
The Stone & Marble Supermarket, 3 - 89
UCSMB, 3 - 93
UGIMA, 3 - 93
Vermont Soapstone Co., 3 - 95
Vetter Stone Co., 1 - 36
Walker & Zanger, 3 - 95

Stool

Anger Mfg. Co., Inc., 6 - 4

Index

Storm – Supply

Candlertown Chairworks, 6 - 14
D & L Mfg., Co., 6 - 21
Essential Items, 6 - 27
Jr Ross Ltd., 6 - 41
Mark Sales Co. Inc., 6 - 50

Storm

(Doors, Windows, etc.)
A & C Metal Products Co. Inc., 12 - 1
A.R. Perry Glass Co., 12 - 1
AAA Aluminum Stamping, Inc., 12 - 1
Advantage Window Systems Inc., 12 - 2
Allied Window Inc., 12 - 2
American Screen & Door Co., Inc., 12 - 3
Anaconda Aluminum, 12 - 4
Cole Sewell Corp., 4 - 4
EMCO, 4 - 6
Grand Era Reproductions, 4 - 8
J. A. Dawley Fine Woodworking, 7 - 3
Petit Industries Inc., 12 - 19
Taylor Brothers Inc., 4 - 16
The Alternative Window Co., 12 - 24
Thermo-Press Corp., 12 - 25
Touchstone Woodworks, 4 - 17

Stove

(Antique, Coal, Gas, Reproductions, Wood, etc.)
AGA Cookers, 10 - 1
Appalachian Stove & Fab, 3 - 8
Barnstable Stove Shop, 10 - 1
Brown Stove Works Inc., 3 - 17
Bryant Stove Works, 3 - 17
Butler Stove Co., 3 - 18
Ceramic Radiant Heat, 3 - 22
Dovre, 3 - 32
Elmira Stove And Fireplace, 10 - 4
Englander Wood Stoves, 3 - 34
Erickson's Antique Stoves, 10 - 4
Frizelle Enos Co., 3 - 38
Garland Commercial Industries, Inc., 10 - 5
Glo King Woodstoves, 3 - 41
Good Time Stove Co., 3 - 41
Hayes Equipment Corp., 3 - 44
Heat-Fab Inc., 3 - 44
Heatilator Inc., 3 - 45
Heating Research Co., 3 - 45
Heritage Energy Systems, 3 - 45
Jotul USA, 10 - 6
Keokuk Stove Works, 3 - 52
Kickapoo Diversified Products Inc., 3 - 52
Lehman Hardware, 3 - 54
Meeco Mfg. Co., 3 - 59
Mohawk Industries Inc., 3 - 61
NHC Inc., 3 - 62
New Buck Corporation, 3 - 64
New-Aire Mfg. Co., Inc., 3 - 64
O'Dette Energies of Canada Ltd., 3 - 66
Portland Stove Company, 3 - 71
Rayburn, 10 - 8
Taylor Manufacturing, Inc., 3 - 86
The House of Webster, 10 - 10
Thermal Control Co., 3 - 90
Vermont Castings, 3 - 95
Viking Range Corporation, 10 - 10
Woodstock Soapstone Co., Inc., 3 - 100

Stucco

Dryvit Systems, Inc., 3 - 32
Stuc-O-Flex International Inc., 3 - 83

Stud

Dale Incor, Inc., 3 - 29

Sunroom

Abundant Energy, Inc., 2 - 1
Advance Technologies, Inc., 3 - 4
Amdega Ltd., 3 - 6
Circle Redmont Inc., 3 - 24
Four Seasons, 3 - 38
Lindal Cedar Sunrooms, 3 - 55
Pella Corporation, 12 - 19
Regal Manufacturing Co., 3 - 74
Southeastern Insulated Glass, 7 - 6
Sun Room Company, 7 - 7
Westview Products, Inc., 3 - 98

Sunscreen

Courtaulds Performance Films, 12 - 7

Supply

(Building, Craft, Electrical, Garden, Plumbing, etc.)
Abatron Inc., 3 - 3
Acme Plumbing Specialties, 3 - 3
Addington-Beamon Lumber, 6 - 2
Albeni Falls Building Supply, 3 - 5
All-Phase Electric Supplies, 3 - 5
Alro Plumbing Specialty Co. Inc., 3 - 5
American Brass Mfg., 10 - 1
American Energy Technologies Inc., 3 - 6
American Solar Network, 3 - 7
Antioch Building Materials, 3 - 8
Appalachian Stove & Fab, 3 - 8
Aylward Products Co., 3 - 11
B & P Lamp Supply Inc., 11 - 4
B. F. Gilmour Co., 3 - 11
BMC West Building Materials, 3 - 11
Badgerland Building Material, 3 - 11
Barrel Builders, 3 - 12
Bay Shore Light & Elec. Supply, 11 - 4
Beautyware Plumbing Products, 3 - 13
Bohemia Plumbing Supply Co. Inc., 3 - 15
Bootz Plumbingware, 3 - 16
Builders Bargains, 3 - 17
Builders Square, 3 - 17
Building Products of America Corp., 3 - 17
CBS Home Express, 3 - 18
CGM Inc., 3 - 18
CPN Inc., 3 - 18
Cane & Basket Supply Company, 6 - 14
Cisco, 3 - 24
Coker's Wholesale Building Supply, 3 - 25
Colonial Building Supply, 3 - 25
Complete Carpentry Inc., 3 - 26
Condar Company, 3 - 26
Consolidated Electrical Distributor, 3 - 27
Country Plumbing, 3 - 27
Craft King, 8 - 19
Crest/Good Mfg. Co., Inc., 3 - 28
Daniels-Olsen Building Products, 3 - 29
De Best Mfg. Co., Inc., 3 - 30
Deutscher & Sons, Inc., 3 - 31
Devine Lumber Do-It-Center, 3 - 31
Donald Durham Co., 3 - 31
Dried Flower Creations, 6 - 24
Dundee Manufacturing Co., 3 - 32
E.L. Hilts & Company, 3 - 32
Electrical Wholesale, 3 - 33
Energy Pioneers, 3 - 34
Fafco Inc., 3 - 35

The Complete Sourcebook

Index - 79

Supply – Supply

Index

Fahrenheat Heating Products, 3 - 35
Fastenation, 1 - 16
Forest Siding Supply Inc., 3 - 38
Freundlich Supply Co., 3 - 38
G S Energy Industries Inc., 3 - 38
Gas Appliance Manufacturers, 3 - 39
General Building Products Corp., 3 - 39
Genova Products, 3 - 39
George Wells Rugs, 8 - 30
Gold Bond Building Products, 3 - 41
Grand Brass Lamp Parts, 11 - 14
Granville Manufacturing Co. Inc., 3 - 42
Greeter Building Center, 3 - 42
H. H. Robertson Co., 3 - 43
H. M. Stauffer & Sons Inc., 3 - 43
HCP Solar Div., 3 - 43
Hancock Gross Inc., 3 - 43
Heat-N-Glo Fireplace Products Inc., 3 - 45
Heckler Brothers, 3 - 45
Home Electric Supply, 3 - 47
Home Improvement Supply, 3 - 47
Home Quarters Warehouse, 3 - 47
Home Warehouse Inc., 3 - 47
Honani Crafts, 8 - 34
Hopi Arts & Crafts, 8 - 34
Housecraft Associates, 3 - 47
ITT Rayonier Inc., 3 - 49
Indiana Brass, 10 - 5
International Manufacturing Co., 8 - 36
International Supply Co., 2 - 6
Island Lumber Co., Inc., 3 - 50
J & L Floral, 8 - 36
Jack's Upholstery & Caning Supplies, 8 - 37
Jameco Industries Inc., 3 - 50
Kallwall's Solar Components Center, 3 - 51
Kanebridge Corp., 3 - 51
Kelly & Hayes Electrical Supply Inc., 3 - 52
Kennedy Electrical Supply, 3 - 52
Lakeland Builders Supply, 3 - 53
Lemee's Fireplace Equipment, 3 - 54
Livingston Systems Inc., 3 - 55
Lotus Water Garden Products Ltd., 7 - 4
M & H Design & Home Center, 2 - 7
M & S Systems, 3 - 56
Mac The Antique Plumber, 3 - 56
Mansfield Plumbing Products, 3 - 57
Marion Plywood Corp., 3 - 58
Marjam Supply Company, 3 - 58
Marque Enterprises, 3 - 58
Marsak Cohen, Cohen Corp., 3 - 58
Maryland Lumber Co., 3 - 59
Meadow Everlasting, 8 - 45
Meeco Mfg. Co., 3 - 59
Meyer Furnace Co., 3 - 60
Midwest Lumber & Supply, 3 - 60
Moller's Building & Home Centers, 3 - 61
Mount Baker Plywood Inc., 3 - 62
Mutual Screw & Supply, 3 - 62
Nashville Sash & Door Co., 3 - 63
National Concrete Masonry Assoc., 3 - 63
National Solar Supply, 3 - 63
Nevada County Building Supply, 3 - 63
New York replacement Parts Corp., 12 - 17
Old Home Building & Restoration, 3 - 66
Olderman Mfg. Corp., 3 - 66
PDC Home Supply, 3 - 67
PGL Building Products, 3 - 68
Patterncrafts, 8 - 52
Payless Cashways, 3 - 68
Pecora Corporation, 3 - 69
Price Pfister Inc., 2 - 9

PriceKing Building Supply Inc., 3 - 71
Pukall Lumber Co., 3 - 72
R & R Crafts, 7 - 5
Real Goods Trading Corp., 3 - 73
Rennovator's Supply, 1 - 29
Reservation Creations, 8 - 55
Rho Sigma Inc., 3 - 75
Richmond Foundry & Mfg. Co., 3 - 75
Rockford-Eclipse, 3 - 76
Roofmaster Products Company, 3 - 76
Royal Brass Mfg. Co., 3 - 76
S. Scherer & Sons Water Gardens, 7 - 6
Samson Industries Inc., 3 - 77
Sanders Building Supply Inc., 3 - 77
Sav On Discount Material, 3 - 77
Sayville Plumbing Go., 3 - 77
Schmitt Builders Supply, 3 - 78
Seelye Equipment Specialists, 3 - 78
Shakertown Corp., 3 - 78
Sioux Chief Mfg. Co. Inc., 3 - 79
Solar Development Inc., 3 - 80
Solar Heating & Air Conditioning Corp., 3 - 80
Solar Innovations Inc., 3 - 80
Solar Oriented Environmental Systems, 3 - 80
Solarmetrics Inc., 3 - 80
South & Jones Lumber Co., 3 - 80
Southland Building Inc., 3 - 81
Specification Chemicals Inc., 3 - 81
Sun Ray Solar Heaters, 3 - 84
SunEarth Inc., 3 - 84
Sundance II Fireplace Distributors, 3 - 84
Sunelco, 3 - 84
Sunheating Mfg. Co., 3 - 84
Supply Line, 3 - 85
T & S Brass & Bronze Works Inc., 2 - 11
TJ International Inc., 3 - 86
The 18th Century Company, 3 - 87
The Caning Shop, 6 - 75
The Majestic Co., 3 - 56 , 7 - 8
The Sun Electric Co., 3 - 89
Thermomax USA Ltd., 3 - 90
Thompson Lumber Co., 3 - 90
Thorn Lumber Co., 3 - 90
Tri-City Lumber/Building Supplies, 3 - 92
Trimall Interior Products Inc., 3 - 92
Trus Joist Corporation, 3 - 92
Tuff-Kote Company, 3 - 92
U.S. Electricar Co., 3 - 92
United Solar Technology Inc., 3 - 93
United States Gypsum Company, 3 - 93
Urdl's Waterfall Creation Inc., 7 - 7
Valley Builders Supply, 3 - 94
Valley Lumber & Hardware, 3 - 94
Vermont Frames, 1 - 36
Vestal Mfg., 3 - 95
Wallace Supply & Wholesale Distributor, 3 - 96
Watco Mfg. Co., 3 - 96
Water Works, 7 - 8
Waterford Gardens, 7 - 8
West Michigan Nail Co., 3 - 97
Westinghouse Electric Supply, 3 - 98
Wiggins & Son Inc., 3 - 98
Wilco Building Material Distributors, 3 - 98
Wolohan Lumber & Improvement, 3 - 100
Woodward-Wanger Co., 3 - 100
Worm's Way, 7 - 8
Wrightway Mfg. Co., 3 - 101
Wyoming Lumber & Supply Co., 3 - 101
Yellow Jacket Solar, 3 - 101

Index

Surround

Aagard-Hanley Ltd., 11 - 1
Accents In Stone, 3 - 3
Architectural Heritage, 1 - 6
Axon Products, 1 - 7
BD Mantels Ltd., 1 - 7
Browne Winther & Co. Ltd., 1 - 9
Emsworth Fireplaces Ltd., 1 - 15
Feature Fires Ltd., 1 - 16
Gawet Marble & Granite Inc., 3 - 39
Maple Grove Restorations, 1 - 22
Minuteman International Co., 3 - 61
Roger Pearson, 1 - 30
The Structural Slate Co., 3 - 89

Swag

Designs for Living Inc., 11 - 9
Dana's Curtains & Draperies, 8 - 21

Swing

Adirondack Designs, 6 - 3
Alfresco Porch Swing Company, 6 - 3
Anger Mfg. Co., Inc., 6 - 4
Gazebo & Porchworks, 7 - 3
Masterworks, 6 - 51
O'Connor's Cypress Woodworks, 6 - 56
The Rocker Shop of Marietta, 6 - 76

Switch

Classic Accents, 3 - 25
Jackson Mfg. Co., 11 - 17
Olivers Lighting Company, 11 - 24
Pass & Seymour, 11 - 25
Precision Multiple Controls, Inc., 3 - 71

System

(Door, Heating, Irrigation, Security, Vacumn, Wall, etc.)

ABCO Supply Company, 9 - 1
Advanced Security, 9 - 1
Alarm Supply Co., 9 - 1
Allister Door Control Systems Inc., 4 - 1
Bedquarters, 6 - 8
Blanco America, 10 - 2
Burdex Security Co., 9 - 1
Burnham, 3 - 18
Caberboard Ltd., 3 - 18
Carrier Corp., 3 - 20
Deeprock, 3 - 30
Dow Chemical USA, 3 - 32
Enerjee International, 2 - 4
HCP Solar Div., 3 - 43
Harden Furniture Inc., 6 - 34
Heath Zenith, 9 - 2
Hillaldam Coburn Topdor Ltd., 4 - 9
Home Automation, Inc., 9 - 2
Honeywell Inc., 9 - 2
Hudevad Britain, 3 - 47
Hydrotherm Inc., 3 - 48
Kallista, 2 - 6
Lennox International Inc., 3 - 54
Omar's Built-In Vacuum Systems, 3 - 66
Premier Communications Company, 9 - 3
RainDrip Water Systems, 7 - 5
Schlage, 9 - 3
Security Link Corporation, 9 - 3
Stanley Door Systems, 4 - 16
Submatic Irrigation Systems, 7 - 7
The J. Goodman Co., 9 - 3
Unity System Inc., 9 - 3

Vision Security Inc., 9 - 3
Wal-Vac Inc., 3 - 95
Wanda Mfg. Co. Inc., 3 - 96
Weil-McLain, 3 - 97
Wellington Hall, Ltd., 3 - 97
Westco Security Systems Inc., 9 - 3
Yellow Jacket Solar, 3 - 101

Table

AMCOA Inc., 6 - 1
Arrben Di O. Benvenuto, 6 - 5
Art In Iron, 6 - 5
Artemide, 11 - 3
Athens Furniture, 6 - 6
Baker Chair Co., 6 - 7
Charles Co., Inc., 11 - 7
Ciro Coppa, 6 - 16
Comoexport-Divisione Di Cantu, 6 - 18
Coppa Woodworking, 6 - 18
Cornucopia, Inc., 6 - 19
Country Bed Shop, 6 - 19
Designs for Living Inc., 11 - 9
Dominion Chair, Ltd., 6 - 24
Dynasty Classics Corp., 11 - 9
Elk Valley Woodworking Inc., 6 - 26
Execulamp Inc., 11 - 11
Fine Arts Furniture Co., 6 - 28
Flexform, 6 - 28
Flexform, 6 - 28
Frederick Duckloe & Bros., 6 - 30
Glober Mfg. Co., 6 - 32
Good Tables Inc., 6 - 32
Grange Furniture, Inc., 6 - 32
Great Paines Glassworks, 4 - 8
Howard's Antique Lighting, 11 - 16
Imperial Marble, Inc., 3 - 49
J. F. Orr & Sons, 10 - 6
Jones' Oak Furniture, 6 - 41
Kenneth Winslow Furniture, 6 - 41
Kings River Casting, 6 - 42
Klein Design Inc., 6 - 43
Kopil & Associates Timeless Furniture, 6 - 43
La Barge Mirrors, Inc., 8 - 41
Marble & Tile Imports, 3 - 57
Marion Travis, 6 - 49
Mark Dahlman Wood Products, 6 - 49
Mark Sales Co. Inc., 6 - 50
Masterworks, 6 - 51
Messer Industries, Inc., 8 - 45
Milano Marble Co., Inc., 2 - 7
Minic Custom Woodwork, Inc., 6 - 53
Minton Corley Collection, 3 - 61
Miya Shoji & Interiors Inc., 8 - 47
Nicola Ceramics & Marble, 3 - 64
Norman Perry, 11 - 23
Old Hickory Furniture Co. Inc., 6 - 56
Ottawa Brass Ltd., 6 - 57
Pottery Barn, 6 - 60
Prochnow & Prochnow, 7 - 5
Queen City Glass Ltd., 8 - 54
Room & Board, 6 - 64
Rose Hill Furniture, 6 - 64
Shaker Shops West, 6 - 67
Shaker Workshops, 3 - 78
Shushan Bentwood Co., 6 - 68
Silhoutte Antiques Inc., 6 - 68
Taos Drums, 6 - 73
The Brass Collection, 6 - 75
The Keeping Room, 6 - 75
The Linen Gallery, 8 - 67
The Shop Woodcrafters, Inc., 6 - 76

The Complete Sourcebook

Index - 81

Tap – Tile

Tidewater Workshop, 6 - 78
Victorian Attic, 6 - 80
Victorian Brass Works Ltd., 6 - 80
Vitra Seating Inc., 6 - 81
Weru (UK, etc.) Ltd., 10 - 11
Wheeler Woodworking, 6 - 83
Windspire, 6 - 85
Wood Goods Inc., 6 - 85
Zanotta, S.p.A./Palladio Trading Inc., 6 - 87

Tap
(Kitchen, Bathroom, etc.)
Astracast PLC, 12 - 4
Barber Wilsons & Co. Ltd., 2 - 2
Hans Grohe Ltd., 2 - 5
Ideal-Standard Ltd., 2 - 6
Meynell Valves Ltd., 2 - 7
Trevi Showers, 2 - 11

Tapestry
Heath Sedgwick, 11 - 14
Hines of Oxford, 3 - 46
Karen Nelson, 8 - 39
Lovelia Enterprises, 8 - 43
Peerless Imported Rugs, 8 - 52
Sanderson, 8 - 58

Teakwood
(Decking, Furniture, Lumber, etc.)
BRE Lumber, 3 - 11
Bangkok International, 5 - 2
Barlow Tyrie, 6 - 8
Blake Industries, 6 - 10
British-American Marketing Services, 6 - 12
Country Casual, 6 - 19
Design Furniture Mfg. Ltd., 6 - 23
Fong Brothers Company, 6 - 29
Indian Ocean Trading Co., 6 - 38
Kingsley-Bate, Ltd., 6 - 42
Lister Teak, Inc., 6 - 46
Maurice L. Condon Co., 3 - 59
Midwest Dowel Works, Inc., 3 - 60
Quality Woods Ltd., 5 - 8
The Natural Woodflooring Company, 5 - 10
Wood Classics, 6 - 85

Telephone
(Antique, etc.)
Mahantango Manor Inc., 8 - 44

Terracotta
Albert Gunther, 3 - 5
Amaru Tile, 3 - 6
American International, 3 - 6
Angelo Amaru Tile & Bath Collection, 3 - 8
Ann Sacks Tile & Stone, 3 - 8
Boston Valley Pottery, 3 - 16
Cancos Tile Corporation, 3 - 19
Ceramiche Brunelleschi S.P.A., 3 - 22
Cisa-Cerdisa-Smov, 3 - 24
Country Floors, 5 - 3
D & B Tile Distributors, 3 - 29
Domus Linea S.P.A., 3 - 31
Hastings Tile & Il Bagno Collection, 3 - 44
Hutcherson Tile, 3 - 48
Impronta S.P.A., 3 - 49
International Terra Cotta, 7 - 3
Kris Elosvolo, 3 - 53
Nemo Tile Company, Inc., 3 - 63
Origines, 6 - 57

Paris Ceramics, 3 - 68
Syracuse Pottery, 8 - 65
The Merchant Tiler, 3 - 88

Terrazzo
H. B. Fuller Co./TEC Incorporated, 3 - 43
Midwestern Terrazzo corp., 5 - 7
Vassallo Precast Mfg. Corp., 2 - 12

Textile
D.L. Couch Contract Wallcovering, 8 - 21
Jameson Home Products, 3 - 50

Threshold
Cumberland Lumber & Manufacturing, 5 - 3
MacBeath Hardwood Co., 1 - 22

Tibetan
Jacqueline Vance Oriental Rugs, 8 - 37

Tiffany
Century Studios, 11 - 6
Dale Tiffany Inc., 11 - 9
EMC Tiffany, 11 - 10
Lundburg Studios, 11 - 21
Nova, 11 - 24
Renaissance Marketing, 11 - 26
Studio Design, 11 - 30
Uroboros Glass Studios Inc., 1 - 36

Tile
ACIF Ceramiche S.R.L., 3 - 2
Actiengesellschaft, 3 - 3
Agrob-Wessel-Servais AG, 3 - 4
Albert Gunther, 3 - 5
Alfa Ceramiche, 3 - 5
Amaru Tile, 3 - 6
American International, 3 - 6
American Marazzi Tile, 3 - 7
American Marble Co., Inc., 3 - 7
American Olean Tile Co., 3 - 7
Amsterdam Corporation, 3 - 7
Andrews & Sons (Marbles & Tiles), 3 - 7
Angelo Amaru Tile & Bath Collection, 3 - 8
Ann Sacks Tile & Stone, 3 - 8
Antiche Ceramiche D'Talia (ACIT) S.R.L.3 - 8
Arius Tile Co., 3 - 9
Armstar, 3 - 9
Arnold-Missouri Corp., 3 - 9
Art on Tiles, 3 - 9
Artesanos Imports, Inc., 6 - 6
Ashfield Stone Quarry, 3 - 9
Association of Greek Heavy Clay Mftrs.,3- 10
Associazione Nazionale degli Industriali,3- 10
Badger Tiles, 3 - 11
Baukeramik U., 3 - 12
Bel Vasaio Ltd., 3 - 13
Belfi Bros. & Co., Inc., 3 - 13
Bellegrove Ceramics Ltd., 3 - 13
Bender Roof Tile Ind.Inc., 3 - 14
Bertin Studio Tiles, 3 - 14
Bettina Elsner Artistic Tiles, 3 - 15
Bisazza Mosaico S.P.A., 3 - 15
Blackland Moravian Tile Works, 3 - 15
Booth-Muirie Ltd., 1 - 8
Boston Tile Company, 2 - 3
Boston Valley Pottery, 3 - 16
Brooklyn Tile Supply Co., 3 - 17
Bundesverband der Deutschen, 3 - 18
Busby Gilbert Tile Co., 3 - 18
Calendar Tiles Ltd., 3 - 19
California Tile Supply, 3 - 19

Index

Tile – Tile

California Wholesale Tile, 3 - 19
Cambridge Tile Mfg. Co., 3 - 19
Cancos Tile Corporation, 3 - 19
Candy Tiles Ltd., 3 - 20
Cedir S.P.A., 3 - 21
Cedit S.P.A., 3 - 21
Celadon Ceramic Slate, 3 - 21
Cemar International S.P.A., 3 - 21
Central Distributors Inc., 3 - 21
Century Floors Inc., 5 - 3
Ceramica Candia S.P.A., 3 - 22
Ceramica Colli Di Sassuolo S.P.A., 3 - 22
Ceramica Del Conca S.P.A., 3 - 22
Ceramica Ilsa S.P.A., 3 - 22
Ceramica Panaria S.P.A., 3 - 22
Ceramiche Atlas Concorde S.P.A., 3 - 22
Ceramiche Brunelleschi S.P.A., 3 - 22
Ceramiche Cuoghitalia S.P.A., 3 - 22
Ceramiche Edilcuoghi S.P.A., 3 - 23
Ceramiche Edilgres-Sirio S.P.A., 3 - 23
Ceramografia Artigiana S.P.A., 3 - 23
Cerdomus Ceramiche S.P.A., 3 - 23
Cerim Ceramiche S.P.A., 3 - 23
Charles Rupert Designs, 3 - 23
Cisa-Cerdisa-Smov, 3 - 24
Co-Em S.R.L., 3 - 25
Colonial Marble Products Ltd., 3 - 25
Color Tile Ceramic Mfr. Co., 3 - 26
Color Tile Inc., 3 - 26
Conservation Building Products Ltd., 3 - 26
Continental Ceramic Tile, 3 - 27
Continental Clay Company, 3 - 27
Cooperativa Ceramica D'Imola Soc ARL,3 - 27
Country Floors, 5 - 3
Crest Distributors, 3 - 28
Croonen KG, 3 - 28
Crossville Ceramics, 3 - 28
D & B Tile Distributors, 3 - 29
Dado Ceramica S.R.L., 3 - 29
Dal-Tile, 3 - 29
Deer Creek Pottery, 3 - 30
Designer Ceramics, 3 - 30
Designs in Tile, 3 - 31
Domus Linea S.P.A., 3 - 31
Dutch Products & Supply Co., 3 - 32
D'Mundo Tile, 3 - 29
EPRO, Inc., 3 - 33
East Coast Tile Imports Inc., 3 - 33
Elon Inc., 3 - 33
Endicott Tile Ltd., 3 - 34
Fergene Studio, 3 - 35
Fierst Distributing Co., 3 - 36
Firebird Inc., 3 - 36
Fired Earth Tiles PLC, 5 - 4
Flooring Distributors, 5 - 4
Florano Ceramic Tile Design Center, 3 - 37
Florian Tiles, 3 - 37
Florida Brick & Clay Co.,Inc., 3 - 37
Florida Ceramic Tile Center, 3 - 37
Florida Tile Industries, Inc., 3 - 37
Focus Ceramics Ltd., 3 - 37
GMT Floor Tile, Inc., 3 - 38
GTE Products Corp., 3 - 39
Gabbianelli S.R.L., 3 - 39
Georgia Marble Company, 3 - 39
Gercomi Corp., 3 - 40
Globe Marble & Tile, 3 - 41
Granite Lake Pottery, 2 - 5
Granitech Corp., 3 - 41
Groupement National de l'Industrie, 3 - 42
Gruppo Elba S.P.A., 3 - 42

H & R Johnson Tiles, 3 - 42
Handcraft Tile Inc., 3 - 43
Hastings Tile & Il Bagno Collection, 3 - 44
Helen Williams - Delft Tiles, 3 - 45
Hilltop Slate Co., 3 - 46
Humes, 3 - 48
Huntington/Pacific Ceramics, Inc., 3 - 48
Hutcherson Tile, 3 - 48
I. C. R. S.P.A. (Appiani, etc.), 3 - 48
IMPO Glaztile, 3 - 48
Idaho Quartzite Corp., 3 - 49
Ideal tile of Manhatttan Inc., 3 - 49
Illahe Tileworks, 3 - 49
Impronta S.P.A., 3 - 49
Italian Tile Center, 3 - 50
Julius Seidel & Company, 3 - 51
KPT, Incorporated, 3 - 51
Kalk-og Teglvaerksforeningen af 1893, 3 - 51
Keniston Tile & Design, 3 - 52
Klingenberg Dekoramik GmbH, 3 - 53
Koninkijk Verbond van Nederlandse, 3 - 53
Kraftile Company, 3 - 53
Kris Elosvolo, 3 - 53
La France Architectural Stone & Design,1- 21
La Luz Canyon Studio, 3 - 53
LaFaenza America Inc., 3 - 53
Latco Ceramic Tile, 3 - 54
Laticrete International Inc., 3 - 54
Laufen International, Inc., 3 - 54
Laura Ashley, 8 - 41
Leonardo 1502 Ceramica S.p. A., 3 - 54
Lifetile, 3 - 55
Lifetime Rooftile Co., 3 - 55
Lone Star Ceramics Company, 3 - 55
Ludowici Celadon Co. Inc., 3 - 56
L'esperance Tile Works, 3 - 53
Mannington Ceramic Tile, 3 - 57
Marble Concepts, 3 - 57
Marcello Marble & Tile PLS, 2 - 7
Marlborough Ceramic Tiles, 3 - 58
Marley Roof Tiles, Canada Ltd., 3 - 58
Maruhachi Ceramics of America Inc., 3 - 58
McIntyre Tile Co. Inc., 3 - 59
Meissen-Keramik GmbH, 3 - 60
Metco Tile Distributors, 3 - 60
Metropolitan Ceramics, 8 - 46
Millen Roofing Company, 3 - 60
Mission Tile West, 3 - 61
Monarch Tile Inc., 3 - 61
Monier Roof Tile Inc., 3 - 61
Moretti-Harrah Marble Co., 3 - 62
Mosaic Supplies Inc., 3 - 62
Motawi Tileworks, 3 - 62
National Ceramics of Florida, 3 - 63
National Ceramics, 3 - 63
Nemo Tile Company, Inc., 3 - 63
Norges Teglindustrieforening, 3 - 64
Novatile Ltd., 3 - 65
Nuove Ceramiche Ricchetti, S.r.l., 3 - 65
Old & Elegant Distributing, 2 - 8
Old Country Ceramic Tile, 3 - 66
Onyx Enterprises of America, 3 - 67
Origines, 6 - 57
Orignial Style, 3 - 67
Ostara-Fliesen Gmbh & Co. KG, 3 - 67
Paris Ceramics, 3 - 68
Peter Josef Korzilius Soehne GmbH, 3 - 69
Pewabic Pottery Co., 3 - 69
Pioneer Roofing Tile Inc., 3 - 70
Pipe Dreams, 2 - 9
Plain and Fancy Ceramic Tile, 3 - 70

The Complete Sourcebook

Index - 83

Tin – Treatment

Ply-Gem Mfg., 3 - 70
Porcelanosa, 3 - 71
Praire Marketing, 3 - 71
Quality Marble Inc., 3 - 72
Quarry Tile Company, 3 - 73
Raleigh Inc., 3 - 73
Rams Imports, 3 - 73
Red Clay Tile Works, 3 - 73
Richmond Ceramic Tile Distributors , 3 - 75
Ro-Tile Inc., 3 - 76
Rocktile Specialty Products Inc., 3 - 76
San Do Designs, 3 - 77
Santa Catalina, 3 - 77
Santa Fe Trading Co., 3 - 77
Shelly Tile Inc., 3 - 78
Sherle Wagner, 2 - 10
Sikes Corp, 3 - 79
Simpson Tile Co., 3 - 79
Snelling's Thermo-Vac, Inc., 3 - 79
South Side Roofing Co. Inc., 3 - 80
Southampton Brick & Tile Co., 3 - 81
Spiegelwerk Wilsdruff GmbH, 3 - 81
Staco Roof Tile Manufacturing, 3 - 81
Staloton - Die keramiker H.H., 3 - 82
Standard Tile Distributors Inc., 3 - 82
Starbuck Goldner Tile, 3 - 82
Stonelight Tile Co., 3 - 83
Stoneware Tile Company, 3 - 83
Structural Stoneware Inc., 3 - 83
Summitville Tiles Inc., 3 - 84
Sun House Tiles, 3 - 84
Suomen Tiiliteollisuusliitto r.y., 3 - 85
Swedecor Ltd., 3 - 85
Tarkett Ceramic Inc., 3 - 86
Tarkett Inc., 5 - 9
Terra Designs, Inc., 3 - 87
The Brick Development Association, 3 - 87
The Decorative Tile Works, 3 - 88
The Merchant Tiler, 3 - 88
The Northern Roof Tile Sales Co., 3 - 89
The Roof, Tile & Slate Co., 3 - 89
The Shop, 3 - 89
The Tile Collection, 3 - 89
The Tileworks, 3 - 89
The Willette Corporation, 3 - 90
Tile & Marble Designs, 3 - 90
Tile Creations, 3 - 90
Tile Emporium International, 3 - 90
Tile Mart International, 3 - 91
Tile Promotion Board, 3 - 91
Tile West Distributors, 3 - 91
Tile and Designs Inc., 3 - 91
Tile with Style, 3 - 91
Tilepak America Inc., 3 - 91
U.S. Ceramic Tile Co., 3 - 92
United Ceramic Tile Corp., 3 - 93
United States Ceramic Tile Co., 3 - 93
Vande Hey-Raleigh Manufacturing Inc.,3 - 94
Verband Schweiz. Ziegel, 3 - 95
Victorian Collectibles, 8 - 72
Victory Tile & Marble, 3 - 95
Villeroy & Boch (USA, etc.) Inc., 2 - 12
Villeroy & Boch AG, 2 - 12
Villeroy & Boch Ltd., 2 - 12
Walker & Zanger, 3 - 95
Wandplattenfabrik Engers GmbH, 3 - 96
Wayne Tile Company, 3 - 96
Western Oregon Tile Supplies, 3 - 97
Western Tile, 3 - 98
Wilh. Gail'sche Tonwerke KG a.A., 3 - 99
Williams & Sons Slate & Tile Inc., 3 - 99

Winburn Tile Manufacturing Co., 3 - 99
Wirth-Salander Studios, 2 - 13
World's End Tiles, 3 - 101
Yulix Inc., 3 - 101

Tin

A A Abbingdon Affilliates, Inc., 1 - 1
Classic Ceilings, 1 - 11
Country Accents, 12 - 7

Toilet

Clivus Multrum, Inc., 2 - 4
Crane Plumbing, 8 - 19
McPherson Inc., 2 - 7
Ohmega Salvage, 2 - 8
Sun-Mar Corp., 7 - 7

Torchier

American Marble Co., Inc., 3 - 7
Colonial Marble Products Ltd., 3 - 25
Gawet Marble & Granite Inc., 3 - 39
Imperial Marble, Inc., 3 - 49
Lighting Source of America, 11 - 20
Lippert Corp., 2 - 7
MDM Marble Co. Inc., 2 - 7
Messer Industries, Inc., 8 - 45
Milano Marble Co., Inc., 2 - 7
Queen City Glass Ltd., 8 - 54
Tomlin Industries Inc., 2 - 11

Track

All-Lighting, 11 - 2
Conservation Technology Ltd., 11 - 7
Eurofase Inc., 11 - 11
Halo Lighting Products/Cooper Ind, 11 - 14
Harry Horn, Inc., 11 - 14
Lighting Source of America, 11 - 20
Martin's Discount Lighting, 11 - 22
National Industries, 11 - 23
NuMerit Electrical Supply, 11 - 24
Track & Plus, 11 - 33
WAC Lighting Collection, 11 - 35

Treatment

*(Blinds, Curtains, Drapery, Jabots,
Shades, Swags, Valances, etc.)*

$5 Wallpaper & Blind Co., 8 - 1
3 Day Blinds, 8 - 1
A. Weldon Kent Emterprises, 8 - 1
A.J. Boyd Industries, 8 - 1
ADO Corp., 8 - 2
ALCO Venetian Blind Co. Inc., 8 - 2
Abbey Shade & Mfg. Co. Inc., 12 - 2
Ace Blinds Inc., 8 - 2
Acme Window Coverings Ltd., 8 - 2
Advance Carpet Decorating Ctr., 8 - 3
Advanced Consumer Products, 8 - 3
Age Craft Mfg. Inc., 8 - 3
Alabama Venetian Blinds Co. Inc., 8 - 3
All Cedar Venetian Blind Mfg. Co., 8 - 3
All-States Decorating Network, 8 - 3
Allison Window Fashions, 8 - 4
American Blind & Wallpaper Factory, 8 - 4
American Window Corp., 8 - 4
American Window Creation, 8 - 4
Around the Window, 8 - 5
Artifacteria, 8 - 5
Atlantic Venetian Blind & Drapery Co., 8 - 6
Avondale Distributors Inc., 8 - 7
Aye Attracting Awnings, 3 - 11
Bali Blinds Midwest, 8 - 7

Index

Treatment – Treatment

Bamboo Abbott Florida Corp., 8 - 8
Barker Supply & Window Coverings, 8 - 8
Beacon Looms, Inc., 8 - 8
Beauti-Vue Products Inc., 8 - 9
Bedroom Secrets, 8 - 9
Berkshire Mfg. Inc., 8 - 9
Best Blinds, 8 - 9
Blind Brite Corp., 8 - 10
Blind Busters, 8 - 10
Blind Center USA, Inc., 8 - 10
Blind Design Inc., 8 - 10
Blind Design, 8 - 10
Blinds 'N Things, 8 - 11
Bradd & Hall Blinds, 8 - 11
Broward Window Products, Inc., 8 - 12
CSS Decor Inc., 8 - 13
Caroline Country Ruffles, 8 - 14
Caroline's Ruffled Curtains, Inc., 8 - 14
Century House of Drapes, 8 - 15
Charles W. Rice & Co. Inc., 8 - 16
Colorel Blinds, 8 - 18
Conrad Imports, 8 - 18
Contemporary Interiors, Inc., 8 - 18
Country Curtains, 8 - 19
Country Ruffles & Rods, 8 - 19
Covington Fabrics Corp., 8 - 19
Curtain Cottage, 8 - 20
Custom Laminations Inc., 8 - 20
Custom Windows & Walls, 8 - 20
Daisy Decorative Products, 8 - 21
Dana's Curtains & Draperies, 8 - 21
Davidson-Bishop Corp., 8 - 22
De La West Draperies, 8 - 22
Del Mar Window Coverings, 8 - 22
Designer Secrets, 8 - 23
Designer Window Decor/Truview, 6 - 23
Devenco Products Inc., 12 - 8
Dianthus Ltd., 8 - 23
Distinctive Window Fashions, 8 - 23
Domestications, 8 - 23
Dorothy's Ruffled Originals, Inc., 8 - 23
Duratex Inc., 8 - 24
E. D. I., 8 - 24
Endisco Supply Co., 8 - 25
Especially Lace, 8 - 25
Faith's Lacery, 8 - 27
Fara Mfg.Co., Inc., 8 - 27
Fashion Tech, 8 - 27
Florida Blinds, 8 - 28
Florida Shades Inc., 8 - 28
G & L Shades Inc., 8 - 29
Gamrod-Harman Co., 8 - 30
Global Blind Express, 8 - 30
Goodman Fabrications, 12 - 10
Gra-Mar Window Treatment, 12 - 10
Graber Industries, 12 - 10
Gulf Coast Window Covering Inc., 8 - 31
Harding's Custom Sheers, 12 - 10
Harmony Supply Inc., 8 - 32
Headquarters Window & Walls, 12 - 11
Helm Products Ltd., 8 - 32
Heritage Imports, Inc., 8 - 33
Home Fashions, Inc., 8 - 33
Hornick Industries, 8 - 34
House of Blinds, 8 - 34
Hudson Venetian Blind Service Inc., 8 - 34
Hunter Douglas Window Fashions, 8 - 35
J. M Mills, 2 - 6
Jag Corp., 8 - 37
Jastrac Mfg., 8 - 37
Jayson Window Fashions, 8 - 37

Jencraft Corp., 8 - 38
John Dixon Inc., 8 - 38
Judkins Co., 8 - 38
K & R Custom Interiors, 8 - 38
Kaleidoscope Ind. Inc., 8 - 38
Kemp Stuttbacher Designs, 8 - 39
Ken Jordan Shutters, 12 - 13
Kirsch, 8 - 40
Lace Country, 8 - 41
Lafayette Venetian Blind Inc., 8 - 41
Laura Copenhaver Industries Inc., 8 - 41
Laurel Mfg. Co. Inc., 8 - 41
Le Lace Factory, Inc., 8 - 42
Linen & Lace, 8 - 42
Linen Lady, 8 - 42
London Lace, 8 - 43
M.A. Bruder & Sons Inc., 8 - 43
MDC Direct Inc., 8 - 43
Mather's Department Store, 8 - 44
McInnis Industries, 8 - 45
Merit Window Fashions, 8 - 45
Metro Blind & Shade, 8 - 46
Morantz Inc., 8 - 47
Mutual Wallpaper & Paint Co., Inc., 8 - 48
Nanik, 12 - 17
National Blind & Wallpaper Factory, 8 - 48
Nationwide Wholesalers, 8 - 48
New Home Window Shade, 8 - 49
New Scotland Lace Co., 8 - 49
New View Blinds Mfg. Ltd., 8 - 49
Newell Window Furnishings, 8 - 49
Old Manor House, 8 - 50
Parker Window Covering, 8 - 51
Peerless Wallpaper, 8 - 52
Penn Needle Art Co., 8 - 52
Perkowitz Window Fashions, 8 - 52
Pintchik Homeworks, 8 - 53
Plastic Sun Shade Co. Inc., 8 - 53
Quix Window Visions & Fabric Works, 8 - 54
Qwik Blinds, 8 - 1
Rochester Drapery Inc., 8 - 56
Royal Crest Inc., 8 - 56
Rue De France Inc., 8 - 57
S. Morantz Inc., 8 - 57
Sebring & Co., 8 - 59
Shades & Verticals & Miniblinds Center, 8 -60
Shutters & Shades, 8 - 61
Silver Wallpaper & Paint Co., 8 - 61
Skandia Industries, 8 - 61
Southwest Florida Blinds Inc., 8 - 62
Spring Lace Two, 8 - 62
Stanwood Drapery Co. Inc., 8 - 62
Temple Producst of Indiana Inc., 8 - 65
Tentina Window Fashion, 8 - 65
The Blind Factory, 8 - 65
The Blind Maker, 8 - 66
The Curtain Collection, 8 - 66
The Decorators Outlet, 8 - 66
Tiffany Wholesale Supply Inc., 8 - 69
Triangle Window Fashions, 8 - 69
USA Blind Factory, 8 - 70
Unique Wholesale Distr. Inc., 8 - 70
United Designs Inc., 8 - 70
United Supply Co., 8 - 71
Versol USA, Inc., 8 - 71
Verticals Inc., 8 - 72
Viking Distributors Inc., 8 - 72
Vintage Valances, 8 - 72
Vista Products Inc., 8 - 72
WallpaperXpress, 8 - 74
Wells Interiors, 8 - 75

The Complete Sourcebook

Index - 85

Tree — Tub

Index

Wesco Fabrics Inc., 8 - 75
West Coast Windows Inc., 12 - 28
Westport Mfg. Co. Inc., 8 - 75
Whiting Mfg. Co. Inc., 8 - 76
Wholesale Verticals, Inc., 8 - 76
Win-Glo Window Coverings, 8 - 76
Winco Window Coverings, 8 - 76
Windo-Shade Distributors Inc., 8 - 76
Window Covering Dist. Inc., 8 - 77
Window Coverings Inc., 8 - 77
Window Modes, 8 - 77
Wisconsin Drapery Supply Inc., 8 - 77
Wrisco Industries Inc., 8 - 77

Tree

TIF Nursery, 7 - 7

Trim

Accents In Stone, 3 - 3
Adelmann & Clark Inc., 3 - 4
American Wood Column Corp., 1 - 4
B.A. Mullican Lumber & Manufacturing, 5 - 1
Central Brass Mfg. Co., 3 - 21
De Best Mfg. Co., Inc., 3 - 30
Fypon Molded Millwork, 1 - 17
House of Fara Inc., 3 - 47
Mad River Woodworks, 1 - 22
Monticello Flooring & Lumber Co., 5 - 7
Northern Moulding Co., 1 - 25
Razorback Hardwood, Inc., 5 - 8
Robbins Inc., 5 - 8
The Bank Architectural Antiques, 1 - 34
The Wood Factory, 1 - 35

Truss

A. Moorhouse Co., 3 - 1
Able Fabricators Inc., 3 - 3
AcuTruss Industries Ltd., 3 - 4
Adam Lumber Inc., 3 - 4
Ailene Lumber Inc., 3 - 4
Alpine Engineer Products Inc., 3 - 5
American Building Component, 3 - 6
Beachwood Lumber & Mfg., 3 - 13
Carolina Components Corp., 3 - 20
Carolina Truss Mfg. Co., Inc., 3 - 20
Causeway Lumber Co., 3 - 20
Enterprise Industries, Inc., 3 - 34
Fabricated Wood Products, 3 - 35
Hamrick Truss, Inc., 3 - 43
Heart Truss & Engineering, 3 - 44
Hjelmeland Truss Corp., 3 - 46
Hughes Roof Truss Co. Ltd., 3 - 48
Idowa Timber, 3 - 49
John Carr Joinery Sales Ltd., 12 - 13
Keen Building Components Inc., 3 - 52
Kent Trusses Ltd., 3 - 52
Kilian Industries Ltd., 3 - 52
Kunico Truss & Prefab Ltd., 3 - 53
Lampe Lumber Co., 3 - 53
Landmark Truss, Inc., 3 - 53
Leduc Truss, 3 - 54
Loredo Truss Co. Inc., 3 - 56
Lumber Specialties, 3 - 56
M & H Truss Co. Inc., 3 - 56
Mays Lumber Co., 3 - 59
McLaughlin Roof Trusses Ltd., 3 - 59
Mid-State Truss Co., Inc., 3 - 60
Northern Michigan Truss Co., 3 - 65
Nuttle Lumber, 3 - 65
OK Truss Co. Inc., 3 - 66
Olympic Structures Inc., 3 - 66

P. B. Trusses Ltd., 3 - 67
Paulis Co., 3 - 68
Perfection Truss Co. Inc., 3 - 69
Pryor Truss Co., 3 - 72
Pueblo Truss Co., 12 - 20
Quality Truss, 3 - 72
Quality-Line Truss Mfg. Co., 3 - 72
Read Bros. Building Supply, 3 - 73
Red Deer Truss Systems, 3 - 74
Reid Building & Truss Co., 3 - 74
Ridgway Roof Truss Co. Inc., 3 - 75
Rimbey Truss Systems Inc., 3 - 75
Riverside Roof Truss Inc., 3 - 76
SRI, 3 - 77
Schubert Lumber Co., 3 - 78
Shoffner Industries Inc., 3 - 79
Silver State Components, 3 - 79
Southern Components Inc., 3 - 81
Standard Building Systems, 3 - 82
Stark Truss Co. Inc., 3 - 82
Stone Door & Truss, 3 - 83
Superior Truss & Components Inc., 3 - 85
Tacoma Truss Systems, 3 - 86
Textruss Inc., 3 - 87
Thorn Lumber Co., 3 - 90
Tilton Truss Mfrs. Inc., 3 - 91
Timber Tech Truss Systems Ltd., 3 - 91
Timber Top Truss Ltd., 3 - 91
Tri State Truss Co., 3 - 92
Tru-Truss Inc., 3 - 92
Trusses Inc., 3 - 92
Uniflor, 3 - 93
Universal Forest Products, 3 - 94
Valley Truss Co., 3 - 94
Villaume Industries Inc., 3 - 95
Warren Truss Co. Inc., 3 - 96
Wascana Wood Components Ltd., 3 - 96
Weems Roof Truss Co., 3 - 97
Wendricks Roof Trusses, 3 - 97
Western Archrib, 3 - 97
Western Wood Fabricators Inc., 3 - 98
Wm. D. Bowers Lumber Co., 3 - 100
Wood Structures Inc., 3 - 100
Youngstown Roof Truss Co., 3 - 101

Tub

A-Ball Plumbing Supply, 2 - 1
Ace Shower Door Co. Inc., 2 - 1
American Marble Co., Inc., 3 - 7
Aqua Glass Corporation, 2 - 2
Beach Craft, Inc., 2 - 3
DuraGlaze Service Corp., 2 - 4
Fleurco Industries 1963 Ltd., 10 - 4
Garofalo Studio, 2 - 5
H & W Plastics Inc., 2 - 5
Keller Industries Inc., 4 - 10
Kimstock Inc., 2 - 6
Lippert Corp., 2 - 7
MDM Marble Co. Inc., 2 - 7
Midland Manufacturing Corp., 2 - 7
Milano Marble Co., Inc., 2 - 7
Ohmega Salvage, 2 - 8
Ole Fashion Things, 2 - 8
Omega Too, 2 - 8
Pipe Dreams, 2 - 9
The Faucet Factory, 2 - 11
The Fixture Exchange, 2 - 11
Thermo Spas Inc., 2 - 11
Tomlin Industries Inc., 2 - 11
Universal Bath Systems, 2 - 12
Valley Fibrebath Ltd., 2 - 12

Index - 86

The Complete Sourcebook

Tumbler
Kemp, 7 - 4

Turkish
A Candle In The Night, 5 - 1
Asia Minor Carpets, 8 - 6
Azar's Oriental Rugs, 8 - 7

Twig
Tiger Mountain Woodworks, 6 - 78

Umbrella
Aberdeen Mfg. Corp., 8 - 2
Basta Sole, 7 - 1
Boswell Roberts Gardens, 7 - 1
Indian Ocean Trading Co., 6 - 38
Macon Umbrella Corp., 6 - 47
Oryx Trading Ltd., 7 - 5

Unfinished
Anderson Furniture, 6 - 4
Country Workshop, 6 - 19
Titan Wood Products Ltd., 6 - 78
Vargas Furniture Manufacturing, 6 - 80

Unit
(Door, Wall, Window, etc.)
Deltacrafts Mfg. Ltd., 6 - 23
Design Furniture Mfg. Ltd., 6 - 23
Doors, Inc., 6 - 24
Edward P. Schmidt Cabinetmaker, 6 - 25
Enhanced Glass Corp., 3 - 34
Good Tables Inc., 6 - 32
John Carr Joinery Sales Ltd., 12 - 13
National Woodworks, Inc., 1 - 25
Pilliod Cabinet Co., 6 - 59
Riverside Millwork Co. Inc., 1 - 29
Suburban Manufacturing Company, 3 - 84

Upholstery
Brentwood Manor Furnishings, 6 - 11
Fabric Shop, 8 - 26
Frissell Fabrics, Inc., 8 - 29
Glammar Mills Ltd., 8 - 30
Jack's Upholstery & Caning Supplies, 8 - 37
Jacquard Fabrics Co., 8 - 37
Joan Fabrics Corp., 8 - 38
Kalkstein Silk Mills, Inc., 8 - 39
Klemer & Wiseman, 8 - 40
Mastercraft, 8 - 44
Mercer Textile Mills, Inc., 8 - 45
Minette Mills, Inc., 8 - 47
Quix Window Visions & Fabric Works, 8 - 54

Vacumn
Nutone, 3 - 65
Omar's Built-In Vacuum Systems, 3 - 66
Wal-Vac Inc., 3 - 95
Wanda Mfg. Co. Inc., 3 - 96

Valance
Stencils & Seams Unlimited, 8 - 63
Vintage Valances, 8 - 72

Valve
Barber Wilsons & Co. Ltd., 2 - 2
Hans Grohe Ltd., 2 - 5
Meynell Valves Ltd., 2 - 7
Trevi Showers, 2 - 11

Vanity
American Marble Co., Inc., 3 - 7
Boulton & Paul PLC, 3 - 16
Colonial Marble Products Ltd., 3 - 25
Doors, Inc., 6 - 24
Gawet Marble & Granite Inc., 3 - 39
Gibraltar, 3 - 40
Imperial Marble, Inc., 3 - 49
Kinzee Industries Inc., 12 - 14
Lippert Corp., 2 - 7
MDM Marble Co. Inc., 2 - 7
Merit Cabinet Distributors, 2 - 7
Milano Marble Co., Inc., 2 - 7
Nicola Ceramics & Marble, 3 - 64
Tomlin Industries Inc., 2 - 11

Varnish
Behr Process Corp., 3 - 13
Color Your World Inc., 8 - 18
Epifanes USA, 3 - 34
Morris Paint & Varnish Co., 3 - 62
Old Western Paint Co. Inc., 6 - 56
Standard Paint Co., 3 - 82
Waterlox Chemical & Coating Corp., 3 - 96

Vase
H. Grabell & Sons, 11 - 14

Veneer
A & M Wood Specialty Inc., 3 - 1
Artistry in Veneers Inc., 1 - 7
Certainly Wood, 3 - 23
Henegan's Wood Shed, 3 - 45
Woodcrafters Supply, 3 - 100

Vertical
Advanced Consumer Products, 8 - 3
USA Blind Factory, 8 - 70
Verticals Inc., 8 - 72

Victorian
*(Architectural Details, Bathroom Fixtures,
Cabinetry, Doors, Furniture, Lighting,
Millwork, Paint, Stoves, etc.)*

A A Abbingdon Affilliates, Inc., 1 - 1
Acorn Antique Doors, 4 - 1
American Furniture Galleries, 6 - 4
American Liberty Furniture, 6 - 4
Andreas Lehman Fine Glasswork, 1 - 4
Anthony Wood Products Inc., 1 - 4
Antiquaria, 6 - 5
Antique Baths & Kitchens, 2 - 2
Architectural Antiquities, 1 - 5
Aunt Sylvia's Victorian Collections, 11 - 3
Baldwin Hardware Corp., 3 - 12
Bathroom Machineries, 2 - 3
Baths From The Past Inc., 2 - 3
Berridge Manufacturing Co., 3 - 14
Brassfinders, 11 - 5
Burdoch Victorian Lamp Company, 11 - 5
California Glass Bending Corp., 12 - 6
Campbell Lamp Supply, 11 - 6
Campbellsville Industries, 3 - 19
Cape May Millworks, 1 - 10
Carol Mead Design, 8 - 14
Classic Designs, 12 - 6
Creative Openings, 4 - 4
Crown Point Cabinetry, 10 - 3
Cumberland Woodcraft Co., 1 - 13
Custom Ironworks Inc., 7 - 2

The Complete Sourcebook

Vinyl – Wall

DS Locksmithing Company,   3 - 29
Davis Cabinet Company, 6 - 22
Deep River Trading Company,   6 - 22
Deer Creek Pottery,   3 - 30
Ellenburg's Furniture,   6 - 26
Empire Woodworks,   1 - 15
Epoch Designs, 8 - 25
Faith's Lacery, 8 - 27
Fantasy Lighting, Inc., 11 - 11
Fox Woodcraft, 10 - 4
Fritz V. Sterbak Antiques,   1 - 17
Fuller O'Brien Paints,   3 - 38
GT Doors & Locks,   4 - 8
Georgia Lighting Supply Co.,   11 - 13
Grand Era Reproductions,   4 - 8
Green Enterprises,   6 - 33
Greystone Victorian Furniture, 6 - 33
H & R Johnson Tiles,   3 - 42
Hallelujah Redwood Products,   1 - 19
Heath Sedgwick, 11 - 14
Heirloom Reproductions, 6 - 35
Heritage Fence Company, 7 - 3
Herwig Lighting Inc.,   11 - 15
Holloways,   6 - 36
Insites,   11 - 17
Jeannie Serpa Stencils, 8 - 37
Kimball Furniture Reproductions,   6 - 42
Kramer Brothers,   6 - 43
Lehman Hardware,   3 - 54
Lexington Furniture Industries, 6 - 46
Magnolia Hall, 6 - 48
Martha M. House,   6 - 50
May's Architectural Detailing,   7 - 4
Old World Hardware Co., 3 - 66
Ole Country Barn,   3 - 66
Ornamental Mouldings, 1 - 26
Park Place,   6 - 58
Pipe Dreams,   2 - 9
Prince Albert's,   6 - 61
Rejuvenation Lamp & Fixture,   11 - 26
Restoration Hardware,   3 - 74
Roy Electric Co. Inc., 11 - 27
San Francisco Victoriana,   1 - 30
Satin and Old Lace Shades,   11 - 28
Southhampton Antiques, 6 - 70
Statements In Design,   11 - 30
Stenart Inc., 8 - 63
Sunflower Shower Company,   2 - 10
Sunrise Specialty,   2 - 10
Taylor Brothers Inc.,   4 - 16
Texas Standard Picket Company Inc.,   7 - 7
The Brass Light Gallery,   11 - 31
The Old Wagon Factory, 4 - 17
The Porch Factory,   1 - 34
The Shop,   3 - 89
The Victorian Merchant, 6 - 77
The Yorkshire Door Company Ltd.,   4 - 17
Turn Of The Century Lampshades, 11 - 33
Victorian Brass Works Ltd.,   6 - 80
Victorian Classics Inc.,   6 - 81
Victorian Classics Lampshades, 11 - 34
Victorian Collectibles, 8 - 72
Victorian Lightcrafters Ltd.,   11 - 34
Victorian Lighting Works,   11 - 34
Victorian Revival,   11 - 34
Victorian Sampler,   6 - 81
Vintage Valances,   8 - 72
Vintage Wood Works,   1 - 36
Welsbach,   11 - 35
Wooden Nickel Architectural Antique,   1 - 38
Woodnorth,   7 - 8

Yestershades,   11 - 36

Vinyl
(Wallcover, Siding, etc.)

ACRO Extrusion Corp.,   12 - 1
ALCOA Building Products,   3 - 2
ALCOA Vinyl Windows,   12 - 1
Allied Building Products Corp., 3 - 5
Alside, 3 - 5
Aluminum Industries of Arkansas,   3 - 6
Atelier H. Juergen Oellers,   8 - 6
Beaver Industries,   3 - 13
Berger Building Products Corp., 3 - 14
Bufftech,   7 - 1
Carpet Express, 8 - 14
Color Your World Inc., 8 - 18
Cross Industries,   3 - 28
D.L. Couch Contract Wallcovering,   8 - 21
Domco Floors,   5 - 3
Elixer Vinyl Siding,   3 - 33
Genova Products,   3 - 39
Heritage Fence Company, 7 - 3
Master Shield, 3 - 59
Mastic Corp.,   3 - 59
National Floor Products Co., Inc.,   5 - 7
Nebraska Plastics Inc., 7 - 5
Parker's Carpets Inc.,   8 - 52
Peerless Wallpaper,   8 - 52
Pro-Glass Technology/Vinyl Tech Inc., 12 - 20
Prototech Polyvinyl Fencing Systems,   7 - 5
Reynolds Metals Company,   12 - 21
Sellers & Josephson,   8 - 59
Singer Wallcoverings,   8 - 61
Tarkett Inc.,   5 - 9
The Amtico Co., Ltd.,   5 - 9
Toli International,   5 - 10
Vinyl Building Products Inc.,   12 - 27
Vinyl Therm Inc.,   12 - 27
Wolverine Technologies Inc.,   3 - 100

Wall
(Furniture, Lighting, Tile, Units, etc.)

Abet Laminati, 3 - 3
Accents In Stone,   3 - 3
Actiengesellschaft,   3 - 3
Agrob-Wessel-Servais AG,   3 - 4
Albert Gunther, 3 - 5
Alfa Ceramiche, 3 - 5
Amaru Tile,   3 - 6
American International, 3 - 6
Angelo Amaru Tile & Bath Collection,   3 - 8
Ann Sacks Tile & Stone, 3 - 8
Antiche Ceramiche D'Talia (ACIT) SRL, 3 - 8
Armstar,   3 - 9
Artemide,   11 - 3
Artistic Surfaces,   8 - 6
Baukeramik U., 3 - 12
Bedquarters,   6 - 8
Bisazza Mosaico S.P.A., 3 - 15
CPN Inc.,   3 - 18
California Tile Supply, 3 - 19
Cambridge Tile Mfg. Co.,   3 - 19
Cancos Tile Corporation,   3 - 19
Ceramica Candia S.P.A., 3 - 22
Ceramica Colli Di Sassuolo S.P.A.,   3 - 22
Ceramica Ilsa S.P.A.,   3 - 22
Ceramica Panaria S.P.A.,   3 - 22
Ceramiche Brunelleschi S.P.A., 3 - 22
Cerim Ceramiche S.P.A., 3 - 23
Charles Street Supply Co.,   3 - 24

Index

Wallboard — Wallcover

Cisa-Cerdisa-Smov, 3 - 24
Crest Distributors, 3 - 28
D & B Tile Distributors, 3 - 29
Deltacrafts Mfg. Ltd., 6 - 23
Design Furniture Mfg. Ltd., 6 - 23
Doors, Inc., 6 - 24
Dynasty Classics Corp., 11 - 9
East Coast Tile Imports Inc., 3 - 33
Edward P. Schmidt Cabinetmaker, 6 - 25
Execulamp Inc., 11 - 11
Fabby, 11 - 11
Florida Ceramic Tile Center, 3 - 37
Good Tables Inc., 6 - 32
H & R Johnson Tiles, 3 - 42
Handcraft Tile Inc., 3 - 43
Harden Furniture Inc., 6 - 34
Hastings Tile & Il Bagno Collection, 3 - 44
Hines of Oxford, 3 - 46
Hutcherson Tile, 3 - 48
Klingenberg Dekoramik GmbH, 3 - 53
Latco Ceramic Tile, 3 - 54
Maurer & Shepherd Joyners Inc., 1 - 23
Metco Tile Distributors, 3 - 60
Milano Marble Co., Inc., 2 - 7
Mosaic Supplies Inc., 3 - 62
National Ceramics of Florida, 3 - 63
Nemo Tile Company, Inc., 3 - 63
New England Slate Company, 3 - 64
Ostara-Fliesen Gmbh & Co. KG, 3 - 67
Pass & Seymour, 11 - 25
Payne's Ristras De Santa Fe, 8 - 52
Pilliod Cabinet Co., 6 - 59
Santa Catalina, 3 - 77
Sligh Clocks, 8 - 61
Spiegelwerk Wilsdruff GmbH, 3 - 81
Staloton - Die keramiker H.H., 3 - 82
Summitville Tiles Inc., 3 - 84
Tile West Distributors, 3 - 91
Wandplattenfabrik Engers GmbH, 3 - 96
Wayne Tile Company, 3 - 96
Wellington Hall, Ltd., 3 - 97
Wilh. Gail'sche Tonwerke KG a.A., 3 - 99

Wallboard

Allied Building Products Corp., 3 - 5

Wallcover

Allison T. Seymour, Inc., 8 - 3
American Wallcovering Distributors, 8 - 4
Angelo's Wallcoverings of Puerto Rico, 8 - 5
Archetonic, 8 - 5
Arlin Wallcoverings USA Inc., 8 - 5
Ashley Wallcoverings, 8 - 6
Atelier H. Juergen Oellers, 8 - 6
Atlas Wallpaper & Paint Co., 8 - 7
Atrium Industries/Triumph Designs, 8 - 7
BMI Home Decorating, 8 - 7
Bamboo & Rattan Works Inc., 8 - 8
Barra U.S.A. Inc., 8 - 8
Bassett & Vollum, 8 - 8
Bayview Wallcoverings, 8 - 8
Beegun's Galleries of Chicago, Inc., 8 - 9
Ben James Ltd., 8 - 9
Bentley Brothers, 8 - 9
Best Discount Wallcoverings, 8 - 10
Best Wallcoverings Inc., 8 - 10
Beverly Stevens Ltd., 8 - 10
Bill Villetto Designs, 8 - 10
Birge Wallcoverings, 8 - 10
Blautex, 8 - 10
Bob Mitchell Designs, 8 - 11

Bolta Wallcoverings, 8 - 11
Borden Home Wallcoverings, 8 - 11
Borges GmbH, 8 - 11
Brewster Wallcovering Co., 8 - 12
Bridge Wallcoverings, 8 - 12
Brod Dugan, 8 - 12
C & A Wallcoverings Inc., 8 - 12
Camelot Design Studio, 8 - 13
Canada Wallcoverings Corp., 8 - 13
Cape Breton Wallcoverings, 8 - 13
Capital-Asam, Inc., 8 - 14
Cavalier Prints Ltd., 8 - 15
Century Wallcoverings Inc., 8 - 15
Chambord Prints Inc., 8 - 16
Charles Graser North America Inc., 8 - 16
Chelsea Enterprises, 8 - 16
Chemrex Inc., 8 - 16
Chesapeake Bay, 8 - 16
Classic Ceilings, 1 - 11
Codis House S.P.A., 8 - 17
Collins & Aikman Corp., 8 - 17
Color Your World Inc., 8 - 18
Columbus Wallcovering Co., 8 - 18
Comark Wallcoverings, 8 - 18
Combeau Industries, 8 - 18
Contract Wallcoverings, 8 - 18
CoverAge Inc., 8 - 19
Coverwalls, Inc., 8 - 19
Crown Corp. D/B/A Mile Hi Crown, 8 - 20
Crown Wallcovering, 8 - 20
Crown Wallpaper Co., 8 - 20
Crutchfield Wallcoverings Inc., 8 - 20
Custom Laminations Inc., 8 - 20
Custom Windows & Walls, 8 - 20
Cynthia Gibson, Inc., 8 - 20
D.L. Couch Contract Wallcovering, 8 - 21
Dae Dong Wallpaper Co. Ltd., 8 - 21
David & Dash, 8 - 21
Daycor West Wallcoverings, 8 - 22
Decor International Wallcovering Inc., 8 - 22
Dekortex Co., 8 - 22
Designer Handprints, 8 - 22
Domus Parati S.P.A., 8 - 23
Dunn-Edwards Corp., 8 - 24
Duron Paints & Wallcoverings, 8 - 24
Edward Laurence & Co., 8 - 24
Egan-Laing Inc., 8 - 24
Eisenhart Wallcoverings Co., 8 - 25
Enterprise Wallcoverings, Inc., 8 - 25
Essex Wallcoverings, 8 - 25
Eurotex, 8 - 25
Exeter Wallcovering, 8 - 26
Eykis Inc., 8 - 26
FSC Wallcoverings, 8 - 26
Fabra-Wall Ltd., 8 - 26
Fashion Wallcoverings, 8 - 27
Fashion Wallcoverings, Inc., 8 - 27
Faux Effects Inc., 8 - 27
Fibreworks Corp., 8 - 27
Fidelity Industries, 8 - 27
Fine Art Wallcovering Ltd., 8 - 27
Fine Art Wallcovering, Ltd., 8 - 28
Forbo Wallcoverings Inc., 8 - 28
Foremost Wallcoverings, 8 - 28
Four Seasons Wallcoverings, 8 - 29
Frankford Wallcovering Inc., 8 - 29
Fred Cole Factory Inc., 8 - 29
Fred G. Anderson, Inc., 8 - 29
Gagne Wallcovering Inc., 8 - 29
Galaxie Handprints Inc., 8 - 29
Gamrod Harman/Shaheen Wallcovering,8-30

The Complete Sourcebook

Index - 89

Wallcover — Wallcover

Gencorp Polymer Products, 8 - 30
Gilman Wallcoverings, 8 - 30
Graham & Brown Ltd., 8 - 31
Groff's, 8 - 31
Groundworks Unlimited, 8 - 31
Hamilton Adams Imports Ltd., 8 - 32
Hampton Wallcovering, 8 - 32
Hang-It-Now Wallpaper Stores, 8 - 32
Hardware + Plus Inc., 3 - 44
Hawthorne Prints Inc., 8 - 32
Hickory Wallcovering, 8 - 33
Hirshfield's, Inc., 8 - 33
Hoffman Mills, 8 - 33
Holvoet NV, 8 - 33
Hunter & Co., Inc., 8 - 34
Hunting Valley Prints, 8 - 35
I. Gottlieb & Associates, 8 - 35
IRM/Queens, 8 - 35
Images Wallcoverings Ltd., 8 - 35
Imperial Mfg. Co., 8 - 35
Imperial Paper Co., 8 - 35
Imperial Wallcoverings Inc., 8 - 35
Impressions Handprinters, Inc., 8 - 35
Innerlimits Inc., 8 - 36
International Wallcoverings Ltd., 8 - 36
J. C. Prints, 8 - 36
J. Josephson Inc., 8 - 36
J. M. Lynne Co., Inc., 8 - 36
Jacaranda, Inc., 8 - 37
Jolie Papier Ltd., 8 - 38
Katzenbach & Warren Inc., 8 - 39
Kayser & Allman, Inc., 8 - 39
Kev Don Industries, 8 - 40
Key Wallcoverings, Inc., 8 - 40
Kimberly Clark Corp., 8 - 40
Kinney Wallcoverings, 8 - 40
Kobe Fabrics Ltd., 8 - 40
Kravet Fabrics, 8 - 41
Kwal-Howells, 8 - 41
Laue Wallcoverings Inc., 8 - 41
Lee Jofa, 8 - 42
Len-Tex Inc., 8 - 42
Lennon Wallpaper Co., 8 - 42
Limonta USA Inc., 8 - 42
Lin-Gor Wallcovering, 8 - 42
Long Island Walls, 8 - 43
M. A. Baskind Co., 8 - 43
M.A. Bruder & Sons Inc., 8 - 43
MDC Wallcoverings, 8 - 43
Marburg Wallcoverings Inc., 8 - 44
Masureel International NV, 8 - 44
Mayfair Wallcoverings, 8 - 45
Mei Bei International Enterprises Corp.,8 - 45
Metro Wallcoverings, 8 - 46
Michele Wallpaper, 8 - 46
Milan Schuster Inc., 8 - 46
Milbrook Wallcoverings, 8 - 46
Mills Wallcoverings, 8 - 47
Mission Wallcovering Distributors, 8 - 47
National Wallcovering, 8 - 48
Nationwide Wholesalers, 8 - 48
Nels Thybony Co., 8 - 49
Newmarket Limited, Inc., 8 - 49
North American Decorative Products , 8 - 49
Northern California Imports, Inc., 8 - 49
Norton Blumenthal Inc., 8 - 49
Norwall Group, 8 - 49
Odyssey Design Products Ltd., 8 - 50
Olney Wallcoverings, 8 - 50
Ontario Wallcoverings, 8 - 51
Ozite Corporation, 8 - 51

P & M Consumer Products Inc., 8 - 51
Pantasote, Inc., 8 - 51
Paramount Interior Products Corp., 8 - 51
Patrick J. Mitchell, 8 - 52
Peerless Wallpaper, 8 - 52
Pettigrew Associates Inc., 6 - 59
Philip Graf Wallpapers, 8 - 53
Pickhardt & Seibert (USA, etc.) Inc., 8 - 53
Plaid Enterprises Inc., 8 - 53
Planox B.V., 8 - 53
Playfield International, 8 - 54
Porter Wallcoverings, 8 - 54
Quality House, Inc., 8 - 54
Quality Wallcovering Inc., 8 - 54
Quest Wallcoverings Ltd., 8 - 54
Rainbow Creations, 8 - 55
Redona Wallcovering S.P.A., 8 - 55
Republic Midwest Inc., 12 - 21
Richard E. Thibaut, Inc., 8 - 55
Rivalba S.P.A., 8 - 55
Robert Crowder & Co., 8 - 56
Rosco Wallcoverings, Inc., 8 - 56
Rosecore Carpet Co. Inc., 8 - 56
Roysons Corp., 8 - 57
Rubin Design Studio Inc., 8 - 57
Rutherford Wallcovering, 8 - 57
S R Wood, Inc., 8 - 57
S. A. Maxwell Co., 8 - 57
S. M. Hexter & Co., 8 - 57
Sancar Wallcoverings Inc., 8 - 58
Sanitas Wallcoverings, 8 - 58
Satex Textile Mural, 8 - 58
Scancelli, 8 - 58
Scandecor Inc., 8 - 59
Schooner Prints, 8 - 59
Seabrook Wallcoverings Inc., 8 - 59
Select Wallcoverings, 8 - 59
Sellers & Josephson, 8 - 59
Shaheen Wallcoverings, 8 - 60
Sharp's Pen Wallpapers, Inc., 8 - 60
Shelbourne Wallcoverings, 8 - 60
Sherburne Ewing Wallcovering Co., 8 - 60
Sherle Wagner, 2 - 10
Shibui Wallcoverings, 8 - 60
Shriber's, 8 - 61
Sinclair Wallcovering, 8 - 61
Singer Wallcoverings, 8 - 61
Sommer UK Wall and Floorcoverings, 8 - 61
Southern Discount Wallcovering, 8 - 62
Southland Wallcoverings, 8 - 62
Steven Linen Associates Inc., 8 - 63
Stroheim & Romann, 8 - 63
Studio 4 Inc., 8 - 63
Sunnyside Corp., 8 - 64
Sunnyside Prints, 8 - 64
Sunrise Designs, 8 - 64
Sunwall Fine Wallcovering, 8 - 64
Sunworthy Wallcoverings, 8 - 64
Surface Materials, Inc., 8 - 64
Tasso, 8 - 65
Taylor Wallcoverings, 8 - 65
Technique Textiles, 8 - 65
Texile Wallcoverings International Ltd., 8 - 65
The Blonder Co., 8 - 66
The House of Mayfair Ltd., 8 - 67
The Maya Romanoff Corp., 8 - 67
Thomas Ray Designs Inc., 8 - 68
Thomas Strahan Co., 8 - 68
Tiara Wallcoverings, 8 - 68
Tower Paint Mfg., 3 - 91
Trendsetters by Magden Ltd., 8 - 69

Index

Wallpaper — Wallpaper

Index

Twil, 8 - 70
Ultima Wallcoverings, 8 - 70
Unique Wall Fashions Inc., 8 - 70
United Coated Fabrics Corp., 8 - 70
United Wallcoverings, 8 - 71
Van Luit Wallcoverings, 8 - 71
Victorian Showcase, 6 - 81
Vision Wallcoverings Ltd., 8 - 72
Vogue Wall Covering Inc., 8 - 72
Vornhold Wallpaper Inc., 8 - 72
Wall Fashions Unlimited, 8 - 73
Wall Trends International, 8 - 73
Wall Visions Inc., 8 - 73
Wall-Decor, Inc., 8 - 73
Wallcoverings North, Inc., 8 - 73
Walldesigns, 8 - 73
Wallpaper Cottage, 8 - 73
Wallpaper Imports Inc., 8 - 73
Wallpaper Warehouse Inc., 8 - 74
Wallquest Inc., 8 - 74
Walter L. Brown Ltd., 8 - 74
Washington Wallcoverings, 8 - 74
Waterhouse Wallhangings Inc., 8 - 74
Waverly Fabric, 8 - 75
Wolf-Gordon, Inc., 8 - 77
Worldwide Wallcoverings & Blinds, 8 - 77
York Wallcoverings Inc., 8 - 78
Zina Studios Inc., 8 - 78

Wallpaper

$5 Wallpaper & Blind Co., 8 - 1
Advance Wallcovering, 8 - 3
Alexander Wallpaper, 8 - 3
American Blind & Wallpaper Factory, 8 - 4
American Discount Wallcoverings, 8 - 4
Angelo's Wallcoverings of Puerto Rico, 8 - 5
Arlin Wallcoverings USA Inc., 8 - 5
Atlas Wallpaper & Paint Co., 8 - 7
Bailey & Griffin Inc., 8 - 7
Barra U.S.A. Inc., 8 - 8
Bassett & Vollum, 8 - 8
Bayview Wallcoverings, 8 - 8
Beegun's Galleries of Chicago, Inc., 8 - 9
Benington's, 8 - 9
Best Discount Wallcoverings, 8 - 10
Best Wallcoverings Inc., 8 - 10
Birge Wallcoverings, 8 - 10
Bob Mitchell Designs, 8 - 11
Bolta Wallcoverings, 8 - 11
Borg Textile Corp., 8 - 11
Borges GmbH, 8 - 11
Bradbury & Bradbury Wallpapers, 8 - 11
Brandt's, 8 - 11
Brewster Wallcovering Co., 8 - 12
Brod Dugan, 8 - 12
Brunschwig & Fils, 8 - 12
C & A Wallcoverings Inc., 8 - 12
Canada Wallcoverings Corp., 8 - 13
Cape Breton Wallcoverings, 8 - 13
Capital-Asam, Inc., 8 - 14
Carol Mead Design, 8 - 14
Carole Fabrics Inc., 8 - 14
Cavalier Prints Ltd., 8 - 15
Century Wallcoverings Inc., 8 - 15
Chambord Prints Inc., 8 - 16
Charles Rupert Designs, 3 - 23
Chelsea Enterprises, 8 - 16
Chemrex Inc., 8 - 16
Chesapeake Bay, 8 - 16
Classic Revivals, Inc., 8 - 17
Cole & Son (Wallpapers, etc.) Ltd., 8 - 17

Collins & Aikman Corp., 8 - 17
Colonial Wallcovering, 8 - 17
Columbus Wallcovering Co., 8 - 18
Comark Wallcoverings, 8 - 18
Combeau Industries, 8 - 18
Contract Wallcoverings, 8 - 18
CoverAge Inc., 8 - 19
Crown Wallcovering, 8 - 20
Crown Wallpaper Co., 8 - 20
Crutchfield Wallcoverings Inc., 8 - 20
D.L. Couch Contract Wallcovering, 8 - 21
DMI Drapery Mfg., 8 - 21
Dae Dong Wallpaper Co. Ltd., 8 - 21
Daycor West Wallcoverings, 8 - 22
Designer Handprints, 8 - 22
Designer Secrets, 8 - 23
Direct Wallpaper, 8 - 23
Duron Paints & Wallcoverings, 8 - 24
East Carolina Wallpaper Market, 8 - 24
Egan-Laing Inc., 8 - 24
Elizabeth Eaton Ltd., 8 - 25
Enterprise Wallcoverings, Inc., 8 - 25
Essex Wallcoverings, 8 - 25
Exeter Wallcovering, 8 - 26
Eykis Inc., 8 - 26
F. Schumacher, 8 - 26
Fabric Fair, 8 - 26
Fashion Wallcoverings, 8 - 27
Fashion Wallcoverings, Inc., 8 - 27
Fibreworks Corp., 8 - 27
Fidelity Industries, 8 - 27
Fine Art Wallcovering Ltd., 8 - 27
Forbo Wallcoverings Inc., 8 - 28
Foremost Wallcoverings, 8 - 28
Four Seasons Wallcoverings, 8 - 29
Frankford Wallcovering Inc., 8 - 29
Fred Cole Factory Inc., 8 - 29
Fred G. Anderson, Inc., 8 - 29
Gagne Wallcovering Inc., 8 - 29
Galacar & Co., 8 - 29
Galaxie Handprints Inc., 8 - 29
Gamrod Harman/Shaheen Wallcovering, 8-30
Gencorp Polymer Products, 8 - 30
Gilman Wallcoverings, 8 - 30
Golden Wallpaper, 8 - 31
Graham & Brown Ltd., 8 - 31
Gramercy, 8 - 31
Greeff Fabrics Inc., 8 - 31
Groff's, 8 - 31
Groundworks Unlimited, 8 - 31
Hallie Greer, 8 - 31
Hampton Wallcovering, 8 - 32
Hang-It-Now Wallpaper Stores, 8 - 32
Harmony Supply Inc., 8 - 32
Hawthorne Prints Inc., 8 - 32
Headquarters Window & Walls, 12 - 11
Hickory Wallcovering, 8 - 33
Hinson & Co., 8 - 33
Hirshfield's, Inc., 8 - 33
Hoffman Mills, 8 - 33
Hunter & Co., Inc., 8 - 34
I. Gottlieb & Associates, 8 - 35
Images Wallcoverings Ltd., 8 - 35
Innerlimits Inc., 8 - 36
International Wallcoverings Ltd., 8 - 36
J. C. Prints, 8 - 36
J. Josephson Inc., 8 - 36
J. R. Burrows & Company, 8 - 37
John Perry Wallpapers Ltd., 8 - 38
Jolie Papier Ltd., 8 - 38
Kayser & Allman, Inc., 8 - 39

The Complete Sourcebook

Index - 91

Walnut – Water

Kev Don Industries, 8 - 40
Key Wallcoverings, Inc., 8 - 40
Kimberly Clark Corp., 8 - 40
King, 10 - 6
Kinney Wallcoverings, 8 - 40
Kwal-Howells, 8 - 41
Laue Wallcoverings Inc., 8 - 41
Len-Tex Inc., 8 - 42
Lennon Wallpaper Co., 8 - 42
Limonta USA Inc., 8 - 42
Lin-Gor Wallcovering, 8 - 42
Long Island Walls, 8 - 43
M. A. Baskind Co., 8 - 43
Marburg Wallcoverings Inc., 8 - 44
Mary's Discount Papers, 8 - 44
Mei Bei International Enterprises Corp.,8 - 45
Metro Wallcoverings, 8 - 46
Michele Wallpaper, 8 - 46
Milan Schuster Inc., 8 - 46
Mills Wallcoverings, 8 - 47
Mission Wallcovering Distributors, 8 - 47
Motif Designs, 8 - 48
Mutual Wallpaper & Paint Co., Inc., 8 - 48
National Wallcovering, 8 - 48
Nels Thybony Co., 8 - 49
North American Decorative Products , 8 - 49
Northern California Imports, Inc., 8 - 49
Norwall Group, 8 - 49
Number One Wallpaper, 8 - 50
Odyssey Design Products Ltd., 8 - 50
Old Deerfield Wallpapers, 8 - 50
Olney Wallcoverings, 8 - 50
Ontario Wallcoverings, 8 - 51
P & M Consumer Products Inc., 8 - 51
Paramount Interior Products Corp., 8 - 51
Philip Graf Wallpapers, 8 - 53
Pickhardt & Seibert (USA, etc.) Inc., 8 - 53
Pintchik Homeworks, 8 - 53
Plaid Enterprises Inc., 8 - 53
Porter Wallcoverings, 8 - 54
Quality House, Inc., 8 - 54
Quality Wallcovering Inc., 8 - 54
Rainbow Creations, 8 - 55
Raintree Designs, Inc., 8 - 55
Republic Midwest Inc., 12 - 21
Richard E. Thibaut, Inc., 8 - 55
Robert Crowder & Co., 8 - 56
Robinson's Wallcovering, 8 - 56
Rosco Wallcoverings, Inc., 8 - 56
Rosedale Wallcoverings Inc., 8 - 56
Roysons Corp., 8 - 57
Rutherford Wallcovering, 8 - 57
S. A. Maxwell Co., 8 - 57
Sancar Wallcoverings Inc., 8 - 58
Sanderson, 8 - 58
Sanz International, 8 - 58
Satex Textile Mural, 8 - 58
Scalamandre Inc., 8 - 58
Scancelli, 8 - 58
Scandecor Inc., 8 - 59
Schooner Prints, 8 - 59
Schumacher & Co. Inc., 8 - 59
Scroll Fabrics Inc., 8 - 59
Seabrook Wallcoverings Inc., 8 - 59
Select Wallcoverings, 8 - 59
Shaheen Wallcoverings, 8 - 60
Sharp's Pen Wallpapers, Inc., 8 - 60
Sherburne Ewing Wallcovering Co., 8 - 60
Shibui Wallcoverings, 8 - 60
Shriber's, 8 - 61
Silver Wallpaper & Paint Co., 8 - 61

Sinclair Wallcovering, 8 - 61
Smart Wallcoverings, 8 - 61
Stencils & Seams Unlimited, 8 - 63
Studio 4 Inc., 8 - 63
Style Wallcovering, 8 - 64
Summer Hill Ltd., 6 - 72
Sunnyside Corp., 8 - 64
Sunnyside Prints, 8 - 64
Sunrise Designs, 8 - 64
Sunwall Fine Wallcovering, 8 - 64
Surface Materials, Inc., 8 - 64
Tasso, 8 - 65
The Blonder Co., 8 - 66
The Classic Coverup Inc., 8 - 66
The House of Mayfair Ltd., 8 - 67
The Maya Romanoff Corp., 8 - 67
The Shop, 3 - 89
The Warner Company, 8 - 68
Thomas Ray Designs Inc., 8 - 68
Thomas Strahan Co., 8 - 68
Tiara Wallcoverings, 8 - 68
Timeless Design, Inc., 8 - 69
Trendsetters by Magden Ltd., 8 - 69
Twil, 8 - 70
Ultima Wallcoverings, 8 - 70
Unique Wall Fashions Inc., 8 - 70
V A Wallcoverings, 8 - 71
Victorian Collectibles, 8 - 72
Victorian Interiors, 8 - 72
Vision Wallcoverings Ltd., 8 - 72
Vornhold Wallpaper Inc., 8 - 72
Wall-Decor, Inc., 8 - 73
Wallcoverings North, Inc., 8 - 73
Wallpaper Outlet, 8 - 73
Wallpaper Warehouse Inc., 8 - 74
WallpaperXpress, 8 - 74
Wallquest Inc., 8 - 74
Walter L. Brown Ltd., 8 - 74
Warner Wallpaper Co., 8 - 74
Washington Wallcoverings, 8 - 74
Waterhouse Wallhangings Inc., 8 - 74
Waverly Wallcoverings, 8 - 75
Yankee Wallcoverings, Inc., 8 - 77
Yield House, 6 - 86
York Wallcoverings Inc., 8 - 78
Yorktown Wallpaper Outlet, 8 - 78

Walnut

American Starbuck, 6 - 4
DeSoto Hardwood Flooring Company, 5 - 3
Larkin Company, 1 - 22
Livermore Wood Floors, 5 - 6
Maple Grove Restorations, 1 - 22
Maurice L. Condon Co., 3 - 59
Midwest Dowel Works, Inc., 3 - 60
Murphy Furniture Mfg. Co., Inc., 6 - 54
Osborne Wood Products Inc., 6 - 57
P. W. Plumly Lumber Corporation, 1 - 26
Pacific Burl and Hardwood, 3 - 68
Rural Hall Inc., 4 - 14
The Burruss Company, 5 - 10
Trott Furniture Co., 6 - 79
Waterford Furniture Makers, 6 - 82

Water

American Energy Technologies Inc., 3 - 6
American Solar Network, 3 - 7
Continental Custom Bridge Co., 7 - 2
Crane Plumbing, 8 - 19
DeepRock, 3 - 30
Dolphin Pet Village, 7 - 2

Index

Wax – Window

Gallery of H B, 6 - 31
Hermitage Garden Pools, 7 - 3
Kester's Wild Game Food Nurseries, 7 - 4
Lilypons Water Gardens, 7 - 4
Lochinvar Water Heater Corp., 3 - 55
Lotus Water Garden Products Ltd., 7 - 4
Maryland Aquatic Nurseries, 7 - 4
Paradise Water Gardens, 7 - 5
Pumphouse, 3 - 72
Radco Products Inc., 3 - 73
Rheem Mfg Co., 3 - 75
S. Scherer & Sons Water Gardens, 7 - 6
Slocum Water Gardens, 7 - 6
Solar Depot, 3 - 80
Solar Water Heater, 3 - 80
State Industries Inc., 3 - 82
Thermal Energy Systems Inc., 3 - 90
Urdl's Waterfall Creation Inc., 7 - 7
Van Ness Water Gardens, 7 - 8
Vaughn Mfg. Corp., 3 - 94
Water Works, 7 - 8
Waterford Gardens, 7 - 8
Wicklein's Aquatic Farm & Nursery, 7 - 8
William Tricker, Inc., 7 - 8

Wax

The Butcher Company, 6 - 75

Weathervane

Adornments for Architecture, 1 - 2
Cape Cod Cupola Co., Inc., 1 - 9
Country Cupolas, 1 - 12
Ives Weathervanes, 7 - 3
Wind & Weather, 7 - 8

Well

DeepRock, 3 - 30

Western

Bones Creek Designs, 8 - 11
Franklin Custom Furniture, 6 - 30
Galeria San Ysidro, Inc., 6 - 31
New West of Jackson, 6 - 55
Onate's Cupboard, 8 - 50
Sweet Water Ranch, 6 - 73
The Lamp House, 11 - 32
Western Log Furniture, 6 - 82

Whirlpool

H & W Plastics Inc., 2 - 5
Kallista, 2 - 6
Plastic Creations Inc., 2 - 9

Wicker

Catherine Ann Furnishings, 6 - 15
Dovetail Antiques, 1 - 15
Ellenburg's Furniture, 6 - 26
Fran's Basket House, 6 - 29
LaMont Ltd., 2 - 6
Lloyd/Flanders, 6 - 47
Michael's Classic Wicker, 6 - 52
Second Impression Antiques, 6 - 66
Shelby Williams Industries, Inc., 6 - 68
The Wicker Garden, 6 - 77
Walters Wicker, 6 - 82
Wicker & Rattan, 6 - 83
Wicker Fixer, 6 - 83
Wicker Gallery, 6 - 83
Wicker Ware Inc., 6 - 83
Wicker Warehouse Inc., 6 - 84
Wicker Works, 6 - 84
Wickerworks, 6 - 84

Willow

Country Store, 6 - 19
Northern Rustic Furniture, 6 - 55
The Willow Place Inc., 6 - 77

Window

$5 Wallpaper & Blind Co., 8 - 1
1 Day Blinds, 8 - 1
3 Day Blinds, 8 - 1
A & C Metal Products Co. Inc., 12 - 1
A & S Window Associates, Inc., 3 - 1
A-J Industries Inc., 4 - 1
A. Weldon Kent Emterprises, 8 - 1
A.J. Boyd Industries, 8 - 1
A.R. Perry Glass Co., 12 - 1
A.W.A., 12 - 1
AAA Aluminum Stamping, Inc., 12 - 1
ACRO Extrusion Corp., 12 - 1
ADO Corp., 8 - 2
ALCAN Building Products, 12 - 1
ALCO Venetian Blind Co. Inc., 8 - 2
ALCOA Vinyl Windows, 12 - 1
AMFT, 12 - 1
AMSCO Windows, 12 - 2
APCA, 12 - 2
APL Window & Door Company, 12 - 2
ARMAC Brassfounders Group Ltd., 3 - 2
AWSCO, 3 - 2
Abbey Shade & Mfg. Co. Inc., 12 - 2
Ace Blinds Inc., 8 - 2
Acme Window Coverings Ltd., 8 - 2
Acorn Window Systems Inc., 12 - 2
Acrymet Industires Inc., 1 - 2
Adams Rite (Europe, etc.) Ltd., 12 - 2
Adkins Architectural Antiques, 1 - 2
Advance Carpet Decorating Ctr., 8 - 3
Advanced Aluminum Products, 12 - 2
Advanced Consumer Products, 8 - 3
Advantage Window Systems Inc., 12 - 2
Age Craft Mfg. Inc., 8 - 3
Alabama Venetian Blinds Co. Inc., 8 - 3
Albert Marston & Co. Ltd., 4 - 1
All Cedar Venetian Blind Mfg. Co., 8 - 3
All-States Decorating Network, 8 - 3
Allied Building Products Corp., 3 - 5
Allied Window Inc., 12 - 2
Allison Window Fashions, 8 - 4
Allmetal, Inc., 12 - 2
Alpine Windows, 12 - 3
Alside Window Company, 12 - 3
Aluma-Craft Corporation, 12 - 3
Aluma-Glass Industries, Inc., 12 - 3
Alumaroll Specialty Co., Inc., 12 - 3
Alumax, 12 - 3
Aluminum Products Company, 12 - 3
Aluminum Specialties Mfg. Co., 12 - 3
Alwindor Manufacturing, Inc., 12 - 3
American Blind & Wallpaper Factory, 8 - 4
American Door Co. of Michigan Inc., 4 - 1
American Screen & Door Co., Inc., 12 - 3
American Window Corp., 8 - 4
American Window Creation, 8 - 4
Amerlite Aluminum Co., Inc., 12 - 3
Amerock Corporation, 3 - 7
Anaconda Aluminum, 12 - 4
Andersen Windows Inc., 12 - 4
Appropriate Technology, Corp., 12 - 4
Arcadia Mfg. Inc., 1 - 5
Architectural Artifacts, 1 - 5
Architectural Components, 1 - 5

The Complete Sourcebook

Index - 93

Window – Window

Architectural Detail In Wood, 12 - 4
Arctic Glass & Window Outlet, 12 - 4
Around the Window, 8 - 5
Arrow Aluminum Ind., Inc., 12 - 4
Art Glass Unlimited Inc., 12 - 4
Arthur Shaw Manufacturing Ltd., 9 - 1
Artifacteria, 8 - 5
Artistic Doors and Windows, 4 - 1
Arvid's Historic Woods, 1 - 7
Asefave, 12 - 4
Atlantic Venetian Blind & Drapery Co., 8 - 6
Atrium Door and Window Co., 4 - 2
Avondale Distributors Inc., 8 - 7
Aye Attracting Awnings, 3 - 11
B & G Custom Window, 12 - 4
B. Lilly & Sons Ltd., 3 - 11
Bali Blinds Midwest, 8 - 7
Bamboo Abbott Florida Corp., 8 - 8
Barker Supply & Window Coverings, 8 - 8
Barnett Millworks, Inc., 1 - 8
BayForm, 12 - 5
Baydale Architectural Metalwork Ltd., 1 - 8
Beacon Looms, Inc., 8 - 8
Beauti-Vue Products Inc., 8 - 9
Bedroom Secrets, 8 - 9
Berkshire Mfg. Inc., 8 - 9
Best Blinds, 8 - 9
Better Bilt Aluminum Products Co., 12 - 5
Better-Bilt Aluminum Products Co., 12 - 5
Bevel Glass & Mirror, 4 - 2
BiltBest Windows, 12 - 5
Binning's Bldg. Products Inc., 12 - 5
Black Millwork Co. Inc., 4 - 3
Blaine Window Hardware, 12 - 5
Blair Joinery Ltd., 12 - 5
Blind Brite Corp., 8 - 10
Blind Busters, 8 - 10
Blind Center USA, Inc., 8 - 10
Blind Design Inc., 8 - 10
Blind Design, 8 - 10
Blinds 'N Things, 8 - 11
Blum Ornamental Glass Co., Inc., 12 - 5
Boise Moulding & Lumber, 3 - 15
Boulton & Paul PLC, 3 - 16
Boyd Aluminum Mfg. Company, 12 - 5
Bradd & Hall Blinds, 8 - 11
Brass Tacks Hardware Ltd., 3 - 16
Broward Window Products, Inc., 8 - 12
Burch Co., 12 - 5
Burt Millwork Corp., 1 - 9
C & S Distributors, Inc., 12 - 6
C. V. Aluminum, Inc., 12 - 6
CSS Decor Inc., 8 - 13
Cain Inc., 12 - 6
California Glass Bending Corp., 12 - 6
California Window Corporation, 12 - 6
Cape May Millworks, 1 - 10
Caradco, 12 - 6
Care Free Aluminum Prod., Inc., 12 - 6
Carolina Components Corp., 3 - 20
Caroline Country Ruffles, 8 - 14
Caroline's Ruffled Curtains, Inc., 8 - 14
Cego Limited, 12 - 6
Century House of Drapes, 8 - 15
CertainTeed Corp., 3 - 23
Chamberlain Group, 12 - 6
Charles W. Rice & Co. Inc., 8 - 16
Cherry Creek Enterprises Inc., 4 - 3
Chubb Lock Company, 9 - 2
Classic Designs, 12 - 6
Coast to Coast Manufacturing Ltd., 12 - 6

Collingdale Millwork Co., 1 - 11
Colorel Blinds, 8 - 18
Columbia Glass & window Company, 12 - 7
Columbia Metal Products Co., 12 - 7
Combination Door Company, 4 - 4
Conrad Imports, 8 - 18
Consolidated Aluminum, 12 - 7
Consolidated American Window Co., 12 - 7
Contact Lumber Company, 3 - 27
Contemporary Interiors, Inc., 8 - 18
Corn Belt Aluminum Inc., 12 - 7
Cotswold Architectural Products Ltd., 1 - 12
Country Curtains, 8 - 19
Country Ruffles & Rods, 8 - 19
Courtaulds Performance Films, 12 - 7
Covington Fabrics Corp., 8 - 19
Cox Studios, 12 - 7
Creative Woodworking Ltd., 12 - 7
Crompton Ltd., 12 - 7
Crown Mfg. Corp. of Missouri, 12 - 8
Curtain Cottage, 8 - 20
Custom Laminations Inc., 8 - 20
Custom Window Co., 12 - 8
Custom Windows & Walls, 8 - 20
DAB Studio, 12 - 8
Daisy Decorative Products, 8 - 21
Dana's Curtains & Draperies, 8 - 21
Davidson-Bishop Corp., 8 - 22
De La West Draperies, 8 - 22
Deacon & Sandys, 6 - 22
Del Mar Window Coverings, 8 - 22
Delsan Industries, Inc., 12 - 8
Designer Secrets, 8 - 23
Designer Window Decor/Truview, 6 - 23
Devenco Products Inc., 12 - 8
Dianthus Ltd., 8 - 23
Dilworth Manufacturing Co., 12 - 8
Distinctive Window Fashions, 8 - 23
Domestications, 8 - 23
Donat Flamand, Inc., 4 - 5
Dor-Win Manufacturing, 4 - 5
Dorothy's Ruffled Originals, Inc., 8 - 23
Down River Intl. Inc., 12 - 8
Dryad Simplan Limited, 12 - 8
Duraflex Systems Ltd., 4 - 6
Duratex Inc., 8 - 24
E. D. I., 8 - 24
ENJO Doors and Windows, 4 - 6
Eagle Window & Door, 12 - 8
Empire Pacific Industries, 12 - 8
Endisco Supply Co., 8 - 25
Energy Arsenal, 12 - 9
Energy Saving Products, 12 - 9
Englander Millwork Corp., 12 - 9
Entrances Inc., 4 - 6
Especially Lace, 8 - 25
Faith's Lacery, 8 - 27
Fara Mfg.Co., Inc., 8 - 27
Fashion Tech, 8 - 27
Fenebee Inc., 4 - 7
First American Resources, 12 - 9
Fleetwood Aluminum Products, Inc., 12 - 9
Flex Trim, 12 - 9
Florida Blinds, 8 - 28
Florida Shades Inc., 8 - 28
Frank Allart & Co., Ltd., 4 - 7
Fuji Hardware Co., Ltd., 2 - 4
Fypon Molded Millwork, 1 - 17
G & L Shades Inc., 8 - 29
G & T Woodworking Ltd., 4 - 7
G-U Hardware Inc., 12 - 9

Index

Window – Window

G. R. Theriault Ltd., 4 - 7
Gamrod-Harman Co., 8 - 30
Garran Mfg. Ltd., 4 - 8
General Aluminum Corporation, 12 - 9
Georgia Palm Beach Alum.Window,12-19
Geze UK, 12 - 9
Glashaus Inc., 3 - 40
Glass Block Co., 3 - 40
Glass Blocks Unlimited Inc., 1 - 18
Global Blind Express, 8 - 30
Golden Gate Glass & Mirror Co., 12 - 10
Goodman Fabrications, 12 - 10
Gra-Mar Window Treatment, 12 - 10
Graber Industries, 12 - 10
Great Gatsby's Auction Galley, 1 - 18
Great Lakes Window, 12 - 10
Great Paines Glassworks, 4 - 8
Gulf Coast Window Covering Inc., 8 - 31
H-R Windows, 12 - 10
Hahn's Woodworking Co., 12 - 10
Hanover Wire Cloth, 12 - 10
Hara's Inc., 12 - 10
Harding's Custom Sheers, 12 - 10
Harmony Supply Inc., 8 - 32
Harry G. Barr Company, 12 - 10
Hayfield Window & Door Co., 12 - 11
Headquarters Window & Walls, 12 - 11
Helm Products Ltd., 8 - 32
Heritage Imports, Inc., 8 - 33
Hess Manufacturing Company, 12 - 11
Historic Window & Door Corp., 12 - 11
Home Fashions, Inc., 8 - 33
Home Window Systems Ltd., 12 - 11
Hope Works Ltd., 12 - 11
Hornick Industries, 8 - 34
House of Blinds, 8 - 34
Howard Industries Inc., 12 - 11
Hudson Venetian Blind Service Inc., 8 - 34
Hunt Windows and Doors, 12 - 11
Hunter Douglas Window Fashions, 8 - 35
Hurd Millwork Company, 3 - 48
IJ Mfg. Ltd., 12 - 12
Imperial Screen Company Inc., 9 - 2
Insulate Industries, Inc., 12 - 12
International Window Corporation, 12 - 12
Irreplaceable Artifacts, 1 - 20
Italian Glass Block Designs Ltd., 1 - 20
J. M Mills, 2 - 6
J. R. Burrows & Company, 8 - 37
J. Ring Glass Studio, 12 - 12
J. W. Window Components, Inc., 12 - 12
J. Zeluck Inc., 1 - 21
Jack Wallis Doors, 4 - 9
Jag Corp., 8 - 37
James Gibbons Format Ltd., 12 - 12
Janik Custom Millwork, 12 - 12
Jastrac Mfg., 8 - 37
Jayson Window Fashions, 8 - 37
Jelco Windows & Doors, 12 - 12
Jeld-Wen, 4 - 10
Jencraft Corp., 8 - 38
Joe-Keith Industries, Inc., 12 - 12
John Carr Joinery Sales Ltd., 12 - 13
John Dixon Inc., 8 - 38
John F. Lavoie Windows, 12 - 13
JonCo Manufacturing, Inc., 12 - 13
Jones Paint & Glass, Inc., 12 - 13
Judkins Co., 8 - 38
K & R Custom Interiors, 8 - 38
Kaleidoscope Ind. Inc., 8 - 38
Kansas Aluminum, Inc., 12 - 13

Kawneer, 12 - 13
Keller Aluminum Products, 12 - 13
Keller Industries Inc., 4 - 10
Kemp Stuttbacher Designs, 8 - 39
Ken Jordan Shutters, 12 - 13
Kinco Corporation, 12 - 13
Kinco, Ltd., 12 - 13
Kinro, Inc., 12 - 14
Kirsch, 8 - 40
Kolbe & Kolbe Millwork Co. Inc., 1 - 21
Lace Country, 8 - 41
Lafayette Venetian Blind Inc., 8 - 41
Laflamme & Frere, Inc., 4 - 11
Laura Copenhaver Industries Inc., 8 - 41
Laurel Mfg. Co. Inc., 8 - 41
Lawson Industries Inc., 12 - 14
Le Lace Factory, Inc., 8 - 42
Leicester Joinery Co., 4 - 11
Leslie-Locke Inc., 3 - 55
Lincoln Wood Products, Inc., 12 - 14
Linen & Lace, 8 - 42
Linen Lady, 8 - 42
Linford Brothers/Utal Glass Co., 12 - 14
Living Windows Corporation, 12 - 14
London Lace, 8 - 43
Louisiana-Pacific Corporation, 3 - 56
M F F, 12 - 14
M.A. Bruder & Sons Inc., 8 - 43
MBS Manufacturing West, Inc., 12 - 15
MDC Direct Inc., 8 - 43
MQ Windows ofEurope&The Americas,12-15
MacDonald Stained Glass, 3 - 56
Made-Rite Aluminum Window Co., 12 - 15
Magnet Trade, 4 - 11
Major Industries Inc., 12 - 15
Malta, 12 - 15
Marvin Windows and Doors, 12 - 15
Marvin Windows, 12 - 15
Mason Corporation, 12 - 15
Masterview Window Company, 12 - 15
Mather's Department Store, 8 - 44
McInnis Industries, 8 - 45
Mercer Industries, Inc., 12 - 15
Merit Window Fashions, 8 - 45
Metal Exchange Corp., 12 - 15
Metal Industries Inc., 12 - 15
Metal Industries, Inc., 12 - 16
Metro Blind & Shade, 8 - 46
Michael's Fine Colonial Products, 1 - 24
Midwest Wood Products, 12 - 16
Milgard Manufacturing, Inc., 12 - 16
Miller Industries, Inc., 12 - 16
Millwork Supply Company, 4 - 12
Modu-Line Windows, 12 - 16
Moeller-Reimer Company, 12 - 16
Mon-Ray Windows, Inc., 12 - 16
Morantz Inc., 8 - 47
Moss Supply Company, Inc., 12 - 16
Mutual Wallpaper & Paint Co., Inc., 8 - 48
NT Jenkins Manufacturing Co., 12 - 17
Nanik, 12 - 17
Napco, 12 - 17
National Blind & Wallpaper Factory, 8 - 48
National Screen Company, Inc., 4 - 12
National Woodworks, Inc., 1 - 25
Nationwide Wholesalers, 8 - 48
New Home Window Shade, 8 - 49
New Morning Windows, Inc., 12 - 17
New Panes Creations, 12 - 17
New Scotland Lace Co., 8 - 49
New View Blinds Mfg. Ltd., 8 - 49

The Complete Sourcebook

Window – Window

New York Wire Company, 12 - 17
Newell Window Furnishings, 8 - 49
Newpro, 12 - 17
Nichols-Homeshield, Inc., 12 - 18
Norandex, Inc., 12 - 18
Norco Windows Inc., 12 - 18
North Star Company, 12 - 18
Northwest Aluminum Products, 12 - 18
Nottingham Gallery, 4 - 12
Nu-Air Mfg. Co., 4 - 13
Old Manor House, 8 - 50
Omega Too, 2 - 8
Optimum Window Mfg. Corp., 12 - 18
Oxford Sash Window Company, 12 - 18
P. C. Henderson Ltd., 12 - 18
Pacesetter Building Systems, 12 - 19
Pacific Industries/Pl. Inc., 12 - 19
Parker Window Covering, 8 - 51
Paulson's Stained Glass Studio, 12 - 19
Peachtree Doors, Inc., 4 - 13
Peerless Products Inc., 12 - 19
Peerless Wallpaper, 8 - 52
Pella Corporation, 12 - 19
Penn Needle Art Co., 8 - 52
Pennco, Inc., 12 - 19
Perfection Metal & Supply Co., 3 - 69
Perkins & Powell, 2 - 8
Perkins Manufacturing & Distributing, 12 - 19
Perkowitz Window Fashions, 8 - 52
Perma Window & Door Service, 12 - 19
Peterson Window Corp., 12 - 19
Petit Industries Inc., 12 - 19
Phillips Industries Inc., 3 - 70
Pintchik Homeworks, 8 - 53
Pittsburgh Corning, 3 - 70
Plains Plastics Inc., 12 - 20
Plastic Sun Shade Co. Inc., 8 - 53
Plunkett - Webster Inc., 12 - 20
Point-Five Windows, 12 - 20
Pompei & Company Art Glass, 12 - 20
Portal Inc., 12 - 20
Pozzi Wood Windows, 12 - 20
Pro-Glass Technology/Vinyl Tech Inc., 12 - 20
Public Supply Company, 12 - 20
Quaker Window Products Co., 12 - 20
Quantum Wood Windows, 12 - 21
Quix Window Visions & Fabric Works, 8 - 54
R & R Lumber & Building Supply Corp.,1 - 28
R. Cartwright & Co., Ltd., 12 - 21
R. Lang Co., 12 - 21
Ralston Regulux Inc., 12 - 21
Rasmussen Millwork/Colonial Craft,12 - 21
Ray Tenebruso, 4 - 14
Remington/Div. of Metal Ind., Inc., 12 - 21
Republic Aluminum Inc., 12 - 21
Reynolds Aluminum Building, 12 - 21
Reynolds Metals Company, 12 - 21
Reynolds Mfg. Company, Inc., 12 - 22
Richard Blaschke Cabinet Glass, 3 - 75
Riverside Millwork Co. Inc., 1 - 29
Rochester Drapery Inc., 8 - 56
Rockwell Window Co. Inc., 12 - 22
Roddiscraft Inc., 12 - 22
Rogow Window/Ideal Aluminum, 12 - 22
Rolladen Inc., 12 - 22
Rollyson Aluminum Products, 12 - 22
Royal Crest Inc., 8 - 56
Royal Plastics, Inc., 12 - 22
Rue De France Inc., 8 - 57
S. D. Davis, Inc., 12 - 22
S. Morantz Inc., 8 - 57

S.N.F.A., 12 - 22
S.Z.F.F./C.S.F.F., 12 - 22
Schuco International, 4 - 15
Seal-O-Matic Industries Inc., 12 - 23
SealRite Windows, Inc., 12 - 23
Season-All Industries Inc., 12 - 23
Seaway Manufacturing Corp., 12 - 23
Sebastapol Wood Windows, 12 - 23
Sebring & Co., 8 - 59
Securi Style Ltd., 11 - 28
Setzer Forest Products, 3 - 78
Shades & Verticals & Miniblinds Cntr, 8 - 60
Sholton Assoc., 3 - 79
Shutters & Shades, 8 - 61
Silver Wallpaper & Paint Co., 8 - 61
Simonton Building Products, Inc., 12 - 23
Skandia Industries, 8 - 61
Skotty Aluminum Prod. Co., 12 - 23
Solartechnic 2000 Ltd., 8 - 61
Southwest Florida Blinds Inc., 8 - 62
Southwood Door Company, 4 - 15
Sovereign Group Ltd., 4 - 15
Sovereign Wright, 4 - 16
Spring Lace Two, 8 - 62
Stanwood Drapery Co. Inc., 8 - 62
Structural Slate Co., 3 - 83
Sun Control Center Of Indiana, 12 - 24
Sun Room Company, 7 - 7
Sun Window Company, Inc., 12 - 24
Sunburst Shutters Inc., 12 - 24
Sunburst Stained Glass Co. Inc., 3 - 84
Superior Metal Products Co., 12 - 24
Supro Building Products Corp., 3 - 85
Swish Products Ltd., 4 - 16
T. Saveker Ltd., 11 - 30
Tafco Corp., 3 - 86
Temple Producst of Indiana Inc., 8 - 65
Tentina Window Fashion, 8 - 65
Teskey Enterprises Inc., 12 - 24
The Alternative Window Co., 12 - 24
The Blind Factory, 8 - 65
The Blind Maker, 8 - 66
The Blount Lumber Company, 12 - 24
The Curtain Collection, 8 - 66
The Decorators Outlet, 8 - 66
The Gerkin Company, 12 - 25
The Joinery Company, 5 - 10
The Jordan Companies, 12 - 25
The Loxcreen Company, Inc., 12 - 25
The Smoot Lumber Co., 4 - 17
Therma-Tru Corporation, 12 - 25
Thermal Windows, Inc., 12 - 25
Thermo-Press Corp., 12 - 25
Tiffany Wholesale Supply Inc., 8 - 69
Torrance Steel Window Co. Inc., 12 - 25
Traco, 12 - 26
Triangle Window Fashions, 8 - 69
Trico Mfg./Div. of Tri-State, 12 - 26
U.T.M.M./T.U.M.S., 12 - 26
USA Blind Factory, 8 - 70
Uncsaal, 12 - 26
Unique Art Glass Co., 12 - 26
Unique Wholesale Distr. Inc., 8 - 70
United Designs Inc., 8 - 70
United States Woodworking, Inc., 1 - 35
United Supply Co., 8 - 71
Universal Components, 12 - 26
Urban Artifacts, 1 - 35
VMRG, 12 - 26
Velux America Inc., 4 - 17
Vent Vue, 12 - 26

Index - 96

The Complete Sourcebook

Index

Windsor – Wood

Verband der Fenster, 12 - 27
Versol USA, Inc., 8 - 71
Verticals Inc., 8 - 72
Vetter Mfg. Co., 12 - 27
Victorian Stained Glass Illusions, 12 - 27
View Guard, 8 - 72
Viking Distributors Inc., 8 - 72
Viking Industries, Inc., 12 - 27
Vintage Valances, 8 - 72
Vinyl Building Products Inc., 12 - 27
Vinyl Therm Inc., 12 - 27
Vista Products Inc., 8 - 72
W & F Mfg. Inc., 12 - 27
WallpaperXpress, 8 - 74
Walsh Screen & Window Inc., 12 - 27
Wartian Lock Co., 9 - 3
Weather Shield Mfg., Inc., 12 - 27
Weathervane Window Company, 12 - 27
Wells Aluminum, Inc., 12 - 28
Wells Interiors, 8 - 75
Wenco Windows, 12 - 28
Wesco Fabrics Inc., 8 - 75
West Coast Windows Inc., 12 - 28
Western Insulated Glass co., 12 - 28
Westport Mfg. Co. Inc., 8 - 75
Whiting Mfg. Co. Inc., 8 - 76
Wholesale Verticals, Inc., 8 - 76
Willard Shutter Co. Inc., 12 - 28
Williams Art Glass Studios, 12 - 28
Win-Glo Window Coverings, 8 - 76
Winco Window Coverings, 8 - 76
Windo-Shade Distributors Inc., 8 - 76
Window Covering Dist. Inc., 8 - 77
Window Coverings Inc., 8 - 77
Window Modes, 8 - 77
Wing Industries Inc., 4 - 18
Winter Seal of Flint, Inc., 1 - 37
Wisconsin Drapery Supply Inc., 8 - 77
Wizard Windows, 12 - 28
Woodgrain Millwork, Inc., 4 - 18
Woodstone Company, 1 - 38
Wrisco Industries Inc., 8 - 77
Yale Ogron Mfg. Co. Inc., 12 - 28

Windsor

Cornucopia, Inc., 6 - 19
Michael M. Reed, 6 - 52
River Bend Chair Company, 6 - 63
Robert Barrow Furniture Maker, 6 - 63
Straw Hill Chairs, 6 - 72
Windsor Chairmakers, 6 - 85

Wine

I. F. M. Co. Ltd., 10 - 5

Wood

ACCRA Wood Products Ltd., 1 - 1
ADI Corporation, 1 - 1
Absolute Coatings Inc., 3 - 3
Adams Stair Works Carpentry Inc., 3 - 4
Aetna Plywood, Inc., 3 - 4
All American Wood Register Co., 3 - 5
Alpine Engineer Products Inc., 3 - 5
American Drew, 6 - 3
American Wood Column Corp., 1 - 4
Andrews Custom Woodworking, 1 - 4
Architectural Detail In Wood, 12 - 4
Arvid's Historic Woods, 1 - 7
Athens Furniture, 6 - 6
Atlanta Furniture Craftsmen, 6 - 6
Basic Coatings, 3 - 12

Bel-Air Door Co., 4 - 2
Bend Millwork Systems Inc., 4 - 2
Berea Prehung Door, Inc., 4 - 2
Berke Door & Hardware, Inc., 3 - 14
Better Trees, 3 - 15
Big Country, 6 - 9
Bonakemi USA, Inc., 5 - 2
Brent Materials Co., 3 - 17
Brooks Furniture Mfg. Inc., 6 - 12
CMF Colonial Moulding, 1 - 9
Caberboard Ltd., 3 - 18
Cabot Stains, 3 - 19
Cal-Wood Door Inc., 4 - 3
Carrier Furniture Inc., 6 - 14
Carver Tripp, 5 - 2
Castle Burlingame, 5 - 2
Century Wood Door Limited, 4 - 3
Ceramic Radiant Heat, 3 - 22
Certainly Wood, 3 - 23
Charles Webb Furniture, 6 - 16
Cider Hill Woodworks, 1 - 10
Coast Trim Company, 3 - 25
Collingdale Millwork Co., 1 - 11
Colonial Stair & Woodwork Co., 3 - 26
Cooper Stair Co., 3 - 27
Craftline, 4 - 4
Creative Structures, 3 - 27
Crown Door Corp., 4 - 4
Cumberland Lumber & Manufacturing, 5 - 3
Dahlke Stair Co., 1 - 13
Daly's Wood Finishing Products, 3 - 29
Danbury Stairs Corp., 1 - 13
Defiance Forest Products, 4 - 4
Deft, Inc., 5 - 3
Delta Door Co., Inc., 4 - 5
Diamond K. Co., Inc., 5 - 3
Diamond "W" Floor Covering, 5 - 3
Dominion Chair, Ltd., 6 - 24
DoorCraft Manufacturing Co., 4 - 5
Doorcraft Mfg. Ltd., 4 - 5
Doorland 2000 Inc., 4 - 5
Doormen, 4 - 5
Doors, Incorporated, 4 - 5
Down River Intl. Inc., 12 - 8
Dura Seal, 5 - 4
Dwight Lewis Lumber Co., Inc., 3 - 32
Dynasty Wood Products Inc., 6 - 25
Eagle Plywood & Door Mftrs. Inc., 4 - 6
Eggers Industries, 4 - 6
Elof Hansson, Inc., 3 - 33
Energy Pioneers, 3 - 34
Englander Millwork Corp., 12 - 9
Enterprise Lumber Co., 3 - 34
F. E. Schumacher Co., Inc., 4 - 7
Fenestra Wood Door Div., 4 - 7
Filmore Thomas & Co., Inc., 4 - 7
Finishing Products, 3 - 36
Flood Company, 3 - 37
Floors By Juell, 5 - 4
Florian Greenhouse Inc., 7 - 2
Fritz V. Sterbak Antiques, 1 - 17
Gilmer Wood Co., 3 - 40
Glidden Co., 3 - 40
Goddard Manufacturing, 1 - 18
Gotham Inc., 1 - 18
Governor's Antiques & Arch. Materials, 1 - 18
Graham Mfg. Corp., 4 - 8
Grande Entrance Door Company, 4 - 8
Granville Manufacturing Co. Inc., 3 - 42
Hale Mfg. Co., 6 - 34
Haley Bros.,Inc., 4 - 8

The Complete Sourcebook

Index - 97

Wood – Wood

Index

Hamrick Truss, Inc., 3 - 43
Harco Chemical Coatings, 3 - 43
Harris Marcus Group, Inc., 11 - 14
Hartco/Tibbals Flooring Company, 5 - 5
Hendricks Woodworking, 4 - 9
Heritage Woodcraft, 1 - 20
Hiskson Corporation, 3 - 46
Historic Floors of Oshkosh, 5 - 5
Hoboken Floors Inc., 5 - 5
Hudson Venetian Blind Service Inc., 8 - 34
Hunt Country Furniture, 6 - 37
IJ Mfg. Ltd., 12 - 12
ITT Rayonier Inc., 3 - 49
Ideal Wood Products, 4 - 9
J. H. Monteath, 3 - 50
J. H. Wood Shake Inc., 3 - 50
JJJ Specialty Co., 4 - 9
Janik Custom Millwork, 12 - 12
Jarabosky, 6 - 40
Jeffries Wood Works Inc., 1 - 21
Jessup Door Company, 4 - 10
Johnsonius Precision Millwork, 3 - 50
Jr Ross Ltd., 6 - 41
Kakabeka Timber Ltd., 3 - 51
Karona Inc., 4 - 10
Kaylien, 4 - 10
Kentucky Wood Floors, 5 - 5
Keokuk Stove Works, 3 - 52
Kincaid Galleries, 6 - 42
Kountry Kraft Hardwoods, 3 - 53
L.D. Brinkman & Co. Inc., 5 - 5
Laflamme & Frere, Inc., 4 - 11
Lamson-Taylor Custom Doors, 4 - 11
Landquist & Son, Inc., 4 - 11
Lanier Furniture Company, 6 - 44
Larue Products, 8 - 41
Liberty Cedar, 3 - 55
Lincoln Wood Products, Inc., 12 - 14
Livermore Wood Floors, 5 - 6
Louisiana-Pacific Corporation, 3 - 56
Lynden Door, Inc., 4 - 11
Madawaska Doors Inc., 4 - 11
Majestic Co., 3 - 56
Malta, 12 - 15
Manchester Wood Inc., 6 - 48
Manivalde Woodworking, 6 - 48
Mansion Industries, Inc., 8 - 44
Maple Grove Restorations, 1 - 22
Maui Trading Co., 3 - 59
Maurice L. Condon Co., 3 - 59
Maywood Inc., 4 - 12
McInnis Industries, 8 - 45
Michael Farr Custom Woodworking, 1 - 24
Midwest Dowel Works, Inc., 3 - 60
Miller Shingle Co., Inc., 3 - 61
Millwork Specialties, 1 - 24
Millwork Supply Company, 4 - 12
Minic Custom Woodwork, Inc., 6 - 53
Mitchell Moulding Co., 1 - 24
Mohawk Flush Doors, Inc., 4 - 12
Moorwood, 1 - 24
Morgan-Bockius Studios Inc., 4 - 12
Nanik, 12 - 17
Nashotah Moulding Co., Inc., 1 - 24
Native American Hardwoods, 3 - 63
New Morning Windows, Inc., 12 - 17
Nord Company, 4 - 12
North Central Door Co., 4 - 12
Nuttle Lumber, 3 - 65
Ohline Corp., 12 - 18
Olympic Structures Inc., 3 - 66

Oregon Wooden Screen Door Co., 4 - 13
Ostermann & Scheiwe, USA, Inc., 1 - 26
Overhead Door Corp., 4 - 13
Pacific Burl and Hardwood, 3 - 68
Perkins Manufacturing & Distributing, 12 - 19
Perma-Door, 4 - 13
Peterson Wood Div., 7 - 5
Pixley Lumber Co., 4 - 13
Pozzi Wood Windows, 12 - 20
Putnam Rolling Ladder Company Inc., 3 - 72
Rackstraw Ltd., 6 - 62
Rasmussen Millwork /Colonial Craft,12 - 21
Readybuilt Products Co., 1 - 28
Ridgway Roof Truss Co. Inc., 3 - 75
Robert M. Albrect Hardwood, 6 - 63
Rockwell Window Co. Inc., 12 - 22
SNE Enterprises, Inc., 4 - 14
Sauder Door Corporation, 4 - 14
SealRite Windows, Inc., 12 - 23
Sebastapol Wood Windows, 12 - 23
Semling-Menke Company, Inc., 4 - 15
Seybold Industries Inc., 6 - 67
Sierra Pacific Industries Millwork Div., 1 - 31
Simpson Door Company, 4 - 15
Smith Millwork, Inc., 1 - 31
Southern Staircase Co., 1 - 31
Specialty Woodworks Co., 4 - 16
Spiral Stairs of America, 1 - 32
Stair Parts Ltd., 3 - 81
Stair Specialist Inc., 3 - 81
Stairways Inc., 1 - 32
Stanley Furniture, 6 - 71
Star Bronze Co., 3 - 82
Starling Inc., 1 - 32
Steves & Sons, 4 - 16
Stuart Flooring Corp., 5 - 9
Stuart Lerman Inc., 5 - 9
Superior Fireplace Co., 3 - 85
Talarico Hardwoods, 3 - 86
Temple Products, Inc., 4 - 16
The Berea Hardwoods Co., 3 - 87
The Blount Lumber Company, 12 - 24
The Furniture Shoppe Inc., 6 - 75
The Golden Rabbit, 6 - 75
The Old Wagon Factory, 4 - 17
The Roane Co., 5 - 10
Thermal Control Co., 3 - 90
Through The Barn Door Furniture Co., 6 - 78
Touchstone Woodworks, 4 - 17
Treske, 6 - 78
Tru-Test General Paint & Chemical, 3 - 92
United Coatings Co., 3 - 93
United Stair Corp., 1 - 35
V-T Industries Inc., 4 - 17
Valley Mouldings Inc., 1 - 36
Vancouver Door Co. Inc., 4 - 17
Vaughan Furniture Co. Inc., 6 - 80
Vetter Mfg. Co., 12 - 27
Walter Norman & Co., 3 - 96
Watson Furniture Shop, 6 - 82
Weathervane Window Company, 12 - 27
Wendover Woodworks, 3 - 97
Western Oregon Doors, Inc., 4 - 18
Weyerhaeuser Company, 3 - 98
Wholesale Door Company, 4 - 18
Will Kirkpatrick, 8 - 76
Willamette Industries Inc., 3 - 99
Willard Brothers Woodcutters, 3 - 99
William H. James Co., 6 - 84
Wood Kote, 3 - 100
Woodgrain Millwork, Inc., 4 - 18

Index - 98

The Complete Sourcebook

Index

Woodstove – Wrought

Woodland Industries, Inc., 4 - 18
Woodworkers, 3 - 100
Woolums Mfg. Inc., 6 - 86
Zimports Collection, 6 - 87

Woodstove

Bryant Stove Works, 3 - 17
Energy Etcetera, 3 - 34
Englander Wood Stoves, 3 - 34
Frizelle Enos Co., 3 - 38
Glo King Woodstoves, 3 - 41
Hayes Equipment Corp., 3 - 44
Heatilator Inc., 3 - 45
Heritage Energy Systems, 3 - 45
Kickapoo Diversified Products Inc., 3 - 52
Lehman Hardware, 3 - 54
Martin Industries Inc., 3 - 58
Mohawk Industries Inc., 3 - 61
NHC Inc., 3 - 62
New Buck Corporation, 3 - 64
O'Dette Energies of Canada Ltd., 3 - 66
Technical Glass Products, 3 - 86
Vermont Castings, 3 - 95
Woodstock Soapstone Co., Inc., 3 - 100

Woodwork

Ability Woodwork Co. Inc., 1 - 2
Accent Millwork Inc., 1 - 2
Anthony Wood Products Inc., 1 - 4
Architectural Salvage Company, 1 - 6
Berbaum Millwork Inc., 3 - 14
Cheyenne Company, 1 - 10
Constantine's, 1 - 12
Cumberland Woodcraft Co., 1 - 13
Detail Millwork Inc., 1 - 14
Drums Sash & Dove Co., 1 - 15
Hallelujah Redwood Products, 1 - 19

Kneeshaw Woodworking Installations, 1 - 21
Marion H. Campbell, 1 - 23
Maurer & Shepherd Joyners Inc., 1 - 23
Old Kentucky Wood Products, 1 - 26
Pridgen Cabinet Works, Inc., 1 - 28
Reeves Design Workshop Ltd., 1 - 28
Riverview Millworks Inc., 1 - 29
Rutt Cabinetry, 10 - 9
Taconic Architectural Woodworking, 1 - 33
Tatem Mfg. Co. Inc., 1 - 33
The Wood Factory, 1 - 35
United States Woodworking, Inc., 1 - 35
Vicor Corp., 1 - 36
Woodstone Company, 1 - 38

Wreath

J & L Floral, 8 - 36
Meadow Everlasting, 8 - 45
Schoenly's Floral Designs, 8 - 59

Wrought

Architectural Iron Company, 1 - 6
Art In Iron, 6 - 5
Arte de Mexico, 6 - 6
Cambridge Smithy, 3 - 19
Gaby's Shoppe, 6 - 31
Goddard Manufacturing, 1 - 18
Kenneth D. Lynch & Sons, Inc., 6 - 41
Lee L. Woodard Sons Inc., 6 - 45
Lyon-Shaw, 6 - 47
Mallin Co., 6 - 48
O.W. Lee Co., Inc., 6 - 56
Precision Furniture Corp., 6 - 60
Sak Industries Inc., 6 - 65
The Heveningham Collection, 6 - 75
Thermal Control Co., 3 - 90
Williamsburg Blacksmiths Inc., 3 - 99

The Complete Sourcebook

NOTES